The Grid: Blueprint for a New Computing Infrastructure

Second Edition

The Elsevier Series in Grid Computing

Series Editors: Ian Foster, Agonne National Laboratory & University of Chicago, and Carl Kesselman, Information Sciences Institute, University of Southern California

The Grid is a rapidly developing computing structure that allows components of our information technology infrastructure—computational capabilities, databases, sensors, and people—to be shared flexibly as true collaborative tools.

The Elsevier Series in Grid Computing examines how the Grid Computing vision is being made a reality and the implications of Grid technologies for computing, industry, science, and society. Titles in the series are authored by leading experts and make the necessary connections between Grid Computing and Networking; Information Technology; Database Management; Programming Languages, Tools and Compilers; Security; Artificial Intelligence, Computer Architecture and Design and other computing disciplines.

Series Editors Ian Foster and Carl Kesselman are the editors of *The Grid 2*, the premier and flagship volume in this series.

The Grid:

Blueprint for a New

Computing Infrastructure

Second Edition

Edited by

Ian Foster

Argonne National Laboratory
and the University of Chicago

Carl Kesselman

Information Sciences Institute,
University of Southern California

AMSTERDAM • BOSTON • HEIDELBERG • LONDON
NEW YORK • OXFORD • PARIS • SAN DIEGO
SAN FRANCISCO • SINGAPORE • SYDNEY • TOKYO
Morgan Kaufmann Publishers is an imprint of Elsevier

ELSEVIER

Morgan
Kaufmann

Publishing Director   Diane Cerra
Senior Acquisitions Editor   Denise E. M. Penrose
Editorial Coordinator   Alyson Day/Emilia Thiuri
Publishing Services Manager   Simon Crump
Senior Project Manager   Angela G. Dooley
Cover Design   Ross Carron Design
Cover Image   Minoru Toi/Photanica
Composition   Integra Software Services Pvt Ltd, Pondicherry, India
Technical Illustration   Dartmouth Publishing
Interior printer   The Maple-Vail Book Manufacturing Group
Cover printer   Phoenix Color Corp.

Morgan Kaufmann Publishers is an Imprint of Elsevier
500 Sansome Street, Suite 400, San Francisco, CA 94111

This book is printed on acid-free paper.

Library of Congress Cataloging-in-Publication Data
Application submitted

ISBN: 1-55860-933-4

For all information on all Morgan Kauffman publications
visit our website at *www.mkp.com*

Printed in the United States of America

03 04 05 06 07   5 4 3 2 1

Dedication

For Alexander and Imogen, who have already enjoyed a lifetime of the Grid—Ian

To Phyllis for enduring the process, and Squirrel for keeping me company in the early morning hours—Carl

Editors

Dr. Ian Foster was born in Wellington, New Zealand. He has a bachelor of science (Hons I) degree in computer science from the University of Canterbury in Christchurch, New Zealand, and a doctorate in computer science from Imperial College, London. Foster is Associate Division Director and Senior Scientist in the Mathematics and Computer Science Division of Argonne National Laboratory, and Professor of Computer Science at the University of Chicago. Foster's research interests are in innovative technologies and applications of large-scale distributed computing. An internationally recognized researcher and leader in the area of Grid computing, he has published five books and over 200 articles and technical reports in parallel computing, distributed systems, and advanced applications. Foster is a fellow of the American Association for the Advancement of Science and of the British Computer Society, which recognized his work on the Strand parallel programming language with its 1989 award for technical innovation.

Dr. Carl Kesselman is the Director of the Center for Grid Technologies at the University of Southern California's Information Sciences Institute and an Information Sciences Institute Fellow. He is also a Research Associate Professor of Computer Science at the University of Southern California. He received a Ph.D. in Computer Science from the University of California at Los Angeles, a Master's of Science in Electrical Engineering from the University of Southern California, and Bachelors in Electrical Engineering and Computer Science from the University of Buffalo. Kesselman's research interests are in all aspects of Grid computing, and his research contributions in this area are internationally recognized. He has published over 100 articles and papers in the area of high performance and distributed computing. He is a fellow of the British Computer Society.

Foster and Kesselman have worked together since the late 1980s, collaborating first on projects in parallel computing and more recently within the context of the Globus Project®, which they established with their colleague Steven Tuecke in 1996. One significant product of their joint work has been the Globus Toolkit®, the open source software that has emerged as the *de facto* standard for Grid computing in both e-business and e-science. Their contributions have been recognized by numerous awards, including the 1997 Global Information Infrastructure Next Generation Internet award, a 2002 R&D 100 award, the 2002 R&D Editor's choice award, and the 2002 Ada Lovelace Medal from the British Computing Society.

They have recently begun to edit a new series entitled *The Elsevier Series in Grid Computing* that will explore all aspects of Grids from standards to applications. Designed for researchers and professionals, the books will be authored by the foremost experts in the field. This second edition of *The Grid* is the first title in this new series.

Contents

PART IV　ARCHITECTURE　　　　　　　　　　　　　213

17　The Open Grid Services Architecture　　　　　215

Ian Foster, Carl Kesselman, and Steven Tuecke

18　Resource and Service Management　　　　　259

Karl Czajkowski, Ian Foster, and Carl Kesselman

19   Building Reliable Clients and Services   285

Douglas Thain and Miron Livny

20   Instrumentation and Monitoring   319

Jeffrey Hollingsworth and Brian Tierney

21   Security for Virtual Organizations: Federating Trust and Policy Domains   353

Frank Siebenlist, Nataraj Nagaratnam, Von Welch, and Clifford Neuman

PART V   DATA AND KNOWLEDGE   389

22   Data Access, Integration, and Management   391

Malcolm Atkinson, Ann L. Chervenak, Peter Kunszt,
Inderpal Narang, Norman W. Paton, Dave Pearson,
Arie Shoshani, and Paul Watson

23   Enhancing Services and Applications with
           Knowledge and Semantics   431

Carole A. Goble, David De Roure, Nigel R. Shadbolt,
and Alvaro A. A. Fernandes

Preface to the Second Edition

The *Grid* is an emerging infrastructure that will fundamentally change the way we think about—and use—computing. The word *Grid* is used by analogy with the electric power grid, which provides pervasive access to electricity and, like the computer and a small number of other advances, has had a dramatic impact on human capabilities and society. Many believe that by allowing all components of our information technology infrastructure—computational capabilities, databases, sensors, and people—to be shared flexibly as true collaborative tools, the Grid will have a similar transforming effect, allowing new classes of applications to emerge.

This is the second edition of *The Grid: Blueprint for a New Computing Infrastructure*. Writing this preface brings home to us just how much has happened since the first edition was published, how much has been learned, and how much new information there is to communicate about Grid technologies, their application, and likely future evolution.

When we started planning the first edition early in 1997, we believed that Grids were destined to be important, but we would not have predicted the impact that Grid technologies have had on the practice of science and industry in the five years since the book appeared in mid-1998. Rereading the first edition, we are delighted with how much of what we wrote back then still applies. However, it is certainly also the case that much has been learned and much is new.

Our understanding has evolved tremendously with respect to the nature both of the opportunities offered by Grid computing and of the technologies needed to realize those opportunities. We now see far more clearly the revolutionary impacts of large-scale resource sharing and virtualization within both science and industry, the intimate relationships between organizational and resource-sharing structures, and the new technologies required to enable secure, reliable, and efficient resource sharing on a large scale.

This understanding has emerged from aggressive and imaginative application experiments conducted by talented research and development teams around the world. We report on some highlights of this work here, and these stories have much to say concerning the excitement that Grid technologies generate within application communities, the successes that have been achieved, and (we must not lose sight of this perspective) the obstacles that remain to be overcome.

The technology has evolved, too, in both its implementation and its specification. The open source Globus Toolkit® was only just emerging five years ago, when the first edition appeared, and it has now been widely adopted as a de facto standard infrastructure with a substantial international contributor and user base: truly the "Linux of the Grid." Meanwhile, work within the Global Grid Forum has produced specifications defining the Open Grid Services Architecture, a Grid standard that is seeing broad adoption within industry and research, with implementations available from multiple sources, including the Globus Toolkit. Other complementary technologies—such as Condor, portal tools, and various commercial offerings—have matured to the point where they form vital parts of the overall Grid software ecosystem. Thus, we are able to describe not only what might be but what is, and the architectural framework within which future developments will occur.

Equally remarkable is the flowering of the Grid community. The Global Grid Forum now regularly welcomes close to a thousand participants at its triennial meetings to discuss and define the technical standards required for further evolution of the Grid. Large international science Grid projects in astronomy, physics, biology, and other fields are well under way, and hundreds of smaller projects are developing Grid technologies, deploying Grid infrastructures, and applying Grids to a wide range of challenging applications. In Asia, Europe, and North America, major government initiatives are being established to create the Grid infrastructures required to support twenty-first-century science and engineering. Meanwhile, a growing number of both large companies and startups (several featured in this book) are investing large sums in the technology and, increasingly, selling Grid solutions to companies with challenging information technology requirements.

Goals of This Book

Our goal in the second edition of *The Grid* is to present an up-to-date view of Grids that reflects this progress and that both reports on real experiences and explains the technologies available today and emerging from labs, companies, and standards bodies. Achieving this goal without at least doubling the size of the book would have been impossible if it were not for the miracle of the Web, and our enlightened editor at Morgan Kaufmann. Fortunately, for your backs and wallets, we have been able to place much of the material from the first edition on the Web, allowing us to focus the second on what is new.

The development of this new edition has thus been an ambitious undertaking, involving substantial revisions to some chapters and a large number of entirely new contributions. In fact, there can be few sentences that remain the same from first edition to second. Nevertheless, the old content remains accessible on the Web, and we refer to it frequently here, using the notation "Chapter 1:N" to refer to Chapter N in the first edition.

This edition, like the first edition, is intended to serve simultaneously as a manifesto, design blueprint, user guide, and research agenda for future Grid systems.

As a *manifesto*, the book seeks to make the case for Grids, explaining why they are important and why we should be concerned with making them a reality.

As a *design blueprint*, the book is intended for software engineers, computing center managers, technology program managers, chief information officers, and other professionals who will be tasked with developing and deploying Grids. This blueprint is intended to describe what Grids will look like, how they will be constructed, and how they will operate.

As a *user guide*, the book is intended for scientists, engineers, and programmers who will develop applications for Grids. For these users, we want to explain what Grid applications will look like, how they will be developed, and what new ways of thinking and programming they will require.

As a *research agenda*, the book is intended for students, researchers, and research managers who want to understand the state of the art in relevant disciplines and the areas in which gaps in our knowledge demand further research. We hope thus to broaden the engagement of researchers in distributed systems, security, collaborative work, and other relevant domains whose engagement is vital to the long-term success of the Grid agenda.

Clearly, we cannot expect to do justice to all four goals in a single book. However, we do believe that we have succeeded in taking useful steps toward each goal, and in so doing we hope to advance understanding of the technologies needed to create the Grids of the future and the implications of these technologies for future applications of computers.

The construction of Grids draws upon expertise from many diverse branches of computer science, including distributed systems, networking, computer and network security, electronic commerce, information systems, databases, operating systems, high-performance computing, and algorithms. Hence, in preparing this book we have assembled a distinguished set of authors, each recognized as an authority in one or more of these fields. We have asked these authors to

summarize concrete achievements and the state of the art in their particular technology area, indicating where further developments will likely take place and the
achievements expected within the next five to ten years. We have also asked them
to identify the primary obstacles to progress—the areas in which focused research
efforts can be expected to make a significant difference. The result, we hope, is a
book that, like the first edition, will be valuable for years to come, both as a summary of where we are and as a road map for where we need to go to make Grids
a reality.

Structure and Content of This Book

As summarized in Table 1 we have divided this second edition into seven parts
comprising a total of 30 chapters. We lead off in Part I with three personal statements by influential thinkers on the significance of Grids, from the perspectives of
infrastructure, science, and industry, respectively. This material provides context
for Part II, which comprises a single scene-setting chapter that lays out central Grid
concepts and architectural principles upon which the rest of the material in the
book is based. Part III is concerned with applications. Building on the first edition's
discussion of compute-intensive, data-intensive, teleinstrumentation, and collaborative applications (Chapters 1:3–6, respectively), this edition's 12 application
vignettes each present a substantial application success story. Parts IV, V, and VI
expand upon the architectural presentation of Part II by providing detailed discussions of core architecture and services, data and knowledge management, and
higher-level tools, and Part VII addresses production Grid deployment, the computing platforms on which Grids are constructed, peer-to-peer technologies, and
network infrastructure.

As this brief preview indicates, this book covers a tremendous amount of
material, more than we expect most readers to handle in one sitting. Thus, we
have structured chapters so that each can be read in isolation, while also providing (through careful editing and numerous cross references) the structure that
ensures that the whole is indeed more than the sum of its parts.

Text Use

The book is designed to be used by the practicing professional or as a text for a
senior undergraduate- or graduate-level course in advanced networking, distributed computing, or Grids. In a quarter-length course, one lecture can be spent on

Section	Topic	Chapter
Perspectives	Grids in Context	1
	The Scientific Imperative	2
	The Industrial Imperative	3
Framework	Concepts and Architecture	4
Applications (brief "vignettes")	Predictive Maintenance: Distributed Aircraft Engine Diagnostics	5
	Distributed Telepresence: The NEESgrid Earthquake Engineering Collaboratory	6
	Scientific Data Federation: The World-Wide Telescope	7
	Medical Data Federation: The Biomedical Informatics Research Network	8
	Knowledge Integration: In Silico Experiments in Bioinformatics	9
	Distributed Data Analysis: Federated Computing for High-Energy Physics	10
	Massively Distributed Computing: Virtual Screening on Desktop Computers	11
	Enterprise Resource Management: Applications in Research and Industry	12
	Interactivity with Scalability: Infrastructure for Multiplayer Games	13
	Service Virtualization: Infrastructure and Applications	14
	Group-Oriented Collaboration: The Access Grid Collaboration System	15
	Collaborative Science: Astrophysics Requirements and Experiences	16
Architecture	The Open Grid Services Architecture	17
	Resource and Service Management	18
	Building Reliable Clients and Services	19
	Instrumentation and Monitoring	20
	Security for Virtual Organizations: Federating Trust and Policy Domains	21
Data and Knowledge	Data Access, Integration, and Management	22
	Enhancing Services and Applications with Knowledge and Semantics	23
Tools	Application-Level Tools	24
	Languages, Compilers, and Runtime Systems	25
	Application Tuning and Adaptation	26
Infrastructure	Production Deployment: Experiences and Recommendations	27
	Computing Elements	28
	Peer-to-Peer Technologies	29
	Network Infrastructure	30

1 Book Structure

TABLE

each chapter, and a project may be assigned based on one of the Grid programming systems described in the book. In a semester-length course, some topics can be covered in greater depth. Each chapter includes recommendations for further reading.

In addition, we maintain a Web site that provides pointers to relevant Web resources, including online documents and information about projects described in the book. The URL for this Web site is *www.mkp.com/grid2*. Questions or comments about this book or the Web site should be directed to the book's general editors at *Gridbook@globus.org*.

Acknowledgments

It is with great pleasure that we acknowledge the efforts of the many people who have contributed to the development of this book. First and foremost, we thank the contributors, who despite busy schedules devoted much effort to planning the book, writing their chapters, and responding to numerous comments and suggestions from the editors and reviewers. In addition to the distinguished authors from the first edition, most of whom also contribute here, we welcome new contributors from many countries (the Grid is truly an international undertaking) and from industry.

We also thank the many colleagues and supporters who have contributed to the progress that we report in this second edition. Here, our acknowledgments must unfortunately be far from complete. However, we must certainly recognize the visionary and dedicated government program managers who funded early research and development work that has made Grid computing possible: notably, Mary Anne Scott and Tom Kitchens at the U.S. Department of Energy Office of Science; Gary Koob at DARPA; Alan Blatecky, Frederica Darema, Dick Hilderbrandt, and Rich Hirsh at the National Science Foundation; Kyriakos Baxevanidis at the European Union; and Tony Hey and John Taylor in the UK eScience programme. We also thank the pioneers who have adopted, applied, promoted, or otherwise advanced the work: David Abramson, Malcolm Atkinson, Paul Avery, Fran Berman, Charlie Catlett, Tom DeFanti, Bill Feireisen, Fabrizio Gagliardi, Lennart Johnsson, Bill Johnston, Ken Kennedy, Miron Livny, Satoshi Matsuoka, Mirco Mazzucato, Paul Messina, Jeff Nick, Dan Reed, Ed Seidel, Satoshi Sekiguchi, Larry Smarr, Rick Stevens, and Irving Wladawsky-Berger, to name just a few. And last but not least, this work would not have been possible without the support of our colleagues at Argonne National Laboratory, the University of Chicago, and the University of Southern California's Information Sciences Institute.

Finally, we gratefully acknowledge the expert help we received during the preparation of the manuscript. Gail Pieper of Argonne National Laboratory once again provided invaluable editing assistance, working far beyond the call of duty to enable us to submit a high-quality manuscript. Julie Wulf-Knoerzer of Argonne handled many aspects of the manuscript production process in her usual efficient manner. Also, as was the case with the first edition, we have been fortunate to work closely with an outstanding team at Morgan Kaufmann Publishers. Denise Penrose, Emilia Thiuri, Alyson Day, Angela Dooley, and the rest of the team at Morgan Kaufmann Publishers were everything we could want from a publisher: professional, efficient, and a delight to work with.

Ian Foster and Carl Kesselman

PERSPECTIVES

PART I

Why is the Grid important? We asked some distinguished thinkers to provide us with their perspectives on this question, and their thoughtful responses form the first section of this book.

Larry Smarr, in his chapter "Grids in Context," analyzes the emergence of the Grid as a new infrastructure. He compares Grids with other major infrastructures, such as the railroad, using historical analogies to provide perspectives on both the complexity of such developments and the widespread impact of the associated changes. He also considers how individuals and groups working in computational science and engineering, experimental and observational science, industrial engineering, and corporate communications can use the Grid today to solve immediate and urgent problems.

Fran Berman and Tony Hey speak to "The Scientific Imperative" in Chapter 2, reviewing the revolutionary changes in technology and methodology driving scientific and engineering communities to embrace Grid technologies. They discuss the challenging and interrelated demands of data-, compute-, and instrumentation-intensive science and also the increased importance of large-scale collaboration. They also outline the ambitious new government programs being created to support these new approaches, and thereby the scientific breakthroughs of the twenty-first century.

Irving Wladawsky-Berger addresses "The Industrial Imperative" in Chapter 3, explaining by analogy and analysis how advances in computing technology are driving an unprecedented integration of technologies, applications, and data that enable global resource sharing beyond what has been possible with the Web alone. He introduces the important concepts of virtualization and on-demand access, and argues that these and other concepts enabled by the Grid are driving information technology infrastructure into a "post-technology" phase in which it has become so ubiquitous as to be invisible.

Grids in Context

Larry Smarr

*T*his second edition of *The Grid* marks a major turning point in the evolution of the Grid concept. The notion of linking people, computers, sensors, and data with networks is decades old, and we have seen increasingly sophisticated Grid applications in recent years. However, here we have for the first time a coherent description of the hardware, software, and applications required to create a functioning and persistent Grid.

For the Grid to be successful, we must consider not only technologies but also the *social aspects* of what will induce researchers, educators, businesses, and consumers to use the Grid as an everyday part of their work. One approach is to study the development of previous infrastructures, such as railroads and the electrical power distribution system, for clues as to how they were jump-started. Another approach is to envision how diverse subgroups of our society would benefit from the Grid and how people would change their working environment as a result of the new enabling technologies. I briefly pursue both approaches in this chapter.

1.1   LESSONS FROM HISTORY

To understand the future of the Grid, it helps to study the history of other infrastructures. The Corporation for National Research Initiatives has specifically considered the development of infrastructures for railroads, telephones and telegraphs, power and light, and banking (293–296). These are a few examples of infrastructures that are distributed, have different end-user devices and intermediate reservoirs, and have created hundreds of billions of dollars in today's world market. Without such infrastructures, life as we know it would be impossible. As we study these infrastructures, which are all quite different on the surface, we begin to notice that they have in common a number of striking features.

The evolution of each infrastructure was incredibly complicated. There is no simple story of how each came into being; indeed, there is a good deal of disagreement on the historical details. However, one point is clear: these infrastructures did not come into being just because a bunch of researchers got together and thought it would be a cool thing to do. Private market forces and the government played fundamental roles, as did invention, research, and standardization. These infrastructures had an important local/global ordering to their time development that is not necessarily apparent, but was critical to the dynamics. When these infrastructures started, almost all traffic was local. For instance, there were robust city telephone systems, but long distance was rare. County roads were prevalent for many decades before the interstate highway system was started in the mid-1950s.

Also critical is a distribution of capacity throughout the infrastructure. When we think of the physical distribution of goods, there are local warehouses, regional warehouses, and national warehouses to enable efficient just-in-time resupply. This distributed system can work only because of the regional "caching" or storing of physical goods. The same is true, for example, in the national electrical distribution system, which ranges from huge-capacity cables leaving dams and nuclear reactors, to cross-country power lines, to local neighborhood lines, to the 110-V lines in private homes.

Such a capacity distribution is already becoming apparent in the developing Grid. In the United States, the Extensible Terascale Facility (ETF) is a good example, with five supernodes at the National Center for Supercomputing Applications (NCSA), the San Diego Supercomputer Center (SDSC), the Pittsburgh Supercomputing Center, Argonne National Laboratory, and the California Institute of Technology, with plans to extend it to a broad range of regional centers, hosting medium-sized nodes with capacity and functions integrated across the ETF by a common Grid middleware infrastructure. Networking capacity is also distributed, or hierarchical—with a 40 gigabit/sec network connecting major supercomputer centers, while the average person is using 50 kilobit/sec over a dial-up modem—a span of almost one million-fold in bandwidth. Similar structures are found within the UK, EU, Japanese, Chinese, and other national Grids. Such distributed differential capacity is characteristic of many of these other infrastructures.

Grids are almost fractal in nature: we need only to look at the billions of appliances in homes worldwide and work upward to the nuclear power generators. Grids are not flat.

1.1.1   Why Is There Chicago?

We tend to think of the world into which we were born as the way it always was, yet history reveals that this is not the case. Much of the development of societal structures is bound up with the development of infrastructure. A fascinating book on this topic is *Nature's Metropolis: Chicago and the Great West* (1992), written by William Cronon, a professor of history at Yale University. Cronon is a quantitative historian— a historian who takes data from shipping records, land sales, and so forth and reconstructs what actually happened. The issue he addresses is "Why is there Chicago?"

Chicago is an artifact of the emergence of infrastructure. Until the early 1800s, Chicago was a small field of onions on a very large lake with a lot of mosquitoes. The development of the modern metropolis of Chicago is a microstudy in the phenomenal story of how the emergence of railroads, enabling the movement of physical goods around the country, completely changed the United States in a few short decades. Cronon emphasizes that we cannot study the development of Chicago in isolation; rather, we must take a national viewpoint to capture the scale of the phenomenon. Specifically, Chicago can be understood only by considering the total transformation of the West.

Just as is happening in Brazil today, the native ecosystems of the center of the United States were rapidly annihilated and replaced by artificial ones in the last half of the nineteenth century. Bison were killed and replaced by cattle. The prairie was destroyed and replaced by monoculture agriculture (wheat or corn). The northern forests were destroyed to provide wood to build homes on the prairie where there were no trees. Cronon points out that none of this could have happened had it not been for the new railroad transportation infrastructure that allowed for goods to be shipped from deep inland to markets far away.

The Great Lakes and the rivers were the previous transportation infrastructure. St. Louis was the dominant midwestern city for a long time before Chicago came into existence. Yet as the railroads emerged and linked with the Great Lakes lines, Chicago grew much more rapidly than St. Louis did. Chicago emerged first of all as an intermediate "cache" for agricultural products. Before then, each farmer would grow his or her own corn, take bags on a wagon to a levee in St. Louis, and sell the bags individually. Chicago enabled farmers to pool their corn into a common elevator.

This fundamental change of pooling and "caching" mixed-origin grain allowed for new groups of middle people who bought and sold goods that they had not grown themselves. Financial institutions, such as the Chicago Board of Trade, came into being because a new class of financial instruments and interactions was required. Stockyards arose for the same "caching" purpose, but with livestock instead of grain. Inventions of "Grid technology" like the refrigerated railroad car, without which meat would spoil before it got from the Chicago stockyards to the eastern consumers, allowed meat for the first time to be sold far from where the livestock was raised or butchered.

The new "middleware" infrastructure enabled the creation of new industries that were not anticipated and not derivative. For example, Chicago quickly became one of the great retailing centers of the world. Today, Chicago hosts the largest number of corporate headquarters outside New York City. Chicago has the world's second busiest airport, which emerged out of the rise of the air transport infrastructure. If there was ever an example of a city that came into existence as a result of the emergence of infrastructure, it is Chicago.

1.1.2   Why Is There Champaign–Urbana?

Champaign-Urbana, located in east central Illinois, had an analogous history. One-hundred and fifty years after the laying of the railroad tracks through Champaign County, we can find the living reminders of the social impact of the railroad infrastructure. Across Champaign County, a number of small towns are strung along the railroad track: Homer, Sydney, Philo, Tolono, Savoy, St. Joseph, Thomasboro, Rantoul, and Mahomet, each located where the grain elevators were built as grain "caches" along the railroad track. Their spacing was set by a one-day's wagon drive to bring corn to the grain elevator.

And how did Champaign-Urbana come into being? Urbana townspeople and the Illinois Central could not agree on a price for the railroad station, so the railroad simply built its station a few miles to the west of Urbana and went on south. That railroad station grew into Champaign. Today a number of shipping companies locate in Champaign–Urbana because it is on the intersection of two major east–west and north–south interstate highways. Again and again, when we look through the "lens" of infrastructure development, we understand just how powerful a social force it is.

1.2   THE GRID ON STEROIDS

We see that infrastructure has serious social consequences. Grids are going to have a similar revolutionary effect as railroads. However, instead of waiting 30 or 40 years to see the changes brought about by this infrastructure, we are seeing the changes much faster. It is not clear that people are sociologically ready to deal with this rate of change.

The world's computer and communications infrastructure is driven by exponentials: it's on steroids. Every aspect—the microprocessor, bandwidth and fiber, disk storage—is all on exponentials, a situation that has never happened before in the history of infrastructure. For example, NCSA's first Cray X-MP, purchased in 1986, cost $8 million, had its own electrical line to the Illinois Power substation, had special cooling, and had absolutely no graphics. It was connected to other supercomputers by the first National Science Foundation (NSF) network backbone with a capacity of only 56 kilobit/sec. A child's video game, such as a Microsoft Xbox, has an MIPS microprocessor with roughly 20 times the compute power of an X-MP processor and has a list price of $200. It uses 250 W, instead of 60,000. It has incredibly interactive three-dimensional graphics. Those who have 500 kilobit/sec DSL in their homes have more computer power and bandwidth than did all five NSF supercomputer centers put together only 17 years ago.

This situation is not like the railroads. It is not like anything in history. So, while we look back on history to get some guiding principles, we need to be a little humble in the face of what we are launching. Grids are going to change the world so quickly that we are not going to have much of a chance—on a human, political, or social time scale—to react and change our institutions. Therefore, there will be a lot of noise, a lot of angry people, and a lot of controversy.

1.3   FROM NETWORKS TO THE GRID

ARPANET, the precursor of the Internet, which forms backbone for the emerging information Grid, started in the early 1970s. ARPANET was an experimental network used by a few computer scientists and the Department of Defense (DoD) community. It developed critically important protocols such as TCP/IP and the notion of packet switching (analogous to the standardization of the electrical power distribution industry on AC versus DC). Various production and research networks evolved from this beginning. One of these was NSFNET, created in 1986 with a 56 kilobit/sec backbone that tied together the five (then new) NSF supercomputer centers. The backbone bandwidth of 56 kilobit/sec was upgraded to 1.5 megabit/sec, and then to 45 megabit/sec during the late 1980s and early 1990s. In 1995 the NSF transferred NSFNET to the commercial sector, which evolved it into today's Internet.

The Internet could never have arisen so quickly had it not been for the federal government funding 100% of the NSFNET backbone, partially funding the regionals, and occasionally funding the academic networking efforts. Within five years, however, the total funding by everybody else involved in the Internet was probably a hundred times more than the federal government's initial investment. (How this worked in the case of railroads is still controversial, but the federal funding for the land ultimately turned out to be a fairly small percentage of the private funding (293).) Thus, I believe that the federal government has a critical role in bringing today's Grid into being.

Similarly, high-performance Grids will not spring into being just by waiting for private industry to do it. In 2002, NSF funded the creation of the TeraGrid, which links five major supercomputing sites with a 40-gigabit/sec dedicated optical network. With its Extensible Terascale Facility program, it is now looking to expand this new infrastructure to other research institutions. Major projects are also under way in Europe and Asia-Pacific to establish the necessary network and computational infrastructure. The cycle of initial government funding leading to a new set of commercial services has started again.

1.4   WHO WILL USE THE GRID?

We cannot assume that the Grid we are building is just going to work and instantly fill with users. We cannot make a *Field of Dreams* assumption: Build it and they will come. If nobody shows up to use it, the Grid is going to be a failure. People will use it only because they want to communicate with resources or people that they care about and need to do their work. This is an example of the local/global phenomenon mentioned in regard to previous infrastructures.

We must stimulate the use of the Grid by applications researchers, drawn from both computational science and experimental and observational science, as well as educators and visionary corporations. We must find groups of people who are globally or nationally dispersed but who have a preexisting need to interact with each other or remote resources—and are totally committed to doing so over the Grid. Their use of the Grid from the beginning will greatly shorten the time it takes for this new infrastructure to develop. If we rely on natural evolution, as witnessed by the other major infrastructures, we will wait decades for new capabilities to appear.

Computational scientists and engineers need the Grid.   Computational scientists and engineers would like to visualize their applications in real time and, for many applications, steer or navigate the computation as well. It is still common practice for computational scientists to transfer the results of complex simulations by shipping tapes—and as a result, it can take days from when a simulation starts to when an error is detected. This is unacceptable. Many other researchers just cannot get access to enough computational horsepower. They need the ability to reach out across the Grid to remote computers.

Experimental scientists need the Grid.   It is important to remember that for every theoretical or computational scientist, there are 10 experimental and observational scientists. If we wish to generally influence science, we need to influence experimental and observational science. Experimental scientists want to hook up their remote instrumentation to supercomputers or to advanced visualization devices, and to use advanced user interfaces, such as Java or voice command for instrumental functions. Thus, for example, brain surgeons in Chicago could control MRI machines in Urbana and collaborate with colleagues in San Francisco while viewing and manipulating the data in real time in three dimensions.

The Berkeley–Illinois–Maryland Radio Telescope Array (BIMA), the fastest millimeter radio telescope array in the world, is located in the high desert of northern California. It is a beautiful region but quite remote from research universities. BIMA uses networks to send data to NCSA supercomputers, which effectively become the computational "lens" of this telescope. Because BIMA is an aperture synthesis telescope, the phase shifts of the radio waves coming in arrive slightly differently at each of the antennas, and a supercomputer is needed to reconstruct what the original object in the sky must have looked like. The telescope takes 1000 two-dimensional images of the sky at one time at different wavelengths, and the computer produces data cubes from them (two dimensions of space and one dimension of frequency). These visualizations can be used, in turn, to steer the instrument or to create a digital library on the fly, which people can look at remotely through Web browsers. This is a perfect example of the type of science that we would like to be able to do at much higher bandwidth, with much more robust software for a broad range of scientific instruments.

Corporations need the Grid.   Most large corporations today are global in extent. While the Web has allowed for corporate intranets to arise, these are still fairly primitive in terms of the types of functionality this book discusses. For example, in the 1990s NCSA worked for several years with Caterpillar on the development of virtual environments to support virtual prototyping. Linking to computer-aided design files that define new heavy earth-moving equipment, Caterpillar has moved from standard computer graphics to heads-up displays to single stereo walls to full CAVE virtual worlds. Caterpillar prototyped teleimmersion with multiple sites, including some internationally. They have suppliers, manufacturers, and customers spread out all over the world and could imagine linking these people over the Grid.

Allstate Insurance, another NCSA industrial partner, has explored using high-speed networks to link its Menlo Park research lab with the data-mining activities going on at NCSA, where large-claims datasets reside on high-performance computers. Such a link would allow for new types of pattern recognition using a total corporate database approach. Given that Allstate has 15,000 claims offices, it imagines using Grid capabilities to unite the company into a single collaborative team. Similar stories will arise for almost any large corporation.

The environment needs the Grid.   Although society is becoming politically ready to deal with large-scale environmental problems such as ozone depletion, global warming, and air and water pollution, researchers are lagging in creating trusted interactive knowledge bases that integrate all known science about these issues. Given the multidisciplinary nature of such problems, it is clear that to gather all the experts needed to study the problem, we will need the Grid.

For example, the dominant environmental threat to the Chesapeake Bay system has moved from industrial pollution to agricultural runoff. Farmers put fertilizer on their fields, which runs off in the spring into the rivers, which feeds large algae blooms, which later produce massive decaying organic masses near the bottom, which ultimately reduce the dissolved oxygen for the shellfish. This is a dynamic, nonlinear, highly coupled, multitimescale, and multispacescale multidisciplinary problem, and the only possible way to deal with it scientifically is computationally. In fact, researchers should be able to work in a collaborative computational framework that links researchers and remote sensors with the Grid, allowing for the integration of much more detailed models of chemical, biological, and physical effects and the testing of the model against field data.

Training and education need the Grid.   One of the first applications of Grid technologies will be in remote training and education. Imagine the productivity gains if we had routine access to virtual lecture rooms! Currently, we often must spend several days flying across the country to deliver a lecture using an antiquated viewgraph projector in a meeting room with only 20 people in the audience. What if we were able to walk up to a local "power wall" and give a lecture fully electronically in a virtual environment with interactive Web materials to an audience gathered from around the country—and then simply walk back to the office instead of going back to a hotel or an airplane?

Given the rapid rate at which K–12 schools are joining community colleges and universities online, it will not be long before some of the more advanced schools begin to use these Grid technologies. The question is not how we use these technologies to redo classic education but what new types of collaborative education will arise using a national-scale Grid? Informal social experiments that show how easily children can work together over the Internet are being run today with shared virtual world games, such as "Quake." The immersive game world has exploded (see Chapter 13). Children may teach us more about collaboration than we learn from university research scientists!

Nations and states need the Grid. Many countries are installing dedicated fiber or "lambda" networks internally, as if the rest of the world were not there. Within the United States, for example, states are installing "dark" fiber networks without regard for the rest of the country. As discussed previously, that is how infrastructure developments start—locally. As these regional "Tera POPs" and national and state dark fiber networks come online, the next question is "Can we interconnect them?" In the early days of the railroad, a number of different track gauges were adopted. When the train tracks extended from their local strongholds, trains could not pass from one system to another. People who are part of the statewide University of California system can interact at high speed with one another today over experimental fiber networks because they are linked institutionally by CENIC. However, what if they need to interact with researchers across the country using experimental networks? This is one of the first capabilities that a continental-scale LambdaGrid will bring to university researchers.

Of course, the Grid will rapidly evolve from research into the private sector. Already, massive networks linking supplier chains are being constructed in industries such as automobile manufacturing, and wireless extensions using RFID tags are exploding. Electronic commerce is just beginning to take off, and eliminating "speed bumps" from one state to the other will be essential for the free flow of information on which commerce is based.

The world needs the Grid. Naturally, Grid development will not stop at national boundaries. Recent proposals have advocated that goods traded over the Internet should be made tax and tariff free. Such a situation could radically change the patterns of world trade over the next few decades. Thus, there is great interest internationally in bringing advanced Grid technologies to all countries. NSF initiatives such as STAR-TAP and StarLight are facilitating the long-term interconnection and interoperability of advanced international networking in support of applications, performance measuring, and technology evaluations, while bodies such as the Global Grid Forum are establishing connections at the levels of protocols and software.

Consumers need the Grid. The functions described previously will all gradually move down the exponential to the consumer. Already we can enter virtual stores, click on merchandise, and find information about various items. Soon we will be able to click on "Sales Help" to have a live streaming video of a store person come up on our screen, from anywhere in the country. Serious research is under way on personal avatars that, given personal measurements, can try on clothes (on a three-dimensional computer screen) to help a customer decide whether to buy an item.

1.5   SUMMARY

All the projects described in this chapter are under development and will come together as part of the Grid projects described in this book. The Grid, however, will require that we adopt new ways of working. The Grid is about collaboration, about working together. Fortunately, there is a whole new set of information technologies that come from the Web and from companies building tools to enable us to work together in collaborative online spaces. Old technologies such as proprietary video teleconferencing are giving way to open-system versions linked over the Internet, surrounded by white boards, interactive software, and recording capabilities.

More advanced efforts tailored to the needs of researchers also are under way, such as the Access Grid technology developed at Argonne National Laboratory. This technology enables shared collaborative spaces. A Web site allows all Access Grid software developers or users to interact with each other via hypernews, application galleries, and shared programs. This new approach to creating a virtual community of software developers working on a common software system (in this case, the Access Grid libraries) allows all participants to work together regardless of place. Presumably participants in these virtual communities can have a rate of progress far greater than by working in isolation.

As the new Grid technologies come into widespread use, we must shift our social patterns of interaction and our reward structure so that we can realize the potential gains from the nonlinear advancements that collaboration will create. Collaboration can be an almost magical amplifier for human work. The success of the Grid will both enable and depend on this amplification.

The Scientific Imperative

Fran Berman and Tony Hey

*L*ike many significant concepts and technologies that we now take for granted, Grid ideas have been inspired by, and were first applied to, problems faced by researchers tackling fundamental problems in science and engineering. Building on ideas first expounded in the 1960s and given concrete form by Grid pioneers in the 1990s, the scientific community continues to lead the development of Grid technologies and is now poised to leverage those technologies to create a computational and data management infrastructure that will act as a key enabler for twenty-first-century science and society.

The origins of the idea of a "Grid" to support scientific research can be traced back to the Internet pioneer J. C. R. Licklider. Licklider began his career as an experimental psychologist studying "psychoacoustics"—how the human ear and brain convert air vibrations into the perception of sound. In the 1950s, he was a human factors researcher on the famous SAGE project at MIT: an air defense system designed to use real-time information on Soviet bombers. As a result of this experience, Licklider wrote a groundbreaking paper (441) in which he argued that computers should be developed:

> [T]o enable men and computers to cooperate in making decisions and controlling complex situations without inflexible dependence on predetermined programs. (441)

In 1962 Licklider was asked to head up two ARPA departments, Behavioral Sciences and Command and Control. He brought to ARPA a vision of a future computer network that was inspired by an analysis of the large amount of time he spent in organizing and manipulating experimental data in his research. Licklider described his hypothetical network in the following terms:

> If such a network as I envisage nebulously could be brought into operation, we could have at least four large computers, perhaps six or eight small computers, and a great assortment of disc files and magnetic tape units—not to mention remote consoles and teletype stations—all churning away. (669)

Lacking the means to implement this vision, he awarded contracts to some leading embryonic computer science research institutions—including Stanford, UCLA, MIT, and Berkeley—to work on the problem. Licklider called this group his "Intergalactic Computer Network," and these researchers later formed the core of the team that would implement the ARPANET. By then, Licklider had left ARPA, and it was left to his successors to realize his vision. Larry Roberts, the principal ARPANET architect, recalled the importance of Licklider's ideas:

> Lick had this concept of the intergalactic network which he believed was everybody could use computers anywhere and get at data anywhere in the world. He didn't envision the number of computers we have today by any means, but he had the same concept—all of the stuff linked together throughout the world, that you can use a remote computer, get data from a remote computer, or use lots of computers in your job. The vision was really Lick's originally. None of us can really claim to have seen that before him nor [can] anybody in the world. Lick saw this vision in the early sixties. He didn't have a clue how to build it. He didn't have any idea how to make this happen. But he knew it was important, so he sat down with me and really convinced me that it was important and convinced me into making it happen. (559, p. 40)

Since the early days of the ARPANET much has changed. The Internet has become a reality, and e-mail and Web browsers have emerged as killer applications. Moore's law has prevailed for more than 30 years, with the result that computers are no longer scarce, expensive resources. Nonetheless, Licklider's vision of a global network of computers and data resources that can be accessed seamlessly from anywhere in the world remains valid. The Grid is our latest and most promising attempt to realize Licklider's vision.

In the rest of this chapter, we review some of the novel scientific problem-solving methodologies that make the large-scale development, deployment, and application of the Grid critical for future science—and that will, we believe, drive the development of the Grid to the next level.

2.1   NEW MODES OF SCIENTIFIC INQUIRY

Continued exponential technology improvements, new collaborative modalities enabled by the quasi-ubiquitous Internet, and the demands of increasingly complex problems have, over recent decades, fueled a revolution in the practice of science and engineering. Today's science is as much based on large-scale numerical simulation, data analysis, and collaboration as it is on the efforts of individual experimentalists and theorists. We review in broad strokes some of the new modes of inquiry that increasingly define twenty-first-century science and engineering.

2.1.1   Data-Intensive Science

Dramatic improvements in the capability and capacity of sensors, storage systems, computers, and networks are enabling the creation of data archives of enormous size and value. Multipetabyte (10^{15} bytes) archives will soon be in place in fields as diverse as astronomy, biology, medicine, the environment, engineering, and high-energy physics (359). Analysis of these vast quantities of data can yield profound new insights into the nature of matter, life, the environment, or other aspects of the physical world.

The sources of these large quantities of data span a wide spectrum. At one extreme, we have individual, highly specialized, and expensive scientific devices that generate large quantities of data at a single location. For example, the worldwide particle physics community is planning an ambitious set of experiments at the Large Hadron Collider (LHC) experimental facility under construction at CERN in Geneva. The goal of this work is to find signs of the Higgs boson, key to the generation of mass for both the vector bosons and the fermions of the standard model of weak and electromagnetic interactions. Particle physicists are also hoping for indications of other new types of matter—such as supersymmetric particles—that may shed light on the "dark matter" problem of cosmology. These LHC experiments are on a scale never before seen in physics, with each experiment involving a collaboration of hundreds of institutions and over 5,000 physicists around the globe.

When operational in 2007, each of the four LHC experiments will generate several petabytes of experimental data per year. This vast amount of data needs to be preprocessed and distributed for further analysis by all members of the consortia to search for signals betraying the presence of the Higgs boson or other surprises. The physicists need to put in place an LHC Grid infrastructure (see Chapter 10) that will permit the transport and data mining of extremely large and distributed datasets. The creation of this infrastructure is being pursued in collaboration with major Grid projects in the United States (NSF Grid Physics Network (93), DOE Particle Physics Data Grid (30), NSF International Virtual Data Grid Laboratory (94)) and Europe (the EU DataGrid project (12) and national Grid projects such as the UK GridPP, Italian INFN Grid, and NorduGrid). The importance of transoceanic bandwidth is recognized via the EU-funded DataTAG project (36) for trans-Atlantic networks and the U.S.-funded STAR-TAP and StarLight (43) international interconnection point.

Another vitally important source of vast quantities of data is the monitoring of industrial equipment. For example, pressure, temperature, and vibration sensors in each of the many thousands of Rolls-Royce engines currently in service generate about a gigabyte of data per engine on each trans-Atlantic flight, which translates to petabytes of data per year. The UK e-Science Distributed Aircraft Maintenance Environment project (Chapter 5) is working to aggregate these data so that they can be mined to detect indications of potential problems. The goal is to transmit a subset of the primary data for analysis and comparison with engine data stored in one of several data centers located around the world. By identifying the early onset of problems, Rolls-Royce hopes to be able to lengthen the period between scheduled maintenance periods, thus increasing profitability. Decisions need to be taken in real time as to how much of the petabytes of data to analyze, how much to transmit for further analysis, and how much to archive.

Similar (or larger) data volumes are being generated by other high-throughput sensors in fields as varied as environmental and earth observation, astronomy, and human health-care monitoring. For example, in astronomy, individual "digital sky surveys" are creating data archives that will scale from a maximum of 10 terabytes today to petabytes within the decade (619). It is estimated that the U.S. National Virtual Observatory project alone will store 500 terabytes per year from 2004 (21). Similarly, the Laser Interferometer Gravitational Observatory project is estimated to generate 250 terabytes per year beginning in 2002 (98). A new generation of astronomical surveys such as the VISTA project in the visible and infrared regions (46) will also contribute to the transformation of the data requirements of the astronomy community. The VISTA telescope will be operational in 2004 and will generate 250 gigabytes of raw data per night and around 10 terabytes of stored data per year. There will be several petabytes of data in the VISTA archive within 10 years. Although these data volumes are impressive, what has astronomers really excited is the prospect of federating many such archives to create a uniformly accessible, globally distributed repository of astronomical data spanning all wavelengths, from radio waves to X-rays. As discussed in Chapter 7, the worldwide astronomy community is working to create such a globally distributed, multiwavelength "virtual observatory." At present, astronomical data using different wavelengths are captured by different telescopes and stored in a variety of formats. The creation of such a multiwavelength "data warehouse" for astronomical data will enable new types of astrophysical studies.

Similar opportunities beckon in medicine, where all-digital scanning technologies are allowing mammograms, MRI scans, and other medical images to be stored online rather than in film libraries. Multiterabyte databases being assembled within hospitals and research laboratories are making it far easier to compare images both across time for individuals and across populations. The linking of these databases with advanced analytical tools offers the potential for automated diagnosis in support of the individual physician, while the federation of multiple databases—potentially on a national or international scale—promises to enable epidemiological studies of unprecedented scope and scale that will provide new insights into the impact of environment and life cycle on disease.

The UK e-Diamond project is one project working to exploit these opportunities. Others include the Biomedical Informatics Research Network, discussed in Chapter 8; the U.S. National Digital Mammography Archive; and the EU MammoGrid. e-Diamond brings together medical image analysis expertise from Mirada Solutions Ltd and the MIAS Interdisciplinary Research Collaboration, computer science expertise from IBM and the Oxford e-Science Centre, and clinical expertise from hospitals in London, Oxford, and Scotland. The goal is to provide an exemplar of the dynamic, best-evidence-based approach to diagnosis and treatment made possible through a Grid middleware infrastructure. The scope of the project is broad, embracing not only distributed data management and analysis but also ontologies and metadata to describe both the physics underpinning the imaging process and the key features within images, as well as the capture of relevant demographic and clinical information. Technologies for data compression and data transfer that allow rapid data mining of the resulting large, federated databases of both metadata and images are also a key research area. Security and privacy are of paramount importance, and any Grid infrastructure must be able to combine databases of information based in hospitals protected by firewalls. The creation of such a large federated database of annotated, digitized, and standardized mammograms will provide the basis for new applications in teaching, aiding detection, and aiding diagnosis that will be developed as part of the project.

2.1.2   Simulation-Based Science

Numerical simulation represents another new problem-solving methodology in its own right, which continues to grow in importance (404). The extensive use of supercomputers (an important class of "central power plant" in a scientific Grid) has of course long been fundamental to scientific disciplines such as climatology and astrophysics in which physical experiments cannot easily be performed but computational simulations are feasible.

Indeed, ultrafast supercomputers have emerged as an important class of "extreme scientific instrumentation." For example, the Japanese Earth Simulator was in 2003 running numerical simulations of Earth's climate at a sustained rate of 40 teraflop/sec, allowing simulations to be performed at an unprecedented 10-km horizontal resolution and generating many tens of terabytes of data in a single run. Other extremely capable systems are being operated by the U.S. ASCI program, DOE and NSF supercomputer centers in the United States, and super-computer centers in Europe and elsewhere.

These tremendous investments in high-end supercomputers are just one indication of a broad phenomenon, which is that as a result of advances in computer performance and computational techniques, computational approaches are increasingly being applied even in fields long dominated by experiment. For example, in chemistry, combinatorial methods provide new opportunities for the generation, via computation rather than experiment, of large amounts of new chemical knowledge. The UK Comb-*e*-Chem project (5) is illustrative of what is being done to exploit this opportunity. The goal of this project is to "synthesize" large numbers of new compounds by high-throughput combinatorial methods and then map their structure and properties. Such a parallel synthetic approach creates hundreds of thousands of new compounds at a time, leading to an explosive growth in the volume of data generated. Each new compound needs to be screened for potential usefulness, and properties and structure must be identified and recorded for promising candidates. Thus, an extensive range of primary data needs to be accumulated, integrated with information in existing databases, and enhanced with accurate models of the various relationships and properties. Comb-*e*-Chem is developing an integrated platform that combines existing structure and property data sources within a Grid-based information- and knowledge-sharing environment.

Similar transformations are occurring in the life sciences, as illustrated by the U.S. Encyclopedia of Life (EOL) project, which seeks to produce a database of putative functional and 3D structure assignments for *all* known publicly available complete or partial genomes. Considerable computational capacity is required to update data as new genome sequences become available. This computation converts the rather sparse information contained in the linear sequence of DNA bases into human-readable information that can be inferred by conversion to the amino acid sequence. Each genome must be subjected to a computation that is built up from loosely structured workflow, with analysis performed by a collection of algorithms that build on information in the EOL database.

2.1.3   Remote Access to Experimental Apparatus

The increasing prominence of simulation- and data-driven science does not mean that experimental science has become less important. On the contrary: the advance of technology is also producing revolutionary new experimental apparatus, and the emergence of high-speed networks makes it feasible to integrate those apparatus into the scientific problem-solving process in ways not previously conceivable.

Thus, for example, we see the earthquake engineering community deploying telepresence capabilities that allow remote participants to design, execute, and monitor experiments without traveling to experimental facilities. As described in Chapter 6, the National Science Foundation's George E. Brown Jr. Network for Earthquake Engineering Simulation (NEES) is an ambitious national program whose purpose is to advance the study of earthquake engineering and to find new ways to reduce the hazard earthquakes represent to life and property. Its goal is to encourage the use of both physical and numerical simulation to develop increasingly complex, comprehensive, and accurate models of how the built infrastructure responds to earthquake loadings. NEESgrid is integrating and deploying Grid technologies to link earthquake engineering researchers across the United States with shared engineering research equipment, data resources, and leading-edge computing resources. The NEESgrid middleware infrastructure allows collaborative teams (including remote participants) to plan, perform experiments, and publish and share their data and results. Collaborative tools aid in experiment planning and allow engineers at remote sites to perform teleobservation and teleoperation of experiments, and enable access to computational resources and open source analytical tools for simulation and analysis of experimental data. The middleware also supports the publishing of results in a curated data repository using standard data and metadata vocabularies and formats.

Similar technologies have been applied successfully for some time to the remote operation of specialized scientific instrumentation (345, 393, 622) (see Chapter 1:4). Grid technologies introduce the possibility of making these specialized usage scenarios routine.

2.2   VIRTUAL COMMUNITY SCIENCE

We have introduced some of the new modes of inquiry enabled by flexible and pervasive access to massive amounts of data, large amounts of computation, and specialized experimental apparatus. Equally important to twenty-first-century science and engineering is the increasingly collaborative and distributed nature of the teams that form to exploit this potential. Indeed, as the NEES example shows, the collaborative nature of science is in many respects inseparable from new capabilities. The most significant impact of Grid technologies on science may be global virtual communities of scientists able to address the fundamental problems of today and tomorrow.

In data-driven science, the high scientific value of large data archives means that they are, increasingly, viewed as major strategic assets by their user communities, who devote considerable effort to establishing, managing, controlling, and exploiting those archives. Similar to the Encyclopedia of Life project mentioned previously, the UK eScience ^{my}Grid project (Chapter 9) is working to design, develop, and demonstrate higher-level Grid middleware to support the use of complex distributed resources for bioinformatics, with specific applications being the analysis of functional genomic data and the annotation of a pattern database. The ^{my}Grid project is developing an e-Scientist's workbench to support experimental investigation, evidence accumulation, and result assimilation. The goal is to help scientists use community information (e.g., "gray literature") and enhance scientific collaboration by assisting the formation of dynamic groupings to tackle emergent research problems. Personalization facilities relating to resource selection, data management, and process enactment allow for the dynamic creation of personal datasets and personal views over repositories, as well as the addition of personal annotations to datasets and a personalized notification service about changes in relevant databases. The ^{my}Grid project is also developing tools and techniques to support the creation of personalized workflows that capture the biologist's know-how and enable reuse of patterns of knowledge discovery. These services can also associate base resources with the derived data, an aspect of the important area of provenance (Chapter 22). The project is developing mechanisms to track the creation of knowledge, to automate the association of metadata with the production of primary experimental data, and to develop ontologies (Chapter 23) to enable automated reasoning about information from different communities.

Similar observations can be made of large-scale experimental and simulation science: increasingly large teams devote considerable effort to establishing and operating diverse apparatus, such as particle accelerators and climate simulation codes. This trend shows no signs of slowing. For example, both the fusion and high-energy physics communities are planning future experimental facilities of unprecedented international scope and scale, and featuring "distributed control rooms" that allow control of long-running experiments to be passed from one time zone to another over the course of a day.

The Comb-*e*-Chem project introduced previously illustrates some of these issues. As much attention is given to the needs of the end-user community as to basic computational issues. Thus, work on the collection of new data addresses support for both process and product data, and integrates electronic laboratory and e-logbook facilities. Also, interfaces are being developed to provide the user community with a unified view of resources and transparent access to data retrieval, online modeling, and experiment design tools. The Comb-e-Chem service-based infrastructure extends to devices in the laboratory as well as to databases and computational resources. An important component of the project is the support of remote users of the UK National Crystallographic Service, physically located in Southampton. The service extends not only to portal access to the apparatus but also to support for the resulting workflow. This scientific workflow corresponds to the chain of linked operations necessary to achieve the desired result—use of the X-ray "e-Laboratory," access to structures databases, and access to computing facilities for simulation and analysis in a specified sequence of operations. The goal is to provide shared, secure access to all of these resources in a supportive collaborative e-science environment.

The EOL project has similar goals. Information produced by EOL software is being stored in a data warehouse and served to the public through the "EOL notebook," which accesses subservient, high-performance MySQL data marts. The EOL notebook portal provides users with data-mining capability that allows extensive, distributed data analyses. Users can gather information with regard to protein function over a wide variety of species and then run complex analysis applications on the combined dataset. An example could be an analysis of variations in structure and function over the evolutionary history of organisms. Such applications require high rates of data transfer and access to a large amount of computation, and thus EOL is both data- and compute-intensive. Because of the sheer number of current and future genomes available and the need for constantly up-to-date and synthesized information, EOL represents a growing class of applications for which a global Grid infrastructure could be critical to enabling new advances in biology.

2.3   INVESTING IN NEW INFRASTRUCTURE

The new modes of inquiry and application scenarios introduced in preceding sections will transform the practice of science and engineering. However, achieving these transformations requires major investments in physical infrastructure (petabyte archival storage, terabit networks, sensor networks, teraop supercomputers), software infrastructure (Grid middleware, collaboratories), and new application concepts and software. Governments are realizing the importance of these investments as a means of enabling scientific progress and enhancing national competitiveness. To this end, major initiatives are under way worldwide, aimed variously at supporting major science and research Grid projects, establishing and enhancing national Grid resources and instruments, developing Grid and middleware technologies, and/or coordinating and facilitating Grid technologies and activities.

John Taylor, Director General of the United Kingdom's Office of Science and Technology, was an early proponent of this idea, coining in 1999 the term *e-science* to denote a new field of endeavor, writing that "e-science is about global collaboration in key areas of science and the next generation of infrastructure that will enable it." He was also successful in obtaining significant funding to realize his concept. The first phase of the UK e-Science programme, launched in 2001 with a budget of £120 M over three years, has established projects spanning many areas of science and engineering (358). A key feature of the program is the active engagement of early adopters from industry: over 80 companies are contributing a total of £30 M in collaborative e-science projects. The industries represented range from IT, pharmaceutical, engineering, and petrochemical companies to financial modeling and media. These projects define middleware infrastructure requirements that far exceed the capability of present Grid middleware. The UK e-Science Core Programme is tasked with identifying the elements of a generic Grid middleware stack that will not only support UK science but also be of interest to industry. The UK program received in 2003 a second investment of about £120 M for a further three years, till 2006.

In the United States, a National Science Foundation (NSF) Blue-Ribbon Advisory Panel chaired by Professor Dan Atkins of the University of Michigan was convened in 2001 to inventory and explore advances in computational technology and to make strategic recommendations on the nature and form of programs that the NSF should take in response to converging technology trends. In their 2003 report (37), the Panel observed that digital computation, data, information, and networks are now increasingly replacing and extending traditional methods of science and engineering research. *In silico* simulation and modeling at new levels of resolution and fidelity are providing a complementary approach to scientific exploration to contrast with the traditional theoretical/analytical and experimental/observational modes. The Panel states that "a new age has dawned in scientific and engineering research, pushed by continuing progress in computing, information and communication technology, and pulled by the expanding complexity, scope, and scale of today's challenges." The report concludes that new technologies have progressed to the extent that it is now possible to envisage creating a global "cyberinfrastructure" on which new types of scientific and engineering knowledge environments and "virtual organizations" can be built. The realization of such cyberinfrastructure would allow research to be pursued in new ways and with increased efficiency. The blue-ribbon report recommends that NSF should lead a large ($1 billion per year), interagency and internationally coordinated Advanced Cyberinfrastructure Program (ACP) to "create, deploy, and apply cyberinfrastructure in ways that radically empower all scientific and engineering research and allied education."

The European Union's "6th Framework" program also devotes substantial sums to research infrastructure and Grid computing, and similar initiatives are underway in Japan, Singapore, and China.

2.4 SUMMARY

Licklider's vision of man-machine symbiosis and a global communication network came from the scientific community. Today, the scientific community still leads the way, as early attempts in Grid computing evolve to the more sophisticated and ubiquitous "virtual organization" concept described in this book, in which Grid middleware enables "coordinated resource sharing and problem solving in dynamic, multi-institutional organizations" [281] (Chapter 4). The UK e-Science concept, the NSF vision of a global cyberinfrastructure, and NASA's IPG all recognize that—following a decade of pioneering work in computational science, data technologies, supercomputing, and networking linked with Grid technologies—computational and data management infrastructure has become a global phenomenon that is poised to evolve as a key enabler for science and society.

The new modes of inquiry outlined in this chapter constitute an ambitious vision for the future of science and engineering. The realization of this vision will require long-term investments of financial resources by governments and of intellectual resources by those who must build and apply the necessary global information infrastructure. We should not underestimate the difficulty of the technical challenges that must be overcome before we can fully realize the vision of a robust middleware infrastructure capable of supporting true virtual organizations. However, we hope that we have communicated just how critically important the realization of this goal is for the future of science and engineering.

ACKNOWLEDGMENTS

We are grateful to a number of people for substantive discussions and assistance with this chapter, including Alan Blatecky, Reagan Moore, Chaitan Baru, Phil Papadopoulos, Mark Miller, Phil Bourne, Susan Rathbun, and Kim Baldridge.

FURTHER READING

For more information on the topics covered in this chapter, see *www.mkp.com/grid2*.

The Industrial Imperative

Irving Wladawsky-Berger

*A*ny sufficiently advanced technology is indistinguishable from magic.

— Arthur C. Clarke

Technology may be the product of knowledge and hard work. Nevertheless, people want it to work like magic. And when technology users want to accomplish something, the last thing they want to think about is how to do it.

That is why the scientific community and increasingly the business world are welcoming Grid computing with the sort of excitement inspired by the Internet not long ago, when its standards and technologies began the march toward near-universal connectivity, broad access to content, and a new model of commerce called e-business. That development was remarkable in many respects, not least because it was a major step in information technology's historic evolution toward total integration into society. And in that passage of Information Technology (IT) to mass adoption, Grid computing could be as consequential as the Internet itself.

Internet standards made possible the Web, which enabled the near-global access to and sharing of content. Open Grid protocols hold the promise of fostering unprecedented integration of technologies, applications, files, and just about any other IT resource, enabling global sharing of these resources beyond what has been possible with the Web. Those same protocols will also virtualize those resources, shielding users from their complexity and allowing them to focus on what they wish to do, rather than how the technology can get it done. Likewise, they will permit management tools to range over that vast heterogeneous infrastructure, rendering it tractable and delivering a quality of service consistent with mass adoption. Finally, having standardized the infrastructure, open Grid protocols will permit the delivery of computing services when and where needed—*on demand*.

In enabling all these capabilities, Grid computing is establishing the conditions necessary for IT to approach mass adoption, or what can be called without too much irony a "post-technology" era.

3.1 THE EVOLUTION OF A TECHNOLOGY: PHASE I

The evolution of a technology can be divided into two fairly distinct phases. In the first—the developmental stage—the primary concern is the technology itself: how it is built and how it works. Initially, the users of the technology are the experts—technical virtuosi or perhaps gifted amateurs—who are comfortable with the technology, can make it perform, and can even build it.

One of the more prominent examples of this evolution is the automobile. In 1885 Gottlieb Daimler became the first to develop a workable internal combustion engine that could propel a vehicle, and his design became the basis of most subsequent engines. As development continued, the automobile began to emerge from the lab, and early adopters began tooling around on dirt roads and solid tires. The difference between a motorist and a mechanic was not great. After all, the probability of the car's breaking down was so high that a fair degree of mechanical skill was needed if one planned on traveling any distance.

Soon the industry agreed on standards, like using a wheel rather than a tiller to steer, and mounting it for the most part on the left. Further design improvements and standards made it more desirable, and the Model T started a process of commoditization. An infrastructure began to evolve around the automobile. The marketplace grew, and the automobile and modern society became indivisible.

Successful technologies, like the automobile and electricity, follow the same basic evolutionary trajectory. They begin with a developmental phase that is often quite long. (The principle of internal combustion, for example, was known as long ago as the seventeenth century. The intended fuel was to be gunpowder, perhaps the reason that an internal combustion engine never got off the drawing board until the nineteenth century.) Then the technology's popularity grows with increasing standardization and declining costs, until finally the technology is adopted throughout society.

3.2   THE EVOLUTION OF A TECHNOLOGY: PHASE II

In the process of this mass adoption, something interesting occurs. People begin to adopt a kind of post-technology perspective. Certainly, the technology is still important, being after all the enabler of everything that follows. However, no longer is the technology pleasing in itself. Increasingly, the application of the technology matters most, along with ease of use, reliability, availability, and cost.

For example, we are surrounded by electrical appliances. We plug one into the wall to make coffee, another to make toast. A stereo provides us with music and the TV with visual entertainment. Rare is the person who, when making coffee, consciously marvels at the vast, complex infrastructure that transports coal perhaps hundreds of miles to a generating plant, uses it to make steam to turn a turbine and produce electricity, then transmits the power across more hundreds of miles to an apartment in a metropolis or an isolated farmhouse on the prairie.

We know the infrastructure is there, but we know it primarily through its effects: a hot cup of coffee, a piece of toast, or the thrilling notes of Lucia—unless, as recently happened, a tree falls across a power line and a large part of the power grid is compromised. Paradoxically, the better the technology, the more obscure it is, its complexity hidden from us, its infrastructure in the hands of experts, the user simply enjoying its benefits. In the post-technology world, the general public simply assumes the technology.

3.3   INFORMATION TECHNOLOGY

Viewed from a historical perspective, information technology (IT) has clearly been in the developmental stage of its evolution. IT began with mainframes and super-computers sheltered in the "glass house." Expensive and complex, these early systems yielded results only to highly trained specialists steeped in the mysteries of programming. With the advent of personal computers and local area networks, millions of people began to use the technology; and since the emergence of network computing and the Internet, hundreds of millions more have come to use it.

Information technology, like electricity and automobiles before it, is fast approaching its own post-technology phase—a time when the application will be dominant and the technology will gradually sink into the background of our lives and be integrated into society. The signs are all there.

One of the major heralds of this new phase is the increasing commoditization of information technologies. Microprocessors, storage, DRAMs, bandwidth, and all sorts of other information technologies, year in and year out, are improving by 50,

60, even 70%, becoming much less expensive, with much more power packed into a smaller unit. Obviously, powerful technologies that are less expensive and smaller are more easily hidden in the environment. Commodity IT, therefore, is potentially ubiquitous, like the little electric motors found throughout our homes and in our cars.

Another indication that IT is headed toward mass adoption is the incessant and incredible increase in the power of systems. That same inexpensive commodity technology is being aggregated into larger and more powerful computers. Soon blades—servers on inch-thick cards—will let us cluster systems by the thousands. In the not-too-distant future, we will see systems with tens of thousands— eventually even hundreds of thousands—of blades or similar small components, all collaborating, all solving unimaginably sophisticated problems, all supporting hundreds of millions of users.

In sum, technologies are becoming commoditized to such a degree that we can afford to have billions of them in the environment, while systems are growing so incredibly potent that we can build a commensurately powerful and connected infrastructure to support them.

Properly handled, this rich lode promises a brilliant future. What will it look like? For one, it will be thoroughly integrated: systems, business processes, organizations, people—everything required for a smoothly functioning whole—will be in close dynamic communication. In addition, the infrastructure will reach much higher levels of efficiency, with all the enterprise's resources fully employed rather than the current spotty, uneven, piecemeal application of these costly assets. The quality of service will be vastly improved, as the infrastructure becomes more self-configuring, self-optmizing, self-healing, and self-protecting. Finally, much greater degrees of flexibility will emerge, leaving people free to make technology choices based on business needs rather than architectural "issues."

3.4   INTEGRATION

The profusion of powerful technologies emanating from the industry's laboratories will let us do new and marvelous things, but realizing that potential depends on our ability to integrate these technologies. Such integration will grow increasingly easier as open standards become more and more common.

Historically, the success of most technologies has depended on the availability of a small number of commonly agreed-upon standards. Total uniformity is not essential. For example, electric standards in France, the United Kingdom, and the United States differ, but only slightly, and with adapters one can live with the differences. The success of electricity is directly related to its standardization, as is the success of automobiles, telephones, broadcasting, and many other technologies.

IT today is moving in that same direction, especially with the rise of open standards and the growing trend toward open source software—be it Linux or Grid protocols or Web services. Standardization has the feel of historical inevitability about it, because standardization is the only way to integrate that incredibly diverse profusion of technologies. Standards bring the kind of flexibility and modularity that allow technology to be absorbed and managed smoothly, that make it commonplace and unremarkable and permit people to pay attention to what it does, rather than what it is.

The cause of Grid standards took a major step forward in 2002, as open Grid protocols were brought together with Web services in the Open Grid Services Architecture (OGSA) described in this book. Web services' XML-based technologies, such as WSDL, UDDI, and SOAP, can now be used as the language in which to express Grid protocols. Clearly, this development portends levels of integration inconceivable just a few years ago—integration at every level, integration that is increasingly dynamic.

Such integration will be a major step forward for e-business. Departments and divisions, people and processes will be united as never before. Together, they will be capable of speedy action and reaction, of quickly forming alliances with other companies or individuals in search of temporary advantage, or more stable partnerships in pursuit of longer term interests. An automaker, for instance, may automatically connect to suppliers offering the best quality and deals on parts, while the suppliers in turn automatically connect with other manufacturers needing similar parts.

Standardization and integration, however, are not synonymous with simplicity. The ever-growing volume of technology and the constant expansion of a heterogeneous infrastructure, no matter how smoothly integrated, lead to profound levels of complexity. And while the availability of technology and growing standardization continue to push IT toward mass adoption in a post-technology era, the industry must find ways to deal with that complexity, keep it from intruding on the user, and make the infrastructure perform efficiently.

3.5 EFFICIENCY

Efficiency poses the same challenge, on a smaller scale, that the IT industry faced in earlier times, when systems like mainframes addressed one job at a time and operating systems were relatively simple (as was life). However, computers and their applications eventually had to be shared among many users, and with sharing the efficient allocation of physical resources became a nightmare.

The solution to this problem stands as one of the more powerful break-throughs in the history of computer science. It was the notion of virtualization that, abetted by increasingly powerful and sophisticated operating systems, provided people with their own machines—virtual systems, consisting of virtual I/O, virtual memory, and virtual storage. Virtualization enabled people to share an expensive and complex resource, as well as the applications and data they were all working with, without worrying about what was there physically, how it did what it did, or even where it was. Increasingly sophisticated operating systems allowed users to invoke a service that then provided and managed the resources needed by these users.

Thirty or so years ago, virtualization within a single system capitalized on a very expensive resource by making it available to users without their needing a deep knowledge of programming in order to use it. Today, the challenge is to virtualize computing resources over the Internet. This is the essence of Grid computing, and it is being accomplished by applying a layer of open Grid protocols to every "local" operating system, for example, Linux, Windows, AIX, Solaris, and zOS. Thus, we will make the sharing of resources over the Internet (or through a private intranet) a reality, while also hiding the vast, complex, global infrastructure supporting the user.

That transparency is essential to accelerate the move to the post-technology era while enabling businesses and other institutions to make the most of substantial investments in heterogeneous systems. Moreover, since Grids bring to bear not just the resources immediately at hand but also those that are distributed all over the world, users can become more productive, paying further dividends on an enterprise's investment in people and technology.

Increased efficiency is the reason so many are turning to open Grid protocols to share resources, as is discussed in later chapters that describe Grid deployments focused on pooling computing resources (see, for example, Chapters 10 and 12). Other chapters are concerned primarily with pooling information (e.g., Chapters 7 and 8) or with accessing specialized instrumentation (e.g., Chapter 6). Major deployment/s are occurring not only in education and government but also within the energy industry, life sciences, manufacturing, and financial services.

Life sciences and the health-care industry will be among the first to benefit from Grid computing (see Chapter 8, and the discussion of e-Diamond in Chapter 2). Hospital complexes, one in Pennsylvania that potentially involves thousands of hospitals and the other at Oxford University in the United Kingdom, are collecting and storing mammograms, so radiologists and physicians can use them to improve the diagnosis and treatment of their patients. Another early commercial user is the gaming industry. Butterfly.net is using Grid technologies to distribute high-performance 3D games online to millions of players, allowing the most efficient use of computing resources (see Chapter 13). With multiple concurrent games running on one Grid, publishers can dynamically allocate resources to more popular games, launch new ones more quickly, and offer flexible and innovative subscription plans to drive revenue growth.

As complexity recedes and global sharing of computing resources becomes commonplace, the effect of Grids on e-business should be as dramatic as when the Internet gave birth to that business model. In addition to a much more integrated environment and marked increases in efficiency attributable to a shared infrastructure, we can expect considerable, though gradual, gains in the quality of service provided to the enterprise. This will be due primarily to the increasingly autonomic characteristics that will characterize the infrastructure.

3.6   GRIDS AND QUALITY OF SERVICE

For the colossal volumes of technology being produced every year to be useful to a business, all this new and sophisticated technology must be manageable. It must hum along smoothly and quietly, unnoticed because it is delivered with a superb quality of service. Grids, because their open standards are running on every system in the infrastructure, will enable increasingly sophisticated levels of management for distributed resources, and the delivery of a quality-of-service characteristic of a mass adoption phase.

Certainly, the level of management today leaves much to be desired, especially in the world of distributed computing and the Internet. In fact, it is a grand challenge for the industry, which must bring to bear more and more sophisticated technologies to provide a very high quality of service at an affordable price.

The answer lies in creating highly sophisticated, end-to-end resource management. The system itself should be able to schedule not just one computer at a time but multiple computers along the path of a particular transaction, enabling truly global collaboration.

Clearly, such work needs to proceed on the basis of OGSA. For the different nodes to collaborate (whether for availability, scheduling, or anything else), they must exchange information. All the nodes in the infrastructure must be addressed as if by a single operating system managing the resources under its control, the difference being that, unlike the resources addressed by a conventional operating system, these are distributed *and* heterogeneous. They come from different vendors, are the products of different architectures, and are totally reliant on a common set of open protocols to feed back information about the state of the system.

OGSA, and the sophisticated software that IT vendors will build around it, will be the equivalent of a virtual operating system applied to all the local operating systems and permitting the resources of the entire aggregation of heterogeneous architectures to be managed in an automated fashion. Its open protocols will allow management to become more autonomic in nature and be carried out much the way biological systems regulate themselves—unconsciously and autonomically. It will configure, optimize, heal, and protect itself with minimal human intervention. In short, it will be self-managing.

Greater integration, efficiency, and a far higher quality of service are some of the more significant ways in which e-businesses will benefit from Grid computing. They are the direct result of the Grid's ability to balance infrastructure needs and costs and to deliver a quality of service that truly unlocks the substantial, unrealized value of the infrastructure. These vast new levels of integration, efficiency, and resiliency will combine to bring a new, far more flexible computing model to e-business.

3.7   THE NEW MODEL: ON-DEMAND COMPUTING

On-demand computing means virtualizing machines, servers, and indeed the entire data center and being able to focus instead on business needs. The ensuing flexibility will allow an e-business to own its own infrastructure (an intra-Grid) or subscribe to the services of an external service provider, or both. That is, it can decide with relative ease whether to make or buy. In fact, it can decide to make *and* buy, choosing to build its own infrastructure for the efficient delivery of mission-critical applications (its baseload, as it were), while drawing on a service provider for more common business processes, such as accounts receivable; for variable infrastructure needs, such as storage; for peak-load computing power; or for advanced capabilities for which it lacks the needed skills.

With computing resources shared globally and managed end to end, the data center can be anywhere—in the enterprise, outside the enterprise, or shared between the two. Where it is installed does not matter. Any authorized user can reach this pool of resources from anywhere—on demand. In an on-demand future, a company might respond to the increasing need for computing resources first with spillover services from their own IT infrastructure and, if that is not sufficient, with capacity from a service provider, purchasing only as much additional capacity as is needed at the moment.

Today, when an enterprise turns to a provider, it must buy information technology services in large blocks, essentially purchasing physical assets over the life of a contract, which may run anywhere from 3 to 10 years. The provider, in turn, is scrambling to respond to the customer's business spikes by buying more physical assets, undermining their own efficiency and increasing the costs to customers. However, with provider and customer sharing common, open protocols, and using Grid and autonomic technologies, service can be provided dynamically in the smallest blocks possible. The customer can then take advantage of virtual services in on-demand fashion.

In this on-demand environment, the customer's data centers need not be recreated physically. The entire data center can just be stored in backup and recreated virtually in the event of a disaster. Virtualization makes the cost to the customer far lower than having to physically mirror the data center. In this future environment, a company can buy computer or data services for applications and consume them only when business demands require it. Applications can request more processing power or data from a provider after they have consumed the internal corporate resources. In either case, the company pays only for increments as used, instead of contracting long term for large volumes. The potential impact on budgets and the bottom line is huge.

As open Grid and Web services protocols become prevalent, more business processes (such as customer relationship management or enterprise resource planning) will become available on demand. These applications will simply be put out for bid by the IT staff, and the best supplier will be chosen.

On-demand computing is the foundation of a business that is far more efficient, far less complex, and extraordinarily flexible. Today, a company has little flexibility with regard to its service providers and, for that matter, its own IT infrastructure. Almost the only way to respond to spikes in demand—expected or unexpected—is to buy new equipment and deploy it. When a company does this, the enterprise has taken ownership of the asset, compounded the complexity of its infrastructure, and compromised its efficiency.

In the new environment, as the focus over time turns more toward the application and the business rather than the infrastructure, the question will become "Do I really need all that infrastructure?" To put it another way, "Do I want to generate my own electricity, with all the investment in people and equipment that entails? Or am I comfortable leaving the generation of electricity to the experts and IT to the IT professionals?"

None of this will happen overnight. However, the planets are aligning: open standards are becoming more prevalent, Grids are appearing in the research community and making their way swiftly into the commercial arena, and on-demand services are appearing in vendor portfolios. It is only a matter of time before information technology achieves the kind of productive anonymity that electricity did when standards made it ubiquitous and routine (if occasionally troublesome).

Arthur Clarke may have been right. As we become capable of doing more and more with our advanced technologies and as we hide those technologies and their complexities from users, the result will indeed seem like magic. Making that magic convincing is one of the most complex and exciting challenges facing our community, as we move IT into its post-technology phase.

FURTHER READING

For more information on the topics covered in this chapter, see *www.mkp.com/grid2.*

PART II

FRAMEWORK

We are now past the preliminaries and ready to dive into the technical meat of *The Grid*. We lead off with Part II, which comprises just the single scene-setting Chapter 4, "Concepts and Architecture." This chapter introduces the central Grid concepts and architectural principles upon which the rest of the book is based. Its purpose is to orient the reader by presenting the concepts and terminology required to understand the material that follows. This is the chapter that should be read before any other.

Concepts and Architecture

Ian Foster and Carl Kesselman

*I*n this scene-setting chapter, we provide an overview of the purpose, evolution, architecture, and implementation of Grid systems—a picture that will then be filled out in the chapters that follow. This chapter thus both introduces Grids and provides a road map for the rest of the book.

The term "the Grid" was coined in the mid-1990s to denote a (then) proposed distributed computing infrastructure for advanced science and engineering. Much progress has since been made on the construction of such an infrastructure and on its extension and application to commercial computing problems. And while the term "Grid" has also been on occasion conflated to embrace everything from advanced networking and computing clusters to artificial intelligence, there has also emerged a good understanding of the problems that Grid technologies address, and at least a first set of applications for which they are suited.

Grid concepts and technologies were originally developed to enable resource sharing within scientific collaborations, first within early gigabit/sec testbeds (161, 163) and then on increasingly larger scales (108, 137, 394, 610). As discussed in Chapter 2, applications in this context include distributed computing for computationally demanding data analyses (pooling of compute power and storage; e.g., Chapter 10), the federation of diverse distributed datasets (e.g., Chapters 7–9), collaborative visualization of large scientific datasets (pooling of expertise), and coupling of scientific instruments with remote computers and archives (increasing functionality as well as availability, e.g., Chapters 1:4 and 1:6).

A common theme underlying these different usage modalities is a need for *coordinated resource sharing and problem solving in dynamic, multi-institutional virtual organizations* (281). More recently, it has become clear (see Chapter 3) that similar requirements arise in commercial settings, not only for scientific and technical computing applications (where we can already point to success stories; e.g., Chapters 11 and 12) but also for commercial distributed computing applications (e.g., Chapter 13), including enterprise application integration (Chapter 14) and business-to-business partner collaboration over the Internet. Just as the Web began as a technology for scientific collaboration and was adopted for e-business, we see a similar trajectory for Grid technologies.

We thus argue that both science and industry can benefit from Grids. However, at the risk of stating the case too broadly, we make a more comprehensive statement. A primary purpose of information technology and infrastructure is to enable people to perform their daily tasks more efficiently or effectively. To the extent that these tasks are performed in collaboration with others, Grids are more than just a niche technology, but rather a direction in which our infrastructure must evolve if it is to support our social structures and the way work gets done in our society.

The success of the Grid to date owes much to the relatively early emergence of clean architectural principles, de facto standard software, aggressive early adopters with challenging application problems, and a vibrant international community of developers and users. This combination of factors led to a solid base of experience that has more recently driven the definition of the service-oriented Open Grid Services Architecture that today forms the basis for both open source and commercial Grid products. In the sections that follow, we expand upon these various aspects of the Grid story and, in so doing, introduce the principal issues to be addressed in the rest of the book.

4.1   VIRTUAL ORGANIZATIONS AND THE GRID

Consider the following scenarios:

✦ A company needing to reach a decision on the placement of a new factory invokes a sophisticated financial forecasting model from an application service provider (ASP), providing it with access to appropriate proprietary historical data from a corporate database on storage systems operated by a storage service provider. During the decision-making meeting, what-if scenarios are run collaboratively and interactively, even though the division heads participating in the decision are located in different cities. The ASP itself contracts with an on-demand cycle provider for additional "oomph" during particularly demanding scenarios, requiring of course that cycles meet desired security and performance requirements.

✦ An industrial consortium formed to develop a feasibility study for a next-generation supersonic aircraft undertakes a highly accurate multidisciplinary simulation of the entire aircraft. This simulation integrates proprietary software components developed by different participants, with each component operating on that participant's computers and having access to appropriate design databases and other data made available to the consortium by its members.

✦ A crisis management team responds to a chemical spill by using local weather and soil models to estimate the spread of the spill, determining the impact based on population location as well as geographic features such as rivers and water supplies, creating a short-term mitigation plan (perhaps based on chemical reaction models), and tasking emergency response personnel by planning and coordinating evacuation, notifying hospitals, and so forth.

✦ Thousands of physicists at hundreds of laboratories and universities worldwide come together to design, create, operate, and analyze the products of a major detector at CERN, the European high-energy physics laboratory. During the analysis phase, they pool their computing, storage, and networking resources to create a "data Grid" capable of analyzing petabytes of data (178, 368) (see Chapter 10).

✦ A large-scale Internet game consists of many virtual worlds, each with its own physical laws and consequences. Each world may have a large number of inhabitants that interact with one another and move from one world to another. Each virtual world may expand in an on-demand basis to accommodate population growth, new simulation technology to model the physical laws of the world will need to be added, and simulations need to be coupled to determine what happens "when worlds collide" (see Chapter 13).

✦ A biologist wants to understand how changes in neuron synapse response induced by a drug impact the performance of specific brain functions. To answer this question, he needs to perform low-level chemical simulations of the synapse and then map this information upward in the structural hierarchy of the brain. This analysis requires mapping simulation across many different databases, each containing information about different levels of the biological system.

These examples differ in many respects: the number and type of participants, the types of activities, the duration and scale of the interaction, and the resources being shared. However, they also have much in common. In each case, mutually distrustful participants with varying degrees of prior relationship (perhaps none at all) want to share resources in order to perform some task. Furthermore, sharing is about more than simply document exchange (as in "virtual enterprises" (148)): it can involve direct access to remote software, computers, data, sensors, and other resources. For example, members of a consortium may provide access to specialized software and data and/or pool their computational resources.

More abstractly, what these application domains have in common is a need for *coordinated resource sharing and problem solving in dynamic, multi-institutional virtual organizations*. The sharing that we are concerned with is not primarily file exchange but rather direct access to computers, software, data, and other resources, as is required by a range of collaborative problem-solving and resource-brokering strategies emerging in industry, science, and engineering. This sharing is, necessarily, highly controlled, with resource providers and consumers defining clearly and carefully just what is shared, who is allowed to share, and the conditions under which sharing occurs. A set of individuals and/or institutions defined by such sharing rules form what we call a *virtual organization* (VO), a concept that is becoming fundamental to much of modern computing. VOs enable disparate groups of organizations and/or individuals to share resources in a controlled fashion, so that members may collaborate to achieve a shared goal.

As these examples show, VOs can vary greatly in their purpose, scope, size, duration, structure, community, and sociology. Nevertheless, we can identify a broad set of common concerns and technology requirements. In particular, we see a need for highly flexible sharing relationships, ranging from client-server to peer to peer; for sophisticated and precise levels of control over how shared resources are used, including fine-grained and multistakeholder access control, delegation, and application of local and global policies; for sharing of varied resources, ranging from programs, files, and data to computers, sensors, and networks; for virtualization of resources as services, so that diverse capabilities can be delivered in standard ways without regard to physical location and implementation; and for diverse usage modes, ranging from single-user to multiuser and from performance-sensitive to cost-sensitive and hence embracing issues of quality of service, scheduling, co-allocation, and accounting.

Resource sharing, virtual organization, and virtualization are not new concepts. For example, in 1965 the designers of the then-revolutionary Multics operating system wrote that "the time-sharing computer system can unite a group of investigators . . . one can conceive of such a facility as an . . . intellectual public utility" (665), and in 1969 Internet pioneer Len Kleinrock suggested, presciently if prematurely upon the installation of the first ARPANET node, that "we will probably see the spread of 'computer utilities,' which, like present electric and telephone utilities, will service individual homes and offices across the country" (415). And of course the distributed systems, networking, operating systems, collaborative work, and security communities have worked for more than 30 years on the principles and mechanisms required to support distributed resource sharing. What is new today is that, as a result of work by these and other pioneers, the Internet is by now quasi-ubiquitous, devices and networks are far more capable, and distributed computing technologies have advanced to the point where it has become practical to think about realizing resource sharing, virtual organization, and virtualization scenarios on a large scale.

4.1.1   Technical Challenges in Sharing Relationships

Depending on context, the virtual organizations with which we are concerned can be small or large, short- or long-lived, single or multi-institutional, and homogeneous or heterogeneous. Individual VOs may be structured hierarchically from smaller systems and may overlap in membership. Furthermore, regardless of these differences, developers of applications for VOs face common requirements as they seek to deliver QoS—whether measured in terms of common security semantics, distributed workflow and resource management, coordinated fail-over, problem determination services, or other metrics—across a collection of resources with heterogeneous and often dynamic characteristics.

We use the example in Figure 4.1 to illustrate some complexities that we face in addressing these issues. The figure depicts three physical organizations, AirCar, Goeing, and CyclesRUs, each of which participates in various virtual organizations that involve controlled sharing of its computational and data resources. In particular, AirCar and Goeing (fierce competitors in the aerospace industry) both collaborate within an international virtual organization, VO-Space, on the design of an advanced space vehicle. In addition, Goeing participates in a regional cycle-sharing consortium, VO-Cycles, in which it pools unused cycles with a local service provider, CyclesRUs, for computationally intensive rendering tasks.

Resource sharing is often conditional: each resource owner makes resources available, subject to constraints on when, where, and what can be done. (In the figure, the text in quotes denotes the policies that apply for each resource or service.) For example, AirCar might allow its VO-Space partners to invoke a simulation service only for "simple" problems (according to some agreed-upon definition). Resource consumers may also place constraints on properties of the resources they are prepared to work with. For example, a participant in VO-Cycles might accept only pooled computational resources certified as "secure." The implementation of such constraints requires mechanisms for expressing policies, for establishing the identity of a consumer or resource (authentication), and for determining whether an operation is consistent with applicable sharing relationships (authorization).

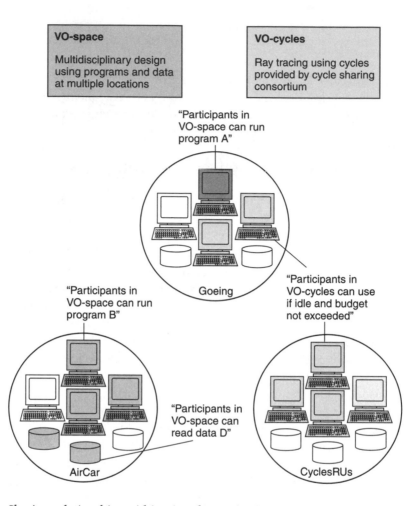

VO-space Multidisciplinary design using programs and data at multiple locations	**VO-cycles** Ray tracing using cycles provided by cycle sharing consortium

"Participants in VO-space can run program A"

"Participants in VO-cycles can use if idle and budget not exceeded"

Goeing

"Participants in VO-space can run program B"

"Participants in VO-space can read data D"

AirCar

CyclesRUs

4.1

Sharing relationships within virtual organizations.

FIGURE

Sharing relationships can vary dynamically over time, in terms of the resources involved, the nature of the access permitted, and the participants to whom access is permitted. Also, these relationships do not necessarily involve an explicitly named set of individuals, but rather may be defined implicitly by the policies that govern access to resources. For example, CyclesRUs might allow access to anyone who can demonstrate that he is a "customer." Thus we require mechanisms for discovering and characterizing the nature of the relationships that exist at a particular point in time. For example, a new participant joining VO-

Cycles must be able to determine what resources it is able to access, the "quality" of these resources, and the policies that govern access.

Sharing relationships are often not simply client-server, but peer to peer: providers can be consumers, and sharing relationships can exist among any subset of participants. Sharing relationships may be combined to coordinate use across many resources, each owned by different organizations. For example, in VO-Cycles, a computation started on one pooled computational resource may subsequently access data or initiate subcomputations elsewhere. The ability to delegate authority in controlled ways becomes important in such situations, as do mechanisms for coordinating operations across multiple resources (e.g., coscheduling; see Chapter 18).

The same resource may be used in different ways in different contexts. For example, a computer might be used only to run a specific piece of software in one sharing arrangement, but provide generic compute cycles in another. This lack of a priori knowledge about how a resource may be used means that performance metrics, expectations, and limitations may be part of the conditions placed on resource sharing or usage.

In addition to such issues of security and policy, Grid users are often vitally concerned with achieving various *qualities of service (QoS)* in the virtual systems formed by integrating distributed components. This concern is fundamental not only within the distributed virtual organizations discussed previously but also, increasingly, within a single enterprise. In the past, computing typically was performed within highly integrated host-centric enterprise computing centers. The rise of the Internet and the emergence of e-business have, however, led to a growing awareness that an enterprise's IT infrastructure is becoming increasingly decomposed, both externally (as it extends to encompass external networks, resources, and services) and internally (as enterprise IT facilities become more heterogeneous and distributed). The overall result is a decomposition of highly integrated internal IT infrastructure into a collection of heterogeneous and fragmented systems.

Enterprises must then reintegrate (with QoS) these distributed servers and data resources, addressing issues of navigation, distributed security, and content distribution inside the enterprise, much as on external networks. Enterprises are also now expanding the scope and scale of their enterprise resource planning projects as they try to provide better integration with customer relationship management, integrated supply chain, and existing core systems. The aggregate effect is that *qualities of service traditionally associated with mainframe host-centric computing* (503) *are now essential to the effective conduct of e-business across distributed compute resources, inside as well as outside the enterprise.* In many ways, this requirement is simply a restatement of the need for infrastructure that facilitates controlled sharing of resources across organizational boundaries, that is, the Grid.

4.1.2   Evolution of Grid Technologies

Grid technologies provide mechanisms for sharing and coordinating the use of diverse resources and thus enable the creation, from geographically and organizationally distributed components, of virtual computing systems that are sufficiently integrated to deliver desired qualities of service (281). These technologies include security solutions that support management of credentials and policies when computations span multiple institutions; resource management protocols and services that support secure remote access to computing and data resources and the co-allocation of multiple resources; information query protocols and services that provide configuration and status information about resources, organizations, and services; and data management services that locate and transport datasets between storage systems and applications.

Grid technologies have emerged from some 10 years of research and development in both academia and industry, which furthermore continues today. As illustrated in Figure 4.2, we can distinguish four distinct phases in this evolution.

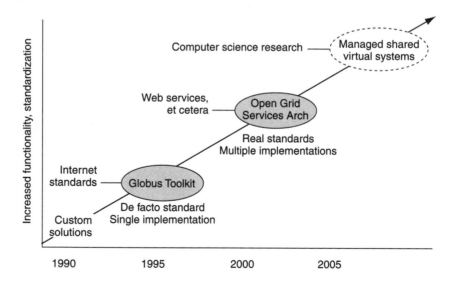

4.2   The evolution of Grid technologies.

FIGURE

Custom solutions. Starting in the early 1990s, work in "metacomputing" and related fields involved the development of custom solutions to Grid computing problems (161, 163). The focus of these often heroic efforts was on making things work and exploring what was possible. Applications were built directly on Internet protocols with typically only limited functionality in terms of security, scalability, and robustness. Interoperability was not a significant concern.

Globus Toolkit. From 1997 onward, the open source Globus Toolkit version 2 (GT2) (276) emerged as the de facto standard for Grid computing. Focusing on usability and interoperability, GT2 defined and implemented protocols, APIs, and services used in thousands of Grid deployments worldwide. By providing solutions to common problems such as authentication, resource discovery, and resource access, GT2 accelerated the construction of real Grid applications. Also by defining and implementing "standard" protocols and services, GT2 pioneered the creation of interoperable Grid systems and enabled significant progress on Grid programming tools. The GT2 protocol suite leveraged existing Internet standards for transport, resource discovery, and security. Some elements of the GT2 protocol suite were codified in formal technical specifications, reviewed within standards bodies, and instantiated in multiple implementations: notably, the GridFTP data transfer protocol (65) and elements of the Grid Security Infrastructure (660). However, in general, GT2 "standards" were neither formal nor subject to public review. Similar comments apply to other important Grid technologies that emerged during this period, such as the Condor high-throughput computing system.

Open Grid Services Architecture. The year 2002 saw the emergence of the Open Grid Services Architecture (279) (OGSA, Chapter 17), a true community standard with multiple implementations, including, in particular, the OGSA-based GT 3.0, released in 2003. Building on and significantly extending GT2 concepts and technologies, OGSA firmly aligns Grid computing with broad industry initiatives in service-oriented architecture and Web services. In addition to defining a core set of standard interfaces and behaviors that address many of the technical challenges introduced previously, OGSA provides a framework within which one can define a wide range of interoperable, portable services. OGSA provides a foundation on which can be constructed a rich Grid technology ecosystem comprising multiple technology providers.

Managed, Shared Virtual Systems. The definition of the initial OGSA technical specifications is an important step forward, but much more remains to be done before the full Grid vision is realized. Building on OGSA's service-oriented infrastructure, we will see an expanding set of interoperable services and systems that address scaling to both larger numbers of entities and smaller device footprints, increasing degrees of virtualization, richer forms of sharing, and increased qualities of service via a variety of forms of active management. This work will draw increasingly heavily on the results of advanced computer science research in such areas as peer-to-peer (Chapter 29), knowledge-based (115) (Chapter 23), and autonomic (365) (Chapter 26) systems.

We define a Grid as a system that coordinates distributed resources using standard, open, general-purpose protocols and interfaces to deliver nontrivial qualities of service. We examine the key elements of this definition:

+ *Coordinates distributed resources.* A Grid integrates and coordinates resources and users that live within different control domains—for example, the user's desktop versus central computing, different administrative units of the same company, and/or different companies—and addresses the issues of security, policy, payment, membership, and so forth that arise in these settings. Otherwise, we are dealing with a local management system.

+ *Using standard, open, general-purpose protocols and interfaces.* A Grid is built from multipurpose protocols and interfaces that address such fundamental issues as authentication, authorization, resource discovery, and resource access. As we discuss in material to follow, it is important that these protocols and interfaces be *standard* and *open*. Otherwise, we are dealing with an application-specific system.

+ *To deliver nontrivial qualities of service.* A Grid allows its constituent resources to be used in a coordinated fashion to deliver various qualities of service—relating, for example, to response time, throughput, availability, and security—and/or coallocation of multiple resource types to meet complex user demands, so that the utility of the combined system is significantly greater than that of the sum of its parts.

The second point is of particular importance. Standard protocols (and interfaces and policies) allow us to establish resource-sharing arrangements dynamically with *any* interested party and thus to create something more than a plethora of balkanized, incompatible, noninteroperable distributed systems. As we discuss at greater length in the following, relevant standards are being developed rapidly within the Global Grid Forum and other bodies. For an entity to be part of *the* Grid it must implement these "inter-Grid" protocols, just as to be part of the Internet an entity must speak IP (among other things). Both open source and commercial products can interoperate effectively in this heterogeneous, multivendor Grid world, thus providing the pervasive infrastructure that will enable successful Grid applications.

In the Internet, it is not uncommon that a specific set of hosts is disconnected from other hosts within an intranet. However, this partitioning occurs as a result of policy and not because of implementation. In general, all networked computers use TCP/IP and its associated protocols; and despite these policy restrictions, we still talk about a single Internet.

Similarly, we speak about *the Grid* as a single entity, even though different organizations and communities use Grid protocols to create disconnected Grids for specific purposes. As with the Internet, it is policy issues (e.g., security, cost, operational mode), not implementation issues, that prevent a service or resource from being accessible.

4.2 GRID ARCHITECTURE

We have argued that the establishment, management, and exploitation of dynamic, cross-organizational VO sharing relationships require new technology. We present a *Grid architecture* that identifies fundamental system components, specifies the purpose and function of these components, and indicates how these components interact with one another. Our goal is not to provide a complete enumeration of all required components but to identify requirements for general component classes. The result is an extensible, open architectural structure within which can be placed solutions to key VO requirements. Our architecture and the subsequent discussion organize components into layers, as shown in Figure 4.3. Components

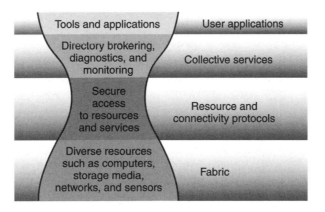

4.3   The layered Grid architecture.

FIGURE

within each layer share common characteristics but can build on capabilities and behaviors provided by any lower layer.

Our Grid architecture is based on the principles of the "hourglass model" (34). The narrow neck of the hourglass defines a small set of core abstractions and protocols (e.g., TCP and HTTP), onto which many different high-level behaviors can be mapped (the top of the hourglass), and which themselves can be mapped onto many different underlying technologies (the base of the hourglass). By definition, the number of protocols defined at the neck must be small. In our architecture, the neck of the hourglass consists of *resource* and *connectivity* protocols, which facilitate the sharing of individual resources. Protocols at these layers are designed so that they can be implemented on top of a diverse range of resource types, defined at the *fabric* layer, and can in turn be used to construct a wide range of global services and application-specific behaviors at the *collective* layer—so called because they involve the coordinated ("collective") use of multiple resources.

4.2.1   Fabric: Interfaces to Local Control

The Grid fabric layer provides the resources to which shared access is mediated by Grid protocols, for example, computational resources, storage systems, catalogs, network resources, and sensors. A "resource" may be a logical entity, such as a distributed file system, computer cluster, or distributed computer pool; in such cases, a resource implementation may involve internal protocols (e.g., the NFS storage access protocol or a cluster resource management system's process management protocol), but these are not the concern of Grid architecture.

Fabric components implement the local, resource-specific operations that occur on specific resources (whether physical or logical) as a result of sharing operations at higher levels. There is thus a tight and subtle interdependence between the functions implemented at the fabric level, on the one hand, and the sharing operations supported, on the other. Richer fabric functionality enables more sophisticated sharing operations; at the same time, if we place few demands on fabric elements, then deployment of Grid infrastructure is simplified. For example, resource-level support for advance reservations (i.e., the ability to request and obtain a commitment for access at a future time; see Chapter 18) makes it possible for higher-level services to aggregate (coschedule) resources in interesting ways that would otherwise be impossible to achieve. However, as many resources do not support advance reservation "out of the box," a requirement for advance reservation would increase the cost of incorporating new resources into a Grid.

Experience suggests that, at a minimum, resources should implement *intro-spection* mechanisms that permit discovery of their structure, state, and capabilities (e.g., whether they support advance reservation), on the one hand, and *resource management* mechanisms that provide some control of delivered quality of service, on the other, as in the following examples:

✦ *Computational resources.* Mechanisms are required for starting programs and for monitoring and controlling the execution of the resulting processes. Management mechanisms that allow control over the resources allocated to processes are useful, as are advance reservation mechanisms (see Chapter 18). Introspection functions are needed for determining hardware and software characteristics as well as relevant state information such as current load and queue state in the case of scheduler-managed resources.

✦ *Storage resources.* Mechanisms are required for putting and getting files. Third-party and high-performance (e.g., striped) transfers are useful (652). So are mechanisms for reading and writing subsets of a file and/or executing remote data selection or reduction functions (118). Management mechanisms that allow control over the resources allocated to data transfers (space, disk bandwidth, network bandwidth, CPU) are useful (587), as are advance reservation mechanisms (see Chapters 18 and 22). Introspection functions are needed for determining hardware and software characteristics as well as relevant load information such as available space and bandwidth utilization.

✦ *Network resources.* Management mechanisms that provide control over the resources allocated to network transfers (e.g., prioritization, reservation) can be useful (see Chapter 1:19). Introspection functions should be provided to determine network characteristics and load (682).

Other important classes of resources include database systems used to store structured data (see Chapter 22) and sensors of various kinds.

4.2.2 Connectivity: Communicating Easily and Securely

The connectivity layer defines core communication and authentication protocols required for Grid-specific network transactions. Communication protocols enable the exchange of data between fabric layer resources. Authentication protocols build on communication services to provide cryptographically secure mechanisms for verifying the identity of users and resources.

Communication requirements include transport, routing, and naming. Although alternatives certainly exist, it is common to assume that these protocols are drawn from the TCP/IP protocol stack: specifically, the Internet (IP and ICMP), transport (TCP, UDP), and application (DNS, OSPF, RSVP, etc.) layers of the Internet-layered protocol architecture (96). This is not to say that in the future, Grid communications will not demand new protocols that take into account particular types of network dynamics—for example, on high-performance optical networks or wireless networks.

The complexity of the security problem makes it important that any connectivity layer security solutions be based on existing standards whenever possible. As with communication, many security standards developed within the context of the Internet protocol suite are applicable. Chapter 21 provides a comprehensive discussion of the security demands of VO environments (146), so we note here just some of the more important requirements:

+ *Single sign-on*. As Grid users frequently want to initiate computations that access multiple remote resources, a user should be able to "sign on" (authenticate) just once, rather than once per resource or administrative domain accessed.

+ *Delegation* (280, 303, 371). A user must be able to endow a program with the ability to run on the user's behalf, so that the program is able to access the resources on which the user is authorized. The program should (optionally) also be able to delegate a subset of its rights to another program: what is sometimes referred to as restricted delegation.

+ *Integration with local security solutions*. In a heterogeneous Grid, each site or resource provider may employ any of a variety of local security solutions. Grid security solutions must be able to interoperate with these various local solutions. They cannot, realistically, require wholesale replacement of local security solutions but rather must allow mapping into the local environment.

+ *User-based trust relationships*. For a user to use resources from multiple providers together, the security system must not require each of the resource providers to cooperate or interact with each other in configuring the security environment. For example, if a user has the right to use sites A and B, the user should be able to use sites A and B together without requiring that A's and B's security administrators interact.

Grid security solutions should also provide flexible support for communication protection (e.g., control over the degree of protection, independent data unit protection for unreliable protocols, support for reliable transport protocols other than TCP) and enable stakeholder control over authorization decisions, including the ability to restrict the delegation of rights in various ways.

We discuss briefly in the following and in far more detail in Chapter 21, how these and related requirements can be addressed using a relatively small set of standard connectivity protocols.

4.2.3   Resource: Sharing Single Resources

Having established identity, the Grid user needs to be able to interact with remote resources and services. This is the role of the resource layer, which builds on connectivity layer communication and authentication protocols to define protocols for the secure negotiation, initiation, monitoring, control, accounting, and payment of sharing operations on individual resources. Resource layer implementations of these protocols call on fabric layer functions to access and control local resources. Resource layer protocols are concerned entirely with individual resources and hence ignore issues of global state and atomic actions across distributed collections; such issues are the concern of the collective layer discussed next.

Two primary classes of resource layer protocols can be distinguished:

+ *Information protocols* are used to obtain information about the structure and state of a resource, for example, its configuration, current load, and usage policy (e.g., cost).

+ *Management protocols* are used to negotiate access to a shared resource, specifying, for example, resource requirements (including advanced reservation and quality of service) and the operation(s) to be performed, such as process creation or data access. Since management protocols are responsible for instantiating sharing relationships, they must serve as a "policy application point," ensuring that the requested protocol operations are consistent with the policy under which the resource is to be shared. Issues that must be considered include accounting and payment. A protocol may also support monitoring the status of an operation and controlling (for example, terminating) the operation.

Although many such protocols can be imagined, the resource (and connectivity) protocol layers form the neck of our hourglass model and as such should be limited to a small and focused set. These protocols must be chosen so as to capture the fundamental mechanisms of sharing across many different resource types (for example, different local resource management systems), while not overly constraining the types or performance of higher-level protocols that may be developed.

The list of desirable fabric functionality provided in Section 4.2.1 summarizes the major features required in resource layer protocols. To this list we add the need for "exactly once" semantics for many operations, with reliable error reporting indicating when operations fail.

4.2.4   Collective: Coordinating Multiple Resources

The collective layer contains protocols and services not associated with any one specific resource but instead capturing interactions across collections of resources. Because collective components build on the narrow resource and connectivity layer "neck" in the protocol hourglass, they can implement a wide variety of sharing behaviors without placing new requirements on the resources being shared. For example:

- *Directory services* allow VO participants to discover the existence and/or properties of VO resources. A directory service may allow its users to query for resources by name and/or by attributes such as type, availability, or load (204). (See, in particular, Chapters 22 and 23—and the discussion of MDS-2 in Chapter 27.)

- *Coallocation, scheduling, and brokering services* allow VO participants to request the allocation of one or more resources for a specific purpose and the scheduling of tasks on the appropriate resources. Examples include AppLeS (114), Condor-G (292), Nimrod-G (57), and the DRM broker (108). (See Chapters 18, 24, and 1:12.)

- *Monitoring and diagnostics services* support the monitoring of VO resources for failure, adversarial attack ("intrusion detection"), overload, and so forth. (See Chapter 20).

- *Data replication services* support the management of VO storage (and perhaps also network and computing) resources to maximize data access performance with respect to metrics such as response time, reliability, and cost (66, 368). (See Chapter 22.)

Programming models and tools (discussed at length in Chapter 24) often define and/or invoke collective layer functions.

- *Grid-enabled programming systems* enable familiar programming models to be used in Grid environments, using various Grid services to address resource discovery, security, resource allocation, and other concerns. Examples include Grid-enabled implementations of the Message Passing Interface (300, 403) (Chapter 24) and manager–worker frameworks (156, 443) (Chapters 19 and 24).

✦ *Workflow systems* provide for the description, use, and management of multi-step, asynchronous, multicomponent workflows (see Chapter 24).

✦ *Software discovery services* discover and select the best software implementation and execution platform based on problem parameters; for example, see NetSolve (153) and Ninf (497), described in Chapter 24.

✦ *Collaboratory services* support the coordinated exchange of information within potentially large user communities, whether synchronously or asynchronously; for example, see CAVERNsoft (220, 437), Access Grid (182) (Chapter 15), Butterfly.net (Chapter 13), and commodity groupware systems.

Collective layer services must also address security, policy, and accounting issues:

✦ *Community authorization servers* enforce community policies governing resource access, generating capabilities that community members can use to access community resources (519). These servers provide a global policy enforcement service by building on resource-layer information and management protocols and security protocols in the connectivity layer. Akenti (648) addresses some of these issues. See Chapter 21 for further discussion.

✦ *Community accounting and payment services* gather resource usage information for the purpose of accounting, payment, and/or limiting of resource usage by community members.

These examples illustrate the wide variety of collective layer protocols and services that are encountered in practice. Note that whereas resource layer protocols must be general in nature and are widely deployed, collective layer protocols span the spectrum from general purpose to highly application- or domain-specific, with the latter existing perhaps only within specific VOs.

Collective functions can be implemented as standalone services or as libraries designed to be linked with applications. In both cases, their implementation can build on resource layer (or other collective layer) protocols and APIs. For example, given a collective coallocation API that uses a resource layer management protocol to manipulate underlying resources, we can define a co-reservation service protocol and implement a co-reservation service that speaks this protocol, calling the coallocation API to implement coallocation operations and perhaps providing additional functionality, such as authorization, fault tolerance, and logging. An application might then use the co-reservation service protocol to request end-to-end network reservations.

Collective components may be tailored to the requirements of a specific user community, VO, or application domain, for example, a library that implements an application-specific coherency protocol, or a co-reservation service for a specific set of network resources. Other collective components can be more general-purpose, for example, a replication service that manages an international collection of storage systems for multiple communities or a directory service designed to enable the discovery of VOs. In general, the larger the target user community, the more important it is that a collective component's protocol(s) and API(s) be standards based.

4.2.5   Applications

The final layer in our Grid architecture comprises the user applications that operate within a VO environment. Applications are constructed in terms of, and by calling upon, services defined at any layer. At each layer, we have well-defined protocols and APIs that provide access to some useful service: resource management, data access, resource discovery, and so forth.

We emphasize that—as is discussed in more detail in Chapter 24—what we label "applications" and show in a single layer in Figure 4.3 may in practice call upon sophisticated frameworks and libraries (e.g., the Common Component Architecture (88), SciRun (517), Cactus (110), workflow systems (130)) and feature much internal structure that would, if captured in our figure, expand it out to many times its current size. These frameworks may themselves define protocols, services, and/or APIs, for example, Web service orchestration frameworks.

4.3   IMPLEMENTING GRID ARCHITECTURE

As discussed in the introduction, the technologies used to implement Grid architecture concepts have evolved over time, from a de facto standard in the form of the Globus Toolkit version 2 to the more formal standard Open Grid Services Architecture (OGSA), implemented by the Globus Toolkit version 3 (GT3) as well as other open source and commercial systems.

We briefly review here the principal features of GT2 and explain both how these features address the Grid technology requirements introduced previously and how they fit into our Grid architecture. We then introduce OGSA. We start with some general remarks concerning the utility of a service-oriented Grid architecture, the importance of being able to virtualize Grid services, and essential service characteristics. Then we define what we mean by a *Grid service*. Technical details on OGSA are provided in Chapter 17 and subsequent chapters.

GT2 has proven to be effective and influential not only because it provides technical solutions to challenging problems encountered when building Grids, such as authentication and secure resource access, but also because it does so by defining standard protocols that enable interoperability. Both advantages have proven important in practice, with many developers writing tools and applications that assume the basic functions introduced in the following (GSI security, GRAM resource access, GridFTP data access, etc.) and large numbers of sites deploying GT2 services in support of these tools and applications (see Chapter 27).

4.3.1   Globus Toolkit Version 2

GT2 (276, 281) is a community-based, open-architecture, open source set of services and software libraries that support Grids and Grid applications. GT2 addresses issues of security, information discovery, resource management, data management, communication, fault detection, and portability. GT2 is the foundation for thousands of major Grid projects worldwide in both academia and industry. Several of these projects are discussed in Chapter 27, which discusses practical issues that arise when deploying GT2 services.

4.3.1.1   Fabric

GT2 is primarily concerned with implementing Grid protocols, not fabric-level behaviors, and as such assumes the existence of suitable software on fabric elements for such purposes as local CPU scheduling, file system management, and system monitoring. However, the toolkit does include some components designed to facilitate interfacing to resource-level protocols. For example, software is provided for discovering structure and state information for various common resource types, such as computers (e.g., OS version, hardware configuration, load (230), scheduler queue status), storage systems (e.g., available space), and networks (e.g., current and predicted future load (451, 681)), and for packaging this information in a form that facilitates the implementation of higher-level resource-layer protocols. Resource management, on the other hand, is generally assumed to be the domain of local resource managers, although the General-Purpose Architecture for Reservation and Allocation (GARA) (283) prototyped a "slot manager" that can be used to implement advance reservation for resources that do not support this capability. Others have developed enhancements to the Portable Batch System (PBS) (31) and Condor (446) that support advance reservation capabilities; see Chapter 27.

4.3.1.2   Connectivity

GT2's connectivity layer is defined by the public-key-infrastructure (PKI)-based Grid Security Infrastructure (GSI) (280) protocols, which provide for single sign-on authentication, communication protection, and some support for restricted delegation. In addition, standard Internet protocols are assumed. In brief:

+ *Single sign-on* allows a user to authenticate once and then create a proxy credential that a program can use to authenticate with any remote service on the user's behalf. A *proxy credential* is a digitally signed certificate that grants the holder the right to perform operations on behalf of the signer, typically only for a limited period of time. Proxy credentials are critical to Grid computing because they allow a user to initiate a computation that accesses multiple remote resources—without having to hand over sensitive credentials (such as a private key in a PKI-based system) to that computation.

+ *Delegation* allows for the creation and communication to a remote service of a delegated proxy credential that the remote service can use to act on the user's behalf, perhaps with various restrictions; this capability is important for nested operations.

GSI addresses interoperability by defining a credential format and an authentication and remote delegation protocol for transmitting those credentials to remote services. The credential format is an extended form of the X.509 certificate, a widely employed standard for PKI certificates. The remote delegation protocol is based on the transport layer security (TLS) protocol (the follow-on to the popular secure socket layer, SSL), although other public key-based authentication protocols can also be used by GSI. In addition, GSI addresses application programmability and portability by defining extensions to the generic security services application programming interface (GSS-API) so that applications can invoke authentication operations conveniently using a high-level API, rather than performing protocol operations directly. Technical specifications define the credential (660), protocol, and GSS-API extensions (470). Further details on GSI design and implementation, including the techniques used to map to local security mechanisms, are provided in Chapter 21.

4.3.1.3   Resource

We now discuss those GT2 resource layer protocols used for remote invocation of computation, resource discovery and monitoring, and data transport.

The Grid Resource Allocation and Management (GRAM) protocol provides for the secure, reliable creation and management of remote computations (205). A two-phase commit protocol is used for reliable invocation, based on techniques used in the Condor system (446) (see Chapter 19 for details). GSI mechanisms are used for authentication, authorization, and credential delegation to remote computations. Multiple interoperable implementations of the GRAM protocol have been constructed (205, 386, 429), but there is no formal protocol specification.

GT2's implementation of the GRAM protocol uses a small, trusted "gatekeeper" process to initiate remote computations, a "job manager" to manage the remote computation, and a "GRAM reporter" to monitor and publish information about the identity and state of the local computation.

The Monitoring and Discovery Service (MDS-2) (204) provides a uniform framework for discovering and accessing configuration and status information such as compute server configuration, network status, and the capabilities and policies of services. The framework defines both a *data model* for representing information about resources and services, and resource-level *protocols* for disseminating and accessing this information. The data model and protocols are described in Chapter 27.

The GT2 MDS-2 implementation provides two main components: a configurable *local registry* or data publisher used to manage the collection and dissemination of information at a particular location, and an index node or *collective registry* used to maintain and support queries against information from multiple locations. Both the local and collective registries perform caching so as to reduce the frequency with which requests for information must be communicated to the original source. Experimental studies show that this caching can be important in high-load situations (698).

The third GT2 component that we describe is GridFTP. This extended version of the file transfer protocol (FTP) is used as a management protocol for data access; extensions include use of connectivity layer security protocols, partial file access, and management of parallelism for high-speed transfers (64). FTP is adopted as a base data transfer protocol because of its support for third-party transfers and because its separate control and data channels facilitate the implementation of sophisticated servers. See Chapter 22 for more details.

Figure 4.4 shows these various GT2 resource layer protocols in action. We first see the user authenticating and generating a proxy credential for User

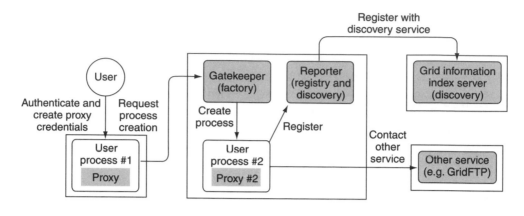

4.4   Selected Globus Toolkit mechanisms.

FIGURE

process #1, thus allowing that process to act on the user's behalf. That process then uses the GSI-authenticated GRAM protocol to request the creation of a new process at a remote location. This request is processed by the Gatekeeper process at the remote location, which creates the new User process #2 along with a new set of proxy credentials, which the new process can use to issue requests to other remote services. The existence and other properties of the new process are registered with the MDS-2 information infrastructure.

4.3.1.4   Collective and Tools

The GT2 software distribution provides only a limited number of collective layer capabilities: the DUROC resource coallocation library (206) is one example. Many GT2-compatible collective layer services and libraries, as well as programming and system tools that depend on those libraries, have been developed by others. Some of these systems have been mentioned in previous sections.

4.3.2   Open Grid Services Architecture

By 2001, the rapidly increasing uptake of Grid technologies and the emergence of the Global Grid Forum as a standards body made it timely and feasible to undertake a standardization (and, in the process, a significant redesign) of the core GT protocols. The following design goals drove this activity, which ultimately produced the Open Grid Services Architecture:

✦ *Factoring of component behaviors.* GT2 protocols such as GRAM combined several functions (e.g., reliable messaging for at-most-once invocation of remote services, and notification for monitoring) that ended up being either reimplemented or unavailable to other functions such as GridFTP or application programs. Thus, a goal in OGSA was to identify essential Grid functions and then to express them in a way that would allow their use in different settings.

✦ *Service orientation.* A *service* is a network-enabled entity with a well-defined interface that provides some capability. While GT2 defined service interfaces to specific resource types (e.g., GRAM for compute resources), service orientation was not consistently applied, and it did nothing to facilitate the definition of arbitrary services or service composition. A goal in OGSA was to enable a uniform treatment of all network entities so that, for example, collective layer behaviors could be expressed as virtualizations of underlying resource layer protocols.

✦ *Align with Web services.* GT2 builds on a mix of low-level protocols and did not provide any standard interface definition language. With the emergence of Web services as a viable Internet-based distributed computing platform, a design goal for OGSA was to leverage the Web services standards (e.g., the Web Services Definition Language, or WSDL), application platforms, and development tools.

The result of this design activity is a service-oriented framework defined by a set of standards being developed within the Global Grid Forum (GGF). A fundamental OGSA concept is that of the *Grid service*: a Web service (see Chapter 17) that implements standard interfaces, behaviors, and conventions that collectively allow for services that can be transient (i.e., can be created and destroyed) and stateful (i.e., we can distinguish one service instance from another). The foundational Open Grid Services Infrastructure (OGSI) specification defines the interfaces, behaviors, and conventions that control how Grid services can be created, destroyed, named, monitored, and so forth. OGSI defines a set of building blocks that can then be used to implement a variety of resource layer and collective layer interfaces and behaviors.

OGSA then builds on this OGSI foundation by defining the services and additional interfaces and behaviors required in a functional Grid environment. For example, interfaces are required for discovery, data management, resource provisioning, and service virtualization. Other services are required for security, policy, accounting, and billing. Service orchestration provides for the coordination of service workflow. GGF working groups are engaged in identifying required functions, rendering these functions as OGSI-compliant interfaces, and defining relationships among the resulting service definitions.

From an organizational perspective, these OGSA services can be viewed within the context of the layered architecture of Figure 4.3. At the connectivity layer, we have a small number of service definitions that address critical issues of authentication, credential mapping, and policy verification, while at the resource level we can identify another small set of service definitions, for data access, job submission, bandwidth allocation, and so on. In a virtualized environment, we find that interfaces defined at the resource layer can reappear at the collective layer as interfaces to virtualized services that from their observable behavior are indistinguishable from resource layer services. Our Grid architecture is thus recursive, with services being composed of services.

OGSA has been broadly adopted as a unifying framework for Grid computing with backing from major scientific and academic Grid communities as well as significant acceptance in the commercial section, from vendors to end users. There are multiple interoperable implementations of this common standards-based, protocol-oriented approach to infrastructure, including GT3, an open source reference implementation of the OGSI and basic OGSA services. A more detailed discussion of OGSA and OGSI can be found in Chapter 17 and in subsequent chapters that discuss specific functionalities and services.

4.4   THE GRID COMMUNITY

In the five years that have passed since the first edition of this book, the development of Grid technologies and applications has grown to become a worldwide effort. Participation in the Global Grid Forum (GGF) has multiplied more than ten-fold since its inception as the U.S. Grid Forum in 1998. Today, delegates from over 400 organizations in over 50 countries attend the thrice-yearly GGF meetings to participate in working groups defining technical specifications or in research groups discussing future directions in Grid technologies and applications, or simply to learn about the technology.

A major impetus for this surge of interest is certainly the needs of the scientific community, which, as discussed in Chapter 2, has urgent demands across a broad range of fronts for more effective and large-scale integration of resources and services. Both grass-roots efforts and major government-funded Grid activities in Japan, Australia, Singapore, China, Europe, North America, and other places have spawned literally thousands of projects on Grid technologies and applications. Given the complexity of the overall problem and the international dimension of many scientific collaborations, the development of common technical standards and collaborative development of key software is vital to success. Thus, GGF fills an important role in the coordination of international Grid efforts.

Industrial involvement in GGF also continues to grow, with around one-third of GGF participants now coming from industry. Both established technology companies such as Fujitsu, HP, Hitachi, IBM, NEC, Microsoft, Oracle, Platform, and Sun and startups such as Avaki, DataSynapse, and United Devices participate in working groups. In addition, we see an increasing number of commercial end-users at GGF meetings.

Another major forum for discussion of Grid technologies is the annual GlobusWorld event, a combined user and technical training meeting for users of the Globus Toolkit.

4.5   FUTURE DIRECTIONS

The tools and experience established over the past five years provide a solid foundation for future developments in Grid applications and technologies. However, success in the ultimate goal of a global infrastructure for distributed system integration and resource sharing will require significant progress in standards, social and business models, and basic research. The sustained collaborative engagement of scientific application groups, industry, and the computer science community is vital.

OGSA stands poised to become the dominant infrastructure for Grids, with significant consolidation around both the general approach and specific specifications such as OGSI. The next major hurdle is to continue refinement of the OGSA model and specifically to define and develop the additional building block services (e.g., end-to-end provisioning, global service discovery, service virtualization) that will raise the level of abstraction for all Grid applications. If we take the Internet as an analogy, then OGSI provides us with TCP/IP; now we need to create the domain name service, routing protocols, and ultimately HTTP analogs. Later chapters discuss specific capabilities and services that, collectively, define a good part of what we expect to be the research, development, product, and application agendas for the next five years.

The development of new application paradigms is a major focus of current work and can be expected to expand in the future. Predictions by industry analysts have focused primarily on commercial intranet deployments with a particular emphasis on increasing resource utilization. Yet this perspective only scratches the surface of the Grid's capabilities. The flexible formation of dynamic collaborations can have a profound effect on organizational structure. However, to achieve this potential, we need advances in the way applications are structured, standardization of associated service definitions, and in some cases new business models as well. For example, dynamic federation requires not only services for dynamically evaluating and enforcing trust relationships but also a dynamic provisioning and payment model to produce a federated (or virtualized) service set that maps to the requirements of the collaboration.

There is an urgent need for program development and execution tools for Grid environments: compilers, debuggers, performance monitors, and libraries. High-level languages and programming paradigms suitable for dynamic environments are required. Grid-enabled libraries (Chapters 16 and 24) and workflow systems are important, but more sophisticated autonomic techniques should also be pursued (Chapters 25 and 26). We require an improved understanding of correctness, performance, troubleshooting, and optimization in dynamic environments. Users need to be able to assemble multiple services to create both Grid infrastructure and Grid applications that meet requirements. The cost of assembling these services must be sufficiently low that users can focus on their goals rather than on building customized infrastructure. Research is required on theories and techniques to describe and reason about the semantics and behavior of services and the compositional effects of putting services together. New tools to support the discovery, composition, and use of services based on high-level descriptions of requirements must also be developed.

We need to understand how to scale the Grid both to larger numbers of entities and to smaller devices. The future pervasive digital infrastructure will seamlessly combine reliable high-performance computing systems, communication networks, and variable low-performance embedded or portable devices with integrated wireless facilities. Resources will vary in their availability, quality, and reliability. Fundamental computing research is needed to enable the realization of trusted ubiquitous systems formed from the coalition of these potentially uncertain components. Effective solutions to these scaling problems must inevitably involve the development of infrastructure elements capable of adapting to changes in application or user needs without undue human intervention: what IBM has termed "autonomic computing" (365), a term that encompasses automated management, configuration, optimization, healing, and protection.

The social, economic, and political aspects of Grids are going to become increasingly important. (The third edition of this book will surely feature authors from the social sciences.) We envision a wide variety of different Grids ranging from highly controlled "intra-Grids" using secure private networks to spontaneous community Grids using the global Internet. The large number of users, cultures, and usage modalities will demand not only new policy specification, monitoring, and enforcement mechanisms but also an improved understanding of the social and economic issues that influence stability and productivity. Social scientists also have much to contribute to our understanding of issues of trust (301, 321, 416) and usability (511, 676).

Another area in which fundamental research is required relates to the role of knowledge systems and services, not only for future Grid applications, but also for the effective functioning of the Grid itself. As discussed in Chapter 23, we need to be able to manage the traceability and integrity of information and to trace provenance, all the way from initial data through information to knowledge structures. New theories and techniques are required to allow tolerant, safe, and scalable reasoning over uncertain and incomplete knowledge that embraces data, metadata, and knowledge activities.

4.5   SUMMARY

We have introduced the principal topics to be discussed at greater length in the chapters that follow. We provided a concise statement of the "Grid problem," which we define as controlled and coordinated resource sharing and resource use in dynamic, scalable virtual organizations. We have also both motivated and defined a Grid architecture, in which are identified the principal functions required to enable sharing within VOs and the key relationships that exist among these different functions. Finally, we have introduced the open source Globus Toolkit that has enabled the rapid adoption of Grid technologies and the Open Grid Services Architecture specifications now supporting the continued expansion of Grid technologies and applications.

FURTHER READING

For more information on the topics covered in this chapter, see *www.mkp.com/grid2* and the following references:

+ Much of the material in Chapter 1:2 is not repeated here, and remains highly relevant.

+ Two recent articles in *Physics Today* (269) and *Scientific American* (270) provide good high-level introductions to Grid computing and its applications.

+ The 2003 report of the National Science Foundation's Blue Ribbon Panel on Cyberinfrastructure summarizes the scientific motivation for Grids (37).

+ A recent book edited by Berman, Fox, and Hey provides good coverage of research in Grid computing (113). See also the proceedings of the annual IEEE Symposium on High Performance Distributed Computing (HPDC).

APPLICATIONS

Our interest in Grids is motivated above all by the prospect of innovative new uses of computers. Hence, applications form a good starting point for more detailed discussion, allowing us to examine simultaneously Grids and future demands that we may expect on technologies.

Each of the 12 chapters in Part III covers a particular application, presenting the motivation for using Grid technologies, the architecture and approach adopted in an implementation, and (where appropriate) experiences and results obtained. These applications come from science and industry, from academia and laboratories, and from large corporations and startups. They cover compute-, data-, sensor-, knowledge-, and collaboration-intensive scenarios and address problems ranging from multiplayer video gaming, fault diagnosis in jet engines, and earthquake engineering to bioinformatics, biomedical imaging, and astrophysics. Collectively, these case studies provide a good introduction to the broad spectrum of usage scenarios driving Grid adoption and development.

In Chapter 5, "Predictive Maintenance: Distributed Aircraft Engine Diagnostics," Jim Austin and his colleagues discuss the application of Grid technologies to the challenging and broadly important problem of computer-based fault diagnosis, an inherently distributed problem in many situations due to the range of data sources and stakeholders involved. They describe, in particular, a UK e-Science project that is applying Grid technologies to the problems of diagnosing faults in Rolls-Royce aircraft engines based on sensor data recorded during flight.

In Chapter 6, "Distributed Telepresence: The NEESgrid Earthquake Engineering Collaboratory," Carl Kesselman, Ian Foster, and Tom Prudhomme describe a collaboratory and telepresence infrastructure developed for the National Science Foundation's Network for Earthquake Engineering Simulation, an ambitious project to transform the specialized equipment used to design earthquake-resistant buildings into remotely accessible facilities. NEESgrid supports telepresence for remote participation in experiments, distributed archiving of experiment data, and the coupling of experiments with numerical simulations.

In Chapter 7, "Scientific Data Federation: The World-Wide Telescope," Alex Szalay and Jim Gray describe the revolutionary changes in astronomy resulting from advances in digital astronomy and the application of Grid concepts. What they call the "World-Wide Telescope" federates data from hundreds of individual instruments, allowing a new generation of armchair astronomers to perform analyses of unprecedented scope and scale. They describe both the opportunities and obstacles associated with this new mode of science.

In Chapter 8, "Medical Data Federation: The Biomedical Informatics Research Network," Mark Ellisman and Steve Peltier describe a project aimed at federating biomedical imaging data. BIRN is deploying compute-storage clusters at research and clinical sites around the United States and is deploying Grid middleware to enable the integration of image data from multiple locations for the purposes of research and, ultimately, improved clinical care.

In Chapter 9, "Knowledge Integration: *In Silico* Experiments in Bioinformatics," Carole Goble and her colleagues present a somewhat different (although complementary) perspective on the data federation and analysis problem. Their ᵐʸGrid project focuses on the semantically rich problems of dynamic resource discovery, workflow specification, and distributed query processing, as well as provenance management, change notification, and personalization.

In Chapter 10, "Distributed Data Analysis: Federated Computing for High-Energy Physics," Greg Graham and his colleagues present a detailed analysis of the technologies and effort required to complete a challenging data generation and analysis task for a high-energy physics experiment. They explain how they harnessed computing and storage resources at six sites to generate 1.5 million simulated events during a two-month run.

In Chapter 11, "Massively Distributed Computing: Virtual Screening on Desktop Computers," Andrew Chien describes the execution of a drug discovery application, virtual screening, on an intra-Grid composed of desktop PCs. Chien discusses how an existing molecular docking application was integrated into a commercial Grid environment to achieve a significant increase in processing power over what drug companies would typically have dedicated to compound screening.

In Chapter 12, "Enterprise Resource Management: Applications in Research and Industry," Wolfgang Gentzsch uses three case studies involving the use of Grid resource management technologies to improve the efficiency and flexibility of resource usage within an enterprise. He presents the design criteria, technologies, and experiences gained in one commercial and two academic settings.

In Chapter 13, "Interactivity with Scalability: Infrastructure for Multiplayer Games," David Levine and Mark Wirt present a service provider scenario from the multiplayer videogaming industry, describing how Butterfly.net is using Grid technologies to deliver scalable hosting services to game developers. These applications are particularly interesting because of the potentially huge number of participants in a game coupled with the need for interactive response.

In Chapter 14, "Service Virtualization: Infrastructure and Applications," Ming Xu and his colleagues explore the increasing role of virtualization in the enterprise information technology infrastructure. They investigate software and infrastructure trends toward virtualization. The chapter concludes with a case study, showing how resource and service virtualization delivered by Platform Symphony resulted in significant performance improvements for a global investment bank.

In Chapter 15, "Group-Oriented Collaboration: The Access Grid Collaboration System," Rick Stevens introduces a rather different application domain for Grid technologies, namely, high-end collaboration and conferencing environments. He describes, in particular, the Access Grid system, its technical requirements, and plans for far more extensive use of Grid technologies.

Finally, in Chapter 16, "Collaborative Science: Astrophysics Requirements and Experiences," Ed Seidel and Gabrielle Allen summarize their pioneering work in the exploration, development, and application of Grid technologies to a range of problems in high-end collaborative science.

Despite the diversity of applications considered, we see clear and consistent themes arising. Grids do enable qualitatively new approaches to problem solving. There are early successes and definite paths to improved future capabilities. Rich middleware services are required if application development is to be manageable. These topics are addressed in later chapters.

The material in this section is entirely new and complements, rather than replaces, Chapters 1:3, 1:4, 1:5, and 1:6 in the first edition, which provided a survey of four general classes of application: distributed supercomputing (also known as metacomputing), real-time widely distributed instrumentation systems, data-intensive applications, and teleimmersive collaboration systems. Although that material of course reflects a 1998 perspective and experience, much of its content stands the test of time and provides a valuable reference. We provide brief summaries of this material.

In Chapter 1:3, "Distributed Supercomputing Applications," Paul Messina discusses distributed supercomputing applications. The chapter first reviews the motivations for using multiple computers, including a need for greater power, the coupling of software at different sites, and performance gains that can result from use of heterogeneous architectures. Then techniques for developing such applications are described, including latency-tolerant algorithms, bandwidth-minimizing decomposition techniques, adaptive scheduling techniques, and fault recovery mechanisms. The practical implications of these issues are illustrated by means of three case studies: a computational chemistry application, a coupled climate model, and a distributed interactive simulation system.

In Chapter 1:4, "Realtime Widely Distributed Instrumentation Systems," William Johnston casts light on numerous practical issues that arise when building Grid applications, particularly those that involve real-time data sources. He describes four such systems: a remotely controlled beamline at a particle accelerator, a cardioangiography system that depends on real-time data cataloging, a high-energy physics data processing architecture that supports very high data rates and volume, and a remote-control system for an electron microscope. These systems are then used to motivate discussions of distributed-storage architecture, network-based caches, agent-based monitoring and management, and generalized access control mechanisms. An overarching theme is the importance of careful architecture design if a Grid system is to meet performance and reliability goals.

In Chapter 1:5, "Data-Intensive Computing," Reagan Moore and his colleagues discuss applications that are both data and compute intensive. In these applications, the focus is on processing and analyzing information rather than simulating a physical process. They first examine both contemporary examples (data assimilation in the earth sciences and digital sky surveys in astronomy) and planned future digital libraries and knowledge networks. Then they review the developments in software infrastructure required to support these applications. They emphasize the need to support not only distributed processing but also distributed caching of data, as well as the demands that will be placed on generic Grid services (e.g., archival storage and resource location) and the need for specialized services for organizing and accessing distributed data.

In Chapter 1:6, "Teleimmersion," Tom DeFanti and Rick Stevens discuss teleimmersion systems, in which advanced display technologies, computers, and networks are used in concert to create shared virtual environments for collaborative design, education, entertainment, and other purposes. They argue that teleimmersive applications will be the Grid's most demanding users, serving not only as early adopters for the technology but also as a primary driver for their future development. They review current and expected future teleimmersive applications and provide a detailed analysis of their networking requirements, characterizing nine types of flow in terms of seven different performance metrics.

Predictive Maintenance: Distributed Aircraft Engine Diagnostics

Jim Austin, Tom Jackson, Martyn Fletcher, Mark Jessop, Peter Cowley, and Peter Lobner

We present an exciting and novel application domain for Grid technologies, namely, the development of an improved computer-based fault diagnosis and prognostic (DP) capability and the integration of that capability with a predictive maintenance system. We describe, in particular, the Distributed Aircraft Maintenance Environment (DAME), a pilot project involving Rolls-Royce, Data Systems and Solutions, and other commercial and academic partners in the UK that is applying Grid-based technologies to the problems of aircraft engine DP and maintenance.

Fault DP problems arise in many domains, including medicine, engineering, transport, and aerospace. Regardless of domain, fault diagnosis systems share a number of operating and design constraints. Specifically, DP systems

+ are data centric: monitoring and analysis of sensor data and domain-specific knowledge are critical to the DP process;

+ typically require complex interactions among multiple agents or stakeholders;

+ are often distributed;

+ need to provide supporting or qualifying evidence for the DP offered; and

+ can be safety or business critical and typically have high dependability requirements.

In some contexts, detection thresholds and intervals enable active fault diagnosis and prognosis that can then allow remedial action to be taken at a safe and convenient time when the impact of maintenance is minimized. In such cases, we say that DP systems can drive "predictive maintenance."

In the sections that follow we first elaborate on the various aspects of DP systems listed previously and then describe the DAME project, its target real-world operational maintenance environment, and its progress to date.

5.1   GRID SERVICES FOR DIAGNOSTIC PROBLEMS

The emerging Grid computing paradigm offers an inherently practical framework to address the design and operational constraints listed in the introduction, as we explain in the rest of this section. We note that some of this material is also relevant to the NEESgrid earthquake engineering collaboratory discussed in Chapter 6.

Data Centricity.   Fault diagnosis is fundamentally based on the monitoring and analysis of sensor data through the application of declarative and procedural knowledge. Data from sensors must be captured, often in real time, and made available to analysis systems, either remote or local. Root cause determination and prognosis may require integrating data from several different systems to build a pattern or a case that is reusable in subsequent diagnoses. To extend the capabilities of fault DP systems, it is also beneficial to archive data such that an operational log of system performance or fault conditions can be maintained. Fault trend analysis and data-mining operations can then be used to reevaluate historical data periodically as the DP knowledge base improves. Archived sensor data may be stored locally to a monitoring system or remotely, although it is typical to store data remotely from the point of monitoring in data archive systems that are extendable and more easily maintained within a controlled environment. Depending on the nature of the system being monitored, the volumes of data being captured can be substantial, requiring vast data repositories. The types of data collected can also be highly diverse; in addition to static numeric, text, and image data, dynamic data are often involved, and thus granularity can vary from milliseconds to days and years.

DP systems must capture not only sensor data but also nondeclarative knowledge, such as procedures for diagnosing the current condition and then developing a prognosis of the future outcome(s). Data capturing the possible faults, past faults, histories of past diagnostic methods, and other heuristic information must be managed and stored. The interpretation of the knowledge can vary among the entities involved, requiring the use of intermediary systems to translate and unify differing viewpoints—with support from ontologies and other systems (Chapter 23). Emerging Grid technologies seem likely to provide solutions for the management and archiving of large data repositories, remote collection and distribution of data, and the coherent integration of information from diverse databases (Chapter 22).

Thus, the Grid represents a promising platform on which to address data management issues relevant to information technology (IT)-based fault DP systems.

Multiple Stakeholders.   Most DP problems involve a number of stakeholders: the system owner or operator, experts that diagnose potential problems, the commercial service provider, and system maintainers as well as organizations associated with each of them. The design of any DP system should accommodate all of the relevant stakeholders (648). The concept of multiple stakeholders requiring interaction to diverse parts of an IT system is inherent within the Grid computing model, and these capabilities can be exploited.

Distribution.   DP systems are typically distributed, such that data monitoring and collection, data storage, data mining, and fault diagnosis may take place at different locations or across diverse IT systems, some of which are not Grid-resident systems. The systems can also be highly dynamic: the processes of DP can be seen as building an organization, involving a number of disparate entities to solve the problem. This organization is virtual, since it may not be permanent and may change often. Distribution is often desirable, or at times unavoidable; but the communications and interoperability issues involved in managing diverse data systems, diverse systems applications, and diverse actors or system stakeholders in a dynamic way add a significant level of computational complexity to the development of DP systems. The standardization of communication and application protocols within the Grid paradigm should help resolve many of these design complexities and support effective interactions with users who do not work within the Grid environment or have direct access to a Grid portal.

Data Provenance.   The motivation for the use of computers to mediate DP systems is clear. IT-based systems can provide automated, rigorous, and procedural solutions for system monitoring and analysis. Within the fault analysis and related prognosis processes, however, it is essential to establish transparency and trust in the results. The steps that have been taken to arrive at a decision are often as important to an end user as the diagnosis and prognosis themselves; end users need the ability to qualify the steps taken to reach a decision or to challenge the reasoning or the data sources. Hence, data provenance (141, 284) is essential. The Grid community is developing open data communication protocols and meta-labeling schemes suited to this task.

Dependability.   DP systems are often business or safety critical. This feature can place high dependability requirements on the design and operation of a DP system, including issues of guaranteed service availability, data security, and system security. When systems are distributed, these requirements become all the more stringent. Grid computing offers a security model tailored to secure distributed computing (Chapter 21), with both data access and data confidentiality being addressed. Guaranteed service and quality-of-service issues are not yet fully defined in the Grid model; however, these concepts are emerging (Chapter 18) and will require assessment.

For these requirements, Grid services offer considerable support. Grid middleware has the potential to mediate the process of DP, within complex and dynamic operational business and engineering processes. Moreover, the Grid can provide service on demand, offering computing resources for computationally intensive applications in the DP process, such as simulation and modeling. Fault DP in complex systems presents many other challenges. Typically, however, two issues are foremost: (1) handling the data (which may be noisy, uncertain, or ambiguous) and (2) mining the data (which may be in large, distributed data repositories) in a timely manner.

5.2 THE AERO-ENGINE DP PROBLEM

We examine these issues within the context of the Distributed Aircraft Maintenance Environment, a project focused on an aero-engine DP problem. Modern aero-engines must operate in highly demanding environments with extremely high reliability. To this end, jet engines combine advanced mechanical engineering systems with tightly coupled electronic control systems. As one would expect, such critical systems are fitted with extensive sensing and monitoring capabilities for performance analysis. In order to facilitate engine fleet management, engine sensor data are routinely analyzed using the COMPASS health monitoring application developed by Rolls-Royce and prognostic applications employed by Data Systems and Solutions. The resulting commercial DP services are subscribed to by many commercial airlines. The goal of monitoring is to detect the earliest signs of deviation from normal operating behavior. To this end, COMPASS compares snapshots of engine sensor data with ideal engine models. The relatively small datasets may be transmitted in flight or downloaded to the ground.

To further increase the effectiveness of data monitoring, QUOTE, an advanced on-wing monitoring system developed by Rolls-Royce and Oxford University (495), performs engine analysis on data derived from continuous monitoring of broadband engine vibration and fuses this data with instantaneous performance data. QUOTE has access to more information than a ground-based system collecting narrow-band performance data. However, it cannot store data from many flights or cross-reference data from the rest of an aircraft fleet; whereas a ground-based system can maintain fleetwide databases of historical information and perform various ad hoc analyses that enable anomalies to be correlated to root causes and appropriate remedial actions to be taken.

Recent advances in communications technologies in the commercial aerospace domain now make it economically viable to consider downloading high-volume engine sensor data during flight. The DAME project, however, permits an alternative. By improving the fault-detection threshold and detection interval, DAME provides ample time for downloading high-volume data *after* the aircraft has landed.

Developing a Grid-based DP system to process the data in such a ground-based system presents the DAME project with three principal challenges:

✦ The type of data captured by QUOTE primarily involves real-valued variables monitored over time. An example is shown in Figure 5.1. Each flight can produce up to 1 gigabyte of data, which implies many terabytes of data across a fleet per year. The storage of these data will require vast data repositories, which will be distributed across many geographic and operational boundaries and must be accessible for health monitoring services.

✦ In order to detect features and analyze the type of data produced by the engine, advanced pattern-matching and data-mining methods must be developed. These methods must be able to operate on terabytes of data with response times that meet the operational demands of the DP tasks.

✦ The DP processes will require collaboration among a number of diverse actors within the stakeholder organizations, who may need to deploy a range of different engineering and computational tools to analyze a problem. Thus, any Grid-based solution must allow a virtual organization to support the services, individuals, and systems involved in DP processes.

To address these challenges, the DAME system is developing a number of core functional services and tools. Beneath these services are other Grid middleware applications that support the integration of tools and functions.

Engine Data Service.   This service controls the interactions between the on-engine monitoring system QUOTE and its communications to a ground station, which establishes the link to Grid data repositories. Since aircraft land in many parts of the world, there will be many replications of this service, each of which will be highly transient, existing only long enough for the flight and monitoring data to be transferred from the aircraft to a ground station.

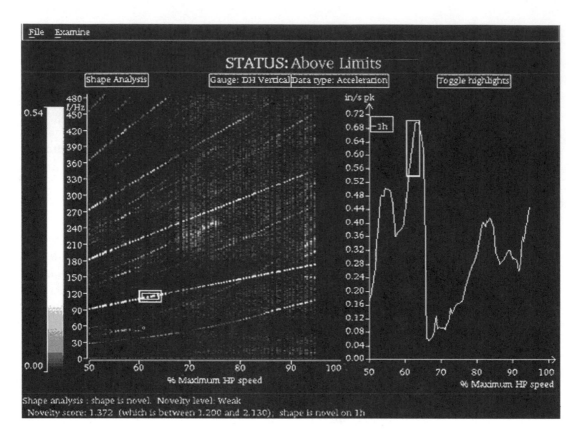

5.1

FIGURE

Typical vibration data captured from a Rolls-Royce aero-engine. On the left is a plot of vibration against shaft speed. The graph shows a box where there is an anomaly, expanded on the right. The right plot shows one "tracked order" and the same anomaly as indicated on the left. © 1996–1999 Oxford University, used with permission.

Data Storage and Mining Service.   This service consists of the AURA pattern-matching engine system (3), which uses specialized methods to rapidly search both raw and archived engine data. The architecture resembles that of a data-mining service (495). The learning achieved with AURA supports continuous improvement of the diagnostic process.

Engine Modeling Service.   This service takes parameters from flight data and runs models of the engine. The main aim is to infer the current state of the engine—in effect, to perform model-based data fusion. This is intended to improve the engine modeling service currently employed in COMPASS.

Case-Based Reasoning Support. This tool uses case-based reasoning (CBR) (430) to improve the knowledge base and captures fault DP methods in a procedural way. One potential application is to manage workflows associated with DP operations. A second is to build and maintain the DAME knowledge base that correlates observed QUOTE engine anomalies with the results of root cause investigations by the various organizations that perform engine maintenance, repair, and overhaul. The learning achieved with CBR tools supports continuous improvement of both of the DP processes.

Maintenance Interface Service. This service organizes all interactions with stakeholders involved in taking remedial actions in response to a diagnosis and prognosis. It captures information that helps validate or refine the output from the preceding DP processes. This link to maintenance, repair, and overhaul stakeholders is essential for "closing the loop," capturing lessons learned, and driving continuous improvement of the DAME DP processes.

These services are supported by (1) autonomous services that capture and check data as they arrive, and notify users that data have arrived and that new diagnostic or prognostic operations might be required, and (2) operations on data using the tools and functions outlined previously.

5.3   OPERATION AND USE OF THE DAME GRID SERVICE

The DAME project, under way since January 2002, has defined the generic system requirements and the deployment and data-mining scenarios. Technology development has commenced with initial focus on implementing the core data analysis functions described previously, and in particular the AURA data-mining pattern-matching Grid service needed to support commercial aero-engine aftermarket services.

The functional operation of the pattern-matching scenario is shown in Figure 5.2. The scenario demonstrates the process of matching anomalous engine data identified by the QUOTE system against the archived database of fleet engine data. This operation involves some of the most critical actions within the aero-engine demonstrator problem, requiring coding and search of terascale engine datasets and compute-intensive processing of the data retrieved. The White Rose Grid (Chapter 12) is used for distributed compute-intensive processes.

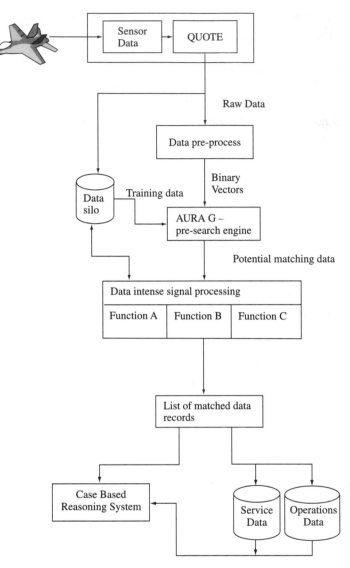

5.2 FIGURE Functional diagram of the pattern-matching scenario within the DAME demonstrator.

The operation starts by using the QUOTE system to identify possible abnormal vibration data. Figure 5.1 shows an example in which QUOTE has highlighted a possible abnormality in the data. When abnormal data are detected that cannot be classified locally by the QUOTE system, then the sensor data are passed to the ground-based diagnostic system and storage facility, where they are stored and held for further processing.

Simultaneously, the system reports the possible abnormality to interested stakeholders (i.e., the airline operator, Rolls-Royce, and Data Systems and Solutions). A search against the archived fleet engine data can be performed automatically or as an ad hoc search initiated by a qualified user. This fleet engine database may contain previous instances of the abnormality that can assist in the diagnosis of the current condition.

The vast data-mining activity to recover related events from the flight archives is facilitated by a Grid-enabled version of the AURA system, AURA-G (3). This pattern-matching engine supports distributed search on massive data collections using scalable, neural-network-derived methods (60).

AURA provides search techniques for terascale datasets that are designed to retrieve a small relevant subset of that data for further processing. In the DAME demonstrator context, the system returns possible vibration data that match the anomaly conditions found on the engine. If similar abnormal events are found in the data archive, then any supporting information relating to these events, such as maintenance steps or remedial corrective action, can be recovered from the appropriate operations databases that are visible on the Grid from within the DAME portal. Where similar events are not detected, or when further processing of the anomalous datasets may be required for fault identification, then further detailed analysis of the data can be performed by using a number of compute-intensive signal analysis modules available within the DAME portal. To do this, a Grid service creates new instantiations of the modules on a set of registered computers. These are passed the data, the module, and the parameters for undertaking the operation. Since the AURA search may return thousands of potential data items, the use of distributed resources is vital to achieve a timely delivery of information.

The diagnostic process is completed with distribution of DP results to the appropriate airline and MRO (maintenance, repair, and overhaul) stakeholders. Remedial action can then be scheduled and a work package prepared. When the pattern-matching provides multiple candidate matches, the CBR element will suggest the most probable diagnosis based on the cases stored in its database and may provide instructions on how to confirm the specific fault.

This example identifies requirements for several fundamental Grid service operations, including simulation of a virtual organization to undertake the analysis operations, invocation of nonpersistent services for compute-intensive operations, use of persistent data storage and data-mining services, creation of temporary data stores, and workflow/taskflow management. Several of these capabilities are already supported by the Globus Toolkit, while others are under development within the OGSA context (see Chapter 17).

5.4   FUTURE DIRECTIONS

The DAME system is developing technology at a number of levels. The base services consisting of AURA-G, QUOTE, CBR, and data storage provide universal components that will be used in many other applications. In particular, Cybula is committed to providing Grid-enabled versions of the AURA search engine for applications as diverse as biometrics to engineering. The composition of these core services into a diagnostic/prognostic workbench or portal is another development level, which deploys Grid middleware services for the management of workflows through the DP services in the demonstrator domain. At the top level, the approach is being applied to Rolls-Royce and Data Systems and Solutions aero-engine DP applications and is being considered for application in medical and other similar diagnostic applications. In addition to the demonstrator, which delivers proof of concept for Grid computing in the DP domain, the project will also deliver to the wider Grid community, via the problems and lessons that we have learned in building a complex DP virtual organization based on Grid services.

DAME is particularly focused on developing a proof-of-concept prototype using the Globus Toolkit and other emerging Grid service technologies to provide input for developing standards in areas such as data mining and core Grid services. In addition, we are using our prototype to explore the functionality and timeliness of a Grid-based DP system in meeting the needs of our industrial partners.

We are also developing models of the performance properties of Grid-based systems with the goal of identifying areas in which improvement may be needed. The scale of the aircraft engine DP problem makes the DAME demonstrator an extremely demanding example in this respect. The dependability of the system is also a prime concern, as is the security of the system when scaled to global level. These issues will be addressed in the near future as the testbed evolves and as a quality-of-service measurement framework is implemented.

ACKNOWLEDGMENTS

This work was performed by the DAME team at the Universities of York, Leeds, Sheffield, and Oxford, with assistance from Rolls-Royce, Data Systems and

Solutions, and Cybula, and was supported by Grant GR/R67668/01 from the Engineering and Physical Research Council in the UK.

FURTHER READING

For more information on the topics covered in this chapter, see *www.mkp.com/grid2*.

Distributed Telepresence: The NEESgrid Earthquake Engineering Collaboratory

Carl Kesselman, Ian Foster, and Tom Prudhomme

*I*n this chapter we describe NEESgrid, a Grid-based system that supports a broad range of activities performed by a community of engineers and researchers engaged in improving the performance of buildings and other structures when subjected to the effects of earthquakes. This earthquake engineering community has some requirements that have much in common with those of other disciplines, such as the need to federate multiple data sources. It also introduces unique challenges that derive from the fundamental role physical experiments play in the design process. We focus our discussion here on the latter topic and describe how NEESgrid integrates a range of earthquake engineering test apparatus into the Grid infrastructure.

6.1   COLLABORATORIES FOR EARTHQUAKE ENGINEERING

A diverse community of scientists and engineers study the impact and aftermath of seismic events on the physical infrastructure of modern society—buildings, bridges, and roads—with the goal of making them safer. Within the field of earthquake engineering, structural engineers focus on the performance of the structures themselves, while geotechnical engineers study the response of soils and landforms to earthquakes, and still another branch of earthquake engineering seeks to understand the nature of tsunamis. However, regardless of the research focus, the earthquake engineering community has historically gained understanding of how structures or soils perform by measuring the response of physical models or soil samples subjected to simulated earthquake loads via the use of specialized testing platforms such as shake tables, reaction walls, and centrifuges.

Advances in understanding the responses of structures or soils are directly linked to access to testing facilities. Sharing of both facilities and the resulting experimental data across the earthquake engineering community can enhance the utility of the experimental facilities and produce improved engineering results. Equally important is the need for experts from the separate domains within the earthquake engineering research community to collaborate and share knowledge. Often, structures researchers are focused on component testing, and geotechnical researchers on the responses of soil samples to experimentally generated earthquake forces. Collaboration among these domain specialists might provide new understanding about the interaction between, for example, structures and soils, or between tsunami activity and the soils or structures that exist on shorelines.

Regardless of subdiscipline, earthquake engineers are focused increasingly on augmenting or replacing experimental methods with computational approaches, developing numerical models that can predict the response of a structure, material, or soil under various loadings. Computational methods can offer deeper insight into structural behavior, help drive design activities, and provide a lower-cost solution than experimental analysis. When used in conjunction with experimental techniques, computational methods can enable entirely new approaches to engineering analysis in which experiments combine both physical and simulated components. However, progress in computational methods is being held back by limited access to the experimental data required to validate numerical models, by an inability to share and compare results for various computational simulations, and by a limited ability for the experimental and computational communities to interact. Thus, in addition to needs for increased access to computational facilities and the need to couple these facilities on demand to experimental apparatus, progress in the use and utility of computational methods in earthquake engineering can also be advanced by enabling the sharing of codes and data between computational scientists and enhancing the ability of the experimental and computational communities to share and exchange information.

6.1.1   NEES and NEESgrid

For the aforementioned reasons, the National Science Foundation recognized that significant advances in earthquake engineering could be achieved by introducing advanced networking, distributed computing, and collaboration technologies to the practice of earthquake engineering. This led to the creation, in 1999, of the George E. Brown Network for Earthquake Engineering and Simulation (NEES) program. This activity comprises three components:

✦ A major investment in earthquake engineering test facilities such as shake tables, reaction walls, and wave tanks, all of which are required to be network accessible, so as to support broad community access to these expensive instruments.

✦ A system-integration activity whose role is to construct the necessary information technology infrastructure for integrating test equipment, simulation, data repositories, and collaboration tools.

✦ A community-wide consortium whose function is to manage the overall infrastructure.

Although the equipment acquisition and consortium development activities are clearly significant to the overall success of the program, it is the system integration part of the project that is most germane to the topic at hand. Hence we focus only on this aspect in the following discussion.

At the core of NEES requirements is the desire to knit the equipment sites, data repositories, and broad earthquake engineering community (experimentalists, researchers, and practicing engineers across the entire disipline) into a more cohesive *virtual organization*. The capabilities offered by Grid infrastructure are a natural fit to the requirements of the NEES program, which led us to create a deployment of Grid technologies called *NEESgrid*. NEESgrid builds on top of standard Grid infrastructure (specifically the Globus Toolkit), augmenting it with services and end-user tools specialized toward the earthquake engineering community and deployed in a manner that exploits the special structure of the NEES experimental environment. NEESgrid is designed to address four high-level requirements:

✦ Increase the effectiveness of the major equipment investment in earthquake engineering test facilities by increasing access to new test platforms and integrating these platforms with simulation and storage resources.

✦ Increase the use of computational methods in earthquake engineering by facilitating shared access to and use of simulation codes, the data and models needed to drive simulations, and the computational and storage resources needed to execute the codes.

✦ Accelerate the development of new earthquake engineering methods by increasing the opportunity for members of the community to collaborate in designing and undertaking research investigations.

✦ Drive the development of new engineering methods in which computational and experimental methods are tightly coupled.

6.1.2   New Modes of Working Enabled by NEESgrid

By creating a collaborative environment that integrates experimental, simulation, and archived data, NEESgrid can provide easier access to computers and storage systems, provide collaboration infrastructure over which existing collaborations can communicate, and enhance the capabilities of existing Web-based tools and, in doing so, improve the current practice of earthquake engineering in the short term. However, the true promise of NEESgrid is that it can stimulate the development of entirely new methods of earthquake engineering, as illustrated by the following three scenarios.

Distributed Pseudodynamic Testing of Structures.   In pseudodynamic testing, a test structure is loaded with forces that are dynamically recomputed as the stiffness of the structure decreases during the test. NEESgrid collaboration and teleoperation facilities, when deployed at multiple test facilities and supercomputer simulation facilities, can enable a new distributed approach that expands substantially the range of structures that can be tested with this method. In this new approach, separate components of a structural system are tested individually at different sites. A computational model is used to control the loads on each component. For example, a number of large-scale reaction wall experiments can be performed simultaneously to investigate behavior of a complex structural system, such as a highway overpass structure with multiple height piers.

Tsunami Inundation Early Warning.   NEESgrid access to deep-ocean sensors, tsunami simulations, and an online archive of inundation maps can enable the creation of an early warning system for tsunami inundation. The initiation of a tsunami would be determined by detecting a seismic event. Based on parameters of this event, online tsunami models are invoked and the inundation archive accessed to identify potential inundation sites. As deep-ocean sensors measure actual tsunami activity, the parameters to the model are adjusted and updated inundation reports generated.

Real-Time Parameter Estimation Using Field Data Analysis.   NEESgrid access to simulation models can be used to improve dramatically the efficiency of field data collection. Rather than collect data and analyze it after the fact, field-test data can be passed to system identification modules in the simulation environment. These modules calculate model parameters in real time; model output is then used to guide further field measurements. For example, an analyst might detect a critical sensitivity of the model to certain vibration modes. The field team can then extract information regarding these modes as the model is being built, rather than having to return later to obtain the required information.

6.2   NEESGRID SYSTEM OVERVIEW

NEESgrid forms a common infrastructure that is shared across the earthquake engineering community. The design of this infrastructure is complicated by the community's diversity, the need to support both experimental and simulation-based investigations, and the need to evolve the system over time as new approaches to earthquake engineering develop. For these reasons, we avoided constructing NEESgrid as a set of "stovepipe" applications but instead have adhered to a layered architecture based on common services, specialized domain-specific toolkits and libraries built on these services, and end-user applications built on the toolkits and libraries.

Our approach to the NEES system integration problem has been simultaneously to *build on proven, existing Grid technology* and to *integrate existing best-practice tools from the commercial and research sectors*. The result is a layered, modular architecture that provides a highly extensible and flexible solution to the full range of NEES problems that enables rapid development of new end-user applications, the incremental introduction of new services, and the integration of new simulation software and experimental apparatus as they are developed. This flexible, extensible framework enables NEESgrid to incorporate new sites and integrate new technologies and future applications as they are developed.

NEESgrid builds on standard Grid infrastructure, specifically the Globus Toolkit. However, the specific requirements of the earthquake engineering community are reflected in the way in which this infrastructure is deployed and in the types of higher-level services layered on top of the basic Grid infrastructure. NEESgrid spans five basic functional components:

+ *Experimental facilities* enhanced with *collaborative technologies* to enable collaborative planning and teleobservation of experiments as they are taking place, *data management* to enable remote archiving and integration of experimental data with simulation capabilities, and *control interfaces* to enable teleoperation where appropriate.

+ *Information management systems* that enable the curation and sharing of data and metadata through centralized and distributed repositories, including storage systems at experimental facilities and other remote sites, enhanced with data management software to enable rapid and controlled publication of and subsequent remote access to experimental and simulation data. This requirement is similar to that encountered in other disciplines (e.g., see Chapter 9), so we do not discuss it here in detail.

+ *Simulation systems* and associated *software repositories* that enable a wide range of earthquake engineers to exploit powerful simulation codes at high speeds, whether on centralized supercomputers or on high-end clusters at user sites.

✦ *User sites*, with *NEESgrid-enabled user desktops* that provide individual users with access to the experimental, collaborative, simulation, and data archive capabilities of the entire collaboratory.

✦ *Support node(s)*, which maintain *online knowledge bases* containing tutorial and other information concerning the effective operation of the many components of the NEESgrid collaboratory and which operate *help desk(s)* that provide access to assistance with the technologies that underlie the NEESgrid collaboratory, whether collaborative tools, data archives, or the underlying networks.

A summary of these components and how they relate to one another is shown in Figure 6.1. Support for information management, simulation, user sites, and support nodes leverage standard deployments of Grid infrastructure. As it is the equipment sites that really set NEESgrid apart from most other Grid deployments, we will focus on their structure in the following discussion.

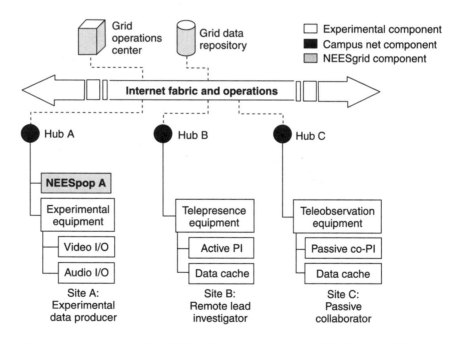

6.1

FIGURE

Main components of the NEESgrid system. The legend indicates which parts of the system are specific to NEESgrid, which parts belong to the existing IT infrastructure, and which parts are specific to a NEEgrid experiment.

6.2.1   NEESgrid Equipment Sites

A variety of experimental equipment is used in earthquake engineering. To test structures, one can build a scale model and measure its dynamic response by placing it on a *shake table* that can be accelerated in any combination of one to six degrees of freedom. Figure 6.2 shows a picture of a shake table along with a scale model that is tested on it. Static loading can be measured by attaching parts of a structure to a rigid *reaction wall* and using hydraulics to apply forces to specific elements of the structure. Soil mechanics are often studied under scale by subjecting a test apparatus (e.g., a small shake table), but subjecting the soil sample to scaled gravity by placing it in a *centrifuge*. The behavior of tsunami waves, caused by earthquakes in the ocean, can be studied by creating waves in large *wave tanks*. There are many other types of test facilities, but these capture the main types of equipment. A given test facility may have one or more of these types of equipment.

The response of the structure under test is measured by instrumenting the model with sensors such as accelerometers, displacement gauges, and strain gauges. In addition, structure response may be captured by still or video images. Currently, most of the sensors produce analog outputs, and these must be connected to an analog-to-digital converter to capture digital data. A data acquisition system is used to then collect the resulting data, while an experiment control system is used to control the actuators such as the hydraulics that drive a shake table. A wide variety of data acquisition and control systems are used, ranging from commercial off-the-shelf systems (such as the National Instruments LabView system) to fully customized systems developed by the equipment sites themselves.

6.2

FIGURE

Two views of a "shake table," one type of equipment to which NEESgrid provides access. The picture on the left shows the three biaxial shake tables located at James E. Rogers and Louis Wiener, Jr., Bridge Structures Laboratory at the University of Nevada, Reno. The picture on the right shows a scaled concrete bridge deck, which can be positioned on two of the tables for testing.

Experiments tend to follow the same general model in which the experiment is broken down into a series of *trials*. One typical sequence is to subject a model to scaled-down versions of earthquakes, gradually increasing the scale factor until the model fails. During a trial it is desirable to observe the progress of the experiment, either via video or by having access to the measured values recorded by the sensors. We refer to this ability as *teleobservation*. At the conclusion of the trial, all measured data need to be available, as some data analysis may be required to calculate the parameters for the next trial. Finally, there are situations in which it is desirable to remotely control the actuators used to drive the experimental platform, for example, when experiments are coupled or in pseudodynamic testing in which a simulation determines trial parameters. This function is called *telecontrol*. Health and safety issues prevail in telecontrol, and one must carefully design a range of safety interlocks for telecontrol to be feasible. Together, teleobservation and telecontrol provide *teleoperation* of NEES equipment sites.

6.2.2 The NEESPoP

Equipment sites are a central component of NEESgrid; and thus, in designing the overall NEESgrid architecture, it was desirable to develop a structure that would minimize the complexity of the NEESgrid/equipment site interface. In designing this interface, we needed to consider the diversity of equipment that would be accessed, the fact that each facility tended to use different data acquisition hardware, the need to ensure common minimal functionality across NEESgrid, and the need to minimize the operational overhead that NEESgrid would impose above and beyond that of a non-Grid-enabled equipment site.

In light of these factors, it was decided to place a dedicated computer system with a standard software and hardware configuration at each experimental facility. This system, called a NEESPoP (NEES point of presence), provides a standard set of Grid services including

+ site status and configuration information, published via the monitoring and discovery service (MDS) (204);

+ teleoperation services, supporting streaming of observational data and remote control of actuators;

+ collaboration services, providing discussion forums, calendaring, electronic notebook, and so on;

+ metadata services and editing and publishing of metadata associated with experimental and simulation data;

+ remote administration services, including monitoring, configuration management, and software update; and

+ data access services based on the GridFTP protocol (65), where for performance reasons equipment sites typically deploy this service on a separate computer.

Each of these services is required at all NEESgrid equipment sites. In addition, a site may optionally support job submission, for analysis and simulation services, via the GRAM resource management protocol (205).

6.2.3   Teleobservation

A central element of the NEESgrid is the integration of experimental facilities in such a way as to facilitate remote operation of an experiment. Remote observation of experimental data can provide a remote observer with the same experience as a local observer. Although some experiments may be short, and it would be acceptable to wait until the end of a trial before looking at the results, there is a general requirement for streaming of some observed data as the trial is being conducted.

A number of factors must be considered in designing the teleobservation services for NEESGrid. Remote observers will be separated from the remote equipment site by an undetermined network connection, with limited bandwidth and unknown delay. Hence, true real-time observation is not actually possible, and bandwidth constraints may make it impossible to observe all of the acquired data remotely. Finally, the actual data being sent may have a variety of data types. Simple sensors such as displacement, acceleration, and stress/strain gauges produce simple three-component time-stamped values (x, y, z, and time). These data may be easily transmitted using simple protocols. However, more complex data streams, such as video, have their own optimized data formats (e.g., MPEG), and these formats should be used.

These considerations motivated the design of the NEESgrid streaming data services (NSDS) protocol. NSDS is a subscription-based protocol that allows a data channel to be first configured and then, in a separate protocol operation, claimed. Access control and policy enforcement are applied at the point of channel configuration. Separation of subscription from data channel claiming allows NSDS to be used to gain access to data channels encoded in a data-type-specific format, and that may even be generated by a server different from that hosting the NSDS. NSDS makes no commitment about timeliness of delivery, but rather streams the data, one element at a time in a best-effort manner.

Each remote experiment is defined by an NSDS configuration file that specifies what sensor data will be made available, the "logical sensor name" under which the data are published, and the policy associated with the particular data stream. Depending on the configuration file, NSDS may make all or a subset of the sensors available for remote data streaming. NSDS can also be configured to create *virtual sensors* whose data stream does not correspond to any direct measurement. For example, only a subsampled version of a high-data-rate channel may be made available, or multiple channels could be combined to produce a stream of the maximum value of the streams. By combining virtual channels with access control, one can create a range of remote usage scenarios. For example, the head of an experiment can see a high-resolution data feed, while other, less-critical, participants have access only to subsampled versions of the same streams.

Although virtual channels help address network bandwidth management, remote observers still need to be able to access the actual measurements associated with an experiment. For this reason, the NEESgrid experimental model asserts that at the conclusion of every trial the full dataset associated with the trial must be available on a *local repository* associated with the equipment site. Remote access to this repository is provided via the GridFTP protocol. The movement of the data to the local repository is implicit, so the remote user does not need to know any details of the underlying data acquisition system. By definition, at the termination of the trial, the data will be available via the repository.

The NSDS server is implemented as an Open Grid Services Architecture (OGSA) service (see Chapter 17) using the Globus Toolkit Version 3. A wide variety of data acquisition systems are in use at different sites. Thus, the server implements a plug-in architecture in which data acquisition system-specific code can be integrated into the server.

6.2.4   Telecontrol

Earthquake engineering experimental platforms tend to be large and expensive facilities. Remote control of a platform holding several tons of concrete or steel is not to be taken lightly! In addition to ensuring that ill-advised commands are not sent to the test apparatus, any control structure must be robust in terms of the wide array of failures that may occur. Poor and variable network qualities of service (e.g., latency, reliability) make tight-loop real-time control difficult at best, and impossible in many situations.

Real-time control issues can be addressed by the use of hierarchical control algorithms (Chapter 1:4). However, perhaps more promising is the application of control to pseudodynamic tests such as those described in Section 6.1.2. In these experiments, the dynamic response is computed based on observed data and then used to determine a static force to be applied to the structure in order to compute the next time step of the dynamic response. In these experiments, the time at which a control signal is applied does not matter, only the *order* in which successive signals are applied is important.

Issues of reliability and health and safety can be addressed by the careful design of the control protocol. NEESgrid has defined a two-phase, transaction-oriented protocol called the NEES Telecontrol Protocol (NTCP). During the first phase of the protocol, actuator movements (control signals) are *proposed*. A proposal may be rejected for a number of reasons. For example, the requestor may not be entitled to perform the requested operation, the requested operation may be inconsistent with the safety parameters of the equipment, or the requested operation may result in undesirable damage to the specimen. Note that the rejection does not necessarily have to be the result of an automated validation process: we anticipate that for many experiments, human-in-the-loop approval may be required before a proposal may be accepted. Once a proposal has been accepted, a subsequent *execute* command causes the proposed action to be performed. A proposal can also be canceled.

To accommodate potential failures, both *propose* and *execute* messages have timeout values. Sequence numbers and transactional semantics are used to ensure at most one execution of any request. (See Chapter 19 for more information on these techniques.) We emphasize that even careful design of the NTCP protocol cannot completely address all failure issues: one must also be careful in the details of the control language. For example, relative rather than absolute position commands (move 5 cm to the left rather than move to position 0.25 m from origin) can result in unknown behavior, depending on how the state is checkpointed in the client and server.

The NTCP server, like the NSDS server, is implemented as an OGSA service in GT3. The use of a plug-in architecture has interesting ramifications, as it allows us to use NTCP to control not only physical experiments but also simulations. Thus, we can easily create hybrid experiments that combine real and simulated components. We have used this approach to construct a distributed experiment in which two parts of a bridge are located in facilities thousands of miles apart, and coupled via a simulated component.

6.2.5 Collaboration

A critical challenge in NEESgrid is not just to create an infrastructure but to deliver the capabilities of that infrastructure to the broad engineering community—who are, obviously, more interested in engineering than in Grids. Thus, NEESgrid provides a standard set of collaboration services built on the *Comprehensive Collaborative Framework* (CHEF), an extensible collaboration framework for creating application- and domain-specific portals that can be accessed via standard Web browsers.

CHEF is extended by creating domain-specific *portlets* that can combine to create a complete end-user environment. New portlets created for NEESgrid include the following:

+ An authentication portlet that provides a Web interface to certificate-based Grid single sign-on capabilities.

+ A streaming data viewer that subscribes to NSDS data streams and displays the resulting values in a variety of different formats.

+ A metadata browser for identifying data files of interest.

+ A GridFTP download portlet that provides point-and-click access to data stored in NEESgrid repositories.

These and other CHEF portlets provide NEESgrid users with simple, Web-based access to all NEESgrid functions. Figure 6.3 shows two screen shots from a NEESgrid collaboration environment that has been created using CHEF portlets.

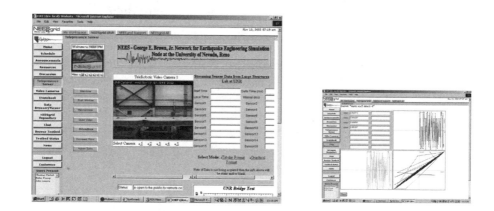

6.3

FIGURE

The CHEF collaborative framework provides a collaboration environment for participating in remote experiments. The screen shot to the left shows a video image of the current experiments, and configuration options for plotting live streaming data feeds from the experiment. The screen shot to the right shows streaming data being plotted.

6.3   SUMMARY

NEESgrid can be thought of as an *infrastructure* for integrating equipment sites, simulation, and data repositories. Although this view is accurate, it tends to obscure a fundamental point: NEESgrid is not just about linking experimental apparatus but is itself a fundamentally new type of "experimental equipment" on which entirely new types of earthquake engineering experiments can be conducted. This perspective is typified by experiments such as that described previously, in which simulation and distributed experimental are seamlessly integrated to create an experiement of scale and complexity previously not possible. As such, NEESgrid has the potential to be transformative, enabling earthquake engineers to address problems of a scope and scale that cannot be considered in the non-Grid environment of today.

ACKNOWLEDGMENTS

This material is based on work supported by the National Science Foundation under Award CMS-0117853. Any opinions, findings, conclusions, or recommendations expressed in this material are those of the authors and do not necessarily reflect the views of the National Science Foundation. NEESgrid is a joint project between the University of Illinois at Urbana-Champaign, the University of Southern California, Argonne National Laboratory, and the University of Michigan. Many people have worked on NEESgrid; this chapter relies particularly on the contributions of Laura Perlman, Shridhar Gullapalli, Paul Hubbard, Nestor Zaluzec, Gaurang Mehta, Charles Severance, Lars Schumann, and Joe Futrelle.

FURTHER READING

For more information on the topics covered in this chapter, see *www.mkp.com/grid2*.

Scientific Data Federation: The World-Wide Telescope

Alexander S. Szalay and Jim Gray

Astronomy is a wonderful Grid application because datasets are inherently distributed and yet form a fairly uniform corpus. In particular:

+ The astronomy community has a fairly unified taxonomy, vocabulary, and codified definition of metrics and units (471).

+ Modern data are carefully peer reviewed and collected with rigorous statistical and scientific standards.

+ Data provenance is tracked, and derived datasets are curated fairly carefully.

+ Most data are publicly available and will remain available for the foreseeable future.

+ Even though old data are much less precise than current data, old data are essential when studying time-varying phenomena.

Each astronomy archive covers part of the electromagnetic spectrum for a period of time and a subset of the celestial sphere. All the archives are from the same sky and the same celestial objects, although different observations are made at different times. Increasingly, astronomers perform multispectral studies or temporal studies, combining data related to the same objects from multiple instruments and archives. Cross-comparison is possible because data are well documented and schematized with a common reference frame and have clear provenance.

The scale of the data—terabytes now, petabytes soon—means that most data must reside in archives managed by the teams gathering and publishing the data.

An astronomer wanting to study a particular kind of object or phenomenon cannot download a full copy of each archive for local processing—both because the scientist does not have a spare local petabyte and because it would take too long to do the download. Rather, the scientist must request small (gigabyte-sized now, terabyte-sized in the future) subsets from each archive that represent the few million objects of interest out of the billions at the archives.

7.1   THE VIRTUAL OBSERVATORY

The Virtual Observatory—sometimes also called the World-Wide Telescope—is under construction in many countries (1, 2, 17, 21, 47). It seeks to provide portals, protocols, and standards that unify the world's astronomy archives into a giant database containing all astronomy literature, images, raw data, derived datasets, and simulation data—integrated as a single intelligent telescope (619).

7.1.1   Living in an Exponential World

The amount of astronomical data is growing at an exponential rate, doubling approximately every year as Moore's law improvements in semiconductors provide better computers and detectors. Once a new detector is deployed, data from that detector keep accumulating at a constant rate. The exponential growth in data volumes arises from the continuous construction of new facilities with ever better detectors. New instruments emerge ever more frequently, so the growth of data is a little faster than the Moore's law prediction. Therefore, while every instrument produces a steady data stream, there is an ever more complex worldwide network of facilities with large output datasets.

How can we cope with this exponentially growing data avalanche? The data pipeline processing that analyzes the raw detector data and the data storage is linearly proportional to the amount of data. The same technology that creates better detectors also creates the computers to process the data and the disks to save the data. For any individual project, the pipeline-processing task gets easier over time: the rate at which it produces data stays constant, while the cost of the computers required to analyze the data decreases by Moore's law. The first year is the most expensive for pipeline processing. Later the pipeline becomes increasingly trivial as the hardware performance improves with Moore's law and as the software performance bugs are fixed. The data storage costs peak in year two, when the storage demand doubles. Thereafter, the storage demand grows at less than

33% per year, while unit storage costs continue to drop. Thus, the community's total processing, networking, and storage costs are likely to remain stable over time, despite exponential growth in data volumes.

In contrast, the astronomy community's software costs seem to be exploding. Software used in astronomy today has its roots in Fortran, with C, C++, and Java emerging. Components are rarely reused among projects: projects tend to write their own software and use few common libraries. Thus, software costs are claiming a growing share of project budgets. Software costs are typically 25 to 50% of the total project cost. For example, the software investment of the Sloan Digital Sky Survey (620) was about 30%. Much of the work was invested in building the processing pipeline, special data access methods, and Web services. We estimate that more than half of this work is generic. The use of tools such as Condor (446) (Chapter 19), Globus Toolkit (276) (Chapter 4), and Open Grid Services Architecture (279) (Chapter 17); virtual data systems such as Chimera (284); SQL databases; and development environments such as .Net and Websphere would have made the task much simpler. One challenge the Virtual Observatory faces is to build reusable or prototypical subsystems that subsequent surveys can adapt to their needs.

7.1.2 Making Discoveries

The strongest motivation for building new sky surveys is to make new discoveries. It is important, therefore, to consider when and where new discoveries are made. We believe that new discoveries are almost always made at the edges or frontiers. Either we need to look much deeper and detect fainter objects, or we must go to extreme colors, by selecting the edges of a color distribution. We can search for objects of extreme shape (gravitationally lensed arcs) or time-domain behavior (supernovae, microlensing).

When the Internet was in its infancy, Bob Metcalfe postulated Metcalfe's law: *The utility of a computer network is proportional to the square of the number of nodes.* It is the number of different connections one can make that matters. A variant of this law seems to apply here: *The utility of N independent datasets is approximately N^2 independent of the information content of each of the datasets in isolation.* It is the number of connections we can make between fundamental properties that enables us to make new discoveries. A new observation of the sky in a previously unobserved wavelength or a new epoch for time-domain astronomy enables new connections to be made. The utility of a collection of independent observations is proportional to the number of nontrivial connections among them. This nonlinear payoff is the motivation behind building multiwavelength sky surveys. By federating datasets from multiple, independent projects, we can make new connections. The early successes of today's sky surveys, Sloan Digital Sky Survey (SDSS) and the Two-Micron All Sky Survey (2MASS), prove this point. The number of discoveries made after the first few hundred square degrees of observations (high redshift quasars, brown dwarfs) was far out of proportion to the area of sky. The magnitude of the new results can be explained only when we include the possible number of pairwise comparisons between filters.

7.1.3   Publishing Scientific Data

It is generally believed that scientific data publishing is well understood. There are the *authors*, mostly individuals or small groups, who create the experiments that provide data. Traditionally, authors have written papers that contain and explain the data. There are the *publishers*, the scientific journals, which print the papers and nowadays also make them available in an online version. There are the *curators*, whose role is filled today by libraries, which organize and store the journals and make them available for consumers. *Consumers* are scientists who want to use and cite the data in their own research.

This model worked well when all the scientific data relevant to the research could easily be included in the publication. The model breaks down, however, with the emergence of large datasets. This breakdown is not unique to astronomy. Particle physics has even larger quantities of data, and a similarly complex picture is emerging in genomic and biology research and in many other disciplines (329).

The author, publisher, and curator roles are clearly present in data-intensive science, but they are performed in different ways. The role of author belongs to collaborations, such as the Sloan Digital Sky Survey, the Human Genome Project, and the Large Hadron Collider at CERN. It takes 5 to 10 years to build the experiment before the author starts producing data. The data volume is so large that it will never be contained in journals—at most, small summaries or graphs will be printed. The data are published to the collaborations (and the world) through Web-based archives. During the project lifetime, curation responsibility rests with the projects themselves. When the collaboration dissolves, the published data are either discarded or moved to a national archive facility for long-term curation. Consumers must deal with the data from these many sources, often obtaining data from publishers not eager to support them. The economic model for long-term curation is difficult because the costs fall to one group and the benefits to others.

7.1.4 Changing Roles

The exponential growth in both the number of data sources and individual dataset sizes puts a particular burden on the projects that generate the data: they have the additional roles of data publisher and data curator. It makes sense to spend six years to build an instrument only if one is ready to use the instrument for at least the same amount of time. This means that during the data-production phase of a six-year project, the volume of data grows at a linear rate. Hence, the mean time the data spends in the project archive before moving to the centralized facility is about three years. Turning this around, the national facilities will have all the data that are more than three years old. If the amount of data is doubling every year, in three years the volume of data grows by eightfold. Thus, the archives have only 12% of the total data and less than 25% of the public data (data are typically made public after a year). The vast majority of the data and almost all the "current" data will be decentralized among the data sources—the new publishers. This is a direct consequence of the patterns of data-intensive science. These numbers were taken from astronomy; the rates may be different for other areas of science, but the main conclusions remain the same.

Thus, the projects are much more than just authors: they are also publishers and, to a large extent, curators. Although scientists understand authorship well, they are less familiar with the responsibilities of the other two roles. These new roles are making many projects spend large amounts of funds on the software to document, publish, and provide access to the data. Such tasks go far beyond the basic pipeline reductions. Since many projects are experimenting with these roles, effort is duplicated, and development time is wasted. We need to identify the common design patterns in the publishing and curation process and to build reusable components and prototypes that others can adopt or adapt.

7.1.5 Metadata and Provenance

As more and more data access is through automated facilities, it is increasingly important to capture the details of how the data were derived and calibrated. This information must be represented in a form that is easy to parse. Even the meaning of data columns can be confusing. One common measure of flux of celestial objects, the so-called Johnson magnitude, has over 150 naming variants, which all denote the same essential concept but with some subtle differences. Unified content descriptors (UCDs) (471) were introduced to address this problem. UCDs are words in a compressed dictionary derived by automatically detecting the most commonly used terms in over 150,000 tables in the astronomical literature. Using a UCD designator can be helpful in finding common and comparable attributes in different archives and serves as a unifying force in data publication.

Archived astronomy data are usually the end product of a complicated processing pipeline, within which the details of the processing (e.g., detection thresholds for objects) are carefully tuned by each project. Currently much of this information is captured in the form of published papers in the literature. There is a slowly emerging trend to describe the processing pipelines in terms of directed acyclic graphs (DAGs; see Chapter 19) and to create a proper workflow for the data reduction. Once DAGs are widely implemented, they will be the proper way to preserve the data provenance. Custom reprocessing of the data will then be quite easy: one will simply feed different parameters to the workflow. We expect this to be an important part of the Virtual Observatory—Grid interface.

During the loading of objects into a database, a similar problem arises. One needs to track the heritage of each object, what version of the processing software has created it, and at what date. This requirement leads to yet another workflow system closely linked to that of the processing.

Most large astronomy datasets are generated by large collaborations. Typically, these collaborations have a good initial project design document, but as the projects progress, much information exchange is through e-mail exploders. E-mails get archived, but not in a formal sense. Thus, once projects go dormant, these e-mails are deleted. Since most technical decisions during the lifetime of projects are contained only in the e-mails, these must be carefully archived and indexed; otherwise, much of the metadata and provenance information is irretrievably lost.

7.2   WEB SERVICES: USING DISTRIBUTED DATA

These problems are not unique to science. Similar issues are emerging in the business world, where companies need to exchange information not only inside their corporate firewalls but also with others. Exchanging and automatically reading data in various formats has haunted application developers for many years. Finally, a worldwide standard is emerging for data representation: the *Extensible Markup Language* (XML; see Chapter 17).

XML is rather complex and was not designed to be human readable. Nevertheless, there are clear grammatical rules for encapsulating complex information in a machine-readable form, and there are style sheets that render XML data to various easily understandable formats.

The most recent XML developments are related to Web services (Chapter 17): a standardized way to invoke remote resources on the Web and to exchange complex data. Web services define a distributed object model that lets us build Internet-scale software components and services. The Simple Object Access Protocol (SOAP) specifies how to invoke applications that can talk to one another and exchange complex data. The Web Service Description Language (WSDL) enables an application to find out the precise calling convention of a remote resource and to build a compatible interface. Toolkits, many freely available, link Web services to most modern programming languages and hardware platforms.

7.2.1   Web Services in the Virtual Observatory

Many of the expected tasks in the Virtual Observatory (VO) map well to Web services. Astronomers are already accustomed to various analysis packages, such as IRAF, IDL, and AIPS++, that have multilayer APIs (197, 655). These packages start with a layer of simple image processing tasks and then build a layer of more complex processing steps on top of that first layer. The packages assume that the data reside in FITS files in the local file system (673), and the processing is done on the workstation itself.

In the Virtual Observatory, most of the data will be remote. As a result, data access to remote resources needs to be as transparent as if it were local. The remote data volume may be huge; therefore, it makes sense to move as much of the data processing as near the data as possible, because in many cases after the first few steps of processing the output volume is dramatically smaller (e.g., extracting object catalogs). In many cases the data not only are remote but do not even exist at the time of the request. The data may be extracted from a database with a query. One can carry this situation even further: The requested data may be created by a complex pipeline on the fly, according to the user's specification, like a recalibration and custom object detection run on an image built as a mosaic from its parts. The GriPhyN project (93) calls this concept "virtual data" (284, 285)—data created dynamically from its archived components.

7.2.2   Everything for Everybody?

We believe that a multilevel layering of services is the correct VO architecture. IRAF and AIPS++ are prototypes, but the concept needs to be extended to handle remote and virtual data sources. The core will be a set of simple, low-level services that are easy to implement even by small projects. Indeed, we expect that there will be reference implementations of these services that can serve as proto-types for publishing new archives. Thus, the threshold to join the VO will be low. Large data providers will be able to implement more complex, high-speed services as well.

These core services can be combined into more complex portals that talk to several services and create more complex results. Such a design will have modular components, standard interfaces, and access to commercially built toolkits for the lowest-level communication tasks. We need to focus on the astronomy-specific issues, and not reinvent the wheel.

We need to carefully define the VO framework and core services. Development resources are scarce and must be used efficiently. It would be a mistake to try to build everything for everybody; it is impossible to make everybody happy. How, then, to choose? A well-known design rule states that 20% of the effort covers 80% of the needs. If the Virtual Observatory builds the right 20% and satisfies 80% of the astrophysics community's needs, it will be counted a success. There is no need to build all possible complex applications—our colleagues have been resourceful in building quite complex applications out of IRAF modules. The VO need only provide clear standards, interfaces, documentation, and reference implementations in order to have most data providers adopt a set of core services. The VO must not lose sight of the ultimate goal: to create a powerful system that is simple to use.

7.3   HIERARCHICAL ARCHITECTURE

Several independent efforts to build these archives are under way, but all seem to be converging on a common architecture and common core technologies. The emerging themes are as follows (see Fig. 7.1).

+ *Archives*. The archives each store text, images, and raw data in blobs or files and store their schematized data in relational databases. They provide data-mining tools that allow easy search and subsetting of the data objects at each archive. They also contain metadata about their contents, describing not only their physical units but also the provenance of the data.

+ *Web services*. The archives provide Web service interfaces for on-demand queries and a file transfer service for answers that involve substantial computation or data transfer. These Web services all support a common core schema that extends the VOTable data model (48). The VOTable model specifies a standard coordinate system, standard representations for core astronomical concepts, and standard ways to represent both values and errors. All of this is built atop SOAP and XML Schema Definitions (XSDs). Some of these Web services are OGSA services to run long-running analysis jobs on the archive's data and to produce derived datasets—but most are interactive tasks that extract data on demand for portals and for interactive client tools.

✦ *Registries and portals.* Each archive declares its services with one or more registries. Registries record what kinds of information the archive provides—the sky coverage, temporal coverage, spectral coverage, and resolution. These registries will be widely replicated, and given the overlaps of astronomy with other disciplines, it seems likely that there will be many different kinds of registries and that a particular service will be registered with many of them. Registries will be used by portals, which serve to answer user queries by integrating data from many archives. We expect that eventually many individuals will build their own custom portals, specializing in solving particular problems.

MAST, GLU, and AstroGrid are sample portals (1). As one of the first experiments of the international Virtual Observatory effort, more than 50 different archives over the world provide a cone search interface for a Web search (6). Each of these services, given a point in the sky and a radius (a cone), returns the archives'

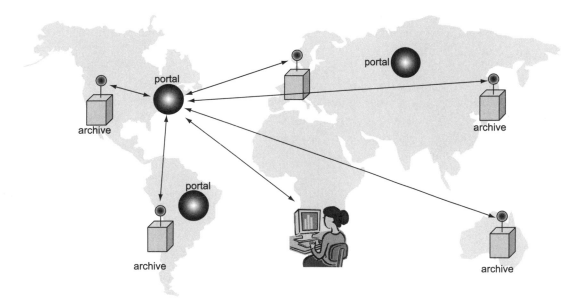

7.1

FIGURE

Portals answer user queries by integrating data from many archives. The archives present their data as Web services.

objects that fall within that cone. The response returns both the metadata (XML schema) and the data as an XML document format called the VOTable data model. The cone service request allows the user to optionally specify the *verbosity* level that controls how much detailed information is returned in the VOTable structure.

SkyQuery is another example of a portal (458). It integrates five different Web services: SDSS, 2MASS, Faint Images of the Radio Sky at Twenty-cm, and the Isaac Newton Telescope Wide Field Survey, along with an image Web service. These archives are located on two continents at several geographic locations. Additional archives are currently being integrated. The portal accepts queries specifying the desired object properties. It then decides which archives have relevant data (by querying each of them) and calculates an optimal query plan to answer the question, doing a Bayesian spatial cross-correlation among the objects in each archive. The resulting answer set is delivered to the user in tabular form along with images of the objects. SkyQuery is itself a Web service and can be used as a component of some other portal that renders the information in better ways or combines these answers with other datasets.

SkyQuery was built using SQL and the .NET tools by four part-time employees in less than two months. The use of XML, SOAP, and Web services made it possible to easily plug together Web services that were running at three different sites. Subsequently, the Isaac Newton Telescope in Cambridge, UK, was able to join the federation with a few days' work. The service has operated without problems for a year since then. This experience has made us very enthusiastic about the advantages of Web services and good tools to build them.

SkyQuery and its component services are both I/O and CPU intensive. They lend themselves to database and compute farms enabled by Web and Grid services. Indeed, some queries cannot be answered interactively; they require reading huge amounts of data or doing extensive calculations. These complex SkyQuery jobs are excellent applications for facilities for submitting, executing, and managing batch computations, and other facilities for bulk data transfer of results.

7.4   THE VIRTUAL OBSERVATORY AND THE GRID

Many potential astronomy applications require access at the granularity of objects rather than entire files. Thus, astronomy data on the Grid will generally reside in read-intensive databases that will be accessed by associative query interfaces that subdivide the data. Comparing multiple observations of the same object taken by different instruments at different times requires accessing and comparing individual records in several different archives. These processes imply a massive use of spatial and other indices, which in turn means a heavy use of databases. The huge data volumes require a parallel search capability with direct random access of certain objects.

Since the same sky is covered by many different surveys, at many different wavelengths, and at many different times, we also need to search and correlate the metadata. Archives and datasets are constructed with great effort and are peer reviewed, so there will be less than a thousand of them. However, each archive has fairly extensive metadata. One or more registry services are needed to gather these data together and to provide queries against the metadata. Again, these tasks are best suited to databases.

These are not the only Grid issues important to astronomy. Access control must be addressed but is less important for astronomical datasets than in other sciences. The data have no commercial value, and astronomers are fairly good about sharing—much of the world's astronomy archives are, in fact, public. Resource management, on the other hand, is likely to be important: if remote users can pose complex queries (which presumably will be desirable), then mechanisms will be required to determine who gets to use how much of scarce bandwidth and computing resources.

7.4.1 Data, Networking, and Computation Economics

With the falling costs of computer hardware, projects are able to provide limited public access to their archives at a modest cost. However, where do they draw the line? How much pro bono processing and search should an archive provide to its data?

A simple calculus can be used to decide the least expensive way to structure a distributed archive. First, with progress in disk technology, all data can be kept online, rather that putting it in near-line tape archives. The data and derived products were collected at great expense, so the data should be safely stored at two or more locations. When a user has a new query or computation, several choices exist.

If the query is small, it can just be sent to one of the archive servers. Today "small" means less than 10 hours of computation ($1 of computing), less than a terabyte of disk and LAN bandwidth, and less than 10 gigabytes of network data movement ($10 of network traffic).

When the query exceeds these limits, some planning is required. With current economics, there is rough parity between (1) one database access, (2) 10 bytes of network traffic, (3) 100,000 instructions, (4) 10 bytes of disk storage, and (5) a terabyte of disk or LAN bandwidth. Most astronomy calculations are data intensive. It is rare to find computations of more than 10,000 instructions per byte. This argues strongly for doing the computation near the data. That in turn means that the publishers should provision a Beowulf cluster near the data for large jobs (those costing more than $100) and develop some form of chargeback for such services. If that is infeasible, then one alternative is to get a copy of the database either over the Internet or via sneakernet (325). Paradoxically it can be faster and cheaper to send a terabyte via a storage brick than via the Internet.

7.4.2   Compute-Intensive Tasks

The transformation of raw instrument data into calibrated and cataloged data is a demanding computational task. For example, about 25% of the Sloan Digital Sky Survey (SDSS) budget went into building the software pipelines that process the photographic and spectroscopic data and produce catalogs of stars, galaxies, quasi-stellar objects, spectrograms, spectral lines, and redshift estimates. This work produced over a million lines of code that continuously transform the raw data into the SDSS catalogs. This software is constantly being refined and improved, so all the old data need to be reprocessed about once a year to produce a new dataset that includes all the data processed in the new and better way. These algorithms consume between 1,000 and 10,000 instructions per byte of input data. Hence, reprocessing the data consumes about 10^{17} instructions—100 exa-instructions operating on about 15 terabytes of source data. With current processors, that is about 10 CPU-years. However, we need to do the computation several times per year. The solution is to use computer clusters to process the data in parallel. Indeed, the current Beowulf cluster at Fermilab can reprocess the entire SDSS dataset in about six weeks, and the resulting data can be loaded into databases in a few days.

This pipeline processing is a natural candidate for Grid services and particularly the Virtual Data Toolkit. The SDSS had to build its own batch job scheduler, its own data lineage tracker, and its own operations interfaces. The European Southern Observatory (ESO) built an even more elaborate and functional system (11). Today, both of these efforts could exploit systems such as the Chimera virtual data toolkit (284) (which in turn builds on the Globus and Condor toolkits) to save a great deal of effort.

7.4.3   Data Mining and Statistics of Terabytes

Although much of the pipeline processing of the data into catalogs stored in archives is linear and has the cost of a few thousand instructions per byte, there are also complex statistical analyses that needs to be performed on the archives subsequently.

In January 2003 both the United States and the European community demonstrated several functional research scenarios using the Virtual Observatory. These scenarios covered a wide spectrum: (1) dynamically cross-correlating the SDSS and 2MASS catalogs; (2) scanning hundreds of thousands of files in order to find clusters of galaxies, and testing Grid tools in the process (81); and (3) multiple interfaces rendering the same complex VOTable document created in response to a transient event (gamma-ray burst). These computations demonstrate the enormous diversity of problems the VO needs to address. The SDSS–2MASS cross-correlation found several previously undiscovered rare objects in the process.

One major impediment to such spatial and multispectral cross-correlations is that our current correlation algorithms involve the computations of pairwise distances. Brute-force algorithms would have quadratic computational and I/O complexity (compare all pairs of objects). Hypothesis testing over a large feature vector has typically cubic computational and I/O complexity, because of the scaling of matrix inversion. Typical matrix sizes today are in the range $10,000^2$ to $1,000,000^2$. Such algorithms are workable for small datasets, but even $N \log N$ algorithms are infeasible for datasets involving billions of objects. We must move from these exact solutions to approximate and heuristic algorithms that have linear and sublinear computational and I/O costs. Even then, the computations will have to be performed over large numbers of CPUs—for a billion objects even $\log N$ is about 30. The creation of such algorithms stands as a major challenge to the data-mining and statistical community.

7.5   OUTREACH USING THE VIRTUAL OBSERVATORY

The World-Wide Telescope is also an excellent laboratory to teach computational science. It presents a well-documented spatial, temporal, and image database that is geographically distributed. Students can rediscover classical astronomy results using real data and real Grid analysis tools, or they can explore new hypotheses and perhaps make new discoveries. The SkyServer project site shows an example of this (328). Over the past two years the student project part of the site has received more than a million Web hits. We estimate the total at more than 10,000 hours of student instruction in astronomy and computational science.

The Virtual Sky (679) provides image navigation over the whole sky, covering many different surveys with the ease of MapQuest. Through its intuitive interface, one can easily compare images from the different surveys with a large dynamic range of magnifications.

7.6   SUMMARY

The World-Wide Telescope is an outstanding Grid application. It involves the federation of many distributed terascale data sources. The astronomy community is interested in mining the individual datasets looking for patterns, but there is even greater interest in cross-correlating the datasets to find new phenomena. The construction of each archive involves massive calculations that ingest, analyze, and categorize the instrument data, producing databases and files. Cross-correlation introduces enormous requirements for data movement and computation.

The emergence of these huge datasets changes the roles of authors, publishers, and curators. Science projects become data authors and publishers and must also do the curatorial work that will allow archives to accept and preserve the data once the project is complete.

Each project will likely publish a database externalized as a set of Web services. The astronomy community is in the midst of defining and prototyping these core services. Portals will federate these Web services to provide uniform access to the archives as though they are a single distributed database. Cross-identifications of objects across multiple archives and searches involving both spatial and time-domain constraints are typical tasks for the Virtual Observatory. Because of the large sizes of the datasets, their distributed nature, and their rapidly varying content, these tasks need an architecture that is inherently distributed and scalable—the Grid. We view the Virtual Observatory as a small part of the larger effort of defining and applying an Open Grid Services Architecture and creating an international Grid infrastructure.

FURTHER READING

For more information on the topics covered in this chapter, see *www.mkp.com/grid2.*

Medical Data Federation: The Biomedical Informatics Research Network

Mark Ellisman and Steve Peltier

*T*he National Institutes of Health (NIH) is pioneering the use of Grid infra-structure for medical research and patient care through the Biomedical Informatics Research Network (BIRN) project. Started in September 2001, BIRN is developing and evolving the hardware, software, and protocols necessary to share and mine data for both basic and clinical research. Central to the project is the establishment of a scalable infrastructure consisting of advanced networks, federated distributed data collections, computational resources, and software technologies (see Figure 8.1) to meet the evolving needs of investigators who have formed testbed scientific collaborations.

By pooling domain expertise, specialized research facilities, instrumentation resources, advanced applications, and regional information, these investigators are tackling disease studies of greater scope and complexity than are independently pos-sible. The development of BIRN is driven by three neuroimaging testbed activities focused on (1) studying disease states and relationships to human brain morphology (Human Structure BIRN), (2) functional imaging analysis of schizophrenia (FIRST BIRN), and (3) multiscale analysis of mouse models of disease (Mouse BIRN). Each testbed serves as a guide for the development of a persistent infrastructure to facili-tate collaborative biomedical research across multiple disciplines.

The immediate objectives of BIRN are as follows:

✦ Establish a stable, high-performance network, linking key NIH biotechnology centers and general clinical research centers.

✦ Develop technologies to federate multiple data collections or databases from distributed partnering centers.

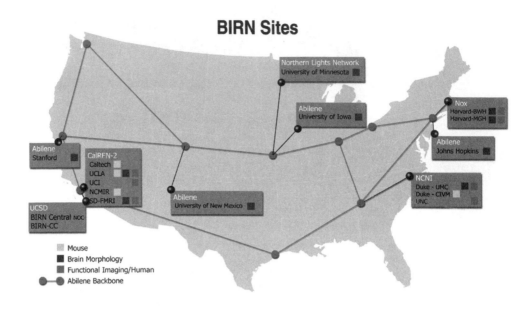

8.1   Participating BIRN sites interfacing on the Internet2/Abeline network.

FIGURE

◆ Enable collaborative data mining of these federated collections or databases.

◆ Leverage distributed computational resources to facilitate collaborative visualization, data refinement, and analysis.

◆ Address project-wide issues relating to reliability, quality of service, performance, scalability, security, and ownership.

◆ Build a stable software and hardware communications infrastructure to enable the coordination of large studies across sites.

As expansion of this project creates additional biomedical research and clinical care testbeds, BIRN is expected to stretch the boundaries of information technology infrastructure, enriching the global Grid movement by providing "application pull" from several biomedical domains.

8.1   NEUROIMAGING DRIVING BIRN

Neuroimaging is one of the most rapidly advancing fields in biological science. Progress has come as a result of advances in imaging methods, instrumentation, computing, telecommunications, and information technology. The integration of these advances provides researchers a powerful new arsenal to investigate previously intractable problems. For example, researchers can now cross-correlate functional and structural brain data captured by various technologies to develop a more complete understanding of brain function. Computational techniques combined with new and existing imaging devices (e.g., magnetic resonance imaging, magnetoencephalography, optical recording, multiphoton microscopy, and high-voltage electron microscopy) provide unprecedented opportunities to correlate brain structure and patterns of neural activity in living subjects, specify the spatial and temporal dynamics of signal transduction processes in individual and groups of neurons, and investigate the fine structural organization of neuronal processes and their constituent proteins.

Neuroimaging data are being collected across multiple scales—from angstroms to cubic centimeters—to understand how molecular interactions give rise to such complex neural processes as thought and memory. If one considers biological activity as a continuum, it will soon be possible to demonstrate how cellular behavior emerges from the molecular level, how tissue behavior emerges from the cellular level, and so on up to the level of the whole organism, ultimately demonstrating cause and effect between activity at the smallest scale and behavior at the largest.

Explosive growth has also occurred in the development, refinement, and application of techniques for functional imaging of the brain. Just as magnetic resonance imaging (MRI), computed tomography (CT), and other "structural" neuroimaging techniques have revolutionized biomedical research and clinical practice, "functional" neuroimaging techniques (e.g., functional magnetic resonance imaging, or fMRI, and positron emission tomography) have revolutionized basic research on human sensory, motor, and cognitive processes by allowing the noninvasive visualization of neural activity in living human subjects. These techniques are now poised to have a profound effect on clinical research and medical practice.

With such advances, however, there arises the increasingly daunting challenge of efficiently storing, managing, curating, accessing, visualizing, and analyzing the volumes of data being collected. A typical project's data collection consists of multiple terabytes. Advances in imaging technologies will surely expand these collection sizes to hundreds of terabytes in less than five years. Compounding the problem is the fact that these data are being collected by disparate technologies (with appreciable variances even in the data collected by like technologies) at different spatial and temporal scales. The material in Chapter 9 is relevant here, speaking to the challenges imposed by the properties of biological data (scale, complexity, instability, etc.) as well as by the extreme distribution, fragmentation, and heterogeneity of biological data collections.

The explosion of such rich multiscale and multimodal data will surely exceed the capabilities of the information technology and infrastructure currently available to biomedical researchers. Managed properly, however, such data present a unique opportunity to accelerate the pace of scientific discovery. Clearly, the availability of such a multitude of data from a geographically distributed set of collections would be of enormous value (statistically, comparatively, and qualitatively) to neuroimaging groups willing to collaborate with their colleagues. However, enabling such usage is not straightforward. Groups who normally compete for recognition and funding need to foster collaborations in which data and technologies are openly shared. Issues such as data ownership, attribution, accuracy, security, authenticity, and veracity must all be considered side by side with the development of technologies and infrastructure. In the case of neuroimaging studies of human disorders, collaborative data sharing is further complicated by the strict requirements of the Health Insurance Portability and Accountability Act (HIPPA) of 1996, which provides guidelines to protect the privacy of patient health information. All of these challenges motivate BIRN.

8.2   BIRN TESTBEDS

Although each testbed shares the common BIRN infrastructure, each also imposes unique requirements derived from the science pursued, as we now explain.

8.2.1   Brain Morphology Testbed (Human Structure BIRN)

A team of research institutions (Duke; Harvard; Johns Hopkins; the University of California, Los Angeles; and the University of California, San Diego) is examining neuroanatomical correlates of neuropsychiatric illnesses, including unipolar depression, early-stage Alzheimer's disease, and mild cognitive impairment. Each group has traditionally conducted independent investigations across relatively small patient populations, using site-specific software tools. The ability to integrate data across independent resources for collaborative data refinement is enabling the Human Structure BIRN to test previously intractable hypotheses.

This testbed is comparing findings across illnesses to identify common and distinctive properties, leveraging the increased statistical power of integrated datasets from geographically distributed resources, the increased analytical scope of combined analysis tools, and the establishment of a federated database between sites. The high-level goals of the project are to determine whether structural differences in the brain contribute to symptoms such as memory dysfunction or depression and whether specific differences distinguish diagnostic categories.

Since these studies involve human patient data, the entire BIRN architecture must adhere to HIPAA regulations for protecting patient confidentiality. These regulations necessitate the use of deidentified data and metadata, architecture-wide encryption, secure data pathways across applications and resources, and strictly enforced control polices for access to protected information. A second challenge is that because of inhomogeneous magnetic fields across scanners, all data are produced with instrument-specific distortions. These distortions necessitate the use of project-wide data normalization, where datasets are warped according to instrument-specific distortion patterns characterized by imaging calibration "phantoms."

8.2.2   Functional Imaging Research of Schizophrenia Testbed (FIRST BIRN)

A second team (Duke; Harvard; Stanford; the University of Iowa; the University of Minnesota; the University of North Carolina; the University of New Mexico; the University of California, Irvine; the University of California, Los Angeles; and the University of California, San Diego) is developing a common functional MRI protocol to study regional brain dysfunction related to the progression and treatment of schizophrenia. The ultimate scientific goal is to attack the underlying causes of schizophrenia and to develop new treatments for the disease. This effort has brought together leaders in different areas of functional neuroimaging to investigate the neural substrates of schizophrenia through the coordination of several recently developed imaging techniques. BIRN infrastructure enables these researchers to exploit large functional imaging databases at the participating sites, to design and execute new cooperative studies across sites, and to develop and distribute techniques to ensure interoperability of existing tools for multimodal analysis.

This testbed is building on the system requirements of the Human Structure BIRN, imposing a more extensive usage model. There are twice as many sites in FIRST BIRN as in the Human Structure BIRN, amplifying the requirements of the BIRN architecture to handle data mining across a greater number of distributed collections. Time series (as opposed to static anatomical imaging) data are being gathered across distributed scanners by using a multitude of scan protocols and a number of common and site-specific experimental paradigms, considerably amplifying the variability to be considered in the normalization process. In addition, FIRST BIRN is correlating functional data with anatomical data acquired from the Human Structure testbed to study whether there are neuroanatomical correlates with cognitive dysfunction across disorders. This activity is accelerating efforts to standardize protocols and formats, and it is driving the modification and development of tools that interoperate (concomitantly increasing coordination, scheduling, quality-of-service requirements, etc.).

8.2.3 Multiscale Mouse Models of Disease Testbed (Mouse BIRN)

A third team (Caltech; Duke; the University of California, Los Angeles; and the University of California, San Diego) is studying animal models of disease across dimensional scales to test hypotheses associated with human neurological disorders. The aim of Mouse BIRN is to share and mine multiscale structural and functional data and to integrate these with genomic and gene expression data on the mouse brain. The initial framework for this area of research has been constructed to enhance the productivity of two collaborations in basic mouse models of neurological disorders:

+ The experimental allergic encephalomyelitis mouse models (both chemically induced and transgenic) undergo episodic weakness and demyelination characteristic of multiple sclerosis.

+ The DAT knockout mouse, with alterations in the dopaminergic system, is an ideal candidate for studies of schizophrenia, Parkinson's disease, attention-deficit hyperactivity disorder, Tourette's disorder, and substance abuse.

Correlated multiscale analysis of these data promises to provide a basis upon which to interpret signals from the whole brain relative to the tissue and cellular alterations characteristic of the modeled disorder.

The Mouse BIRN is pushing the boundaries of handling massive datasets, from common animal subjects, assembled by correlating data acquired at different spatial scales and using different imaging modalities. For example, multi-wavelength 4D datasets acquired with a real-time multiphoton laser-scanning microscope at UCSD can generate greater than 50 gigabyte/hour, producing single multiterabyte datasets with image fields containing hundreds of millions of pixels of information. Mouse BIRN is building technologies to correlate these massive datasets with magnetic resonance data (Duke), histological data (UCLA), diffusion tensor data (Caltech), and high-resolution electron tomography data (UCSD), generating huge multiresolution scenes of incredible detail and perspective, while placing significant demands on the underlying architecture for managing, visualizing, and refining that data in a collaborative and meaningful manner.

8.3 THE BIRN GRID

Although neuroimaging technology has generated remarkable progress in understanding how mental and neurological diseases develop, progress has been hampered by the inability for one laboratory to share findings with others. A lack of coordinated networks and limitations in compatible computer hardware and software have isolated scientists, excluding them from collaborative efforts that could provide the sufficient number of test subjects needed for a comprehensive look at brain dysfunction. The BIRN architecture is being designed to remedy this problem.

Each testbed presents practical requirements for performing large-scale bioinformatics studies, characterizing a multitude of usage cases for computation and data in an inherently distributed environment. As the global Grid community moves forward with the development and standardization of Grid technologies, this project brings forth domain-specific issues of practical value to biomedical informatics research. Specifically, this project motivates the development of services for biomedical resource "virtualization," providing multiple real-world scenarios in which aggregations of BIRN researchers (many of whom participate in multiple areas) benefit from a common national infrastructure while adhering to testbed-specific policy controls for access, ownership, and security. As BIRN infrastructure is realized, each testbed is becoming a functional virtual organization, marshaling a coordinated pool of technologies, resources, and expertise to solve key challenges in biomedical research.

The architecture to accomplish this goal is designed around a flexible, large-scale Grid model, where network-connected component resources (data, computation, instrumentation, and visualization) are tightly integrated by an evolving abstraction layer of Grid middleware technologies, including the Globus Toolkit (276) (Chapter 4) and the Storage Resource Broker/metadata catalogue (SRB/MCAT) (535) (Chapter 1:5).

Globus Toolkit technologies are incorporated in four main areas: security, information services, resource management, and data management. The Grid Security Infrastructure (GSI) (280) (Chapter 21) is a fundamental component of the system architecture, providing authentication and authorization services using public key certificates. The Grid Resource Allocation Management (GRAM) (205) service (Chapter 18) is used to remotely launch computationally intensive neuroscience applications. Prior to being launched, many applications require parameters in the form of small text configuration files (e.g., XML tags, shell scripts). These parameter files are delivered to applications via Globus Toolkit data Grid services (64, 178). Since the BIRN architecture is inherently distributed, dynamic resource scheduling is necessary and will be even more important as additional Grid resources are incorporated. Information services, such as the Globus Toolkit's Monitoring and Discovery Service (MDS) (204) and Network Weather Service (NWS) (682), are being investigated as solutions for making dynamic scheduling decisions based on server usage patterns and the geographic proximity of resources and users.

BIRN also includes technologies to mediate real-world queries across multiple, heterogeneous distributed databases. Central to this data integration and federation effort is the development of knowledge-based information mediation technology, where domain knowledge from each project is used to semantically correlate the data sources. A toolkit layer of APIs and Grid services is also under development to enable myriad BIRN visualization and data refinement applications to be incorporated into the emerging architecture, interfacing with the Grid as needed.

GridPort (646) services have been heavily leveraged to extend these middleware services to the Web interface layer via the development of a BIRN portal. This portal provides a centralized execution environment that can be dynamically customized for each user and in which all resources, applications, and control policies are presented with minimal administrative overhead (single log-in and passphrase). The architecture of the evolving BIRN Grid is shown in Figure 8.2.

A homogenously equipped rack of hardware provides each BIRN site with its data resource and network point of presence. This use of a uniform base configuration dramatically increases the efficiency of project-wide system administration, performance monitoring, and upkeep. The use of new technologies for reproducibly deploying, maintaining, upgrading, and operating the production distributed Grid environment from a remote network operations center (NOC) is also facilitated. A key ingredient is the use of "Rocks" technology (38) as a robust mechanism for producing customized distributions (with security patches and custom system parameters preapplied) of all required software.

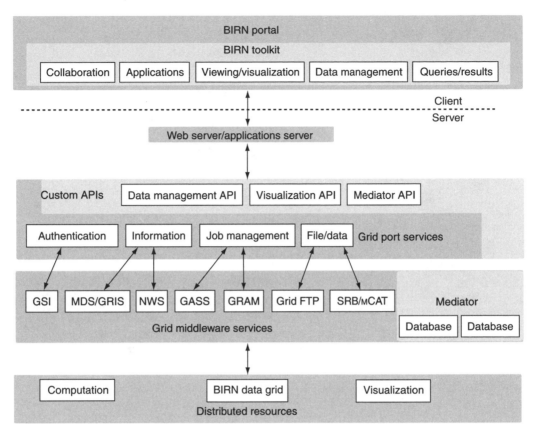

BIRN Grid architecture.

8.4   INFORMATION MEDIATION

The primary motivation for integrating data from multiple BIRN sites is to gain a deeper understanding of a scientific problem than would have been possible with any individual site's data. The mediation architecture deployed can link multiple databases with different schemas, maintained at different research institutions, into a data federation. It allows individual researchers to manage their own data in databases tailored to meet their specific needs. Those searching the system, however, interface to the BIRN data federation as if it were a single database. Queries are issued against a "mediator," a virtual database that combines the individual data sources in meaningful ways. This combination is achieved by using

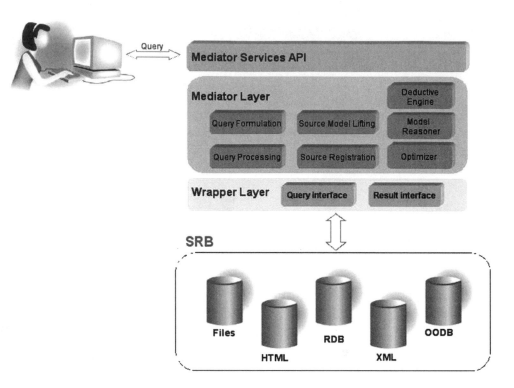

Information mediation architecture.

"integrated view definitions," which describe how the mediator represents the source databases.

A user submits a query to the mediator—or, more precisely, to one of the integrated views the mediator can expose. A mediation engine then evaluates the queries with the domain knowledge metadata—a potentially compute-intensive process—and retrieves query results and/or "handles" for relevant datasets. The dataset handles are then used to search the metadata catalog and retrieve the actual data.

The BIRN mediation architecture (see Figure 8.3) incorporates additional knowledge in the form of ontologies and brain atlases to provide the necessary "glue knowledge" to integrate data across scales, disciplines, and species (341, 453). To accomplish this semantic (i.e., ontology-based) information integration, the BIRN mediator accepts conceptual models containing schemas, their semantic properties, and constraints, rather than only logical models. The conceptual models from data and knowledge sources can be specified in any form of logic language, including description logic derivatives (335) typically used in the XML/RDF-based "semantic Web" languages discussed in Chapter 23. We view the BIRN mediation task as a premier example of how the semantic Web will actually be deployed for the management of distributed scientific information over a large network.

8.5 DRIVING THE DEVELOPMENT OF GRID TECHNOLOGIES

The general requirements for BIRN are great, considering the complexity and extent of the data. The datasets are large and cover a broad spectrum of multidimensional file formats, describing images, volumes, surfaces, time-series representations, and so forth. The cumulative data-generation rate can be as high as 100 gigabyte/day at a steady rate, with burst loads exceeding 500 gigabyte/day. As NIH adds additional testbed partnering groups to BIRN and expands to other organ systems and disease loci (heart, liver, diabetes, cancer, etc.), the data rate is projected to grow by two orders of magnitude over the next five years.

Interacting with these data involves computationally intensive tasks such as volume and surface rendering, much of which will need to happen in real time to allow for steering and navigation of data within a collaborative environment among multiple sites. Although client-side computer resources may be adequate to work with low-resolution datasets, extensive resources will be routinely needed to refine massive multiscale and multimodal datasets, or to render high-resolution images and movies. Such requirements will require transparent access to computational resources (e.g., the NSF TeraGrid (162) and iVDGL (94)) beyond the client workstation or single utility server included with each BIRN site installation.

A key goal for the continued development of the BIRN Grid is to enrich and simplify the expansion of such an integrated collaborative environment, providing customized and secure access to all necessary applications, appropriate data, and resources available across the network. A desirable method for providing this level of integration will be to implement a series of platform-independent services to allow seamless connections to all application resources. Thus, we expect that the BIRN Grid architecture will transition toward a set of BIRN Grid Services Compliant with the Open Grid Services Architecture (278) (OGSA, Chapter 17), so that BIRN developers are freed from the many security and management issues resolved within OGSA standards. The integration of OGSA technologies will thereby propel the development of a stable and secure service-oriented architecture, within which developers can extend applications to BIRN with minimal understanding of the complexities of interfacing with the Grid.

Despite the emergence of new Grid-based solutions, the expertise to deliver sufficient performance, reliability, quality of service, scalability, and security for BIRN is outside the interests and capabilities of most domain scientists. The unique requirements of the biomedical sciences, however, have yet to be sufficiently communicated to IT professionals building next-generation collaborative and resource-sharing technologies. BIRN is integrally tied to both efforts, building persistent, production-level infrastructure, middleware "glue" technologies, interactive (site-independent) tools, and collaboration systems that extend the state of the art for each beyond their own understanding of what is possible. Neuroimaging is a perfect application for driving the integration of technologies. Cutting-edge imaging resources are well established; the data and computation usage models associated with disease studies are extensive; the data are massive, have many forms and formats, and are growing beyond the capabilities of the current IT infrastructure in place to manage and use them effectively; and data integration across wide geographic areas is of critical relevance to biomedical research. Thus, this area presents a unique opportunity for the global Grid community to steer middleware technologies into the hands of domain scientists to address applications with pervasive impact and relevance to the global populace. Strides in this direction are well under way at the interface of BIRN and the emerging OGSA.

ACKNOWLEDGMENTS

We acknowledge the contributions of Maryann Martone, Jeffrey Grethe, Amarnath Gupta, Mark James, Philip Papadopoulos, Abel Lin, and Tomas Molina of the BIRN-CC staff. This work is supported in part by the National Institutes of Health (BIRN Coordinating Center 3P41-RR08605; National Center for Microscopy and Imaging Research 3P41-RR04050).

FURTHER READING

For more information on the topics covered in this chapter, see *www.mkp.com/grid2* and also visit the BIRN Web site *www.nbirn.net*.

Knowledge Integration: *In Silico* Experiments in Bioinformatics

Carole Goble, Chris Greenhalgh, Steve Pettifer,
and Robert Stevens

An *in silico* experiment is a procedure that uses computer-based information repositories and computational analysis to test a hypothesis, derive a summary, search for patterns, or demonstrate a known fact. The ᵐʸGrid project is developing high-level service-based middleware to support the construction, management, and sharing of data-intensive *in silico* experiments in biology.

Biologists, aided by bioinformaticians, have become knowledge workers, intelligently weaving together the information available to the community, linking and correlating it meaningfully, and generating even more information. Many bio-Grid projects focus on the sharing of computational resources, large-scale data movement and replication for simulations, remote instrumentation steerage, high-throughput sequence analysis, or image processing, as in the BIRN project (Chapter 8). However, much of bioinformatics involves a scientific process with relatively modest computational needs but significant semantic and data complexity. Consequently, ᵐʸGrid is building high-level services for integrating applications and data resources, concentrating on dynamic resource discovery, workflow specification and dynamic enactment, and distributed query processing. These services merely *enable* experiments to be formed and executed. Thus, ᵐʸGrid's second category of services supports the scientific method and best practice found at the bench but often neglected at the workstation, specifically provenance management, change notification, and personalization.

Figure 9.1 shows the life cycle of *in silico* experiments and the core activities of ᵐʸGrid:

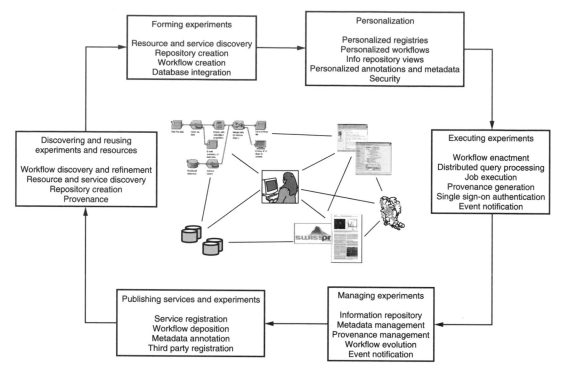

9.1

The cycle of ᵐʸGrid *in silico* experiments.

FIGURE

◆ *Experimental design components* can be shared and reused: workflow
  specifications, query specifications, notes describing objectives, applications,
  databases, relevant papers, the Web pages of important workers, and so on.

◆ *Experimental instances* are records of enacted experiments: data results, a history of services invoked by a workflow engine, instances of services invoked,
  parameters set for an application, notes commenting on the results, and
  so on.

◆ *Experimental glue* groups and links design and instance components: a query
  and its results, a workflow linked with its outcome, links between a workflow
  and its previous and subsequent versions, and a group of all these things
  linked to a document discussing the conclusions of the biologist.

◆ Scientists should be able to discover, use, and pool experiments and their
  components.

ᵐʸGrid has a service-based architecture, prototyping on top of Web services, and intercepting the Open Grid Services Architecture (279) (OGSA; Chapter 17) and in particular OGSA data access and integration services (Chapter 22). Its services can be described as semantically aware, as the project is pioneering semantically rich metadata expressed using ontologies, which are used to discover and select services and components, compose services, and link components together. All components, including workflows, notes, and results, are stored in the ᵐʸGrid Information Repository and are annotated with semantic descriptions so that the knowledge encapsulated within can be more effectively pooled and reused. The technologies draw from the Semantic Web (115) initiative; thus, ᵐʸGrid is an early example of a "Semantic Grid" (Chapter 23).

Our target users are bioinformaticians, tool builders, and service providers who build applications for biologists. The target environment is open, by which we mean the services and their users can be decoupled. Services are not just used solely by their publishers but by users unknown to the service provider, who may use them in unexpected ways. Scientists may opportunistically use services as they are made available, but must adapt to the services as they are published and cope with their evolution and withdrawal. This situation contrasts with a closed domain (such as a drug company) in which resources may be prescribed, adapted, and stabilized. Our scientists work in a mix of local, personal, and public facilities, covering a spectrum of control that both the user and the service provider can exert over the services. Thus we must be flexible enough to be usable within the closed domains of private organizations, and also in hybrids where both private and public data resources can be accessed.

ᵐʸGrid development is being steered by two testbed problems: (1) the functional analysis of clusters of proteins identified in a microarray study of circadian rhythms in the model organism *Drosophila melanogaster* (fruit flies) and (2) the efficient design of genetics studies of Graves disease (an immune disorder causing hyperthyroidism).

The immediate objectives of ᵐʸGrid are to enrich the global Grid movement by

+ developing services for data-intensive integration, rather than computationally intensive problems;

+ developing high-level services for e-science experimental management;

+ investigating the use of semantic Grid capabilities and technologies, such as semantic-based resource discovery and matching; and

+ providing an example of a "second generation" service-based Grid project, specifically a testbed for OGSA base services.

We are producing an assembly of the components (myGrid-in-a-box) with reference implementations, a demonstrator application (an e-lab workbench EStudio), and a demonstration of third-party applications using some of the components, for example, Talisman, an application builder for the InterPro database annotation pipeline (510).

9.1   MOTIVATION: BIOINFORMATICS *IN SILICO* EXPERIMENTS

Biology is emerging from its sequencing to its post-genomics period. Instead of studying one gene we study the whole genome. Instead of one cell cycle we study the whole organism. Instead of one organism we compare organisms. We are moving from what the genome is (though this is still to be completed) to what the genome does and how it does it. Instead of inferring knowledge from fundamental "laws" (there are few in biology), biologists collect, compare, and analyze information arising from "wet" bench observations and instruments, and nowadays also derived by complex queries, algorithms, and computational models applied to large distributed experimental datasets. Connections are made between different pieces of evidence, and these add to the overall body of knowledge. Computationally generated results are tested at the bench, and these results are in turn fed back into the knowledge pool.

Bioinformatics faces computationally intensive problems, such as running tens of thousands of similarity comparisons between protein sequences or simulating protein folding. However, it also has numerous semantically complex information-intensive applications and problems that drive the architecture and services of myGrid. Data are deposited in public databases as a condition of funding and publication and are increasing exponentially—currently a new genome sequence is deposited every 10 seconds. Thanks to high-throughput experimental techniques such as DNA microarrays that generate tens of gigabytes of numerical data, the discipline is becoming less descriptive and more quantitative. Even so, crucial information is commonly encoded using descriptive text (e.g., gene names, gene product functions, anatomy, and phenotypical phenomena) or is published in the literature.

Semistructured data are commonplace because they are adaptable when scientists are uncertain about what they are collecting. Similarly, controlled vocabularies and shared ontologies are flexible when a scientist is unsure about what they are describing. However, this uncertainty leads to volatility in database schema and database contents. It is also common practice to publish and use "gray" information, which is speculative or only partially complete. Rapid advances in the science and knowledge of how to analyze data mean the information is open to continual change (extensions, revisions, reinterpretations)—even to the raw data itself if mistakes are found in sequences, for example. New versions of algorithms may well generate different results when replayed over the same datasets. Database curators infer or copy data from other, equally evolving, databases, forming complex interdependencies between resources that are exacerbated by the practice of replicating resources locally for performance, security, and reliability or taking a snapshot of a database. Results derived from unstable information are themselves subject to uncertainty but often enter the "scientific pipeline" with few of the necessary health warnings. Coping with this viral propagation of data between databases requires support for security, controlled collaboration, authentication, provenance, and digital watermarking.

More problematic still is that the community is globally distributed and highly fragmented. Different communities act autonomously, producing applications and data repositories in isolation. Few centralized repositories exist except for critical resources replicated for improved performance and reliability. Most biological knowledge resides in a large number of modestly sized heterogeneous and distributed resources (over 500 publicly available at the time of writing). The different communities produce a range of diverse data types such as proteome, gene expression, sequence, structure, interactions, and pathways. The data cover different scales and different experimental procedures that may be challenging to interrelate. The different databases and tools have different formats, access interfaces, schemas, and coverage and are hosted on cheap commodity technology rather than in a few centralized and unified superrepositories. They commonly have different, often homegrown, versioning, authorization, provenance, and capability policies.

Despite this fragmentation, the post-genomic era of research is about crossing communities: whole genome analysis rather than an individual gene, comparing the genomes of different species, and investigating the whole cell life cycle and not just a component. Finding appropriate resources and discovering how to use and combine them are serious obstacles to enabling a biologist to make the best use of the available specialist resources and the information from different communities. Technologies for intelligent information integration and data federation are increasingly important.

Biologists record the "who, why, what, when, where, and how" of bench experiments they perform. However, the *in silico* experiments themselves—the workflows, queries, the versions of resources, the thoughts and conclusions of the scientist—are generally not recorded by users, or are set down in an unsystematic way in "Readme" files. This *provenance* information is essential in order to promote experimental reuse and reproducibility, to justify findings or provide their context, and to track the impact of changes in resources on the experiment.

Results and their workflows ought to be linked. Sharing experimental know-how would raise the quality of *in silico* experiments and the quality of data by reducing unnecessary replication of experiments, avoiding the use of resources in inappropriate ways, and would improve understanding of the quality of data and practice. However, it is time consuming to record the large amounts of metadata and intermediary results with enough detail to make the process repeatable by another user unless it is automated or incidentally gathered. The history and the know-how behind the generation of information are as valuable as the information itself; however, best practice is poorly shared in e-biology despite the fact that experimental protocol is highly developed for bench experiments.

Finally, biology is a discipline in which small teams or individuals make a difference, especially when they are able to use the same resources as larger players. The division between providers (a few) and consumers (many) of resources is indistinct. Specialists produce highly valued "boutique" resources because Web-based publication is straightforward and expected. This openness pervades biology and partially accounts for the success of the Human Genome project and the rapid impact of findings on genomics.

myGrid focuses on speculative explorations by a scientist to form *discovery experiments*. These evolve with the scientist's thinking and are composed incrementally as the scientist designs and prototypes the experiment. Intermediate versions and intermediate data are kept, notes and thoughts are recorded, and parts of the experiment and other experiments are linked to form a network of evidence, as we see in bench laboratory books. Once the experiment is settled, it may be run continuously and repetitively, in production style. Discovery experiments by their nature presume that the e-biologist is actively interacting with and steering the experimentation process, as well as interacting with colleagues (in the simplest case by e-mail). An individual scientist keeps personal local collections, makes personal notes, and has personal preferences for resources and how to use them. We contrast this with *production experiments* that are prescriptive, predetermined, and not open to change, for example, streaming data from an instrument and automatically processing it and placing it into a database, where performance and reliability are more significant. Experiments are made by individual scientists, harnessing resources that they do not own, published by service providers without a priori negotiation or agreements with their users, and without any centralized control (147).

This state of the art in information-intensive bioinformatics brings many challenges. The process is knowledge intensive, and that knowledge is tacit or encoded in semistructured texts; the environment and resources are changeable and unpredictable; the capabilities and methodology of scientists vary; and biological questions require complex interactions between resources that are independent yet interdependent. There is little prescription, lots of sharing, and a great deal of change.

9.2 myGRID ARCHITECTURE AND TECHNOLOGIES

In the service-oriented myGrid architecture (Figure 9.2), networked biological resources are services, as are the components themselves. Our high-level services sit on top of OGSA technologies such as lifetime management of service instances

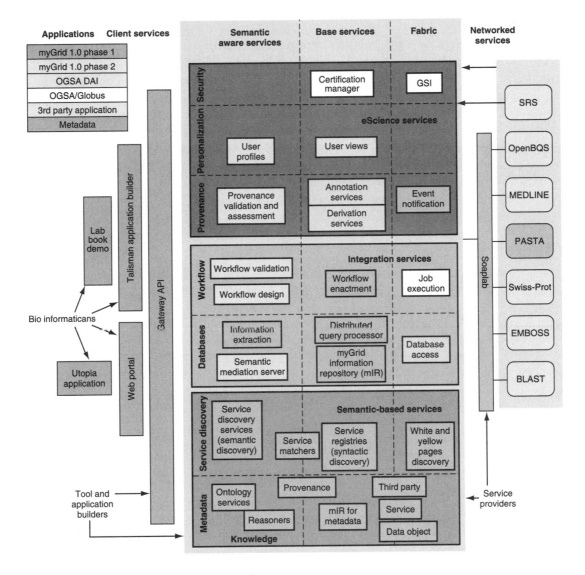

9.2   The myGrid service stack.

FIGURE

and job execution. To cope with the volatility of legacy services, we adopt two layers of abstraction. A *nested component model* abstracts over the many service delivery mechanisms used by the community (of which OGSA is one) to allow service developers and providers to separate concerns in their business logic from on-the-wire protocol specifications, and to allow service providers to configure service behavior, such as fault tolerance and security. Clients interact with services in a protocol-independent manner.

The second layer of abstraction is the *Gateway*, which provides an optional unified single point of programmatic access to the whole system, for ease of use, especially from diverse languages and legacy applications. This construct isolates the end user (and client software) from the detailed operation and interactions of the core architecture and adds value to myGrid in respect of support for collaboration, provenance, and personalization. The Gateway deals with single sign-on and certification (Chapter 21), thus avoiding the need to repeatedly perform authorization as a workflow executes. It overlays distinctive elements such as provenance metadata and semantic relationships on non-myGrid services (such as legacy Web services). Thus, when accessed through the Gateway, normal Web services may appear to expose metadata in a myGrid-compliant manner when in fact these metadata are added in transit through the Gateway. Applications can interact with services directly or via the Gateway.

9.2.1   Semantic Discovery and Metadata Management

A myGrid object can be defined as any identifiable entity that plays a role in an experiment. Thus, a data entry in a database, a workflow specification, a concrete workflow template, a workflow instance bound to services, a service, an annotation on a result, and a link between an executed workflow and the resulting data collection are all objects. A bioinformatician needs knowledge to find and use these objects and to form workflows or distributed queries efficiently and effectively.

A key feature is the incorporation of some of this specialist knowledge into semantically rich descriptions of services and the objects they exchange and act upon. This knowledge is used throughout: for example, to link together components or find links, to validate workflows or find them, to intelligently integrate databases, and to drive portal interfaces. Services and objects carry a range of descriptions: "operational" metadata detailing their origins, quality of service, and so on; structural descriptions detailing their types (string, sequence, collection, etc.) or signatures (inputs, outputs, portTypes); and semantic descriptions that cover what they mean (an enzyme, an alignment algorithm). We are experimenting with metadata attached to objects, so that it becomes possible to determine what can be done with an object regardless of how it was produced. Metadata are also attached to services, to determine the types of objects consumed and produced. Additionally, the model is obliged to cope with the many (de facto) standards in biology that make the type scheme rather open. Early versions circumvent this problem by using the EMBOSS application suite operating in a predetermined-type system.

Providers publish their services, and consumers find and match services and objects, by a range of mechanisms such as name, words, signatures, types, and, in particular, ontological descriptions. For semantic service and object discovery the project is pioneering the use of techniques from the Semantic Web (115) (Chapter 23). Both data objects and services are semantically annotated using ontologies represented in the RDF/XML-based semantic Web ontology languages DAML+OIL (366) and its follow-up OWL (662). Using automated classification-based reasoning over concept descriptions, one can classify and match services (with degrees of imprecision), negotiate service substitutions, and relate database entries to service inputs and outputs based on their semantics. Services (and, for that matter, objects) may be described using (multiple) ontologies, and descriptions by third parties for users who wish to personalize their choice of services, including those they do not own. This work extends the registry specification in OGSA and other cataloging schemes such as MCAT (536), UDDI, and the Globus Toolkit's Monitoring and Discovery Service (204, 264) (MDS-2: Chapter 4).

Service registration uses a multilevel service model distinguishing between "classes" of services and "instances" of services. The latter are real services (e.g., the protein database SWISS-PROT) that may have many copies distributed across the Grid, whereas the former are abstract notions of services (e.g., protein sequence databases) (683) (see Chapter 23). ᵐʸGrid presumes the existence of multiple registries—personal, local, enterprise, or specific community—that can be federated. These register service instances (e.g., a specific version of SWISS-PROT running at *http://ebi.ac.uk*). A *view* is a service that allows discovery of services over a set of service descriptions stored in the registries. Views are currently implemented using an RDF-based UDDI scheme, and carry metadata about location, quality of service, access cost, owner, version, authorization, etc., of service instances. A view may be created and owned either by a single person or an organisation, and the discovery process can be personalized by attaching third-party metadata to service descriptions in the view. A *semantic find service* provides discovery over views by reference to semantic descriptions defined using domain ontologies expressed in OWL (662). Thus services can be described and classified at a more abstract level to enable a more general class of queries such as "all protein databases," allowing workflow specifications to be composed that can be bound at run time with any available and "semantically" suitable services.

Workflow templates and instantiated workflows can also be advertised and discovered in the same way as service classes and service instances.

The ᵐʸGrid Information Repository (mIR) lies at the heart of the architecture.
This stores any kind of object: data generated by experiments along with any
metadata describing the data, biologists' personal annotations of objects held in the
mIR and other external repositories, provenance information, workflow specifications, etc. Metadata, represented using a resource description framework (RDF), is
used to aggregate provenance, registry, personalization, and other metadata to give
information such as who was using which service and why. All components attract
annotation by metadata. DAML+OIL ontologies are used not only to describe the
services but also to annotate entries in databases with concepts. Connections
between components and services are generated by shared ontological terms, for
example by using the COHSE ontology-based open hypermedia system (150).

An organization would typically have a single mIR, which would be shared
by many users, each using it to store their provenance, data, and metadata.
Different users can be provided with different views of the information it contains. These types of views are enforced by exploiting the security features of the
database server on which the mIR is built. The organization uses such security
settings to enforce rules on modification and deletion of data. Because not all
data used in experiments will be local to an installation, users are also able to
augment data in a remote repository, with their own annotations stored locally
in the mIR. The mIR is an early adopter of OGSA-DAI services (27) (Chapter 22),
using it to make the repository accessible to local and remote components over
a Grid. The OGSA-DAI distributed query-processing service allows data from the
mIR and one or more remote data repositories to be federated, producing unified
information views to the biologist. Users can also register their interest in an
object in the mIR and be notified of any relevant new information. Notifications
may also be used to automatically trigger workflows to analyze new data.

9.2.2   Forming Experiments: Knowledge-Based Mediation

SoapLab is a universal connector for legacy command-line-based systems. The vast
majority of services that we want to be able to make use of are shell scripts, PERL
fragments, or compiled architecture-specific binaries rather than Web services;
SoapLab provides a fairly universal glue to bind these into Web services. Current
services include NCBI and WU BLAST sequence alignment tools, the complete
EMBOSS application suite (an independent package of high-quality free open source
software for sequence analysis), MEDLINE (498), and the Sequence Retrieval
System (251). ᴹʸGrid regards *in silico* experiments as combinations of distributed

queries and workflows over these bioservices. Handling *descriptive narrative* in semistructured annotations within these services is a particular problem in bioinformatics. A small team is working on information extraction, exploiting work in PASTA (375). Initially, text services will be integrated as another Web service, but a more ambitious idea is an "ambient text" system where potential search terms are gleaned from the enacting workflow and the user interface to silently provide a library of useful texts on the user's desktop through the gateway.

Service mediation is primarily workflow-based rather than being mediated via a virtual database as in BIRN (Chapter 8). A workflow enactment engine enacts workflows specified initially in IBM's Web Service Flow Language and latterly our own language Scufl. Workflow descriptions are both syntactic and semantic. Syntactic descriptions apply to workflows where the user knows that the operations and the data passed between services matched at a type level. Workflow templates and their semantic descriptions capture the properties of a service rather than specific instances of services. *At the time of enactment*, available services are dynamically discovered, procured, and bound by the enactment engine, with optional user intervention. Workflows specified semantically are more resilient to failures of specific instances of services since alternatives that match the same profile can be discovered. A challenge is that abstract workflows require the resolution of types between services and metadata descriptions so that a user can identify appropriate workflows based on experimental goals such as analysis of microarray data. Creating services dynamically, data streaming for large volumes of data, suspension and resumption of workflows, and user involvement with enacting workflows are further challenges for supporting discovery.

OGSA-DAI and ᵐʸGrid are together building a distributed query-processing system (DQP) that will allow the user to specify queries across a set of Grid-enabled information repositories in a high-level language (initially OQL). Queries are compiled, optimized, and executed on the Grid, supported by a run-time infrastructure. Complex queries on large data repositories may result in potentially high response times, but the system can address this through parallelization, as parts of the query—for example, join operators—can be spread over multiple Grid nodes to reduce execution time (596). As the query language is based on OQL, it allows calls to Web services to be included in queries (e.g., to apply biological computational services such as BLAST to data retrieved from repositories). This enables an important symmetry: workflows can include calls to information services, and queries over information repositories can include calls to services that are implemented as workflows. We believe that DQP will be a powerful tool for many Grid-based e-science applications, freeing the user from concerns over scheduling, optimization, and data transfer. It could underpin, for example, the query-processing and optimization components of BIRN's knowledge-based Information Mediation Architecture.

9.2.3   Managing and Sharing Experiments

One aim of the project is to automate the incidental collection of *provenance* metadata (141, 284). Provenance comes in two forms: *derivation paths*, which track how a result was generated (the query or the workflow) or how a workflow (or query) has evolved; and *annotations*, which augment components with "who, what, where, why, when, and how" metadata that may be structured, semistructured, or free text. When a workflow is executed, the workflow enactment engine provides a record of the provenance of results, automatically generating a trace of the service operations that have been used in the derivation of each result. This provenance dependency graph can be played backward to track the origin of data and played forward to define an impact analysis of changes to base data, to be managed by the *event notification service*. In discovery experiments, workflows evolve incrementally—substituting one database for another or altering the parameters of an algorithm, while a workflow is being enacted. Workflows are derived from other workflows or based on workflow templates, and this provenance is valuable knowledge to share in the evolution of experimental practice. The gateway adds value to services that do not provide their own provenance data by logging service invocations itself.

Personalization capabilities are extended to all components and services. ᵐʸGrid registries are personalized with third-party descriptions and multiple views; the workflows are stored so that they can be edited, and specialized; preferences for databases and parameters for tools are kept as part of provenance records in the mIR. The mIR view mechanism described earlier is core to personalization.

The volatility of bioinformatics data means that the tracking of changes to resources is crucial for forming a view on their validity and freshness. The *event notification* services accept events on any component and route them to consumers. Notification events are filtered by the notifying service and by user agents based on the user preferences. Users register their interests via metadata that describe resources or services to a fine granularity, and are alerted when new, relevant information becomes available. The type and granularity of notification can be indicated via ontological descriptions provided by the metadata services. An OGSA-compliant notification server has been prototyped. OGSA-DAI plans to support data source-change notification that will be integrated with other components via this server. Notification applies to all aspects of ᵐʸGrid—for example, a registry is notified when a service comes online, and an application is notified when a service is registered in a registry visible to the current user.

9.3   SUMMARY

^{my}Grid is building the services needed for a personalized problem-solving environment for a bioinformatician. Its open framework is intended to be sufficiently agile and adaptable to cope with the bioinformatics environment and the independence of bioinformaticians and service providers. We seek to make it easier to construct *in silico*, ad hoc experiments within virtual organizations; to execute and reexecute these experiments over long periods; to find and adapt the experiments of others; to store partial results in local data repositories and provide personal views on public repositories; and to track the provenance and the currency of the resources directly relevant to a user's specific experimental space.

We are developing *high-level services for data-intensive integration*, including an event notification system, distributed query processor, workflow enactment engine, and the ^{my}Grid information repository.

We are developing *high-level services for e-science experimental management*, in such areas as personalization and provenance. Experiments on simple annotation and workflow logging have begun, and the canonical model and APIs are active areas of research. Dependencies are frequently not some mechanistic algorithm but copies of parts of other annotation entries or direct references to other database entries. Curated databases accumulate *copies* (possibly corrected, often editorialized, sometimes transformed) of information from the databases they draw from. This *viral propagation* of information raises issues of provenance/data migration, provenance aggregation, and credit for originating sources. Scientists need to receive not only notifications of changes but also *explanations* for changes to results in which they have registered a specific interest.

We are developing *semantic Grid capabilities and technologies* by extending OGSA's simple registry specification with semantic service descriptions and reasoning, and the deployment of service ontologies and distributed ontology services based on DAML+OIL and RDF. An early version of the ontology of bioinformatics and services is being investigated by the BioMOBY and I3C bioinformatics Web services registry efforts.

We are providing *a "second-generation" service-based Grid and an immediate testbed* for OGSA. ^{my}Grid and OGSA-DAI (Chapter 22) are Grid-service-based open frameworks, meaning that there are well-defined interfaces on which can be built higher-order frameworks (e.g., DQP or provenance management). Being service-based, the components are dynamically discoverable via registries, enabling run-time interrogation of published metadata, thereby facilitating dynamic composability of services. Wrappers specific around bioservices and generic wrappers technologies such as those for databases provide a means to operate with legacy applications. The framework and gateway reduce the complexity of third-party service providers integrating applications.

The ᵐʸGrid-in-a-Box Developer's Toolkit will provide a shrink-wrapped version of the middleware, including open source versions of the software, guidelines for use, and a report on existing experiences. A number of common bioinformatics resources, wrapped as Web services, have been made available to the life sciences community. Sufficient performance, fault tolerance, security, and scalability are all to be addressed.

By making an extensible platform that directly supports *in silico* experimentation, and by sharing all components of an experiment as first-class objects, we hope to improve both the quality of data and the quality of the experiments. Bioinformatics represents a perfect opportunity for the global Grid community to direct middleware developments to really help scientists undertake e-science.

ACKNOWLEDGMENTS

We acknowledge the contributions of Luc Moreau, Paul Watson, Matthew Addis, Mark Greenwood, Norman Paton, Alvaro Fernandes, and Milena Radenkovic to this chapter. The consortium comprises the Universities of Manchester, Southampton, Newcastle, Nottingham, and Sheffield and the EMBL-European Bioinformatics Institute. Other project members include Nedim Alpdemir, Vijay Dialani, David De Roure, Justin Ferris, Rob Gaizauskas, Kevin Glover, Claire Jennings, Peter Li, Xiaojian Liu, Phillip Lord, Darren Marvin, Simon Miles, Tom Oinn, Juri Papay, Simon Pearce, Angus Roberts, Alan Robinson, Tom Rodden, Martin Senger, Nick Sharman, Neil Davis, Anil Wipat, and Chris Wroe. This work is supported by UK e-Science program EPSRC GR/R67743, with contributions from the DARPA DAML subcontract PY-1149, through Stanford University.

FURTHER READING

For more information on the topics covered in this chapter, see *www.mkp.com/grid2*.

Distributed Data Analysis: Federated Computing for High-Energy Physics

Greg Graham, Richard Cavanaugh, Peter Couvares, Alan De Smet, and Miron Livny

CMS (Compact Muon Solenoid) is a high-energy physics detector planned for the Large Hadron Collider (LHC) at the European Center for Nuclear Research (CERN) near Geneva, Switzerland. CMS is currently under construction and is expected to be completed in 2007, at which time it will begin to record data from the highest-energy proton-proton collisions ("events") yet produced. Data from these collisions will shed light on many fundamental scientific issues, including a definitive search for the Higgs particle and the possible origin of mass in the universe, the existence of a new fundamental symmetry of nature called supersymmetry, and even the possible discovery of new spatial dimensions. The data will contain information from potentially millions of individual elements within the detector itself, which will be used to reconstruct the actual collision. Even though these data will be filtered online before analysis, it is still expected that CMS will produce up to several petabytes of data per year.

Although the CMS detector will not begin taking data until after 2007, hundreds of physicists around the world, members of the CMS collaboration, are currently taking part in compute-intensive Monte Carlo simulation studies of the detector and its potential for uncovering new physics. Monte Carlo simulation studies integrate clean theoretical predictions of underlying physics against all of the efficiencies and electronic noise of the millions of detector elements in order to produce realistic simulation data. The simulation data can be used to help predict the impact of detector design on discovery potential. Once the CMS detector is functioning, the output of simulation studies will be compared directly against actual data. Such comparisons provide improved detector calibrations, measurements of physical processes, and indications of possible scientific discoveries.

The scientists and institutions participating in the CMS collaboration are located throughout the world. These scientists are not expected to live at CERN for the duration of its expected 15-year lifetime, but rather need to make significant contributions to the scientific process "from a distance." Therefore, even before the completion of the CMS detector, and then throughout its lifetime, there will be a need to knit scientists together worldwide and put large heterogeneous worldwide-distributed institutional compute and storage resources at their disposal in an organized way. In this regard, Grid technology has shown great promise to

+ manage effectively the addition and removal of heterogeneous institutional resources in a dynamic virtual organization;

+ expose these resources to the entire worldwide collaboration with a consistent set of protocols and APIs; and

+ provide mechanisms to control and optimize the enormous flow of data from the CMS detector to scientists working around the world.

To address these issues, the U.S. participants in the CMS collaboration (US-CMS) began exploring Grid technology in the autumn of 2002 to accomplish an official production request of Monte Carlo simulation data. One of these efforts is the US-CMS Grid. Participating Grid sites include the California Institute of Technology; the Fermi National Accelerator Laboratory; the University of California, San Diego; the University of Florida, and the University of Wisconsin, Madison. For a period of time, a group from CERN also joined the US-CMS Grid effort. Table 10.1 shows the resources of the US-CMS Grid (90). Sites were linked

Site	Number of worker CPUs
Caltech	40 (0.75 GHz)
	40 (2.4 GHz)
Fermilab	80 (0.85 GHz)
University of Florida	80 (1 GHz)
UC San Diego	40 (0.75 GHz)
	40 (2.4 GHz)
CERN	72 (2.4 GHz)
UW Madison	5 (0.85 GHz)

10.1   US-CMS Grid Resources.

TABLE

by high-bandwidth Internet connections, typically OC12 or higher, with giga-bit/sec or 100-megabit/sec connections to each computer. Our goal was to complete an assignment of 1 million "events" requiring roughly 200,000 CPU-hours in a 60-day timeframe. This is roughly the amount of time it took for these same sites to complete an assignment of this size in the past, managing their own computations using existing non-Grid technology.

The participating sites are typically organized as cluster farms with server nodes and worker nodes. The worker nodes were either on the public Internet or behind a NAT firewall.

10.1   IMPLEMENTATION

We chose to base the US-CMS Grid on the basic functionality provided in early versions of the GriPhyN Virtual Data Toolkit, which is in turn based on the Globus Toolkit (276) (Chapter 4) and the Condor High-Throughput Computing System (446) (Chapter 19), including the Condor-G (292) job submission inter-face to the Globus Toolkit. In addition, we employed rudimentary software to manage the US-CMS Virtual Organization. This approach toward basic middle-ware functionality allowed rapid middleware deployment and facilitated a rel-atively high level of fault tolerance by reducing the variety of possible failure modes.

10.1.1   The Virtual Data Toolkit

The Virtual Data Toolkit (VDT) is produced by GriPhyN (93) and includes the core Grid middleware necessary to deploy and operate a computational Grid. In add-ition, the VDT employs a packaging manager known as Pacman for automated installation of Grid middleware to the various US-CMS Grid sites. Once installed, the Grid site administrator is able to manually configure the VDT to fit the appro-priate local compute cluster architecture.

The US-CMS Grid evolved over several VDT releases, each time providing useful scalability information back to the middleware developers. We relied on the VDT for all Grid components, which allowed for simple and consistent man-agement of the middleware across the entire Grid.

This is not to say that Grid middleware deployment was never problematic. There were problems from time to time with low operating system resource defaults for file handles and inodes, for example. There were also problems with unreliable

Virtual data toolkit components	Version	Comments
Server		
Globus Tookit	2.0	Modified GASS cache/jobmanager
Condor	6.4.3	Includes DAGMan
Fault Tolerant Shell	0.99	Provided fault tolerant data transfers
Client		
Globus Clients	2.0	GSI, GridFTP
Condor-G	6.4.3	—

10.2

TABLE

Software from the VDT 1.1.3, Currently Installed on the US-CMS Grid.

file transfers. However, none of these problems proved to be showstoppers, and—more important—all provided important feedback to the middleware developers themselves.

The particular versions deployed on the US-CMS Grid for the production run described here were VDT 1.1.3 and 1.1.4, which included core client and server components from the Globus Toolkit and Condor (see Table 10.2).

10.1.2   CMS-Specific Software

The physics simulation software used by CMS is complicated and has evolved over years—in some cases decades—to embody a great deal of accumulated knowledge and problem-solving experience. Furthermore, it has taken time for scientists to trust the core software to perform correctly. For these reasons, it was important to adapt existing simulation software to the Grid as much as possible, rather than rewrite it from the ground up as a Grid application.

This approach presented challenges, however. Specifically, past practice had been to run the software in much smaller and more controlled environments than the Grid. For example, shared-file systems and common user databases were assumed to exist between submission and execution machines, and the necessary software was assumed to be installed locally beforehand. Also, the standard methodology for running the CMS software had evolved over time from systems managed by hand on individual computers by a few researchers or small clusters of loosely managed computers, to large batch systems utilizing large clusters of largely homogenous resources.

Several layers of management software had therefore been written to help automate the process of running the multiple computations in order on multiple computers and organizing the results. In CMS, this included a legacy, Bash-script-based, job-tracking system (IMPALA), which provided a relatively robust system for declaring, creating, executing, and tracking large numbers of individual jobs through a variety of locally resident batch systems. The more recent MCRunjob (319) package provides a metadata-based approach for specifying more complex workflow patterns, translating them into a set of submittable jobs in a variety of environments, including virtual data language, DAGMan directed acyclic graphs, and the legacy IMPALA environment.

To get early buy-in from CMS, we utilized as much of the existing scientific and production-management software as possible, while enabling it to run on the Grid. This approach enabled direct comparisons between Grid and non-Grid methods. To produce these results as quickly as possible, we chose to insert an adapter layer of software into the existing system, called MOP, and reengineer the existing layers as little as possible. See Table 10.3.

Actual Monte Carlo production depends most critically on the size of each "event" at the CMKIN stage (which simulates the "event"): the more by-product particles produced after the initial proton—proton collision translate into higher processing times for later stages of computation. The CMSIM stage simulates the CMS detector's response to the particles produced in the CMKIN stage and is the most CPU intensive of all stages. CMS Monte Carlo production consists of pipelining several stages together where the output of one stage serves as the input to the next (434). The longest stages are typically CPU bound, but some are I/O bound, and some vary depending on the data. Table 10.4 summarizes the typical characteristics of the stages used in CMS Monte Carlo production.

Condor/FBS	Local-site batch system
Globus Toolkit	Security, I/O, GRAM resource allocation protocol and services, GridFTP
Condor-G	Grid job management
DAGMan	Job dependency management
MOP	Grid "wrapper" generation for non-Grid jobs
IMPALA/MCRunJob	Job creation layer
CMSIM	Physics simulation code

10.3

TABLE

Post-Grid Software Layers.

Step	CPU time (sec/event)	Output size (megabyte/event)	Bound
Stage 1 (CMKIN)	0.05	0.05	CPU
Stage 2 (CMSIM)	350	2.0	CPU
Stage 3 (writeHits)	0.05	1.0	I/O
Stage 4a (writeDigis No PU)	2.0	0.3	CPU
Stage 4b (writeDigis 10^{34} PU)	10.0	3.0	CPU and I/O
Stage 5 (ntuple)	<1	0.05	CPU and I/O

10.4

TABLE

CMS Computation Stages and Their Typical Characteristics (Approximate).

Note that actual performance can be highly variable depending on the physics process being simulated.

Quality assurance considerations require that all productions run uniformly and utilize specific versions of the CMS software. In order to create a "sandbox" environment for the CMS binary executables, a distribution after release (DAR) packaging and deployment mechanism was developed for CMS software. DAR bundles all shared object libraries (including any necessary gcc libraries) along with scripts for setting up the necessary environment variables for job execution. The DAR release version corresponding to the particular production run described in Section 10.2 was then uniformly preinstalled across all US-CMS Grid sites.

CMS Monte Carlo production normally proceeds by breaking up production requests into 250-event collections and processing each collection serially through all stages. For the US-CMS Grid production during autumn 2002, there were two requests for events. The first request was for 1 million events processed through all steps. The second request was for 500,000 events processed only through the CMSIM stage.

10.1.3   Integration Software—MOP

MOP (short for Monte Carlo Production) is a "Grid adapter" developed for CMS by Particle Physics Data Grid (PPDG) that sits between the job creation step and the Grid middleware in the Virtual Data Toolkit and adds necessary subtasks to each job to enable it to run on the Grid without modification. As such, MOP provided a Grid interface similar to that of a traditional batch system.

The jobs, as produced for the US-CMS Grid production run, were not themselves particularly "Grid aware." MOP represented each generated job as directed acyclic graphs (DAGs), using four DAG node types: stage-in nodes to transport the execution environment to the worker node, run nodes to run the executables on remote resources using the Globus Toolkit GRAM interface, stage-out nodes to transport results back to the submit site, and cleanup nodes to remove any leftover job state from the worker nodes. From the standpoint of the CMS software, the jobs are still "local jobs," and MOP takes care of the Grid issues of staging, data transfer, and cleanup.

During production Grid runs, MOP was invoked to create DAG representations of each job at submit time. Once a DAG was produced, MOP submitted the DAG to the DAGMan package of Condor, which ran the DAG nodes using the Condor-G gateway, allowing DAGMan to run DAG nodes on remote compute sites running Globus Toolkit jobmanagers. In turn, these Globus Toolkit jobmanagers are able to run jobs using local batch queues.

10.1.4 The Virtual Organization

Much like local networks of machines, worldwide networks of Grid resources require some kind of centralized user database management. The Globus Toolkit provides a local mechanism for each system to map Grid user certificates to local users (280) (Chapter 21) but provides no way to synchronize or automatically distribute this information among multiple systems.

To automate the process of adding and removing users from the US-CMS Grid, we used the Caltech Virtual Organization Group Manager, which stores the user information in a central LDAP database and allows an administrator to create groups and populate users.

10.2 THE PRODUCTION RUN

In large collaborative environments, such as that associated with the CMS experiment, the stress of running large-scale MOPs can approach stresses not encountered anywhere outside of running the actual experiment. The consequences of failure in large-scale MOP do not approach those associated with the loss of actual data. However, they include missing important deadlines set by funding agencies, failure to validate fundamental computing models, and in the era of data taking the possibility of falling behind competitors in the race for scientific discoveries. In this modern age of high-energy particle physics, computing is seen more and more as a critical extension to detectors themselves.

The emerging US-CMS Grid entered this highly charged environment during the spring 2002 CMS Monte Carlo production, in support of the technical design report of the data acquisition system, and quickly fell to its knees! Close inspection of the middleware revealed that, although the underlying Grid computing model was sound, several key components were lacking in the implementation. After a six-month period of reengineering, the US-CMS Grid reemerged in the autumn of 2002. After breezing through an initial 50,000-event test run in September, the US-CMS Grid was ready to participate in a 10-million-event study of the backgrounds in the CMS detector. The part assigned to the US-CMS Grid consisted of a 1-million-event request processed through all steps (excepting pileup) plus a 500,000-event request to be processed through the CMSIM stage only.

CMS Monte Carlo production is highly organized. Conveners of special-purpose groups (organized around specific physics topics) enter production requests into a reference database at CERN. Production staff at CERN review new requests and break them up into smaller parts. Each part is assigned to a participating CMS regional center. Regional centers receive requests for production by e-mail, with each request including a key into the assigned part of the production in the reference database.

The US-CMS Grid was set up as a virtual regional center in order to participate in the CMS production. After receipt of an e-mail request, the CMS job creation tools were invoked with the given key. The tools then contacted the reference database at CERN and downloaded all necessary parameters via HTTP. Each created job consisted of executable scripts with parameters to generate 250 events (using the CMKIN stage) and process them through the CMSIM, writeHits, writeDigis (No PU), and n-tuple-making stages for the 1-million-event request; MCRunJob also created a different, simpler script performing just the CMKIN and CMSIM steps for the 500,000-event request.

During the running of the US-CMS Grid, the operator would typically generate a few hundred jobs at a time and assign them to different Grid sites by hand. This approach did not attempt to use a scheduler or resource broker because we felt that there were still lessons to be learned lurking in the middleware itself. Job submission involved the invocation of MOP, which took the job scripts and wrapped them into DAG nodes as described previously. DAGMan then took these DAGs and, using Condor-G as a backend, was able to run the DAG nodes on remote Globus Toolkit jobmanagers. In the US-CMS Grid, these jobmanagers were configured to use either regular Condor or the Fermilab Farm Batch System as queue managers on local clusters. Information and job output were sent back to the submit site by the "stage-out" DAG node.

We encountered many problems during the run and fixed many of them, including integration issues arising from the integration of legacy CMS software tools with Grid tools, bottlenecks arising from operating system limitations, and bugs in both the Grid middleware and application software.

Every component of the software contributed to the overall "problem count" in some way. However, with the current level of functionality, we were able to operate the US-CMS Grid with 1.0 FTE of effort during quiescent times over and above normal system administration and up to 2.5 FTEs during crises. This compares favorably with the official spring 2002 Monte Carlo production of CMS, but concrete comparisons are hard to draw because of the looser organization of the spring 2002 effort, as discussed in the next section. The following are examples of the problems encountered:

✦ (Pre-Grid) During spring 2002, the Globus Toolkit 2.0 GASS Cache (117) was found to not support the required level of performance for CMS production. The software was reengineered in consultation with Condor developers and Globus Toolkit developers over the summer of 2002, and released in GT 2.2.

✦ Many simultaneous globus-url-copy operations originating from the MOP master site when submitting many jobs would cause some globus-url-copy operations to hang. Globus-url-copy operations were wrapped in Fault Tolerant Shell (FTSH) scripts. FTSH contains semantics to time out and retry shell commands; we found that it could be applied to many other places to add fault tolerance to existing applications (see Chapter 19).

✦ Condor was configured to resubmit failed jobs in some instances. We did not have sophisticated problem-tracking tools during this run, and therefore there was often an inability to realize that something was wrong when problems were occurring.

✦ Jobs sometimes failed because of application code problems. During one episode in November, middleware was suspected of causing disk cache over-runs. A "war room" of middleware developers was organized to create a problem tree and explore all of its branches. Eventually, after three days, the bug was traced to incorrect but innocuous-looking program input from the job creation step and given to a developer of the job creation software, after which the problem was diagnosed and fixed within 90 minutes. More sophisticated error analysis is needed to sort bugs correctly to the right people.

✦ Condor-G running on the MOP master site uses a "gahp_server" to handle its communication with processes running under the Globus Toolkit on remote worker sites, one thread per tracked process. With over 400 CPUs available to the US-CMS Grid at later stages of production, running two assignments to produce 1.5 million events, we had to divide production over two physically separate MOP master machines, to avoid the scaling limit of the number of gahp_server threads.

10.3   SUMMARY

The US-CMS Grid was a success in that it produced all required events and provided many useful insights into operating a Grid in production mode (86). Also, many problems were uncovered with the software at all levels. Despite problems, the production was remarkably smooth and sustained for over two months.

Figure 10.1 shows the progress of the US-CMS Grid full n-tuple production during the fall of 2002. The two left plots show throughput as a function of time, with the lower plot also showing a linear fit. The two notable flat spots occur during the SC 2002 conference and the winter holidays, when manpower was not available to submit new jobs. The two right plots express performance measured in average events per day, during each of 12 roughly five-day periods, shown as a function of time (upper) and in histogram format (lower). The theoretical maximum daily rate achievable across the entire US-CMS Grid is 45,000 events per day, and average efficiency was just under 40%.

This performance is comparable to the conventional CMS spring 2002 production. The spring 2002 production was more complicated in that it involved

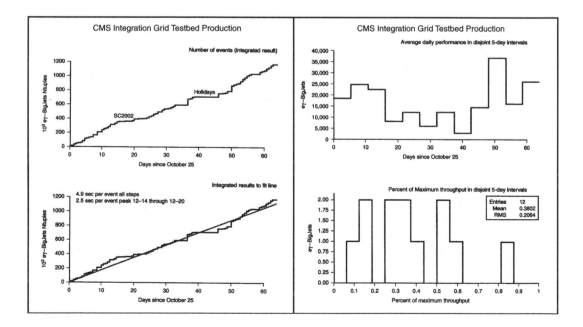

10.1   Performance of the US-CMS Grid. See text for details.

FIGURE

more events with pileup and many more file transfers. Also, it is hard to calculate efficiency of the spring 2002 production because it is hard to determine when a site was unavailable because of problems or just idle for lack of a request. Nonetheless, similar estimates of efficiency range from 30 to 50%.

Scheduling functionality was not implemented in the MOP system during the fall 2002 US-CMS Grid run. Rather, jobs were distributed by direct operator specification at job submission time. MOP was logically divided into the MOP master site and the MOP worker sites. Jobs were created and submitted from the MOP master site, all input files were staged in from the MOP master site, and all output was returned to the MOP master site. No replica catalogs (Chapter 22) were used during the production process itself, but resulting data products were registered in GDMP (612) at the end of processing. These issues are being studied in anticipation of a MOP upgrade. During fall 2002, Fermilab hosted the US-CMS Grid MOP master site.

ACKNOWLEDGMENTS

We acknowledge the CMS Core Computing and Software group and the US-CMS Software and Computing projects for supporting this effort. We especially thank Veronique Lefebure and Tony Wildish of the CMS Production Team for their support and helpful discussions. Also thanks to the US-CMS Grid Team: Erik Aslakson, Julian Bunn, Saima Iqbal, Harvey Newman, Suresh Singh, and Conrad Steenberg of the California Institute of Technology; M. Anzar Afaq, Shafqat Aziz, L. A. T. Bauerdick, Michael Ernst, Joseph Kaiser, Natalia Ratnikova, Hans Wenzel, and Yujun Wu of Fermi National Accelerator Laboratory; James Branson, Ian Fisk, and James Letts of the University of California, San Diego; Adam Arbree, Paul Avery, Dimitri Bourilkov, Jorge Rodriguez, and Suchindra Kategari at the University of Florida; Jaime Frey, Alain Roy, and Todd Tannenbaum at the University of Wisconsin, Madison.

FURTHER READING

For more information on the topics covered in this chapter, see *www.mkp.com/grid2*.

Massively Distributed Computing: Virtual Screening on a Desktop Grid

Andrew A. Chien

*W*e describe an exemplar of an important class of applications for the emerging Grid, namely, coarse-grained task-parallel computations arising from parameter sweeps, Monte Carlo simulations, and data parallelism (see Chapters 10, 19, and 1:13) (56, 444). These applications generally involve large-scale computation to search, optimize, and statistically characterize products, solutions, and design space—all activities critically important in the increasingly information-driven economy. Indeed, the availability and use of increased computation can often directly increase the quality of answers that can be achieved. Our exemplar is a task-parallel drug discovery application. We describe how this application can be supported effectively on what we call *desktop Grids*.

Because desktop resources are pervasive, desktop Grid systems can aggregate thousands to tens of thousands of machines even within a single company. The strategy involves exploiting the availability of idle desktop workstations or PCs—often idle as much as 95% at night and 85% during the day (444, 446). These machines, and their software, typically are extremely heterogeneous and subject to varied management and use regimens. Hence, in order to achieve a high degree of utility, desktop Grid systems must be able to put an application on the platform easily and must secure the data as the application executes on the network. Moreover, such systems must do so without requiring armies of information technology administrators.

The application that we describe here is *virtual screening*: the testing of hundreds of thousands to millions of candidate drug molecules to see whether they block the activity of a protein. We examine, in particular, the deployment of a virtual screening application on the *Entropia* desktop Grid system. The key advantages of Entropia are the ease of application integration and its new model for providing security and unobtrusiveness for the application and client machine. Applications are integrated using binary modification technology without requiring any changes to the source code. This binary integration automatically ensures that the application is unobtrusive, and provides security and protection for both the client machine and the application's data. Other systems require developers to change their source code to use custom APIs or simply provide weaker security and protection. In many cases, application source code may not be available, and recompiling and debugging with custom APIs can be a significant effort.

The remainder of this chapter is structured as follows. First, we describe the computational needs of drug discovery. Next, we discuss the basic characteristics of a desktop Grid and how a virtual screening application is deployed across it. We then describe the delivered performance for virtual screening on a desktop Grid. We conclude with a summary and some future directions. Throughout, we use the Entropia system as an example.

11.1   COMPUTING NEEDS OF DRUG DISCOVERY

With the recent completion of the sequencing of the human genome, the mouse genome, and numerous other genomes, computation is increasingly viewed as a critical tool in the earliest stages of drug discovery. The ongoing identification of new therapeutics is critical to public health and is the subject of significant investment by large pharmaceutical companies, biotech companies, and venture capital firms. The life sciences research market for information technology (excluding health care) is expected to grow to $9 billion by 2003. These investments are predicated on the critical importance of information technology as a method of discovery and evaluation for new drug compounds.

In addition to the explosive growth of genomic information, the amount of proteomic and molecular data available to biotechnologists is growing exponentially, doubling in as little as six months to a year. This rate of growth greatly exceeds the 18-month rate of individual processor power doubling predicted by Moore's law. As a result, researchers are increasingly motivated to use multiprocessor (parallel) systems.

The growth in data is only one of several factors driving the rapid increase in computational demands. Navigating the data has become a critical problem. For example, as Figure 11.1 shows, the National Center for Biotechnology Information (NCBI) GenBank database is doubling in size every 12 months. Many research activities involve sequence searching against this database, the cost of which scales with database size.

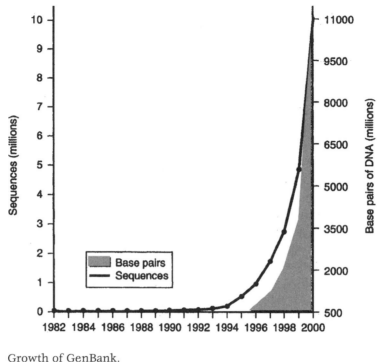

Growth of GenBank.

Combinatorial chemistry raises another computational problem. Combinatorial chemistry can be used to create molecules en masse. However, computers are used to design and select which compounds are *worth* synthesizing. For example, high-throughput virtual screening techniques use computational analysis to select a subset of compounds appropriate for a given receptor. Here the computational demand scales with the number of candidate molecules.

11.2   GRID TECHNOLOGY LEVERAGE AND REQUIREMENTS

Pharmaceutical researchers need to access more data than in the past and to perform more computation on that data. Although modern techniques in combinatorial chemistry and high-throughput screening allow large numbers of molecules to be synthesized and assayed, significant limitations remain because of the time and resources required to complete these experiments in the laboratory. Virtual screening (95, 670) allows one to identify a focused set of compounds, selected on the basis of their properties and those of the target receptor, and leads to an enhanced hit rate in the bioassay. Unfortunately, the size of the computational problem is large, and the number of compounds involved is enormous.

The requirements for virtual screening can certainly be addressed by building larger central computing facilities. However, such facilities are extremely expensive and are often not designed for the specific task at hand. Another approach is to employ specialized high-performance computing systems (404). However, these systems require considerable investment in specialized packaging and interconnection technologies, and thus these systems are commonly reserved for problems that require high interprocessor performance. Still another solution is to use Linux and Beowulf clusters (609). Built from commodity components, these clusters provide significant amounts of compute power at a lower cost per node than mid-range compute servers and have become popular. However, the cost of building, maintaining, and operating these systems can be significant because of the range of open source software and systems involved. Both high-end and Beowulf systems also may require expertise in algorithm parallelization.

Desktop Grid computing provides a good solution for virtual screening problems. These problems do not require high interprocessor performance, and a desktop Grid can deliver significantly more compute power than a central compute server. For example, whereas a typical Beowulf cluster might have 128 processors, a desktop Grid system might have thousands or even tens of thousands of PCs. This increased compute power enables biologists not only to do more virtual screening in less time but also to execute more complex and more accurate methods, in order to reduce the number of false positives. The strategy fits well with a current trend in virtual screening of separating the docking step (that is, identifying the most likely binding mode of this compound to a specific receptor) from the scoring step (that is, determining how tightly this docked molecule binds relative to other molecules), which can involve more complex algorithms than those needed for docking.

11.3   DOCKING ON A DESKTOP GRID

Testing typically involves assessing the binding affinity of the test molecule to a specific place on a protein in a procedure commonly called *docking*. Docking codes (252) are well matched for distributed computing because each candidate molecule can be evaluated independently. The amount of data required for each molecular evaluation is small—basically the atomic coordinates of the molecules—and the essential results are even smaller: a binding score. The computation per molecule ranges from seconds to tens of minutes or more on an average PC. The coordination overhead can be further reduced by bundling sets of molecules or increasing the rigor of the evaluation. Low thresholds can be set for an initial scan to quickly eliminate clearly unsuitable candidates, and the remaining molecules can be evaluated more rigorously.

We implemented the docking step (252) on the Entropia DCGrid 5.0 platform. This application takes as inputs a compound database and a protein receptor or enzyme configuration. The compounds in the database are "docked" against the submitted protein receptor or enzyme, and the resulting configurations scored and ranked. Because each of the compounds in the database can be docked and scored independently, significant parallelism is available. To adapt this program to the Entropia system, we wrote a small piece of code that partitions the compound database into disjoint smaller compound databases. The binary is processed by using Entropia's application preparation tools (fully automatic), which encapsulate the binary in Entropia's virtual machine (180). We term each invocation of the docking binary on a compound database piece and the protein receptor a "subjob" and the docking of the entire compound database against the protein receptor the "job." We also wrote a second piece of code that combines the resulting rankings into a single final ranking for the entire job. The application integration took approximately two hours. The operation of this integrated application is depicted in Figure 11.2.

As Figure 11.3 shows, performance increases linearly to over 500 nodes and compares favorably in performance with both a high-end multiprocessor (an SGI system) and a Beowulf cluster. Nevertheless, the computational demands of virtual screening today are enormous and unlikely to be met soon. Typical cases require thousands of processors. For example, many pharmaceutical libraries have a million potential drug molecules that can be tested against sets of thousands of proteins. Some companies would like to routinely screen 10 or 20 million. Achieving a screen of a million compounds against a single site in 24 hours requires a thousand nodes. Doing so with turnaround within a business day ($\sim$8 hours) requires 5,000 nodes. In the case of 10 and 20 million compounds, the requirements are 50,000 to 100,000 nodes in a desktop Grid.

The virtual screening application can be scaled to a larger numbers of compounds and nodes on a desktop Grid, with performance characteristics as shown in Table 11.1. These characteristics were chosen to achieve turnaround within a day on our local test Grid within Entropia. They reflect a run approximately 200 times smaller than many full-scale production virtual screening environments that involve millions of compounds. Figures 11.4 and 11.5 illustrate the performance

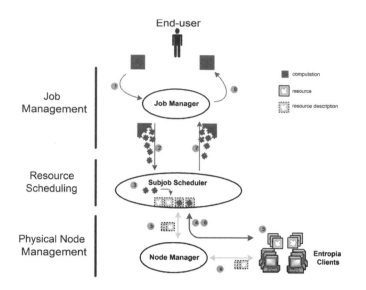

11.2

FIGURE

Docking application on the Entropia desktop Grid. The job manager sends subjobs (dock, compound binary, protein receptor) to the subjob scheduler; these subjobs are then executed on the resources. Results are combined in the job manager to produce an aggregate result to the overall dock job.

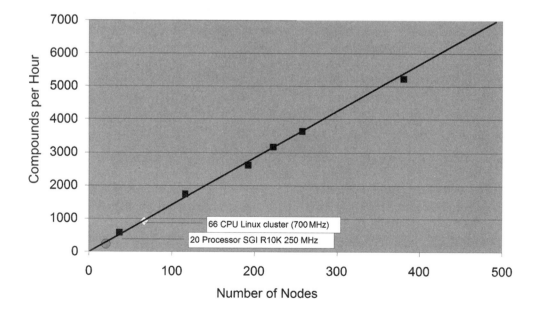

11.3

FIGURE

Docking throughput on a desktop Grid installed in a large pharmaceutical company.

Number of molecules	5,000 (1–10 M is production)
Molecules per subjob	1 (fine-grained stress test)
Execution time	1,357,914 sec, 22,361 min, 377 h, or 15 days
Number of machines used	94 Pentium III and IV machines
Speedup	72 times (18,644 seconds or 5 hours)

11.1 Performance Characteristics of a Virtual Screening Application.

TABLE

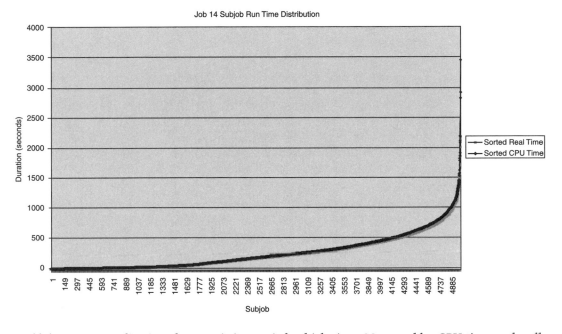

11.4 Application characteristics: varied subjob sizes. Measured by CPU time and wall-clock completion time (upon arrival at the server).

FIGURE

characteristics of the application on the Entropia desktop Grid system. Together, these figures indicate the potential performance for this application on large desktop Grids.

Figure 11.4 plots the sizes of subjobs (the independent executions of docking a single compound against the protein receptor). As the figure shows, the time to completion for the subjobs varies widely because the computation structure is far from uniform. Figure 11.5 shows the evolution of the overall computation, as the independent pieces (subjobs) are scheduled on resources and complete over time.

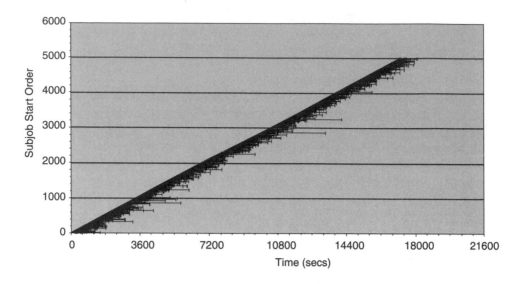

11.5

FIGURE
Timeline of subjob execution. Each subjob is initiated in numerical order, and the black line reflects the execution lifetime of each subjob. The variability in subjob execution time and the excess available parallelism are both readily visible.

This plot shows the variability in subjob time clearly, and the steady progress of the system through the large overall job. The thinness of the band indicates that even in this modest-sized run, there is significantly more parallelism to be exploited. For example, using 1000 nodes (ten times as many) would simply compress this plot in the x dimension by a factor of 10, but there is ample parallelism to achieve that.

11.4   SUMMARY

We have used virtual screening to illustrate the potential of desktop Grid platforms for computationally intensive applications. Desktop Grids are suitable for a wide range of similar applications that exhibit high degrees of task parallelism and scale with dataset size. To support these applications, desktop Grids bring huge computational capabilities of thousands of machines, delivered conveniently for application use. Thus, desktop Grids are changing what is possible—both quantitatively and qualitatively—for the biological sciences.

ACKNOWLEDGMENTS

We gratefully acknowledge the talented engineers and architects at Entropia who contributed to the design and implementation of the Entropia system and its applications: in particular, Wilson Fong and Steve Elbert, who worked on the application described here. The author is supported in part by the Defense Advanced Research Projects Administration through U.S. Air Force Rome Laboratory Contracts AFRL F30602-99-1-0534 and the National Science Foundation through NSF EIA-99-75020 Grads and NSF Cooperative Agreement ANI-0225642 (OptIPuter) to the University of California, San Diego. Support from Hewlett–Packard is also gratefully acknowledged.

FURTHER READING

For more information on the topics covered in this chapter, see *www.mkp.com/grid2* and the following references:

+ Chien et al. (180) gives an in-depth description of the Entropia platform.

+ The book, *Virtual Screening* (414), is a collection of papers discussing high-throughput virtual screening and comparing it to traditional empirical techniques.

+ Dock (252) and Gold (395) are several of the leading high-throughput docking programs.

12 | Enterprise Resource Management: Applications in Research and Industry

Wolfgang Gentzsch

*D*istributed resource management systems can exploit Grid technologies to integrate and map user workloads to computational resources at multiple locations. Such systems can provide numerous benefits, including better resource utilization (increased from 20 to 80% or more in some situations), on-demand access to required resources, virtualization as a means of shielding users from infrastructure details, and automated failover.

In this chapter, we describe three large-scale deployments of such systems: one from industry (GlobeXplorer) and two from academia (University of Houston Campus Grid and UK White Rose Grid). The objective is to illustrate the technical rationales that can motivate the application of distributed resource management systems, implementation approaches that have proved successful in these deployments, and experiences and lessons learned.

These three deployments use a mix of technologies to achieve their goals. Resource management within sites is achieved via the use of Sun Grid Engine (SGE), a cluster management system distributed in both open source and enhanced forms by Sun Microsystems, and deployed in several thousand locations worldwide. The integration of resources at multiple locations is achieved via the Globus Toolkit (276) (Chapter 4).

12.1 GLOBEXPLORER: DIGITAL IMAGE INGEST AND ANALYSIS

Companies such as Mapquest, Yahoo!, Hotmail, and (as discussed here) GlobeXplorer commonly operate centralized cluster computing data centers to support their user workloads. Such centralized clusters represent a

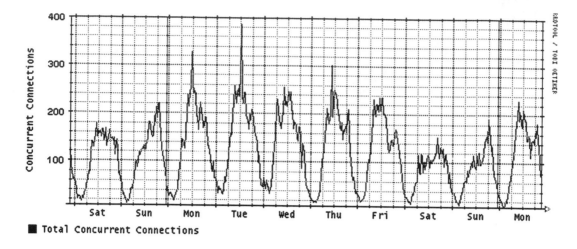

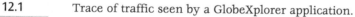

RRDTOOL / TOBI OETIKER

12.1   Trace of traffic seen by a GlobeXplorer application.

FIGURE

well-accepted approach to addressing scalability, modularity, and quality-of-service goals.

Because most traffic to such sites originates in North America, it is common to encounter a regular diurnal pattern, such as that illustrated in Figure 12.1. In addition, such sites may experience traffic spikes caused by fluctuations in user behavior associated with news events, promotional offers, and other transient activity. A rule of thumb is that sites should provision for 10 times normal peak demand, which itself can be two times or more larger than average demand. The result is large amounts of unused capacity.

Single-site Grid computing typically comes as a "Eureka!" event to such Web-based companies when they realize that they own a virtual supercomputer that is often doing nothing (particularly at night) and that can in principle be applied to various projects that had previously been considered impractical. With appropriate support in place, these projects can operate as background jobs on the otherwise idle hardware.

GlobeXplorer, the company that is the focus of this case study, is a leading provider of satellite images and aerial photography via the Internet. It faced in 2002 the problem of ingesting a national archive of several hundred thousand frames of raw aerial photography, each requiring nearly 30 minutes of dedicated CPU time of processing to perform geometric corrections for terrain distortion, color enhancements, and wavelet compressions. Because of the loose-grained parallelism of the core jobs, SGE provided an ideal mechanism to address this problem. SGE transformed the ingest process from being CPU bound to I/O bound: GlobeXplorer could not feed "the beast" fast enough.

At GlobeXplorer, basic precautions were taken from the beginning to ensure that jobs prototyped in the lab were effectively isolated in production in terms of directory structures, prioritization, and permission. Database schemas and workflow have now stabilized to the point that overall utilization of the production machines has increased from 43 to over 85%. Moreover, GlobeXplorer has saved nearly $750,000 in capital and operating expenditures on this project alone. It is by now routine for GlobeXplorer to process several terabytes of imagery each week in addition to production applications.

Admittedly, the move to Grid computing did add some complications. A side effect of full utilization is that site resources are now mission critical to two different business processes: in-line HTTP traffic and content ingest. Intuitive observations of the compute farm statistics must now account for the fact that requests originate from both the Web and the SGE scheduler and must take into account several workflows overlaid on the same compute, networking, and storage resources. Configuration management issues concerning system library versioning, mount points, and licensing face these same considerations.

Another issue of concern is the need for multisite coordination of scheduling, to ensure proper separation of the front office (the HTTP compute farm) and the back office (workflow controller). The Globus Toolkit is used for this purpose, complementing the functionality of SGE.

The tremendous success of this implementation has led GlobeXplorer management to embrace the concept of Grid computing and support the increased use of Grid technologies throughout the enterprise. The data portrayed in the maps served by GlobeXplorer originate from multiple sources, such as population data, street networks, satellite, and aerial archives. The Globus Toolkit is to be used as a framework for supply-chain management of such complex content types that will ultimately become a part of GlobeXplorer's product offerings (see Figure 12.2). Experimentation is under way with remote data centers that have specialized image algorithms, larger content archives, and computing capacity, with the goal of constructing such a supply chain.

Such chains might include coordinate reprojection, format transcodings, false-color lookups for multispectral data, edge enhancements, wavelet compression, buffering zone creation from vector overlays, and cell-based hydrologic simulations. Routines for these operations will exist in binary forms at various locations and will require various resources for execution. It will often be more efficient to migrate an algorithm to a remote archive than vice versa. GlobeXplorer plans to "remotely add value" to previously inaccessible or unusable archived data stores by using OGSA to provide product transformation capabilities on the fly to

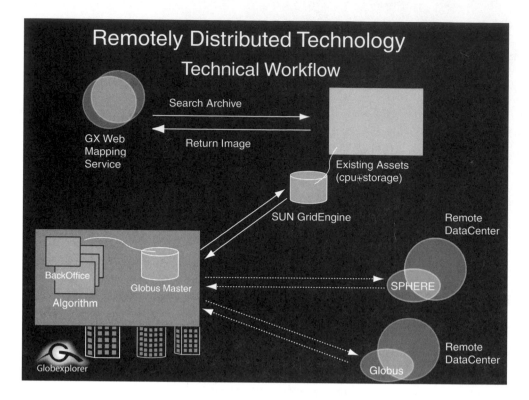

12.2   Globus Toolkit as a framework for a supply-chain management Grid.

FIGURE

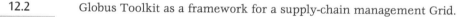

a transient supply chain. The objective is to create derivative product offerings, with guaranteed service-level agreements, to the mission-critical applications of our customers.

This vision (see Figure 12.3) of chained flows of discoverable data and services is shared by other participants in the dominant standards body of geographic information: the OpenGIS consortium (OGC). The intention is that chains themselves will be expressible in emerging standards such as WS-Route, WSFL, and related service-oriented workflow description languages, expressed as trading partner agreements within ebXML registries. Workflow technologies discussed in Chapter 19, including Chimera (284), are also relevant here.

Perhaps the largest challenges to making this vision a reality are standards-based registration and discovery issues and metadata harmonization across disparate, often overlapping, standards at the organizational, local, regional, and national levels, implemented in often overlapping technologies such as LDAP

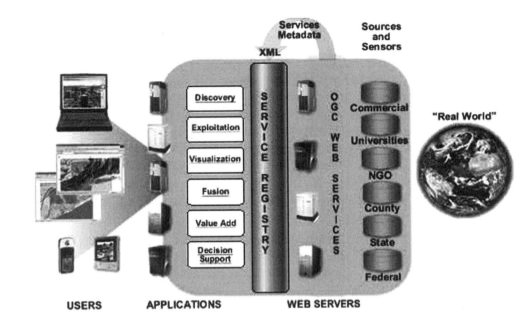

12.3   OGC Web services vision.

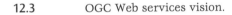

FIGURE

and Z39.50. These issues are actively being addressed in the context of pressing applications such as homeland security, which requires immediate access to critical, often sensitive, data regulated by federal freedom of information and privacy legislation, network security, and privacy issues (public vs private data).

12.2   UNIVERSITY OF HOUSTON CAMPUS GRID

The University of Houston (UH) is typical of many university campuses in that its faculty are engaged in many scientific research projects that require access to significant computational resources: researchers in chemistry, geophysics, mechanical engineering, computer science, and mathematics are among those who routinely perform large amounts of computing.

To support these users, UH operates a number of both large and small computational clusters connected via optical fiber. Its central High Performance Computing Center (HPCC) includes a cluster of Sun Fire 6800 and 880 platforms connected via

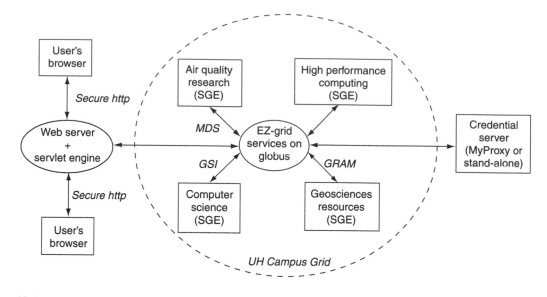

12.4   University of Houston campus Grid.

FIGURE

Myrinet. These systems are available to a broad cross section of faculty and are deployed for both research and teaching. The facility is heavily used, with a high average queue time for submitted jobs. UH therefore exploits the availability of other resources on campus to alleviate this problem by connecting a number of different systems, including those at the HPCC, in a campus Grid (see Figure 12.4).

This Grid is divided into administrative domains corresponding to the owner of the hardware, each of which may contain multiple clusters with a shared file system. All basic Grid services, such as security and authentication, resource management, static resource information, and data management, are provided by the Globus Toolkit (276) (Chapter 4), whose features may be directly employed by accredited users to submit jobs to the various clusters. An independent certification authority is managed by the HPCC. SGE serves as the local resource manager within domains and is thus the software that interfaces with the Globus Toolkit resource manager component. The Globus Toolkit's monitoring and discovery service is used to provide access to information such as operating system version, CPU load, queue information, application profiles (metadata about applications), and job execution histories. Policy-based authorization and accounting services (617) are used to examine and evaluate resource provider usage policies.

Because many application scientists find it daunting to deal with Grid infrastructure, a portal, called EZ-Grid (172), has been created to make it easy for the scientists to interact with Grid services. The Globus Toolkit-based EZ-Grid provides interfaces for authenticating users, accessing information on the system and its status, and scheduling and submiting jobs to resources within the individual domains. The development of EZ-Grid was facilitated by CoG Kits (429), which provide libraries that enable application developers to include the Globus Toolkit middleware in high-level applications in languages such as Java and Perl. The EZ-Grid portal server has been implemented with Java servlets and can be run on any Web server that supports these servlets.

One demanding collaborative research effort supported by the UH Grid involves a team of scientists working on the numerical simulation and modeling of atmospheric pollution, with a special focus on subtropical Gulf Coast regions such as Houston–Galveston–Brazoria. The team uses a parallel version of a community air quality model designed to forecast the impact on atmospheric pollution of various strategies for reducing volatile organic compounds and nitric oxide. The photochemical air quality model consists of a set of coupled partial differential equations, one for each chemical species. The input to these equations is the complete local weather data and concentrations of chemical precursor molecules, ideally from real-time monitoring. The project therefore involves the execution of a limited-area weather model—indeed, multiple limited area models are executed on increasingly smaller, but more closely meshed, domains—in conjunction with the chemical model. It also relies on global weather data automatically retrieved each day. The Grid system is required to start the weather model, once these data are locally available, and to initiate execution of the chemical code, once the weather code has reached a certain phase. Since these are run at separate Grid sites, the files must be automatically transferred.

A second major application domain for the UH Grid involves geophysicists engaged in research, development, and evaluation of seismic processing and imaging algorithms. These algorithms generally involve the handling of very large datasets. Geophysicists use the UH Grid to execute methods for high-resolution imaging of seismic data, in order to better identify and quantify hydrocarbon reserves, and aggressively disseminate results to the oil and gas industry. Industry partners provide real-world data and the opportunity to verify results by testing in a working oil field. Particularly computationally demanding is a Three dimension prestack wave equation depth migration algorithm. Three-dimensional prestack imaging is the most compute-intensive application currently run within the supermajor oil and geophysical service companies, consuming the vast majority of CPU cycles. The workload generated includes both low-priority, long-running jobs and high-priority, short-term imaging algorithms. High-speed access to the storage system is critical for their execution.

12.3   WHITE ROSE GRID

Our third example, the White Rose Grid (WRG) based in Yorkshire, UK, is a virtual organization of three distinct institutions: Leeds, York, and Sheffield universities. WRG comprises four large compute clusters, each named after a white rose: two at Leeds (Maxima and Snowdon) and one each at York (Pascali) and Sheffield (Titania).

The White Rose Grid is heterogeneous in terms of underlying hardware and operating platform. Maxima, Pascali, and Titania are built from a combination of large symmetric memory Sun servers and storage and backup, whereas Snowdon comprises a Linux/Intel-based compute cluster interconnected with Myricom Myrinet.

The four independent clusters are interconnected through open source Grid middleware. To ensure a stable platform for local users at each site, Grid Engine Enterprise Edition, HPC ClusterTool, and Sun ONE Studio provide distributed resource management and MPI support, as well as compile and debugging capabilities. Users at each campus use the Grid Engine interface (command line or GUI) to access their local resource; WRG users also have the option of accessing the facility via a portal.

The White Rose Grid uses share-tree policy mechanisms supported by Grid Engine Enterprise Edition to ensure that 25% of each cluster's compute resource is available to WRG users and the remaining 75% to local users. (This policy causes the scheduler to adjust job resource shares periodically to ensure that users, groups, and projects get close to their allocated share of the system over the accumulation period.) As depicted in Figure 12.5, each WRG cluster hosts a Globus Toolkit GRAM server (205) (Chapter 18). WRG users are registered both with each of these servers (to provide access to remote systems) and with the user set associated with the WRG share (to ensure that total use by WRG users at any node does not exceed 25%).

Web access is provided by a WRG portal constructed with the Grid Portal Development Kit (GPDK), based on the Java CoG Kit (429), Java Server Pages, JavaBeans, and Apache Tomcat. Like many portals, the WRG requires use of the MyProxy online credential repository (507) to store a delegated credential, which is retrieved by the portal server prior to interaction so that the portal can subsequently act on that user's behalf.

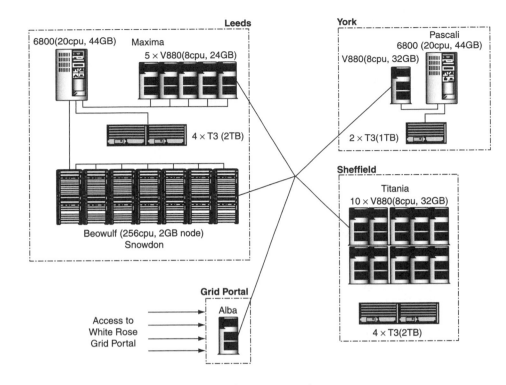

12.5

FIGURE

The four clusters that form the White Rose Grid.

12.4   SUMMARY

We have presented three deployments of Grid technologies aimed at enabling more efficient and flexible use of resources, within a company (GlobeXplorer), university campus (Houston), and multiuniversity virtual organization (White Rose Grid). Each deployment has leveraged open source software such as the Globus Toolkit, Sun Grid Engine, and portal technologies to construct a Grid environment that is being used successfully by a large user community.

These case studies demonstrate that deployment of Grid technologies within campuses can increase resource utilization and enable more convenient access to resources, both by individuals seeking a specific system for an application and by teams of researchers collaborating on a project. In each case, deployment of Grid technologies also increased overall demand for computing.

ACKNOWLEDGMENTS

We thank Suzanne George and Chris Nicholas, GlobeXplorer, for Section 12.1; Barbara Chapman and Babu Sunderam, University of Houston, for Section 12.2; and James Coomer and Charu Chaubal of Sun Microsystems for Section 12.3.

FURTHER READING

For more information on the topics covered in this chapter, see *www.mkp.com/grid2.*

Interactivity with Scalability: Infrastructure for Multiplayer Games

David Levine and Mark Wirt

*P*lanet Earth has approximately 430 million gamers. Some like to walk into arcades, plop quarters into the machine, and rack up the highest score on the boardwalk. Others prefer to quaff Bawls, the high-caffeine guarana drink, and frag their opponents at LAN parties. Then there are the console gamers who sit shoulder to shoulder in the den, shucking and jiving down the court or across the field, defying gravity, living like Mike for a few short hours. Finally, there are the handhelds gamers sitting on the airplane desperately trying to get to the next level before the captain asks that all electronic devices be turned off for landing.

Someday all of those gamers in arcades, on PCs and consoles, or twiddling at handhelds will want to find each other online to match wits and reflexes in thousands of simultaneous sessions. Millions of those gamers will want to play the same game, with each other, at the same time. The potential for online gaming is huge—what game one is in, at any given moment, might someday be more important that what job one holds, what TV show one watches, what sports team one follows, or what country one hails from.

Serving millions of gamers in high-performance, low-latency tournaments requires a distributed infrastructure that can be widely deployed by leveraging commodity hardware that can be racked and stacked, and employing as many free open source components as possible. In this chapter, we describe such an infrastructure, known as the "Butterfly Grid," which supports massive multiplayer (MMP) games via an on-demand service that can expand as the market for online gaming grows.

13.1   DESIGN OF THE BUTTERFLY GRID

The requirements for video game infrastructure are rigorous. Gamers will not tolerate downtime, lag, cheating, or anything else that could get in the way of the ongoing illusion of an immersive game world. To provide high performance, scalability, and reliability, the Butterfly Grid is designed as a fully distributed, multi-tiered system. To leverage the emerging Grid infrastructure, the Butterfly Grid is standards-based, augmenting the best thinking that the academic, research, and commercial computing communities have to offer, with services focused on addressing the unique requirements of the online gaming community.

In formulating the requirements for the Butterfly Grid, we consider not just the gamers who would populate it but also the needs of the game development studios that would create the games, the publishers who would fund the development effort and market the games, and the service providers who would operate the Grid.

13.1.1   Developer Requirements

Developers are focused on performance as well as flexibility. They need to use familiar tools and programming languages, such as C and C++ for high-performance compiled code and Python for scripting game play. Game developers are comfortable with Linux servers for hosting game logic, but they need to be able to use their favorite 3D rendering engines, such as NDL's NetImmerse (23), Criterion's Renderware (35), or Intrinsic Alchemy (18), on the front-end machines on which the users interact. They would also want to write games for dedicated video game consoles such as the PlayStation2, for Windows PCs, and for mobile devices such as the PocketPC, reusing as much of their same code as possible.

Successful developers of single-player, shrink-wrapped games use every available computing resource to optimize game performance by juggling such subsystems as the graphics engine, artificial intelligence routines, and the reading and writing of data to create the illusion of an ongoing, interactive experience without the kind of glitches and lag that would momentarily interrupt the illusion. If Grid-based gaming is to be successful, the developer must have the same fine level of control over how best to allocate the resources that make up the Grid to serve their particular game. Some games would require powerful artificial intelligence driving nonplayer characters, while others would focus on player-versus-player action. Some would want enormous, boundless worlds and vistas with many players in the same scene, while others would want compartmentalized game play with only a few players in each scene.

For this reason, the architecture of the Butterfly Grid currently gives the developer a generic gaming platform, with the ability to allocate dedicated resources to the most important facets of the game. Future platforms will need more sophisticated resource management functions, with the ability to provision resources to specific games, players, or functions within a game. Resource management functions as described in Chapter 18 will be critical to the ultimate success of performance-sensitive interactive applications, such as those supported by the Butterfly Grid.

13.1.2 Publisher Requirements

Publishers are the financiers of the game world. Their primary talent is to cultivate studios, game designers, and franchises that will earn money in the marketplace. If it does not fit on a spreadsheet, the publisher is generally not interested. Therefore, a Grid for gaming must handle multiple games on one resource base, so that publishers can dial up or dial down the infrastructure to support particular games, based on their relative success at generating revenue. This again points to the importance of a pervasive and flexible resource management infrastructure.

13.1.3 Service Provider Requirements

Internet service providers are pushing broadband connections through DSL and cable modems, and gamers are gobbling them up. An interesting phenomenon happens, though, when thousands of gamers on broadband connections are all playing a game hosted on a centralized server farm: the provider hosting the game has to handle enormous amounts of data. It was actually better for game-hosting providers when the gamers were connecting over modems.

The solution is to distribute the game state and associated load to multiple servers. Service providers can then host games close to the place where the DSL or cable connections come together, and not route the traffic all over the Internet. To facilitate this distribution, the game servers should be designed to run on inexpensive commodity hardware, such as blade, so that service providers can easily manage the games and add more computing resources as they grow. Of course, decentralization introduces its own problems, in that game state must be kept consistent across servers. A key element of the Butterfly Grid technology is the services and protocols that maintain the distributed game state.

13.1.4   The Architecture in Practice

To meet all of these requirements, the Butterfly Grid is structured as a multitier, distributed system. The Butterfly Grid builds on core Grid services provided by the Globus Toolkit (Chapter 4), augmented with the specialized services to support multiplayer gaming activities. The major tiers, from front to back, are as follows:

The object management system (OMS).   The OMS provides the first tier of the architecture and is the window into the shared environment. The OMS resides on the client device and appropriately renders data that have been translated into inherent protocols by the middle layer. Within the OMS, the developer can define custom dead-reckoning models to optimize interactive performance by allowing local state updates without requiring network communication.

The network protocol stack (NPS).   The NPS is layered upon UDP/IP and allows packets to be flagged for reliable transmission. The NPS is fairly stateless on the transmission end, which keeps the stack light and easy to implement, even on resource-poor platforms. The receiving end deduces most state information needed by the system through the transmission of heartbeat packets.

Gateway servers.   The Gateway translates the interactions, changes, and actions of game objects into communications protocols understood by the end user's client platform. The Gateway also acts as a single point of entry to a section or region of the game, hiding the internal structure of the game configuration from the game clients outside the firewall.

Daemon controllers.   Daemon controllers are dedicated artificial intelligence processes on dedicated servers that drive the activities of nonplayer characters (NPCs). They are essentially "privileged clients" driven by servers that act like players.

Game servers.   The Game server manages the game as defined by the game rules and logic, the objects and attributes that comprise the game environment, and objects that represent the players themselves as they are involved in game play. Game servers instantiate specific regions of the game, called locales. Game play can move securely across locales and across servers without interruption. Within a game, each player is represented by a single authoritative object called the *embodiment of record*. There may be other copies of this state distributed across the Grid and over the network to many game clients, but those objects are not authoritative ones. The *locale* thread plays a central role in propagating client state by duplicating and distributing state update packets to copies of the embodiment of record located in other game clients. Flow of information is controlled by creating a *region of presence*, which identifies what other objects are within range of a given client (i.e., player). Information about the changing state of the client is transmitted to all other objects whose *area of interest* overlaps the client's region of presence. In this way the client state is propagated throughout the Butterfly Grid.

Datastore.   This stores the persistent information required to define the worlds and objects and to maintain gameplay over time.

Grid services.   Basic resource management, security, and discovery services are based on the Globus Toolkit. This layer provides the lowest level of the infrastructure, monitoring the performance of the hardware and redirecting resources as required.

In May 2002, we introduced the Butterfly Grid to the video game industry at the Electronic Entertainment Expo in Los Angeles. We have game development studios from around the world building and testing new titles on our Grid, and we have been working with service providers to implement Grid nodes for their subscribers. The Butterfly Grid vision is to provide a single, integrated interoperable infrastructure, so that every gamer can play with any other, regardless of physical location, access network, or access device (438).

13.2   THE GLOBUS TOOLKIT AND THE BUTTERFLY GRID

The Butterfly Grid was designed specifically to meet the requirements of the online video game industry's value chain, from developer, through publisher and service provider, to the gamer. Although there are clearly specialized capabilities required to support online gaming (for example, distributed state update), by leveraging existing Grid infrastructure components, we hope to minimize cost of development and deployment, and perhaps most important to gain interoperability with and access to Grid-based resources that we anticipate will be deployed over the coming years.

In the process of developing the Butterfly Grid, questions of resource and environment management came to the forefront. It is easy to maintain an instance of a running executable, but when the application *becomes* the network in some sense, these management functions become harder and more pressing. Many of the core resource management problems associated with online gaming are no different from those associated with any Grid application: discovery and allocation of processing resources, creation and management of executing programs, access to storage systems and databases, and so on. For this reason, we choose to leverage existing Grid infrastructure at the core of the Butterfly Grid.

The current implementation of the Butterfly Grid relies on the Globus Toolkit (276) (Chapter 4) for core Grid functions. As the Open Grid Services Architecture (279) (OGSA, Chapter 17) becomes available, we anticipate migrating to that platform, using OGSA-based versions of the Globus Toolkit and leveraging advanced services for resource provisioning (Chapter 18) and data access (Chapter 22).

13.2.1   Globus Toolkit Services Used by the Butterfly Grid

We have identified three functions that the Globus Toolkit can provide to the interactive gaming application environment:

+ Staging and maintenance of a code base in a distributed environment

+ Scheduling, monitoring, and termination of application process instances in a distributed environment

+ A monitoring framework for real-time instrumentation

The staging and maintenance of code are functions well performed by the Globus Toolkit. Many of the tools (globus-job-submit, globus-job-run, and globus-run) transfer files as part of resource management. Moreover, the files can be staged to cache data and executables in an intelligent way. At the user's discretion, the Globus Access to Secondary Storage (GASS) system can be employed to cache the data (117). Secure checksums are used to compare cached and requested versions of files, which are in turn transferred only when necessary. This caching function can be important in highly replicated environments with large sets of game data.

The scheduling, monitoring, and termination of processes are part and parcel of distributed resource management, and the Globus Toolkit performs these functions well. Of particular interest to us was the Globus Security Infrastructure (GSI) (146), which vastly eased authentication in the distributed environment. Security is important, and it was useful to employ a system in which one authorized credential can function at the authorizing document in many functions on many machines.

Instrumentation is important in both development and deployment environments, but such instrumentation is complex in a highly distributed environment. The Globus Toolkit's monitoring and discovery service (MDS-2) (204) provides an extensible and scalable framework for monitoring. MDS is a hierarchical, LDAP-based service that collects and distributes a plethora of OS-level monitor data (of the type of data normally provided by the simple network management protocol), and can be easily extended to provide application-level data.

13.2.2 Integration with the Higher Tiers of Service

An online game forms a virtual organization consisting of players, the software that defines the world that defines the game, and the Grid-based resources available for hosting the services needed to instantiate the world. Within the Butterfly Grid, these virtual organizations are defined via a *game configuration specification* (GCS), an XML-based specification structure for the description of games.

All data elements for a game are specified within GCS: what objects exist in the game, the properties those objects have or can have, how the game space is partitioned—all the essential properties of a game are distilled and captured within the GCS. Internally, a game's GCS is used to generate and initialize a game's datastore.

GCS was originally developed to describe the structure for nondistributed games. To enable the configuration of a Grid-based gaming environment, we decided to extend the specification to include all data needed to physically instantiate a game instance on a physical Grid. Although a tutorial or detailed explication of the GCS is beyond the scope of this chapter, a description of a few of the document elements is in order:

<GRID>: The Grid is the base (root) node of a GCS document. Everything within a Grid (physical and logical) is contained within a Grid element.

<MACHINE>: The machine element gives names and addresses to physical machines on a game Grid. Multiple addresses are allowed, as these machines can be multihomed.

<ACCOUNT>: An account element is an authentication record for players of games, as well as an authentication record for daemon processes (NPC controllers). This is defined outside the scope of a game because one account could have permission to participate in more than one game. The Account is related to games via a system of <PERMISSION> records (which will not be discussed here).

<SOFTWARE>: The software element defines a version of the game Grid application and relates that version of the software package to physical files within physical storage. Data files, shared libraries, executables, and scripts may all be specified as elements within the <SOFTWARE> tag.

<WORLD>: A World is a game. The objects, properties, and game-specific data of a game are all defined within the <WORLD>. Game designers, for example, would do most of their work within the element <WORLD>.

The <WORLD> tag contains the details of an actual, physical instantiation of a game. This is specified by defining an <INSTANCE> tag that relates the game to user-defined content, physical machines, and specific server and gateway processes. Some of the more important elements that the <INSTANCE> can contain are the following:

<NETWORK>: Specifies multicast information (group and port) so that the Butterfly.net game Grid discovery protocols can be used.

<SERVER>: Specifies a running server process. The element relates the server with the locales it will service, and specifies the machine the instance is to run on.

<CONTENT>: Defines the nondata-driven elements of a game: scripts, datafiles, executables, and shared libraries.

<GATEWAY>: Instantiates a gateway process on a physical machine.

<DATASTORE>: Specifies how an instantiated game will connect to a data store, and contains identifiers, user names, and passwords.

To give an idea of what GCS files look like, we show in Figure 13.1 a small GSC example that instantiates a game on a small Grid of two machines.

Since the GCS <INSTANCE> relates to physical program files, certain information concerning directory structure is included. It is inelegant, but this is unavoidable: If directory structure were not specified, the process of running multiple instances of a game (or different games) on one physical machine would be much more difficult.

13.2.3   Deploying the Game

Although the GCS represents an instantiated game on the Grid, it is not an executable in and of itself. It must still be mapped to the Globus Toolkit services. We do this mapping by parsing the GCS and producing three types of output. First, we produce a game configuration file. The Butterfly Grid is largely data-driven, but a little configuration information is needed to bootstrap the process. Figure 13.2, for example, shows the configuration file for the gateway in the example of Figure 13.1. The configuration allows the networking portion of the Grid to be initialized, and provides information about how to connect to the data store.

```
<ServerEXE name="server"/>
        <GatewayEXE name="gateway"/>
        <SharedSO name="serverc.so"/>
        <SharedSO name="serverc2.so"/>
        <script name="server.py"/>
     </Software>
     <world game="1" version="1">
       <Instance>
            <Software version="1.2"/>
            <Network multicastAddress="224.0.0.1" multicastport="4444" gameport="9632"/>
            <Remotebase name="/usr/local/instance1"/>
            <Datastore name="gbase1">
                 <UID value="db1"/>
                 <Password value="PASSWORD"/>
            </Datastore>
            <Server machine="grid1">   <!--One server process-->
                 <locales>1,2</locales>
            </Server>
            <Gateway machine="grid2"/>   <!--One gateway process-->
            <Daemon machine="grid1">   <!--Daemon. Relates to Content EXE-->
                 <UID value="daemon1"/>
                 <Password value="PASSWORD"/>
                 <Executable name="daemon"/>
                 <Host machine="grid2"/>   <!--Gateway to which to connect-->
            </Daemon>
            <Content base="/home/game1/content">
                 <script name="Interactions.py"/>
                 <script name="Utilities.py"/>
                 <Executable name="daemon"/>
                 <SharedSO name="serverc.so"/>
                 <Datafiles remote="terrain"><!--Remote directory, relative to base-->
                        <Datafile name="terrain.nrm" type="read"/>
                        <Datafile name="terrain2.nrm" type="execute"/>
                 </Datafiles>
            </Content>
       </Instance>
     </world>
</Grid>
```

13.1   An example of a game configuration specification file.

FIGURE

```
database     =gbase1
username     =db1
password     =PASSWORD
system_host  =172.17.0.2
system_port  =9632
active_game  =[1.1.0]
server_host  =224.0.0.1
server_port  =4444
```

13.2   The configuration file for the gateway node defined in Figure 13.1.

FIGURE

```
&
(rsl_substitution=(REMOTE "/usr/local/instance1")
        (LOCALDIR "/usr/local/archive/1.2"))
(executable=$(GLOBUSRUN_GASS_URL)#$(LOCALDIR)/prep.sh)
(arguments="terrain")
```

13.3

FIGURE

A sample Globus Toolkit RSL file.

Second, the parser produces resource specification language (RSL) files. RSL (205) is the runtime specification language used by the Globus Toolkit to specify an application environment, and it is the main interface into the intricacies of the Globus Toolkit resource management (205). Files can be staged, environment variables can be set, and code can be executed. In general, the parser produces several distinct RSL commands that do the following.

✦ Prepare a remote machine, creating any directories necessary to implement the GCS. This is done by transferring a small UNIX shell script to the remote machine and calling it with arguments describing the directories to be created. Figure 13.3 is an example of one such file.

✦ Stage the necessary files and change the execution bits on any executable. The Globus Toolkit assumes that data files are nonexecutable, so a shell script is called to give files executable permission when needed.

✦ Execute the code on the remote machine. Of the RSL files, this is the only type that needs to be called in batch submission mode.

Finally, the parser produces glue scripts that execute the RSL on the appropriate machines and capture the job submission ID for subsequent status monitoring and termination. Application-specific information is coded into these processes, parsers, and scripts. Because we have kept them small and modular, however, they have proved to be flexible and maintainable. We have taken the toolkit approach, and we have been happy with the results.

13.2.4   Future Work

The integration of our GCS, application software, and the Globus Toolkit's resource management function works well, and we will continue to use it in the way it was designed. Looking forward, we see two thrusts to pursue.

First, we will be integrating into MDS the increasing instrumentation information produced by the Butterfly Grid. The approach we are taking is to produce small, lightweight instrumentation probes for the metrics that we are interested in. By formatting the output of these probes into well-formatted information objects, we can easily extend MDS to include game-specific instrumentation. As our instrumentation is extended, *dynamic reallocation* services will be written. What we described previously prebuilds the execution environment, but dynamic reapportionment of resources in a running game is interesting and useful, and as such we are currently devoting much time and effort to their implementation.

Second, as OGSA services emerge, we will cast our services into OGSA-compliant forms. Initially, this effort will take the form of thin, lightweight OGSA wrappers to our existing services; but as the architecture becomes better defined and widely deployed, OGSA functionality will probably be more tightly integrated into our offering. To this end, we have begun a pilot project to provide our services within an e-utility infrastructure. The Web service wrappers developed in this pilot project will be OGSA-compliant when the specification becomes sufficiently rich that compliance becomes possible.

FURTHER READING

For more information on the topics covered in this chapter, see *www.mkp.com/grid2*. In addition, the book *Practical Grid Computing for Massively Multiplayer Games* (438) provides further details on gaming and Grid technologies; *Developing Online Games: An Insider's Guide* (487) also has useful material on game design but does not speak to the use of Grid technologies.

Service Virtualization: Infrastructure and Applications

Ming Xu, Zhenhua Hu, Weihong Long, and Wayne Liu

*D*riven by ever-increasing processing demands, application and infrastructure technologies have evolved from *monolithic* to *open* and then to *distributed* systems. When mainframe computers ruled the enterprise, peaks and valleys in demand for application services could be handled by aggregating applications on a shared infrastructure. However, technology trends such as the emergence of e-business, the introduction of application servers, the shift toward blade computing, the increased distribution of enterprise resources, and the growing importance of multiorganization collaborations (i.e., virtual organizations) have led to a proliferation in the number of servers, services, and organizations that contribute to the execution of any given workflow or task (279). Consequently, there is no longer a single locus of control for the workloads and systems important to an enterprise. The result is a loss of application-level service guarantees and the introduction of inefficiencies in infrastructure utilization. These problems are driving rapid evolution into a new *service virtualization* era. Virtualization has the potential to mitigate workload management problems by reintroducing a single cohesive system view onto the distributed information technology (IT) infrastructure.

Service virtualization is a technical concept, but its purpose is solving *business* problems. It is more than simply balancing the enterprise computing workload. The new rules of the business world dictate that the costs of servicing an organization's IT demands must be reduced, and that IT practices and purchases must measurably contribute to business objectives and priorities. IT managers are faced with the seemingly impossible tasks of maintaining service levels while cutting spending; sharing resources and information while ensuring security; and getting products out the door faster with fewer resources. Along with these internal pressures and competitive pressures, IT managers are charged with improving the responsiveness and agility of the company by organizing their IT infrastructure to adapt to dynamic business objectives and market climates.

In this chapter, we introduce service virtualization, explain its connection with Grid computing, and present a case study that involves the application of virtualization in a commercial computing context.

14.1   APPLICATION AND INFRASTRUCTURE TECHNOLOGY TRENDS

Service virtualization is a consequence of evolutionary trends in both application and infrastructure technologies (Figure 14.1). Looking first at application technologies, we see that over the past 20 years they have become more and more detached from the underlying hardware platform on which they run.

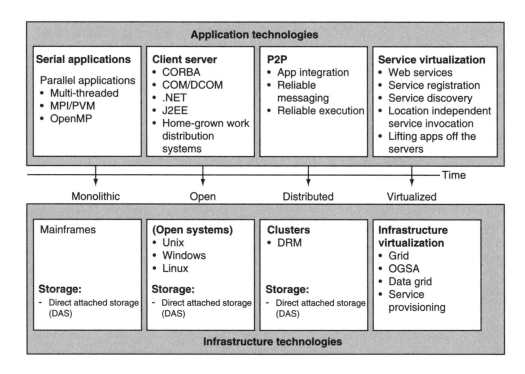

14.1
FIGURE

Application and infrastructure technology trends.

Monolithic applications are statically *bound* to the underlying systems, most often symmetric multiprocessors. Scaling such applications incurs prohibitive cost.

Client/server applications remove dependencies on hardware platforms, but are still dependent on underlying application infrastructures such as .NET, J2EE, or CORBA, all of which have varying degrees of scalability and reliability problems.

Guaranteed distributed computing approaches augment the client/server approach by adding simple job management and reliable messaging and execution mechanisms.

In the *service virtualization* approach, as typified by the Open Grid Services Architecture (279) (OGSA, Chapter 17), applications are encapsulated as services, and a distribution framework is used to disseminate work across service instances. Service virtualization also allows the application developers to treat services from different application domains as building blocks that can be assembled and reassembled to adapt to changing business needs.

These application trends are being driven by both increased user demands and corresponding trends in the underlying infrastructure on which applications are hosted. Here, the starting point is the mainframe, a monolithic and proprietary system, expensive and hard to scale. However, mainframe environments arguably have the most comprehensive resource management system (503) and set the standard by which subsequent infrastructures are judged.

Open systems, such as Unix, Windows, or Linux servers, remove dependencies on proprietary hardware and operating systems, but in most instances are used in isolation. IT infrastructures built during the open systems era are inflexible, complex systems that have difficulty scaling to accommodate expanding business volumes and are slow to respond to new business initiatives. In these infrastructures, each deployed application has its own set of servers purchased for production, failover, staging, testing, and development. Multiple applications rarely share common servers, resulting in silos of statically linked applications and servers. This configuration results in poor server utilization. Since each application runs on its own server, applications are locked into expensive SMP hardware that requires expensive forklift upgrades to accommodate higher peak volumes.

Clusters address the issues of efficiency and the removal of silos within the connected enterprise. As discussed in Chapter 28, clusters can be constructed from machines on desktops or dedicated racks of server blades, usually under a system management domain. The rise of cluster computing has motivated the creation of sophisticated resource management systems that can dynamically allocate and configure cluster nodes for dynamic supply–demand management to optimize IT productivity. Examples of such systems include Platform's LSF (454, 701), Sun Microsystem's Sun Grid Engine (Chapter 12), Veridian's Portable Batch System (31), and various research systems (84, 173). These systems are largely used for batch and end-of-day processing.

The coming area of *infrastructure virtualization* promises an infrastructure that delivers just-in-time compute and storage capacity, reducing management and administration costs through automation, while providing greater control over end-user service levels. The term "utility data center" (84, 322) is sometimes used for such systems, to emphasize the potential economies of scale that can be achieved when a centralized infrastructure is used as a utility. Software partitions map software components to platform resources and allow application components to be isolated from each other, even though they share hardware resources and a single instance of the operating system. Service virtualization decouples applications from the hardware, removing scalability issues and other hardware limitations, while providing flexibility to meet new business opportunities. A virtualized service delivers the best value when it is integrated with a virtualized infrastructure, as shown in Figure 14.2.

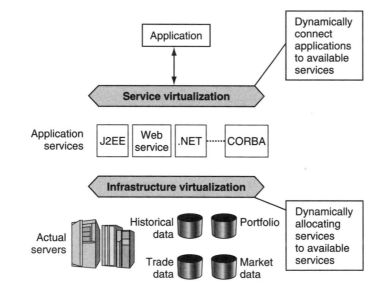

14.2

FIGURE

Service and infrastructure virtualization.

14.2   THE THREE LAYERS OF VIRTUALIZATION

Implementations of virtualized services can be decomposed into *application, orchestration*, and *infrastructure* layers (Figure 14.3). Application layer programs send inputs (or work units) through the orchestration layer to infrastructure layer services. Results are returned to the application layer via the orchestration layer. The interactions between these three layers are the domain of Grid technology, which by defining standard interfaces and behaviors for service creation, monitoring, management, and so forth facilitates the creation of scalable, interoperable virtualization infrastructures.

14.2.1   Application Layer

Front, middle, and back office applications are often complex and GUI based; the applications themselves can range from traditional workflows to massively parallel applications. We thus face the task of mapping a set of work units onto a virtualized service infrastructure. The application layer provides a set of APIs, a

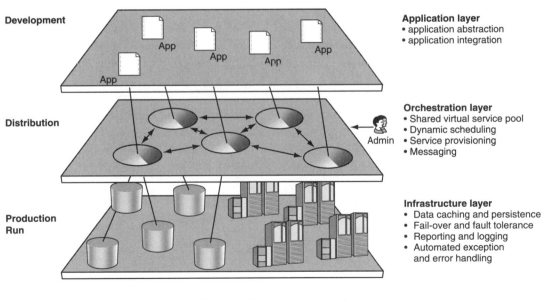

14.3   The three layers of a virtualized service implementation.

FIGURE

development and testing environment, and run-time monitoring tools to help the user submit work units into the virtualized service environment for execution.

Grid technologies provide appropriate abstractions for encapsulating the required analytics services, work units, and application data, and for disseminating data, collecting results, exception handling, and logging. Thus, they facilitate flexibility in how work units are executed, especially those with critical-response-time constraints: for example, pricing applications in the financial services industry.

14.2.2   Orchestration Layer

The orchestration layer provides intelligent policy-driven work and data-routing capabilities. Like a packet-forwarding router, it sends inputs to services and returns results to requesters. However, the orchestration layer is not a *blind* forwarder. It is responsible for distributing processing demands (potentially from multiple applications, users, business units, and virtual organizations) to services in a manner that meets organizational priorities, risk, and productivity goals. To this end, it carefully monitors—and may model—both the application load vector and server load metrics. Hence, the orchestration layer is the key component for integrating service and infrastructure virtualization. It fulfills the roles of resource manager and master scheduler across the entire infrastructure.

The orchestration layer is also responsible for managing the mapping of services to resources, a mapping that can change over time in response to changing application workloads. The orchestration layer performs *load balancing* to optimize execution turnaround times by mapping services to the least-loaded servers and *resource matching* to speed time-to-results by matching application services to the most appropriate servers.

Organizations can leverage a variety of advanced scheduling policies to align resource usage to business objectives based on competing priorities, deadlines, and demands. *Prioritized scheduling* can be used to guarantee that mission-critical tasks finish executing as quickly as possible by giving them preference over lower-priority tasks that might otherwise compete for resources. *Fairshare scheduling* apportions the resource usage of different business units to ensure that their resource consumption does not impact the performance of other business units. *Execution preemption* suspends low-priority jobs, freeing resources for more pressing tasks that require timely responses. *Advance reservation and backfill* policies increase the throughput and reliability of critical tasks by providing application services with unimpeded access to specific resources at specific times. *Deadline scheduling* guarantees that batch tasks, such as end-of-day reports, have access to all resources needed to meet deadlines.

We note that effective implementation of these policies requires that the orchestration layer be able to negotiate and monitor appropriate service-level agreements (Chapter 18) with both the submitters of applications and the resources that will execute those applications. Many front-, middle-, or back-office applications consist of work units with a wide spectrum of run-time and memory requirements. Considerable intelligence and knowledge about application and service capabilities are required to satisfy policies. In this respect, service virtualization systems can require considerably more sophistication than high-throughput or cycle-scavenger models (449) (see Chapters 1:13 and 11) that focus on maximizing throughput.

14.2.3 Infrastructure Layer

The infrastructure layer manages the production run of the work on heterogeneous servers, including PCs, high-powered blades, and high-end SMP machines. These nodes may be either dedicated servers in the data center or desktop workstations in use by other users. Services are dynamically loaded and invoked based on application requests. The status and resource usage of these services are collected for accounting purposes. Should a server fail, the work is rerouted to other servers to be reprocessed.

The infrastructure layer consists of three functional parts: service deployment and operation, service monitoring, and data cache management. The management of these parts ensures that services are deployed and published correctly and provisioned at the right time in the right places with the right resources. Services are operated on demand and in line with business objectives, providing constant monitoring to ensure that the services are running at optimal levels. In the case of a service failure, issues are alarmed and/or corrected.

14.3 A VIRTUALIZATION CASE STUDY

We present a case study to illustrate the application and benefits of service virtualization. This case study involves a global investment bank. Financial institutions rely heavily on complex, compute-intensive applications that are often critically time dependent. Delivering accurate and timely end-of-day, intraday, and real-time reports or analysis of complex scenarios is crucial to successful management of day-to-day operations in competitive global markets. Increasing volumes of complex transactions, simulations, and risk analyses need to be processed quickly, reliably, and efficiently by an investment bank's IT infrastructure.

To maintain its high performance level in competitive global markets, a world-class investment bank was faced with the challenge of aggressively managing costs involved with application development, maintenance, and operations. The bank investigated the possibility of developing and implementing a shared computing utility for certain capital markets applications that would be supported by its business technology group. The bank's business technology group is a global operation that supports front-office operations in three major locations (New York, London, and Tokyo), along with a host of smaller offices. This group consists of approximately 2000 IT professionals who support lines of business around fixed-income derivatives, credit markets, foreign exchange, emerging markets, and equities.

14.3.1   The Challenges

The bank has seen a dramatic increase in its high-performance computing (HPC) requirements over the past few years, due to increased complexity of derivative valuation models, increased volume of the bank's derivatives portfolios, the introduction of new complex financial products, and entry into new markets, such as credit.

In response to this rapid change, a number of business units and their associated teams in the business technology group built their own HPC solutions to perform risk management calculations and other compute-intensive tasks required to support their businesses. The computation engines for these applications were tightly coupled to the overall risk management system. Often, all these executable programs ran on the same physical machine, and, at times, the same machine functioned as the database server. This monolithic architecture was suitable in an era when networks were slow and one SMP machine with 20 to 50 processors could handle overall CPU demands.

This infrastructure design approach forced technology groups in each of the bank's lines of business to develop and maintain their own applications and HPC hardware. The result was high operational costs, as financial application developers had to develop distribution mechanisms and load-balancing schemes for internal HPC solutions, and HPC solutions were duplicated across each line of business. In addition, each team required staff to operate its HPC services and perform service maintenance, such as repairs and capacity planning, while tuning and upgrading systems.

Having each business unit attempt to improve quality of service and performance levels in its isolated HPC environment was inefficient, time-consuming, and expensive. Providing support for dynamic scaling, optimization, accounting services, and fail-over/redundancy in each area was also problematic.

14.3.2 The Solution

The bank selected Platform Symphony™, a real-time application execution solution, to achieve its goal of delivering compute power where and when needed by the different lines of business, thereby reducing the cost of high-performance computing through more efficient use of servers. Platform Symphony would allow the bank to aggressively manage its portfolio of applications to gain economies of scale through widespread sharing of HPC resources.

The bank's risk management applications and other HPC consumers were organized in terms of four layers: user interface and ad hoc calculation tools, business logic, persistence, and high-performance computing. Using Platform Symphony, the compute-intense HPC layer was made available as a common service. Platform Symphony replaced the various incompatible, homegrown HPC solutions and now handles global data management, master–slave interprocess communications, high-speed caching, hardware partitioning, and distribution management for applications across all lines of business. The other existing layers of the bank's applications remained unchanged, except at the interface with the HPC layer.

In the bank's new Platform Symphony-enabled infrastructure, financial applications automatically register with the workload and service scheduler to obtain a list of currently available services. Based on the type of task to be executed, the applications request the type of service needed from the published directory, and the workload and service scheduler ensures that enough host service masters are invoked to execute the job according to service-level agreements, work priority, or deadlines.

Using Platform Symphony's common API, the bank's existing applications plug right into the new infrastructure architecture, automatically registering for high-performance computing services on demand and releasing them when execution is completed.

Applications throughout the bank now share one set of generic services and are controlled by the Grid-enabled infrastructure. Instead of each application running on its own HPC solution, they now all connect to a central HPC service. Application developers are more productive now that they no longer need to create "plumbing" code to handle distribution management. They are free to focus on adding value by improving the business logic of the applications.

The common infrastructure prioritizes requests received from application clients according to predetermined policies and allocates hardware and software resources to ensure that the proper valuation engine processes the requests and returns the results to the calling application. Platform Symphony's automated and self-healing commodity hardware management has also enabled the bank to reduce operational costs dramatically. When faults arise, corrective actions are initiated without the need for staff intervention. If the problem cannot be resolved by restarting the server or restoring its image, the hardware is simply replaced, eliminating staff costs, which account for the bulk of operation expenses.

Creating a centralized compute layer based on commodity hardware has allowed the bank to remove applications from expensive dedicated hardware and reassign them to vast banks of cheap, commodity hardware that can be reprovisioned dynamically with the services required to meet demand and fulfill business objectives. These commodity servers can be quickly reassigned to new services when conditions change, thus achieving more effective utilization of assets. Scaling the computing capabilities of every application across every line of business is now as simple as adding more servers to the infrastructure's pool.

Virtualization has thus enabled better hardware utilization, less redundant software development, lower support costs, and economical quality of service.

14.4   SUMMARY

Application and infrastructure virtualization can allow organizations to meet business objectives for cost, contingency, and consolidation. From an application perspective, virtualization technologies can turbo-charge applications by providing access to more computational capacity; from an infrastructure perspective, virtualization can allow for more efficient use of resources via optimized workload orchestration and service provisioning.

The benefits of virtualization are most apparent if realized through standard tools and infrastructure services. It is here that Grid technologies enter the picture. Standard approaches to service definition, creation, health monitoring, failover, service-level agreement negotiation, and so forth allow enterprises to replace homegrown, poorly documented, high-maintenance distribution infrastructures. As we saw in our case study, this transition to standard infrastructure can bring significant benefits to end users, business units, and enterprises.

In the longer term, we expect virtualization to enable three paradigm shifts: (1) the pay-per-use (utility data center) model, (2) disposable computing, and (3) the move to customer-focused sets of services. With the pay-per-use model, overprovisioning is eliminated. Each virtual organization can potentially access thousands of processors during peak processing periods, while only paying for the average demand, making high-performance computing increasingly affordable.

ACKNOWLEDGMENTS

This work and this chapter were done on behalf of Platform Computing Inc.

FURTHER READING

For more information on the topics covered in this chapter, see *www.mkp.com/grid2*.

15

Group-Oriented Collaboration: The Access Grid Collaboration System

Rick Stevens and the Futures Lab Group

*A*n important class of Grid applications aimed at supporting wide-area, real-time, computer-mediated communications has begun to emerge. The Access Grid is an example of such an application.

The Access Grid project grew out of research in Argonne's Futures Laboratory (234, 282), which began in 1994 to develop collaboration environments based on two assumptions: (1) over time, the amount of bandwidth and computing available to research groups would become virtually limitless; and (2) most scientific collaborations involve groups of people at each collaborating institution, not just single individuals.

Although a number of researchers were exploring the feasibility of connecting users via desktop services, the Access Grid project took two important steps away from this tradition. The first step was to focus on environments for *small groups of users* rather than individual users. Large-scale scientific collaborations often involve dozens of institutions and hundreds of researchers. Within these large projects, however, one can often identify core groups of researchers and institutions. The Access Grid targets such core groups of 3 to 20 users per site at about eight sites. The second step was to build into the Access Grid framework the idea of *persistent* virtual venues—network-based virtual meeting points suitable for supporting multiday meetings or long hours of joint work.

The result is the *Access Grid*—an ensemble of network, computing, and interaction resources that support group-to-group human interaction across the Grid.

15.1   THE CURRENT SITUATION

In designing the first Access Grid (AG), we focused on basic enabling infrastructure, using open source software wherever possible, avoiding commitment to a particular vendor, and encouraging participants to contribute to research and development of AG technology. We borrowed ideas from the LabSpace (234), MOOs (202), Jupiter (201), ManyWorlds (236), and CAVERNsoft projects (437) and adopted a strong spatial metaphor for resource organization similar in spirit to that of some text-based virtual reality environments (227, 575, 658).

The current Access Grid comprises large-format multimedia displays, presentation and interactive software environments, and interfaces to Grid middleware and remote visualization environments. Once an exploratory development platform, it now has hundreds of users and is being used on a daily basis around the world for production group-oriented collaboration (Figure 15.1). These users access the AG through Access Grid Nodes connected via the Internet, typically using multicast video and audio streams. Users can also participate in AG sessions from multimedia PCs, and we are exploring the use of commodity technologies such as game consoles, which provide more advanced graphics than do most PCs and are beginning to support virtual environments.

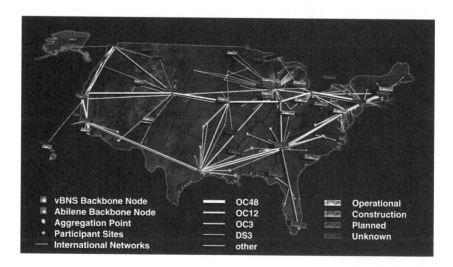

■	vBNS Backbone Node	━━	OC48		Operational
■	Abilene Backbone Node	━━	OC12		Construction
●	Aggregation Point	━━	OC3		Planned
●	Participant Sites	━━	DS3		Unknown
━	International Networks	━━	other		

15.1

FIGURE

A snapshot of Access Grid deployment status in January 2001, when 40 institutions had nodes. There were more than 200 by mid-2003, making the Access Grid the largest group-oriented collaboration testbed in existence.

15.2   THE ACCESS GRID VISION

We want the Access Grid to be a space where users can both "hang out" comfortably with colleagues at other places and also attend and participate in structured meetings such as site visits, remote conferences, and lectures. The space should support the same capabilities that we have now in face-to-face meetings—the ability to share ideas, thoughts, experiments, applications, and conversation. In addition, the space should be "smart" enough to allow participants to export items from PCs to other individuals or groups.

We see the Access Grid as a first step toward room-based computing (298) that will challenge desktop metaphors in the decades ahead. This paradigm shift raises numerous research challenges. Our strategy (similar in spirit to the Linux open source model) is to support production use of the Access Grid while we experiment with new ideas. Some of these research efforts are supported by industry. For example, the Access Grid has recently become the subject of human factors studies at Motorola and elsewhere (19) aimed at understanding how to make group-to-group collaboration more effective. Other work is funded by federal programs, with the DOE-funded Group-to-Group Middleware project (part of the SciDAC program) working to improve the software framework on which the Access Grid depends.

In the remainder of this chapter, we discuss five main areas of Access Grid research: virtual venues, security, workspace docking, node management, and asynchronous collaboration.

15.3   THE VIRTUAL VENUES SERVICE

The current Access Grid implementation uses a spatial metaphor (a set of "rooms" mapped to multicast addresses) to control the interaction and to provide simple persistence. We are generalizing this concept in the next-generation AG2 implementation to support a peer-to-peer model that operates much like the Web, in the sense that anyone can host a server (a virtual space) that anyone on the network can visit. The goal is to create a peer-to-peer architecture (Chapter 29) that can scale to thousands of nodes, with no centralized services, in which anyone can trivially create new spaces and link them into the overall peer-to-peer infrastructure. All spaces are fully connected, modulo security permissions and restrictions. To date, we have created a set of interface specifications and an open source reference implementation.

The AG2 architecture (Figure 15.2) comprises four types of service. *Security services* provide for a single global authentication for use within specific domains, key

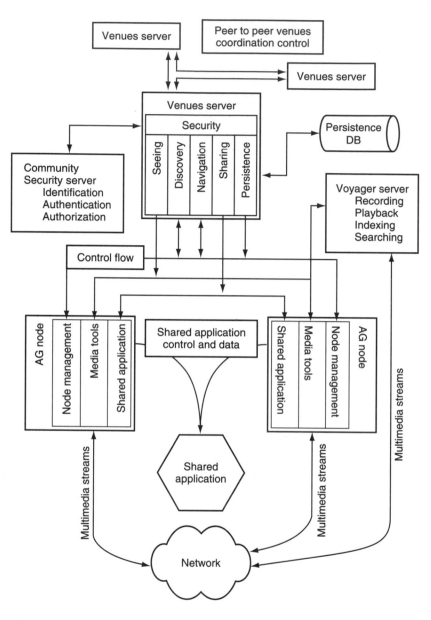

The next-generation AG2 architecture.

management and certificate authority, and stream encryption. *Persistence services* allow users to create persistent project spaces where critical objects (data, media streams, applications, post-it notes, etc.) can be stored, viewed, and manipulated. The *spatial metaphor* is expanded with a more complex set of interconnections and with a more sophisticated navigation and discovery mechanism based on new registration and discovery services built into the venues services. A *facsimile service* supports the execution of existing applications in a shared mode. We also plan to create a new programming interface for writing AG collaboration-aware applications.

15.4 SECURITY

Based on an analysis of the security required by the Access Grid community, we have defined multiple levels of security, ranging from no restrictions at all (akin to free browsing of Web pages) to tight security. We now are evaluating the vulnerability of each mechanism implemented as part of the Access Grid architecture (577). The security model is being developed in collaboration with emerging Grid security projects (146, 280, 648), particularly the Globus Toolkit (276) (Chapter 4), and will be fully integrated with the Grid services model (279) (Chapters 17 and 21). We are also addressing noncryptographic issues, including end-system security, physical security, and human-in-the-loop social engineering attacks.

15.5 WORKSPACE DOCKING

Access Grid users often desire to "share" some portion of their personal workspace (current desktop applications and data) with other AG users, nodes, or sites, both local and remote. We call this "workspace docking" (Figure 15.3). We are investigating several approaches. One of the most compelling involves dragging the windows from one's laptop onto the shared space in the room space; mouse and keyboard control of the application remains with the user who shared the application, and can be passed around as desired. Another option involves a global-shared document space and clipboard, in which one drags data regions or entire documents and applications to the shared space.

Most desktop application-sharing systems replicate the display primitives of the server's application on the client display. This approach can provide low to moderate performance, with applications served directly from the desktop into the Access Grid via a multicast-enabled AG client application. The downside is that the data are not made available to the remote users for later use, nor does

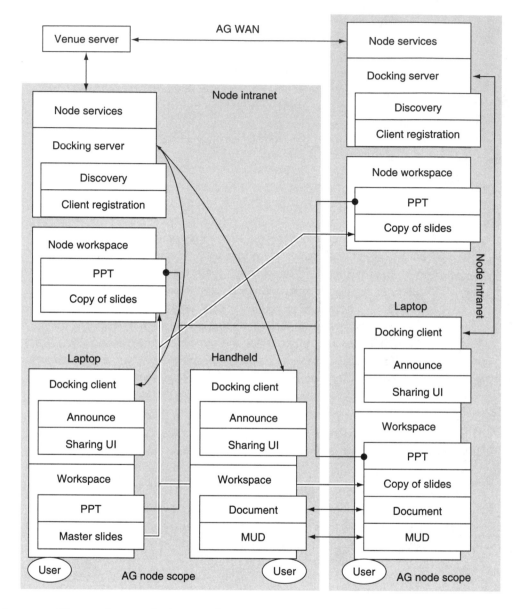

The workspace docking architecture. We see several user devices docked to Access Grid nodes.

the approach permit asynchronous investigations. Furthermore, since the client application typically is provided as pixels only, there may be color depth and color mapping compatibility problems. We believe this approach will be most useful for the occasional sharing of an application to a limited number of sites. A variation of this approach can be implemented by using a modified WireGL (374) for OpenGL applications. All X-Windows-based applications and some client-server based Windows applications admit a better solution for workspace docking. With the same general model, the application can be served from the user's desktop system; the communication to the display client is not necessarily limited to display primitives. The docking step entails migrating or launching one or more application clients (linked with multicast as needed) onto the AG displays and attaching them to the user's server.

15.6   NODE MANAGEMENT

We are developing an AG2 software services layer that will improve node operations through simplified user interfaces, automated node configuration, and node management functions. We plan to conduct a human factors analysis of Access Grid use to identify key areas of future research to improve the user experience.

The current software components and services available for AG events include vic (467), rat (355), distributed PowerPoint (307), MOO (202), multicast beacon (174), virtual venues services, remote visualization application control, scheduling, and the Voyager multimedia recording system (235). Many of these services are not fully exploited, however, because they are hard to use or poorly integrated. To address this situation, we have created a configuration specification for all AG 2.0 Node services and interfaces. The configuration database based on this specification is hosted on the Access Grid Node control computer and includes static information (e.g., graphics and network capabilities, audio and video capture hardware, software revisions) and dynamic information (e.g., current node operator, venue, and docked users). The database will also provide resource labeling, so that resources can be quickly found by function.

One AG2 core service being implemented is the node control service: an extensible interface for starting, stopping, and configuring components and services to the Access Grid. The interface specification will include a mechanism for registering new components and services with the node configuration database (39, 208, 316, 580). The interface will be network accessible through multiple mechanisms: custom software clients, Web pages, and perhaps hardware solutions such as the Crestron Control System.

To test our system, we are prototyping the integration of a new AG device—a custom-built 3D scanner, comprising commodity digital cameras and software that processes the images. The 3D scanner has reasonably simple control and data acquisition interfaces. We will integrate this scanner into a local node and develop example client applications that can be used to operate the scanner and interact with the scanner data.

15.7   ASYNCHRONOUS COLLABORATION

As the size and scope of wide-area collaborations grow, participants need to interact asynchronously. This requirement has traditionally been addressed by mechanisms such as written minutes, videotapes, and audiotapes. These mechanisms are one dimensional, however, and do not capture the nuances of personal interplay that happen during meetings. In addition, AG-based collaborative sessions contain too many data streams to capture via a traditional single-stream recording. The Voyager multistream recording system (235) provides the core of a solution. Currently Voyager 1.0 can record and play back the many RTP-encoded audio and video streams that form the foundation of AG collaborations. On the other hand, slide shows, spreadsheets of experimental data, and distributed visualizations of terascale datasets do not map directly to the streaming data types supported by Voyager. Although one can archive streaming video from screen captures or camera views of the visualizations, such mechanisms capture neither the full resolution of the images nor relevant semantic data.

To address this issue, we are extending Voyager to include streams of control information used for distributed slide shows or Web-browsing, high-resolution lossless encodings of experimental data or simulation output, and streams of navigation information from distributed exploration of datasets. We will also expand Voyager to include management of nonstreaming data such as meeting documents, along with their associated streaming control data for applications acting on these documents. To archive such data, we will leverage existing mechanisms such as Web servers for archiving slide show documents and Web pages, hierarchical storage systems associated with large-scale supercomputer systems and Grid data-management systems (64, 178) (Chapter 22).

Integration of Voyager and the Access Grid requires high-level coordination of system resources. Where possible, Voyager will use management services provided by the virtual venues software. We also will develop Voyager plug-in modules for the venues server that will enable Voyager to leverage Access Grid security mechanisms, providing a secure authentication, authorization, and encryption services programming interface with which a user can add support for archiving custom streaming data types and can link archived control data with large-scale datasets on remote storage servers.

15.8   SUMMARY

Immersive virtual reality (VR) technology (199), first developed in the mid-1980s, has been used to realize a range of advanced multiuser wide-area collaboration scenarios (226, 563) (see Chapter I:6). Such pioneering efforts revealed several limitations for work environments. Of most concern was the fact that users tire of spending extended time in the dark spaces needed for projection VR or of being immersed in a completely synthetic world without access to high-resolution text displays or high-quality interactions devices. During this same time desktop multimedia technology capabilities grew considerably, to the point that all modern desktop systems can easily handle video and audio, and desktop PCs have exceeded dedicated graphics systems in rendering performance and pixel bandwidth.

The Access Grid project builds on these experiences and technology. Unlike earlier efforts, however, the Access Grid is explicitly targeted at group-to-group collaborations in high-end workspaces. It provides persistent virtual project rooms that enable groups to maintain project-related materials and applications in a form that is continuously available to team members. Users have also designed studio-like spaces for Access Grid deployment that give participants control over lighting, sound quality, and video; the more professional the video and audio, the more effective the user experience. The Access Grid also is being used to explore collaborative modalities that enable groups to share visualization experiences critical in the analysis of complex phenomena.

Our vision of the Access Grid reflects the belief that, within the near future, bandwidth, computing, and imaging power will become effectively free and that high-quality audio and video capture will be increasingly inexpensive. The challenge will be how to organize these capabilities to support high-end scientific work—to create environments that people want to spend time in and that encourage experimentation and growth.

FURTHER READING

For more information on the topics covered in this chapter, see *www.mkp.com/grid2*.

16 Collaborative Science: Astrophysics Requirements and Experiences

Gabrielle Allen and Edward Seidel

*A*strophysics is a natural driver for extreme computing technology. From simulations of the universe and its constituents to analysis of vast amounts of data collected by observatories of various kinds, astrophysics has always been at the forefront of computation. Calculus itself was developed by Newton as a "computational technology" to understand the dynamics of the solar system, and astrophysicists led the creation of the U.S. supercomputing centers program in the early 1980s (404). Thus, it is not surprising that astrophysicists are today a driving force behind the development of the Grid. In this chapter, we explain how this symbiosis between astrophysicists and Grid technologists contributes to the development of both disciplines.

Astrophysicists use computational tools to understand exotic processes in the universe, from localized processes (star formation, solar physics, supernovae, collisions of or accretion around neutron stars and black holes, gravitational waves, and γ-ray bursts) to collections of all these (the formation and interactions of galaxies) to dynamics of and structure formation in the universe itself. Each process is complex, drawing from a vast fundamental knowledge base that includes nuclear, atomic, and particle physics, astrochemistry, relativistic magnetohydrodynamics, radiation transport, and general relativity. In some problems (e.g., γ-ray bursts), *all* of these elements may be needed to describe the real-universe processes. Modeling these different processes requires a wide range of both physical theory and algorithmic techniques (e.g., finite differences, finite elements, spectral methods, N-body approaches, smooth-particle hydrodynamics). Processes may occur on multiple and dynamically changing time and length scales that are intricately intertwined.

The resulting computational problems are immense; a realistic calculation capable of predicting what actually happens in nature dwarfs the capacity of existing supercomputers. Most of these problems are intrinsically large scale and three dimensional and thus require highly parallel codes to run efficiently on advanced computer architectures. When 3D astrophysical processes are modeled on large-scale computers, they usually generate huge amounts of output data. Storing, managing, visualizing, analyzing, and ultimately understanding the output—and its relevance to any observational data—can be overwhelming.

Astrophysics is also increasingly collaborative: the physics is often so rich and varied that no single group or community has enough expertise to tackle every part of a problem. Larger and larger collaborations among groups with different expertise are required to give a realistic description of these processes. As a result, astrophysicists are heavily involved in collaborative virtual organizations (281) (VOs, Chapter 4), with distributed colleagues sharing (usually in ad hoc ways) resources, data, codes, knowledge, and expertise.

Astrophysics is also an observational science (Chapter 7). A large and varied array of detectors, satellites, and observatories is creating a vast amount of data. These data sources need to be linked and, ultimately, connected to simulations of the sources from which data are collected. This interplay between a multitude of prodigious data sources (both archived and live from different experiments) and both simulation and analysis processes (that themselves may require computational power that dwarfs what is available on today's largest systems) is what makes Grids so important to the astrophysics communities. The available computing power of any single site is too limited to properly consider many important problems, and the widely distributed communities and data present major difficulties. An environment of seamlessly integrated computational resources, continuously updated data archives, and communities of scientists and engineers are exactly what is required for the astrophysics and many other disciplines—and exactly what is promised by the Grid.

16.1   NUMERICAL RELATIVITY AND ASTROPHYSICS

To provide a definite focus (and to draw on our own expertise), we concentrate on Grid approaches being used and developed *now* in the numerical relativity community. The approaches and tools we describe are, however, applicable across a wide range of applications in computational astrophysics and beyond.

Numerical relativity, the numerical solution of Einstein's equations for general relativity, is demanding computationally and requires a broad expertise base drawing from large, dispersed collaborations of both physics and computer scientists (73). Interest in the field is currently high, since we will soon be observing gravitational waves with large-scale laser interferometric detectors (98).

Today, crude simulations of sources of gravitational waves, such as colliding black holes or neutron stars, supernova explosions, and other phenomena, are barely within reach of available computational resources and the communities that use them. Large groups and collaborations, such as those clustered around the European Astrophysics Network, run simulations on a daily basis on both workstations and supercomputing resources worldwide. Sharing a common code base (based on the Cactus framework; see the following section), groups of researchers create simulation codes by assembling modules, for example, for evolving the gravitational field, hydrodynamics, analysis of gravitational waveforms, parallel I/O and communication, and remote control and visualization. These codes must be extremely portable: the same code must run equally well on an unnetworked home laptop in Greece for development and testing, a workstation in Germany, or on any subset of a dozen large (1000 + processor) supercomputers worldwide. Such needs motivate interdisciplinary and international common formats, protocols, and access, especially for data and information (Chapters 22 and 23).

Computational resource needs will increase far beyond those just described as projects move from development to real production, for example, to calculate accurate waveforms for gravitational wave observatories. Such projects will also require even larger collaborations, because the mathematical, physical, and computational knowledge needed to perform a single simulation—with as much realistic physics as is required to model a real astrophysics event—is so vast. The difficulties just described all then increase dramatically, and functioning Grid technologies and tools will be crucial for success.

Computational astrophysicists have different requirements for the Grid according to whether they *develop* or *run* codes. Those developing Grid-enabled codes need tools and procedures for diagnosing and solving the problems that arise in this complex environment. Those running codes are more interested in reliability, ease of use, and new functionality such as remote techniques for interaction and collaboration. For example, a user simulating some exotic astrophysical process must be able to submit a job to an appropriate resource. When the job starts, it must be able to notify interested users distributed across the world; while it runs, various users may need to monitor its status and change the parameters; and after it has completed, the potentially huge amounts of data generated must be archived, visualized, and analyzed, again by many scientists. We emphasize that technologies that meet some of these needs exist. They were used, for example, in one of the largest simulations to date of two orbiting, coalescing black holes: see Figure 16.1.

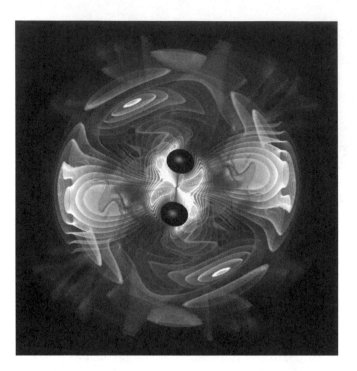

16.1

FIGURE

Two orbiting black holes, at center, are about to collide in this visualization of one the largest simulations to date of this process. The emitted gravitational waves (which researchers hope to detect this decade) are shown as different shades of grey. This simulation required well over 100 gigabytes of memory, generated a terabyte of output data, and required more than a day on thousand-processor machines at the National Center for Supercomputing Applications (NCSA) and the National Energy Research Scientific Computing Center (NERSC). Grid technologies were used to remotely monitor and perform basic visualizations of this production simulation, while it was running, by a collaboration of astrophysicists in different countries. (Image provided by AEI/ZIB.)

16.2   CACTUS: AN APPLICATION FRAMEWORK FOR THE GRID

Developing large codes is challenging even on today's independent resources because of the need to understand the different problems potentially arising on different architectures or different numbers of processors. On the Grid, the problems are multiplied. We require clear and complete logging information, the ability to recreate a specific environment in order to reproduce specific results, and

Grid-enabled frameworks and toolkits that hide the complexity of the Grid and provide application-oriented APIs for functionality. The Cactus application framework that we describe here addresses some of these concerns. Others are being addressed in the European GridLab project (71, 581), which is developing a "Grid Application Toolkit" that will provide abstract APIs for common Grid operations, such as moving and archiving files, searching for suitable machines, and migrating running codes.

Although Grid technologies should work with legacy codes and current working practices, ultimately applications need to be written and developed in new ways if they are to fully leverage the potential of the Grid. Further, the way that we as scientists use our codes, utilize our resources, and conduct our collaborations also needs to be rethought. The Cactus application framework (318) includes features suitable both for prototyping Grid use and for exploiting the Grid as technologies mature. We find that many capabilities needed for Grid execution coincide with those required for running and working successfully in today's computing collaborative environments, such as abstraction, portability, modularity, checkpointing and restart, flexible I/O, information interfaces, and parameter steering.

Cactus is an open source, generic problem-solving environment designed to provide scientists and engineers with a portable and collaborative framework for high-performance computing. Cactus emerged from the numerical relativity community but is now used by a growing number of applications in science and engineering. The simulations of black hole collisions presented in Figure 16.1 were performed using a code developed in the Cactus framework.

The Cactus design was motivated primarily by computational issues facing researchers needing large scale resources and involving sizable development and user teams. Its resulting modular structure easily enables parallel computation across different architectures and collaborative code development between different groups. Modules, or "thorns" in Cactus nomenclature, can implement different parts of custom-developed scientific or engineering applications, such as numerical relativity. Other thorns from standard computational toolkits provide a range of computational capabilities, such as parallel I/O, data distribution, or checkpointing.

Although Cactus is used today mainly in traditional supercomputing environments, many of its design features enable it to make good use of Grid technologies and to prototype new Grid scenarios. In particular, Cactus is highly portable (for example, it runs on iPAQs and Playstations) and has a configurable and scriptable build system, a built-in information Web server and steering API, and robust platform-independent checkpointing and restart capabilities.

The Cactus I/O layer maps parallel I/O to different libraries and new file formats. HDF5 support for platform-independent hyperslabbing and downsampling has proved particularly useful for Grid work. We describe Grid usage scenarios requiring these capabilities in Section 16.6. The parallel driver layer is implemented by a thorn, and the default MPI-based PUGH driver can be replaced by drivers based on other paradigms. PUGH can be linked with MPICH-G2 (403) (Chapter 24) for distributed computing (see Section 16.5).

16.3   RESOURCE SHARING WITHIN VIRTUAL ORGANIZATIONS

In the remainder of this chapter, we use a series of usage scenarios to illustrate opportunities for Grid usage in computational science. Although motivated by computational astrophysics, these scenarios are applicable across many disciplines. In each scenario, we ground our presentation firmly in reality by describing how today's technologies have been used to enable the activity now, and then present our vision of how the activity can evolve as Grid technologies are fully deployed. Based on what is possible now, and sometimes even in prototype form, we believe that these apparently futuristic scenarios are not far from being realized.

We first consider issues relating to resource sharing within collaborative communities. The VO concept introduced in Chapter 4 is central to our work. We consider a VO as a collection of resources managed independently, but cooperatively, and available to some user community. Effective organization and use of these resources are of prime importance to this community.

The simplest and currently most important usage scenario for computational astrophysics on the Grid is probably that of *resource discovery and job submission*. A scientist in the European Astrophysics Network has prepared an executable and input parameter file to simulate a black hole merger. With access to many large-scale computing facilities around the world, typically all with different user IDs, passwords, operating, queuing, and file systems, simply choosing where to run this simulation is complicated. Often researchers will use the resource they used the day before, regardless of whether it is the *best* available now (e.g., least loaded, most appropriate for current job).

Grid technologies simplify the process of accessing these resources. As discussed in Chapter 4, certificate-based authentication allows users to access all systems in their VO with a single log-in, which is then mapped to their local account. Similarly, other local idiosyncrasies can be removed: common Grid-enabled interfaces to local batch systems, file systems, data archiving, and so forth create the notion of unified user commands for all resources. At present the basic Grid technologies to support this process are well developed and robust in the Globus Toolkit and are rapidly being deployed across many sites.

Going one step further, it is natural to provide access to, and interaction with, all the resources in one's VO through a Web-based *portal* (Chapter 24). Once authenticated, the user can in principle see all available resources and submit preconfigured jobs to a given machine. We use such a portal developed within the NSF Astrophysics Simulation Collaboratory project (567) to perform these and other functions.

A unified, single Grid log-in system, with all relevant information and job submission mechanisms collected in a point-and-click Web interface, is a major step forward. The next step is to allow the user to formulate a resource request (generated manually or automatically, based, for example, on statistics of the last similar job) that is then forwarded to a VO-aware resource broker service (Chapter 18) that can automatically route the job to the *most appropriate* resource. If these resource-brokering services can be accessed by the applications themselves, then changing application needs or machine loads can trigger requests for other resources, to be found and used on demand, as we describe next.

16.4 INTERACTING WITH GRID JOBS

Traditionally, the computational scientist running a large simulation first submits a job to the batch system on a remote machine and then periodically logs onto that machine to check status. Maybe the job is still waiting in the queue, maybe it is actually running, or—as frequently occurs—maybe it has been terminated for an unexpected reason. Such working practices are frustrating for users. A job sits in a queue for days and then fails upon execution because of a simple error in initialization. Or perhaps it runs for 72 hours and then aborts because it had been preset to output too much data and a disk quota was exceeded. Worst of all, it may have used 100,000 CPU-h but produced nonsensical results because of an incorrect parameter setting. These considerations motivate the development of more sophisticated interactive job monitoring and steering that will soon enable much more innovative Grid applications, such as those described in the following.

An information and steering interface has been developed for Cactus that allows any user with a Web browser to interact with a running job. The HTTPD Cactus thorn is a Web server that can display all current information about the running job, including active routines, their version numbers, time step, estimated time to completion, and written data files and can even include visualizations embedded in the Web pages. Any parameters declared *steerable* can be changed on the fly through a Web form interface; I/O frequency, variables output, downsampling, and any other such parameter can be changed at will, allowing the

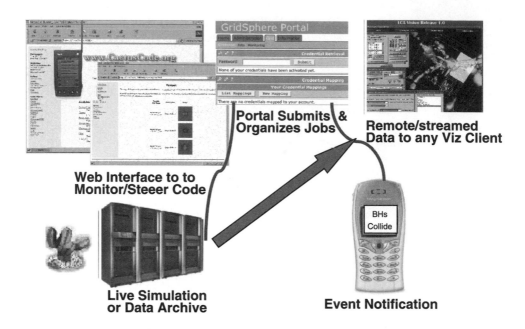

**Portal Submits &
Organizes Jobs**

**Remote/streamed
Data to any Viz Client**

**Web Interface to to
Monitor/Steeer Code**

**Live Simulation
or Data Archive**

Event Notification

16.2

FIGURE

A user can submit jobs from a portal, and jobs are registered with the portal when they start, allowing access by all participating collaborators. Jobs can be monitored, and steered or their output data visualized, either live or from data archives. Important events in the life of a job trigger notification to various types of devices.

user to correct many problems, *without having to restart*. When a job starts, its URL is broadcast to a portal, which then notifies a user-defined group of collaborators via e-mail or SMS message with contact information that they can then use to access the simulation from a browser. Significant simulation events, such as the merging of two black holes, can be programmed to trigger notification of a user or group of collaborators.

A portal thus becomes the organizing instrument for *collaborative* computational science. Jobs can be grouped by collaboration, by topic, by status (currently running or archived output data), and so forth. Hyperlinks to data produced by the simulation provide instant access for visualization. When such links are clicked, data residing in a file is downloaded from the remote site to the local user machine, and the appropriate visualization client is automatically launched. If, on the other hand, the data reside in memory allocated to a running simulation, it will be streamed over a socket directly to the local visualization client. The overall picture of interactions with remote data or running jobs is shown in Figure 16.2.

These technologies are seeing a growing use in numerical relativity projects. Several problems must be addressed, however, before such interaction mechanisms are fully embraced. First, firewall issues often conflict with the user's need to interact directly with remote data or simulations from any location. Second, such tools need to be enhanced to exploit Web and Grid services mechanisms (Chapter 17) so that, for example, applications can announce themselves, not just to a portal, but to any other compliant information servers or applications, exchanging data, contacting resource brokers to find new resources, starting other applications, notifying users or other applications when certain events take place, and so forth.

16.5   DISTRIBUTED COMPUTING

We describe various methods for distributing applications across resources: task farming, metacomputing, migration, and spawning.

Task farming involves farming out (a great many) independent or loosely coupled tasks to resources scattered across a VO (see Chapters 1:13, 19, and 24). Typically, tasks require little or no communication between tasks, and often return little data. Task farming can be used in our community for parameter studies, both to tune theoretical and computational parameters and to vary physical parameters over a large range of possibilities to search for the most interesting regime to be studied in depth. For example, the investigation of critical phenomena for a pure gravitational wave collapsing to form a black hole requires knowledge of the precise critical value for the amplitude of the initial wave. Slightly above this amplitude, the wave will collapse to a black hole; slightly below, it will disperse. Dozens or hundreds of jobs may be needed to find the critical value to sufficient accuracy. Grid task farming makes use of underlying Grid technologies to discover appropriate resources in a VO, to handle the staging and starting of a set of tasks, and to archive task results, all in as short a time as possible.

Metacomputing involves the distribution of one or more tightly coupled tasks across a number of large machines (72, 110). Metacomputing can be used to increase not only peak capability but also available capacity: if, say, 1024 processors are needed but not immediately available on any one machine, four machines might be able to provide 256 processors each. We have demonstrated the feasibility of metacomputing with real production applications, on production machines and networks, and with no special conditions being created to enhance performance. For example, in 2001, we ran a simulation of colliding black holes across multiple remote machines, running on different operating systems, using adaptive techniques that automatically adjust messages sent across the network between machines to increase the efficiency, from 15 to over 70% *as the simulation ran* (72). A *Grid-enabled* version of the message-passing layer (403) (Chapter 24) allowed the Cactus-based application code to be run without modification. Such experiments show that such Grid-based metacomputing scenarios can be run with a high degree of efficiency even for tightly coupled simulations such as Einstein's equations requiring many communications. Although these technologies are quite advanced and robust, they are used primarily for development—but only because of infrastructure deployment and scheduling issues. As Grid technologies are deployed across production sites, these capabilities can become a regular mode of operation.

More complex distributed computing scenarios build on the technologies described so far. *Migration* involves moving a simulation from one site to another (239), for example because contention slows the simulation, or because the simulation needs more memory as adaptive meshes resolve a developing black hole. Migration proceeds with the help of a resource brokering service. If a new resource is found, a checkpoint file is written and transferred, a new executable is started, and the portal is notified of the new location. Robust prototypes of migration (69) use unmodified Cactus-based relativity applications.

A variation on migration is *spawning*, which involves moving just a *part* of an application to an appropriate remote resource. For example, when simulating black hole collisions, analysis tasks must be carried out to locate the black hole horizons or compute the gravitational waves emitted. These time-consuming tasks may not feed back to the main simulation or be easily parallelized and hence can be spawned to a more appropriate resource, allowing the primary resource to concentrate on advancing the main simulation. We demonstrated spawning scenarios in 2001, with a black hole simulation running in Germany spawning analysis tasks to resources in Europe, Asia, and North America.

16.6   DATA MANAGEMENT

The large 3D simulations that we have been considering here generate correspondingly large amounts of output data, which must be analyzed, visualized (often by several different members of a VO), and archived for later use. Each simulation can generate hundreds of files with different file formats, and the discovery and manipulation of these files are complicated by the fact that users are running on different machines, with different file systems, quotas, and archiving capabilities. For Grid applications, the data management problem is exacerbated—users may not even know on which machine their simulation is running, or the simulation may be moving between resources and leaving data in multiple locations.

Even when the location of a file is known, its size may make moving the file to a local machine for analysis inconvenient or impossible. This was the case for the huge black hole collision simulations described previously (see Figure 16.1). Although Grid technologies were important for the international group of astrophysicists to remotely and collaboratively run, monitor, and adjust those simulations while they were running, the huge output generated could not be transported to local sites in other countries for analysis; instead, a team of scientists flew from Berlin to the United States to visualize and retrieve the data!

This problem is rapidly being solved. Tools for manipulating remote data are already being used by astrophysicists. One example is GridFTP servers (64) (Chapter 22), containing extensions from the German GriKSL project. When run on the file systems of machines holding data, these servers allow remote HDF5 data files to be analyzed with local visualization systems. Downsampling or zooming can be used to match the amount of transported data to the available bandwidth. Any visualization systems incorporating a GridFTP client along with the usual HDF5 reader can display these remote data, and such readers already exist for OpenDX and Amira software. These tools address the remote data problem and can be used to create, from thousands of miles away, the visualization such as the one shown in Figure 16.1.

16.7   SUMMARY

We have outlined how Grid technologies are being used in computational astrophysics today and how we expect these technologies to be used in the future. Although we have focused on the needs and applications of the numerical relativity community, the tools and experiences that we describe are quite general and apply to many other computational science disciplines. All of these scenarios are motivated by the needs of present-day astrophysicists, are working now in prototype form, and have been tested on real codes and in real production environments using today's Grid technologies.

The best way to bring these scenarios into everyday production use is to develop Grid applications in close collaboration with Grid infrastructure developers. Such a partnership ensures that application requirements found by prototyping and testing scenarios are addressed and solved and that the applications are ready to exploit the Grid as soon as possible. We envision that the scenarios described here will be running in production within a few years at most.

Still more advanced scenarios will become reality when applications take full advantage of a more mature Grid. Dynamic applications will themselves become Grid services, interacting with other services, moving about, expanding and contracting, adapting to their needs and to local resource and Grid conditions. Huge amounts of data will be collected from experiments and sensors around the world. In gravitational wave astronomy, Grid applications may process these data as they are collected, using Grid-enabled data analysis applications, then simulate the astrophysical sources of the data using Cactus-based applications, which in turn steer astronomical observatories generating the data, tuning their frequency characteristics to be more sensitive to a signal expected in a few hours. Likewise, other Grid-enabled applications will warn forecasters of impending earthquakes based on recent data acquired from satellites and ground-based geodetic data collected just hours before (581).

ACKNOWLEDGMENTS

Many colleagues contributed to the work and ideas presented here, in particular Werner Benger, Thomas Dramlitsch, Tom Goodale, Gerd Lanfermann, Andre Merzky, Thomas Radke, Michael Russell, and John Shalf, as well as our friends in the ASC, GriKSL, and GridLab projects. We are pleased to acknowledge support from NSF PHY-9979985 (ASC), DFN-Verein TK 6-2–AN 200 (GriKSL), and EU IST-2001-32133 (GridLab). Black hole simulation images resulted from computations at NCSA and NERSC.

FURTHER READING

For more information on the topics covered in this chapter, see *www.mkp.com/grid2*.

IV PART

ARCHITECTURE

The Grid architecture that we introduce in Part IV defines a standard, service-oriented approach to structuring Grid systems. In this architecture, system and application functions are organized as modular, interoperable, reusable services, which can then be composed to create increasingly sophisticated systems. The five chapters in Part IV (and indeed also the two chapters on data and knowledge in Part V) are concerned with the design and implementation of this architecture and various of its central services.

Chapter 17, "The Open Grid Services Architecture," by Ian Foster, Carl Kesselman, and Steven Tuecke, leads off with a description of the Open Grid Services Architecture (OGSA), the standards-based Grid computing framework that underlies much of the technology presented in this book. They first introduce the service-oriented architecture principles that underlie OGSA, and then proceed to provide a detailed description of the Web services mechanisms and the Open Grid Services Infrastructure specification that together define the core interfaces and behaviors that underlie OGSA. Numerous examples and a case study depict how these mechanisms are used to construct applications. The chapter concludes with a discussion of higher-level OGSA services.

A defining feature of Grids is the sharing of networks, computers, and other resources and services. This sharing introduces a need for resource and service management. User requirements for performance must be translated into resource requirements, and conflicting resource requirements must be resolved. In Chapter 18, "Resource and Service Management," Karl Czajkowski, Ian Foster, and Carl Kesselman provide a broad perspective on the management of Grid resources and services. They describe requirements, present a general Grid resource and service management framework, and explain how various contemporary resource management systems fit this framework.

Another defining feature of distributed systems is, unfortunately, the inevitability of failure. In Chapter 19, "Building Reliable Clients and Services," Douglas Thain and Miron Livny present a range of principles and techniques that can be used to construct Grid services and clients that execute reliably (from a client perspective) despite various classes of failures. They illustrate their presentation with numerous examples, many based on the large-scale distributed systems that they have built in recent years, including Condor and Condor-G.

In Chapter 20, "Instrumentation and Monitoring," Jeff Hollingsworth and Brian Tierney address issues relating to the instrumentation and monitoring of Grid resources and services for purposes such as discovery, troubleshooting, performance tuning, accounting, and auditing. They describe a range of practical techniques, as well as systems that incorporate these techniques, and illustrate the application of their techniques with case studies.

Finally in Chapter 21, "Security for Virtual Organizations: Federating Trust and Policy Domains," Frank Siebenlist and his colleagues discuss the challenging security requirements encountered in distributed, multi-institutional Grid environments and techniques that can be used to address these requirements. They discuss current trends in security technologies and their relationship to the Grid. They also introduce work on an OGSA security model, describe a Grid security implementation, and summarize expectations for future developments.

The material in these five chapters is almost entirely new, reflecting the tremendous advances that have been made in Grid architecture and services since the first edition appeared. However, as was the case with applications, much of the material from the first edition remains relevant. In particular, Chapter 1:12, "High-Performance Schedulers," provides a valuable survey of scheduling techniques and systems, Chapter 1:13, "High-Throughput Resource Management," provides a detailed description of high-throughput computing and the Condor system (described only briefly here in Chapter 19), and Chapter 1:16, "Security, Accounting, and Assurance," presents a valuable introduction to many security issues discussed with a more distinct Grid focus in Chapter 21. Chapter 1:14, on instrumentation and measurement, is superseded by Chapter 20, and Chapter 1:11, which introduces the Globus Toolkit and its applications, is superseded by material in Chapters 4 and 27 and by the application chapters.

The Open Grid Services Architecture

Ian Foster, Carl Kesselman, and Steven Tuecke

*T*he past several years have seen a remarkable maturation and standardization of Grid technologies around the banner of the Open Grid Services Architecture (OGSA) (279). We first touched on OGSA in Chapter 4, and most of the application chapters have referred to it. We now drill down on the details of what OGSA is and its central role in Grid computing. Our goals are not only to communicate the key concepts but also to indicate how OGSA mechanisms can both simplify the development of secure, robust systems and enable the creation of interoperable, portable, and reusable components and systems. Although this chapter is certainly not a programming manual, we do provide enough technical detail to allow readers to start down the path of designing OGSA-based systems.

Our presentation follows a staged approach. After reviewing the principles of service-oriented architecture, we introduce the primary elements of the core service interfaces and behaviors that constitute OGSA and an example that we use throughout the chapter to illustrate the use of OGSA mechanisms. Then we introduce, in a staged fashion, the various elements of OGSA. First, we review the Web services technologies on which OGSA is based, focusing on the Web Services Description Language (WSDL) (183) that OGSA adopts as an interface definition language. Then we describe the foundational Open Grid Services Infrastructure (OGSI) (659), a set of WSDL interfaces and associated conventions, extensions, and refinements to Web services standards designed to support basic Grid behaviors. We review the higher-level interfaces, models, and behaviors likely to complete OGSA, pointing to subsequent chapters for more detailed discussion in many cases. We complete the chapter with a detailed application case study, a discussion of OGSA implementation strategies, and thoughts on future directions.

17.1   SERVICE-ORIENTED ARCHITECTURE

OGSA Grid technologies are based on a *service-oriented architecture*. We describe here what this term means and why it is important.

A service is an entity that provides some capability to its clients by exchanging messages. A service is defined by identifying sequences of specific message exchanges that cause the service to perform some *operation*. By thus defining these operations only in terms of message exchange, we achieve great flexibility in how services are implemented and where they may be located. A service-oriented architecture is one in which all entities are services, and thus any operation visible to the architecture is the result of message exchange.

The following three examples emphasize the generality and broad applicability of the "service" concept, which can encompass, as shown here, functionalities ranging from low-level resource management (e.g., the storage service) to high-level system-monitoring functions. (In the language of Chapter 4, a "service" can implement both resource- and collective-level functions.)

+ A *storage service* might provide operations for storing and retrieving data, reserving space, monitoring the status of the storage service, and querying and defining the policies that govern who is allowed to access the service.

+ A *data transfer service* might provide operations for requesting the transfers of data from one storage service to another, managing and monitoring the status of such transfers, and querying and defining the policies that govern how different transfer requests are prioritized.

+ A *troubleshooting service* might monitor the status of various other services, such as storage and data transfer services, and provide operations allowing other entities to request notification on various error conditions and to query and define the policies that determine who is allowed to receive such notifications.

The examples also introduce two important themes that we will revisit later in detail. First, we see that common behaviors, such as "monitor status" and "query and define policy," can reoccur in different contexts. A goal of the OGSA design is to allow these behaviors to be expressed in standard ways regardless of context, so as to simplify application design and encourage code reuse. To achieve this reuse of behaviors, operations are often grouped together to form a service *interface*. Interfaces can then be combined to specify a service with the desired behaviors. Second, we see an example of a higher-level service behavior (data transfer) being implemented via the composition of simpler behaviors (storage service). Ease of composition is a second major design goal for OGSA.

By encapsulating service operations behind a common message-oriented service interface, service-oriented architectures encourage *service virtualization*, isolating users from details of service implantation and location (see Chapter 14).

For example, consider the storage service mentioned previously, which presents the user with an interface that defines, among other things, a "store file" operation. A user should be able to invoke that operation on a particular instance of that storage service without regard to how that instance implements the storage service interface. Behind the scenes, different implementations may store the file on the user's local computer, in a distributed file system, on a remote archival storage system, or in free space within a department desktop pool—or choose from among such alternatives depending on context, load, amount paid, or other factors. Regardless of implementation approach, the user is aware only that the requested operation is executed—albeit with varying cost and other qualities of service, factors that may be subject to negotiation between the client and service (Chapter 18).

Interaction with a given service is facilitated by using a standard *interface definition language (IDL)*, such as WSDL (183), to describe the service's interface(s). An IDL defines the operations supported by a service, by specifying the messages that a service consumes and produces. An interface specification describes the messages the service expects but does not define what the service does in response to those messages (i.e., its *behavior*). Behavior can be specified either informally through human-readable specification documents or (in principle at least) via a formal semantics description (211, 468). In either case, an important role of an IDL is to provide well-known names to which such semantics can be attached, in order to facilitate discovery of services that perform desired functions.

A well-defined interface definition language and a separation of concerns between service interface and implementation simplify the manipulation and management of services in four important respects: service discovery, composition, specialization, and interface extension.

Service discovery is important in distributed computing because we frequently must operate in unfamiliar environments in which the identity and detailed characteristics of available services are unknown to us. In a service-oriented architecture, we can easily create registries containing information about the interfaces of available services, which users can query to find suitable candidates.

Service composition is important because it enables code reuse and the dynamic construction of complex systems from simpler components. A well-defined interface definition language simplifies composition because a client need only know a service's interface to invoke it. Support for multiple protocol bindings (discussed in the following) can be important for service composition, by allowing for optimizations designed to reduce the cost of service invocation within specialized settings, such as a single address space.

Specialization refers to the use of different implementations of a service interface on different platforms; see, for example, our prior discussion of the storage service. This strategy can facilitate seamless overlay, not only to native platform facilities, but also to virtual ensembles of resources via the nesting of service implementations.

Interface extension is an important feature of an interface definition language, as it allows for specialized implementations to add additional, implementation-specific functionality, while still supporting the common interface. This strategy is important because it allows for the development of standard service interfaces, without requiring a "least common denominator" approach to implementation. Implementations can, instead, compete through value-added extensions to a standard interface, in addition to value-added implementation of the standard interface (e.g., better qualities of service).

17.2   A SERVICE-ORIENTED GRID ARCHITECTURE

We describe in this book a specific practical realization of a service-oriented architecture, namely, that provided by the Open Grid Services Architecture. We focus our attention in this chapter on the core OGSA components.

As illustrated in Figure 17.1, the three principal elements of OGSA are the *Open Grid Services Infrastructure, OGSA services*, and *OGSA schemas*, which we characterize briefly in the following paragraphs and describe in more detail later in the chapter. Furthermore, OGSA builds on *Web services*, a standards-based, widely deployed distributed computing paradigm (320) that provides the basic mechanisms used to describe and invoke Grid services. OGSA services may be hosted in a variety of different environments and may communicate via different protocols, as we describe in the following.

Web services provide important machinery, but current Web service standards do not address important issues related to basic service semantics: how services are created, how long they live, how to manage faults, and how to manage long-lived state, to name a few. These and other important service behaviors must be standardized to enable service virtualization and service interoperability. These issues are addressed by a core set of interfaces called the Open Grid

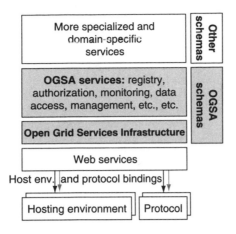

The core elements of the Open Grid Services Architecture (shaded).

Services Infrastructure (OGSI) (659). A Web service that adheres to OGSI standards is called a *Grid service*.

OGSI defines essential building blocks for distributed systems, including standard interfaces and associated behaviors for describing and discovering service attributes, creating service instances, managing service lifetime, managing groups of services, and subscribing to and delivering notifications. However, OGSI does not define all elements that arise when creating large-scale systems. We also need to address many other issues, both fundamental and domain-specific, of which the following are just examples:

+ How do I establish identity and negotiate authentication?

+ How is policy expressed and negotiated?

+ How do I discover services?

+ How do I negotiate and monitor service-level agreements?

+ How do I manage membership of, and communication within, virtual organizations?

+ How do I organize service collections hierarchically so as to deliver reliable and scalable service semantics?

+ How do I integrate data resources into computations?

+ How do I monitor and manage collections of services?

Without standardization in such areas, it is hard to build large-scale systems in standard fashions, to achieve code reuse, and to achieve interoperability among components—three distinct and important goals. Thus, OGSA must also define additional services in these and other related areas.

Interoperability is about more than a common language: one also needs a common vocabulary for describing objects of common interest. Thus, OGSA must also define standard schema for describing properties of common Grid entities.

17.3   AN EXAMPLE

We use a single example throughout this chapter to illustrate both the principles and the details of OGSA as described here and in subsequent chapters. Here we set the scene by introducing the example. As illustrated in Figure 17.2, we consider a system comprising the following components:

✦ Multiple storage services each implement a standard storage service interface. (Further to our discussion of virtualization, note that each storage service instance may be implemented in a different way and provide different qualities of service to users. For example, one implementation might encapsulate a simple local file system, while another distributes user files across free storage on desktop systems, while yet another interfaces to a mass storage system.)

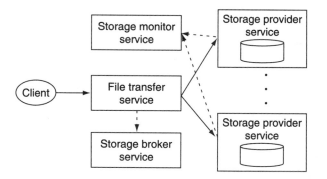

17.2

FIGURE

The various services involved in our example.

+ One or more *file transfer services* handle requests to perform transfers from one storage service to another. (Again, different file transfer service instances might implement the same interface in different ways, with the same or different qualities of service.)

+ Various other services provide additional functionality, such as discovery (brokering) and troubleshooting (monitoring).

+ Various clients access these services.

The arrows in the figure indicate some of the interactions that occur between the various components. A client communicates requests to the file transfer service, asking it to oversee a transfer from one storage service to another. The file transfer service may in turn communicate with the storage broker to schedule access to the storage services, and then with various storage services to affect the transfer. Meanwhile the monitoring service receives and processes status updates from the various storage providers.

As we proceed through the chapter, we shall see how various OGSA features can be used to implement increasingly functional versions of this basic scenario. The various elements are brought together in Section 17.7, which provides an integrated discussion of the scenario.

17.4   WEB SERVICES

We provide some background on Web services, which, as noted previously, describes an emerging distributed computing paradigm based on standard techniques for describing interfaces to software components, methods for accessing these components via interoperable protocols, and discovery methods that enable the identification of relevant service providers. These techniques are programming language-, programming model-, and system software-neutral. Web services standards are being defined within the World Wide Web Consortium (W3C) and other standards bodies and form the basis for major new industry initiatives such as Microsoft (.NET), IBM (e-Business on Demand), and Sun (Sun ONE). From the perspective of OGSA, the Web services standard of most interest is WSDL.

The Web services framework has two advantages for our purposes. First, our need to support the dynamic discovery and composition of services in heterogeneous environments necessitates mechanisms for registering and discovering interface definitions. WSDL supports this requirement by providing a standard mechanism for defining interface definitions separately from their embodiment within a particular binding (transport protocol and data-encoding format). Second, the widespread adoption of Web services mechanisms means that a framework based on Web services can exploit numerous tools and extant services, such as WSDL processors that can generate language bindings for a variety of languages (e.g., JAX-RPC (583); Web Services Invocation Framework, WSIF (486)), workflow systems that sit on top of WSDL, and hosting environments for Web services (e.g., Microsoft .NET, IBM WebSphere, BEA Weblogic, and the open source Apache Axis.

In addition to WSDL, the Web services community has defined or is defining a variety of other standards concerned with such issues as service registry (44), security (381) (see also Chapter 21), policy (380), service orchestration (53) and— as we describe in Section 17.5, Grid services. These definition activities are taking place within W3C, GGF, OASIS, and other standards bodies.

Above all, OGSA makes use of WSDL (183), a standard under development within the W3C for describing software components or services in a manner independent of any particular programming language or implementation approach. A WSDL service definition is a document encoded using the W3C standard extensible markup language (XML) (134, 253). XML syntax features potentially recursively defined elements, each with the format

```
<element-name optional-parameters> list-of-zero-or-more-elements
</element-name>
```

A WSDL service definition describes a Web service as a set of *endpoints* operating on messages containing payloads conforming to a schema defined using the W3C standard XML Schema. Service interfaces (or portTypes, in WSDL terminology) are defined abstractly in terms of message structures and sequences of simple message exchanges (or operations, in WSDL terminology), and then bound to a concrete network protocol, data-encoding format, and endpoint address. Related concrete endpoints are bundled to define abstract endpoints (services). WSDL is extensible to allow a description of endpoints and the concrete representation of their messages for a variety of different message formats and network protocols.

A WSDL definition comprises a *service description*, which defines the service interface, and *implementation details*, which describe how the interface maps to protocol messages and concrete endpoint addresses. Figure 17.3 shows an example of a WSDL service description, which has elements as follows.

The <portType> element defines an interface (here, the StorageService interface) by specifying the zero or more operations supported by a Web service that implements the interface. Each operation is specified by an <operation> element, which defines the messages used to implement the operation. In Figure 17.3, a single operation, getFile, is specified; this has an input message getFileRequest and

```
<wsdl:definitions xmlns:tns="…" targetNamespace="…">
  <message name="getFileRequest">
    <part name="term" type="xs:string"/>
  </message>

  <message name="getFileResponse">
    <part name="value" type="xs:string"/>
  </message>

  <portType name="StorageServicechange">
    <operation name="getFile">
      <input message="getFileRequest"/>
      <output message="getFileResponse"/>
    </operation>
  </portType>
</wsdl:definitions>
```

17.3   WSDL example, showing the portType, operation, and message elements.

FIGURE

output message getFileResponse. (This example involves a request-response exchange between client and service. A WSDL operation definition can also omit the output message to implement an asynchronous communication.)

The <message> element defines a message used by the Web service to implement an operation. A message element defines the parts of a message and the associated data types. Both the input and output messages specified in Figure 17.3 compose a single part, with type xs:string referring to a string type defined in a system library.

A WSDL definition can also include <types> elements to define data types used by the Web service. In object-oriented terms, one can think of a <portType> as a class, an <operation> as a method, and a <message> as a method argument.

The details of WSDL implementation descriptions are not particularly relevant to our discussions here, but in brief, the <binding> element is used to specify the messaging protocol, data-encoding model, and transport used for communicating messages, while the <service> element defines concrete endpoint addresses for a set of bindings. The example in Figure 17.4 specifies the commonly used simple object access protocol (SOAP) (41) and HTTP as messaging and transport protocols, respectively; document (rather than RPC) messaging style; and literal rather than SOAP encoding.

The separation of abstract interface (portTypes and messages) from concrete encodings (binding) is an important aspect of Web services, and hence OGSA.

```
<binding type="glossaryTerms" name="b1">
  <soap:binding style="document"
          transport="http://schemas.xmlsoap.org/soap/http" />
    <operation>
      <soap:operation soapAction="http://example.com/getFile"/>
      <input>
        <soap:body use="literal"/>
      </input>
      <output>
        <soap:body use="literal"/>
      </output>
    </operation>
</binding>
```

17.4   WSDL example, showing the binding element.

FIGURE

A service-oriented system that defines a single "standard" mechanism for invoking service operations can suffer from performance problems in certain settings. For example, a standard mechanism based on SOAP (41) or other Internet protocol communications (486) may be unacceptably slow when a client and the service that it wants to access are located on the same physical computer.

By separating abstract and concrete descriptions, WSDL allows multiple bindings for a single interface. Thus, for example, a single service implementation might support both one or more distributed communication protocols (e.g., SOAP over HTTP, and/or some more optimized protocol) and a locally optimized binding (e.g., local IPC) for interactions between request and service processes on the same host. Other binding properties may include reliability (and other forms of QoS) and authentication and delegation of credentials. The choice of binding should always be transparent to the requestor with respect to service invocation semantics—but not with respect to other things: for example, a requestor should be able to choose a particular binding for performance reasons.

As an example of when this capability is important, consider a workflow service that coordinates multiple application tasks, including file transfers. Support for multiple protocol bindings can allow this service to interact with a file transfer service located on the same machine via in-memory operations rather than more expensive TCP/IP communications. As a second example, a storage service might support two different protocol bindings for its data transfer operations: a generic protocol based on a general-purpose transport and an optimized data channel protocol that supports more rapid data movement.

Web services thus partition the specification of the "protocol" used to interact with a service into the interface (the abstract messages communicated), the message protocol (e.g., SOAP), and the transport protocol (e.g., HTTP).

17.5   OPEN GRID SERVICES INFRASTRUCTURE

Our ability to virtualize and compose services depends on more than a standard interface definition language (i.e., WSDL). We also require standard interface definitions and associated semantics for common service interactions. Without these, it is impossible to build interoperable, reusable components. To give just one example, different services should follow the same conventions for error notification, so that consumers of multiple services can process error notifications uniformly from all of those services, regardless of source.

These standard interfaces and semantics are provided in OGSA by the Open Grid Services Infrastructure. Using a combination of WSDL interface descriptions and human readable specifications, OGSI defines mechanisms for creating, naming, managing lifetime, monitoring, grouping, and exchanging information among entities called Grid services. These conventions provide for the controlled, fault-resilient, and secure management of the distributed and often long-lived state commonly required in distributed applications. OGSI also introduces standard factory and group registration interfaces for creating and discovering Grid services. The paragraphs that follow summarize these features, most of which are also illustrated in Figure 17.5.

Grid service descriptions and instances.   In a system in which services can be instantiated dynamically, we need terminology that allows us to distinguish between the *definition* of a service definition and an *instantiation* of that service definition in the form of an executing service. Thus OGSI introduces the twin concepts of the Grid service description and Grid service instance as organizing principles for distributed systems.

Service state, metadata, and introspection.   OGSI defines mechanisms, called *service data,* for representing metadata and state data related to a service as part of its description, and for accessing (via both queries and subscriptions) that information from a service instance. This uniform mechanism for accessing the publicly visible state of a service instance supports introspection, monitoring, and discovery. A client application can ask a Grid service instance to return information describing itself, such as the collection of interfaces that it implements, when the

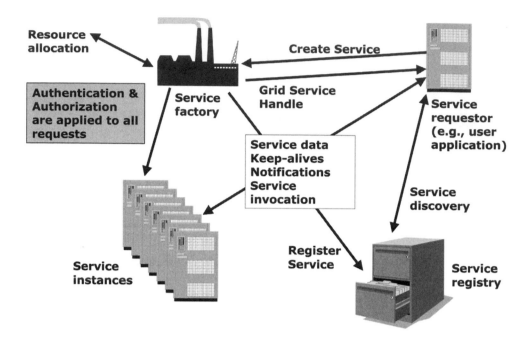

17.5

FIGURE
Important OGSI concepts and interactions, including the factory (used to create service instances) and registry (used to discover service instances), and the standard messages used to query service data associated with service instances and to manage service instance lifetime. All interfaces are defined in standard WSDL.

service expects to terminate, and interface-specification information about the current state of the instance.

Naming and name resolution.   OGSI defines a two-level naming scheme for Grid service instances. An instance may have one or more *Grid service handles*, which are simple, abstract, long-lived names for that instance, in the form of Uniform Resource Identifiers (URIs). Handles can be mapped by HandleResolver services to concrete but potentially less-long-lived *Grid service references* containing protocol binding and endpoint addressing information.

Service life cycle.   OGSI defines mechanisms for managing the life cycle of a Grid service instance, including both explicit destruction and soft-state lifetime management functions, and Grid service factories that can be used to create instances implementing specified interfaces.

Fault type. OGSI defines a standard base type for all fault messages that may be returned by a Grid service. This simplifies problem determination by having a common base set of information that all fault messages contain. The base type includes the originator and time of the fault, an optional human readable description, an optional legacy fault code, and an optional list of faults describing the underlying cause.

Service groups. OGSI defines a means of representing and managing groups of service instances. These mechanisms may be used for a variety of purposes, including collective information management (e.g., registries) and collective operations (e.g., group lifetime management).

OGSI defines several interfaces (i.e., WSDL portTypes), summarized in Table 17.1. Each of these portTypes defines a set of operations and the OGSI specification defines the expected behavior for each of these operations. In the rest of this section, we expand on these various aspects of OGSI.

Of the portTypes listed in Table 17.1, the GridService portType holds special significance. Although the other portTypes may be optionally included, the GridService portType defines operations so fundamental that every OGSI compliant service must support them. These operations, summarized in Table 17.2, provide mechanisms for inquiring about service state and managing service

portType name	Description
GridService	Encapsulates the root behavior of the service model, including service data and lifetime management
HandleResolver	Mapping from a GSH to a GSR
NotificationSource	Allows clients to subscribe to notification messages
NotificationSubscription	For managing the lifetime and other properties of a subscription
NotificationSink	Defines a single operation for delivering a notification message to the service instance that implements the operation
Factory	Standard operation for creation of Grid service instances
ServiceGroup	Service data for representing a group of service instances, and the policies associated with group membership
ServiceGroupRegistration	Allows Grid services to be added and removed from a ServiceGroup
ServiceGroupEntry	For managing the lifetime and other properties of a registration to a ServiceGroup

17.1   Standard Interfaces Defined by the OGSI Specification.

TABLE

Operation	Description
findServiceData	Query information about the Grid service instance
setServiceData	Modify service data values
requestTerminationAfter	Specify earliest desired termination time
requestTerminationBefore	Specify latest desired termination time
destroy	Terminate Grid service instance

17.2

TABLE

Operations Defined by OGSI GridService Interface.

lifetime. We discuss these operations in more detail in Sections 17.5.2 and 17.5.4.2, respectively.

17.5.1   Grid Service Descriptions and Instances

In the basic Web services model, services are assumed to be created (and destroyed) by mechanisms that are out of the scope of the Web services standards themselves. Yet applications often need to instantiate new transient services dynamically—for example, to handle the management and interactions associated with the state of particular requested activities. When the activity's state is no longer needed, the service can be destroyed. For example:

✦ In a videoconferencing system, the establishment of a conferencing session might involve the creation of services at intermediate points to manage end-to-end data flows according to quality-of-service constraints.

✦ In a Web-serving environment, we might want to vary the number of request-processing services, so as to provide for consistent user response time by managing application workload through dynamically added capacity.

✦ In the example of Figure 17.2, each "storage service" would be an instance of the Grid service description, StorageService. Each StorageService instance has a unique local state (Section 17.5.2), has a unique name (Section 17.5.3), and can be managed independently of other StorageService instances—but implements the same interfaces and behaviors. As we will see in the following, our implementations of this and other services in Figure 17.2 can themselves involve the creation of additional service instances used to represent various transient state components.

Other examples of transient services might be a query against a database, a data-mining operation, a network bandwidth allocation, a running data transfer, and an advance reservation for processing capability. As these examples emphasize, services can be extremely lightweight entities, created to manage even short-lived and large numbers of activities.

Transience has significant implications for how services are managed, named, discovered, and used. One immediate consequence is that we need to distinguish between the definition of a Grid service and an instance of that definition. A Grid service description consists of the WSDL (with OGSI extensions) that defines the Grid service's interfaces and associated semantics; a Grid service instance is an addressable, potentially stateful, and potentially transient instantiation of such a description.

These concepts provide the basic building blocks used to build OGSA-based distributed systems: Grid service descriptions define interfaces and behaviors, and a distributed system comprises a set of Grid service instances that implement those behaviors, have a notion of identity with respect to the other instances in the system, and can be characterized as state coupled with behavior published through type-specific operations.

17.5.2   Service Data

Standard WSDL has no formalized concept of service state. Any state encapsulated by the service is implicit in the service implementation and the semantics of its operations, and the service's interface must include operations for accessing that state. It might appear that this is not too onerous: for example, if a service has internal state elements A, B, and C, one can easily provide external access to that state by defining additional operations GetA, GetB, and GetC—and similarly, SetA, SetB, and SetC, if desired. However, these operations are insufficient if transactional or join semantics are required, for example, if we want to determine whether a service has certain values for A and B at the same time, or to ask a question of a service that combines multiple values. We could presumably define a "GetAB" operation, but the number of such operations tends to grow combinatorially with the number of discrete bits of state.

OGSI addresses these issues by defining WSDL extensions that allow for the explicit declaration of publicly visible state associated with an interface (called service data), and by defining standard operations for accessing (via both queries and subscriptions) that state. Each interface defined in the service description can specify zero or more *service data elements* (SDEs), which are named, typed XML elements, with additional properties such as how they may be modified during the lifetime of the instance. All SDEs defined within a service description's interface(s) are combined to form a logical XML document associated with each service instance that implements that service description. OGSI defines standard operations for accessing an instance's service data document. OGSI also defines standard attributes that can be attached to an SDE to convey additional information about the SDE's lifetime, which are useful when SDE values are propagated to other entities.

SDEs can be used to represent a wide variety of information, including relatively static characteristics of a Grid service instance (e.g., capacity, location, speed), more dynamic state information (e.g., freeSpace, load), information about error conditions (e.g., outOfSpaceError), access control policies, and currently active transfers.

In addition, OGSI service data mechanisms can be used for a wide variety of purposes, such as introspection, discovery, and monitoring. For example, a client may query (introspect) SDEs representing static and dynamic characteristics of a service instance to determine whether the service instance meets its requirements. Or, as we discuss in greater detail in the following, a service instance might be configured to communicate this information using notification operations to one or more registry services so as to support more efficient discovery. Notification mechanisms can also be used to communicate changes in values representing service status (e.g., error conditions and load) to management applications configured to monitor services, thus allowing them to detect and respond to erroneous conditions.

Figure 17.6 provides an example of service data for a simple storage service. Note the gwsdl name on the portType definition, indicating that we are using Grid-extended WSDL. OGSI requires WSDL features planned in the still-in-progress (as of mid-2003) WSDL v1.2, and so this interim gwsdl approach has been adopted until WSDL v1.2 is finalized. Specifically, the gwsdl:portType extends the WSDL v1.1 portType with an *extends* attribute for portType composition and extension, and an open extensibility model that allows for service data elements to be declared as part of the portType.

As this example shows, SDEs are defined in the WSDL that describes a Grid service interface. The standard OGSI interfaces define SDEs, too: for example, Table 17.3 summarizes the SDEs defined in the GridService interface. Note that some SDEs can appear multiple times in an instance's service data document.

17.5.2.1 *Accessing Service Data Elements*

OGSI defines both pull- and push-mode mechanisms for accessing service data. The findServiceData operation associated with the GridService interface provides "pull-mode" access, allowing clients to query a Grid service instance's service data. This operation can accept an extensible set of query expressions, from simple searches for a particular named element, to complex queries containing

```
<wsdl:definitions xmlns:tns="…" targetNamespace="…">
  <gwsdl:portType name="StorageService" extends="ogsi:GridService">
    <wsdl:operation name=getFile>
      …
    </wsdl:operation>

    <sd:serviceData name="capacity" type="xsd:integer" />
    <sd:serviceData name="location" type="xsd:string" />
    <sd:serviceData name="speed" type="xsd:integer" />
    <sd:serviceData name="freeSpace" type="xsd:integer" />
    <sd:serviceData name="load" type="xsd:integer" />
    <sd:serviceData name="outOfSpaceError" type="ogsi:FaultType"
                    minOccurs="0" />
    <sd:serviceData name="accessControlPolicy"
                    type="tns:PolicyType"/>
    <sd:serviceData name="activeTransfer"
                    type="tns:ActiveTransferType"
                    minOccurs="0" maxOccurs="unbounded"/>
  </gwsdl:portType>
</wsdl:definitions>
```

17.6   OGSI WSDL definitions for service data in a simple Grid service.

FIGURE

SDE	#	Description
Interface	1+	Names of the interfaces (portTypes) supported by the Grid service instance
ServiceDataName	0+	Names of the service data elements contained in the instance's service data values document
FactoryLocator	1	The factory that created the instance, or NIL if none
GridServiceHandle	0+	GSHs for the Grid service instance
GridServiceReference	1+	GSRs for the Grid service instance
FindServiceDataExtensibility	1+	Query expression types that can be passed to the findServiceData operation
SetServiceDataExtensibility	2+	Update expression types that can be passed to the setServiceData operation
TerminationTime	1	Earliest and latest termination times of the Grid service instance

17.3   Service Data Elements Defined in the GridService Interface.

TABLE

multiple conditions (e.g., XPath or Xquery). OGSI requires that every service support one simple "by name" query expression, but allows for services to extend this with other query expressions.

OGSI also defines standard mechanisms to "push" delivery of service data elements, for example, notification. Unlike pull-mode access, which is a required operation, push-mode delivery is supported via a set of optional OGSI interfaces: NotificationSource, NotificationSubscription, and NotificationSink.

The OGSI notification framework allows clients to register interest in being notified of particular messages (the *NotificationSource* interface) and supports asynchronous, one-way delivery of such notifications (*NotificationSink*). If a particular service wishes to support subscription of notification messages, it must support the *NotificationSource* interface to manage the subscriptions. A service that wishes to receive notification messages must implement the *NotificationSink* interface, which is used to deliver notification messages.

To start notification from a particular service, a client invokes the subscribe operation on the notification source interface, specifying the notification sink (perhaps different than the client) and an initial lifetime for the subscription (lifetimes are discussed in detail in Section 17.5.4.2.) The notification source creates a Grid service instance that implements the NotificationSubscription portType, which may be used by clients to manage the (soft-state) lifetime of the subscription, and to discover properties of the subscription. A stream of notification messages then flows from the source to the sink, while the sink (or some other client) sends periodic "keepalive" messages to the subscription instance to notify the source that it is still interested in receiving notifications. If reliable delivery is desired, this behavior can be implemented by defining an appropriate reliable protocol binding for this service.

We illustrate the use of these mechanisms by describing how they can be used by a monitoring service to request notifications of excessive load conditions on a storage service. A subscription request issued by the monitoring service to the storage service specifies the following:

+ A *subscription expression*, which describes (a) the content(s) and type(s) of the XML element(s) to be sent from the notification source to the notification sink (e.g., the "load" service data element), and (b) when messages should be sent, based on changes to values within a service instance's service data (e.g., whenever the load value exceeds a threshold).

+ The Grid service instance (the sink) to which notification messages should be delivered (in this example, the monitoring service).

+ An initial lifetime for the subscription. Here, as elsewhere in OGSI, soft-state lifetime management mechanisms are supported.

The OGSI notification framework allows both for direct service-to-service notification message delivery and for integration with various third-party services, such as messaging services commonly used in the commercial world, or custom services that filter, transform, archive, or specially deliver notification messages on behalf of the notification source. Notification semantics are a property of the protocol binding used to deliver the message. For example, a SOAP/HTTP protocol or direct UDP binding would provide point-to-point, best-effort notification, while other bindings (e.g., some proprietary message service) would provide better than best-effort delivery. A multicast protocol binding would support multiple receivers.

17.5.2.2   Service Data Element Schema

OGSI service data and associated operations provide basic machinery for monitoring and managing Grid service instances. Given these mechanisms, one needs to define appropriate service data (and policies for governing who can access the service data) and then link this service data to the appropriate service state; authorized clients can then query the service data, request notifications when it is modified, and/or change the service data's value. Underlying monitoring and management functions can be implemented via application-specific mechanisms or via standards such as CIM (233), SNMP (562), or LDAP (372), as discussed in Chapter 20.

These mechanisms introduce the need for standard schema, and a variety of such standard schema are being defined within OGSA. One area in which discussion has already started concerns *common management models*, a term used to denote an abstract representation of a resource such as a node, interface adaptor, disk, file system, or IP address. Such a model can map directly to a physical resource or alternatively serve as an abstract representation of a logical resource constructed from multiple physical resources to build higher-level services and applications.

Management is the active process of monitoring, modifying, and making decisions about a resource, including the capabilities that use manageability information to perform activities or tasks associated with managing resources. Manageable entities are exposed as Grid services in OGSA. A manageable Grid service (resource) implements the GridService interface plus additional interfaces for the purpose of being used from or included in an application or management tool. Information relevant to the management of a resource is published as service data elements, using schema defined by the common management model and queried through use of the GridService interface's query and subscription operations. Additional interfaces provide manageability interfaces to facilitate traditional systems management disciplines such as performance monitoring, problem determination, configuration, operational support, event notification, discovery, and life-cycle management.

17.5.3   Naming

Because Grid services are dynamic and stateful, we need a way to distinguish one dynamically created service instance from another. For example, we might use this information to communicate to other Grid entities the information needed to access a specific service. Thus, we need a naming scheme for Grid service instances. Such a naming scheme should allow Grid services to be upgraded during their lifetime, for example to support new protocol versions or to add alternative protocols. It is also desirable that a naming scheme not require a fixed mapping of service instances to network addresses, since that would make it difficult to relocate a service instance, as might be required for failover, load balancing, or replicated implementations for scaling.

OGSI addresses these requirements by defining a two-level naming scheme for Grid service instances based on simple, abstract, long-lived Grid service handles (GSH) that can be mapped by handle resolution services (i.e., services that implement the OGSI-defined HandleResolver interface) to concrete but potentially shorter-lived Grid service references.

A Grid service handle is a globally unique name that distinguishes that specific Grid service instance from all other Grid service instances that have existed, exist now, or will exist in the future. (If a Grid service fails and is restarted in such a way as to preserve its state, then it is essentially the same instance, and the same GSH can be used.) A GSH is represented using a Uniform Resource Identifier.

A GSH carries no protocol- or instance-specific information such as network address or supported protocol bindings. Instead, this information is encapsulated, along with all other instance-specific information required to interact with a specific service instance, into a single abstraction called a Grid service reference (GSR). The format and content of a GSR are dependent on the underlying protocol binding, but in a SOAP environment one can expect to see GSRs represented as WSDL documents containing <service> and <binding> elements. Unlike a GSH, which is invariant, the GSR(s) for a Grid service instance can change over that service's lifetime. A GSR may have an explicit expiration time or may become invalid at any time during a service's lifetime, and OGSI defines handle resolution mechanisms for obtaining an updated GSR from the more stable GSH.

GSRs are basically network-wide pointers to specific Grid service instances hosted in (potentially remote) execution environments. A client application can use a GSR to send requests (represented by the operations defined in the interfaces of the target service) directly to the specific instance at the specified network-attached service endpoint identified by the GSR. The result of using a GSR whose lifetime has expired is undefined. Holding a valid GSR does not guarantee access to a Grid service instance, local policy or access control constraints (for example, a maximum number of concurrent requests) may prohibit servicing a request. In addition, the referenced Grid service instance may have failed, preventing the use of the GSR.

The OGSI specification states that a GSH must globally and for all time refer to the same Grid service instance. This statement does not imply that the GSH must always refer to the same or a single network address. A service instance may be implemented in any way, as long as it obeys the semantics associated with its service description, that is, the portType(s) that the service instance implements. Thus, for example (see Figure 17.7), a service instance may be migrated from one location to another during its execution: the handle resolver simply returns different GSRs before and after migration. (If migration is anticipated at a particular time in the future, the lifetime associated with the service instance's GSR(s) can be set appropriately.)

On the other hand, the implementation of a service may be distributed or replicated across multiple resources, as long as it obeys the semantics associated with its service description. A single GSH would be associated with this service, though that GSH may resolve to different GSRs referring to different resources, based on such factors as resource availability and utilization, locality of a client, and client privileges. Some service descriptions may require tight state coherency between any such replicated implementations. For example, the semantics of the service

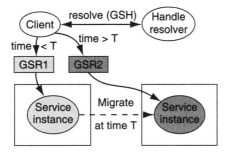

17.7

FIGURE

A GSH resolves to a different GSR for a migrated service instance before and after migration occurs, at time T.

description may require that the service move through a series of well-defined states in response to a particular sequence of messages, thus requiring state coherence regardless of how GSHs are resolved to GSRs. In that case, constructing such a replicated implementation might be difficult. However, other service descriptions that allow for looser consistency between the various members of the distributed service implementation may be defined.

17.5.4   Service Life Cycle

One of the major distinctions between a Grid service and an ordinary Web service is the underlying assumption that Grid services may be transient, created as part of the normal operation of the infrastructure. This assumption has two consequences: we must have mechanisms to create new services, and we must be able to specify assertions about the lifetime of a service. We address these two factors in the following sections.

17.5.4.1   Creating Transient Services: Factories

Grid service instances may be created either via manual out-of-band mechanisms (like any Web service) or via a request to a *factory* operation. Although there are expected to be a variety of domain-specific factory operations in various interfaces, OGSI defines a standard, extensible Factory interface to accommodate many common and simple cases. The Factory interface's createService operation creates a requested Grid service with a specified interface and returns the GSH and initial GSR for the new service instance. It should also register the new service instance with a handle resolution service.

Returning to our file transfer service of Figure 17.2, recall that this service fills requests to perform data transfers. We can implement the file transfer service as a factory that responds to a request to perform a transfer by creating a new instance of a PerformTransfer service that is then responsible for monitoring and managing the progress of the requested transfer. This representation of the file transfer as a service instance has the advantage that normal OGSI naming, service data, and lifetime management mechanisms can be used for subsequent management.

This example emphasizes that different hosting environments may implement Grid service instances in different ways, depending on their own capabilities and/or the characteristics of the service instances being created. In some circumstances, Grid service instances may be heavyweight entities corresponding to operating system processes; in others (including, probably, the file transfer example just discussed), a Grid service instance may be represented simply by an entry in

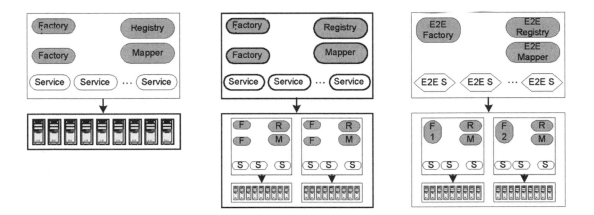

17.8

FIGURE

Three different hosting environment structures, as described in the text. From left to right: simple, virtual hosting, and multicomponent.

a table. The point of this discussion is that the OGSA programmer should not assume that creating a Grid service instance is an expensive operation, but should nevertheless be aware that costs may vary significantly between implementations.

Like any OGSA interface, the Factory interface can be virtualized in various ways. Figure 17.8 depicts three possible approaches. First, the Factory interface can be implemented directly by a hosting environment (e.g., .NET, J2EE, Linux system) that provides mechanisms for creating and subsequently managing new service instances. Such a factory processes a client createService request by invoking hosting-environment-specific capabilities to create the new instance. For example, a J2EE-based factory might create a new Enterprise Java Bean for the new instance, while in a high-performance computing environment the factory might map createService requests into requests to an underlying scheduler able to start jobs on a Linux cluster. Services may be implemented in different ways in these two cases, but such differences are transparent to service requestors, who see only the factory and service interfaces.

Second, one can construct a *virtual hosting environment* that creates services by delegating the request to other factory services. This strategy could be useful in a Web serving environment, in which a new computer is integrated into the active pool by asking an appropriate factory service to instantiate a "Web-serving" service on an idle computer.

The third approach depicted in Figure 17.8 shows a virtual hosting environment that defines new semantics by creating higher-level "virtual services" comprising multiple components. A request to create an instance of such a service is implemented by asking lower-level factories to create multiple service instances and by composing the behaviors of those multiple lower-level service instances into that single, higher-level service instance.

In each case, the "hosting environment" that implements the factory interface is responsible not only for creating the new service instance but also for registering it with a handle resolution service, obtaining a GSH, and performing other house-keeping tasks required to manage the new service instance. The factories would also, presumably, be registered with appropriate discovery services so that clients could discover their existence.

These examples illustrate how Grid service mechanisms can provide uniform interfaces to collections of distributed resources. Implementations that map to native platform resources and APIs enable seamless integration of higher-level Grid ser-vices such as those just described with underlying platform components. Furthermore, service sets associated with multiple virtual hosting environments can map to the same underlying physical resources, with those services represented as logically distinct at one level but sharing physical resource systems at lower levels.

17.5.4.2 Service Lifetime Management

The introduction of transient service instances raises the issue of determining the service's lifetime: that is, determining when a service can or should be terminated so that associated resources can be recovered. Under normal operating condi-tions, a transient service instance is created to perform a specific task and termin-ates either on completion of this task or via an explicit request from the requestor or from another service designated by the requestor. In distributed systems, how-ever, components may fail and messages may be lost. One result is that a service may never see an expected explicit termination request, thus causing it to consume resources indefinitely.

OGSA addresses this problem through a soft-state approach (189, 697) in which Grid service instances are created with a specified lifetime. The initial life-time can be extended by a specified time period by explicit request of the client or another Grid service acting on the client's behalf (subject of course to policy). If that time period expires without having received a reaffirmation of interest from a client, either the service instance's hosting environment or the service instance itself is at liberty to terminate the service instance and release any asso-ciated resources. The OGSI mechanisms used to manage the life cycle of a Grid service instance in this way work as follows.

Negotiating an initial lifetime. When requesting the creation of a new Grid ser-vice instance through a factory's createService operation (Section 17.5.4.1), a client indicates earliest and latest acceptable initial termination times. The factory selects an initial termination time and returns this to the client with the GSH. The termination time of "infinity" indicates that the Grid service instance plans to exist indefinitely and is therefore not subject to soft-state lifetime management.

Explicit termination.   The Grid service interface's destroy operation allows a client to request that a Grid service instance terminate immediately.

Requesting a lifetime modification.   A client requests a lifetime modification by directing keepalive messages, as implemented by the GridService interface's requestTerminationBefore or requestTerminationAfter messages, to the Grid service instance. These messages specify a maximum and minimum acceptable new lifetime, respectively; the service instance responds by selecting a new lifetime and returning this to the client. Note that such messages are effectively idempotent: the result of a sequence of requests is the same, even if intermediate requests are lost, as long as not so many requests are lost that the service instance's lifetime expires.

The periodicity of keepalive messages can be determined by the client based on the initial lifetime negotiated with the service instance (and perhaps renegotiated via subsequent keepalive messages) and knowledge about network reliability. The interval size allows trade-offs between currency of information and overhead.

These mechanisms might be used in the data transfer example of Section 17.3 as follows. A long-lived data transfer can represent a substantial investment of resources, and so we might well want to use lifetime management mechanisms to ensure that these resources are recuperated in the event of client failure. Thus, we treat a file transfer service instance as an entity subject to lifetime management. Things then proceed as follows:

1. A request to initiate a transfer (i.e., to create a file transfer service instance) leads to the negotiation of an initial lifetime. This lifetime will presumably represent a compromise between the potentially competing goals of the client and service, with each being concerned either to make the lifetime as long as possible, to reduce or eliminate the need for subsequent lifetime extensions, or alternatively to make the lifetime short, so as to reduce wasted resources in the event of failure.

2. The client sends periodic keepalive (requestTerminationAfter) requests to indicate its continued interest in the transfer.

3. At some point, one of three things happens:

   a. The transfer completes, and the file transfer service instance terminates.

   b. The client fails, and its failure to send further keepalive messages leads to the destruction of the transfer service instance once its lifetime expires.

   c. The client decides that it is no longer interested in the transfer and, to conserve resources, performs an explicit destroy of the transfer service instance.

The OGSI approach to lifetime management has the desirable property that a client knows, or can determine, when a Grid service instance expects to terminate. Thus, a client can determine when a service instance has terminated and its resources have been recovered, even in the face of system faults (e.g., failures of servers, networks, clients). The client knows how long it has to request a final status from the service instance or to request an extension to the service's lifetime. Moreover, it also knows that if system faults occur, it need not continue attempting to contact a service after a known termination time, and that any resources associated with that service would be released after that time—unless another client succeeded in extending the lifetime. In brief, lifetime management enables robust termination and failure detection, by clearly defining the lifetime semantics of a service instance. Similarly, a hosting environment is guaranteed that resource consumption is bounded, even in the face of system failures outside its control. If the termination time of a service is reached, the hosting environment can reclaim all associated resources.

At the same time, this approach to lifetime management provides a service with considerable autonomy. Lifetime extension requests from clients are not mandatory: the service can apply its own policies on granting such request. A service can decide at any time to change its lifetime, either in response to a lifetime extension request by a client or for any other reason. A service instance can also cancel itself at any time, for example if resource constraints and priorities dictate that it relinquishes its resources. Subsequent client requests that refer to this service will fail.

17.5.5 Fault Model

Automatic adaptation to faults, as can be required in a Grid setting, requires the ability to return faults (also called exceptions in some programming languages) that are not only rich with information about the cause of the fault but also consistent in their content, semantics, and means of delivery. Thus, OGSI defines a common approach for conveying fault information from operations. This common approach is used consistently within OGSI itself and is recommended for use within other OGSA components and applications.

The OGSI fault model comprises a standard XSD type, ogsi:FaultType, which defines two required elements, the originating service and a time stamp, and several optional elements, including plain language description(s) of the fault, further ogsi:FaultType element(s) describing an underlying cause for the fault, a fault code to provide support for legacy fault-reporting systems, such as POSIX errno, and extensibility elements that can be used to communicate arbitrary additional information.

It is expected that a Grid service operation will define one XSD type for each fault it returns, where that type is an extension of the ogsi:FaultType. For example, the HandleResolver::findByHandle operation, which accepts a Grid service handle as input and returns a Grid service reference as output, defines faults including InvalidHandleFault, NoReferencesAvailableFault, and RedirectionFault. The RedirectionFault extends ogsi:FaultType with a reference to another handle resolver.

17.5.6   Service Groups

The final three OGSI interfaces that we describe, ServiceGroup, ServiceGroupEntry, and ServiceGroupRegistration, are concerned with organizing groups of service instances. A service group is a Grid service that maintains information about a group of Grid service instances. Any arbitrary collection of service instances can be grouped in this way; they need not have the same interface, creator, lifetime, purpose, or any other point in common. The only requirement is that someone wants to group them. Examples of situations in which service group mechanisms might be used include the virtual hosting environments of Figure 17.8, the monitor and broker of Figure 17.2, and a registry service used to keep track of service instances created within a particular VO.

The basic ideas underlying the service group construct are illustrated in Figure 17.9, which shows a factory that uses service group mechanisms to maintain a registry of the service instances that it creates. The ServiceGroup portType defines entry service data elements to represent the zero or more member service instances that form a service group. Other service group features not shown here include the following:

✦ The ServiceGroup portType also defines an optional SDE, membershipContentRule that can be used to define constraints on the service instances allowed as members.

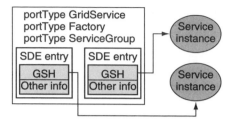

17.9

FIGURE

Using the ServiceGroup interface to manage a group of service instances created by a factory.

◆ Each entry SDE may also contain a reference to a service instance implementing the ServiceGroupEntry portType. The ServiceGroupEntry portType provides independent lifetime management functions for individual entries and a unique key (GSH) for each entry, and can be extended to provide more advanced entry management functions.

◆ The ServiceGroupRegistration portType defines add and remove operations that can be used to add and remove ServiceGroupEntry instances from a ServiceGroup.

As elsewhere in OGSI, the basic functionality is limited, providing just a basic service grouping framework. The true power of this framework emerges when it is specialized in various ways, for example by extending ServiceGroupEntry to provide specialized entry management functions.

17.6   OGSA SERVICES AND SCHEMA

OGSI is the foundation upon which OGSA services are built. OGSI mechanisms for creating, managing, and exchanging information among Grid services are useful in and of themselves. However, their true value to the programmer emerges when they are used to construct higher-level interfaces and associated behaviors that provide functionalities not supported directly within OGSI.

A wide variety of functionality can and presumably will be defined by many different developers to meet various specific application requirements. What we term here "OGSA services and schema" are those Grid components that are sufficiently broadly applicable that we can expect to see them in essentially any Grid system: for example, service discovery, service management, monitoring, security, data access, and messaging. The definition of standard interfaces, behaviors, and schema for such components facilitates the development of reusable components and interoperable systems by making it possible, for example, for a service implemented by one developer to be discovered via a registry produced by another, for services from different sources to communicate faults in a consistent fashion, and for common monitoring and management capabilities to work across a wide variety of services.

The potential range of OGSA services is vast, and at the time of writing (mid-2003) we are just now beginning to understand the best ways to factor Grid functionality into OGSA services and define the appropriate interfaces. However, we are able to outline the principal elements as defined or planned at the time of writing (mid-2003), and we also refer the reader to later chapters for additional details. We group services into three broad groups: core services, data- and information-related services, and computation management services. Not all of those described here may eventually become standardized as part of OGSA, but all provide useful capabilities.

17.6.1   Core Services

Core services address such fundamental issues as name resolution, service discovery, security, policy, and messaging. In our view, these services are so fundamental that some variant of them must eventually be supported by any OGSA-compliant service. Needless to say, additional domain-specific specializations and variants of these core service functionalities may also be defined.

Name resolution and discovery.   OGSI's two-level name space requires HandleResolver services capable of resolving from GSHs to GSRs. Standard behaviors must be defined for the OGSI HandleResolver interface to permit GSH resolution in various settings. In addition, we expect to see standard service registration and discovery interfaces for maintaining and querying mappings from semantic information (e.g., key words or directory structures) to GSHs. These latter interfaces can build on OGSI ServiceGroup mechanisms.

Service domains.   It is common practice for an OGSA-compliant "service" to be implemented via a collection of internal services managed in some coordinated fashion. Service domain interfaces and behaviors facilitate the creation and operation of, and the integration of new services into, such *service domains*.

Security.   This category is wide-reaching, encompassing issues relating to the management and verification of credentials; privacy and integrity; and policy (see next item). Security services are discussed in more detail in Chapter 21.

Policy. A policy is a definitive goal, course, or method of action based on a set of conditions to guide and determine present and future decisions. Policies are implemented or executed within a particular context, such as security, workload management, and qualities of service, and provide a set of rules to administer, manage, and control access to Grid resources. OGSA policy interfaces can provide a framework for creating, managing, validating, distributing, transforming, resolving, and enforcing policies within a distributed environment.

Messaging, queuing, and logging. Messaging and queuing functions must be exposed via appropriate OGSA interfaces, which will presumably include publication-subscription (pub-sub), topic-based messaging, and queue-based messages. A logging service is a form of mediator between message producer and message consumer that can provide archival storage for message streams. Defining standard interfaces to logging services is important because it allows different clients to exploit the same common logging service implementations.

Events. An event is a representation of an occurrence in a system or application component that may be of interest to other parties. Standard means of representing, communicating, transforming, reconciling, and recording events are important for interoperability.

Metering and accounting. Accounting mechanisms are used to collect, deliver, reconcile, store securely, and manage information about resource usage and/or charges. Accounting often involves extracting information that may come from a logging service to determine billing. Accounting schemas are also needed.

17.6.2   Data and Information Services

This second set of anticipated OGSA services is concerned with the management of data and information. A broad review of Grid data and knowledge management functions is provided in Chapters 22 and 23. In brief, interfaces are required for the following functions:

Data naming and access. The need to be able to access, federate, and integrate into computations diverse forms of remote data leads to a need for interfaces for naming and accessing data resources consistently across relational databases, XML databases, and file systems. These interfaces provide the foundation upon which higher-level data management and integration capabilities are built.

Replication. Standard interfaces must be defined for tracking, discovering, and performing replication of data resources. As discussed in Chapter 22, it is anticipated that standard interfaces can be defined for basic functions (e.g., for replica location (176)) upon which can be defined various higher-level and domain-specific functions.

Metadata and provenance. Standard interfaces are also required for maintaining various forms of metadata about data resources (see Chapter 23). One important class of metadata is concerned with provenance, describing and tracking how data are created, and recreating the steps required to regenerate data on demand (141, 285).

17.6.3 Resource and Service Management

Another set of standard interfaces is concerned with the management of resources, or as we may also say in a service-oriented framework, *services*. Required functionality includes provisioning, orchestration, transactions, administration, and deployment.

Provisioning and resource management. As discussed in greater detail in Chapter 18, standard interfaces are required for negotiating service-level agreements (SLAs) between resource consumers and resource providers and for dynamic resource allocation and redistribution consistent with SLA policy.

Service orchestration. Standard interfaces that can allow for service-independent mechanisms for describing and managing the choreography of a set of interacting services are required. The DAGman and Chimera systems discussed in Chapter 19 are relevant here, and we can expect to see Web service choreography systems (53) extended to deal with Grid services.

Transactions. Transaction interfaces encapsulate protocols used to assure all parties that transactions have executed correctly in a distributed environment. As discussed in Chapter 19, transactions are both important and problematic in Grid environments. Again, proposals for Web services standards in this area may be relevant to Grids.

Administration and deployment. Standard interfaces are required for such tasks as software deployment, change management, and identity management and for deploying needed software (operating system, middleware, application) and data into hosting environments.

17.7   CASE STUDY REVISITED

We return to our storage services example and present a more complete picture of its implementation, expanding in particular on aspects relating to SLA negotiation and enforcement. Recall from Section 17.3 that the example involves the movement of files from one storage system to another, an operation that needs to be performed reliably and in a timely fashion. To minimize the potential for problems, the framework allows for the reservation of storage space on the destination storage system. Because a file transfer can be a long-running operation, the framework also addresses monitoring of transfer progress and notification in the event of problems. The overall framework, illustrated in Figure 17.10, comprises four different types of factory service (shaded) and one registry service (not shaded).

Each distinct factory service type illustrated in Figure 17.10 supports one or more interfaces that allow for the creation of dynamic service instances that are then used to maintain SLAs, perform transfers, or monitor transfer status:

✦ The *storage service* supports two factory interfaces, for storage management and data transfer, that define operations to create service instances for managing a disk space reservation and an individual transfer (via, for example, GridFTP), respectively.

✦ The *reliable transfer service* supports one factory interface, for the creation of file transfer service instances that in turn actually initiate and perform file transfers.

✦ The *storage broker service* supports one factory interface, for the creation of storage broker service instances responsible for negotiating end-to-end quality-of-service guarantees (via, specifically, the negotiation of storage reservations at the source and destination storage system).

✦ The *monitoring service* supports one factory interface, for the creation of a monitoring and notification service instance responsible for monitoring an individual transfer.

We discuss the purpose and functioning of these various components in more detail in the following. However, we note briefly here that a complete transfer will involve negotiation with a storage broker service (for an end-to-end reservation) followed by a request to a transfer service (to initiate the storage-service–to–storage-service transfer, plus an associated monitoring service).

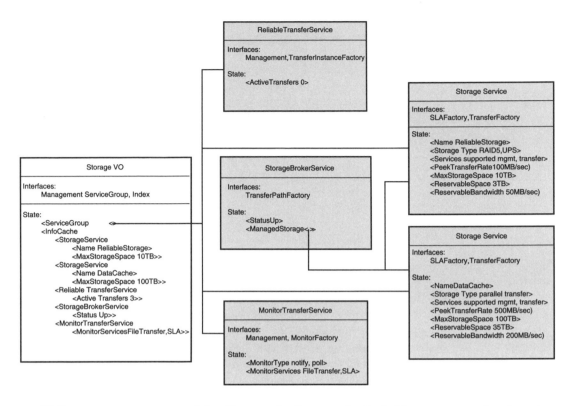

17.10

FIGURE

Components of the file transfer framework. Shaded boxes are service factories; unshaded boxes are instances created by a factory.

The registry service (*StorageVO*) is used to keep track of and support discovery of the various factory services depicted in Figure 17.10. Whereas in this simple example we have only five services to keep track of, we might reasonably have hundreds or thousands in a real Grid environment. One simple way to enable service discovery is to collect relevant service data elements from all available services. Then a single query can be used to identify which services may address application requirements. In our example, the StorageVO service instance fills this function. This service uses OGSI's ServiceGroup mechanism to keep track of the services considered to be available to the VO. In practice, an OGSA implementation such as GT3 will provide a sophisticated *IndexService* that augments the basic ServiceGroup with a variety of caching mechanisms, cache update policies, and rich mechanisms for sorting and indexing the resulting service data elements.

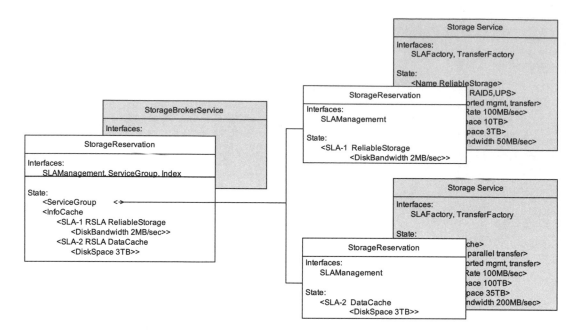

17.11

FIGURE

The result of negotiating an SLA with the storage system. White boxes are service instances produced by underlying shaded factory services.

We now describe in more detail the function of the other services illustrated in Figure 17.10. Prior to initiating a transfer, we may want to allocate storage space at the file destination to ensure that we will not run out of disk space. Similarly, for performance reasons we may want to ensure that we will have a minimal amount of disk bandwidth at the source. Both objectives can be realized by negotiating an advance reservation with the storage systems in question. As we discussed earlier, this agreement can take the form of an SLA between the storage system and the consumer of the service capability. One approach to obtaining the required SLAs would be for the application to negotiate directly with each underlying service. However, it is often advantageous for the negotiation process to be delegated to a third party, called a broker, to achieve a more modular application design and perhaps also for reasons of policy. For example, to ensure that resource usage is consistent with community goals, a VO might require that all resource negotiation take place via a community broker.

The result of this SLA negotiation process is shown in Figure 17.11. Each storage system now has an SLA instantiated on it, represented by an instance of a

StorageReservation service. To represent the SLA in its entirety, the *StorageBrokerService* creates a single virtual SLA, which responds to the same interface as the component SLAs and uses the Index interface to create a unified view of the SLA state. We have in effect used a single collective layer OGSA service to virtualize a set of underlying resource layer services.

Once the resources for the transfer have been allocated, it is time to initiate the transfer. A single file transfer will require the interaction of two different types of services. The actual transfer is performed by a data movement service while a higher reliable data transfer service initiates the data connections, monitors its progress, and keeps persistent data on the transfer to provide robust behavior across failure.

With this model in mind, we can now go through the steps required to initiate the file transfer. The first step is to locate the *ReliableTransferService* and use its interface to create an instance of a *DataTransfer* service. This service is intended to be highly reliable and may use methods such as checkpoint/restart to increase its robustness. The definition of service semantics and service naming in OGSI was crafted so as to allow a single service interface to be implemented via a replicated service implementation, so a replicated implementation is also possible.

Before it can initiate the transfer, the DataTransfer service must create the service endpoints for the data movement. It does this by invoking the appropriate factory methods in the storage service to create a *Delivery* service instance that can access data located on the storage service. These Delivery services (shown in Figure 17.12, labeled GridFTP after a commonly used delivery mechanism) provide a control interface that can be used to create a data channel between two servers, and to cause a data blob (e.g., file) to be transferred over this data channel. The data transfer service uses the control interface to monitor the progress of the transfer.

Once the Delivery services have been created, we need to associate the previously negotiated SLA with the services. This information could be passed in as an argument to the factory method when the Delivery services are created. An alternative approach would be to go back to the storage system management interface and present it with a handle to both the service and the SLA and have it bind the two together. The advantage of this approach is that it provides a means of rebinding the service to a different SLA should this become necessary at some point during the execution. SLAs and binding are discussed in greater detail in Chapter 18.

At this point, we have initiated the desired file transfer between the two storage systems. The final step is to set up a monitoring infrastructure so that we can be notified when something goes wrong. Each instance of a monitor behaves like

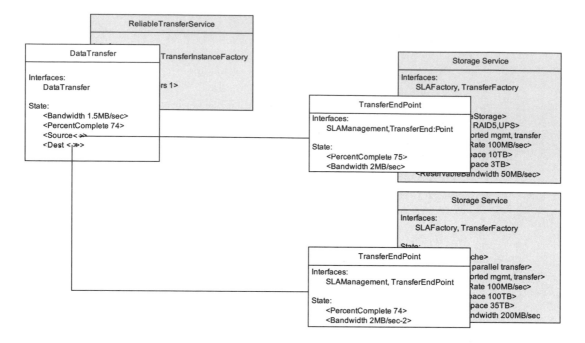

17.12

FIGURE

Establishment of delivery service instances to effect the data transfer.

an index service, allowing other services to register to it and collecting service data. The resulting structure is shown in Figure 17.13.

This collecting of service status data into a single location allows us to synthesize complex conditions to which the end user can then subscribe (using OGSI notification mechanisms) in order to be notified if the collection of services enters a state of interest. For example, a user (or other system component, such as a fault determination or performance-monitoring system) might want to be notified of transfer failures, transfer performance levels that violate specified bounds, or preempted storage reservations.

A final observation is that we have now created a somewhat complex arrangement consisting of many distributed service instances. While the factory services are shared across the VO, and hence have long lifetimes, the dynamically created services are all of use only to this application. Hence, it is desirable to have a safe way of shutting down the entire assembly regardless of the state of any of its pieces. This is where OGSI's soft-state lifetime management mechanisms come into play. With appropriate nesting of service lifetimes, the task of maintaining lifetimes can be distributed in a hierarchical fashion. For example, the lifetime of

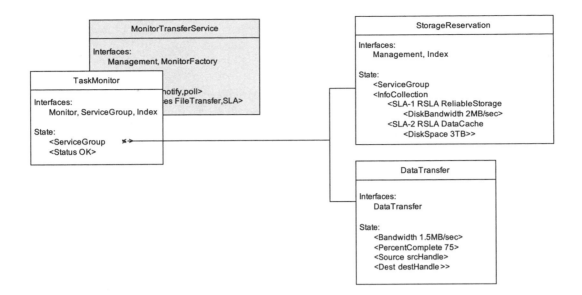

17.13

Monitoring infrastructure for the case study.

FIGURE

the Delivery services is scoped by the lifetime of the *TransferService*. Therefore, a reasonable strategy would be for the TransferService to send lifetime extension requests to the Delivery services. A similar approach can be taken with the *SLAService*. For example, one could have the lifetimes of both the SLAService and the TransferService extended by the *MonitorService*. Finally, updating the lifetime of the MonitorService should be the responsibility of either the application or the user that requested the transfer in the first place.

17.8   OTHER ISSUES

Typed interfaces and other features of service-oriented architectures are frequently cited as fundamental characteristics of so-called distributed object-based systems. However, various other aspects of distributed object models (as traditionally defined) are specifically not required or prescribed in the service-oriented architecture used for Grid computing: specifically, implementation inheritance, service mobility, development approach, and hosting technology. Thus, OGSI and other aspects of OGSA neither require nor prevent implementations based on object technologies that support inheritance at either the interface or the implementation level. There is no requirement in the architecture to expose the notion of implementation inheritance at either the client side or the service provider side of the usage contract. In addition, the Grid service specification does not prescribe, dictate, or prevent the use of any particular development approach or hosting technology for the Grid service. For example, there is nothing about OGSI that is Java-specific: one can implement OGSI behaviors in C, C#, Python, or other languages, and indeed implementations in these languages are appearing.

We also point out that service-oriented architectures are not without potential problems. For example, the interface definition language may be insufficiently expressive to allow for the convenient representation and invocation of interesting services and associated operations; features of the interface definition language and/or its implementation may hinder high-performance execution; critical aspects of the service-oriented architecture (e.g., security) may be left unspecified, or may be limited in their capabilities; and/or there may not be the critical mass of users and developers for the other benefits listed previously to apply. It appears that the Web services base and the derivative Open Grid Services Architecture described in this chapter and book may have overcome these potential limitations in ways that previous distributed systems technologies (e.g., CORBA, DCE, COM) have not. However, despite promising early results, it is still relatively early in the adoption and application of this technology, and surprises may lie ahead.

17.9   OGSA IMPLEMENTATIONS

We first make some general observations concerning OGSA implementation techniques and then describe specific approaches adopted in OGSI implementations.

17.9.1   Principles

The following observations are based on material in the OGSI specification (659). OGSA (and, in particular, OGSI) does not dictate a particular implementation architecture for OGSA services and the service provider "hosting environments" that support their execution. A variety of approaches are possible, ranging from implementing the Grid service instance directly as an operating system process to a more specialized component model such as J2EE. In the former case, most or even all support for standard Grid service behaviors (invocation, lifetime management, registration, etc.) is encapsulated within the user process (for example,

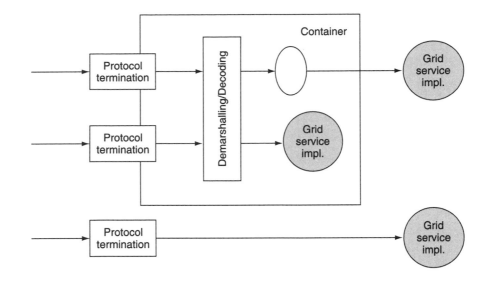

17.14

FIGURE

Two alternative approaches to the implementation of argument demarshaling functions in a Grid service hosting environment.

via linking with a standard library); in the latter case, many of these behaviors are supported by the hosting environment.

Figure 17.14 illustrates these differences by showing two different approaches to the implementation of argument demarshalling functions. We assume that, as is the case for many Grid services, the invocation message is received at a network protocol termination point (e.g., an HTTP servlet engine) that converts the data in the invocation message into a format consumable by the hosting environment. At the top of the figure, we show two Grid service instances (the circles) associated with container-managed components (for example, Enterprise Java Beans within a J2EE container). Here, the message is dispatched to these components, with the container providing facilities for demarshaling and decoding the incoming message from a format (such as an XML/SOAP message) into an invocation of the component in native programming language. In some circumstances (the lower circle), the entire behavior of a Grid service is completely encapsulated within the component. In other cases (the upper circle), a component will collaborate with other server-side executables, perhaps through an adapter layer, to complete the implementation of the Grid service behavior.

At the bottom of the figure, we depict another scenario in which the entire Grid service behavior, including the demarshalling/decoding of the network message, is encapsulated within a single executable. Although this approach may have some efficiency advantages, it provides little opportunity for reuse of functionality between Grid service implementations.

A container implementation may provide a range of functionality beyond simple argument demarshaling, such as lifetime management, authentication and authorization, and request logging. For example, the container implementation may provide lifetime management functions, intercepting lifetime management messages and terminating service instances when a service lifetime expires or an explicit destruction request is received. Thus, we can avoid the need to reimplement these common behaviors in different Grid service implementations.

17.9.2   Globus Toolkit Version 3 and Other OGSI Implementations

As discussed in Chapter 4, the Globus Toolkit is an open source software product that has been developed since 1996 to provide middleware services and libraries for the construction of Grid applications. It comprises components for authentication and authorization, communication, job submission, data transfer, resource monitoring and discovery, and so forth. In other words, it implements many of the OGSA functions described previously.

The recently released Globus Toolkit version 3.0 (GT3) provides a complete implementation of OGSI, and has refactored many of its capabilities into OGSI-compliant services. For example, GT3 defines OGSI-compliant services for discovery of services, submission and monitoring of program execution jobs (671), and reliable file transfer. Other GT capabilities, such as data delivery, replica location, and community authorization, are being refactored to be OGSI compliant. Although these services cannot yet be properly termed OGSA services, since they have not yet been standardized, they nonetheless begin to demonstrate the power of OGSI. We expect that many GT3 services will provide a basis for the definition of OGSA standard service interfaces.

Several other OGSI implementations have been or are being developed. For example, the pyGlobus package has been extended to implement OGSI within a Python environment (386), while the UNICORE project [560] has a Java implementation.

17.10   FUTURE DIRECTIONS

We review briefly some key areas in which further research and development is required to advance the development and range of applicability of OGSA. Further details are provided in later chapters.

Services and tools. The set of OGSA services needs to be expanded in many directions, including but certainly not limited to security (Chapter 21), resource management (Chapter 18), data and knowledge management (Chapters 22 and 23), instrumentation and troubleshooting (Chapter 20), and workflow. New tools are required to facilitate the integration of Grids into different application scenarios.

Implementation. Practical experience with OGSA-based Grids is raising, and will continue to raise, many implementation challenges, relating for example to the need for high-performance protocols, lightweight service instance implementations, and effective sandboxing technologies.

Semantics. Current Web services and OGSA technologies provide an expressive interface definition language for protocol specification, but no formal mechanisms for expressing the behavior of individual services. The development of such mechanisms will certainly be important, at least in certain domains. So will the development of mechanisms for analyzing, and reasoning about, the behavior of service compositions. See Chapter 23 for further discussion of these topics.

Scalability. The future of distributed systems will clearly feature radical scaling in multiple dimensions. Our technologies must be able to deal with increasingly large numbers of entities, with potentially billions being quite feasible in the not-too-distant future. We also need technologies that can scale to increasingly complex communities and interactions, including "service economies" that may feature extremely large numbers of mutually distrustful participants. (Thus, for example, reputation management services are likely to be important.) Also, as embedded and mobile systems become ever-more sophisticated and prevalent, the need to be able to scale down to small footprints will become increasingly important. These and other dimensions of scaling introduce challenging issues. Is the current OGSA framework a good basis for future development? Are alternative, lighter-weight foundations required? Are new or different primitives required to support highly distributed, autonomous infrastructures?

17.11 SUMMARY

We have described in some detail the essential elements of OGSA, which supports, via standard interfaces and conventions, the creation, termination, management, and invocation of *stateful, transient services as named, managed entities with dynamic, managed lifetime.* Although the reader must turn to other sources to learn how to write OGSA services and applications, the level of detail provided here should have provided a good understanding of the purpose and structure of OGSA and of techniques that can be used to apply OGSA to distributed computing problems.

Within OGSA, everything is represented as a Grid service, that is, a (potentially transient) service that conforms to a set of conventions (expressed using WSDL) for such purposes as lifetime management, discovery of characteristics, and notification. Grid service implementations can target native platform facilities for integration with, and of, existing IT infrastructures. Standard interfaces for creating, registering, and discovering Grid services can be configured to create various forms of VO structure.

An important merit of this service-oriented model is that all components of the environment can be virtualized. By providing a core set of consistent interfaces from which all Grid services are implemented, we ease the construction of hierarchical, higher-order services that can be treated in a uniform way across layers of abstraction. Virtualization also enables mapping of multiple logical resource instances onto the same physical resource, composition of services regardless of implementation, and management of resources within a VO based on composition from lower-level resources. It is virtualization of Grid services that underpins the ability for mapping common service semantic behavior seamlessly onto native platform facilities.

The development of OGSA represents a natural evolution of the Globus Toolkit 2.0, in which the key concepts of factory, registry, reliable and secure invocation, and so on exist, but in a less general and flexible form than here, and without the benefits of a uniform interface definition language. In effect, OGSA refactors key design elements so that, for example, common notification mechanisms are used for service registration and service state. OSGA also further abstracts these elements so that they can be applied at any level to virtualize VO resources. The Globus Toolkit provides the basis for an open source OGSA implementation, Globus Toolkit 3.0, which supports existing Globus Toolkit APIs as well as WSDL interfaces. Other implementations are available from other sources.

The development of OGSA also represents a natural evolution of Web services. By integrating support for transient, stateful service instances with existing Web services technologies, OGSA extends significantly the power of the Web services framework, while requiring only minor extensions to existing technologies.

ACKNOWLEDGMENTS

We thank Ravi Madduri for his help with examples, Brian Carpenter for suggesting Figure 17.5, and the contributors to the OGSI specification for their assistance with the development of the material presented here. This work was supported in part by the Mathematical, Information, and Computational Sciences Division subprogram of the Office of Advanced Scientific Computing Research, Office of Science, U.S. Department of Energy, under Contract W-31-109-Eng-38, and by IBM.

FURTHER READING

For more information on the topics covered in this chapter, see *www.mkp.com/grid2* and the Global Grid Forum's OGSA-related working groups. In addition, we recommend the book *Building Web Services with Java: Making Sense of XML, SOAP, WSDL, and UDDI* (320) as an introduction to Web services.

18

Resource and Service Management

Karl Czajkowski, Ian Foster, and Carl Kesselman

*T*he term *resource management* refers to the operations used to control how capabilities provided by Grid resources and services are made available to other entities, whether users, applications, or services. Strictly speaking, resource management is concerned not with the core function of a resource or service—that is, what it does for clients—but rather with the manner in which this function is performed, such as when a requested operation starts or how long it takes to complete.

Early work on resource management in networks and Grids has led to the development of a range of management abstractions and interfaces specialized to the different classes of entities that need to be managed. For example, integrated (133, 697) and differentiated services (124) have been developed for networks (Chapter 1:19), Grid resource allocation manager (GRAM) for computational resources (205), and storage resource manager (SRM) functions for storage (588) (Chapter 22). However, these domain-specific approaches become increasingly unwieldy and inappropriate as more sophisticated applications demand increased levels of control. In future Grids, resource management functions must permeate the Grid infrastructure, and we will require broadly applicable basic management functions that can be applied to a range of resources and services in a uniform fashion.

In this chapter, we both define the Grid resource management problem and present a set of general mechanisms that can be used to address the challenges just noted. Our approach is to introduce a generalized resource management framework and use it as a basis for characterizing existing approaches and for defining a direction for resource management development, particularly as framed within the Open Grid Services Architecture (279) (OGSA, Chapter 17).

18.1   RESOURCE MANAGEMENT ON THE GRID

At the heart of the Grid is the ability to discover, allocate, and negotiate the use of network-accessible capabilities—be they computational services offered by a computer, application services offered by a piece of software, bandwidth delivered on a network, or storage space provided by a storage system. Although there are many facets to acquiring capabilities for a Grid application, we use the term resource management to describe all aspects of the process: locating a capability, arranging for its use, utilizing it, and monitoring its state.

Traditionally, the term "resource" has been interpreted narrowly as denoting a physical entity, such as a computer, network, or storage system. In contrast, we use the term here in a highly generic sense, to denote any capability that may be shared and exploited in a networked environment. This more general definition is consistent with a service-oriented architecture (Chapter 17), within which both traditional resources and virtualized "services" (e.g., database, data transfer, simulation) may differ in the function they provide to users but are consistent in the manner in which they deliver that function across the network. From this perspective, we could quite reasonably have titled this chapter "Service Management." In the interest of retaining established terminology, however, we continue to use the term resource management but with the understanding that we are applying it in this more general context.

Resource management in traditional computing systems is a well-studied problem. Resource managers exist for many computing environments and include batch schedulers, workflow engines, and operating systems. These systems are local, have complete control of a resource, and thus can implement the mechanisms and policies needed for effective use of that resource in isolation.

What distinguishes resource management in the Grid environment from these local systems is the fact that the managed resources span administrative domains. This distribution can present problems due to heterogeneity in the way that similar resources are configured and administered. For example, cluster schedulers such as Platform's Load Sharing Facility and Sun's Grid Engine have incompatible interfaces for submitting jobs to a compute platform. Thus, much early work in Grid resource management focused on overcoming these issues of heterogeneity, for example through the definition of standard resource management protocols (205, 206) and standard mechanisms for expressing resource and task requirements (539).

More important than such issues of "plumbing," however, is the fact that different organizations operate their resources under different policies; the goals of the resource user and the resource provider may be inconsistent, or even in conflict. Further complicating the situation is the fact that Grid applications often require the concurrent allocation of multiple resources, necessitating a structure in which resource use can be coordinated across administrative domains (206, 272). Much current activity in Grid resource management is focused on understanding and managing these diverse policies from the perspective of both the resource provider and the consumer.

In this chapter, we take a broad look at Grid resource management. We first examine the basic requirements for a Grid resource management system and then present a generic resource management model that addresses these requirements. This model provides a general framework for describing resource management independent of the type of resource that is managed. We use this model to describe several existing Grid resource management systems and to place current and future directions in Grid resource management in context.

18.2   REQUIREMENTS

The core goal of resource management is to establish a mutual agreement between a resource provider and a resource consumer by which the provider agrees to supply a capability that can be used to perform some task on behalf of the consumer.

This perspective on resource management is somewhat unconventional. Traditionally, tasks have been handled through job submission, while resource capabilities have been handled through specialized quality-of-service interfaces. As we shall explain, however, a unified approach offers significant advantages.

Grid systems and applications encompass a rich variety of both tasks and resources. Hence, it is not surprising that Grid resource management encompasses a wide range of different scenarios. The following examples capture some of the diverse resource management situations that can arise:

+ Task submission, in which the resource accepts responsibility to perform a specified task, for example, execute a program, move a file, or perform a database lookup. This is the most basic type of resource management agreement, in which the provider simply commits to perform the agreed-upon function without necessarily committing to when the task will start and finish, how many additional tasks the resource would be able to take on for the user, how many other tasks it might take on in the future, and so forth.

+ Workload management, in which the task submission scenario described previously is extended by *provisioning* a service to provide tasks with a specified *level* of capability, such as processors on a computer, threads or memory in a server, bandwidth on a network, or disk space on a storage system. Workload management enables the client to control not only what task will be done but also aspects of *how* tasks are performed. Levels of capability might be expressed as maximum task turnaround time, average turnaround time, task throughput, and so forth.

✦ On-demand access, in which resource capability is made available at a specified point in time, and for a specified duration. This type of resource management can be particularly important in so-called online applications, such as teleoperation in NEESgrid (Chapter 6).

✦ Coscheduling (206, 277), in which a set of resources is made available simultaneously by coordinating on-demand agreements across the required resources. Use of this type of management function is typified by data transfer services (Chapter 23), in which source and sink storage systems must be coordinated along with network bandwidth, or distributed parallel computations (Chapter 24), in which multiple compute resources are to be made available at the same period of time.

✦ Resource brokering scenarios, in which a broker service acts as an intermediary to a set of resource capabilities and directs tasks to appropriate resources based on broker-specific policy. One such policy is to maximize total job throughput. (Brokers are discussed in more detail in Chapter 19.)

As these examples illustrate, resource agreements can encompass not only a commitment to perform a task but also commitments to level of performance, or *quality of service*. Creating agreements of this type is sometimes called *provisioning*. For example, an database service can be provisioned to support 100 simultaneous queries, with an average throughput of 10 queries per second; file space within a storage system can be provisioned to support data transfers of up to 10 terabytes; or a computer system can be provisioned to allow submission of jobs requiring up to 200 processors. The timing and duration of the agreement provide a third dimension to a resource management agreement. By creating different combinations of *what, how*, and *when* agreements are held, one can address a range of resource management paradigms.

We note that Grid-based resource management systems generally cannot create quality-of-service agreements without cooperation from the resource being managed. The reason is that a resource is typically not dedicated to a specific virtual organization (VO) but rather is shared across VOs—or, as is often the case, between Grid and non-Grid users. Unless the resource has provisioning as a fundamental capability, predictable quality of service cannot be delivered to a Grid consumer of such a resource. To date, provisioning capabilities have been limited to fairly localized and tightly coupled resources and services. However, as we discuss further in Section 18.5.2, more sophisticated distributed resource management systems oriented toward pools or clusters, such as Oceano (84) and Utility Data Center (322, 419), make available the underlying service behaviors required for Grid-based end-to-end provisioning.

The general case of on-demand access (specifying the time and duration in an agreement) is often referred to as creating an "advance reservation" (221, 261). Advance reservation is particularly important if one wishes to coordinate the use of two or more resources. For example, large distributed simulations (473) can require access to many large computational resources at one time. Online experiments (274) require that computational resources be available when the experiment is being conducted; multimedia applications can require network, CPU, and disk (492); and processing pipelines such as data transfer (283), data analysis (118, 160, 424), and distributed visualization (203) require simultaneous access to a balanced resource set. Having the ability to negotiate an agreement for a specific time enables an application to ensure that the necessary capabilities will be available when required.

Introducing reservation raises the possibility that one knows a resource capability will be required but does not yet know how it will be used. For example, in space-shared supercomputers, nodes may be set aside for special high-priority users without knowing what application (or parameters) will be executed. In utility computing, nodes may be allocated to an enterprise that will specify the software configuration at a later time. In these examples, the resource management paradigm is to obtain commitment for resource capability without expressing the details of how that capability will be used. The converse is also possible: one may wish to specify a task to be performed in the absence of having the capability to perform that task with any given level of performance. An example of this situation is a traditional batch queuing system in which jobs are specified and resource capability is allocated and assigned to the task at a later time.

18.3   A GENERALIZED RESOURCE MANAGEMENT FRAMEWORK

These considerations motivate us to synthesize the uniform view of resource management illustrated in Figure 18.1, in which resource management operations are abstracted in a way that is independent of the type of resource being managed. The basic resource management operations from this figure (submit, acquire, bind) are applicable to any resource type. It is in the details of these agreements

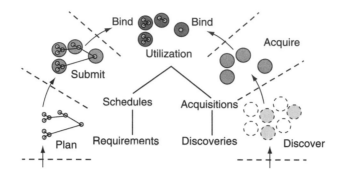

A general resource management framework. Applications apply a submit operation to make tasks available to resources according to an execution schedule that meets application requirements. Available resources are discovered, and capability is obtained via acquire operations. Finally, resources are utilized by associating submited tasks with aquired resources via a bind operation.

that the specifics of the resource utilization (number of processors, amount of bandwidth, name of a program or file, etc.) appear. By identifying an underlying resource management model, we hope to provide a context within which we can characterize and understand the function of different resource management systems as well as provide guidelines as to how resource management systems should be constructed.

In the figure, resource management activities flow bottom up, with the top of the figure representing the eventual goal of resource management: a resource used to perform a task on behalf of a requestor. The two paths flowing toward utilization capture the resource management process from the perspective of the task as presented by resource consumer (left-hand path) and the resource capability as offered by the resource provider (right-hand path).

18.3.1   Service Level Agreements

Underlying the resource management model defined previously is the need to represent agreements negotiated through the submit, acquire, and bind operations. (As we discuss later, planning and discovery are not generally represented through agreements.) Within this model, a resource consumer needs to understand and affect resource behavior, often requiring assurances or guarantees concerning the level and type of service being provided by the resource. Conversely, the owner wants to maintain local control over how the resource can be used and how much service information is exposed to the client.

A common means for reconciling these two competing demands is to negotiate a *service level agreement* (SLA), by which a resource provider "contracts" with a client to provide some measurable capability or to perform a task. Service level agreements explicitly state the terms of the agreement between a resource user and resource provider. SLAs provide a simple abstraction of a resource on the Grid. Local policy, non-Grid usage, detailed configuration information, and so forth all become irrelevant as the resource is defined only by the SLAs it is willing to negotiate. An SLA allows clients to understand what to expect from resources, without requiring detailed knowledge of competing workloads or resource owners' policies. This concept holds whether the managed resources are physical equipment, data, or logical services.

Given that each of the resources in question may be owned and operated by a different provider, establishing a single SLA across all of the desired resources is not possible. Our solution to this problem is to implement the resource management model by decomposing management functions into different kinds of SLAs that can be composed incrementally, allowing for coordinated management across the desired resource set.

More specifically, we express general resource management functions as some combination of three different kinds of SLA:

+ *Task service-level agreements* (TSLAs), in which one negotiates for the performance of an activity or task. For example, a TSLA is created by submitting a job description to a queuing system. The TSLA characterizes a task in terms of its service steps and resource requirements.

+ *Resource service-level agreements* (RSLAs), in which one negotiates for the right to consume a resource. An RSLA can be negotiated without specifying the activity for which the resource will be used. For example, an advance reservation takes the form of an RSLA. The RSLA characterizes a resource in terms of its abstract service capabilities.

+ *Binding service-level agreements* (BSLAs), in which one negotiates for the application of a resource to a task. For example, an RSLA promising network bandwidth might be applied to a particular TCP socket, or a RSLA promising parallel computer nodes might be applied to a particular job task. The BSLA associates a task, defined by its TSLA with the RSLA and the resource capabilities that should be met by exploiting the RSLA.

These SLAs implement the resource management model of Figure 18.1, in which one can submit tasks to be performed, get promises of capability, and lazily bind the two. By combining these agreements in different ways, we can represent

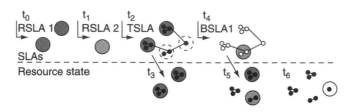

18.2

FIGURE

Three kinds of SLA—RSLA, TSLA, and BSLA—allow a client to schedule resources as time progresses from t_0 to t_6.

a variety of resource management approaches, including batch submission, resource brokering, coallocation, and coscheduling.

Figure 18.2 illustrates how the SLAs can be combined over time to allow a client to schedule resources as time progresses. In this case, at times t_0 and t_1 the client acquires two resource promises (RSLA 1 and RSLA 2) for a future time; at t_2 a complex task is submitted as the sole TSLA, using RSLA 1 to get initial portions of the job provisioned; later, at t_4, the client applies the second RSLA via a BSLA to accelerate provisioning of another component of the job. Finally, at t_6 the resource provider binds the last piece of the job to a capability without an explicit BSLA.

SLAs can be linked to address more complex resource coallocation situations. Consider a job that transfers data from a storage system to an intermediate location, computes on the data, and transfers the results to a final destination. The computation is performed on resources allocated to a community of users. For security reasons, however, the computation is not performed by using a group account. Instead, a temporary account is dynamically created for the computation. In this situation, the activation and persistence of this temporary account are an abstract task and are maintained by establishing a TSLA to which all jobs in the account are linked. (In order for the account to be reclaimed safely, all linked TSLAs must be destroyed.) The resource management activities then map to the following set of SLAs:

+ TSLA1 establishes the temporary user account and initializes it to meet user requirements—for example, by installing and initializing specified software.

+ RSLA1 promises the client 50 gigabytes of storage in a particular file system on the resource.

+ BSLA1 binds part of the promised storage space to a particular set of files within the file system.

+ TSLA2 runs a complex job that spawns constituent parts for staging of input and output data. The job scheduled by TSLA2 might have built-in logic to establish the staging jobs TSLA3 and TSLA4, or this logic might be part of the provider that performs task TSLA2 on behalf of the client.

+ TSLA3 is the first file transfer task, to stage the input to the job site without requiring any additional quality-of-service guarantees in this case.

+ TSLA4 is the second file transfer task, to stage the large output from the job site, under a deadline, before the local file system space is lost.

+ RSLA2 and BSLA2 are used by the file transfer service to achieve the additional bandwidth required to complete the (large) transfer before the deadline.

As mentioned previously, job submission must be done in the context of the temporary account SLA. Consequently, an implementation of the SLAs must have mechanisms for enforcing this nesting, such as triggering recursive destruction of all SLAs from the root to hasten reclamation of application-grouped resources.

18.3.2   Policy and Security in Resource Agreements

Typically, resource policy controls by whom and how its resources may be used. For example, the resource may be used only by certain users or during specific times of the day or may require different levels of payment for different levels of service. Thus, the policy will govern the SLAs to which the resource provider is willing to agree. Policy enforcement is symmetric: it may be applied by both entities entering into an SLA.

Detailed knowledge of the policy is not required to establish an SLA; knowledge of the resource is limited to the terms of the SLA. This aspect is critical in that often a provider may not wish to make its policy public. In practice this means that the provider (or consumer) will publish whatever policy information it wishes to make available to potential consumers for the purposes of service discovery, but private policy may be applied when SLAs are negotiated.

In general, issues of policy enforcement will require mechanisms for authenticating the participants in an SLA negotiation, associating properties to the entities in question (role, group membership, ability to pay, etc.), and providing mechanisms for enforcing restrictions based on identity and attribute. This enforcement can be complicated by the fact that resource agreements sometimes may not be made with the actual consumer of the resource but may be obtained by a third party on behalf of the consumer. This behavior is typical of resource brokers that obtain a commitment of resource capabilities and redistribute them, often applying additional policy or cost functions. A consumer may interact with a broker by requesting submission of the task (expecting the broker to complete it), or the consumer may ask a broker to allocate capability across one or more resources with which the broker has established agreements. In both scenarios, the resource management process is complicated by the introduction of the broker's additional administrative domain (thus, we now have the consumer, the broker, and potentially a different administrative domain for each resource selected by the broker). Of course, brokers can interact with other brokers, adding to the list of administrative domains touched in a single resource management operation. Grid resource management systems must address issues of cross-domain trust and policy and if and how delegation of rights between intermediaries is allowed. The requirements for resource management functions are not unique in this regard, and the techniques discussed in Chapter 21 should be an integral part of the resource management system.

18.3.3   Resource Descriptions

Although the type of agreements established between resource providers and consumers can be generically defined, the exact nature of those agreements is highly dependent on the type of resource being provided. Clients in general must request resources by property, for example, by capability, quality, or configuration. These requirements are expressed through a *resource description language*. This language

+ enables the resource consumer to describe what capabilities are desired, and what they will be used for (e.g., job configuration);

+ enables a resource provider to describe the capabilities that it can offer, and under what terms (this description does not have to completely model the resource being offered; rather, it expresses only those capabilities that the resource is prepared to negotiate);

+ provides a vehicle for the propagation of resource and agreement state through monitoring and discovery data paths of the resource management system.

Experience suggests that a resource description framework should contain the following basic primitives:

+ Parameterized resource attribute metrics describing a particular property of the resource. Examples of such metrics are *bandwidth, latency*, and *space*.

These attribute descriptions can express limits (e.g., between 10 and 100 megabit/s), and they may scope these metrics to a window of time in which the attribute value (or range) is being asserted.

✦ Resource composition operators that allow complex resources to be described as compositions of simpler resource primitives. A resource description language may contain a variety of composition operators, including the following:

- ◆ *Conjunctive sets* that itemize required elements.

- ◆ *Typed sets* that name specific sets of resources for the purpose of associating meaning with a set. For example, the typed set {space, bandwidth}$_{disk}$ tells us that we are constraining the speed and size of a secondary storage device with reusable metrics for space and bandwidth.

- ◆ *Arrays* that are sets of identical elements.

- ◆ *Disjunctive alternatives*, which differ from a resource set in that only one element must be satisfied. Alternatives can be used to express other solution spaces for the application requirements within distinct planning regimes or to phrase similar requirements using basic and specialized metrics in the event that a client could benefit from unconventional extensions, which may or may not be recognized by a given manager.

✦ As with resource metrics, compositions may be required to hold for specific time intervals. Each subgroup within a composite must have a lifetime wholly included within the lifetime of the parent group.

In addition to these basic elements, we may want to intermingle control, or *configuration*, directives within a resource description. In an open environment, this intermingling is notational convenience to avoid presenting two statements—one modeling the requirements placed on the structured resource and one providing control data to the resource manager for the structured resource.

We believe, moreover, that resource descriptions must be *dynamically extensible* and that the correct mechanism for extension is heavily dependent on the technology chosen to implement the resource manager. Sets of clients and resources must be able to define new resource syntax to capture novel devices and services, so the language should support these extensions in a structured way. With the widespread adoption of OGSA as the core Grid infrastructure technology, the resource descriptions and the mechanisms for extension are likely to be rooted in XML schema definitions.

18.3.4   Resource Description Languages

Two major resource description languages are in widespread use in current Grid environments: the Globus Toolkit Resource Specification Language (RSL) and condor classified ads (ClassAds). Both languages provide most of the primitives and composition operators outlined previously. Neither language supports any temporal notation, although either could be easily augmented to support start time and end time as resource metrics.

RSL is the specification language used by the Globus Toolkit to describe task configuration and service requirements. RSL syntax was derived from the search string format for the Lightweight Directory Access Protocol (LDAP) and consists of attribute value pairs combined with a fixed set of composition operators in prefix notation (205). The following example illustrates its major features:

```
+(& (resourceManagerContact=
  "flash.isi.edu/O=Grid/.../CN=host/flash.isi.edu")
(count=1)
(label="subjob A")
(executable= my_app1)
)
( & (resourceManagerContact=
  "sp139.sdsc.edu:2119:/O=Grid/.../CN=host/sp097.sdsc.edu")
(count=2)
(label="subjob B")
(executable=my_app2)
)
```

An attribute/value pair can represent either a resource metric (e.g., "count," which specifies the requested number of processors) or a configuration parameter (e.g., "executable," which specifies the name of a program to execute). Note the alternative representations of conjunction: the "&" operator specifies a conjunction of resource metrics, while the "+" operator is used to express a set of separate resource requests that must be fulfilled. This second notation is particularly useful for specifying coallocation requests (i.e., coordinated resource usage).

In contrast, classified advertisements (ClassAds; see Chapter 1:13) (539) use a symmetric notation to describe both task and resource requirements, thus simplifying the process of matching task and resource requirements. ClassAds descriptions are semistructured, not schema based: the set of attributes in a ClassAd, as well as their names and meaning, is determined by convention, and not by any agreed-upon schema. ClassAds have been extended to support matching with multiple resources (540), sets of resources (448), and matching via constraint solving (447).

Within the commercial sector, significant progress has been made in developing resource models for enterprise system management. The simple network management protocol's management information base and, more recently, the common information model (CIM) (232) are two examples. CIM seems particularly relevant in the Grid environment.

CIM (see also Chapter 20) is being developed by the Distributed Management Task Force, a multivendor standards organization whose goal is to develop interoperable standards for management software. CIM is based on an object-oriented metamodel that enables all of the types of composition described previously, while providing an extensible framework describing new resource types. The metamodel is defined in a syntax-neutral *metaobject format* that can be encoded into a variety of syntactic structures, including XML, thus making CIM-based descriptions attractive to Web-services-based Grid systems, such as those being defined by OGSA (see Chapter 17). CIM also defines a growing set of object definitions for hardware and software resources. At present, this set includes some of direct interest to the Grid community (e.g., descriptions of computing elements, storage systems, and some basic software services) but does not encompass all resources and tasks present in a typical Grid. Hence, significant object development is required before CIM can be used for Grid computing. However, given its broad industry backing and its flexible object model, we believe that CIM offers considerable promise as a description language for resource management agreements.

18.3.5   Resource Discovery and Selection

While resource capability agreements are at the core of the resource management model defined in Figure 18.1, additional functions are specified as part of the model. *Resource discovery* is the process of querying the distributed state of the Grid to identify those resources whose characteristics and state match those desired by the resource consumer. *Resource selection* is the process of choosing from a set of candidates provided by resource discovery. The selection is typically driven by high-level application criteria, such as time to completion, reliability, or cost.

The distributed nature of the Grid environment makes precise determination of the resource state difficult. Furthermore, the introduction of multiple policy domains makes precise control of the resource state difficult by preventing traditional strategies such as transactions with so-called ACID properties. Hence, discovery and selection are often intermingled with resource management activities: one identifies potential resources and then engages in a detailed negotiation with the resource to determine whether the resource provider will make the specific commitments to the resource consumer that will satisfy the application needs.

The separation of discovery from allocation operations has important ramifications. Since discovery does not imply any commitment, we can make it a lightweight, nonauthoritative operation (i.e., not the subject of an SLA negotiation). Service acquisition, on the other hand, implies a guarantee of service and will, in general, be more costly to establish. A second advantage to separating discovery is that the methods used to aggregate resource information for the purposes of Grid-wide discovery can exploit a loose coherency model, further reducing the overhead of collecting and searching information about large, distributed resource sets (204, 264).

Clearly, a relationship exists between the description of the service used for the purposes of discovery and the description used for establishing an SLA with that service. In the Globus Toolkit, this relationship is indirect, since the description language used by the Monitoring and Discovery Service (MDS-2) (204) is based on LDAP object classes, which have a similar but not identical syntax to that used to express job and resource requirements in RSL. Thus, once a desired resource is discovered and selected, information about the resource as well as descriptions of the task must be explicitly mapped into RSL before an SLA can be negotiated. ClassAds take a more symmetric approach, using the same notation for describing task and resource characteristics. As discussed in the next section, this simplifies the process of resource selection, since no transliteration is required when moving from discovery to allocation operations. CIM-based descriptions are not currently being used for resource allocation. However, an approach similar to that being used by ClassAds could be easily taken.

18.3.6   Task Management

Resource management does not stop with the initiation of the requested activity. Typically, we want to monitor task status during execution, as well as the status of the managed resource, if for no other reason than to ensure that the agreed-upon capability is provided. Monitoring can be a complicated activity, both because the environment is distributed and because resources may have been provided via intermediaries such as resource brokers. The view of the resource may have been abstracted, making it difficult for the consumer to know enough about the underlying resource set to directly monitor the environment.

Monitoring is discussed in Chapter 20. However, in addition to the generic functions discussed in that chapter, resource management systems often include resource-management-specific monitoring capabilities, for example, to monitor SLA status (a topic discussed in Chapter 26). Monitoring can be especially important in SLA implementations in which an SLA can be in different states. For example, there may be a delay between when a TSLA is negotiated (e.g., by submitting a program to a batch queue) and when the corresponding task is initiated (i.e., the program starts executing). Thus, we may want to monitor the SLA status to determine when the task was actually initiated.

Based on the results of task and resource monitoring, one may want to perform additional management functions that may alter the state of current SLAs or perhaps negotiate additional agreements. Of course, any SLA modification must be consistent with both the terms negotiated as part of initial SLA establishment and the explicit and implicit policy of parties that entered into that agreement. The following are examples of management functions that we may wish to perform after SLAs have been established, perhaps during task execution:

✦ *Terminate an SLA*. SLAs may be terminated for various reasons, for example, application error, the availability of a better resource provider, or unsatisfactory provider performance (e.g., SLA violation). In the case of nested or linked SLAs, termination of an outer SLA may automatically terminate contained SLAs. Alternatively, premature termination of an SLA may not be allowed until all contained SLAs have terminated.

✦ *Extend SLA lifetime*. In this simple form of renegotiation, the duration of the SLA is extended without modifying any other terms of the agreement. Extension may be necessary because the task has taken longer than expected to complete or because a provider is not willing to give out large resource commitments at once but instead requires periodic update to ensure that the requestor has not failed. This *soft-state* (542) or *leasing* (323) approach to lifetime management is fundamental to the structure of OGSA, and we expect it to be applied to SLAs.

✦ *Renegotiate other SLA terms*. We might change terms, for example, to allocate additional disk space or reduce the upper bound on transaction response time. Or we might add terms, for example, to move from a best-effort arrangement to a guaranteed quality of service on specific resource capabilities.

✦ *Create a new SLA*. If modification of an existing SLA is not appropriate or not allowed, we may wish to create a new SLA. If the SLA is for a different resource or a new type of SLA for an existing resource, normal negotiation mechanisms for establishing an SLA can be used. If the new SLA is to replace an existing one, the ability to create a new SLA may be impeded by the commitments associated with the existing SLA. Hence, a specialized negotiation protocol may be needed to support replacement of one SLA by another.

18.4   GRID RESOURCE MANAGEMENT SYSTEMS

We have identified the basic concepts of a Grid resource management system and defined a general resource management framework that can be used to describe a wide variety of resource management approaches across a broad class of resources. In the rest of this chapter, we use this framework to characterize several resource management systems.

Before looking at specific systems, we make some general observations. Current Grid resource management systems have tended to focus on management of compute resources, with an emphasis on job submission. Although a range of attributes can be specified, start- and end-time constraints generally are not exploited. Thus, whereas current systems can be understood in the context of the resource management framework, in practice they tend to explicitly manage only TSLAs, with the underlying local resource management implicitly provisioning and binding as part of the their implementation.

Perhaps the most significant reason Grid resource managers have been limited in scope is the dearth of functionality in underlying local resource management systems that Grid resource managers must rely on to implement SLAs. Job submission services tend not to support advanced reservation, network quality-of-service support is not widely available, and even storage quality-of-service support is limited. Although sophisticated workload management systems exist in the commercial environment (503), to date these platforms have not been integrated into the Grid environment.

Nevertheless, we have reason to be optimistic. As applications increasingly rely on Grids for their execution environment, there will be pressure to create and deploy richer local resource management solutions and to export their functionality via Grid-based resource management. A case in point is utility computing, which most major computer vendors are advocating as the next step in the evolution of the corporate IT infrastructure. For utility computing to work, service must extend beyond best effort, and end-to-end performance requirements will be essential.

18.4.1   The Globus Grid Resource Allocation Manager

The Globus Toolkit's Grid Resource Allocation Manager (GRAM) (205) is representative of first-generation Grid resource management systems. GRAM defines a layered resource management architecture, following the model presented in Chapter 4. At its core, GRAM defines the resource-layer protocols and APIs that enable clients to securely instantiate a computational task. GRAM itself does not implement any local resource management functionally but instead relies on local resource management interfaces to provide this function. Typically, the GRAM server interfaces to a local job management system such at Platform's Load Sharing Facility, Veridian's Portable Batch System, IBM's LoadLeveler, or Sun's Grid Engine. GRAM can also provide a submission interface into resources managed by the Condor system (Chapter 19).

The GRAM protocol can be layered onto any resource management system that can be abstracted as a job submission. Typically, such an action results in the execution of a specified program, but this is not required by the GRAM protocol. Indeed, the protocol has been used to manage a variety of different resources. For example, Oracle has developed a layering onto Oracle's database products for access to database utilities, invocation of SQL commands, and access to the Oracle scheduler, and the GriPhyN project has developed an interface to the Laser Interferometer Gravitational Wave Observatory (LIGO) Data Acquisition System (217).

GRAM has no notion of advance reservation. Clients submit TSLAs while provisioning and binding are performed implicitly by the resource supporting the GRAM protocol. Coallocation is supported without advance reservation via a light-weight broker called DUROC (206), enabling simultaneous coallocation of distributed resources by layering on top of the GRAM API. Of course, without reservation support, simultaneous access requires luck or out-of-band resource provisioning agreements (essentially, manual creation of an RSLA that is implicitly claimed by the TSLAs through techniques such as dedicated queues or exclusive resource access). DUROC has been used to build parallel message-passing libraries (403), to execute large-scale parallel simulations (99, 138), and to acquire clustered storage nodes for real-time access to large scientific datasets for exploratory visualization (203).

As discussed in Section 18.3.4, the GRAM protocol uses RSL as its resource description language. Because GRAM has no separation of different agreement types, RSL conveys information about resource requirements (resource description) as well as task descriptions (task description). The GRAM implementation defines RSL to contain a specific set of portable resource metrics, and it allows clients to pass through explicit configuration parameters to the local resource management system.

18.4.2 General-Purpose Architecture for Reservation and Allocation

The General-purpose Architecture for Reservation and Allocation (GARA) generalizes the GRAM architecture to provide for advanced reservations and end-to-end management of quality of service on different types of resources, including networks, CPUs, and disks (272, 283). It defines APIs that allow users and applications to manipulate both reservations and allocations of different types of resources in uniform ways.

GARA extends the GRAM resource management model in two ways: by generalizing the API and protocols from managing compute resources into more generic *resource management objects* and by extending the GRAM interfaces and protocols to allow the creation of advance reservations. GARA reservations can be established without indicating what task the reservation is to be used for, thus implementing an RSLA. Subsequent GRAM-style job submissions can be made by providing a reservation handle-created call along with the job description, creating a TSLA. For network flows, clients initiate a similar claiming operation by providing the reservation handle and socket address information, creating a BSLA.

GARA uses a specialized form of RSL for describing reservations. This RSL includes reservation start- and end time parameters, as well as attributes related to the quality of service being reserved, for example network bandwidth, number of processors, fraction of a CPU, and amount of memory.

The terms of a reservation vary from resource to resource. One especially interesting set of experiments focused on the use of GARA to reserve and provide access to network bandwidth (283). In these experiments, we created a *bandwidth broker* architecture that was implemented by creating a *slot manager*: a GARA-enabled resource manager that can set aside fractions of channel capacity for fixed duration. Reserving an end-to-end network path may require spanning network links that are in separate administrative domains. To address the problem of diverse trust relationships and usage policies that can apply in multidomain network reservations, individual bandwidth brokers communicate via bilaterally authenticated channels between peered domains. GARA provides the secure transport of requests from source domain to destination domain, with each bandwidth broker on the path being able to enforce local policies and modify the request with additional constraints. The lack of a transitive trust relationship between source and end domains is addressed by a delegation model where each bandwidth broker on the path is able to identify all upstream partners by accessing the credentials of the full delegation chain (573).

18.4.3   Condor

Condor (291, 446) (Chapters 1:13 and 19) is a widely used high-throughput scheduler that uses ClassAds for discovery and resource matching and an opportunistic scheduling discipline. Like most current resource management systems, Condor explicitly manages TSLAs between a client and the management system. Condor implements client TSLAs by establishing further RSLAs and TSLAs between the submission service and individual resources. These low-level jobs execute user tasks and stage checkpoint data in and out of the resources. Condor also provides a mechanism called a *glide-in* (see Chapter 19), which allows the Condor environment to be established dynamically on a resource using GRAM as a creation mechanism. The glide-in is a GRAM job created by TSLA with the GRAM resource. It virtualizes the compute nodes hosting the GRAM job to provide a Condor RSLA/TSLA manager.

18.4.4 Resource Brokers

Resource brokers, or *metaschedulers*, are commonly used to virtualize the interface to sets of resources. A broker acts as an intermediary between a user community and a set of associated resources by providing a single point of submission for tasks, using standard Grid resource management protocols such as GRAM to forward the task to one or more of the underlying resources for execution. To date, broker implementations have focused primarily on computational jobs or workflows (57, 426) (see also Chapter 1:12), although brokers for other resources such as network bandwidth are also possible (410, 493). Resource brokers can be advantageous for a number of reasons:

+ *Resource virtualization.* One primary virtue of a broker is that it provides a simplified view of a resource set, isolating the end user from having to understand the specifics of the resources available to a virtual organization.

+ *Policy enforcement.* A central function of a broker is to decide onto which underlying resource a task should be directed. Although this decision may be based purely on resource management considerations (e.g., equal distribution of load, or achieving best resource utilization), the broker also offers a control point at which community-based policy can be asserted. This policy can enforce community priorities, the roles of users, cost models, and so forth.

+ *Protocol conversion.* While Grid protocols such as GRAM define standardized methods for remote job submission, a range of legacy tools that do not speak Grid protocols is useful. In these cases, a broker can serve as a protocol converter, in addition to its normal resource selection function. For example, a group at Sandia National Laboratories has developed a resource broker (108) that provides a CORBA submission interface for clients, while using GRAM for actual task submission to the underlying resource.

The algorithms used to distribute work to underlying resources vary from broker to broker and generally consider some utilization model (such as fair share) along with community policy. Usually, however, a Grid resource broker does not control the underlying resources. In the absence of such capability, the broker is limited in the types of guarantees it can make to its clients. These issues are discussed further in Section 18.5.2.

A number of Grid-based brokers for computational resources are in use, for example, Sun Grid Engine (SGE, see Chapter 12) and Platform's Load Sharing Facility. It is important to distinguish between the deployment of such brokers as a *local* resource management solution, using local interfaces and protocols, and their deployment at a Grid level, using GRAM as the underlying protocol.

Brokers that are more specialized, oriented toward stereotypical workflows and deployment environments, have also been developed. For example, the job submission broker developed for the EU Data Grid (EDG) project supports the generic three-step paradigm of (1) stage data, (2) compute on the data, and (3) place the results on a repository. Details about data and computation are provided via a broker submit file. The EDG broker chooses between various compute resources and data sources based on a simple cost-minimization model, which considers the overhead of moving data, the compute resources available for execution, and the network bandwidth connecting storage and compute resources. Information required to drive these decisions is obtained by querying standard Grid information services (204). This broker is deployed as part of the EU Data Grid environment and used to support a range of science-oriented applications.

18.5   THE SERVICE NEGOTIATION AND ACQUISITION PROTOCOL

Future directions in Grid resource management are being driven by three major trends. First is the shift toward service-oriented architecture, specifically the use of OGSA (Chapter 17), as the common foundation on which Grid infrastructure is created.

Second is the extension of management requirements from limited classes of resources (computational, storage, network) to more general management interfaces across all types of services, in addition to traditional hardware resources.

Third is the increased use of provisioned rather than best-effort service. This trend is itself driven by two factors: the need to support more predictable behavior in application-level workflows and the emergence of a utility computing/service model in which sets of services are aggregated and virtualized, presenting them to the network in a manner indistinguishable from a single "basic" service.

Taken together, these trends argue for an implementation of the SLA-based resource management model (as described in Section 18.3) in such a way that they could become part of the basic behavior of any OGSA service. The proposed SLA model is independent of the service being managed—the semantics of specific services are accommodated by the details of the agreement, and not in the types of agreements negotiated. Because of its general applicability, we refer to the protocols used to negotiate these SLAs as the *Service Negotiation and Acquisition Protocol* (SNAP) (207).

18.5.1   SNAP Protocol Elements

The emergence of OGSA as the common means for creating Grid infrastructure has a number of implications for the implementation of the resource management framework. In OGSA, all operations are defined with respect to a *portType*, which defines a set of operations and associated data types. SLA negotiations are fundamentally no different from any other service operations. Consequently, a service can offer resource management functionality by including SLA negotiation portTypes within its service definition.

One can imagine a small number of fairly general SLA negotiation protocols. A very basic negotiation protocol may be for the requestor to send the terms of a desired SLA to a target service, which then accepts or rejects the terms. We anticipate, however, that in many cases it will be desirable to have complex negotiations that more closely reflect the nature of the service being provided. For example, we expect that the following negotiation patterns will be of use:

+ *propose/accept*, an interaction in which a request for an SLA is either accepted or rejected.

+ *(propose/counterpropose)**/*accept*, a generalization of *submit/accept* in which either party may prolong negotiation of SLA terms before accepting.

+ .../*accept/commit*, a protocol in which agreement is reached to establish an SLA, as in the previous patterns, but the SLA is not activated until an explicit *commit* operation is performed. This protocol may be desirable if a cost is associated with creation of the SLA.

In addition to these common negotiation patterns, we expect that specific service types will have their own idiosyncratic negotiation styles that can also be captured as portTypes, perhaps by extending (i.e., inheriting from) one of the common negotiation portTypes. These patterns may in turn be specialized as specific services are instantiated.

In practice, each such negotiation pattern may be preceded by a discovery phase in which a service publishes or advertises what type of SLAs and negotiation patterns it is willing to support, and this information is used by a requestor to select a candidate service provider. SLA advertisements can be represented as service data elements and accessed with standard OGSA mechanisms.

The negotiation protocols as represented by operations and portTypes capture one aspect of SNAP. However, without a means for expressing the requirements and terms of an SLA, these protocols are not very useful. Regardless of the service type, common elements will appear in any SLA: the time period for which it holds, the identity of the negotiating parties, the terms of agreement, and so forth. These structures can be described by a common set of extensible *XML schema definitions* (XSDs), which are included in the definition of an SLA negotiation portType.

Attributes whose type and value must be specialized to the service being managed will also exist. In many instances it will be possible to construct SLA descriptions by combining general and service-specific attributes with a standard set of composition operators as described in Section 18.3.3. Hence, the schema definitions for describing an SLA must be extensible so as to accommodate both additional attribute types and additional operators for combining attributes within an SLA. Moreover, we must also admit the possibility that a service may be so idiosyncratic as to prohibit reuse of any descriptive elements outside of the specification of SLA types (i.e., TSLA, RSLA, and BSLA). Hence, the SLA schemas must be designed to support extensibility with respect to the basic structure of the SLA as well.

SNAP is being used in the design and implementation of GRAM-3, the next generation of job submission protocols for the Globus Toolkit. GRAM-3 recasts the current GRAM job submission mechanism as TSLA negotiation and maps GARA's reservation and claim mechanisms into RSLA and BSLA negotiations when local schedulers can provide such capability. In merging the two models, we find two forms of resource claim: TSLAs claim resources implicitly as part of a task creation, and BSLAs claim resources in order to augment existing tasks.

To summarize, rather than the single-purpose resource management systems and interfaces we see today, we anticipate the next several years will see the widespread application of resource management functionality, with virtually every service subject to task, resource, and binding SLAs. The associated interfaces must be standardized in a community forum to achieve maximum benefit from such ubiquitous deployment.

18.5.2   Interfacing to Local Resource Management Systems

SNAP defines how a service presents resource management functionality to the network. For the resulting SLAs to be more than empty promises, however, the service implementation must provide the mechanisms required to deliver the agreed-upon capabilities. In situations in which a service is structured only for Grid-based operation, support for SLAs is an integral part of the service operation. Alternatively, the service implementation may rely on external mechanisms, namely, local resource managers, to honor SLA commitments.

The SNAP protocol agreements can be mapped onto a range of existing local resource managers. Experience with GRAM shows that TSLAs can be mapped to a range of local job schedulers, as well as simple time-sharing computers (138, 276). GARA has shown how RSLAs and BSLAs can be mapped to contemporary network and CPU quality-of-service systems (272, 277, 283). Following this model, SNAP manager services represent *adaptation* points between the SNAP protocol domain and local RM mechanisms. Although mapping of SLAs onto underlying resource management systems will remain an important vehicle for implementing SLAs in legacy environments, we anticipate that local resource management services will increasingly become Grid-enabled, exporting SLA negotiation interfaces natively. Such native support might improve protocol endpoint efficiency as well as reduce semantic conflicts between global and local management systems.

As discussed previously, support for SLAs with any type of quality-of-service constraints is difficult unless the ability to provision services is supported throughout, since Grid services are shared across virtual organizations as well as with non-Grid users. Historically, local resource management systems have offered little in the way of provisioning. Although tightly coupled, single-system image commercial environments have long offered infrastructure for workload management, these facilities have not be available on larger-scale, more loosely structured resources such as clusters. With the emergence of processor farms, utility computing, and "blades," however, we are seeing the increased availability of local resource managers such as Oceano (84), UDC (322, 419), SRM (587, 588), and MUSE (173) that support more sophisticated provisioning interfaces for both computational and storage resources. In addition, trends in optical networking, specifically in the area of dynamic allocation of whole optical wavelengths (i.e., lambda switching), point toward a similar capability in networking resources.

These advances will ensure that basic functionality needed to implement RSLA agreements will become more widely available. In addition, as Grid services take hold, we expect that Grid-based use will become the main driver for many types of local resource managers and that their implementation will migrate toward being Grid service based. As this happens, the current boundaries between

Grid resource management and local resource management will blur, with Grid-based interfaces being the primary (or sole) interface to a local resource manager. This blurring has the potential to improve the robustness and performance of Grid resource management, as OGSA-based interfaces can have access to internal state and management mechanisms. A second important consequence is that we obtain a completely uniform view of resource and service management, from the local site to the large-scale VOs that result from Grid technology.

18.5.3   The Grid Resource Allocation Agreement Protocol

The Grid Resource Allocation Agreement Protocol Working Group (GRAAP-WG) of the Global Grid Forum is adapting the SNAP model for use as a standard Grid service interface for negotiated resource management. The working group is developing both detailed scenarios and requirements for advance negotiation of traditional jobs as well as a protocol definition.

A draft document entitled WS Agreement exists as of mid-2003. This document describes portTypes that represent as services both individual SLAs and the persistent manager through which negotiations are initiated. The WS-Agreement negotiation model closely models the existing SNAP concepts of SLA formation, while introducing fine-grained negotiation of terms written in an extensible language derived from the proposed WS-Policy language. This model supports all the variations of simple and complex negotiation cycles suggested previously in a single, unified protocol model. The WS-Agreement portTypes make use of many of the advanced features of the Open Grid Services Infrastructure. In addition, they are using management features being designed in the Common Management Models Working Group (CMM-WG) of the Global Grid Forum, to express SLA life-cycle and relationships between SLAs and other services.

18.6   FUTURE DIRECTIONS

The emergence of service-oriented architecture, increased interest in support-ing a broad range of commercial applications, and natural evolution of func-tionality are collectively driving significant advances in resource management capabilities. Although today's Grid environment is primarily oriented toward best-effort service, we expect the situation to become substantially different in the next several years, with provisioning becoming the rule rather than the exception.

We possess a good understanding of the basic mechanisms required for a provisioned Grid. Significant challenges remain, however, in understanding how these mechanisms can be effectively combined to create seamless virtualized views of underlying resources and services. Some of these challenges lie strictly within the domain of resource management: for example, robust distributed algorithms for negotiating simultaneous SLAs across a set of resources, and techniques for renegotiating SLAs to meet changing demands. Other issues, such as expression of resource policy for purposes of discovery, and enhanced security models that support flexible delegation of resource management to intermediate brokers, are closely tied to advances in other aspects of Grid infrastructure. Hence, the key to progress in the coming years is to create an extensible and open infrastructure that can incorporate these advances as they become available. The SNAP approach presented here has these characteristics, and we anticipate that future resource management infrastructure, as being developed in the Global Grid Forum within groups such as GRAAP-WG, CMM-WG, and the proposed Storage Resource Management working group (SRM-WG), will rely heavily on these principles.

ACKNOWLEDGMENTS

This work was supported in part by the Mathematical, Information, and Computational Sciences Division subprogram of the Office of Advanced Scientific Computing Research, Office of Science, U.S. Department of Energy, under Contract W-31–109-Eng-38, and by IBM and Microsoft.

FURTHER READING

For more information on the topics covered in this chapter, see *www.mkp.com/grid2* and the following references:

- ✦ Chapters 1:9 and 1:10 provide good reviews of the Condor resource management system and previous work in scheduling for high-performance computing.

- ✦ The book *Resource Management for Grid Computing* (490) provides more details on many of the technologies and concepts discussed here.

Building Reliable Clients and Services

Douglas Thain and Miron Livny

*T*raditional distributed computing is dominated by a client–server model. File systems, databases, and hypertext systems are all designed with the assumption that a few powerful and reliable servers support a large and dynamic set of clients. Servers are complex and expensive, while clients are lightweight, cheap, and simple. Servers are responsible for persistence, security, and coherence, while clients are responsible for very little. Client software often acts directly on behalf of an interactive user who steers the overall interaction.

Grid computing is different: a single Grid client may harness large numbers of servers over extended time periods. For example, one client may consume more than 100,000 CPU-hours in one week on systems distributed worldwide (443) (see also Chapter 10). As a consequence, both Grid clients and servers are multiplexed, multiprotocol, and multithreaded. This organization could be termed *peer-to-peer* (Chapter 29) to indicate that participants are equals, although it need not be the case that participating systems are poorly connected, particularly unreliable, or mutually untrusting, as is often assumed in peer-to-peer computing. The key point is that multiple parties—both consumers (clients) and providers (servers) of capabilities—must act in concert to achieve an overall goal in a reliable fashion. Each must meet obligations relating to security, performance, and progress. Thus, each requires techniques to overcome various kinds of failure conditions and to track long-lived interactions that may stretch over days or weeks.

Preceding chapters have introduced the basic principles of service-oriented architecture and OGSA (279), explained why future Grid services will have persistent state and active and complex responsibilities (Chapter 17), and introduced the notion of a service-level agreement (SLA) as a means of negotiating expectations concerning the duties that other parties will fulfill (Chapter 18). In this chapter, we introduce *client-oriented architectures* that may be used to achieve reliable distributed execution in complex, distributed, and dynamic Grid environments. Building on experiences within the Condor project—which has specialized in the problem of reliably executing jobs on remote machines for almost two decades—we present specific techniques for use in three different contexts: remote execution, work organization, and data output.

19.1   PRINCIPLES OF RELIABLE SYSTEMS

We first introduce some general design principles that apply to distributed systems and, in particular, to the complex applications often found in Grid computing. We shall encounter applications of each of these principles in our discussion of remote execution, work management, and data output.

Effective operation requires responsible behavior.   Responsibility is a common notion in distributed computing. Random behavior is rarely acceptable; rather, all parties are required to operate within certain limits of decorum. The following are some well-known standards of conduct:

✦ The Ethernet (474) discipline arbitrates access to a shared medium without a central controller. The discipline expressly prohibits transmission at will. Civilized clients must listen for a quiet interval before broadcasting, and then double-check to make sure that transmissions were broadcast correctly. If an accidental collision occurs, a client has the responsibility to inform others that may be affected by using a short attention burst, and then must fall silent again for a specified time. If Ethernet clients simply tried to "shout" louder and faster to drown out everyone else, the medium would be entirely unusable.

✦ The two-phase commit protocol (327) allows for the atomic acceptance of a series of nonatomic operations. This protocol places strong burdens on both coordinators (clients) and servers. During the assembly of a transaction, either side may abort at will. However, once a server accepts a coordinator's request to prepare the transaction, it may not release that transaction of its own accord. Conversely, the coordinator has the obligation to try forever until it successfully completes a prepared transaction. An abdication of responsibility from either side would lead to an inconsistent system and potentially the loss of data.

✦ The Jini (668) resource discovery system allows a client to obtain a lease on a server. Once allocated, the server accepts the responsibility of serving only the lessee. Likewise, the client accepts the responsibility of periodically renewing the lease. If a communication failure prevents renewal, both sides have the obligation to assume the lease is broken, thus preventing waste and inconsistent states.

The client is ultimately responsible for reliability.   This is a restatement of the end-to-end design principle (570). In the final reckoning, the consumer is responsible for his/her own well-being. The careful grocery shopper always checks a carton of eggs for cracked shells. So too must the Grid client verify that job outputs are coherent and complete.

Reliable services are difficult to manage.   This theme is counterintuitive. It would seem that services that make greater efforts to be resilient to failures would be more useful and reliable. Yet, the opposite is frequently true. More reliable services often have more complex and unexpected failure modes. Sometimes the best service is the one that fails frequently in a predictable way.

Soft state simplifies garbage collection.   As discussed in Chapter 17, soft-state mechanisms (e.g., leases (323)) can simplify the recovery of resources following abnormal (as well as normal) task termination.

Logging simplifies persistent state.   Grid services that manipulate persistent state must remember completed actions, track requests in the process of assembly, and deal with requests that were started but perhaps forgotten. A log—a stream of event records that survives crashes—is a standard tool for this job. By using well-known techniques, the history and current state of a service may be easily recovered from the log.

19.2   RELIABLE REMOTE EXECUTION

We next turn to the deceptively simple problem of reliable remote execution. We illustrate our discussion with two examples of large-scale distributed systems—traditional Condor and Grid-enabled Condor-G—that achieve reliable remote execution in different ways. Traditional Condor, designed to deal with opportunistic resources, focuses on the problems of ensuring that failures are detected rapidly and forcing a quick reset to a known state. However, the techniques used to achieve this goal are less well suited for use in a wide-area network in which remote servers are persistent. Condor-G allows for network disconnections while a job is managed by a remote batch system, but this feature introduces new and complex challenges for system coherency.

19.2.1   Condor

The core components of the traditional Condor distributed batch system (Figure 19.1) form the Condor *kernel*. Each component must discharge a certain responsibility, as we now describe:

The *schedd* is a reliable client of Grid computing services. It serves as the entry point for end users, providing a transaction interface for submitting,

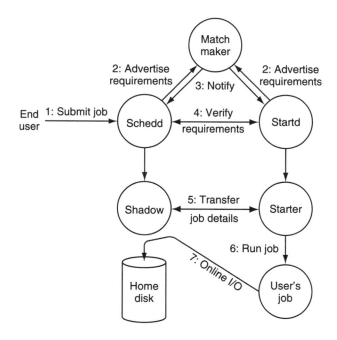

19.1

FIGURE

The Condor kernel: the seven steps to run a Condor job. (1) The user submits the job to a schedd. (2) The schedd and the startd advertise themselves to a matchmaker. (3) The matchmaker notifies two compatible parties. (4) Both parties verify that they match each other. (5) The shadow and starter are created and communicate the details of the job to be run. (6) The starter executes the user's job. (7) If needed, the job performs I/O by communicating with the shadow directly or through a proxy in the starter.

querying, and removing jobs. It is also responsible for persistently storing a user's jobs while finding places for them to execute. The schedd is responsible for enforcing user requirements on job execution. For example, the user may require that jobs run only on machines that have sufficient memory and that are owned by a trusted user.

The *startd* is a reliable Grid computing service. It manages an execution machine and is responsible for finding work to be done within the constraints placed on it by the machine's owner. For example, an owner might permit only jobs submitted by the "physics" group to be run during the day while allowing any sort of job to run at night. Jobs that satisfy these requirements may also be ranked. The same owner might prefer, but not require, jobs from the "chemistry" group at night. When supervising a job, the startd is responsible for monitoring the state of the machine, possibly evicting and cleaning up after a job if the owner's requirements are no longer met.

The *matchmaker* is responsible for introducing potentially compatible consumers (schedds) and producers (startds). The matchmaker accepts *advertisements* from all parties, written in the ClassAd (538, 539, 541) resource description language, describing their current state and the properties of the resources that they seek. Once a potential match is found, both resources are notified. The matchmaker is also responsible for enforcing system-wide policies that cannot be enforced by a single schedd or startd. For example, the matchmaker controls admission to the pool as well as the fraction of machines allocable to any given user. It also performs accounting to track pool-wide resource use.

Although the matchmaker informs compatible parties that they are a potential match, each party still bears a responsibility to enforce its own requirements and to translate the potential of a match into productive work. The match could be bad if it is based on stale information or if the matchmaker is untrustworthy. Thus, schedds and startds contact each other directly to verify that their requirements are still met before attempting to execute a job. Once satisfied, they may begin to work together. However, either side may abort the match at any time if it discovers that its requirements are no longer satisfied.

Two subprocesses—a shadow and a starter—work together to actually execute a job. The *starter* is responsible for creating an execution environment at the remote site. Like a command-line shell, it transforms a job description into the operating system calls that actually execute the job. It creates a working directory, sets up standard I/O streams, and monitors the job for its exit status. Most important, it is responsible for informing the other Condor components whether the job was able to execute in the available environment. Although the starter provides all mechanisms needed to execute a job, it does not provide policies. The starter relies entirely on the shadow to decide what to run and how to do it.

The *shadow* is responsible for making all policy decisions needed by a job. Upon request, it names the executable, arguments, environment, standard I/O streams, and everything else necessary for a complete job specification. When the job terminates, the shadow examines the exit code, the output data, the execution machine, and any other relevant information to determine whether the job has truly run to completion or has simply failed in the current environment. The shadow also serves as a basic data server for the job. It provides a remote I/O channel that the user's job may call either directly or via a proxy in the starter. This channel may be used to fetch the executable from the home site and to perform online input and output. (Note that the data server role may be filled more efficiently by third parties such as storage appliances (637) and checkpoint servers (101). The primary responsibility of the shadow is to control how and when these resources are used.)

We categorize these processes according to their reaction to failures. *Resilient processes* are designed to handle a wide variety of error conditions via standard techniques such as retry, logging, resetting, and notification. *Brittle processes* simply abort and exit upon detecting any sort of unexpected condition. As might be expected, resilient processes can be complex to develop and debug, generally requiring the management of persistent state and logging in stable storage. Brittle processes are easier to create and maintain.

The shadow and starter are brittle processes. Throughout the execution of a job, they maintain a TCP connection with each other that is used for communicating both the job's remote I/O and execution details, such as the exit code and resource use. If either side should detect that the connection is broken, it immediately aborts, killing itself entirely. If the local system is not prepared to execute a job—whether it is due to a lack of memory, an offline file system, a corrupted operating system, or even just a bug in Condor—the same form of abort is used, thus breaking the TCP connection and forcing the peer to take the same action.

Although these processes are brittle, they may still manipulate persistent state. For example, both make use of local logs to record their progress. The shadow even manipulates the job-state database stored in the schedd to indicate the disposition of the job and the amount of resources it has consumed. If either the shadow or starter should fail unexpectedly, the job state does not change. Thus, the mere disappearance of a job cannot be considered to be evidence of its success.

Neither the shadow nor the starter is responsible for cleanup. This task is left to the resilient schedd and startd, which enforce the lease that was negotiated to use the machine. Each process monitors the state of the machine on which it runs as well as the disposition of its shadow and starter children. If any child process should exit, then the resilient processes are responsible for cleaning up by killing runaway jobs, deleting temporary disk space, and discarding unused credentials. Unlike Condor-G, which we describe in Section 19.2.2, no remnant of the job is left behind after a failure.

This enforced cleanup ensures the consistency of the entire system. The startd must not simply restart a job after a failure, because the schedd will not necessarily know (or desire) that the job continued there. Rather, the schedd is left free to choose the next site of the job. It might try again at the location of the last failure, it might attempt to use another known but idle machine, or it may begin matchmaking all over again. The schedd is charged with this responsibility precisely because it alone knows the state of the job.

The matchmaker is also a brittle process, although it has few error conditions to encounter. If the matchmaker process or machine should crash, running schedds and startds will not be affected, although no further matches will be made. Once restarted, a matchmaker will quickly rebuild its state from the periodic updates of startds and schedds, and the pool will operate as before.

Every machine that runs some component of Condor is managed by a resilient *master* process. This process has no duty except to ensure that schedds, startds, and matchmakers are always running. If such a service process should terminate—whether due to a bug, administrative action, or just plain malice—the master logs the event, restarts the process, and may inform the human system administrator. Repeated failures are interspersed with an exponentially increasing delay to prevent busy-looping on unexpected conditions. This ability to start and stop processes is also used as a remote "master switch" to enable and disable Condor simultaneously on large numbers of machines. The UNIX "init" process manages the master process and thus handles system startup, shutdown, and errors in the master itself.

This dichotomy of resilient and brittle processes has several advantages. As an engineering model, it dramatically simplifies the addition of new technologies and features to serve running jobs. The vast majority of these are placed in the brittle processes, where error conditions and even faulty code are cleanly handled by the controlled destruction of the whole process. The resilient processes are naturally more complicated, but take part only in the fundamental matchmaking interaction, which is well debugged and unaffected by the addition of most new features.

However, the brittle interaction between the shadow and the starter has one significant drawback. There must be a reliable network connection between the submission and execution sites for the entire lifetime of a job. If it is broken, the job is not lost, but a significant amount of work must be repeated. To permit temporary disconnections between the two sites requires that both sides become resilient processes with persistent state and a more complex interaction. Exactly this model is explored in Condor-G.

19.2.2   Condor-G

As discussed in Chapter 4, Grid computing technologies developed within the Globus Project (276) provide standard protocols and services for accessing remote resources. In particular, the Grid Security Infrastructure (GSI) (280), Grid Resource Allocation Manager (GRAM) (205), and Global Access to Secondary Storage (GASS) (117) protocols can be used to construct secure remote execution systems that cross institutional boundaries while making use of existing batch systems without modification. However, the successful orchestration of these three protocols is no small matter, requiring a client that can persistently manage a large number of jobs even in the face of complex failures. To fulfil this role, the Condor and Globus projects collaborated to build Condor-G (291), a Grid-enabled agent for accessing remote batch systems.

In the Condor-G architecture (Figure 19.2), as in traditional Condor, the end user interacts primarily with a *schedd*, which keeps all job state in persistent storage. However, rather than specify the general requirements each job has for an execution machine, the user must specify the specific name of a Globus Toolkit GRAM server that represents an entire remote batch system.

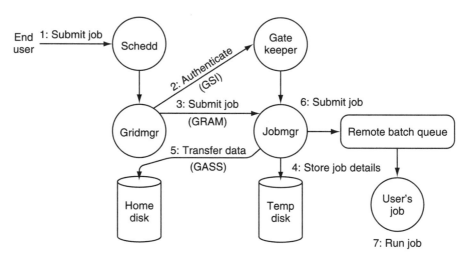

19.2

FIGURE

Condor-G architecture—the seven steps to run a Condor-G job. (1) The user submits a job to the schedd, which creates a gridmanager for the job. (2) The Gridmanager authenticates the user to the gatekeeper, which creates a jobmanager. (3) The Gridmanager transmits the job details to the jobmanager. (4) The jobmanager stores the details. (5) The jobmanager transfers the executables and input data from the home site. (6) The jobmanager submits the job to the remote batch queue. (7) The job executes.

For each job submitted, the schedd creates a process called a *gridmanager*, which is responsible for contacting a remote batch queue and providing the details of the job to be run. The gridmanager is analogous to the shadow in traditional Condor. It is responsible for actively seeking out a remote batch system through its main point of contact, the gatekeeper. Once a job begins running, the gridmanager is also responsible for servicing the job's input and output needs through the GASS protocol.

The *gatekeeper* is responsible for enforcing the admission policies of a remote batch queue. Using GSI, it accepts connections, authenticates the remote user, and maps the remote credentials into a local user ID. Once authenticated, the client may request a particular service, such as access to a batch queue through a jobmanager. The gatekeeper creates the new service process with the local user ID and passes the connection to the remote user.

The *jobmanager* is responsible for creating a remote execution environment on top of an existing batch execution system. A variety of jobmanagers are available for communicating with batch systems such as LoadLeveler (16) (a descendant of Condor), LSF (702), Maui (385), and PBS (31). A jobmanager could even pass jobs along to a traditional Condor pool such as that discussed in the preceding section. The jobmanager bears a responsibility similar to that of the traditional Condor starter, but it differs in one significant way: unlike the starter, it uses the local batch system to hold the details of a job in persistent storage and attempts to execute it even while disconnected from the gridmanager. This strategy permits a system to be more resilient with respect to an unreliable network, but also creates significant complications in protocol design.

We use the GRAM protocol design to illustrate several important issues relating to remote interactions. An early version of the GRAM protocol design, shown in Figure 19.3, used atomic interactions for the submission and completion of jobs. For example, the submission of a job from the gridmanager to the jobmanager consisted of a single message containing the job details. Upon receipt, the jobmanager would create a unique name for the job, store the details under that name, and return the ID to the gridmanager. Thereafter, it would transfer the executable and input files and attempt to submit the job to the remote batch queue.

However, a failure at any of several key points in this interaction would cause trouble. Some crashes would result in an *orphan* job, left running and consuming CPU and storage, but with no way to stop or recover it. Other crashes would result in a *wasted* job, which ran successfully but could not communicate its results back to the submitter. For example:

✦ An orphan would be created if the network connection failed after the jobmanager stored the job details but before it could return the job ID. In this

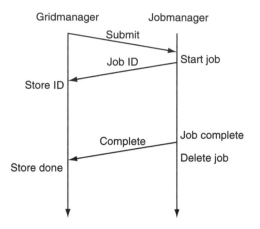

19.3

FIGURE

The original GRAM protocol used between the gridmanager and jobmanager. It consisted of two atomic interactions: one to submit a job and one to indicate job completion. This protocol can lead to orphaned or wasted jobs, as described in the text. A standard solution to this problem is shown in Figure 19.4.

case, the job would run in the batch system, the jobmanager would oversee it, but the gridmanager would not know its ID.

+ An orphan would also be created if the machine running the gridmanager crashed after the job ID was returned. In this case, the job would run in the batch system, and the gridmanager would know its ID, but there would be no jobmanager to oversee it.

+ A job would be wasted if any crash or network failure prevented the job completion message sent by the jobmanager from reaching stable storage at the submitter. In this case, the jobmanager would delete the completion details immediately after sending the message, leaving no possibility for the gridmanager to request them again after a failure.

These problems can be solved by the use of *transactions* for grouping and naming commands and the *two-phase commit* protocol for an orderly completion. A standard two-phase commit protocol is shown in Figure 19.4. Here, the transaction is created by a *begin* message, which causes the server to create a new transaction, naming it with a unique ID that must be logged and is returned to the client, which does the same. The ID is used to identify the transaction in all further messages. One or more following *data* messages fill the named transaction with all of the details the client wishes to provide. A *prepare* message ends the first phase, causing the server to check the transaction's validity and fix it in permanent storage,

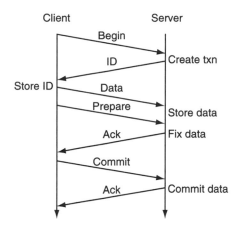

19.4

FIGURE

A standard two-phase commit protocol between a generic client and server. The first phase consists of a begin message to create a transaction, one or more data messages to provide the transaction details, and a prepare message to fix the transaction in persistent storage. The second phase is consummated with a commit message. Condor-G uses a variation of this protocol shown in Figure 19.5.

while stopping short of actually completing the operation. In the second phase, a *commit* message forces the prepared transaction to run to completion and frees the log. An acknowledgment from the server to the client permits the client to free its own log. At any time, an *abort* message (not shown) may be used to destroy the transaction completely.

The two-phase commit protocol allows for easy recovery from a failure of either party or the communication medium. If any message following begin is lost, the client may resend it without harm, using the logged transaction ID to refer to the correct operation. The separation of prepare from commit allows a single client to initiate multiple transactions at multiple servers, committing all of them only if prepare is accepted at all services. The worst loss that can happen with this protocol occurs if the response to begin is lost. Because the transaction ID is unknown to the client, it must start a new transaction, thus wasting a small amount of storage at the server. Such incomplete transactions may be removed periodically by a garbage collector.

These considerations led to a redesign of the GRAM protocol in Globus Toolkit version 2 (GT2). As the introduction of a complete two-phase commit protocol would have involved a costly rewrite of a large portion of the protocol, this redesign reaped most of the benefits by employing a limited form of two-phase commit through small changes to the submission and completion elements of the protocol. These improvements are shown in Figure 19.5.

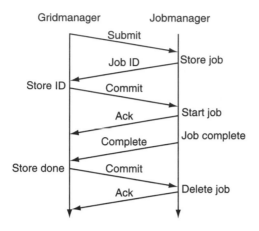

19.5

FIGURE
The improved GRAM protocol, which uses a limited form of the two-phase commit protocol given in Figure 19.4. In the first phase, the gridmanager submits the job details to the jobmanager. In the second phase, the gridmanager issues a commit to complete the transaction. A similar technique is used to indicate job completion.

To submit a job, the gridmanager issues a submit message as before. However, this message is interpreted as a combination of begin, data, and prepare. It requests a new transaction, specifies all of the job details, and forces the data into persistent storage. The jobmanager then responds with a unique job ID. To complete the transaction, the gridmanager issues a commit message that is acknowledged by the jobmanager. A similar convention is used in reverse when the job is complete. The jobmanager sends a complete message to the gridmanager, informing it that the job has completed. The gridmanager responds with another commit message, indicating that it is safe to delete the entire transaction, and the jobmanager acknowledges.

This protocol provides coherence in the event of failures. After the initial submit message, either party or the network may fail, but the protocol may resume by referring to the existing transaction ID. The greatest loss could occur if the submit message is successful but its reply is lost. However, this amount of data is relatively small. Large binary objects such as the executable and input files are transferred asynchronously by the jobmanager only after the submission has been committed.

Another challenge in the early GRAM design lay in the fact that the jobmanager stored locally persistent state and dealt with two other persistent services: the gridmanager and the batch queue. Yet the jobmanager itself is not persistent. If the entire system should lose power and reset, then the gridmanager and batch queue would recover and resume, but there would be no jobmanager to oversee the running job. This is a common and dangerous situation: the schedd is aware that the job is in a remote batch queue, but without the jobmanager it cannot control the job.

To remedy this situation, GRAM in GT2 and in later Globus Toolkit releases is equipped with a restart capability. If the schedd loses its connection with the jobmanager, it restarts another one by contacting the gatekeeper and requesting another jobmanager of the same type. It then asks the newly minted jobmanager to recover the persistent state of job in question and to continue monitoring the running job. Thus, as long as the schedd itself recovers, it can assume responsibility for starting the jobmanager.

We note that this new form of resilience places an important obligation on the jobmanager. Because the schedd creates a new jobmanager whenever needed, any jobmanager has the obligation to destroy itself whenever contact with the schedd is lost. Otherwise, it would be possible for two jobmanagers to oversee the same job. In the same way that the shadow and starter are obliged to be brittle in traditional Condor, the jobmanager is also obliged to be brittle because another process—the schedd—is responsible for its resilience.

This discussion emphasizes the point that resilience introduces complexity. The brittle properties of the traditional Condor system make failure recovery simple. However, the resilient nature of every process in Condor-G makes failure recovery much more complicated. The standard techniques established by highly consistent systems such as distributed databases must not be overlooked when designing computational Grids (327, 537).

19.2.3   Gliding In

Both traditional Condor and Condor-G have distinct advantages and disadvantages. Traditional Condor allows for powerful selection and description of resources and provides specialized environments for checkpointing, remote I/O, and the use of runtime systems such as PVM, MPI, and Java. Condor-G allows a user to reliably harness any remote computation system, even if it is not a Condor pool. The two approaches may be combined to leverage the advantages of both via a strategy called *gliding in,* which builds a traditional Condor pool on top of a Condor-G system.

The glide-in technique is shown in Figure 19.6. First, the Condor software is packaged into a "glide-in job" that is given to Condor-G. Next, the user estimates approximately how many machines he wishes to use, and submits that many glide-in jobs. Once running under the remote batch queue, these processes form an ad hoc Condor pool with an existing public matchmaker or perhaps a private

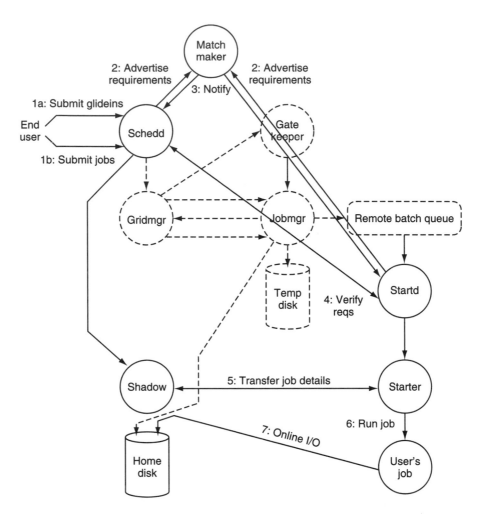

Gliding in Condor via Condor-G. (1a) A user submits a glide-in job to a Condor-G schedd. They are transferred to a remote batch queue as described in Figure 19.2. (1b) A user submits a normal job to the same schedd. (2–7) Jobs execute on the glided-in Condor system as in Figure 19.1.

matchmaker established by the user. Of course, the size of the pool depends on how many glide-in jobs propagate through the remote queue and actually begin running: the user only exercises indirect control through the number of glide-in jobs submitted. Once the ad hoc pool is formed, the same user may then submit jobs of actual work to be done. These jobs perform matchmaking and execute on the glided-in resources just as in traditional Condor.

The glided-in Condor processes make the remote batch queue a more friendly execution environment by providing the specialized Condor tools and language environments. They also allow the user to perform resource management without involving the host batch system; jobs may be preempted, migrated, or replaced at the user's whim without involving the underlying system. The glided-in Condor pool also offers the user some insurance against runaway consumption. If some oversight in the protocol between the gridmanager and jobmanager should accidentally leave a job running in the remote batch queue, it will appear in the roster of the ad hoc Condor pool where the user can either harness it or deliberately remove it. If the glide-in jobs themselves are left behind and unused, they will automatically terminate themselves after sitting idle for a user-defined length of time. Thus, the user need not worry about misplaced jobs.

19.3   WORK MANAGEMENT

So far, we have described a user's needs as simply a *job:* a single process to be executed on one machine. (Of course, a single job might be many tasks destined to run on a multiprocessor. However, such a job and machine would each be represented as one entity within a Grid.) However, most users come to the Grid to accomplish a large amount of work, frequently broken into small independent tasks. They may be performing parameter sweeps, rendering digital video, or simulating a complex system. The performance of such workloads is not measured in traditional microscopic computing metrics (such as floating-point operations per second) but in end-to-end productive terms such as permutations examined per week, video frames rendered per month, or simulations completed per year—what is known as *high-throughput computing* (539) (see also Chapter 1:13).

Users need higher-level software to manage such large-scale activities. Systems such as Condor and Condor-G manage work that is ready to be performed. Users also need to track work that is yet to be done, has already completed, or perhaps needs to be repeated. In addition, they need structures that control the order, priority, and assignment of work to Grid resources. The Condor Project and its collaborators are investigating a number of these structures, which may be divided into two categories: job parallel and task parallel.

A *job-parallel* system considers a body of jobs to be done, chooses the next jobs to execute, and then looks for resources on which to execute them. Job-parallel systems are well suited to workloads where each job requires distinct resources. The primary tool for job-parallel computing in the Condor project is the directed acyclic graph manager, or DAGMan for short. DAGMan is used in several settings, including the Condor and Condor-G systems described previously. With slight variations, it is used in two other Grid systems that we describe in the following.

A *task-parallel* system performs a similar task in the opposite order. It considers the (potentially changing) resources it has currently available, and then assigns a task from a work list to a suitable resource. Task-parallel systems are well suited to workloads in which tasks are small and have similar requirements. We describe a task-parallel framework known as master–worker that has been used in several production settings, most notably to solve a significant optimization problem. A similar task-parallel model is used by the XtremWeb system, which works in concert with Condor.

19.3.1   Job-Parallel Computing

Figure 19.7 shows a *directed acyclic graph*, or DAG for short. A DAG consists of several nodes, each representing a complete job suitable for submitting to an execution system such as Condor or Condor-G. The nodes are connected by directed edges, indicating a dependency in the graph. For example, in Figure 19.7, job A must run to completion before either job B or C may start. After A completes, jobs B and C may run in any order, perhaps simultaneously.

DAGMan is the Condor process responsible for executing a dag. DAGMan may be thought of as a distributed, fault-tolerant version of the standard UNIX

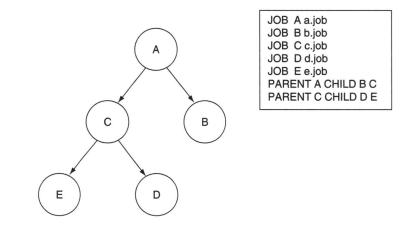

19.7   A directed acyclic graph of jobs, or DAG.

FIGURE

make facility. Like make, it ensures that all components of a DAG run to completion in an acceptable order. Unlike make, it does not rely on the file system to determine which jobs have completed. Instead, it keeps a log to record where jobs are submitted, when they begin executing, and when they complete. If DAGMan should crash, it can replay the log to determine the progress of the DAG.

DAGMan executes jobs by submitting them to a schedd in a Condor or Condor-G pool. As described earlier, the schedd ensures that the jobs are persistently retried, even if system components (including schedds) crash. To provide DAGMan with the same sort of resilience, DAGMan itself is submitted to the schedd, which considers it to be a normal Condor job in every respect, except that it executes under the supervision of the schedd on the submitting machine. Thus, the same transactional interface can be used to submit whole DAGs, inquire about their status, and remove them from the queue.

Each job in a DAG carries its own independent requirements on execution. In a traditional Condor pool, one job in a DAG may require a machine with a large amount of memory, while another may require a machine with a particular type of CPU. In a Condor-G system, different jobs may need to run on entirely different gatekeepers. Each job maintains its own abstract requirements that are not evaluated until the job has been passed to the schedd for consideration by the matchmaker. We call this property *late binding*. The job is not assigned an execution site until the last possible moment. Thus, the system has maximum flexibility in deciding how to execute the job. Other systems have explored the possibility of binding earlier in the lifetime of a job. We discuss two such systems here: the EU DataGrid and the Chimera system.

The planned EU DataGrid (EDG) is a Globus Toolkit-based Grid that links computing centers and data storage centers across Europe to support the computing needs of a variety of data-intensive science projects. In the planned EDG architecture (Figure 19.8), work is expressed as an abstract DAG consisting of jobs with requirements on the site of execution. In addition to the usual requirements such as the necessary CPU or amount of memory, these jobs may also have requirements on relationships between elements. For example, one job may need to execute on a machine with a certain dataset in local storage, while another job may simply need to run at the same site as its predecessor in the DAG. Armed with this information, the schedd evaluates the DAG piece by piece. For each job, it employs the traditional model of consulting with a matchmaker to find an appropriate match for the job. However, instead of matching with a single machine, it matches with an entire batch queue. It then uses the Condor-G mechanisms for executing the job through that queue. This process continues until the entire DAG has been evaluated and executed.

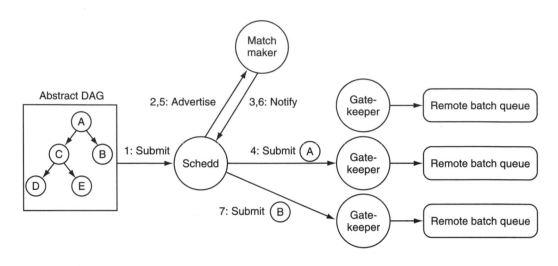

19.8

FIGURE The planned architecture for executing dags in the European DataGrid. (1) The user submits a DAG composed of jobs with abstract requirements. (2) The schedd advertises the requirements of the first job. (3) The matchmaker notifies the schedd of a compatible gatekeeper. (4) The schedd executes the first job via Condor-G as in Figure 19.2. (5) The schedd advertises the second job. (6) The matchmaker notifies the schedd. (7) The schedd executes the second job. This pattern continues until the DAG is complete.

The Chimera system (284, 285) is designed for the production of *virtual data*. Unlike a traditional batch execution system, Chimera does not require the user to specify what programs are to be executed. Rather, it asks the user to specify what data are to be produced. Much like a functional programming environment, Chimera plans what procedures are necessary to realize the data using fundamental inputs. Thus, the user is relieved of the burden of tracking and managing large numbers of batch jobs, while the system can silently optimize caching, data placement, and function shipping. The architecture of the Chimera system is shown in Figure 19.9.

The user interacts with the Chimera system by submitting a request for specific virtual data elements. Chimera consults a *virtual data catalog* to determine whether the data have already been created, and may potentially respond immediately with the result if it is available. Otherwise, Chimera produces a DAG designed to compute the necessary data. This DAG is executed via the use of many of the Condor-G components described previously.

The Chimera architecture admits a variety of scheduling strategies, from early to late binding. The Pegasus planner (216) performs early binding, using

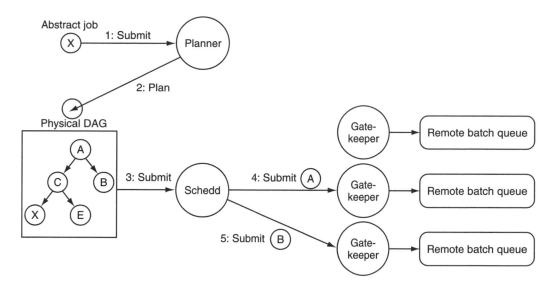

The architecture of the Globus Chimera virtual data system. (1) The user submits an abstract job that describes a data object to be realized. (2) The planner creates a DAG that will realize the data. Each job in the DAG is bound to a physical location. (3) The DAG is submitted to a schedd. (4) Each job in the DAG is executed via Condor-G as in Figure 19.2.

various planning techniques to produce a concrete DAG composed of jobs whose location is already specified in the form of a GRAM gatekeeper name. The whole DAG is passed to a schedd, which then executes each component via Condor-G, as in Figure 19.2. Other approaches (544) that perform late binding via callouts from the Condor-G agent to simple decision makers also are being explored.

All of these examples use DAGMan to manage job-parallel workloads, but they differ in how and when abstract names are assigned to physical resources. The traditional Condor approach of *late binding* defers this decision until the last possible moment. If the job should fail, an entirely new name binding may be attempted and the job sent elsewhere. In the EDG *medium-binding* approach, the user still specifies abstract requirements on when and where each component must be executed, but the schedd makes a single decision regarding which batch queue to use. Once made, the final assignment of compute resource is left to the local batch scheduler. Finally, in the Chimera–Pegasus *early-binding* approach the user is to specify an abstract target of the work, but the planner decides on the entire set of physical resources to use before the work is even submitted to Condor-G. The schedd simply passes the jobs to the named resources.

None of these approaches is universally better than the others. Early name binding is needed when the information needed to make a good placement decision is not integral to the remote execution system. This is appropriate in Chimera because the planner has information about storage resources that is not available to Condor. Late name binding is better when such information is available, because the system is able to make alternate choices when failures and other exigencies thwart the original plan. An example of this is found in the notion of *I/O communities* (637) that integrate the state of storage into an existing matchmaking system. Medium name binding is a compromise that works when storage resources are accessible to the matchmaker but not to the target execution system.

19.3.2   Task-Parallel Computing

The task-parallel model works by first harnessing the necessary workers and then assigning work units as workers are available to process them. This computing model is naturally suited to large problems of indeterminate size that may be easily partitioned. We discuss two task-parallel computing systems: Condor master–worker (Condor-MW) and XtremWeb (XW). See also Chapters 28 and 29.

In the Condor-MW and XW systems (Figure 19.10), as in other similar systems such as Entropia (180), SETI@home (79), and Nimrod (56), one master process directs the computation with the assistance of as many remote worker processes as it needs or the computing environment can provide. The master itself contains three components: a work list, a tracking module, and a steering module. The

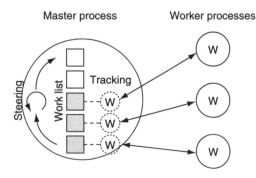

19.10   The master–worker framework.

FIGURE

work list simply records all outstanding work. The *tracking module* accounts for the remote worker processes and the remaining work to be done and assigns workers uncompleted work. The *steering module* directs the computation by assigning work, examining results, and modifying the work list.

Task-parallel computing is naturally fault tolerant. Workers are assumed to be unreliable: they disappear when machines crash and they reappear as new machines become available. If a worker should fail while holding a work unit, the steering module simply returns it to the work list. The steering module may even take additional steps to replicate or reassign work for greater reliability or simply to speed the completion of the last remaining work units near the end of a problem.

Workers themselves must be managed. New workers must be sought out when needed, failed workers must be noted and replaced, and idle workers must be released when no longer needed. These functions can be performed within the system itself or by the user. We explore both possibilities.

The Condor-MW (443) system is a set of C++ classes that encapsulate communication and management facilities needed for task-parallel computing. The programmer extends these classes to construct an application-specific master and worker. The management of workers may be tightly integrated with the work itself. For example, as a computation progresses, the master may want to scale the number of workers with the size of the work list. This capability is supported by the function set_target_num_workers, which the application writer can call at any point in a program (534) to request that the master attempt to adjust the number of workers, using the underlying Condor schedd to request new resources or release old ones. Of course, the number of workers is a goal, not an assertion. The number of workers may be less than the target if there are no more available machines, and may be higher if the master slowly releases workers as they finish their current tasks.

Communication between master and workers is achieved via TCP connections, thus allowing the master to know when a stream has broken, indicating that a worker has disconnected or failed. A distributed file system may also be used as the communication channel, in which case messages between master and workers are placed in a rendezvous directory that serves as a persistent message queue. This approach allows MW to tolerate network outages, relying on the underlying file system for reliable delivery. In this model, timeouts must be used to detect the failure of a worker process. A third option is to use PVM communications.

The master dispatches work units to workers and thus maintains tight control over the disposition of each worker. It knows exactly which are busy and which are idle, and can even deliberately hold workers idle in the expectation of future work or as an instantaneous reserve against failures. (In Condor, a client is "charged" for machines that it claims, whether it uses them or not. Typically, the charge is accumulated only as a convenience figure to measure pool use and control priority, but it could also be turned into a pecuniary debt.) Because the master controls the workers closely, it may distinguish between failed and idle workers and seek out new resources as needed.

The XtremWeb (257) system (XW) is a Java-based system for task-parallel computing. Like Condor-MW, it encapsulates many of the communication and organizational details for task-parallel computing, allowing the programmer to concentrate on application details. XW differs from Condor-MW in several key ways. It is designed to operate over a wide-area network, assuming no underlying remote execution system. Thus, workers operate autonomously, pulling work units from the master. It does not manage the allocation of the workers themselves, but it does provide for security and for operation through network disconnections.

An XW worker manages a machine in a manner similar to a Condor startd. It permits remote processes to run only within the constraints of the machine's owner. For example, it may permit remote users to harness the machine at night or when the console is idle. When available to perform work, the worker contacts a well-known master to obtain a work unit. It is then free to operate while disconnected and may choose to pause or discard work at its discretion. When disconnected, a worker is responsible for sending periodic messages to the master to indicate that it is still alive.

The pull nature of the XW worker is well suited to the realities of the current Internet. Firewalls, address translators, and similar devices often prevent symmetric network connectivity. However, many such barriers permit a TCP connection to be initiated from the private portion to the public network, thus encouraging a design in which the master is placed on a public network and passively accepts incoming connections from workers, which are more numerous and likely to execute on private networks.

XW provides security mechanisms to protect the integrity of the application and the machine owners. For portability, the worker itself is bootstrapped in a Java virtual machine, but end-user computations may be performed in native code. To protect the owners of worker machines, only native code certified by a central authority is accepted for use. A public-key encryption system is used to ensure code authenticity and to protect communications between the master and workers.

Because the XW master manages only work and not the workers themselves, an application has no direct control over the number of workers that it harnesses. However, this task can be performed outside the context of the system. For example, an XW system may be integrated with a Condor pool or Condor-G system by starting an XW master and submitting a number of XW workers to a schedd. As Condor is able to execute the XW workers, they report to the known master, distribute the application code, and go to work.

XW is planned to be used as a distributed resource manager for the Pierre Auger Observatory. This international scientific group aims to study high-energy cosmic rays indirectly by way of their interaction with Earth's atmosphere. To properly calibrate the detector, its behavior to a large number of incident rays must be simulated. Approximately 10 CPU-years (570) of simulation must be performed. To complement the existing standard computing clusters, XW will be used to distribute the FORTRAN simulation code to opportunistic workers.

19.4 THE LAYERS OF GRID COMPUTING

The preceding discussion shows how a complex Grid computing system can be built up in layers, with each layer assuming the responsibility to multiplex resources for a different reason. Figure 19.11 shows these responsibilities. Together, the Condor-G gridmanager and jobmanager form an *inter-Grid* system. They are responsible for bridging the gap between autonomous systems on the Grid and are concerned with matters of security and disconnected operation. They have limited facilities for managing different classes of machines and jobs. These problems are better solved by the Condor schedd and startd, which form an *intercustomer* system. Once connected via the inter-Grid system, they manage all the details of heterogeneous systems and arbitrate requests for service from different customers. However, they do not provide services for managing the order and assignment of work to be done, tasks that are better handled by an *intertask* system such as DAGMan, Condor-MW, or XW.

The most flexible layers of a Grid system are task parallel. The unique feature of a task-parallel system is that it provides separate interfaces for the allocation of resources and the assignment of work. For example, in both Condor-MW and XW the user may manipulate the number of workers available,

Master Process		Worker Process
Gridmanager	**Inter-Grid Layer**	Jobmanager
Schedd	**Inter-Customer-Layer**	Startd
MW-Master XW-Master	**Inter-Task Layer**	MW-Worker XW-Worker

19.11 The layers of Grid computing.

FIGURE

by either calling a procedure (Condor-MW) or invoking new workers externally (XW). This distinction leads to a powerful and robust system design, because the concerns of performance are separated from those of correctness. If higher throughput is needed, more workers may be added. If shorter latencies are needed, nearby or faster workers may be added. The master's work-assignment algorithm is oblivious to what resources are selected, and persists through all failures.

The same distinction between allocation and assignment is found in other layers as well. The traditional Condor intercustomer system is task parallel at heart. The schedd allocates machines using the matchmaking algorithm and then only assigns work in the order of local priority as machines become available. Like a Condor-MW or XW master, the schedd may hold allocated machines idle as hot spares or as a cache for future requests, if it is willing to pay the price.

When allocation and assignment are coupled, the system is less flexible. For example, Condor-G couples machine allocation with job execution. It submits a job to an existing remote batch queue without advance knowledge of whether the job will execute immediately or at all. If multiple queues are available, it must send a job to wait in one queue or the other and may find it difficult to enforce local orderings on job execution. To remedy this problem, we may layer a task-parallel system on top, as is done with gliding in. The task-parallel Condor system multiplexes the job-parallel Condor-G, allowing the user more flexibility in resource allocation.

Thus, rather than place all of these responsibilities in one process or system, each layer is responsible for the needs of one type of element: Grids, customers, or tasks. Depending on the desired functionality, users can assemble an appropriate system by overlaying one layer on top of another.

Exactly such a layered system was built in the year 2000 to attack a series of unsolved optimization problems (443). Using Condor-MW, four mathematicians from Argonne National Laboratory, the University of Iowa, and Northwestern University constructed a branch-and-bound searching algorithm. This technique divided the initial search space into smaller regions, bounding what could be the best possible solution in each. Despite a highly sophisticated solution algorithm, the time required to find a solution was still considerable: over seven years with the best desktop workstation available at the time. This solver was deployed on a layered system consisting of the master–worker framework running on a traditional Condor pool glided in over a Condor-G system. A solution to the NUG-30 facilities assignment first posed in 1968 was found in less than one week by using over 95,000 hours of CPU time on 2,500 CPUs at 10 different physical sites.

19.5   RELIABLE OUTPUT

The final problem that we consider is the following. Jobs placed on remote execution sites may wish to read and write from archival storage, send messages back and forth to other running processes, or read and write intermediate results at known rendezvous points. These activities are known collectively as input and output (I/O). Regardless of destination, most I/O activities are performed via standard file system operations such as open, read, write, and close. As with remote execution, these operations assume a fault-free connection between the application and the target storage device, and reliability is at best an illusion provided to the application. Within a Grid computing system, we must be prepared to deal with all manner of failures.

We focus here on output. Input is a well-studied problem: file systems, databases, and Web browsers have all addressed the difficulties of replicating read-only data for the sake of a migrating client (254, 528). Much of that research is relevant and already implemented for Grid computing systems. Furthermore, output has stricter requirements for consistency. Whereas an already-read input may be discarded with the knowledge that it may be reread at a predictable cost, output data are usually (but not always) a more expensive commodity produced by a careful confluence of inputs with software and hardware. Indeed, some outputs (such as those of a physical measurement) may not be reproducible at all. Finally, output may be considered the simple dual of input. Every reader requires a writer, and the recording of data into stable storage is more complex than its retrieval.

We assume that a running application wishes to record its output in a named storage location. Whether this is an archival device, rendezvous storage, or another running application is a minor detail. The simplest way to accomplish this task is to connect the file system operations of an application by remote procedure call to the storage device. This is known as remote output. As we will see, this method is sensitive to all of the problems of disconnection discussed previously in the context of a remote execution scenario. We present several techniques for making remote output robust against system failures. However, before we embark on that discussion, we must establish several primitives for reliably recording output data in stable storage.

19.5.1   Storage Transactions

Just as execution systems require careful protocols (such as two-phase commit) to provide a reliable service, so too do storage systems require disciplines for ensuring that complete actions are secure and incomplete actions are cleaned up. However, unlike databases, most mass-storage devices do not support the complete notion of a transaction as we explored earlier. Instead of begin, pre-pare, commit, and abort, we have only *fsync*, which forces all previous changes to storage. Nevertheless, we can still perform reliable storage operations if we accept limitations on either the sort of operations performed or on the nature of the transaction itself.

If we limit programs to performing only the storage of complete new files, we can provide reliability through what we call a *delivery transaction*. This disci-pline provides the same guarantees as the ordinary two-phase commit protocol. Suppose that a program wishes to deliver a new file f1. To begin a delivery trans-action, a new file f1.t must be created. The program may then write data into f1.t in any desired order. To prepare the transaction, the write permissions on f1 are checked, the data are fixed to permanent storage by invoking fsync on f1.t, and the file is renamed to f1.p. Finally, to commit the transaction, the file is renamed into f1.

This discipline satisfies the two-phase commit requirements as follows. If the transaction is to be aborted at any time, f1.t may simply be deleted without harm. If either the client or server should crash before the transaction is prepared, the recovery procedure should delete all unprepared transactions by deleting any file ending in .t. Files ending in .p have been fixed to disk and may safely be retained. Finally, if either side should crash while a rename is in progress, the POSIX (32) semantics of file renaming ensure that the entire file will exist under exactly one of the names f1 or f1.p.

Delivery transactions are certainly a dominant mode of interaction in Grid computing, but they are not the only mode. Some users' jobs require more sophis-ticated interactions with storage, sometimes creating and deleting multiple files. A limited form of reliability may still be provided for these jobs without resorting to a full-blown database system. If we limit a job to the use of certain operations and apply the fsync operation as a form of commit, we can provide what we call a *half-transaction*. A half-transaction guarantees that a series of operations, once committed, is safely on stable storage. A half-transaction has no facility for abort-ing incomplete work. It must be carried forward.

When using half-transactions, we must limit a job to idempotent operations. An operation is idempotent if it may be run multiple times, perhaps not even to completion. But if the final execution is successful, then the end effect on storage is the same as if exactly one successful execution occurred. Most file-system oper-ations, if correctly recorded, are idempotent.

For example, the creation of a file by name is idempotent. It may be repeated many times and the file still exists exactly once. Writing data to a file is also idempotent if the write offset is explicitly given. A few key operations are not idempotent. For example, appending to an existing file is not idempotent if the current file size is the implicit write point. Renaming a file from one name to another is also not idempotent. These operations must be avoided when using half-transactions.

Half-transactions are used as follows. A stream of idempotent output operations may be written to storage. To complete the half-transaction, a commit must be issued. A standard file system provides commit by allowing a client to invoke fsync on all files that have been modified. If the client receives an acknowledgment for the commit, then the half-transaction is complete. If the connection between the client and server is lost, then the entire half-transaction must start again. However, it does not matter if any or all of the write operations have succeeded or failed, because the idempotent property guarantees that the end result will be the same. When the likelihood of failure is high, a single half-transaction may be strengthened by adding periodic commit operations before the final commit. If a failure occurs, the half-transaction need only be resumed from the operation following the most recent commit.

19.5.2   Reliable Delivery Techniques

Whether we are performing delivery transactions for whole files or half-transactions for arbitrary updates, Grid computing requires reliable services for delivering the inputs and outputs. However, it is difficult to divorce the completion of output from job execution. The manipulation of storage is an important side effect of execution, and we would be negligent indeed if a job completed reliably without performing its output (or vice versa). Thus we must pay special attention to the integration of job completion with output completion. Where the word commit appears, it may be used to indicate the completion of either a storage transaction or half-transaction, whichever is in use.

The most natural form of output is *direct output* (Figure 19.12). In this model, a job stays in close contact with its target storage. When it requires input or output, it issues a remote procedure call to the target storage to access some limited portion of the data that it needs immediately, perhaps with some ability to cache and buffer expected data. This approach is used in the Condor remote system call facility (602), in which every system call executed by a job is sent home for execution at the shadow. Similar techniques are found in distributed file systems such as NFS (572) and AFS (370).

No matter what type of storage transaction the job employs, it is responsible for seeing that any modifications run to completion. Thus, the job itself is responsible for issuing a final commit to the target storage before indicating a

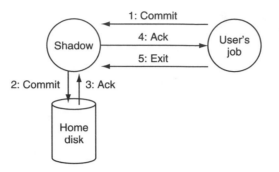

Direct output via remote system calls. When the job is ready to exit, it issues commit to the shadow. The shadow forces all output to the disk, and sends an acknowledgement back to the job. Now satisfied, the job informs the shadow that it is complete.

successful exit to the process that supervises it. In traditional Condor, the roles of storage device and supervisor are both played by the shadow process, but the same principle applies to other systems. If the commit does not succeed, the job is responsible for aborting itself rather than indicating a successful completion.

The direct output technique is easily constructed and well understood. However, it has one major drawback. It holds the job hostage to the whims of the larger system. If the storage device crashes, the network fails, or a temporary load diminishes bandwidth, the job will pause as it waits for the remote procedure call to finish. This is the case regardless of whether the output is performed over a stream connection, as in Condor, or over datagrams, as in NFS. On the other hand, the output might complete, but the job might fail or be evicted before it can record a successful completion.

One technique for insulating the job from these problems is to perform all I/O in large pieces before and after the job executes. This strategy is used, for example, in the Globus Toolkit GASS system (117). It does provide limited insulation but also creates new problems. A job's I/O must be known before it runs, which is not always possible. Also, the user cannot see progressive output, as may be required to determine whether a computation is running correctly. Some jobs may permit limited interactive steering when run in a batch mode, so interactive access may allow more efficient use of resources.

What many jobs and users require is an "interactive when possible" I/O capability that makes a job's inputs and outputs immediately available *when network conditions permit*. Otherwise, output is buffered and performed in the

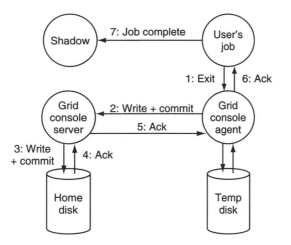

19.13

FIGURE
The Grid Console permits more flexible I/O coupling. As the job runs, it writes output data to the agent, which stores it on the temporary disk or forwards it to the server. When the job wishes to exit, it informs the agent, which must then force all output to the server. If successful, the job is informed and may indicate completion to the shadow.

background so as not to unnecessarily delay execution. The *Grid console* provides this capability. It is composed of two parts, an *agent* and a *server* (Figure 19.13). The agent attaches itself to the job's standard input and output streams using the Bypass (638, 639) interpositioning tool. As the job runs, it traps I/O operations and, if the network is available, passes them to the shadow via remote procedure calls. If the network is not available, output data are simply written to local temporary storage. When the network becomes available again, the agent writes the buffered outputs to the shadow and resumes normal operations. Input data are read on demand from the server. If the network is not available when an input is needed, the job is blocked. When the job wishes to exit, the agent ensures that all buffered data are written and committed, and then permits the job to exit.

The Grid console is an improvement over direct output, as it permits the job to operate even when disconnected from the shadow. This technique is similar to the form of disconnected operation found in file systems such as Coda (413), which permit a client to optimistically operate when disconnected from the home file system. However, when the job exits, it may still be blocked if the network is down—a necessary consequence of the small but vital coupling between the job's exit code and its output side effects.

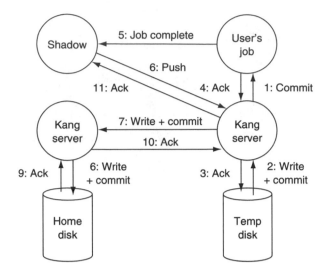

19.14

FIGURE

Kangaroo permits even more flexible coupling. The job writes its output data to the nearest Kangaroo server as it runs. When it wishes to exit, it issues a **commit** to the nearest server. If successful, it indicates completion to the shadow. The shadow must then issue a **push** in order to ensure that all output has successfully been delivered.

We may stretch this coupling even further by using the *Kangaroo* (636) I/O system, shown in Figure 19.14. A Kangaroo system is a peer-to-peer network of identical servers, each providing temporary storage space for visiting jobs. A job may queue output requests as messages at any Kangaroo server, addressing them with the name of the user's home storage. Like Internet mail, these requests proceed to their destination asynchronously, perhaps passing through several servers along the way. Unlike Internet mail, Kangaroo provides two distinct consistency operations. When a job writes data to a nearby server, it uses a commit message to make sure that the data are safe on local storage. Thus, the job may exit with confidence that the data will arrive eventually, although it does not make any guarantees about exactly when it will arrive. The job informs the shadow that it has exited and evacuates the machine, making it available for another job to use. The shadow, knowing the output may still be spooled at the remote Kangaroo server, must use the second consistency operation, push, to ensure that all dirty data are forced back to the home storage site before informing the user that the job has completed.

These three variations on reliable output share many properties with remote execution. The simplest systems involve tight coupling between the submission and execution sites. A more relaxed coupling has advantages, but it demands more complex interactions between client and server.

19.6   FUTURE DIRECTIONS

We have introduced techniques that a client of distributed services can use to deal with disconnections and failures and to ensure that remote services reach an acceptable state. (Just as database system imposes order on unstructured disk drives, so too must Grid clients impose order on unstructured workers.) We conclude by reflecting on the properties of an ideal remote Grid service, one that would be a reliable and effective partner for a Grid client. Although remote services need not be perfect (good clients are prepared to deal with failures), better services can enable more effective and efficient Grid clients.

An ideal remote execution service would have the following features:

+ Powerful ways to asynchronously interact with third parties, such as databases or file systems, on behalf of a job

+ Precise tools for measuring and limiting what resources a job consumes

+ Reliable methods for cleaning up an unmanaged machine before and after each job executes

+ Clear responsibility for dealing with failures and unexpected events without continuous oversight from the submitter

We call this imagined reliable partner the *Grid Shell*. A Grid Shell surrounds a job, insulating it from a hostile environment. Some of this insulation occurs by preparing the execution site appropriately, perhaps by transferring files or installing other software before the job runs. Some might also occur by emulating the necessary services at run time. Whatever the tools available to the Grid Shell for dealing with the complexity of the outside world, it must rely entirely upon an external policy manager (such as a shadow or a gridmanager) to control how and where it uses remote resources.

A Grid Shell does not exist now, although there already exist many pieces of software that provide some of the needed capabilities. Like a traditional command-line shell, it does not perform any of the user's work directly but is an overseer or caretaker responsible for watching a user's job throughout its lifetime. It must locate an executable from a number of choices, given a particular user's preferences and settings. It must set up physical input and output objects and bind them to logical names such as standard input and output streams. It must create the job process and then monitor its completion, detecting whether the job has completed normally or was simply unable to execute in the current environment.

Although a Grid Shell would generally not be an interactive tool, it must follow user commands and policies. As a user will not typically be physically involved in every decision made, the Grid Shell acts as the agent or representative of the user and controls resource consumption decisions made for the user. In Condor, this role is filled by the shadow. Although other components perform all of the complicated roles necessary to carry out distributed computing, the shadow alone is responsible for simply directing what is to be used. The Grid Shell must respect this distinction.

For example, the Globus Toolkit jobmanager satisfies the first requirement for a Grid Shell. It transfers all necessary standard input and output streams before and after a job executes. However, it does not decide where these streams come from on its own. It is informed of this information by the gridmanager, which fulfills the role of the shadow in a Condor-G system. The jobmanager is also an excellent tool for disconnected operation, as it is capable of moving these streams asynchronously and resuming after a failure.

The second requirement is satisfied by the traditional Condor starter. As a job runs, that starter continuously monitors all of its resource use, including CPU time, memory size, and file-system activity. If the job exceeds any limits set by the user, then the starter can cleanly terminate the job. This capability can be used to prevent runaway consumption due to software or hardware failures, or it may simply limit the user's consumption to what is mandated by the community as his or her fair share.

A traditional Condor startd meets the third requirement. When a disconnection or other failure prevents a job from running properly, a Grid Shell must be careful to precisely clean up the execution site in a manner expected by the submitter. This frees the submitter to attempt the job elsewhere without fear of creating conflicts between multiple running jobs and without unnecessary consumption of resources. Of course, a Grid Shell need not be aggressive about cleanup. If the submitter and the shell agree, an appropriate time interval may pass or other conditions may be met before cleanup occurs. As long as the two parties agree on the conditions, a reliable system will result.

The final requirement states that the shell must have some independent facility for retrying failures without oversight from the submitter. We have explored this facility with an experimental piece of software known as the *fault-tolerant shell*. This is a simple scripting language that ties together existing programs using an exception-like syntax for allowing the failure and retry of programs. For example, this script attempts a file copy followed by a simulation for up to five attempts at one hour each. If either should fail, the pair is tried again until a time limit of three hours is reached:

```
try for 3 hours
try 5 times
  copy-data ftp://ftp.cs.wisc.edu/data data
end
try for 1 hour
  run-simulation data
  end
end
```

We imagine the Grid shell as an ideal partner for remote execution in a Grid computing environment. Many of the properties of the Grid shell have been explored in existing software, but work remains to tie these disparate systems together into a coherent whole. If carefully engineered with public interfaces, such a tool would be useful to all manner of remote execution systems, regardless of the vendor of the client or server.

19.7   SUMMARY

Grid computing is a partnership between clients and servers. Grid clients have more responsibilities than do traditional clients and must be equipped with powerful mechanisms for dealing with and recovering from failures, whether they occur in the context of remote execution, work management, or data output. When clients are powerful, servers must accommodate them by using careful protocols. We have described some of the algorithms that may be used to help clients and servers come to agreement in a failure-prone system. Finally, we have sketched the properties of an ideal service for remote execution called the Grid Shell.

Many challenges remain in the design and implementation of Grid computing systems. Although today's Grids are accessible to technologists and other users willing to suffer through experimental and incomplete systems, many obstacles must be overcome before large-scale systems are usable without special knowledge. Grids intended for users of ordinary competence must be designed with as much attention paid to the consequences of failures as the potential benefits of success.

ACKNOWLEDGMENTS

This work was supported in part by Department of Energy awards DE-FG02-01ER25443, DE-FC02-01ER25464, DE-FC02-01ER25450, and DE-FC02-01ER25458; European Commission award 18/GL/04/2002; IBM Corporation awards MHVU5622 and POS996BK874B; and National Science Foundation awards 795ET-21076A, 795PACS1077A, 795NAS1115A, 795PACS1123A, and 02-229 through the University of Illinois, NSF awards UF00111 and UF01075 through the University of Florida, and NSF award 8202-53659 through Johns Hopkins University. Thain is supported by a Lawrence Landweber NCR fellowship and the Wisconsin Alumni Research Foundation.

FURTHER READING

For more information on the topics covered in this chapter, see *www.mkp.com/grid2* and the following:

+ Chapter 1:14 and a series of technical articles describe early Condor development (444, 446, 489), checkpointing (602), and remote system calls (445).

+ Other articles describe the matchmaking model and ClassAd language (538, 539, 541), as well as extensions to the ClassAd language (447, 637).

+ Transactions and reliability in databases and other distributed systems are described in standard texts (327, 537); technical articles describe earlier developments (324, 326).

Instrumentation and Monitoring

Jeffrey Hollingsworth and Brian Tierney

*T*ypical Grid environments are highly distributed and composed of many elements. Grid middleware and tools seek to hide much of the resulting system complexity from the user, which is desirable when things are working fine but can cause difficulties when problems arise. The user then needs a means of seeing precisely what is happening. Also, with the range of resources available, Grid processes need a way to understand the current status of various elements in order to make resource allocation decisions.

Grid monitoring is the measurement and publication of the state of a Grid component at a particular point in time. To be effective, monitoring must be "end-to-end," meaning that all components between the application endpoints must be monitored. This includes software (e.g., applications, services, middleware, operating systems), end-host hardware (e.g., CPUs, disks, memory, network interface), and networks (e.g., routers, switches, or end-to-end paths). Instrumentation is the process of adding probes to generate monitoring event data.

Monitoring is required for a number of purposes, including status checking, troubleshooting, performance tuning, and debugging. For example, assume a job has been submitted to a resource broker, which uses a reliable file transfer service to copy several files to the site where the job will run, and then runs the job. This particular process should normally take 15 minutes to complete, but two hours have passed and the job has not yet completed. Determining what, if anything, is wrong is difficult and requires a great deal of monitoring data. Is the job still running or did one of the software components crash? Is the network particularly congested? Is the CPU particularly loaded? Is there a disk problem? Was a software library containing a bug installed somewhere? Monitoring provides the information to help track down the current status of the job and locate any problems.

This chapter provides background on the challenges of instrumentation and monitoring in Grid systems. We first describe in more detail which Grid components need monitoring data, and why. We then describe the basic pieces of a Grid monitoring system necessary to move monitoring data from where it was measured to the component that needs it. A survey of monitoring tools and frameworks is presented, including Dyninst, Grid Monitoring Architecture, Network Weather Service, NetLogger, Ganglia, the Globus Toolkit's Monitoring and Discovery Service, OGSA-based monitoring, and standards such as Simple Network Management protocol and Common Information Model. Finally, we present some detailed case studies that demonstrate how the various components interact to solve a particular problem.

20.1   CONSUMERS OF MONITORING DATA

The frequently dynamic nature of Grid resources and applications results in many opportunities for the use of instrumentation and monitoring data. The following are some major uses of data monitoring:

Troubleshooting and fault detection.   When a Grid job fails, it can be difficult to determine the source of the failure. Comprehensive monitoring information is needed for both real-time fault detection and for postmortem analysis.

Performance analysis and tuning.   Developers of Grid applications and middleware often observe performance problems such as unexpectedly low throughput or high latency. Determining the source of the performance problems requires detailed end-to-end instrumentation of all components, including the applications, operating systems, hosts, and networks. The case study in Section 20.7.2 illustrates this type of application.

Guiding scheduling decisions.   In an environment in which available communication and computational resources constantly change, measurements of current state can be used to drive resource allocation and scheduling decisions. For example, network monitoring data can be used by Grid data management middleware (Chapter 22) when selecting the best source from which to copy replicated data. Either raw historical data or, when feasible, predictions of future end-to-end path characteristics between the destination and each possible source can be used for this purpose. Accurate predictions of the performance obtainable from each source require measurement of available bandwidth (both end-to-end and hop-by-hop), latency, loss, and other characteristics important to file transfer performance. A resource broker (Chapters 18 and 19) is another example of a middleware component that can exploit monitoring data in order to make intelligent scheduling decisions. Although jobs may be assigned to compute resources based only on relatively static data such as CPU capability, total memory, operating system, and network capacity, better optimization may come from incorporating dynamic monitoring data such as batch queue length, CPU or network load, or local storage system load.

Gathering data to improve the next execution of the program.   Historically, offline refinement has been the primary use of performance instrumentation. Data are gathered during an execution and used by the programmer or the compiler to alter the program so that it will run faster when next executed. Chapter 1:15 discusses how to present performance data to application programmers, and Chapter 25 discusses compiler use of performance data.

Adapting an executing computation.   For long-running programs, the computational resources required or available may change during a single execution. Performance data can be used to guide computational steering (Chapter 24) or to permit applications or run-time libraries to adapt their behavior in response to observations (e.g., the Active Harmony System described in Section 20.7.1; see also Chapter 26).

Debugging.   Complex, multithreaded, distributed programs can often be difficult to debug. The proper instrumentation and analysis tools can aid the debugging process. The case study in Section 20.7.2 illustrates this type of application.

Auditing and intrusion detection.   Security and accounting services are another important consumer of monitoring data (see Chapter 21).

20.1.1   End-to-End Monitoring Components

A complete end-to-end monitoring system has several components, as shown in Figure 20.1. Each is discussed in detail in the following sections.

Instrumentation.   Instrumentation is the process of putting probes into software or hardware to measure the state of a hardware component, such as a host, disk, or network, or a software component, such as operating system, middleware, or application. These probes are often called sensors. Facilities for precision instrumentation

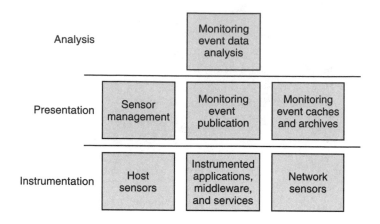

Monitoring components.

FIGURE

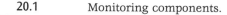

of Grid applications, Grid middleware, and hardware resources are essential to the process of tuning and debugging. It is common for Grid applications to run much slower than expected, and without detailed instrumentation data it is nearly impossible to determine the source of the bottlenecks. Additionally, it can be extremely difficult to debug deadlocked threaded, distributed applications without detailed instrumentation.

Monitoring event publication.   Consumers of monitoring event data need to locate appropriate monitoring event providers. Standard schemas, publication mechanisms, and access policies for monitoring event data are required.

Event archives.   Archived monitoring event data are critical for performance analysis and tuning, as well as for accounting. Historical data can be used to establish a baseline with which to compare current performance.

Sensor management.   As Grid environments become larger and more complex, there are more components to monitor and manage, and the amount of monitoring data produced by this effort can quickly become overwhelming. Some components require constant monitoring, while others are monitored only on demand. A mechanism for activating sensors on demand is required.

Data analysis.   Collecting large amounts of monitoring data is useless unless these data answer the user's questions about their application. Data analysis techniques provide a way to reduce raw data to the salient information. These can include statistical clustering techniques, data mining, or critical path analysis.

Most of these components have existed in one form or another in traditional computing environments. However, several issues make the overall monitoring problem more difficult in a Grid environment. A Grid monitoring service has the following requirements:

+ *Discovery*. The distributed nature of Grid systems makes it difficult to discover what types of components are available and how they are performing. Consumers must be able to find and understand monitoring data. This may involve doing distributed queries over multiple registries of monitoring data sources. Common monitoring event descriptions are required.

+ *Authorization*. A Grid monitoring data publication systems must have a mechanism for controlling who has access to what data. For example, some organizations do not want to publish what version of the operating system a host is running, as that makes it easier to exploit security holes. ISPs never publish routing information, even though Grid middleware could use this information to make scheduling decisions. Monitoring events generated by detailed instrumentation of a Grid middleware component may be useful only to developers, and allowing other access to these data may put unnecessary load on the monitoring system.

+ *Interoperability*. A large number of groups have written a wide assortment of monitoring event producers. For these data to be useful on the Grid, monitoring event consumers must be able to understand the data's contents. Common event formats and types are required.

+ *Intrusiveness*. When monitoring any resource, one must be careful that the act of doing the monitoring does not affect what is being monitored. Intrusiveness has always been critical to instrumentation. However, since a Grid environment includes many shared resources, it is important to ensure that multiple users of a monitoring system do not perturb the system being measured or each other's measurements. For example, running too many CPU or network probes will clearly affect the results.

No current Grid monitoring system satisfies all these requirements. However, there seems to be broad consensus within the Grid community on requirements, and several organizations are working on services to address these requirements.

20.1.2   Monitoring Event Data Representation

The form of the collected performance data has an important effect on the time efficiency of instrumentation, space needed for storage, and the type of analysis that can be performed. Instrumentation data can be divided into finite-sized structures (whose size does not depend on the length of program execution) and trace streams. The finite-sized structures include counters and timers associated with program structures, such as a counter for each procedure or process. These counters or timers are updated at strategic points in the program's execution. Trace streams generate a new datum each time the program executes a traced operation.

20.1.2.1   Scalars: Counters and Timers

The counter is the simplest form of performance data. It is incremented by an appropriate value at appropriate points in execution. Counters may be allocated for software monitoring events, such as procedure calls, or hardware events, such as cache misses. The main efficiency issue associated with counters is the size. A small counter (32 bits) is currently large enough for most software-based operations and can be updated efficiently on current processors. Large counters (64 bits) are needed for low-level and hardware operations that occur at close to processor clock frequency. Unfortunately, not all current processors can efficiently operate on 64-bit integers and as a result must use a sequence of 32-bit operations.

Timers are deceptively complex. The basic and obvious concerns are that they be precise (clock cycle resolution) and fast to access. New processor designs address these issues. Equally important are two additional abilities: providing both *process time* (CPU time of a process or thread) clocks and *wall time* (elapsed time) clocks; and virtualizing clocks, to associate them with individual program or system components.

Process and wall-time clocks measure fundamentally different activities. Computation time is more easily tracked by process time clocks. Wall time is important for measuring such quantities as I/O or synchronization blocking times. If a processor is dedicated to a single thread or process, only one type of clock is needed, but in modern systems with multiple processors or threads, both types of clocks are important. Most operating systems give fast access to cycle counting wall timers but give slow (system call speed) access to coarse-resolution (often 10-microsecond!) process timers.

Clock virtualization can be provided in either hardware or software. Hardware virtual clocks are like wall clocks, except that during a context switch the clock value for the old thread is saved into memory and the value for the thread to be dispatched is loaded into the clock. A software implementation that stores the wall time at dispatch and the total time consumed by previous dispatches of the process is also possible. However, for the clock to meet the low latency requirement, these values must be stored in memory locations readable by a user process. This software approach requires addition and subtraction operations to compute the virtual time. It is easy to implement cheap, accurate process timers, but operating system vendors continue not to do so.

20.1.2.2 Traces

The most general form of performance data is the trace. At selected points in a program's execution, data can be added to a trace stream. These data can include any type of information but are typically split into header information (event type, time stamps, size) and event type-dependent information (such as the number of bytes sent for a message-send event trace).

Although tracing is flexible, the size of the data collected can be problematic because the trace size grows with the length of program execution. The desire for detailed (fine granularity) traces increases the frequency of traced events and the desire to measure long-running programs means increasing the duration of tracing. The combination of these two issues can strain disk sizes or network connections.

PICL (306) was an early and influential tracing package that produced a common (and predetermined) format for trace records. The common format allowed many data analysis and visualization projects to share tools and performance data.

The Pablo tracing system (550) increased the flexibility of tracing by including metadata about the trace format as part of the trace log. This self-describing data format (SDDF) gave programmers and tool writers the flexibility to easily add new trace types and to include new types of performance variables.

20.1.2.3 Vectors: Time Series

A compromise between scalar performance data and traces is a time vector of performance data. The Paradyn *time histogram* introduced this idea to performance tools (478). The time histogram allows for profiling performance behavior over a period of time, yet maintains a finite size.

A time histogram is a fixed-size array whose elements store values of a performance metric for successive time intervals. Two parameters determine the granularity of the data stored in time histograms: initial bucket width (timer interval) and number of buckets. Both parameters can be adjusted to meet the need of the application. If program execution time exceeds the initial bucket width times the number of buckets, new space is freed to store additional data by doubling the bucket width and rebucketing the old data. The longer a program runs, the coarser the granularity of the performance data. For a time interval that needs precise data, a programmer could start a new time histogram for that time interval.

20.2   INSTRUMENTATION

Instrumentation is the process of putting probes into software or hardware to record data. Unless the correct information is gathered at the lowest levels, it is impossible for higher-level software to perform its analysis. This section starts by describing low-level instrumentation (clocks and hardware event counters) and then discusses instrumentation data representation. It also includes information about several existing data collection architectures.

20.2.1   Clocks

A crucial hardware feature for instrumentation is an accurate clock. The quality of the clocks provided by the system can determine whether it is possible to build to some types of instrumentation. There are three aspects of the quality of the supplied clock that affect an instrumentation system: high resolution, low latency access, and multinode synchronization.

To be a useful measure of fine-grained monitoring events, a clock should provide resolution that is approximately the same as the underlying processor clock. This clock must provide enough bits so that it does not roll over in a short amount of time. At least 64 bits are required for current processors. Many recent microprocessors, such as the Intel Pentium (463), SPARC v9, DEC Alpha (7), and Itanium, include high-resolution clocks.

High resolution alone is not sufficient; for a clock to be useful, it must be accessible with low latency to permit the measurement of fine-grained events. Clock operations need to be supported by user-level instructions that execute with similar performance as register-to-register instructions. The Intel Pentium family provides a clock that meets this requirement; however, SPARC v9 does not.

Clock synchronization is an important issue for building instrumentation for a Grid. Single-system multiprocessors provide hardware for clock synchronization; however, this hardware is generally not available for wide-area systems. Two other choices are available for wide-area computing. First, the communication network between nodes can be used to synchronize the clocks. Protocols such as NTP provide a way to synchronize clocks to within the variation between packet arrivals on the network, about 1 microsecond for LANs or 10 microseconds for WANs (479). NTP uses a hierarchy of time servers to distribute clock updates. The top-level (called stratum-1) clocks are synchronized to a variety of highly accurate time sources: radio clocks (e.g., WWV), atomic clocks, or global positioning system (GPS) clocks.

Periodically, each node being synchronized by NTP contacts an NTP time server. By estimating the round-trip delay between the time server and the node, the NTP algorithm is able to compensate for the time it takes a time-stamped response to travel from the server to the client.

A second choice is to use an external time base to synchronize clocks. For example, a highly accurate clock is available from GPS satellite receivers. By using GPS it is possible to synchronize clocks to within a few microseconds (479).

20.2.2 Time Stamps

In a Grid environment, it is important to have high-precision accurate time stamps as part of each monitoring event. Time stamps are simply the current value of a wall clock. In most parallel and distributed systems, time stamps are not used as the primary source of debugging information since it is not generally possible to get sufficiently accurate and synchronized wall clocks to uniquely order high-frequency events. However, the coarser granularity of events across a Grid may make it possible to use time stamps rather than more sophisticated techniques such as Lamport's logical clocks (428) for debugging.

20.2.3 Hardware Counters

To fully understand Grid applications, it is necessary to understand the behavior of the code running on each node. As more and more features are integrated onto a single chip, it is increasingly important that instrumentation be incorporated into the chips, since many useful types of information are no longer visible to an external instrumentation system. Modern processors, such as the Sun UltraSPARC III, Intel Pentium IV, and IBM Power4, provide a rich collection of performance data. For example, the Pentium provides access to its performance data through the model-specific registers (MSRs). These registers include a 64-bit cycle clock and counts of memory read/writes, L1 cache misses, branches, pipeline flushes, instructions executed, pipeline stalls, misaligned memory accesses, bus-locked cycles, and interrupts. The UltraSPARC III and Power 4 provide a similar set of counters. In addition to processor counters, networking devices such as switches, routers, and line cards often contain hardware counters that can be monitored as part of a overall Grid monitoring environment.

A weakness of several current architectures is that their performance registers are protected and accessible only in kernel mode. This restriction means that instrumentation executing in an application program cannot access these registers without an expensive trap into the operating system kernel. Because of these traps, an instrumentation system must collect coarser-grained information to amortize the trap overhead over a sufficiently large code region.

Use of hardware counters by applications (and even tools) has been limited by the difficulty of accessing the counters and the different types of counters that have been provided on different platforms. In fact, even two different versions of a processor chip will have somewhat different counters. The PAPI (136) package from the University of Tennessee helps this situation by providing a single API for accessing hardware performance counters on many different types of platforms. PAPI even provides a way to ask for counters in an abstract way (i.e., floating-point operations per second) and get the appropriate machine counter. However, PAPI is limited by the fact that different hardware companies count events differently. For example, some companies count an FMA (floating-point multiply and add) as one floating-point operation, and others count it as two. These subtle differences are particularly frustrating in a Grid environment where a single application may be running on multiple types of hardware at once.

20.2.4   Overhead

An important issue in data collection is the impact of collecting data. Unless the overhead of instrumentation is kept sufficiently low, the underlying system being measured will be altered to an unacceptable extent by the measurement overhead. The acceptable overhead for an application depends on the type of data being gathered and its use. For example, if data are being gathered for a detailed simulation study, a slowdown of an order of magnitude may be acceptable. However, if the purpose of monitoring is to provide data to a scheduler, an overhead of less than 1% might be required. Somewhere in the middle would be monitoring an application to tune it. In this case, an overhead of 5–15% might be acceptable.

One approach to instrumentation perturbation is to try to subtract the time required for the intrusion. An example is the PREFACE system (116), which assumes programs to be composed of serial and parallel portions. PREFACE instruments the serial portions where the time perturbations can be subtracted without changing event orderings. In the parallel regions, the time necessary for execution of the instrumentation is also subtracted. However, no attempt is made to identify when intrusion introduces changes in the ordering of events. As a result, the approach is not useful in the general case.

Maloney and Reed (459) modeled delays and produced a performance prediction for how the program would behave without instrumentation. They studied the timing delays introduced by intrusion and attempted to quantify changes in the ordering of events. They modeled intrusion as delays and constructively recover the compensated timings. Both *time-* and *event-based* models were developed to compensate for the temporal changes to the application and the order changes possible through differential delays of processes. They developed approximate models of instrumentation intrusion and then refined them until acceptable predictions of performance were possible.

Lumpp applied control theoretic techniques to the perturbation problem in message-passing systems (455). The approach includes requirements on the parallel system, the instrumentation, and the parallel program in order to ensure recovery is possible. Their work differs from previous work in that the correctness of the ordering of events is paramount. Given sufficient trace information, it is possible to recover the timings that would have occurred in the absence of the instrumentation.

The Paradyn Parallel Performance tools take a different approach to controlling overhead and the volume of data collected (362). The unique feature of their approach is that it lets the programmer see and control the overhead introduced by monitoring rather than simply being subjected to it. The cost system is divided into two parts: *predicted cost* and *observed cost*. Predicted cost is computed when an instrumentation request is received, and observed cost while the instrumentation is enabled. Predicted cost is used to decide whether the requested data are worth the cost of collection. For example, if the user requests performance data whose predicted cost of collection is 100% of the application's run time, they might decide that the impact of collecting the data is too high to warrant collection.

20.2.5 Existing Instrumentation Solutions

To collect data about an application, we instrument the application executable so that it generates the desired information when it runs. Program instrumentation techniques vary from completely manual (programmer-inserted directives) to completely automatic (no direct user involvement).

Instrumentation can be inserted into the application source code directly, automatically by the compiler, by placement into run-time libraries, or even by modifying the linked executable. Each approach has advantages and disadvantages.

Figure 20.2 shows the stages of a compilation and a sample of the places that different tools insert their instrumentation. For example, SvPablo (222) and Prophesy (685) instrument source code automatically. This approach provides

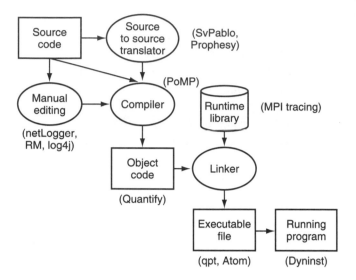

Program instrumentation can be performed at various levels from source code thorough a running program.

maximum portability of source code but requires tools for each source language. Another approach is to instrument run-time library calls. For example, the MPI tracing interface provides a way for a tool to intercept all calls to MPI routines. When an MPI program is compiled using this interface, all calls to the MPI library are routed through a "name-shifted" version of each function. Tools are written as a library of routines that record the desired information for each MPI function. This approach provides easy instrumentation in multiple languages but limits the instrumentation points to library calls. NetLogger (651), ARM (645), and log4j (342) provide routines that application programmers can call to monitor their program. This approach provides maximum flexibility but requires programmers to hand modify their program to be measured. The Dyninst system (139) permits instrumentation to be inserted into running binaries.

For detailed performance analysis, it is sometimes necessary to see inside the host operating system. For example, Web100 exposes the statistics inside the TCP stack itself through an enhanced standard management information base (MIB) for TCP (462). If a network-based application is performing poorly, TCP information from Web100 allows one to determine whether the bottleneck is in the sender, the receiver, or the network itself. Monitoring apparatus for general kernel event tracing (MAGNET) (302) provides a high-fidelity, low-overhead monitoring mechanism for exporting kernel events to user space, while kerninst (625) allows the user program to inject new code into arbitrary points in the kernel to gather statistics.

To illustrate tradeoffs in different styles of instrumentation, we briefly present NetLogger, ARM, and Dyninst.

20.2.5.1   NetLogger Toolkit

Researchers at Lawrence Berkeley National Laboratory have been developing a toolkit for instrumenting distributed applications called NetLogger (651). Using NetLogger, distributed application components are modified to produce time-stamped traces of "interesting" events at all the critical points of the distributed system. Events from each component are correlated, allowing one to characterize the performance of all aspects of the system and network in detail.

All tools in the NetLogger Toolkit share a common monitoring event format and assume the existence of accurate and synchronized system clocks. The NetLogger Toolkit itself consists of four components: an API and library of functions to simplify the generation of application-level event logs, a service to collect and merge monitoring from multiple remote sources, a monitoring event archive system, and a tool for visualization and analysis of log files. To instrument an application to produce event logs, the application developer inserts calls to the NetLogger API at all the critical points in the code and then links the application with the NetLogger library.

NetLogger events can be formatted as an easy-to-read-and-parse ASCII format. To address the overhead issues discussed previously, NetLogger includes a highly efficient self-describing binary wire format, capable of handling over 600,000 events per second (340). NetLogger also includes a remote activation mechanism and reliability support.

The NetLogger Reliability API provides fault tolerance features that are essential in Grid environments. For distributed monitoring, a particular challenge is that temporary failures of the network between the component being monitored and the component collecting the monitoring data are relatively common, especially when several sites are involved. The NetLogger API includes the ability to specify a "backup" (i.e., failover) destination to use. This may be any valid NetLogger destination but typically is a file on local disk. If the primary destination fails, all data are transparently logged to the backup destination. Periodically, the library checks whether the original destination has "come back up." If so, the library reconnects and, if the backup destination was a file, sends over all the data logged during the failure.

The NetLogger Toolkit also includes a data analysis component. One of the major contributions of NetLogger was the concept of linking a set of events together and representing them visually as a "lifeline," as shown in Figure 20.3. Visualizing event traces in this manner makes it easy to see where the most time

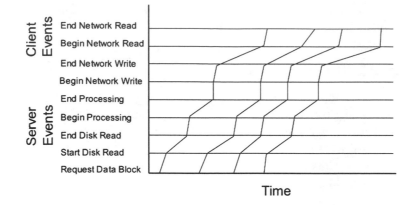

20.3   NetLogger lifelines.

FIGURE

is being spent. The NetLogger visualization tool, *nlv*, provides an interactive graphical representation of system- and application-level events. NetLogger's ability to correlate detailed application instrumentation data with host and network monitoring data has proven to be a useful tuning and debugging technique for distributed application developers.

20.2.5.2   Enterprise Measurement Forum Products

The Open Group's Enterprise Management Forum has two products related to instrumentation. The application response measurement (ARM) API (645) defines function calls that can be used to instrument an application for transaction monitoring. It provides a way to monitor business transactions, by embedding simple calls in the software that can be captured by an agent supporting the ARM API. ARM was originally made available in 1996 by Hewlett–Packard and Tivoli.

The application instrumentation and control (AIC) API provides the facility to instrument an application so that a user of that application will receive real-time information on the progress of work flowing through that application. It also enables the user to exercise control over the work being processed by that application.

20.2.5.3   Dynamic Instrumentation

Dynamic instrumentation (Dyninst) is the process of adding, removing, and changing instrumentation in a running program (139). With dynamic instrumentation, data collection probes are inserted into a program while it is running, applying the changes directly to the executing program. With this technology, decisions as to what kind of instrumentation to use can be deferred until the moment it is needed, and changes to this instrumentation can be made at any time.

In practice, dynamic instrumentation has been a big success. It pushes the technology to its most flexible limits, with many traditionally cumbersome activities becoming simple. Dynamic instrumentation offers several substantial benefits:

+ *Allows changing instrumentation during a program's execution*: Initially data can be collected about high-level, summary characteristics; then the instrumentation can be adjusted to focus on the details of apparent problems. This follows the natural way in which programmers work but avoids the need to rerun lengthy computations.

+ *Allows measurement of large, production-sized applications*: Since instrumentation is inserted dynamically, it can (at run time) systematically work through the critical parts of the program and skip unimportant ones.

+ *Avoids recompiling*: Since changing data collection is much easier than recompiling, the development process is sped up.

+ *Easily integrates new sources of performance data*: Any performance measure that is available from a program's address space easily can be turned into a new metric that can be analyzed and displayed. For example, hardware performance counters that can be mapped into a programmer's address space can be easily used.

The features of dynamic instrumentation are available to tool builders via a C++ API (139). Since the API is the same for all of the supported platforms (currently Solaris/Sparc, x86/Linux, x86/Windows, Power/AIX, MIPS/IRIX, and Alpha/TruUnix64), a Grid monitoring system that has the ability to perform detailed instrumentation no matter where the application is running can be built. Dyninst technology can be used directly via Dyninst or as part of IBM's Dynamic Probe Class Library (DPCL) interface.

20.3   SENSORS AND SENSOR MANAGEMENT

As Grids are becoming larger and more complex, there are more components to monitor and manage, and the amount of monitoring data produced by this effort is becoming overwhelming. Some components require constant monitoring, while others need to be monitored only on demand. Sensors for measuring hosts, networks, and services are required.

An approach to active monitoring specifically designed for Grid-style computing is the Network Weather Service (NWS) (681). NWS uses a collection of monitoring servers that measure network latency and bandwidth between pairs of nodes. These observations are then used to predict future network performance. NWS contains a family of predictors and dynamically selects a prediction function based on throughput and latency.

An important open issue in network prediction for large-scale Grids is the time horizon of a prediction. For a prediction to be useful, it must be issued far enough in advance to permit the system to take appropriate action. If the intended system action is static process placement, the forecast must cover the entire lifetime of the process, which could be several hours. If the goal is to permit process migration, the forecast must be issued in time to permit an orderly migration to take place.

The RMON protocol (667) provides a way for hubs and switches to record and report statistics about the traffic passing through them. The RMON protocol defines a set of simple network management protocol (SNMP) management information base (MIB) variables that can be extracted, and RMON permits gathering statistics about packet counts, a matrix of traffic by sending and receiving hosts, and statistics about selected TCP and UDP ports. Several commercial products use RMON to provide performance information for a network. For example, Visualware's VisualProfile (664) provides a Java-based interface that allows monitoring and traffic measurement.

Ganglia (633) is a monitoring package designed to provide information about the status of nodes in a cluster or Grid. Nodes running Ganglia monitor variables, such as the number of CPUs on a node or 1-minute load average, that are useful for scheduling and monitoring clusters. The key features of this system are a simple monitoring process that runs on each node in the system and an efficient protocol that ensures that timely information is made available without causing excessive data transmission. To do this, Ganglia maintains metadata for each monitored variable with a minimum update interval and a maximum change threshold. Information is propagated only when the monitored variable has changed by more than the threshold or if no message has been sent for the required time interval. Nagios (568) provides similar monitoring to the Ganglia system. Nagios is primarily aimed at system administration and includes features to monitor Unix services, such as SMTP or HTTP, running on each node. Condor (446) (Chapter 19) uses similar monitoring to decide which nodes are available to run jobs.

Figure 20.4 shows the top-level screen for Ganglia running at the San Diego Supercomputer Center. The Grid summary (of 17 clusters) shows the aggregate

20.4

20.4

FIGURE

Sample Ganglia output (courtesy of NPACI, SDSC, UC Berkeley).

status of 487 hosts (with 1010 total CPUs). The top left-hand graph shows the status of the processors on the clusters over approximately a one-hour time interval. The top right-hand graph shows the memory utilization for the same period. The other graphs show the same metrics plotted for the individual clusters. Because of space limitations, only two individual clusters are shown in the figure.

To be useful in a Grid context, monitoring data from tools such as NWS, RMON, and Ganglia must be made available to Grid applications, and middleware via a monitoring data publication service, as described in the next section.

20.4   INFORMATION AND MONITORING EVENT DATA PUBLICATION

In the Grid, a substantial amount of monitoring data must be collected for a variety of tasks such as fault detection, performance analysis, performance tuning, performance prediction, and scheduling. The distributed nature of Grid infrastructure and applications means that these data are themselves distributed. Therefore, to make use of monitoring event data, consumers must first use a monitoring data publication system to locate an appropriate data provider. To publish and interpret monitoring event data, standard schemas and ontologies are required.

Designing such a monitoring-data publication system is challenging given the diversity, size, dynamic behavior, and geographical distribution of the monitored Grid components that may interest the consumer of a single monitoring data event.

20.4.1   Requirements

In a Grid environment, the monitoring service must also be distributed. In fact, a Grid would not typically have one monitoring service but several, unified through a common discovery interface. A Grid monitoring service must be

+ *Reliable*: If one component is down, the rest of the monitoring system must be usable. All components must be distributed.

+ *Timely*: The monitoring data must be "fresh" enough to be useful. Therefore, the latencies required to both locate and access the monitoring data must be bounded appropriately for a given class of monitoring data.

+ *Scalable*: The system must scale to required levels in terms of both number of producers and consumers of monitoring data. Monitoring event rates may vary widely: events may be generated at rates from several thousand per second (e.g., application instrumentation data) to a few times per year (e.g., a "disk full" error message).

+ *Secure*: Only authorized users or groups should be able to access certain types of monitoring data. Different sites and virtual organization policies must be accommodated.

We now describe some examples of existing work in this area: the common information model (CIM), Grid Monitoring Architecture (GMA), Open Grid Services Architecture (OGSA) monitoring services, the Monitoring and Discovery Service

(MDS), and relational GMA (R-GMA). GMA is a general architectural model, OGSA is a detailed technical specification, MDS and R-GMA are actual working systems, and CIM is both a data model and a publication system. Not discussed are a number of other Grid monitoring systems under development, including CODE (599) and Hawkeye (640). Other existing event publication systems not discussed here include the event-handling components of CORBA and JINI.

20.4.2   Common Information Model

Few of the monitoring issues discussed here are unique to Grid environments. The Desktop Management Task Force (DMTF), a consortium of several major industry partners, has a number of initiatives in this area, including Common Information Model, Desktop Management Interface (DMI), Directory Enabled Network (DEN) initiative, Web-Based Enterprise Management (WBEM), and the Alert Standard Format (ASF) (225).

The Common Information Model is an implementation-neutral schema for describing overall management information in a network/enterprise environment (232). CIM paradigms draw from traditional set theory and classification theory. The schemas can be described using UML.

Besides schemas, the CIM specification also includes a monitoring event publication system. Monitoring events are produced by CIM *providers*. The CIM *object manager* (CIMOM) is used to publish the monitoring data and to keep track of who has subscribed to specific events and to forward them to subscribers. Consumers of monitoring data are called *client*s, which can request or search for data stored in the CIMOM's repository and subscribe to be notified of changes to any resource known to the CIMOM. An open source version, called *Pegasus* (644), is being developed.

20.4.3   Grid Monitoring Architecture

In 1999 a working group was formed within the Global Grid Forum with the goal of defining a scalable architecture for Grid monitoring. This group has produced both a set of requirements for Grid monitoring and a high-level specification for a Grid monitoring architecture (GMA).

In GMA, the basic unit of monitoring data is called an event. An event is a named, timestamped, structure that may contain one or more items of data. These data may relate to one or more resources such as memory or network usage or be application-specific data like the amount of time it took to multiply two matrices. The component that makes the event data available is called a producer, and a

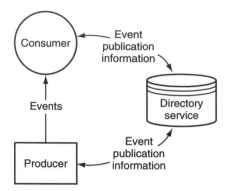

20.5   Grid Monitoring Architecture components.

FIGURE

component that requests or accepts event data is called a consumer. A directory service is used to publish what event data are available and which producer to contact to request it. These components are shown in Figure 20.5.

GMA supports both a subscription model and a request/response model. In the former case, event data are streamed over a persistent "channel" that is established with an initial request. In the latter case, one item of event data is returned per request. The unique feature of GMA is that performance monitoring data travel directly from the producers of the data to the consumers of the data.

A producer and consumer can be combined to make what is called a producer/consumer pipe. This can be used, for example, to filter or aggregate data. For example, a consumer might collect event data from several producers and then use that data to generate a new derived event data type, which is then made available to other consumers. More elaborate filtering, forwarding, and caching behaviors could be implemented by connecting multiple consumer/producer pipes.

The GMA architecture specification omits many details necessary to build interoperable monitoring systems. A number of groups are now developing monitoring services based on this architecture, such as R-GMA (263) (relational GMA, so-called because it uses a relational model for all data and organizes data about Grid entities in tables), Remos (229), and TOPOMON (142).

20.4.4   Monitoring and Discovery Service

The Monitoring and Discovery Service (MDS) (204, 264) is the information services component of the Globus Toolkit. Chapter 27 provides a detailed discussion of MDS deployment and operations issues; we provide here a high-level description of MDS architecture.

MDS defines two fundamental protocols: a soft-state *registration* protocol, which an information provider uses to notify other components of its existence and information, and an *enquiry* protocol, which an information consumer uses to request information from an information provider. These protocols are implemented within two primary components, a configurable information provider component called a Grid Resource Information Service (GRIS) and a configurable aggregate directory component called a Grid Index Information Service (GIIS). MDS version 2 (MDS-2) uses LDAP as its information model and query protocol, and also (optionally) to construct a uniform namespace for resource information across a system that may involve many organizations (see Chapter 27).

A GRIS is a service that can answer queries about a particular resource by directing the query to an information provider for a given Grid resource, and is responsible for authenticating incoming information requests. A GIIS provides a means of combining arbitrary GRIS services to provide a coherent system image that can be explored or searched by Grid applications.

A major focus of MDS's design is on achieving scalability in a system with large numbers of information providers and consumers. Thus, care is taken to associate lifetime information with all data items, and both the GIIS and GRIS are designed to perform caching, so that in a high-load situation a majority of queries can be addressed by a GIIS or GRIS rather than being forwarded to the information provider. Experimental studies (698) demonstrate the effectiveness of this strategy for cachable data when compared with R-GMA and Condor's Hawkeye system, which do not perform caching.

20.4.5 Open Grid Services Architecture

The Open Grid Services Architecture (278) (Chapter 17) incorporates at a fundamental level much of the functionality required to implement a Grid monitoring service. Any OGSA Grid service can have associated with it arbitrary Service Data Elements (SDEs): named and typed data objects that can be both queried and subscribed to by other parties. Subscription is handled via standard notification interfaces that allow clients to register interest in being notified of changes in SDE state via asynchronous, one-way delivery of notifications.

There is a straightforward correlation of GMA concepts and OGSA mechanisms. The GMA producer and consumer are roughly equivalent to the OGSA *notification source* and *notification sink*. The GMA event is equivalent to the OGSA *notification message*, and the GMA directory service is similar to the OGSA *registry*. Thus, it appears that, in principle, the SDE construct and associated interfaces can be used as a universal framework for Grid monitoring, although it remains to be seen whether one can implement these mechanisms with sufficient efficiency in all situations.

The monitoring and discovery services component of version 3 of the Globus Toolkit (GT3) seeks to exploit this promise. GT3 replaces the LDAP-based MDS with a GIIS that uses OGSA mechanisms to provide registration and discovery of Grid information sources, and to provide inquiry- and subscription-mode access to monitoring data.

20.5   MONITORING EVENT DATA ARCHIVES

Monitoring event data archives are critical for performance analysis, tuning, and accounting. In a Grid environment, conditions over which users have no control are constantly changing. Historical data can be used to establish a baseline for analysis of current performance.

As an example, a user of a Grid file replication service (176) notices that it takes much longer to generate replicas this week than it did last week. The user has no idea why performance has changed: is it the network, disk, end host, GridFTP server, GridFTP client, or some other Grid middleware such as the authentication or authorization system?

To determine what changed, the user needs to analyze monitoring data from hosts (CPU, memory, disk), networks (bandwidth, latency, route), and the FTP client and server programs. Depending on the application and systems being analyzed, from days to months of historical data may be needed. Sudden changes in performance might be correlated with other recent changes or may turn out to occur periodically in the past. To spot trends and interactions, the user needs to be able to view historical data from many perspectives.

20.5.1   Archive Requirements

A monitoring archive aggregates monitoring events from different tools, across different systems, over a period of time. Many queries across such an archive will be designed to find relations between the characteristics of these events. Thus, monitoring data archives should support relational queries.

Although different monitoring data archives will have different schemas, some basic characteristics of monitoring events should be preserved by any archive. Each archived monitoring event needs at least a precision timestamp, a global name for the type of monitoring event, an identifier for the "target" of that event, and one or more associated values. The global name is useful because an archive is only one possible place to store a monitoring event, and the event name serves to tie together archives, memory caches, flat files, analysis programs, and so forth, in an implementation-neutral way.

Monitoring archives can, in general, afford to trade off response time for (data update) throughput. Fast response times are usually required only for recent or averaged data, and this problem is best solved with some sort of monitoring data cache. However, aggregate monitoring data may arrive at high rates for an extended period of time, so if the system throughput is too low, it may fall behind, and data in the archive will always be stale.

Given these potentially high monitoring event rates, it is important to ensure that the act of sending monitoring event data to the archive is not intrusive. Monitoring event data should be buffered on disk and sent to the archive in the background. Thus, nodes must have sufficient buffer space to prevent data loss during transient periods of high event frequency.

20.5.2   Example Monitoring Data Archive Systems

The Prophesy project includes a monitoring archive database (685). Prophesy collects detailed predefined monitoring information at a function call level. The data are summarized in memory and sent to the archive when the program completes. In addition, Prophesy includes modeling and prediction components.

Another system that provides access to historical data is PperfDB (400), which provides a way to store performance measurements for different program executions. The system also includes an automatic difference operator that allows programmers to discover what changed between two different executions of a program.

NetLogger includes a relational monitoring event archive, which provides the ability to correlate events and understand performance problems in distributed systems. The NetLogger project has shown how a relational database with historical data allows for the establishment of a baseline of performance in a distributed environment, and finding events that deviate from this baseline is easy with SQL queries.

20.6   DATA ANALYSIS

Collecting monitoring data is only the start of the process. To be useful, data must be analyzed. Several other chapters of this book describe how gathered data can be used by various parts of Grid middleware. For example, Condor

(Chapter 18) and Autopilot (Chapter 26) use monitoring data to make decisions about how to run programs. Those chapters concentrate on how monitoring data are used by the system software to help operate the Grid. In this section, we concentrate on how performance data gathered by a running program can be used to identify bottlenecks in the application. The case studies in the next section (and also see Chapter 26) illustrate another use for monitoring data, namely, the adaptation of program behavior to improve performance.

20.6.1   Automatic Performance Diagnosis

Paradyn's Performance Consultant (PC) (478) can automatically control the dynamic instrumentation. The PC has a well-defined notion of performance bottlenecks, based on identifying the parts of the program consuming the most resources, and then categorizing the type of problem (e.g., synchronization, I/O, memory, and CPU) causing the bottleneck. Using fairly simple heuristics, the PC is able to guide the programmer to the source of many performance problems. The Paradyn system is designed for identifying bottlenecks in parallel programs written using message passing or pthreads.

Combining the PC and dynamic instrumentation allows Paradyn to automatically control the level of instrumentation overhead. It uses a feedback-based model to control the cost of instrumentation. The application programmer sets the threshold (percentage of CPU use) for Paradyn's instrumentation, and the PC automatically controls its rate of searching for bottlenecks based on this value.

The programmer simply tells the PC to start searching for performance problems. The PC will select parts of the program to instrument, evaluate the results from that instrumentation, and then try to refine its instrumentation based on the results. Figure 20.6 shows a search in progress. The dark grey nodes are types of problems or program parts that have been currently identified as bottlenecks, the underlined nodes are ones that have been rejected as bottlenecks, and the rest currently are being evaluated. If one follows the highlighted nodes, one of the problems that the PC found is that there is a "ExcessiveSyncWaitingTime" (i.e., the time spending waiting on synchronization is above the user-specified threshold). This synchronization problem has been localized to module (file) s_msg.o, and further localized to procedure s_recv.

The PC gives the programmer a strong head start in trying to locate performance problems; in many cases, the PC provides sufficient information to completely locate a problem. Once a problem is shown to

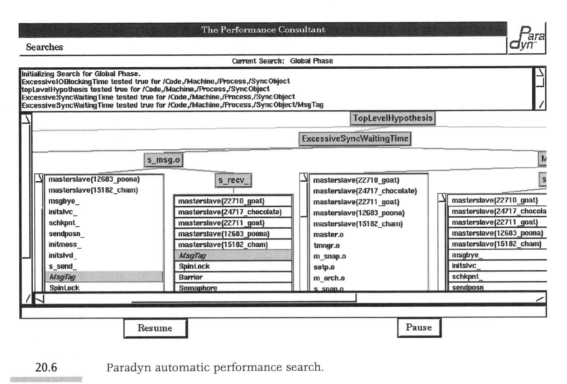

20.6 FIGURE   Paradyn automatic performance search.

programmers, they can use the Paradyn visualizations to quantify the nature of the problem.

20.6.2   Automatic Summarization

Prophesy (686) and SvPablo (222) provide a way to capture summary performance data (rather than event logs) from Grid applications to be used for data analysis. The idea is that rather than recording events of everything that happened during the program's execution, the tool records only the summary information for specific activities. For example, the Prophesy tool records information about communication points (sends and receives), subroutines and loops, and I/O. For each point (e.g., a call to a communication routine or a loop head), the system records information about the frequency and duration of the activity. At the end of the program's execution, data are saved about each point.

20.7   CASE STUDIES

We use two case studies to show how instrumentation and monitoring tools can be used to improve the performance of Grid applications. The first concerns a system called *Active Harmony*, in which applications expose parameters about different configurations and algorithms they support. A run-time layer then monitors application performance and Grid parameters and adjusts the tunable parameters for the harmonized application. The second case study presents a complete end-to-end instrumentation and monitoring use case combining a number of components to collect data for analysis using the NetLogger performance analysis tool.

20.7.1   Dynamic Tuning with Active Harmony

Active Harmony is an infrastructure that allows applications to become tunable by applying minimal changes to the application and library source code. This adaptability provides applications with a way to improve performance during a single execution based on the observed performance. The types of things that can be tuned at run time range from parameters such as the size of a read-ahead parameter to what algorithm is being used (e.g., heap sort vs quick-sort).

Active Harmony demonstrates the use of instrumentation, event publication, and run-time data analysis. In Active Harmony, applications are instrumented to report their performance characteristics and available tuning options. Each program component (library or different coupled applications) then publishes this information to the Harmony server that contains the data analysis modules. The Harmony server has no information about specific applications; instead it is an optimization framework that is able to run any application that can publish monitoring data and tunable parameters.

To illustrate the techniques, we consider a 3D volume reconstruction application (132) built on top of the active data repository (ADR) middleware (425). The 3D volume reconstruction application uses digital images of a space to reconstruct the objects that are visible from the various camera angles. ADR is an infrastructure that integrates storage, retrieval, and processing of large multi-dimensional datasets. ADR provides the user with operations including index generation, data retrieval, scheduling across parallel machines, and memory management. The data are accessed through range queries (i.e., extract all data within a specified region of space). A range query is processed in two steps: query planning followed by query execution. As part of query execution, input and output items are mapped between coordinate systems and the data are aggregated to generate the final result. During the processing phase, a temporary dataset called the accumulator is created to hold the results of the query being processed.

Because ADR is middleware used to build multiple applications, including the Harmony calls in ADR code makes every application built on top of ADR tunable. The parameters used were the following:

+ *tileSize* represents the size of the memory tile used by the ADR back-end to store information before it is aggregated. It is the size of the tiles that the accumulator will be partitioned if it does not fit into memory. This parameter greatly influences query planning and execution since it is somewhat analogous to the block size in a computational code that has been blocked (tiled) to fit into a cache.

+ *lowWatermark* is the upper bound of the number of pending reads and number of ready reads issued to the disk in order to resolve a certain query.

+ *maxReads* is the maximum number of reads issued in order to resolve the current query if the number of pending read operations and the number of ready read operations are below the lowWatermark.

The original version of the volume reconstruction application used values for the parameters provided by the ADR designers. The application was harmonized by adding calls to expose these parameters to the system. The experiments were run on a Linux cluster with 16 machines, each with two 450-MHz processors connected by the 100-megabit/sec Ethernet.

Figure 20.7 presents the improvement obtained in the processing time of each of the queries. The Active Harmony system sped query processing by up to 50%

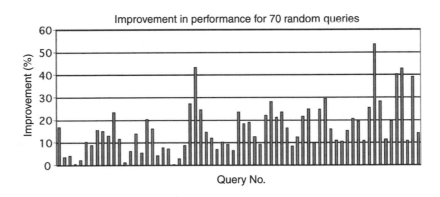

20.7   Performance improvement for the volume reconstruction application.

FIGURE

for the set of 70 random queries that we generated. However, the average improvement was about 10%. This is due to the fact that some of the queries that had the greatest speed-ups were short, compared with others for which the improvement was less than 10%. The performance improvement for the longest query, which took about 10 minutes to be completed, was about 18%.

Active Harmony can use heuristic search techniques to optimize an application when the shape of the performance curve and thus the best value are unknown prior to execution. This ability to optimize a program without detailed knowledge of the full objective function is critical since in a Grid environment components of an application may never have been used together before and may never be used together again.

Figure 20.8 shows how this works. In this illustration, the same query for each tuple of parameter values was submitted to the ADR back-end with different values for the three application parameters. By sweeping through all parameter

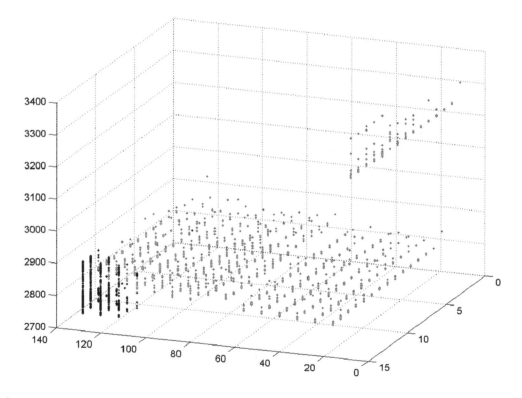

20.8

FIGURE

Performance curve (via exhaustive search) for the volume reconstruction application.

combinations, it is possible to construct a complete performance curve. The complete parameter sweep recorded values for the performance function of up to 25% slower than the optimum, while the range of values explored by the Active Harmony system was within 5% of the minimum. The minimum was reached by exploring only 11 tuples (out of the almost 1,700 possible tuples).

The axes of the graph in Figure 20.8 are as follows: the vertical one represents the performance function, while the horizontal ones are the tileSize and the lowWatermark. The values obtained for different values of the third parameter, maxReads, are stacked one on top of the other in the graph. The lighter points in the graph are from the exhaustive search and are spread on the entire value space. The darker points (lower left-hand corner) trace the path followed by the tuning, and are concentrated near the minimum.

20.7.2   End-to-End Monitoring with NetLogger

Our second case study concerns end-to-end instrumentation and monitoring of a data transfer service. It encompasses all the aforementioned monitoring components: instrumentation, monitoring event publication service, monitoring event archive, sensor management systems, and data analysis.

We consider the problem of developing, tuning, and running a reliable bulk data transfer service for the Grid. The first step is to insert instrumentation code during the development stage to ensure the program is operating as expected. This can be done using an instrumentation package such as ARM or (as used here) NetLogger, and instrumentation code should be added to generate time-stamped monitoring events before and after all disk and network I/O. Most modern bulk data transfer programs, such as GridFTP (64) (Chapter 22) and bbftp, are multi-threaded and support parallel data streams. Such threaded programs can often have hard-to-detect bugs, and instrumentation is important to ensure that the program is behaving properly.

For example, Figure 20.9 shows NetLogger lifelines for the data receiver in an early implementation of a parallel FTP. The three groups of lifelines are traces for each of three separate read sockets and include monitoring events for reading header and data packets. All three streams should always be active, but as shown in the graph, streams 0 and 1 start and stop somewhat erratically. The cause turned out to be a simple logic bug that selected the wrong socket for reading when data were available on multiple sockets. This type of subtle bug could easily remain undetected without this type of analysis and visualization.

Now that the file transfer service is debugged and tested, it is ready for production use. Other monitoring services now become important. The level of

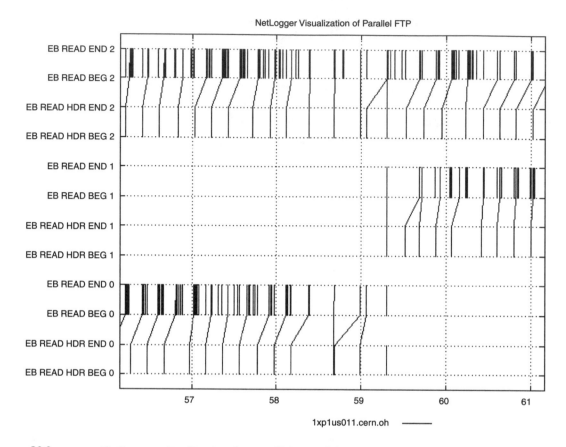

20.9   NetLogger visualization for parallel FTP debugging.

FIGURE

instrumentation required for the debugging scenario previously cited can easily generate thousands of monitoring events per second. Clearly one does not need or want this level of monitoring activated all the time, so some type of monitoring activation service is needed so that a user can turn instrumentation on and off in a running service.

Next, it is useful to establish a performance baseline for this service and store this information in the monitoring event archive. System information such as processor type and speed, OS version, CPU load, disk load, and network load data should be collected during the baseline test runs. Network monitoring data, such as network capacity, available bandwidth, delay, and loss, should also be collected. The sensor management service again may be needed to start system and network sensors before running the baseline tests. If sensors are already running, the monitoring event publication service is needed to locate the sensors and initiate a subscription for the resulting monitoring data. Several tests are then run, sending complete application instrumentation (for clients, servers, and middleware), host, and network monitoring data to the archive. It is probably not possible to establish baseline for all possible network paths that may be used, but it is useful to try to collect baseline data for several paths that represent typical paths in a given Grid.

This data transfer service is then put into production use, and everything works fine for a few months. One day, however, users start complaining that data transfers are taking much longer than previously. Without end-to-end monitoring and instrumentation, it can be hard to track down the cause, which may relate to the software, hardware, and/or network. To collect data for analysis, one must

+ locate relevant monitoring data in the monitoring event publication service and subscribe to that data;

+ activate any missing sensors using the sensor management system, and subscribe to the data they produce;

+ activate instrumentation of the data transfer service, and subscribe to that data; and

+ locate monitoring data in the monitoring event archive for the baseline test from when things were last working.

Data analysis can then begin and will include the following steps:

+ Check the hardware and OS information to see whether anything changed.

+ Look at the application instrumentation data to see whether anything looks unusual.

+ Look at the system monitoring data to see whether anything looks unusual (e.g., unusually high CPU load).

+ Correlate the application and middleware instrumentation data with the host and network monitoring data.

Figure 20.10 shows the result of such an analysis. This plot, generated by the NetLogger visualization tool *nlv*, correlates client and server instrumentation data with CPU and TCP retransmission monitoring data. The events being monitored are shown on the y axis, and time is on the x axis. From bottom to top, one can

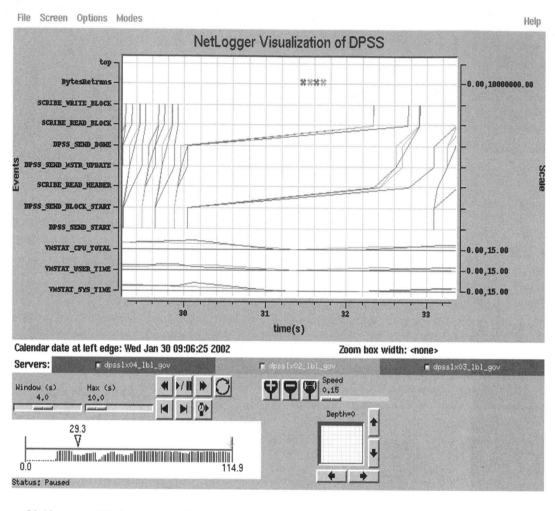

20.10   NetLogger visualization system.

FIGURE

see CPU utilization events, application events, and TCP retransmit events all on the same graph. Each semi-vertical line represents the "life" of one block of data as it moves through the application. The gap in the middle of the graph, where only one set of header and data blocks is transferred in 3 seconds, correlates exactly with a set of TCP retransmit events. The plot makes it easy to see that the "pause" in the transfer is due to TCP retransmission errors on the network. Thus, we determine that our performance problems are due to network congestion.

Tracking down the cause of the network congestion is a difficult problem and requires a large amount of network monitoring data.

20.8   SUMMARY

We have explained why instrumentation and monitoring are so vital to the success of Grid infrastructure and applications, and presented some of the major concepts, systems, techniques, and applications that have been developed to obtain and apply Grid monitoring information.

Many open issues remain to be addressed. For example, standard schema must be defined for many Grid components. CIM provides a good starting point, but important Grid components such as batch schedulers, replica managers, and metrics for network paths are not yet part of CIM. GGF working groups have been formed to develop and define the required new CIM schemas. Similarly, emerging Web services technologies such as OGSA, WSDL, SOAP, XSchema, and UDDI may meet some of the challenges of Grid monitoring interoperability, but much work remains to be done to define a complete Grid monitoring framework that includes common event data descriptions, event dictionaries, and query formats. Also, we are still only in the early stages in the areas of automated problem determination and program adaptation.

Nevertheless, we believe that the pioneering work reported in this chapter puts the Grid community in an excellent position to achieve major advances in the creation of reliable, high-performance, adaptive applications.

FURTHER READING

For more information on the topics presented in this chapter, see *www.mkp.com/grid2* and the following references:

+ The Global Forum Grid Information Systems and Performance Area (311);

+ The Distributed Management Task Force Common Information Model standards Web site *www.dmtf.org/standards* (233); and

+ The Global Grid Forum Grid Management Architecture Web site (312).

Security for Virtual Organizations: Federating Trust and Policy Domains

Frank Siebenlist, Nataraj Nagaratnam, Von Welch, and Clifford Neuman

*T*his chapter discusses the security requirements encountered in Grid environments and how they are being addressed. We begin by describing Grid-specific security and policy challenges. We then discuss current trends in security technologies and their relationship to the Grid. We also introduce the ongoing efforts in the Global Grid Forum to define an Open Grid Services Architecture (OGSA) security model. Using the OGSA (279) (Chapter 17), we illustrate how a Grid security implementation takes shape. We conclude with a brief discussion of the current state of Grid security and the expectations for the near future.

21.1 GRID SECURITY REQUIREMENTS

We focus first on general Grid security requirements, using the notion of a secure Grid society to expose the source of these requirements and how they may be addressed. We also present a real-world example of a Grid application, which demonstrates the nontrivial nature of the security requirements. The virtual organization concept is used to model Grid collaborations and their security challenges.

21.1.1 The Secure Grid Society

To make a society prosper, one needs rules (both written and unwritten), understanding of good and bad behavior with its consequences and account-abilities, acknowledgment of cultural differences in behavior, initial trust and earned trust, identification of the risks associated with transactions, and so on (301). By studying these requirements and possible solutions and their parallels with the Grid, we can better understand how to achieve a "secure Grid society."

The Internet has created a whole new economy and a new society. We commonly order from commercial Web sites with our credit cards, and many have bought and sold goods from auction services such as eBay. These activities depend on our establishing a level of trust that makes us feel comfortable: We have some idea of the risks involved and understand the potential benefits. To help us with that risk-versus-reward determination, we may quantify the risk: vendors are rated for their service, sellers and buyers earn or lose stars through past performance, chat-group gossip conveys the experiences of others, and credit cards have limited liability. This new electronic society is in many ways a mirror of the real one.

As the commercial world moves to electronic business-to-business interactions, the abstraction level of these interactions is raised. Ultimately, the services of many businesses will be found through the equivalents of electronic yellow pages or brokers, and business transactions will be concluded if automated negotiated service-level agreements (SLAs, Chapter 18) are agreed upon. Part of the SLA equation is risk-benefit analysis, which will be facilitated by real-time access to credit bureaus and Dun and Bradstreet-like rating services (427).

We believe that the Grid will evolve in this direction, too, and it may have to use the same kind of business semantics in the SLA negotiation between requesters and providers of Grid services.

We envision a Grid future in which resources are completely virtualized and the identities associated with Grid entities, requesters, and service providers are completely hidden behind services for discovery, matchmaking, negotiation, scheduling, and so forth. The fact that Grids are used to build dynamic cross-organizational collaborations (virtual organizations, or VOs, Chapter 4) further complicates the situation because VOs require the establishment of trust and associated security across multiple organizational boundaries. In this case, a risk management approach that quantifies issues of trust, cost, and benefit will be essential to creating policies that meet VO operational objectives. Although these concepts find use in sitewide security analysis (e.g., in the insurance and financial services industry), techniques for applying risk management principles to dynamic cross-organizational collaborations are in their infancy and require more research. The Grid research community should tackle these complex socioeconomic interactions in collaboration with economists and social scientists.

21.1.2 Grid Security Example

A prime example of a Grid project that shows all challenges in the extreme is the Compact Muon Solenoid experiment (Chapter 10). Data from this experiment at the Large Hadron Collider in the CERN Laboratory in Switzerland will be analyzed by more than 2000 physicists at more than 150 universities and laboratories in 34 countries (see Figure 21.1).

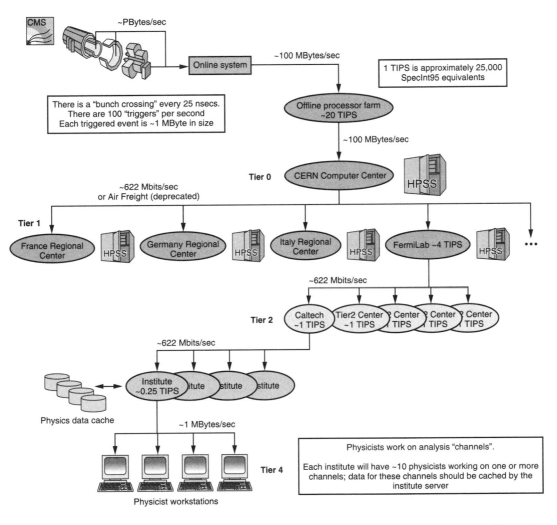

21.1

FIGURE

The global dissemination and sharing of the Compact Muon Solenoid (CMS) experimental data from the Large Hadron Collider in CERN.

The dissemination, processing, sharing, and virtualization of data, as well as the sharing and virtualization of compute resources, networks, and experiments, lead to challenging requirements for storage, network bandwidth, and compute power. The associated security requirements are equally challenging:

✦ Data will move through, and be accessed from, many different centers in different countries with different security mechanisms and policies in place at each center (e.g., one center may use the Grid Security Infrastructure (GSI) (280), whereas another uses Kerberos (501)).

✦ The community requiring access to the data spans multiple organizations and countries. Thus, center administrators need the ability to enforce policy without knowing the individuals that access their resources. For example, a job originally submitted in Switzerland may use compute cycles from the center in Italy, and the Italian center administrator may know the job submitter not as an individual identity but only as a member of a particular research group.

✦ Trust must be established and expressed between different centers, from which remote access policies must be derived. For example, the Italian and Swiss centers need to establish a level of trust expressed in terms of policies that can be used to derive SLAs on submitted jobs.

✦ Data integrity and confidentiality can be crucial: the winning of a Nobel prize may depend on the enforcement of data privacy and fine-grained access control. Creators and owners of data may want to associate policy with the data that is independent of where the data are physically stored. For example, a policy might state that "raw data should be created or modified only by personnel involved in data acquisition. A Swiss scientist's job may run on a computer in Italy, but the data used and generated by the job are sensitive and cannot be accessed by anyone that the scientist does not trust and grant access."

✦ Physicists need the authority to submit jobs that require nontrivial SLAs to match the availability of data, network resources, storage, and CPU cycles, with the associated access rights to each of these resources in different administrative domains.

Many other equally challenging Grid projects are under way. Their common denominator is that they span multiple administrative domains and deal with nontrivial negotiations and agreements of trust and access rights.

21.1.3   Security Challenges and Requirements

Security requirements within the Grid environment are driven by the need to support scalable, dynamic, distributed virtual organizations (281) (VOs, Chapter 4)—collections of diverse and distributed individuals and organizations that seek to share and use diverse resources in a coordinated fashion. The VO concept serves as the basis for the Grid security model that we introduce to support scenarios such as that in Section 21.1.2: Resources from multiple locations are coordinated to serve an even larger, more distributed collection of users.

From a security perspective, a key attribute of VOs is that, in addition to VO-specific policy, participants and resources are governed by the rules and policies of the classical organizations of which they are members. Furthermore, whereas some VOs, such as the multiyear scientific collaboration given in the example, will be large and long-lived (in which case explicit negotiations with resource providers are acceptable), others will be short-lived—created, perhaps, to support a single task, such as two individuals sharing documents and data as they write a proposal—in which case overheads associated with VO creation and operation must be minimal.

A fundamental requirement is thus to enable access by VO members to resources that live within classical organizations and that, from the perspective of those classical organizations, have policies in place that speak only about local users. This VO access must be established and coordinated only through *binary* trust relationships that exist between the local user and their organization and between the VO and the user. We cannot, in general, assume trust relationships between the classical organization and the VO or its external members.

Grid security mechanisms can address these challenges by allowing a VO to be treated as a *policy domain overlay* (see Figure 21.2). Multiple resources or organizations outsource certain policy control(s) to a third party, the VO, which coordinates the outsourced policy in a consistent manner to allow for coordinated resource sharing and use.

Complicating Grid security is the fact that new services (i.e., resources) may be deployed and instantiated dynamically over a VO's lifetime. For example, a user may establish personal stateful interfaces to existing resources, or the VO itself may create directory services to keep track of VO participants. Like their static counterparts, these resources must be securely coordinated and must interact with other services.

This combination of dynamic policy overlays and dynamically created entities drives the need for three key characteristics in a Grid security model:

+ *Enables integration and interoperability*. Organizations participating in a VO often have significant investment in existing security mechanisms and

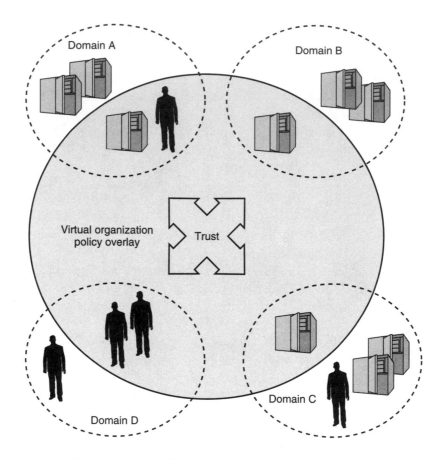

A virtual organization policy domain overlay pulls together participants and resources from disparate domains into a common trust domain.

infrastructure. Grid security, rather than replacing these mechanisms, must enable integration and interoperability between them.

✦ *Enables creation and management of dynamic trust domains.* Not only must parties in a VO be able to interoperate at the level of protocols, but in order to coordinate resources, VOs need to establish trust among VO users and resources. These trust domains can span multiple organizations and must adapt dynamically as participants join or leave the VO.

✦ *Supports dynamic creation of services.* Users must be able to create new services (e.g., "resources") dynamically without administrator intervention. These services need to be coordinated and must interact securely with other services.

Thus, we must be able to name the service with an assertable identity and grant access rights to that identity without contradicting the governing local policy.

Traditional means of security administration that involve manual editing of centralized policy databases or issuance of credentials through elaborate procedures cannot meet the demands of these dynamic scenarios. We require a user-driven security model that allows users to create entities and policy domains in order to create and coordinate resources within VOs.

21.1.3.1 *Implementation Agnostic and Interoperable Architecture*

For both technical and pragmatic reasons, no single security technology that will both addresses all Grid security challenges and can be adopted in every hosting environment can be defined. Even if new standards are adopted, existing security infrastructures cannot be replaced overnight. For example, each domain in a Grid environment is likely to have one or more registries in which user accounts are maintained (e.g., LDAP directories (666)); such registries are unlikely to be shared with other organizations or domains. Similarly, authentication mechanisms deployed in an existing environment reputed secure and reliable will continue to be used. Each domain typically has its own authorization infrastructure that is deployed, managed, and supported. It will not be acceptable to replace any of these technologies with a single model or mechanism.

Thus, to be successful, Grid security architecture must *integrate* with, rather than replace, security architectures, models, and implementations deployed in domains and hosting environments. This means that the architecture must be *implementation agnostic*, allowing it to be instantiated in terms of a variety of existing security mechanisms (e.g., Kerberos, public key infrastructure) and allowing it to incorporate new security services as they become available.

These traits enable the deployment of Grid security in a single domain but do not enable two different deployments to interact. Different domains and hosting environments make different decisions regarding the mechanisms and policies they use. Distributed applications that traverse services, servers, hosting environments, and security domains need to be able to interact with each other, thus introducing the need for *interoperability*.

Interoperability between conversing parties is achieved only if they can interoperate (at least minimally) at every layer involved in a message exchange:

✦ At the *transport layer*, an agreed-upon transport mechanism to send messages is required. For instance, conversing parties need to be able to support a given version of HTTP (e.g., HTTP 1.1.), or, in the case of messaging infrastructure, the messaging end points must be able to converse (e.g., Java messaging services (352)). The selection of a transport layer mechanism may be affected if security is required of the transport layer. For example, if parties required protection of data, they could accomplish this through the use of secured HTTP (HTTPS) as the transport mechanism.

✦ At the *message layer*, mechanisms that allow conversing parties to exchange messages that can be consumed and processed by endpoints (e.g., SOAP messages pertaining to a particular version of SOAP) are required. As with the transport layer, it is possible to implement security in the message layer. For example, if SOAP messages are being exchanged, part of the agreement may be that the message be protected through the use of standard SOAP signing (52, 321) or encryption (321, 383) mechanisms.

✦ At the *services layer*, each party must be able to specify its requirements and policies for quality of protection in order to engage in a secure conversation, and the requirements and policies expressed by different parties must be made mutually comprehensible. For example, in a service-oriented framework, resources are cast as services with service definitions (e.g., WSDL; see Chapter 17). These service definitions can be used to advertise the policies and requirements of the service, such as the fact that it accepts Kerberos credentials as a valid means of authentication. For example, policy and requirements can be stated using tagged components in the CORBA model or by WS-Policy expressions in Web service endpoints.

✦ At the *policy* layer, mechanisms to represent names are needed to facilitate the correct application of policies. Names of entities, services, resources, and operations are all expressed in policies and may be assigned by different authorities in different domains and asserted using different authentication mechanisms. For example, the policy statement "The Kerberos user Alice from domain XYZ is allowed to invoke method foo( ) on resource BigServer in domain ABC" requires that the policy creator and policy enforcer agree on how to express names and who assigns these names for entities ("Alice from domain XYZ"), operations ("method foo( )"), and resources ("BigServer in domain ABC") so that they are unambiguous, consistent, and trusted.

21.1.3.2 Dynamic Trust Domains

The VOs that underlie collaborative work within Grids may form quickly, evolve over time, and span organizations. Their effective operation depends critically on *trust*, the extent to which one participant can rely on others to behave as expected (321).

In the simple case, personal knowledge between parties in the VO allows policies to be derived from identifiable trust "anchors" (parties vouching for other parties). An example in current Grid systems is the use of certificate authorities to root certificate-based identity mechanisms. For these to work, one must "know" about the trustworthiness of the certificate authority used to establish the identity of a party in order to bind it to specific usage policies. Although the direct expression of policies in terms of identities is a nontrivial task, progress in the expressiveness of policy languages may be sufficient to allow this.

However, in a nontrivial VO such as that described in Section 21.1.2, personal knowledge does not scale in terms of either the size of the VO (there are too many members to be known to each other) or the dynamic nature of the VO (members, resources, and even services join and depart too frequently for knowledge to be maintained). In these situations, *delegation* mechanisms (303, 371)—mechanisms that allow one entity to assign rights to another—can provide a means for scalable assertion of policy. However, these mechanisms also require some trust anchor, such as the federation service shown in Figure 21.3. In the most general case, trust relationships may need to be established from "first principles," using techniques such as reputation management (553, 691, 692) to create and monitor trust relationships.

21.1.3.3 *Dynamic Creation of Services*

Over the lifetime of a VO, new services (i.e., resources) may be dynamically created and deployed. For example, a user may establish personal stateful interfaces to existing resources, user jobs will be instantiated as a service to allow for management, or the VO itself may create directory services to keep track of VO participants. Like their static counterparts, these resources must be securely coordinated and interact with other services. To enable this secure interaction and coordination, these services need to be granted rights to allow them to perform actions and establish secure relationships with other entities.

To grant rights to these services, one must be able to identify them. This allows the expression of policy that expresses the services' rights to perform an action, be a member of a group, and so forth. This leads to the requirement to be able to give dynamic services a unique, assertable identity. Since the user may create these dynamic services, traditional manual means of security administration will not suffice. Identity creation and rights granting must be user driven to allow them to occur in real time.

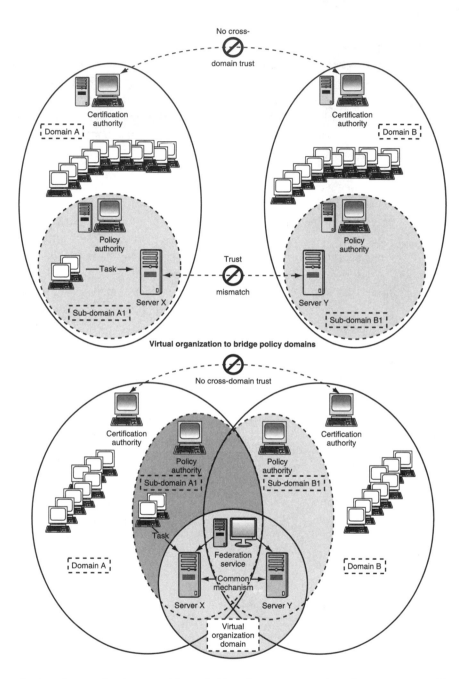

FIGURE

A virtual organization provides a bridge for a community of resource providers and users who belong to separate policy domains.

21.1.3.4   Security Disciplines

In order to address the high-level security requirements, a comprehensive Grid security model must leverage diverse security disciplines (280).

Authentication.   To enable interoperability, we must provide plug points for multiple authentication mechanisms and the means for conveying the specific mechanism used in the authentication operation. The authentication mechanism may be a customized approach or an industry-standard technology. The plug point must be agnostic to any specific authentication technology.

Delegation.   The establishment of dynamic trust domains requires facilities to allow for delegation (303, 371, 500) of access rights from requestors to services, as well as for delegation policies to be specified. In delegating authority from one entity to another, care should be taken that the authority transferred through delegation is scoped only to the task(s) intended to be performed (as in a least-privilege model (571)) and within a limited lifetime, to minimize the misuse of delegated authority.

Single sign-on.   Participants in a Grid environment often need to coordinate multiple resources to accomplish a single task. Having to manually perform an authentication process (e.g., typing in a pass phrase) for each authentication operation is overly burdensome. Security mechanisms must ensure that an entity, having successfully completed the act of authentication once, need not reauthenticate upon subsequent access to Grid resources within some reasonable period of time. Such a mechanism must also take into account that a request may span security domains and hence should factor in federation between authentication domains and mapping of identities. This requirement is important from two perspectives:

+ It places a secondary requirement on a Grid implementation to be able to delegate an entity's rights, subject to policy (e.g., credential lifespan, restrictions placed by the entity).

+ If the credential material is delegated to intermediaries, it may be augmented to indicate the identity of the intermediaries, subject to policy.

Credential life span and renewal.   To limit the risk of compromise in delegation and single log-on, credentials need to be scoped to a reasonable lifetime. It may not always be possible to predict accurately the lifetime required for a particular task, and in many cases a task initiated by a user may take longer than the life span of the user's initially delegated credential. In those cases, the user needs to be notified before the credentials expire or needs to refresh those credentials so that the task can be completed.

Authorization.   Access to Grid services must be controlled based on authorization policies (i.e., who can access a service, under what conditions) attached to each service. In addition to the standard model of policies being specified by the resource owner, policies will come from sources such as the requestor's VO and home organization. Requestors may also specify invocation policies on their requests (i.e., who does the client trust to provide the requested service). Authorization should accommodate various access control models and implementations.

Privacy.   Both a service requester and a service provider must be allowed to define and enforce privacy policies, for instance taking into account personally identifiable information or purpose of invocation. (Privacy policies may be treated as an aspect of authorization policy addressing privacy semantics such as information usage rather than plain information access.)

Confidentiality.   The confidentiality of the underlying communication (transport) mechanism must be protected, as must the confidentiality of the messages or documents that flow over a given transport mechanism. The confidentiality requirement includes point-to-point transport as well as store-and-forward mechanisms.

Message integrity.   Unauthorized changes made to messages or documents must be detectable by the recipient. The use of message- or document-level integrity checking is determined by policy, which is tied to the offered quality of the service.

Policy exchange.   Service requestors and providers must be allowed to dynamically exchange security (among other) policy information to establish a negotiated security context between them. Such policy information can contain authentication requirements, supported functionality, constraints, privacy rules, and so forth.

Secure logging.   Provisions must be made for security services, facilities for time-stamping, and mechanisms for securely logging any kind of operational information or event. The word *securely* in this context means reliably and accurately, that is, so that such a collection is neither interruptible nor alterable by adverse agents. Secure logging is the foundation for addressing requirements for notarization, nonrepudiation, and auditing.

Assurance.   Means must be provided to qualify the security assurance level expected of a hosting environment. This information may include virus protection, firewall usage for Internet access, and internal virtual private network (VPN) usage (310). Users can consider such information when making a decision about the environment in which to deploy a service.

Manageability.   Security management in Grids is needed, for example, in the areas of identity management, policy management, and key management. Security management also includes higher-level requirements such as virus protection and intrusion detection and protection, which are requirements in their own rights but are typically provided as part of security management.

Firewall traversal.   A major barrier to dynamic, cross-domain Grid computing today is the existence of firewalls (179). Although firewalls may provide only limited value within a dynamic Grid environment, they are unlikely to disappear soon. Thus, a Grid security model must take them into account and provide mechanisms for cleanly traversing them—without compromising local control of firewall policy.

As Grid computing continues to evolve to support e-business applications in commercial settings, the requirements and functions discussed in this section will form the foundation for standards-based interoperability not only between real organizations within a VO (intra-VO) but also across organizations belonging in different VOs (inter-VO). On this foundation, applications and infrastructure can be built to establish the trust relationships required for commercial distributed computing, enterprise application integration, and business-to-business partner collaboration over the Internet.

21.2   EMERGING SECURITY TECHNOLOGIES

Over the past 10 years, a number of distributed computing technologies have emerged, such as DCE, DCOM, CORBA, and the Web/HTTP, each with integrated security solutions based on Kerberos, public key, username/password, or other technologies. Experience with early Grid projects indicated that these distributed computing technologies could not meet Grid-specific requirements. As a result, new technologies were developed to address these needs, including Legion (373, 687) (Chapter 1:9), Condor (446) (Chapter 1:13), Sun Grid Engine (Chapter 12), and the Globus Toolkit (276) (Chapters 1:11 and 4).

More recently, Web services have emerged, with a great deal of industry momentum to make the WS framework the distributed computing platform of the future (320). Many associated WS security components are still being designed and standardized. However, it is clear that industry is pushing for a comprehensive security framework that will address many Grid requirements.

The Grid community, within the Global Grid Forum (GGF), has adopted the WS framework as the foundation for the Open Grid Services Architecture (279) (OGSA: Chapter 17), which is projected to be the basis for the next generation of standardized Grid middleware implementations. Building on that WS foundation, OGSA defines and standardizes additional infrastructure features and services that address Grid-specific requirements. GGF working groups are developing standards that leverage and augment the WS security standards (491, 591).

This section discusses the status and trends of a number of the security technologies that are being used to form the basis for the emerging Grid security framework. Relevant Grid-related security projects and tools are discussed briefly, followed by a discussion of the OGSA security architecture.

A number of technologies and trends are emerging in the general security community. We discuss how these relate to the Grid security challenge.

21.2.1   XML-Based Security Protocols

The Web services security community is using XML (Chapter 17) as a foundation for redefining all of the basic security protocols and assertions. Basic primitives for digital signing (52) and encryption (383) have been defined and are being used to compose more complex assertions and protocols, for example for authentication and trust establishment (40, 381). Where previous technologies were tightly coupled with an underlying security framework (e.g., secure socket layer, SSL, with X.509/PKI (228), DCE with Kerberos (501, 643)), WS security components are specified in a manner that is agnostic to the actual mechanism. For example, WS-Security (a draft standard that defines encryption and signing of SOAP messages (381)) specifies how a protected message should be formatted, how the protection mechanisms should be identified, the protecting key material identified, and so forth but does not mandate a particular mechanism to be used for the protection (381). As another example, the XML key markup specification (XKMS) allows for the outsourcing of public-key infrastructure (PKI) and certificate format-specific validation (266), which facilitates the deployment of the same security components in different domains. These mechanism-agnostic approaches allow the same basic assertion formats and protocols to be deployed with different underlying security infrastructures. In addition, they allow an infrastructure to process the formats and protocols without having to be familiar with the mechanism used. These features are important to the Grid security architecture because they provide more flexibility to accommodate a variety of security mechanisms instead of dictating a small set that must be embedded into the infrastructure.

21.2.2   Message-Level Security

Currently, the most popular security protocol, SSL/TLS (228), requires a direct transport layer connection between the endpoints. A secured connection is established between the endpoints and protects the exchanged data. This has the undesirable effect of adding an intermediary in the trust chain; that is, the two endpoints are no longer in direct communication.

Many Grid scenarios require end-to-end message protection over a route that traverses one or more intermediate components. Examples include traversing firewalls or application-level routers. To meet the needs of these scenarios, message protection must be brought from the transport layer into the message layer.

In the context of SOAP message exchanges, message-level security can be achieved through the WS-Security specification. Other proposed specifications, such as WS-SecureConversation and WS-Trust, build on the basic functionality of WS-Security to provide security context establishment, key exchange, and message protection (379, 380).

21.2.3   Group Authentication and Key Exchange

A number of Grid projects require group authentication and key exchange. For example, when a collaborative group wants to ensure privacy while using broadcast technologies such as multicast video (182) (see Chapter 15), a single key must be shared among the group. Depending on the group policy, members of the group may not be allowed to access the group's material from points in time prior to their joining the group or after their departure. Policy of this kind requires that the group generate and distribute a new key after such changes in group membership. These problems of group security are much like the problems faced in supporting dynamic VOs. There has been considerable research regarding protocols and lifecycle management with these dynamic groups, and we expect that these technologies can be leveraged to help address Grid challenges (411, 607).

21.2.4   X.509/PKIX Enhancements and Alternatives

PKI is the general term for a security infrastructure based on public-key cryptography. Such an infrastructure defines message formats and protocols that allow entities to securely communicate claims and statements. The most commonly used assertions are those that bind identity, attributes, and authorization statements either to keys or to identities.

The most popular PKI is defined by the IETF's PKIX working group (369), which defines a security system used for identifying entities (users and resources) through the use of X.509 identity certificates (384). In this PKI, highly trusted entities known as certificate authorities (CAs) issue X.509 certificates where essentially a unique identity name and the public key of an entity are bound through the digital signature of that CA. As a trusted third party, the CA can be used as an introducer: through the proof of private key possession and the validation of the CA's issued X.509 certificates, entities are able to associate a trusted, unique identity name with the communicated claims and statements of others. In similar fashion, attribute authorities (AAs) are defined, which issue attribute certificates that bind attributes to an identity name through the AA's digital signature (256). Although undefined by PKIX, authorization systems are expected to use the asserted identity name and attributes, such as group membership and roles, to express and enforce access control policy.

Although the X.509/PKIX PKI-related technologies have achieved a fair amount of adoption in the Web through the use of X.509 certificates for secured Web servers, they have encountered setbacks outside this space in general adoption and related commercial success. Furthermore, the adoption and support of the X.509 attribute certificates have been very slow.

The emerging XML-based security assertions formats and protocols are providing equivalent technologies to those defined by X.509/PKIX, with the added advantage of being more agnostic toward the underlying public key infrastructure. The latter property will make it easier for organizations to choose or to migrate to public-key technologies that deploy alternative assertion formats and trust models, such as pretty good privacy (PGP) (703) or simple public key infrastructure (SPKI) (247). Having that flexibility is important to Grid security, as identities associated with services can be dynamically created and short-lived and may not have a identity name associated with them—a situation that does not fit the traditional X.509/PKI model well with its centralized CA and its focus on identity assertions.

These XML-based security technologies are being integrated in a variety of emerging XML-based messaging protocols (e.g., SOAP). These allow Grid applications to choose the underlying security technology that best fits the deployment model and still benefit from the ability to use the same message and protocol formats.

To provide an alternative that will address the dynamically created and short-lived identities within the X.509/PKIX framework, the Grid security community is actively involved in the specification of extensions to the X.509 certificate format to use these same certificates for the dynamic issuance of identities and delegation of rights by users (660). The advantage of this approach is that these certificates can be used transparently in existing technologies that use

X.509/PKIX technologies currently, such as the transport security layer (TLS or SSL) (228). Section 21.4.2.3 discusses this approach.

21.2.5 Enforcement of Multiple Policies

As Grid applications traverse more administrative domains and become more virtualized, the number of different policies that must be enforced increases, as follows.

+ The service or resource provider's policy will be the ultimate authority; however, the ability for a resource or service provider to define access policy specific to individual external requesters, groups, or even organizations becomes increasingly difficult as the number of those entities increases.

+ Each administrative domain will have a local policy that applies to individuals and groups within the domain accessing external resources.

+ VOs may define their own access control policies that apply to their members and resources.

+ Entities may empower others to work on their behalf with a policy to limit the delegated rights to the minimum needed for the task(s) in question.

This distribution of policy creation brings with it several challenges. Without standardization, as the number of sources of policy increases, so does the number of policy languages. As a policy evaluator parses and combines policies, the functionality it needs to do so increases. Policies must all be distributed from the creators to the evaluator. Such distribution must be reliable and secure to prevent disruptions or compromises of the systems the policy pertains to.

A number of efforts address one or more of these challenges: Akenti (648), the Virtual Organization Management Service (249), PERMIS (168), the Generic Authorization and Access Control API (GAA-API) (569), the Keynote Trust-Management System (126), the Authorization (AZN) API (125), and the Community Authorization Service (519). At present, lack of agreed-upon standards hampers the interoperability of these solutions. As we move to a WS-based infrastructure, efforts are under way in the Grid community to standardize the authorization service interface (672) and to enable pluggable authorization services for Grid applications. Furthermore, existing and emerging XML-based specifications for authorization rule languages (13) and policy expressions (102) have the potential to express the demanding authorization policy requirements of Grid applications, users, and VOs.

21.2.6   Identity and Credential Federation

Wherever VO members or resources interact, the policies mentioned in the preceding section must be enforced. In general, policy rules are expressed by using identifiers, such as principals, groups, and roles, that adhere to naming schemes and are asserted by identity and naming authorities. The ability to evaluate the policy rules depends on the ability to map or federate these identity assertions to the format used in the policy expressions and through assertion made by an authority trusted in the administrative and application domain of the policy enforcement agent.

The Grid community has developed a number of technologies that address some of the most common federation issues. For example, in order to bridge different administrative domains in which Kerberos and X.509 public key certificates are used for authentication, services allow Kerberos principals to be mapped to X.509 identities (and vice versa) (146, 590, 661).

A number of standardization efforts address the identity and credential federation: the Security Assertion Markup Language (SAML) (40) in conjunction with Liberty-Alliance, Microsoft Passport, the Extensible Access Control Markup Language (XACML) (13) , and WS-Policy/Federation. These efforts are in different states of maturity and address slightly different requirements.

21.2.7   Assertion-Style Authorization

Policies that govern the interactions between VO members need to be expressed in terms of not only the identities of the individuals and resources but also those entities' role in the VO and complex state such as accounting. Simple access control lists (ACLs) are not expressive enough for these complex authorization policies.

A number of authorization languages (e.g., SAML, Extensible Rights Markup Language (XrML) (14), and XACML) that allow for the expression of finer-grained policy assertions that can address the policies on VO-member interactions have been or are currently being standardized. Ongoing work to standardize authorization service efforts within the Grid community (discussed in the preceding section) is expected also to standardize assertion formats and expressions.

21.2.8   OGSA Security

The Open Grid Services Architecture introduces both new opportunities and new challenges for Grid security. In order to address the Grid-specific security requirements of OGSA, it makes sense to leverage as much as possible the existing and emerging Web services security standards, and to augment those only when needed.

Emerging Web services security specifications address the expression of Web service security policy (WS-Policy (102), XACML (13)), standard formats for security token exchange (WS-Security (381), SAML (40)), and standard methods for authentication and establishment of security contexts and trust relationships (WS-SecureConversation (379), WS-Trust (380)). These specifications may be exploited to create standard, interoperable methods for these features in Grid security. However, they may in some cases also need to be extended to address the Grid security requirements listed in the preceding. Clearly, WS security requirements are not fundamentally different from those of the Grid; the differences are more a matter of emphasis and modeling. For example, the fact that Grid applications span multiple administrative domains and that the collaborations are confined to teams of participants leads to requirements that focus on the federation of identities and credentials, and makes the VO a useful modeling abstraction.

Within GGF, an OGSA security working group has been formed with a charter to enumerate and address Grid security requirements in the context of OGSA.

Secure operation in a Grid environment requires that applications and services be able to support a variety of security functionality, such as authentication, authorization, credential conversion, auditing, and delegation. Grid applications also need to interact with other applications and services having a range of security mechanisms and requirements that are likely to evolve over time as new mechanisms are developed or policies change. Hence, Grid applications must avoid embedding security mechanisms statically.

To achieve integration and interoperability in this environment, a given service may need to use a variety of existing security technologies. Exposing security functionality as services (i.e., with a WSDL definition) achieves a level of abstraction that helps provide an integrated, secure Grid environment. Like any other service in the Web services domain, security services should also hide implementation details (see Figure 21.4).

This strategy allows well-defined protocols and interfaces to be defined for these services and permits an application not only to use a security service with a particular implementation to fit its current need but to replace a service as requirements change, without modification to the application.

An OGSA infrastructure may use a set of primitive security functions in the form of services themselves. Such services may include the following:

Authentication service.   An authentication service is concerned with verifying proof of an asserted identity. One example is the evaluation of a user ID and password combination, in which a service requestor supplies the appropriate password for

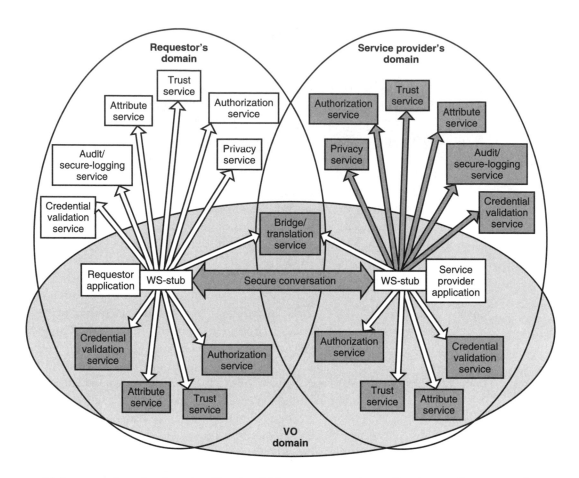

21.4

FIGURE

Security functionality should be cast as services, allowing applications to locate and use the particular functionality they need.

an asserted user ID. Another example involves a service requestor authenticating through a Kerberos mechanism, and a ticket being passed to the service provider's hosting environment, which determines the authenticity of the ticket before the service is instantiated.

Identity mapping service. An identity mapping service provides the capability of transforming an identity that exists in one identity domain into an identity in another identity domain. As an example, consider an identity in the form of an X.500 distinguished name (DN) (167), which is carried within an X.509 V3 digital certificate. The combination of the subject DN, issuer DN, and certificate serial number may be considered to carry the subject's or service requestor's identity. The scope of the identity domain in this example is considered to be the set of certificates issued by the certificate authority. Assuming that the certificate is used to convey the service requestor's identity, the identity mapping service may map the service requestor's identity to an identity that has meaning (for instance) to the hosting environment's local platform registry. The identity mapping service is not concerned with the authentication of the service requestor; rather, it is strictly a policy-driven name mapping service.

Authorization service.   An authorization service is concerned with resolving a policy-based access control decision. The authorization service consumes as input a credential that embodies the identity of an authenticated service requestor and, for the resource that the service requestor requests, determines whether the service requestor is authorized to access the resource. It is expected that the hosting environment for OGSA-compliant services will provide access control functions, and it is appropriate to further expose an abstract authorization service depending on the granularity of the access control policy being enforced.

VO policy service.   A VO policy service is concerned with the management of policies associated with a VO's resources and users. The aggregation of the policies contained within and managed by the policy service composes a VO's policy set. The policy service may be thought of as another primitive service, which is used by the authorization, audit, identity mapping, and other services as needed.

Credential conversion service.   A credential conversion service converts between different types or forms of credential. Conversion may include such tasks as reconciling group membership, privileges, attributes, and assertions associated with entities (service requestors and service providers). For example, the credential conversion service may convert a Kerberos credential to a form required by the authorization service. The policy-driven credential conversion service facilitates the interoperability of differing credential types that may be consumed by services. It is expected that the credential conversion service will use the identity mapping service.

Audit service.   An audit service, similar to the identity mapping and authorization services, is policy driven. The audit service is responsible for producing records that track security-relevant events. The resulting audit records may be reduced and examined to determine whether the desired security policy is being enforced. Auditing and reduction tools are used by the security administrators within a VO to determine the VO's adherence to the stated access control and authentication policies.

Profile service.   A profile (or user attribute) service is concerned with managing service requestor's preferences and data, which may also be consumed by the authorization service. These data may be service requestor-specific that, for example, can be used to tailor the service requestor's experience (if incorporated into an application that interfaces with end users). It is expected that these data will also be used by portal applications that interface with a person.

Privacy service.   A privacy service is concerned primarily with the policy-driven classification of personally identifiable information. Service providers and service requestors may store personally identifiable information using the privacy service. Such a service can be used to articulate and enforce a VO's privacy policy.

21.3   WS SECURITY

Industry has rallied around Web services as an emerging architecture that can deliver integrated, interoperable solutions. Ensuring the integrity, confidentiality, and security of Web services through the application of a comprehensive security model is critical, both for organizations and for their customers. Secure interoperability between virtual organizations demands interoperable solutions using heterogeneous systems. For instance, the secure messaging model proposed by the Web services security road map (381) document supports both PKI and Kerberos mechanisms as particular embodiments of a more-general facility and can be extended to support additional security mechanisms.

The security of a Grid environment must take into account the security of various aspects involved in a Grid service invocation, as depicted in Figure 21.5. We discuss several of these aspects in the following.

21.3.1   Access Control

A Web service can be accessed over a variety of protocols and message formats it supports, as defined by its bindings (278). Given that bindings deal with protocol and message formats, they should provide support for quality of service, including such security functions as confidentiality, integrity, and authentication.

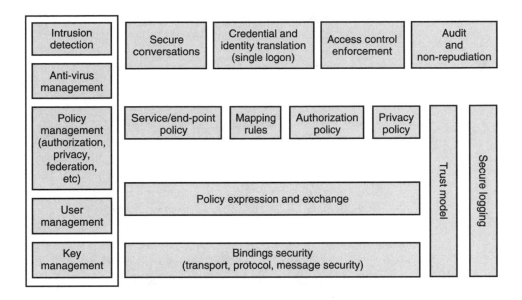

21.5

FIGURE

Components of the Grid security model.

21.3.2   Secure Conversation

Each participating endpoint can express the policy it wishes to see applied when engaging in a secure conversation with another endpoint. Policies can specify supported authentication mechanisms, requirements for integrity and confidentiality, trust policies, privacy policies, and other security constraints. Given the dynamic nature of Grid service invocations, endpoints will often discover the policies of a target service and establish trust relationships with it dynamically.

Once a service requestor and a service provider have determined each other's policies, they can establish a secure channel over which subsequent operations can be invoked. Such a channel should enforce various qualities of service, including identification, confidentiality, and integrity.

21.3.3   Credential Translation

The security model must provide a mechanism by which authentication credentials from the service requestor's domain can be translated into the service provider's domain and vice versa. This translation is required in order for both ends to evaluate their mutual access policies based on the established credentials and the quality of the established channel.

21.3.4   Bindings Security

The set of bindings to be considered includes SOAP (SOAP/HTTP, SOAP over a message queue, or SOAP over any other protocol) and IIOP bindings. The security of a binding is based on the security characteristics of the associated protocol and message format. If new protocols or message formats are introduced, care should be taken to address security requirements in those bindings so that, at a minimum, suitable authentication, integrity, and confidentiality can be achieved.

HTTP is an important protocol to consider because of its transparency to firewalls and its wide adoption. In the case of bindings over HTTP, requests can be sent over SSL (i.e., "https"), and thus SSL can provide authentication, integrity, and confidentiality. However, SSL ensures these qualities of service only among participating SSL connection endpoints. If a request needs to traverse multiple intermediaries (firewalls, proxies, etc.), end-to-end security must be enforced at a layer above the SSL protocol.

Security information can be carried in the SOAP message itself in the form of security tokens defined in the WS-Security specification (381). SOAP messages can also be integrity and confidentiality protected by using XML digital signature and XML encryption support, respectively. Signature and encryption bindings defined in WS-Security can be used for this purpose.

Web services can be accessed over IIOP when the service implementation is based on CORBA (508). In the case of IIOP, the security of the message exchange can be achieved by using the Common Secure Interoperability specification, version 2 (CSIv2) (642). This specification is also adopted in J2EE (616).

In addition to, or in lieu of, binding-level security requirements, network security solutions (e.g., firewalls, the IP security protocol (IPSec) (408), VPN, domain name service security extensions (DNSSec) (87)) remain useful components for securing a Grid environment. Firewalls can continue to enforce boundary access rules between domains, and other network-level security solutions can continue to be deployed in intradomain environments. Grid services deployment can take the topology into consideration when defining security policies. At the same time, deployment assumptions may surface as policies attached to firewalls and network architecture.

The Grid security model must leverage security capabilities of any of these underlying protocols or message formats. For example, in the case of SOAP over HTTP requests, one can use WS-Security for end-to-end security functionality,

HTTPS for point-to-point security, and SSL, TLS, or IPSec for other purposes. Security requirements for a given Web service access will be specified and honored based on the set of policies associated with the participating endpoints. For example, a policy associated with a Web service can specify that it expects SOAP messages to be signed and encrypted. Thus, service requestors accessing that service would be required to use WS-Security to secure their SOAP requests.

Addressing the security of the service bindings will address the requirements related to the integrity and confidentiality of messages, achieving delegation facilities and facilitating firewall traversal.

21.3.5 Policy Expression and Exchange

Web services have certain requirements that must be met in order to interact with them. For example, a service may support specific message-encoding formats or require specific security credentials to perform a specific action. A hosting environment has access to policies associated with a hosted Web service so that it can enforce the invocation requirements when the service is accessed. Once a service requestor knows the requirements and supported capabilities of a target service, it can evaluate the capabilities and mechanisms that the service provider supports. At the end of the evaluation, the service requestor and the service provider together select the optimal set of bindings to converse with one another. Note that the ability to acquire this knowledge is a privilege given by the hosting environment's policy.

In a dynamic environment such as the Grid, it is important for service requestors to discover these policies dynamically and make decisions at run time. Such policies can be associated with the service definition (e.g., WSDL) or service data (i.e., part of Grid service specification), can be exchanged between service requestor and service provider (e.g., service provider can return information about the policy through some negotiation), or can be part of the binding information in the Grid service reference (similar to the CORBA security tagged component).

In addition to service provider policies that need to be exposed to a service requester (or similarly service requestor policies to the service provider), there may be other policies that a service requestor or a service provider's environment needs to know, but not necessarily expose, in order to ensure a secure environment. For example, a service provider may have a set of authorization policies that indicate authorized requestors, and this policy need not be (most likely will not be) exposed to service requestors. Similarly, requestors may have policies specifying the identity of service provider's hosting environments it may trust for certain service invocations.

The emerging WS-Policy specifications may address the requirements for a format, language, and framework for the expression of policy requirements and capabilities of both the requestor and service provider. Additional profiles for SAML assertions and XACML authorization expressions may increase the applicability of this approach.

21.3.6   Policy Enforcement Layer

The bindings and exchange layers discussed so far allow the service requestor and service provider to discover one another's policy. The policy enforcement layer of the model deals with the nature and enforcement of these policies: secure association between service endpoints, mapping of identities and translation of credentials across domain boundaries between them, authorization policies, and privacy policies, which together form the basis for enforcing control of access to protected services. These are reviewed briefly in the following.

21.3.6.1   Secure Association

In many cases, the integrity and privacy protection for the message exchange between requestor and service provider is derived from a security context established at the start of the communication. One reason for the initial context establishment may be that the policy requires the parties to authenticate before any application data are exchanged. Another reason may be the (possibly) improved performance through the use of symmetric session keys for the cryptographic protection. The period of time over which a context is reused is considered a session, or *association*, between the interacting endpoints. Security context establishment and maintenance should be based on a Web service context (to be) defined within Web or Grid service specifications.

The notion of a context is tightly coupled with bindings. Many protocols (e.g., IPSEC, SSL, IIOP) and mechanisms (e.g., Kerberos) already support secure association contexts. In the case of SOAP, the context can be carried and secured as part of the SOAP messages.

The emerging WS-SecureConversation and WS-Trust specifications describe how a service provider can authenticate requestor messages, how service requestors can authenticate service providers, and how (mutually) authenticated security contexts can be established. These mechanisms are designed to operate at the SOAP message layer so that the messages may traverse a variety of transports and intermediaries. Alternatively, other technologies, such as SASL and BEEP, may be used. Therefore, the mechanism used to establish security contexts between endpoints will be based on the bindings used as well as the policy associated with the endpoints.

21.3.6.2 *Identity and Credential Mapping or Translation*

Since the members of a VO belong to different organizations with different security infrastructures and policies, mismatches arise between different members' identities and credentials. In order to be able to use the other party's identity and credentials for the local policy rule evaluations, some form of federation is required. This federation will typically be accomplished through mapping or translation of identities or credentials through proxies, gateways, or trusted intermediaries. The mapping or translation components at this layer are responsible for implementing these functions as directed by corresponding policies. The definition of these policies is the subject of suitable management functions and trust models to be discussed later. The resulting federation framework is the basis for addressing the requirements for single authentication and delegation.

The WS security architecture identifies a WS-Federation component that is expected to define how federated trust scenarios are constructed using the WS-Security, WS-Policy, WS-Trust, and WS-SecureConversation specifications (378). With additional profiles we expect also to leverage SAML and Liberty Alliance federation assertions.

21.3.6.3 *Authorization Enforcement*

The ability to enforce the authorization policy is key to the overall security infrastructure. In an Internet environment, authorization is typically associated with a service provider such that it controls access to a resource based on the identity of the service requestor. The Grid's requirements emphasize that both the requestor and provider have enforcement point: the requestor's policy states whether the provider is allowed to serve the requestor.

The implementation of the authorization engine in each domain may also follow different models (e.g., role-based authorization, rule-based authorization, capabilities, or access control lists).

The WS security architecture includes a WS-Authorization component that is expected to describe how access policies for a Web service are specified and managed. In particular, it will describe how claims may be specified within security tokens and how these claims will be interpreted at the endpoints. Additional profiles are to be defined to leverage existing standardized SAML and XACML authorization assertions and expressions. It should be taken into account that every domain is likely to have its own authorization model, authorization authority, and management facilities. Defining an authorization model will address the requirement to provide a secure Grid environment by controlling access to Grid services.

21.3.6.4 Privacy Enforcement

Maintaining anonymity or the ability to withhold private information is important in certain service environments. Organizations creating, managing, and using Grid services will often need to state their privacy policies and require that incoming service requests make claims about the service provider's adherence to these policies. The WS-Privacy specification will describe a model for how a privacy language may be embedded into WS-Policy descriptions. The general practices and rules defined by the platform for privacy preferences (P3P) effort (196) can prove useful in privacy policy enforcement.

21.3.6.5 Trust

Each member of a VO is likely to have a security infrastructure that includes authentication service, user registry, authorization engine, network layer protection, and other security services. The security policies, authentication credentials, and identities belonging to that member organization are likely to be managed, issued, and defined within the scope of the organization (i.e., a security domain). To securely process requests that traverse between members of a VO, the member organizations must have established a trust relationship. Such trust relationships are essential for services accessed between the members to traverse network checkpoints (e.g., firewalls) and satisfy authorization policies associated with a service achieved by translating credentials from one domain to another (e.g., Kerberos to PKI) and mapping identities across security domains of the security model. Such a model needs to define direct or mutual trust relationships between two domains, as well as indirect trust relationships brokered through intermediaries. These relationships will then often materialize as rules for mapping identities and credentials among the involved organization domains.

The WS-Trust specification describes message formats and processes that can be used to prove and establish trust relationships. Trust can be established and enforced based on trust policies defined a priori. Because of the dynamic nature of Grids, however, trust relationships may also need to be established dynamically, by using trust proxies that act as intermediaries. Once such a model is defined, this will play a role in defining how trust assertions are to be consumed by a service provider or a requester. The model will also form the basis for satisfying the requirements to achieve single log-on based on trust of asserting authority or trust on the requesting member of a VO.

21.3.6.6   Secure Logging

Often, the adherence to stated policy can be checked only through the secure logging of the relevant information used for the evaluation of the policy decisions. The Grid security model explicitly calls for a secure logging functionality as the necessary foundation for many higher-level audit-related services. Similar to the trust model and security management, secure logging is a basic service applicable to other components in the model.

21.3.6.7   Security Management

The Grid security model groups all security management functions applicable to various aspects of binding, policy, and federation. These include key management for cryptographic functions, user registry management, authorization, privacy and trust policy management, and management of mapping rules that enables federation. Security management functions may also include the management of intrusion detection, anti-virus services, and assurance information enabling service requestors to discover what security mechanisms and assurances a hosting environment can offer.

21.4   GSI: AN OGSA SECURITY REFERENCE IMPLEMENTATION

We next present a specific implementation of an OGSA-based Grid security architecture: the Grid Security Infrastructure, which is included as part of the Globus Toolkit Version 3 (GT3). The Grid Security Infrastructure (GSI) is the name given to the portion of the Globus Toolkit that implements the security functionality. GSI is a combination of various existing and custom-developed security technologies that have been carefully integrated to support Grids. In this section we briefly discuss these components and their integration. More details are provided in a longer article (671).

21.4.1   GT2 Grid Security Model

GT3 security has its genesis in the extensive experience gained in the design, implementation, and use of the earlier GSI version included in the Globus Toolkit version 2 (GT2: Chapter 4) (276). All GT2 services use a common GSI (146, 280) for security functionality. The designers of GSI evaluated several related efforts before electing to build on PKI. They noted the following shortcomings in other approaches with respect to Grid security requirements:

✦ Kerberos (501) requires the explicit involvement of site administrators to establish interdomain trust relationships or to create new entities.

✦ The CRISIS wide-area security system (109) defines a uniform and scalable security infrastructure for wide-area systems but does not address interoperability with local security mechanisms.

✦ Secure Shell (SSH) (690) provides a strong system of authentication and message protection but has no support for translation between different mechanisms or for creation of dynamic entities.

The Legion security model (373) is perhaps the most similar to that of GT2, using X.509 certificates for delegation. However, it lacks mechanisms for creation of dynamic entities.

21.4.2   GSI Highlights

At a high level, GT2 GSI ("GSI2") and GT3 GSI ("GSI3") are similar in design and goals. However, largely because of its leverage of Web services technology and its focus on extensibility and pluggability, the GSI3 implementation differs significantly from the earlier GSI implementation. We touch here on the highlights of GSI, pointing out where GSI2 and GSI3 differ.

21.4.2.1   Authentication

GSI defines a credential format based on X.509 identity certificates (164, 660). An X.509 certificate, in conjunction with an associated private key, forms a unique credential set that a Grid entity (requestor and service provider) uses to authenticate itself to other Grid entities (e.g., through a challenge-response protocol such as TLS).

As described in Section 21.2.1.4, each GSI certificate is issued by a trusted party known as a certificate authority, usually run by a large organization or commercial company. A CA acts as a trust root for identity name assertions. In order to trust the X.509 certificate presented by an entity, one must trust the CA that issued the certificate.

X.509 identity certificates are used within GSI because the establishment of trust between two administrative domains through this public key technology is relatively lightweight. In contrast to mechanisms such as Kerberos (501), where interinstitutional trust requires a bilateral agreement at the organizational level, trust in a CA can be established unilaterally. A single entity in an organization can decide to trust any CA, without necessarily involving the organization as a whole. This feature is key to the establishment of VOs that involve only some portion of an organization, where the organization as a whole may provide little or no support for the VO and hence have little or no interest in trusting any CAs used by that VO.

21.4.2.2 Identity Federation

GSI uses gateways to translate between X.509-based identity credentials and other mechanisms. For example, the Kerberos Certificate Authority (KCA) (417, 661) and SSLK5/PKINIT provide translation from Kerberos to GSI and vice versa, respectively. These mechanisms allow a site with an existing Kerberos infrastructure to convert credentials between Kerberos and GSI as needed. For example, users coming into the site with GSI credentials can convert to Kerberos credentials and then use existing site security infrastructure without modification. Likewise, users communicating from the site can convert their Kerberos credentials to GSI identity credentials to authenticate to other Grid sites.

21.4.2.3 Dynamic Entities and Delegation

GSI introduces X.509 proxy certificates, an extension to X.509 identity certificates (660) that allows a user to assign dynamically a new X.509 identity to an entity and then delegate some subset of their rights to that identity. Users create a proxy certificate by issuing a new X.509 certificate signed using their own credentials instead of involving a CA. This mechanism allows new credentials and identities to be created quickly without the involvement of a traditional administrator. Thus, this approach solves the issue of how to delegate rights to entities, both dynamic and static.

21.4.2.4 Message-Level Security

GT3 uses the Web services security specifications to allow security messages and secured messages to be transported, understood, and manipulated by standard Web services tools and software. GT3 offers both stateful and stateless forms of secured communication.

Stateful. GSI supports the establishment of a security context that authenticates two parties to each other and allows for the exchange of secured messages between the two parties. GT2 uses the TLS (228) transport protocol for both security context establishment and message protection. GT3 achieves security context establishment by implementing preliminary versions of WS-SecureConversation (379) and WS-Trust specifications (380), which use SOAP messages to transport context-establishment tokens between the two parties. GT3 messages carry the same context establishment tokens used by GT2 but transport them over SOAP instead of TCP. Once the security context is established, GSI3 in GT3 implements message protection using the Web services standards for secured messages (XML-Signature (321) and XML-Encryption (321)).

Stateless. To allow for communication without the initial establishment of a security context, GT3 also offers the ability to sign messages independent of any established security context, by using the XML-Signature specification. Thus, a message can be created and signed, allowing the recipient to verify the message's origin and integrity, without establishing synchronous communication with the recipient. A feature of this approach is that the identity of the recipient does not have to be known to the sender when the message is sent. As we discuss later, this approach allows for messages to be created by clients and delivered to services whose creation is caused by the message itself.

21.4.2.5 *Management of Overlaid Trust Domains*

The requirement for overlaid trust domains to establish VOs is satisfied by using both proxy certificates and security services such as the Community Authorization Service, or CAS (519). GSI has an implicit policy that any two entities bearing proxy certificates issued by the same user will inherently trust each other. This policy allows users to create trust domains dynamically by issuing proxy certificates to any services that they want to interoperate.

The implicit policy of trust between proxy holders allows for the lightweight, dynamic creation of simple trust domains but has limitations when it comes to complicated trust domains with, for example, limited trust between multiple parties. In that latter case, we can turn to security services such as CAS that allow flexible, expressive policy regarding multiple users in a VO to be created. CAS allows a VO to express the policy that has been outsourced to it by the resource providers in the VO. This process, as illustrated in Figure 21.6, comprises three steps:

✦ The user authenticates to CAS and receives assertions from CAS expressing the VO's policy in terms of how that user may use VO resources.

✦ The user then presents the assertion to a VO resource along with the usage request.

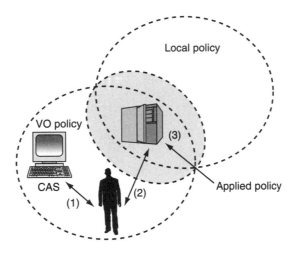

21.6

FIGURE

CAS allows VOs to express policy, and it allows resources to apply policy that is a subset of VO and local policy.

◆ In evaluating whether to allow the request, the resource checks both local policy and the VO policy expressed in the CAS assertion.

CAS allows a resource to remain the ultimate authority over that resource, but it also allows the VO to control a subset of that enforced policy. In turn, the VO can coordinate the policy across a number of resources to control the sharing of those resources by the VO.

21.4.2.6   Security Service Abstraction

A significant difference between GT2 and GT3 is that, in GT3, applications may be contained in sophisticated container-based hosting environments (currently AXIS and J2EE with ongoing work with .NET). These hosting environments provide a high level of functionality and allow for much security implementation complexity to be pulled from applications. Such an approach allows for GT3 security to be instantiated in hosting environments, simplifying application development and enabling security functionality to be upgraded independently of applications.

As GT3 continues to be developed and refined, we envision a rich variety of security functionality instantiated as services available for applications to use. Already in the current GT3 release authentication, authorization, and message protection are all implemented outside the application, as part of the hosting environment and in separate security services.

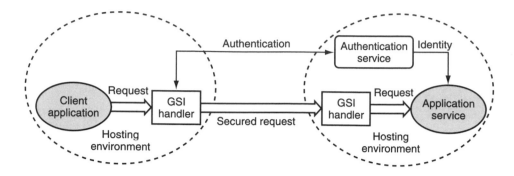

21.7

FIGURE

Authentication handled by the hosting environment in GT3.

As shown in Figure 21.7, when an application in GT3 sends a request, it is sent to one or more software components known as handlers for processing to prepare it for transmission. When the GSI handler is invoked, it determines the destination of the request and authenticates to an authentication service at the destination to establish a security context (subsequent request by the application can reuse this context). The handler then uses the established context to protect the message (confidentiality or integrity protection) as required by the policies of the client and service. A similar handler in the hosting environment on the server side checks and removes the protection and delivers the request to the application service. The identity of the client is also available to the service from the authentication service. This approach allows the application code to be independent of the deployed security. Hence, the security can adapt to different requirements as needed. For example, the GSI handlers could be replaced with Kerberos-based code without having to change the application code.

21.5   SUMMARY

As Grid applications become more sophisticated and complex, so do the associated security requirements. To meet security requirements, one must raise the abstraction level, a process that has consequences for the trust establishment: risk-benefit analysis will become part of the service-level agreement negotiation (Chapter 18). The use of a VO concept helps in understanding and modeling collaborative interactions. VO participants should be able to manage its security policy dynamically within the limits set by the participating organization.

The Grid community is defining the Open Grid Services Architecture as the basis for future applications. OGSA as well as its security components will build on the Web services (WS) foundation. Emerging WS security technologies are expected to cater for most Grid requirements. Observed gaps are in the areas of identity and credential federation, complex delegation of rights, quantification of trust, and the use of VOs as a cross-domain collaboration model.

The Global Grid Forum provides the venue for our community to investigate, discuss, address, and standardize Grid-specific security requirements. The development of GT3, an open source reference implementation of the basic OGSA infrastructure services, facilitates the adoption of its technology by both the Grid community and commercial vendors. The security components of this toolkit, specifically the Grid Security Infrastructure (GSI), already address some of the complex Grid requirements. Many collaborative efforts within the Grid community are developing security technologies, which will result in a comprehensive framework able to tackle the "Grid security challenge."

ACKNOWLEDGMENTS

We are pleased to acknowledge contributions by Jarek Gawor, Sam Meder, Laura Pearlman, and Steve Tuecke. This work was supported in part by the Mathematical, Information, and Computational Sciences Division subprogram of the Office of Advanced Scientific Computing Research, Office of Science, U.S. Department of Energy, under Contracts W-31–109-Eng-38, DE-AC03-76SF0098, DE-FC03-99ER25397, and No. 53-4540-0080; and by IBM.

FURTHER READING

For more information on the topics covered in this chapter, see *www.mkp. com/grid2*. In addition, Bruce Schneier's book *Applied Cryptography* (576) still gives the best comprehensive review of modern cryptography, while his *Secrets and Lies* (577) is written for both technical users and managers and deals with practical security on the higher level of companies, networks, and humans.

V DATA AND KNOWLEDGE

PART

Computing is the science of information processing, and the generation and manipulation of information pervades all aspects of computing. Nevertheless, we feel confident in asserting that information—data and knowledge—is even more important in the Grid environment than in other domains.

We make this assertion for two reasons. First, the virtual organizations that define Grid systems are formed to solve problems too complex or expensive to solve with local resources. Problem solving is concerned with the consumption and production of information. Thus, as we saw in the case studies of Part II, the generation, federation, and manipulation of information are the primary concern for many of the applications that motivate the development and deployment of Grid technologies, and are an important concern for all.

The second connection is more subtle but equally important. The inherent complexity and dynamism of Grid environments mean that we cannot rely on implicit knowledge about system configuration, state, policies, and evolution. Instead, Grid middleware must be able to use and process information about the availability of services; their purpose; the ways in which they can be combined and configured or substituted; and how they are discovered, are invoked, and evolve. The Grid itself is a complex and information-rich environment. Thus, we are concerned not only with information *on* the Grid but also with information *about* the Grid.

The two chapters that constitute Part V address this topic of information in a Grid context from the perspectives of data and knowledge management, respectively. Data and knowledge are vague terms: one person's data is another's knowledge, and thus we find some overlap in concerns and topics between the two chapters. However, they each address distinct and complementary parts of the overall problem.

Chapter 22, "Data Access, Integration, and Management," is concerned with the technical challenges and solutions involved in the integration, analysis, and management of distributed data. Malcolm Atkinson and his colleagues present and analyze application requirements, technical solutions, and open issues associated with maintaining and manipulating information on and for the Grid. Notably, they emphasize the commonality of interest that obtains between the sometimes apparently distinct worlds of structured and file-based data, emphasizing the common requirements for such functions as discovery, transport, and federation.

Chapter 23, "Enhancing Services and Applications with Knowledge and Semantics," is concerned with the particular type of structured data sometimes referred to as knowledge. Carole Goble and her colleagues introduce the motivations, technologies, and research challenges that underlie knowledge both on and for the Grid. In so doing, they define what is involved in building a knowledge-rich Grid in which services and applications are able to benefit at all levels from a coordinated and distributed collection of knowledge services founded upon the explicit representation and the explicit use of different forms of knowledge.

These two chapters significantly extend, but do not supplant, the treatment of data-intensive science provided by Chapter 1:5, "Data-Intensive Computing," which presents a 1998 perspective on the nature of data-intensive science and the role that Grid technologies—in particular, the influential Storage Resource Broker system—can play in its advancement. The most important difference is perhaps the recognition, reflected in the material presented here, that data and knowledge management are so fundamental that they cannot be treated as a vertically integrated "solution" but rather as a set of fundamental interfaces and behaviors that must ultimately permeate every aspect of the Grid.

Data Access, Integration, and Management

Malcolm Atkinson, Ann L. Chervenak, Peter Kunszt, Inderpal Narang, Norman W. Paton, Dave Pearson, Arie Shoshani, and Paul Watson

*D*igital data are now fundamental to all branches of science and engineering; such data play a major role in medical research and diagnosis and underpin business and governmental decision processes. Increasingly, these data are organized as shared and structured collections held in databases, XML documents, and structured assemblies of binary files. Driven by advances in simulation and sensor technology (Chapter 2), data collections have grown to the extent that multiple terabyte-sized, and soon petabyte-sized, collections of data are becoming prevalent (359).

The sheer size of datasets being generated makes the interpretation of the data in any one collection challenging. Analysis may demand teraflops of compute power and require access to terabytes of data distributed across millions of binary files and multiple databases. Furthermore, analysis may require complex series of processing steps, each generating intermediate data products of size comparable to the input datasets. These intermediate data products need to be stored, either temporarily or permanently, and made available for discovery and use by other analysis processes. Effective manipulation, processing, and use of these large-scale, distributed data resources require an infrastructure in which shared data, storage, networking, and compute resources can be delivered to data analysis activities in an integrated, flexible manner.

The advent of ubiquitous network connectivity and the scale of modern challenges, such as deciphering the function of all the genes in a large number of species, have led to widespread collaboration in the creation, curation, publication, management, and exploitation of these structured collections. Moreover, although individual collections are typically specialized to hold data of interest to particular communities, substantial advances can be achieved by combining information from multiple data resources. For example, astronomers are building virtual observatories where data collected at different frequencies (X-ray, radio, optical, infrared, etc.) and at different times can be conveniently combined to discover new properties of the universe (Chapter 7). Similarly, functional genomics requires comparison between species and integration with protein biochemistry and crystallography databases, laboratory phenotypical data, and population studies (Chapter 9). Consequently, data analysis must both deal with issues of large-scale computation and data movement and provide mechanisms to integrate information from diverse, geographically distributed structured collections hosted on a variety of platforms and administered independently according to differing policies.

As collections increase in scale and number, it becomes impractical to arrange for integration of data access and analysis into application workflows through ad hoc schemes. More structured mechanisms for discovering, accessing, analyzing, and integrating data become critical if these important assets are to be shared and exploited to their full potential. The Grid services described in this book provide the necessary foundation for the types of integration needed to meet the data access and analysis needs of science and industry.

The Open Grid Services Architecture (279) (OGSA, Chapter 17) defines basic architectural structure and mechanisms for creating a service-oriented infrastructure and can be applied directly to the challenges associated with the sharing, interpretation, and analysis of data collections. However, the integration of distributed data collections also demands additional Grid services whose function is tailored to the requirements of data-intensive applications. In this chapter, we focus on these services.

Data have a multifaceted relationship with Grid infrastructure. Many Grid applications have significant data access and analysis requirements; virtually every scientific, engineering, medical, and decision-support application depends on accessing distributed heterogeneous collections of structured data. In addition, the Grid itself uses many structured data collections for its operation and administration (Chapter 20); service data elements (see Chapter 17) constitute just one example. As Grid technology becomes more sophisticated and autonomic, the number, volume, and diversity of these collections will increase. Hence, systematic data access and integration methods become important, not only for Grid applications, but for the Grid itself.

The term "data Grid" has sometimes been used to denote Grid architectures oriented toward data-intensive applications. We avoid using this term because it implies a false distinction between "data Grids" and "computational Grids," which in practice build on common infrastructure. Furthermore, any substantial data analysis necessarily requires access to the full range of Grid services, including computing, network, and security. Thus, we use the common term "Grid" in all cases, with the understanding that services oriented to the management of data will be available, along with other services required to support the operation of virtual organizations.

In this chapter we first discuss how data are used by applications and review the various sources and types of structured data that appear in the Grid. We then introduce an architectural framework for structuring data-oriented services and present a number of important data-oriented services, highlighting current solutions and discussing future directions. We conclude with a case study: the Earth System Grid, which uses a variety of data services to address the data analysis requirements of the climate modeling community.

22.1   DATA-INTENSIVE APPLICATIONS

Data-intensive applications for Grids occur within both the scientific and business domains. Scientists require mechanisms to transfer, publish, replicate, discover, share, and analyze data. Business applications in such domains as financial services, pharmaceutical research, and online business services need to maintain database consistency regionally or worldwide, manage data replication, facilitate data discovery, and respond dynamically to changes in the load applied to databases by users.

22.1.1   Scientific Applications

New discoveries become possible as scientists mine correlations and anomalies from multiple data sources. Such data mining is becoming a major *modus operandi* for scientific collaboration (521). As more and more data are recorded and organized as structured data resources available to large communities of scientists from many disciplines, investigations increasingly involve accessing subsets of these resources, extracting specific data from each, and using those data in combination to test or develop some scientific model. In some cases, moderate volumes of data are combined to derive specific results. In other cases, large volumes of data (terabytes to petabytes) are examined in pursuit of more general understanding. In virtually all cases, the integration of the different data depends on scientifically based transformations and comparisons. These operations typically require the execution of complex code, specific to the application or domain, written by the relevant scientists. That code, often encapsulated in a mixture of separate programs and sophisticated query predicates linked by a workflow script, must be executed in conjunction with the data extraction and transfers. The results are often accumulated in other data collections that may be immediately shared or retained by a local team and subsequently contributed to public repositories, perhaps only in digest form or after the scientists have tested and validated the results. Consequently, typical applications use multiple data resources. The following examples illustrate this type of analysis:

+ *Data mining* is used in astronomy to scan data coming from satellites, telescopes, and other instruments for rare objects. In the Sloan Digital Sky Survey project, researchers have used data-mining techniques to identify high-redshift quasars. (See Chapter 7.)

+ *Statistical analysis* is applied in high-energy physics applications to events generated by particle detectors. Using histograms generated from these events, physicists can measure their understanding of the basic forces of nature. (See Chapter 10.)

+ *Simulation and analysis* are used in biological applications such as genomics to combine published data about known genomes into new sequences, which are stored as derived data products and analyzed for their chemical properties. (See Chapter 9.)

In these and many other cases, the communities generating and consuming the data are large, multidisciplinary collaborations, in which participants fill many different roles. *Experimentalists* organize data collection processes, provide records describing how data was collected, interpret the data, and arrange the generation of standard data products. *Theoreticians* create and run simulations that produce data, provide records describing how it was produced, and interpret data. *Data curators* organize, maintain, and publish shared collections of data, including primary data, data products, annotations, and their own interpretations and integrations of data; they also provide so-called metadata that describe the organization of their collection and the policies governing its use. *Database engineers*, *computer scientists*, and *developers* of scientific applications jointly establish and optimize the supporting infrastructure and formulate and develop schemas, queries, and code that represent the science. Collaboration among all of these groups is essential for scientific advancement.

Scientific data exploration consists typically of three phases: data generation, postprocessing, and analysis. Because of the nature of scientific analysis, datasets at all phases are often published by the community and subsequently accessed in a read-only manner. Alternatively, for example when adding new attributes to a structured dataset, the data may be updated rather than augmented, a process that may have ramifications with respect to consistency constraints if data have been replicated. In all cases, keeping a record of what processing steps the data have been subjected to is important to maintain the veracity of any scientific results.

The *data generation* phase may consist of running large simulations that require the full use of a supercomputer for many hours. During this phase, the main concern is storing the resulting data fast enough to avoid slowing the computer simulation run. Current rates of data production often reach 1 gigabyte/sec. Datasets may also need to be moved to archival storage at the same rate to make room for data from the next simulation run. The datasets produced by these simulations may be large. For example, climate models generate terabytes of data per simulation run, and increases in simulation resolution will greatly increase data storage requirements. Even a conservative increase in the granularity of the model meshes—a factor of 2 per dimension of space and time—will generate a factor of 16 more data. Moving such datasets is often prohibitive; rather, a subset selection and filtering of the data need to be performed at the simulation site, and only the results sent to the scientist for further analysis.

In the *postprocessing* phase, data generated during a simulation run are typically validated, subjected to some initial processing and formatting, and annotated with appropriate auxiliary information (i.e., metadata) to form a data collection. The type of postprocessing varies with the application, such as applying scientific codes to interpret the data in fusion applications or generating multiresolution representations of the data for visualization. In some cases, the amount of data generated in the postprocessing phase is equal to or greater than the original data, especially if indexes are built for use in the analysis phase. Postprocessing of the data can be done at multiple computational sites. Thus, large subsets of the original dataset typically are replicated at multiple locations. Today, several high-energy physics experiments need to replicate files at a sustained rate of 1–2 terabytes a day, or about 10–20 megabyte/sec. Hence, access to a robust data replication capability is highly desirable. Services for registering the location of replicas and for discovery of data replicas are also required.

In the *analysis* phase, different combinations of data from one or more data collections must be accessed and processed to provide the desired result. A typical application structure is shown in Figure 22.1. P1 and P2 denote application programs, and DS1 to DS4 denote four data resources held at different sites with different structures that are independently managed. The data flows DF1 to DF5 denote movement of structured data. For example, DF1 and DF2 could be the result of queries sent as part of the workflow organizing the whole computation;

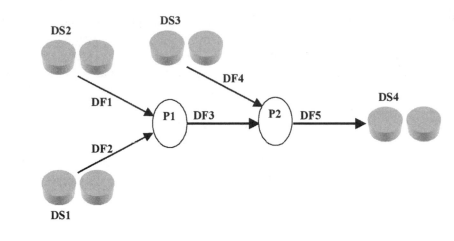

22.1   An example data access and integration application structure.

FIGURE

DF4 could be the result of a query sent by P2, partially determined as a result of the data delivered by DF3; and DF5 could denote the addition of data to DS4. Scientific workflows that access and integrate structured data will often be significantly more complex than this.

22.1.2   Business Applications

Business applications encompass many different usage scenerios. Some commercial applications, in areas such as engineering design and pharmaceutical research and development, are essentially scientific in nature, and hence have much in common with those in the sciences. Others, such as in financial services, have different characteristics, both in their use of data and data volumes. Although use of Grid technologies in the commercial sector is just beginning to take hold, we are starting to see significant application classes emerge.

Data mining plays a significant role in many commercial endeavors. For example, in the financial services sector, data mining is used for fraud detection, while in retail supply chains, data mining is used to detect trends and patterns in purchasing behaviors. In general, the size of the data collections associated with commercial data mining tends to be smaller than that of large-scale scientific applications. Nevertheless, the need to integrate distributed data and compute resources remains just as urgent, or even more so. Industries concerned with capital costs will want to utilize diverse data-processing resources, from desktop machines to data center servers allocated on demand. For this reason, these applications are just as sensitive to issues of discovery, data placement, scheduling, and workflow management as are scientific analysis applications.

A second important class of commercial applications being explored in the commercial space focuses on *integrated data access* both within and among enterprises. Increasingly, data to support business operations are distributed across multiple databases. Some of this distribution is due to the fact that no single database holds all information required by an application. Alternatively, for performance or reliability reasons, applications require local copies of either entire datasets or subsets. Current database federation technology is not sufficient to address these requirements in a general, cross platform manner, and the current approach to application development is either to rely on vendor-specific solutions or to support replication and federation in an ad hoc and application-specific manner. This approach results in both increased fragility of the application code and an underutilization of capital resources due to a lack of sharing. Hence, there is a strong motivation to migrate these applications to an infrastructure in which basic data access, replication, and data integration services are provided by standard infrastructure elements.

These integration applications differ from scientific applications in several respects. Data are almost exclusively structured and stored in databases, rather than in binary files. The total volume of data tends to be smaller than that of scientific datasets: terabytes rather than hundreds of terabytes (with notable exceptions). Finally, while the importance of preserving provenance tends to make updates of scientific datasets rare, commercial datasets may be updated frequently. Updating complicates replication and coherency and often requires some type of transactional semantics. Nevertheless, even in financial datasets, total coherency of all distributed and replicated data products is typically *not* a prerequisite but rather a property that may be enforced to varying extents, depending on application semantics.

22.2   CATEGORIES AND ORIGINS OF STRUCTURED DATA

While different classes of data may be generated at different stages in the scientific process, we focus here on *structured data*. This term denotes data whose structure is explicitly defined in a way that can be exploited by operations: for example, so that queries may extract subsets of data based on that structure. We limit our discussion to structured data because structuring is required to understand data and hence is a prerequisite for sharing data across a collaboration.

Often data are structured using the relational model or, more recently, by XML documents and associated XML schema. Data structured by these mechanisms are often stored or managed in database management systems. Data may also may be binary, however, with an explicit structure definition and software that exploits that structure (such as HDF (22) or NetCDF (24)). Moreover, in many cases, particularly in legacy biological and earth systems databases, data are held as semistructured data, that is, ASCII text data where the structure is represented by formatting conventions (55). This data can be integrated and queried (213, 344), for example, by constructing wrappers that access the relevant data and present it against an agreed schema. In some cases, the data in scientific papers may be extracted automatically and presented with regular structure (361).

Any attempt to define general-purpose data access and integration technology must address diversity in data structure, for several reasons. First, the multiple categories of structured data make it sensible to amortize the costs of developing generic data access and integration technology over a wide spectrum of uses. Second, the many different usage patterns make the technology hard to design. Third, this diversity leads to different and dynamically varying operational loads that require adaptive optimization. To illustrate this diversity, we consider five categories of structured data.

Primary structured data.   Primary structured data are observations and their associated metadata recorded directly into databases. Such data recording supports the highest data rates from digital scanners, which typically deliver binary "images" as multidimensional arrays. (The multidimensional array is itself a structure that can be exploited, for example, to retrieve hypercuboid slices, as in DataCutter (118).) Frequently, these image collections become part of a structured collection after processing (e.g., to achieve normalization, interpretation, and annotation). For example, the primary data from scanning microarrays are collected and shared according to standard structures such as MIAME (135) and MAGE (603). Direct recording in databases supports many other forms of data collection, from a field worker's personal record keeping to the output of highly automated laboratories.

Ancillary data.   Ancillary data are *structured* metadata used to support bulk binary or structured data. Large volumes of such data can be required to enable searching of a body of data for rare events, such as Higgs bosons or gravity waves (98), or for analysis, as in digital sky surveys (619). Metadata are often expressed through *schemas*. A technology-independent *logical schema* describes the logical structure of a database in terms of some data model (e.g., a relational model); a technology-dependent *physical schema* describes the organization of the database, the access policies, and enforced invariants called integrity constraints. Four forms of ancillary data are common:

+ *Organizational metadata* support management technologies that underpin Grid operations, for example by recording the location of copies of a logical file or, as in Chimera (284), maintaining structured data used to plan and record data derivation processes.

+ *Technical metadata* organize the interpretation of the primary data, for example, indexes that accelerate near-neighbor searches in a digital sky survey.

+ *Application metadata* guides the interpretation of the primary data (e.g., by allowing users to select the data catalogued with relevant properties).

+ *Data products*, including summaries, catalogs, and indexes, are produced by successive steps in deriving information from the primary data (e.g., a table of classified astronomical objects found in a digital sky survey). Data products may be treated as primary data by some scientists and as metadata by others.

Collaboration data.   Collaboration data are collected to enable scientific information to be shared quickly and precisely. This class of data accounts for much of the legacy structured data in the sciences and represents an important emergent mode of collaborative behavior. Scientists increasingly collaborate by recording and sharing data via databases, normally using agreed terminologies, a practice that the Grid will encourage. In the life sciences, groups of scientists have communicated for some 20 years by writing to publicly available structured data collections, for example, to record the genetics, phylogeny, ontology, and phenotype of a particular species; to record protein structures and function; and to develop and interpret whole genome sequences. This practice has led to many collections of related data, each curated by a particular group who impose standards and structure. Mechanisms have emerged that allow others to annotate some collections in independently stored databases that refer to data in curated collections (240). Other examples are the MIPS functional genomics database (476) and the Kegg biochemical pathways database (397). Scientific databases need to reflect the complexity of the systems they describe. For example, the PEDRO system (632), integrated with GIMS (195), requires a complex UML schema to represent proteomic data.

Inevitably, as a science progresses, new understanding emerges. Collection entries are added and revised, and the original structures often prove inconvenient or inadequate for holding the new topics of importance. Hence, not only the content of a collection but also its structure evolves with time.

Personal data. Personal data are data assembled by or about individual users. Personal data may include profile data, such as preferences and reusable working methods, digital laboratory notebooks, representations of work in progress, and personalized workflow scripts. These data are typically private, in contrast to collaborative data where the intention is to communicate with other researchers. Personal data may, however, refer to collaboration and primary data, and selections may eventually be transferred to communal data.

Service data. Data used to support Grid operation are known as service data. Examples are data in registries, data describing services, data defining authorization policies, data describing progress enacting workflows, and data defining current system state. The Globus Toolkit's monitoring and discovery service (204, 264) is a system widely used to maintain data about the properties and state of resources and services. Another established example of service data is the catalogs that map logical names to physical names and track the location of physical files. For example, the Replica Location Service (176) (see Section 22.7) uses a distributed database approach, with a uniform schema and soft-state protocols for maintaining consistent catalogs and continuous operation despite partial failures.

22.3   DATA MANAGEMENT CHALLENGES

Generalizing from the examples of Section 22.1, we can identify key application requirements for data management services and the associated challenges that result from those requirements. At a high level, the challenges are driven by three main factors:

+ Diverse usage scenarios that include, for example, both updatable and read-only data, differing consistency requirements, and diverse data-access methods (e.g., binary formatted vs. relational data).

+ Heterogeneity at all system levels, including storage systems, data formats, data access mechanisms, and policy.

+ Performance demands associated with access, manipulation, and analysis of large quantities of data.

We now examine the challenges resulting from these factors.

22.3.1 Data Sources

We use the term *data source* to denote any facility that may accept or provide data. A common instantiation of a data source is software such as a database system, mass storage system, or file system that manages various storage devices including disk cache, network-attached storage, disk array, and robotic tapes. However, the term can also denote a read-only data resource or an instrument or program (e.g., a simulation or distributed query evaluator) that generates structured data.

Not all data sources are long-lived; some can be transient, created and destroyed dynamically. An application may use an internal database or temporary local database to hold progress data or to accumulate results. For example, in a Monte Carlo exploration of a parameter space, a new database may be created on the processor farm dynamically chosen for the model runs by a workload scheduler. At the end of the computation, the key database contents, or derivatives computed from them, may be added to a persistent archive located elsewhere on the network, while the local database is discarded.

Alternatively, a model may require a database defining its boundary conditions. For example, when exploring the likely development of a bush fire, a primary data resource may be queried to access pertinent data regarding terrain and vegetation for the locale and season. That snapshot may be formed into a new read-only database of appropriate structure for the application, which can then be replicated at each computer where the simulation is running, thus avoiding network latency and database contention whenever boundary condition data are queried.

These examples highlight a need for Grid-enabled data sources that can be quickly and automatically installed, configured, and disassembled, along with the need for data movement and replication. Within the OGSA framework, this requirement can be met by ensuring that data sources can be produced via factory operations.

A data source provides access to data, for reading and/or writing. The Grid is likely to contain diverse data resources with different storage systems, data types, data models, and access mechanisms. Storage system types include various file systems, caches, databases, hierarchical storage systems, and directory services. Data types include files, collections of files, tabular data from relational databases, structured data from XML databases, semistructured data, and abstract data concepts such as virtual data. Data models include databases with different schemas, and access mechanisms include file-system-style open/close/read/write versus SQL, XQuery, or XPath query mechanisms. This diversity of access methods can result in undesirable application complexity or can inhibit an application's ability to adapt to new, unanticipated data sources. Thus, we want both uniform methods for accessing a data source and the ability to transform data among types and to mediate among data models.

The consequences of unauthorized access to data resources can be catastrophic, and thus data source stakeholders must be able to control sharing of datasets within a virtual organization. Such sharing requires user authentication and access control mechanisms for enforcing local and community policies for data access and resource usage. For example, when performing a data transfer, users must be authenticated and authorized to access the data being transferred and to consume space on the destination storage system. The efficient and coordinated use of data sources may also require the ability to manage the data source itself: allocating and reserving space for data transfers, staging data from tape systems to disk caches, reserving bandwidth into the storage system, and so forth. Chapter 18 describes a general mechanism for specifying and executing such resource management functions; here, we discuss management functions specific to data sources.

22.3.2   Data Discovery, Movement, and Replication

Users require the ability to *discover* desired data based on metadata attributes rather than knowledge of name or location. Discovery issues for data sources are not that different from those that arise for other Grid resources (Chapter 20), and encompass how to describe relevant attributes of the resource (i.e., metadata) and how to publish, index, and update metadata. Here as elsewhere, it can be important to define metadata conventions that allow a community to share information using common vocabulary and semantics.

Another fundamental operation is *data movement* between storage systems or between programs and data storage. Data movement provides the foundation for replication, caching, and bulk data access. The potentially large size of datasets and wide-area data transfer delays makes the efficiency of data transfer an important concern. Data may be filtered before transfer, effectively running a query or analysis to extract only a desired subset of the data. Many applications are concerned with the reliability of data movement and thus may wish to maintain state on outstanding data transfer operations, retry failed transfers, and/or restart interrupted transfers.

One reason for moving data is to create *replicas* to reduce access latency, maintain local control over necessary data, or improve reliability and load balancing. Thus, we need services for replicating data, locating existing replicas, selecting among available replicas, and proactively replicating data items to satisfy demand.

Replicated data may or may not need to be kept consistent, and consistency requirements can vary widely by application and community. Even within commercial applications with updates, such as financial services, there is a recognition that a one-size-fits-all consistency model is not necessary or even desirable and that some data can be allowed to become inconsistent. Thus, it is desirable that the consistency model be made explicit so that applications have the correct expectations. Guaranteeing consistency among replicated data objects in Grids is challenging, given heterogeneous data resources, wide-area communication delays, and likelihood of resource failures.

22.3.3 Data Analysis and Processing

Figure 22.1 illustrates how data analysis may consist of a series of data-processing and data analysis steps. The construction and subsequent execution of such a complex series of operations can pose difficult planning, scheduling, and monitoring challenges. One approach to managing this complexity is to adopt a *virtual data* abstraction (93), in which desired data collections are specified by name or attributes, and underlying services construct the processing step, taking into consideration preexisting intermediate results, data location, computational resource availability, and so forth. For example, the Chimera virtual data system provides a language for specifying virtual data products, an interpreter that maps from a virtual data description to a plan for creation of the data, catalogs for recording provenance information for newly created data items, and Grid infrastructure that can discover whether the data item exists or can initiate production of the data item (284, 285).

Once an execution graph such as that shown in Figure 22.1 is produced, either as the result of an explicit query or by a virtual data system, one must map the execution of the operations onto available services and resources. Issues here include planning the computation, perhaps breaking it into a series of data movement and computational tasks; selecting the best storage and computational resources to perform each task and scheduling them; and monitoring progress, including recovery from task failures.

We note that for any derived data product, it is important to record information not only about the data but about how the data were produced: what is called *provenance information* (141). Such information includes exact information about the analysis or simulation programs that produced a data item and the inputs to those programs. Although provenance data are another form of metadata, they present unique challenges with respect to how they are structured, obtained, and used to reconstruct data analysis chains.

22.4   ARCHITECTURAL APPROACHES

The design of infrastructure to support data-intensive applications has taken various paths, ranging from monolithic integrated architectures targeted to specific usage scenarios, to layered protocol architectures. The emergence of OGSA (Chapter 17) makes convergence to a standard service-oriented architecture seem likely. Nevertheless, factoring the general space of data-oriented applications into an orthogonal, reusable, efficient, and complete set of data services remains a challenging task. In many ways, design of a good service-oriented architecture for data-oriented applications is no different from service design for the rest of the Grid. We require a set of services that are not overly prescriptive with respect to semantics or implementation, that can be easily reused across a wide range of usage scenarios, and that capture fundamental usage paradigms that can be combined with other services to construct higher-level behaviors.

As of late 2003, only the most basic data-oriented Grid services are being put forward for standardization. However, a rapidly expanding base of practical experience with globally distributed, large-scale, data-intensive application domains, combined with results in building distributed data management systems such as distributed databases and distributed file systems, makes it possible to identify classes of Grid services critical to integrating large, distributed data collections into the Grid environment.

Following a layered service architecture (Chapter 4), we partition data-oriented services into four classes:

+ *Resource-level services for data sources*. We distinguish between data access and data movement services. Access services provide secure, high-performance access to, and update of, structured data and may include support for creating data views, and accessing (and possibly filtering) data through a range of query mechanisms. Movement services are oriented toward data transport and are generally oblivious to the structure of the data once access methods have been determined. Other important data source interfaces include monitoring, auditing, discovery (for characterizing a data source's capabilities), and management (for controlling the quality of service associated with the use of a data source).

+ *Collective services for managing data*. Services in this class provide primitive mechanisms for managing data across more than one data source: for example, third-party data transfer, data discovery, data transformation and filtering, and scheduling.

✦ *Collective services that federate data sources.* Services in this class combine, or federate, two or more data sources, integrating them at some level of functionality. In general, federation services should be structured to support a wide range of integration strategies, from a completely unified and transparent view of the combined data sources (e.g., a virtual data base) to much weaker forms of integration, such as replication without coherency (e.g., a federated namespace only). Federation services may include replication services, data naming and location, data federation (schema mediation), consistency management, and distributed query management.

✦ *Domain-specific services.* Services in this class provide specialized data management, processing, and analysis operations oriented toward specific application domains. For example, specific applications may be able to implement relaxed transactional semantics that exploit domain knowledge to yield good performance.

We emphasize that this categorization is in no way comprehensive. Many non-data-specific services can be used in conjunction with such data services. For example, security (Chapter 21), resource management (Chapter 18), and computational services (Chapter 28) can be combined to create complex data-oriented services such as distributed query processing and data analysis workflow management.

22.5   DATA SOURCE SERVICES

We now examine the basic resource-level services required for managing and accessing data sources. We confine our discussion to data sources, as the representation of computing, networking, security, and other services are discussed elsewhere in this book.

22.5.1   Data Access

We first consider issues relating to data access and the rendering of data sources as Grid services. Note that while data may reside physically on a variety of devices, we are concerned here only with the interfaces presented to users wishing to access data stored on the device and the performance characteristics advertised for those access methods.

We can categorize data sources as either file oriented or database oriented. With few exceptions (e.g., the Storage Resource Broker (100)), most work in data-oriented services has focused on file-oriented data sources. Much of this work was driven by simulation-based science, in which data are typically output to files. Furthermore, database systems often sit on top of file systems, and thus data services that manipulate files without looking at their content (e.g., data transfer) can be applied to database services as well. Nevertheless, current and future directions in data sources are strongly focused on support for database technology and on providing integrated services that accommodate both file- and database-oriented data sources.

This integration of Grid and database technology is motivated first of all by scenarios in which a virtual organization uses Grid technology for some purpose (e.g., for creating, monitoring, and scheduling computational workloads) but also needs to use databases and database management systems. It is infeasible to reimplement the functionality provided by the databases, even if ownership and invested interests permitted this action (unusual, since the cost, delay, unnecessary unreliability, and disruption would be unacceptable). Therefore, access to these existing data resources is essential. This situation is common in today's science projects, and hence the current emphasis is on developing technology to make remote access to databases convenient (520).

Even simple remote database access scenarios tend to generate pressure on database providers, database management system providers, and database platform providers to make changes. For example, the Grid enables the creation of tools and services that rely on a uniform model for charging, metering, and diagnostic probing. As interactions with data resources are intimately connected to the remainder of the computations, operations teams, application developers, and application users will begin to expect this uniform technology to extend to those data management components themselves. Similar pressure will exist to develop consistent authentication and authorization mechanisms, such as single sign-on, acceptable to all parties. The applications will require notifications from databases as a result of triggers. Database management systems may use the Grid's established lifetime management regimes to recover resources (e.g., notification obligations). Database management systems may eventually use Grid infrastructure to implement distributed databases and Grid services to expose data and functionality. At the same time, we can expect that the established security, management, engineering, and diagnostic facilities supported by database management systems will influence the development of Grid services.

A second motivation for integrating Grid and database technologies derives from needs for functionality not yet provided by simple extensions to database technology. For example, the coupling of computations with operations on data resources introduces many new optimization challenges. Short-term optimizations, data location and movement, process location and movement, and scheduling of data operations and computation can, in principle, be brought into the same framework as longer-term optimizations relating to how and where to store data. This holistic and multiscale optimization requires substantial research and development. Radical reengineering of Grid and database technologies may be required. For example, if databases need to be created or moved as part of a Grid application, then database management systems must have their location and lifetime managed by Grid technology.

In the following subsections, we explore services first for file-oriented access and then for database-oriented access.

22.5.1.1   *GridFTP as a File Access Service*

GridFTP (64) was designed as a fundamental data access and data transport service. Its designers sought to create a protocol that would provide a uniform interface to various storage systems, including hierarchical storage systems, disk systems, and storage brokers. Incompatible data access protocols used by these storage systems effectively partition the datasets available on the Grid. Applications must either choose only a subset of storage systems or use multiple methods to retrieve data. GridFTP was designed with the assumption that it would be mutually advantageous to both storage providers and users to have a common but extensible underlying data transfer protocol that provides interoperability between disparate storage systems. Storage providers would gain a broader user base because their data would be available to any client. Storage users would gain secure, efficient access to a broader range of storage systems and data.

GridFTP functionality includes both features supported by the FTP standard and a number of extensions. FTP was chosen as a base because of its widespread use on the Internet and because the FTP protocol provides a well-defined architecture for protocol extensions, and supports dynamic discovery of the extensions supported by a particular implementation. In addition, various groups have already added extensions through the IETF, some of which address Grid requirements. To facilitate interoperation with other Grid services, GridFTP services use the widely deployed Grid Security Infrastructure (280) (GSI, Chapter 21) for robust and flexible authentication, integrity, and confidentiality.

GridFTP can be used both to access specific data values and to move data blobs from point to point. To facilitate its use as a data access protocol, server-side processing allows for the inclusion of user-written code that can process the data prior to transmission or storage. Partial file retrieval is included by default. Its use as a data transport protocol is facilitated by third-party control of data transfer that allows a user or application at one site to initiate, monitor, and control a data transfer operation between two other sites (Figure 22.2).

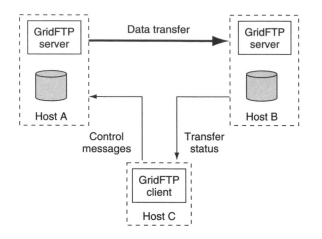

 22.2

FIGURE

A third-party transfer operation is used by a client at one site to initiate a transfer between two GridFTP servers at other sites.

Performance and reliability are critical issues in a protocol for accessing large amounts of data. GridFTP supports parallel data transfers that use multiple TCP streams between a source and destination, and striped data transfers to increase parallelism by allowing data objects to be interleaved across multiple hosts. Large TCP windows are used to improve the efficiency of file transfer for large files, reducing the overhead of control message and TPC synchronization. Also, because large transfers can take a long time and hence are more susceptible to failure, GridFTP contains mechanisms for reliable and restartable data transfer, and user-provided fault recovery algorithms to handle failures such as transient network and server outages.

22.5.1.2   *Data Access and Integration*

Data access functionality in GridFTP is primarily directed toward file-oriented structured data with access primitives to return subsections of files. Although FTP's extended data commands do make it possible to perform "get" operations with complex specifications, a higher-level, more direct query interface is desirable and will facilitate more uniform access to data sources.

Standard interfaces exist for accessing structured data within an enterprise from an application. These typically establish a session and then submit a series of query statements within some transaction regime. Each submission obtains a response, either a result set or a status response indicating whether the execution succeeded or failed. Using standard mechanisms such as ODBC and JDBC, the

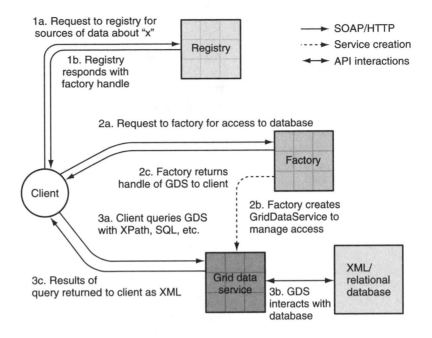

The OGSA-DAI architecture, showing the steps involved in retrieving data from a remote database.

application program is independent of some aspects of the database to which it connects, and remote connection is supported.

Using these standard interfaces as a baseline, the Data Access and Integration (DAI) Services Working Group of the Global Grid Forum is developing specifications for data access and integration (363) appropriate for the Grid environment. OGSA-DAI components will form an open source reference implementation of these specifications. At the time of writing, the UK e-Science Programme project OGSA-DAI has constructed "plug-and-play" data access and integration components (83), the first version of which was released in conjunction with the Globus Toolkit Version 3 (GT3) in June 2003. OGSA-DAI assumes an architecture that matches OGSA (Chapter 17) and provides a simple set of composable components.

As illustrated in Figure 22.3, the client uses a data registry first to locate a Grid data service factory (GDSF) service capable of generating the required access and integration facilities. The information returned allows the client to choose an appropriate GDSF and activate it using its Grid service handle (GSH). The client then asks that GDSF to produce a set (here one) of Grid data services (GDS) that provide the required access to data resources. A GDS may be the data resource itself or a proxy for that data resource, as illustrated here. The client then requests the GDS to perform a sequence of operations, such as update, query, bulk load, and schema edit. To enable an open-ended range of data models and operations, the required operations are requested by using a request document, which specifies a sequence of activities such as database operations defined using standard query languages and data delivery. Additional components required for data translation are included in the DAI architecture.

22.5.2   Managing Data Sources

We now shift our attention from data access to the resource management functions (Chapter 18) used to manage the storage systems holding the data collections being accessed. We are interested, in particular, in managing storage space, which requires not only storage quotas, which limit the total amount of storage that any user, group, project, and so forth may consume, but also storage *reservations*, which ensure that agreed-upon amounts of storage are available for a specified duration of time. We may also want to manage bandwidth and data throughput. However, as discussed in Chapter 18, our ability to manage resources is typically limited by the resource's local management software. Although some real-time operating systems provide guaranteed-rate I/O to storage systems, these functions are not yet generally available.

Any data source must incorporate monitoring and auditing services (Chapter 20) so as to allow local and remote entities to keep track of the resource's state (e.g., available free space), monitor the progress of individual operations, and track resource consumption by users and services.

We now discuss some current solutions to storage resource management.

22.5.2.1   NeST

NeST is a software-only Grid storage appliance developed by the Condor project at the University of Wisconsin at Madison (111). Its developers argue that to be useful in a Grid environment, storage appliances must provide two features. First, they must be able to make guarantees about storage availability so that wide-area schedulers can move large datasets without fear of resource revocation. Second, they must be self-cleaning to ensure that failed operations or misbehaving clients do not permanently fill the storage appliance and prevent other users from accessing it.

NeST provides these two features using a concept, called a *lot*, that provides a specified capacity to a particular user or group and can be also used to logically group sets of files to facilitate sharing, discovery, and removal. Lots can be either

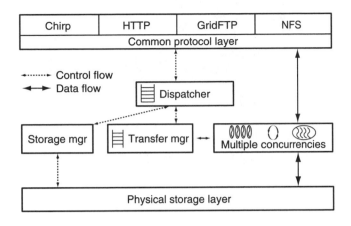

22.4

FIGURE

NeST components.

best effort or guaranteed. Best-effort lots are removed lazily as space becomes scarce. Guaranteed lots have a specified duration that can be renewed as necessary. (Open Grid Service Infrastructure lifetime management functions could be used for this purpose: see Chapter 17.) When its duration expires, a guaranteed lot becomes a best-effort one.

As shown in Figure 22.4, NeST has four main components: storage manager, transfer manager, dispatcher, and protocol layer. The storage manager controls and virtualizes a machine's underlying physical storage and enforces access control and storage space guarantees. The transfer manager asynchronously manages data transfers between protocol connections. The dispatcher is the main scheduler for NeST and controls the flow of information among components. The protocol layer virtualizes specific protocols used by clients to and from a common interface understood by NeST components. Protocols supported by NeST include FTP, GridFTP, HTTP, a subset of NFS, and Chirp (the native protocol of NeST).

22.5.2.2   Storage Resource Managers

While NeST incorporates management functions into the storage system implementation, storage resource manager (SRM) (587, 588) services manage associated storage via a range of techniques, including cache management, preallocation and advance reservation of space for data transfers, staging of data from slow to fast storage in a hierarchical storage system, and scheduling of storage system requests. SRMs can also manage the file content of shared temporary space and use replacement policies to maximize file sharing. SRMs were initially designed to manage file caching for hierarchical storage systems; however, recent work has generalized their functionality.

An SRM typically manages two types of shared resources, files and space. Its basic function is to allocate space to a client upon demand, check that the client has permission to use that space, assign the space to the client for a period of time according to its policy, and release the space either when the client requests its release or when the lifetime assigned to the space expires. When a file is moved into the space managed by an SRM, the file can be "pinned" for a period of time to ensure that the space occupied by the file is not reclaimed before the client that requested the file can complete its operations on that file. By allowing subsequent requests for the same file from different clients to extend the duration of the pinning, the SRM promotes the sharing of files among clients of the storage system. In such cases, the SRM keeps track of the pin lifetime expiration and space consumed by the file with each user for each file. As with NeST, Open Grid Service Infrastructure lifetime management functions could be used for this purpose.

An SRM that manages a disk cache is referred to as a disk resource manager (DRM), to distinguish it from an SRM that manages access to a hierarchical mass storage system, which is called a hierarchical resource manager (HRM). Note that the file in the source location could be managed by another SRM (for example, it could be an HRM accessing HPSS). Therefore, SRMs are designed to communicate with each other using the same interface that a client uses. DRMs have been designed to manage files on behalf of a client even when they do not support explicit space reservation (588). Consider the following scenario. A client needs 500 files but can start processing as soon as one file is available. The client should be able to submit a single request for the 500 files to a DRM that manages a shared disk in its site. The DRM queues the request, assigns a default space allocation to the client, and checks whether any of the files are in its disk cache, perhaps because some client accessed them earlier). If so, it pins the files (up to a total size of the allocation assigned to the client) and returns to the client with this information. The client can then start processing the files and release each file when it is done, so that the DRM can put another file into the released space. If a requested file is not in the disk cache, the DRM uses the information provided in the request to get the file from its source location, using data transport protocols such as GridFTP.

In this situation, the client has an incentive to release files so as to create space for their next file. This behavior helps the DRM manage its space efficiently. If, however, the client neglects to release a file that was pinned for that client, the file will be released after the lifetime of the pin expires. Thus, DRMs perform automatic garbage collection. Files are not removed from the disk cache unless space is needed. The DRM can choose which files to remove from its cache when space is needed, in order to maximize the sharing of files.

HRMs are basically DRMs associated with a mass storage system (MSS), such as HPSS. They usually have a disk cache that they control. When a file is requested from the HRM, the HRM will contact the MSS and get the file transferred into its disk. At this point it can make the file available for transfer with GridFTP. HRMs can act as front-end storage managers to MSSs and usually run on a system at the same site as the MSS, to avoid firewall and security pitfalls.

HRMs are designed to queue multifile requests for putting and getting files into and out of MSSs. They can make such requests concurrently but usually limit the number of concurrent requests to avoid overloading the MSS. Because they maintain a queue, they can reorder file requests so that files stored on the same tape can be read at the same time. This capability avoids unnecessary dismounts and mounts of tape. HRMs also monitor the success of MSS file transfers. If a temporary failure occurs, they wait until the MSS recovers and then reissue the file request.

22.6   COLLECTIVE DATA MANAGEMENT SERVICES

Collective services define functions whose operations span multiple resources or services, including storage services, management services, and computational services. We present here a set of collective data services that have proven to be important, but one can certainly imagine a wider range of such services.

22.6.1   Data Transport Services

A variety of collective services manage the transport of data between data storage services. For example, a *multiple data object transfer service* allows users to submit a large number of simultaneous data transfer operations and monitor and manage the status of each. Another example is *reliable data transfer services*, which maintain the state of outstanding data transfer operations, monitor the progress of transfers, and attempt to restart failed transfers. Reliable data transfer services augment the basic data transfer services described previously (e.g., GridFTP) with enhanced failure semantics and reliability (see Chapter 19).

An OGSI-compliant reliable file transfer (RFT) service, developed as part of the Globus Toolkit, allows monitoring and control of third-party data transfer operations between two GridFTP servers. Figure 22.5 illustrates the structure of

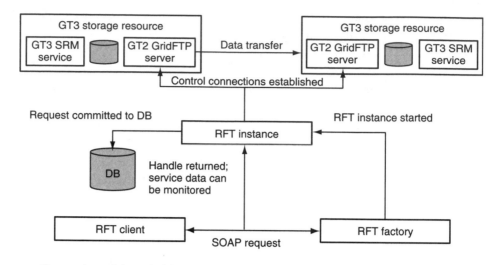

Illustration of the reliable file transfer service.

the RFT service and shows how it constructs a higher-level behavior by combining a set of more basic services. A client issues a request to an RFT factory, which instantiates an RFT service instance. That RFT instance controls the transfer and stores the state of the transfer in persistent storage (in this case a database). The RFT instance communicates with two storage resources running GridFTP servers. The RFT instance initiates a third-party transfer from the source to the destination GridFTP server and monitors the status of the transfer, updating the state describing the transfer in the database. If the transfer fails because the client or one of the storage resources fails, then the transfer state in the RFT database is sufficient to resume or restart the interrupted transfer when all resources become available.

22.6.2   General Data Discovery Services

We must be able to discover relevant data collections before we can access, integrate, and analyze them. Thus, we require *data discovery services* for identifying data items that match specified characteristics or metadata. These characteristics may simply be logical or physical data names but more frequently are high-level attributes that describe the data. Discovery may be based on general attributes that may be common to all data collections, such as information about the creator, owner, and last modifier of the data; physical metadata such as data size and access control information; and information about how the data were generated by an experimental apparatus, simulation, or analysis.

OGSA mechanisms for the publication and discovery of service properties via registries can be applied to data services, if effective approaches can be found to describe, query, and match relevant service properties. The situation is complicated by the number of objects one may wish to discover, the complexity of the data model, and the need to model various subsets and various views of a data collection. A similar problem has been recognized in the Web (115). A promising strategy is to exploit ontological technologies to construct a "Semantic Web/Grid" (215) (Chapter 23).

A number of data discovery services are being developed for Grid environments. Some data discovery services are specialized for a particular application domain or virtual organization. For example, many application domains provide customized *metadata services* that allow attribute-based discovery of data based on community conventions or ontologies for metadata. Ontologies can also form the basis for higher-level services that attempt to extract knowledge from Grid data (482).

The Storage Resource Broker's (100) metadata catalog (MCAT) represents one attempt to provide an application-independent metadata service. MCAT maintains logical and physical metadata attributes in a relational database, enforces access control, and provides consistency among replicated data stored in SRB servers. The Metadata Catalog Service (MCS) (177) represents another approach, in which metadata services are decomposed further so that only relationships between attributes and logical (location-independent) collection names are stored. Both MCAT and MCS provide a general metadata scheme, allow the specification of application-specific attributes, and use standard schemas for data characterization and discovery, such as the Dublin Core (10) produced by the digital library community.

An advantage of services such as MCAT and MCS is that they can maintain automatically the metadata required by Grid registries. However, we must often also integrate existing databases, in which case we require automated mechanisms for registering relevant data. (Here as elsewhere in a Grid, manual mechanisms are too expensive and inaccurate.) Initially, such a system might infer content description from the identifiers and comments in schema or a data dictionary, but ultimately the database description itself must adapt to meet these requirements. This is an issue as much for policy and standards within domain communities as it is for technology. Traditionally, contextual metadata management (521) has been seen to be application-specific, although the common data warehouse model (509) has attempted to address some of these issues in the commercial sector.

22.6.3   Workflow Management, Planning, and Scheduling

Data analysis workflows in Grids are likely to span multiple data sources and computers. They may require that data be shipped from a storage resource to a remote service to perform a required analysis. Alternatively, it may be more economical to ship computation to the data. The decomposition and scheduling of analysis workloads can be complex, and much effort has been devoted to automating these activities.

We focus here on approaches to automating workflow planning and management based on high-level abstractions and languages for composing model parts (284). Eventually, the database management system, data components, and application components may all be decomposable and recomposable under the direction of dynamic optimizers, placement algorithms, and schedulers that can optimize at the scale of the whole system. However, such approaches are not yet practicable.

Some applications require little planning because they perform repetitive tasks according to well-defined workflows. Examples include scientific, diagnostic, and analytic applications such as running similar evaluations for many candidate drugs, making similar comparisons using data from similar equipment, or evaluating phenotypes from genetically related subjects. These repetitive processes generally operate in a relatively stable context with prechosen, mostly read-only, data and established workflows. Such cases are supported today by products such as DiscoveryLink (344), Kleisli and K2 (213), and Polar (596). Established data-mining methods (241, 336, 349, 594, 675) over data warehouses (388) may also suit some of these stable applications and deliver the required virtual database for the application scientists; in these cases, the Grid may be used to operate the workflows that populate the data warehouse and to provide access to the warehouse.

For other applications, significant planning of the execution workflow is required. High-level analysis tasks may be decomposed into subtasks prior to execution. A high-level description of processing steps must then be mapped into an execution sequence consisting of data movements between data sources and the specification of computation services to be used for analysis steps. Planning and mapping can be performed prior to and/or during execution. The dynamic nature of Grid services and the potential for failure can lead to a need for replanning and/or just-in-time task allocation.

Once an initial plan for executing the workflow has been created, a workflow management system is responsible for initiating execution of individual tasks in the specified order. The workflow manager must monitor task status, enforce dependencies specified by the planner, and attempt to restart failed tasks or resubmit them to alternate resources. In the case of task failures, the workflow manager may try various execution options or may notify higher-level planning services to create an alternative workflow or task mapping.

A number of planning and workflow management services have been constructed and early successes obtained with systems targeted to specific usage scenarios. For example, the DataCutter (119) data-filtering service uses a programming model called filter-stream programming that decomposes an application into a set of filters. Filters are connected via a stream abstraction that performs application-specific data processing. The DataCutter planner maps filters to hosts, and the DataCutter execution system follows the plan at run time, instantiating filters on the designated hosts, connecting filters using communication streams, and initiating execution. Filter placement may be recomputed during application execution.

Alternatively, one can develop more general, reusable services that support a range of usage scenarios. For example, the Virtual Data Toolkit (VDT) provides catalog, planner, and workflow management services to support the creation and execution of data analysis tasks. At the core of VDT is the Chimera virtual data system (284, 285) discussed in Section 22.3.3, which allows the user to specify a desired data type and uses a catalog of data transformations to construct an analysis workflow. Chimera can then turn to a range of planning services to map the execution graph onto specific services for execution, including the Pegasus (Planning and Execution in Grids) system (216). Workflow execution within VDT is provided by the Condor DAGMan system (309), which allows users to specify dependencies between tasks that compose a job. Once dependencies are satisfied, the DAGMan submits tasks to Grid resources.

22.7   FEDERATION SERVICES

We start our discussion of federation services by considering what federation means in the context of current database technology. In a *federated database*, many databases contribute data and resources to a multidatabase federation, but each participant has full local autonomy. In a *loosely coupled* federated database, the schemas of the participating databases remain distinguishable, whereas in a *tightly coupled* federated database, a global schema hides (to a greater or lesser extent) schematic and semantic differences between resources (466), mapping a single logical schema mapped to multiple physical schemas. In the Grid setting, federation is more general than integrating databases and attempts to provide a uniform framework in which diverse data sources (be they relational, file-structured, XML, etc.) can be integrated (55).

One approach to integrating across data sources is to create a *virtual database*, wherein a set of databases is presented as a single integrated view with a single *federated schema*, that users then use directly, unaware of the separate databases behind the view. The concept of federated databases was popular in database research, and the logical construction of the single view implemented by distributed queries was shown to be feasible. However, the operational management of such systems has never proved feasible, as autonomous changes in the contributing databases demand costly and continuous maintenance of the view realization (466).

We can deliver aspects of virtual databases by combining specific subdomains of contributing queries required for some specific and limited purpose. This strategy is used in DiscoveryLink (344), Kleisli and K2 (213), and Polar* (596). Further research is needed to improve optimization, automate integration, extend the range of applications, address more complex systems, and automate accommodation of autonomous changes.

The diversity of usage scenarios makes it unlikely that a one-size-fits-all approach to federation is feasible. Instead, many types of loose federations must be constructed, differing according to how aspects of the distributed data sources are federated and to what extent the distribution is made transparent to the user. Application developers must use additional knowledge to decide when the operational cost of delivering a transparency is warranted by savings in development and maintenance costs of higher-level applications or improved user convenience. Loose federations can provide several types of transparency:

+ *Location transparency*. Mechanisms for accessing data are independent of the data's location.

+ *Name transparency*. An application can access data without knowing its name or location; that is, it is possible to discover data using registry queries that describe requirements in terms of data content and operations.

+ *Distribution transparency*. An application can query and update data without being aware that it comes from a set of distributed sources.

+ *Replication transparency*. An application can access data without being aware of replica and caching mechanisms.

+ *Ownership and cost transparency*. Applications are spared from separately negotiating for access to individual sources.

+ *Heterogeneity transparency*. The access mechanism is independent of the actual implementation of the data source.

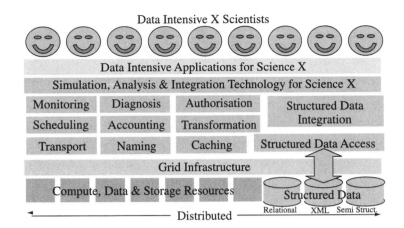

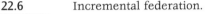

22.6   Incremental federation.

FIGURE

♦ *Schema change transparency.* Data resources are allowed to rearrange their data, for example, across different tables to meet performance requirements or to accommodate new information, without affecting applications.

With the introduction of these diverse, weaker forms of federations, customized integration becomes an alternative to creating a virtual database. Different types of transparency provided by separate specialized federation services (e.g., name federation, replica federation, consistent replica federation) can be combined to construct the specific cost/performance/functionality trade-off appropriate to the application domain. Such domain-independent federation services can also be used to simplify the development and maintenance of applications that for, one reason or another, construct their own project-specific integration systems (queries, programs, data flows, and workflows). Ideally, these services will be accompanied by tools that assist scientists with all steps in the scientific integration application lifecycle.

We expect to see an evolutionary approach to the use of federated data services by applications, as illustrated in Figures 22.6 and 22.7, which show the structure of a typical application in some data-intensive science, X, such as functional genomics, atmospheric systems science, or combustion engineering. The goal is the same in both cases: to provide access to sophisticated analysis and simulation computations using integrated data from multiple resources. Each builds on a standard Grid infrastructure (Chapter 17) and services such as those described previously, as well as basic federation services that we describe in following sections.

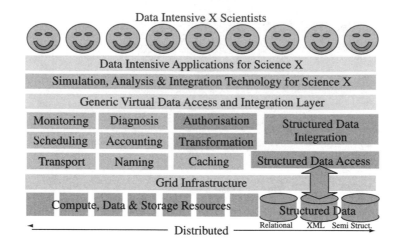

22.7

FIGURE

Generic federation, which includes a generic virtual data access and integration layer.

In current projects, the community of X scientists will typically share common components across many applications (Figure 22.6). Thus, *within their domain* they have established common data representations and function specifications. Particular applications are constructed using this community-developed layer of common components (460) in conjunction with more generic Grid services, data management services, and federation services.

In Figure 22.7, a virtualization layer has been interposed below the common components layer. It should make no difference to code that has already been built using existing community-specific services, that is, following the incremental integration model. Its availability, however, should substantially reduce the cost of building more subject-specific code, by providing *consistent* structured data access, which is difficult to implement. It should also give opportunities for improving efficiency.

The capabilities of the generic virtual data access and integration layer will develop incrementally. More sophisticated federation services will be created, combining federation attributes with planning and workflow services to perform progressively larger tasks expressed in increasingly abstract terms. The factories that create these services may specialize in generic facilities and produce new factories optimized for some particular task. Other strategies of delivering more advanced capabilities (e.g., increasing the sophistication of individual federation services) may prove effective.

Knowledge of applications and data resources will always enable some expert scientific-applications developers to outperform advanced integration services. However, as robust and reusable federation services become more widely available, the majority of application developers will eventually benefit from using automatically supported integration. Just as with database query, in most cases the system-supplied optimizers will (eventually) perform better than application developers because of access to system data and accumulated research.

Services for federating and integrating diverse data resources may include services for mediating among different data models, for accessing data resources with different access methods, and for replicating data and keeping it consistent. (An example of such a service is the Multimission Archive at Space Telescope (184), which provides a uniform interface to retrieve data from many different data sources, databases, or files.) In the following sections, we examine a few of these services in more detail.

22.7.1 Data Mediation

Data mediation services provide transparency with respect to data models. Mediation can be as simple as renaming attributes or as complex as providing sophisticated semantic-based mappings from elements in one data model to one or more elements in a second data model. Combining data mediation with the mechanisms that provide uniform access to data relieves applications from the specifics of how to retrieve data elements of interest.

A simple type of mediation involves services that map data names, and potentially data values, from one data model to another. This approach can be used to provide access to legacy data stored in formats that are not widely supported. IBM's DiscoveryLink (344) is an example of this approach, in which various data sources register to a federation server, providing a source-specific mapping function into a globally defined schema. More sophisticated approaches mediate among data models based on well-defined semantics of the assorted models. Such knowledge-based approaches to mediation are based on the creation of data vocabularies (ontologies) and rules for mapping among terms (Chapter 23).

22.7.2 Replication Services for Location Transparency

Replication services provide for replication transparency. We can decompose replication into three different types of service:

+ *Replica management services* create copies and update location services so that the location of a replica can be identified.

+ *Replica location services* serve as registries to locate where replicas exist by defining a mapping between a data object name (logical name) and the storage services that can provide access to the data object (physical names). With the replication location services, replicas are not constrained as "bitwise" copies.

◆ *Consistency services* manage relationships among the various replicas.

Multiple service definitions may exist for each type of service, each providing different federation semantics.

A replication management service is responsible for creating replicas and potentially supports selection among replicas. Such a service can define a replication policy, based perhaps on dataset popularity (543) or a desired availability (545) (see also Chapter 29). Such a service combines decision-making with interaction to data transport services, replica location services, and consistency services. For example, Reptor (343) provides for the management of data replication operations, controlling the copy of an existing data item and its registration with a replica location service and metadata catalog. An optimization component selects from among existing replicas and picks the best location for creation of new replicas.

A replica location service maintains and provides mappings between logical names for data items and the locations of one or more copies, or *replicas*, of the data. We describe a replica location service developed by the Globus and European DataGrid projects and included in the Globus Toolkit (176). This framework is based on several mechanisms:

◆ *Consistent local state maintained in local replica catalogs (LRCs)*. Local catalogs maintain mappings between arbitrary logical names for data and target names (either logical or physical) associated with replicas of the data.

◆ *Collective state with relaxed consistency maintained in replica location indices (RLIs)*. Each RLI contains a set of mappings from logical names to target names. A variety of index structures can be defined with different performance characteristics, simply by varying the number of RLIs and the amount of redundancy and partitioning among the RLIs.

◆ *Soft-state maintenance of RLI state*. LRCs send information about their state to RLIs using soft-state protocols, which, as discussed in Chapter 17, have many advantages in distributed systems. State information in RLIs times out and must be periodically refreshed by soft-state updates.

◆ *Compression of soft-state updates*. To reduce the amount of soft-state information that must be sent and the storage requirements of RLIs, soft-state updates may be compressed. The current RLS implementation uses bloom filter

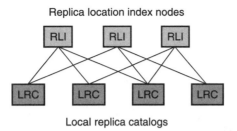

Replica location index nodes

Local replica catalogs

22.8

A replica location service example.

FIGURE

compression for this purpose. A bloom filter is a bitmap constructed by executing a series of hash functions against the logical names registered in an LRC.

The RLS implementation defines a distributed service based on a flexible framework that allows users to make trade-offs among requirements for consistency, space overhead, reliability, update costs, and query costs. Figure 22.8 shows an example of a distributed RLS that consists of four local replica catalogs and three replica location index nodes.

The RLS does not enforce consistency constraints among replicas; rather, it provides a simple distributed registry, allowing clients to register and discover mappings. We now discuss consistency services that can be layered on top of RLS.

22.7.3   Consistency Services

Grid consistency services allow replication of data items, possibly with some level of consistency guaranteed among replicas. Consistency requirements for replicated data in Grid systems vary widely. At one extreme, a Grid that provides read-only access to published data may not require services to maintain consistency among replicas. At the other extreme, a Grid may provide strict consistency with synchronous, transactional semantics for updating replicas, thereby supporting traditional distributed file system or database functionality.

Grids present special challenges for maintaining consistency among replicated data. Because Grid storage resources are widely distributed, the invalidation protocols, distributed locking mechanisms, and two-phase commit protocols used in distributed databases and file systems may experience long delays. In addition, Grid storage resources may fail, and networks connecting storage resources may be partitioned. Thus, it may be difficult to update synchronously all existing replicas in a Grid because some replicas may not be available.

In view of these challenges, many Grid systems are being designed with more relaxed consistency semantics. For example, updates may be restricted to designated master copies of data items; subsequently, these updates are propagated to other replicas with some delay. To facilitate management of these temporary inconsistencies, a Grid may support explicit maintenance of data version information. For example, a financial services company might maintain strict consistency over a database in one geographic region of operations and propagate changes with some delay to database replicas in other regions of the world.

22.8   CASE STUDY: THE EARTH SYSTEM GRID

To illustrate how data services can be combined to deliver integrated data access capabilities, we present a case study: the Earth System Grid (ESG) (271), a project whose participants are shown in Figure 22.9. ESG seeks to enable geographically distributed teams of climate researchers to effectively and rapidly develop new knowledge from massive, distributed data holdings and to share results with a wider community (67). Climate simulation models produce a tremendous volume of data, and this volume will grow rapidly with the increasing data resolution and computational capabilities. For example, a 100-year simulation of the Community Climate Simulation Model (CCSM) produces approximately 0.75 terabytes of data. Improved data resolution is expected to increase output size to approximately 11 terabytes.

ESG's goal is to develop a production system for delivering ESG data to climate scientists, sophisticated metadata services for climate data discovery, and filtering data servers to reduce data transfer requirements. The output datasets of climate model simulations are stored in terabyte- and eventually petabyte-scale data archives, currently using the high-performance storage system (HPSS). HRM middleware (Section 22.5.2.2) is used to manage HPSS storage, schedule data requests, stage data from tape storage to disk cache, manage caches, and copy multiple data files among storage locations.

ESG datasets are accessed and filtered by using the OpenDAP data access protocol. Formerly known as DODS (Distributed Oceanographic Data System), OpenDAP defines both protocols and APIs for accessing elements of streamed data and is widely used in the climate modeling community. The OpenDAP server implementation has been modified to provide authentication of users via the Grid Security Infrastructure, enhanced performance through the GridFTP data transfer

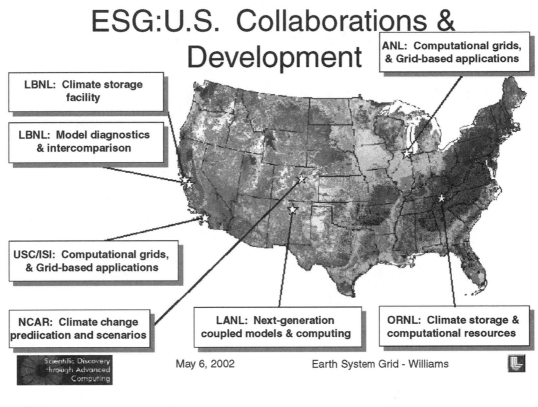

ESG:U.S. Collaborations & Development

ANL: Computational grids, & Grid-based applications

LBNL: Climate storage facility

LBNL: Model diagnostics & intercomparison

USC/ISI: Computational grids, & Grid-based applications

NCAR: Climate change prediication and scenarios

LANL: Next-generation coupled models & computing

ORNL: Climate storage & computational resources

Scientific Discovery through Advanced Computing

May 6, 2002   Earth System Grid - Williams

22.9   ESG partner sites.

FIGURE

protocol, and authorization using the Globus Toolkit's Community Authorization Service (519). This use of OpenDAP as a gateway to Grid data services allows ESG to provide high-performance access to replicated and distributed datasets to end-user analysis tools without modification. This is exactly the incremental integration strategy described in Section 22.7 and illustrated in Figure 22.7.

Metadata services—an important part of the ESG architecture—address the automatic extraction and generation of metadata as well as services for data discovery and query based on metadata attributes. A common ESG metadata schema has been defined, as has the relationship of this schema to other schemas, including federal standards, the NASA Global Change Master Directory, digital library standards such as the Dublin Core, and metadata schemas used by climate researchers in other nations. ESG metadata are stored in the MCS metadata catalog service mentioned previously, and the replica location service is used to track

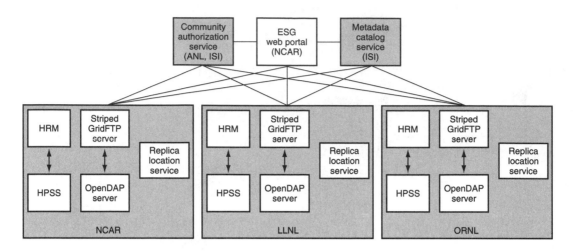

22.10

Components deployed in the ESG infrastructure.

FIGURE

data replicas. An ESG Web portal provides access to published climate datasets and metadata and manages workflow for accessing the various components of the ESG infrastructure. Figure 22.10 shows the Grid services deployed at several ESG sites.

22.9   SUMMARY

Scientific, engineering, and medical research are being revolutionized by new and systematic ways of collecting, managing, sharing, publishing, and exploiting large volumes of data, often within international, multidisciplinary collaborations. Corresponding developments are occurring in industry. These new problem-solving approaches require both new technologies and new behaviors. Great challenges lie ahead for designers of Grid data management technologies as they build on the protocols and services described in this chapter to provide rich higher-level functionality, including data federation, data consistency, workflow management, and knowledge extraction.

The next five years will see a continued evolution of data-oriented Grid services. Many services described here will continue to be refined, and new services will emerge as the data-oriented element of the Open Grid Services Architecture become better understood.

Virtual data abstractions appear to be powerful; and the planners, schedulers, and workflow managers have the potential to become critical components, not only for virtual data, but in making progress toward creating more integrated virtual database abstraction layers. Future work will include improved languages for specifying virtual data and more complete schemas for recording provenance information. We will also witness more sophisticated planners and workflow managers.

Much effort will be focused on "federating" data services to facilitate sharing, integration, and interoperability among diverse data sources. These services must include distributed, heterogeneous *metadata services* that provide query and discovery capabilities across heterogeneous metadata catalogs; *data model federation services* that map among data models; *transformation services* that convert data among diverse formats; and *consistency services* that manage replicated data, providing varying levels of synchronization among replicas.

Database research and experience have much to offer here, and we recommend that researchers not familiar with its achievements invest time in understanding them. The interplay between Grid technology and database technology will spur advances and adaptation on both sides. In the short term, because of the large investment in DBMS and installed databases, the emphasis will be on providing mechanisms that allow Grid applications to connect conveniently to existing database technology, with due concern for performance, accounting, authorization, and notification. The development of these mechanisms poses significant initial challenges because database mechanisms are already sophisticated. In the longer term, a more radical coevolution may be expected. Early stages will include support by DBMS of the monitoring, diagnostic, and lifetime management mechanisms because these are most beneficial to applications when they are uniformly and ubiquitously supported. Gradually, the DBMS will use the uniform platform for dependability, such as load sharing and permitting collocated validated installation of processes to avoid data movement.

A particular challenge is to develop compatible and consistent approaches to metadata. There are two driving forces: facilitating discovery of relevant data, where relevance is defined in some application terms, and facilitating cooptimization of data operations with computational operations. Although such consistent metadata are highly desirable, there is as yet little progress toward specifying its structure, content, and representation.

Once basic access and integration components are robust and the required consistent metadata are in place, more sophisticated access and integration technologies should emerge. Two related avenues of research are required: (1) the development of more abstract notations specifying combinations of computation and data extraction, and (2) the development of models for these combined tasks that permit planning and optimization. These functions may be encapsulated as factory services that build networks of Grid services, including other factories to handle repeated subtasks.

Data is important in science both as a source of information, which can be extracted by data mining and hypothesis testing, and as a mechanism for collaboration based on communication through shared databases. These two facets are spurring advances in data management that will have long-term effects on the arrangements for data access and integration. A few examples follow.

Archiving is already an important activity that has new requirements in the context of scientific data. Decisions, claims, and patents are made on the basis of the state of a scientific database at a particular time. To validate or re-evaluate the science, a normal scientific procedure requires recovery of that particular prior state. Exploiting the structure allows all prior states to be retrieved with little overhead (140).

Annotation associates new data with existing data. It may be produced automatically, for example, as data are generated by instruments and programs to record *derivation* and *provenance*, or it may be added by researchers sharing their understandings and discoveries (141). The technical and social challenges of managing this growing body of data are many. For example, if a scientist attaches annotation to a visualization of some spatiotemporal phenomenon, how is that linked with the primary data and with which subsequent evaluations should it be available?

New *storage structures and indexes* will emerge to support the combinations of computation and data-intensive operations. Data scanning becomes costly at the scales emerging in scientific data. Arrangements that increase parallelism and improve cache use, such as vectorization, will have substantial benefits. Many searches on scientific data involve approximate matching, which poses complex codesign tasks for indexes and algorithms (376). The Grid may be useful in permitting the construction of optimized indexes to be shipped to large memory systems. The resulting index can then be shipped to smaller machines to enable parallel and distributed searching. This strategy exploits the particular update properties of much scientific data. Replication for durability may use different structures at different locations; then the appropriateness of each copy for a particular computation may be considered by optimizers.

As the scale and number of data resources grow, it becomes progressively more difficult for scientists to have reliable intuitions about the quality and relevance of data. For example, humans cannot read more than a small fragment of the contents of the databases they use, and collaborative content construction makes it hard to transfer faith in a fellow scientist to the data collection—no individual takes responsibility. As automation progresses to better support integrated data use, scientists become less aware of which data are used and how they are used. Thus, the danger arises that progress will lead to unreliable inferences and decisions. There exists a responsibility, both on those that construct data access and integration tools and on those who use them, to take due care about the quality and comprehensibility of those tools and processes.

ACKNOWLEDGMENTS

Support was received from the UK e-Science Core Programme through grants to the National e-Science Centre, the North West e-Science Centre, the North East e-Science Centre, and the OGSA-DAI Centre Project and from the EPSRC ^{my}Grid e-Science Pilot project. European Commission funding for the European Data Grid project supported Peter Kunszt. IBM and Oracle supported Inderpal Narang and Dave Pearson, respectively. Comments by Peter Buneman and Christoph Koch on an early draft were particularly helpful. We also gratefully acknowledge support from the National Science Foundation's GriPhyN project and DOE SciDAC program.

FURTHER READING

For more information on the topics covered in this chapter, see *www.mkp. com/grid2* and the following references:

+ A more detailed discussion of the data demands of e-science applications is given by Hey and Trefethen (359).

+ Many of the challenges and techniques associated with Grid data services have their genesis in database technology. Consulting standard texts, such as *Fundamentals of Database Systems* (248), or articles on the current state of the art in database systems (418) can provide valuable insights.

+ Although there have been significant advances since the first edition of this book, Chapter 1:5, "Data Intensive Computing," is still well worth reading.

Enhancing Services and Applications with Knowledge and Semantics

Carole A. Goble, David De Roure, Nigel R. Shadbolt, and Alvaro A. A. Fernandes

What do knowledge and the Grid have to do with each other? The virtual organizations that define Grid systems (Chapter 4) are formed to solve problems, and problem solving is ultimately about the use and generation of knowledge. Knowledge is used to interpret existing information; for prediction; to change the way that scientific research or business is done; and ultimately for the pursuit, creation, and dissemination of further knowledge. Scientists use knowledge to steer instruments or experiments; businesses use knowledge to link data together in new insightful ways. The collaborative problem-solving environments that exploit and generate domain knowledge urgently need the sophisticated resource-sharing modalities supported by Grid technologies (281). Thus, a first connection between knowledge and the Grid concerns what we call "knowledge *on* the Grid," or "knowledge for Grid *applications.*"

A second connection is equally important. Knowledge is crucial for the flexible and dynamic middleware embodied by the Open Grid Service Architecture (OGSA, Chapter 17). The dynamic discovery, formation, and disbanding of ad hoc virtual organizations of (third-party) resources require that Grid middleware be able to use and process knowledge about the availability of services; their purpose; the way they can be combined and configured or substituted; and how they are discovered, are invoked, and evolve. Knowledge is found in protocols (e.g., policy or provisioning) and in service descriptions such as the service data elements of OGSA services. The classification of computational and data resources, performance metrics, job control descriptions, schema-to-schema mappings, job workflow descriptions, resource descriptions, resource schedules, service state, event notification topics, the types of service inputs and outputs, execution provenance trails, access rights, personal profiles, security groupings and policies, charging infrastructure, optimization trade-offs, failure rates, and so on are all forms of knowledge. Thus, knowledge is pervasive and ubiquitous, permeating the Grid. We can characterize this second connection as "knowledge *for* the Grid," or "knowledge for Grid *infrastructure*."

In this chapter we introduce the motivations, technologies, and research challenges that underlie knowledge both on and for the Grid. Our goal is to communicate what will be involved in building a knowledge-rich Grid in which services and applications are able at all levels to benefit from a coordinated and distributed collection of knowledge services founded upon the explicit representation and the explicit use of different forms of knowledge (149, 482).

The chapter is structured as follows. After some introductory examples, we discuss different kinds of knowledge, present our terminology, and consider the need to make knowledge explicit and to use it explicitly (Section 23.2). In Section 23.3, we examine the architectural implications of knowledge orientation in Grid environments, and in Sections 23.4 and 23.5 we describe essential technologies for knowledge representation and processing, including those of the Semantic Web. In Section 23.6, we consider the necessary attributes of knowledge-oriented Grids and examine knowledge-oriented Grid services. In Section 23.7, we review Grid projects that use knowledge. We conclude with a discussion of challenges that arise when deploying knowledge on Grids.

23.1   KNOWLEDGE FOR AND ON THE GRID

We use two examples to illustrate how knowledge can be useful for both Grid *applications* and Grid *infrastructure*. See also Chapter 9 for a third example.

We consider first a portal that supports clients wishing to run a local area weather forecasting model. The client enters the dimensions of the problem in terms relevant to the application, for example "solve on an area from latitude 50° to 51°N, longitude 100° to 101°W with a resolution of 1/8 of a degree and a time period of 6 hours." This description contains (from the user's viewpoint) all the information needed to define the scope of the resources required. The user might also have quality-of-service requirements; for example, "the results are needed within 4 hours." A broker charged with finding suitable resources has to translate this request into terms that can be matched with different machines, which might be described as "128 processors on an Origin3000, 4 gigabytes memory, priority queue" or "256 processors, 16 megabytes memory per processor, fork request immediately on job receipt."

The EuroGrid project (250) has developed a resource broker that can perform this semantic translation but only in the context of the UNICORE middleware (560), which supports the necessary abstractions. In the Grid Interoperability Project (GRIP) (332), this broker is being extended to work with the Globus Toolkit's information publishing model (204) (Chapter 4). In this context, the broker no longer has the support of the UNICORE abstractions but must recreate the translation of the user's request into resource sets that can be matched against MDS-2 descriptions. Mappings between UNICORE and Globus Toolkit resource descriptions can be complex, and currently there is no equivalent translation of some terms between the two descriptions. By capturing their semantics in an ontology that describes Grid resources, we can enrich the translation process between the brokers.

Our second example concerns the Geodise project, which uses knowledge engineering methods to model and encapsulate design knowledge so that new designs of, say, aeroengine components can be developed more rapidly and at a lower cost. A knowledge-based, ontology-assisted workflow construction assistant (KOWCA) holds generic knowledge about design search and optimizations in a rule-based knowledge base. Engineers construct simple workflows by dragging concepts from a task ontology and dropping them into a workflow editor. The underlying knowledge-based system checks the consistency of the workflow, gives the user advice about what should be done next, and tests the workflow during the construction process. The knowledge in KOWCA enables engineers, both novice and experienced, to share and use a community's experience and expertise.

Thus, applications, infrastructure, and knowledge are all interlinked. An optimization algorithm will be executed over brokered computational resources; a design workflow will be executed according to a resource schedule planned according to service policies and availability (175).

23.2 KNOWLEDGE IN CONTEXT

Our vision of the benefits that can ensue from a knowledge-oriented Grid is shown in Figure 23.1, with life sciences being used as a typical e-science application. The figure shows the many entities that can be regarded as knowledge:

1. A workflow specification, which not only defines a protocol and a set of services to execute but also embodies experience.

2. A distributed query, which is a provenance trail and a derivation path for a virtual data product (141, 285).

Database query — Question: What ATPase superfamily proteins are found in mouse?
(know-what)   1. Q9CQ/8 07046814SB_MOUSE from Swiss-Prot version 30,   Provenance
                      05/11/02 16:45 GMT, EBI server.   (know-where
Virtual data   2. 070455, P5477514SB_MOUSE from Swiss-Prot version 29,   -from)
products   05/11/02 16:45 GMT, local copy.   Replicas
(know-how)   3. P43686 and P54775 derived by a distributed query over DB1 (know-which)
                      and DB2.
Workflow   4. InterPro (no particular version) is a pattern database for protein Ontology and
(know-how)   superfamilies and domains for GPCRs but you need an account.   inference
                   5. The publicly available workflow mouseATPase   (know-whether)
Personalized   (http://www.somelab.edu/bio/carole/wf/3345.wsfl) will generate
profile   the result from data in your personal repository and you have Authorization,
(know-whom-to)   permission to run the services it needs. Click to run it.   authentication
                   6. The Attwood lab expertise is in nucleotide binding proteins   and accounting
Collaboration   (ATPase superfamily proteins are nucleotide binding proteins). (know-who)
and community   7. Jones published a new paper on this in Nature Genetics two
(know-where)   weeks ago, and you have an account to access it on-line.   Explanation
                   8. Smith in your lab asked this question yesterday and the answer (know-why)
Digital archive   he got is annotated by a commentary in his e-Log Book.
(know-which   9. P4S686 (human) calculated by applying the algorithm ABC
-when)   located at NCBI using data in database AAA.

                                    Annotation and notes
                                    (know-that)

23.1   The different ways that knowledge could be exploited to increase the potential of
                  the Grid. In this example, knowledge is used for data discovery, to initiate com-
FIGURE   putation, to discover resources, to asset policy, and so on.

3. A provenance record of how a workflow was operated and dynamically changed while it was running, and why.

4. The personal notes by a scientist annotating a database entry with plans, explanations, and claims.

5. The personal profile for the setting of an algorithm's parameters.

6. The provenance of a data entry or the provenance of all the data entries for an aggregated data product.

7. The explicit association of a comprehensive range of the experimental components: literature, notes, code, databases, intermediate results, sketches, images, workflows, the person doing the experiment, the lab that person is in, the final paper, and so forth.

8. Conventions established to describe, organize, and annotate content and processes.

9. Explicit problem-solving services that can be invoked: calling up a service to classify, predict, configure, monitor, and so on.

10. Communities of practice or sets of individuals who share a common set of scientific interests, goals, and experiences.

Note the wide variety of data sources of interest. Points 1–3 describe processes. Points 3–6 describe explicitly recorded knowledge. Point 7 asserts knowledge not of an entity but of how entities are linked together. Point 8 recognizes the importance of shared terminologies and conceptualizations that enable content and processes to be annotated, mapped, and shared. Point 9 emphasizes explicit knowledge-processing services. Point 10 recognizes the importance of understanding and describes the networks that exist between scientific practitioners. All give rise to knowledge descriptions that can be asserted or generated in their own right so that they can be found, linked, and reused.

23.2.1 Definition of Terms

Data, information, metadata, knowledge, and semantics are all related terms. Differentiating between them is difficult and contextual and often leads to confusion: one process's knowledge is another's data. We adopt terminology that is widespread in both knowledge engineering and knowledge management.

✦ *Data* are raw uninterpreted content, for example, a sequence of numbers or alphanumeric characters such as *www.somelab.edu/bio/carole/wf/3345.wsfl*.

✦ *Information* is an interpretation of that content into basic assertions or facts, structured using some data model. It is an organization of raw content establishing relationships and ascribing properties to content. For example, the data string just given denotes a Web services flow language (WSFL) specification for a workflow.

✦ *Metadata* are descriptive information about an entity, for example, that the WSFL specification was written by Professor Goble, that it takes mouse proteins and finds their homologues in humans, that it uses the algorithm BLASTp to compare a protein sequence with others and find those that are homologous to it, and so on.

✦ *Knowledge* is information put to use to achieve a goal or to realize an intention, created as a result of familiarity gained by experience or association with some other knowledge. For example, nucleotide sequences and amino acid sequences are disjoint classes of sequence, any enzyme is a kind of protein, the presence of a particular enzyme will lead to the transfer of a chemical group from one compound to another, and ATPase superfamily proteins are kinds of nucleotide-binding proteins. Some knowledge embodies practice. For example, if two protein sequences in different species are homologous, they might have the same function. Ontologies are one way of representing knowledge, by providing a vocabulary of terms for use by metadata descriptions, an explicit formal specification of the meaning of the terms, and an explicit organization of the way the terms are related that captures the conceptualization of a domain (see Section 23.4).

✦ *Semantic* decisions are based on inference, the logical process by which reasoning procedures are used to derive new facts from known facts (e.g., the properties and behaviors of Grid entities). These reasoning procedures may be rooted in traditional logic and may embody probabilistic methods. We can infer that SwissProt is a source of data for BLASTp, that any ATPase data entry in SwissProt will be supplemented by the more specialist InterPro database, and that http://www.somelab.edu/bio/carole/wf/3345.wsfl can be used to hypothesize human proteins on the basis of homology with mouse proteins using BLASTp.

23.2.2   Making Knowledge Explicit

A knowledge-oriented Grid (and a Semantic Web; see Section 23.5.1) depends on making knowledge *explicit* so that rich semantics can be used in decision-making and in purposeful activity by computational entities provided with a machine-processable account of the meaning of other entities with which they interact. There are two fundamental requirements for such knowledge and machine-processable semantic content:

✦ *Explicitly held and explicitly used knowledge.* Computationally implicit knowledge is knowledge merely embedded in programs or tools in forms such as a signature declaration, database schema, or algorithm. The utility of such implicit knowledge is limited. Thus we stress the need for *computationally explicit knowledge* for which some sort of formal knowledge representation technique exists that can be exposed to discovery, processing, and interpretation (see Section 23.4).

✦ *Computationally accessible and usable knowledge.* Universal description discovery and integration (UDDI) (44) is an example of a service that helps locate Web services by enabling robust queries against rich metadata (see also Chapter 17). A textual note describing a service in a UDDI registry is metadata that embody knowledge. A person can interpret metadata, but a machine finds such interpretation difficult. In particular, it is difficult to assign semantics to the metadata automatically. Informally specified knowledge and

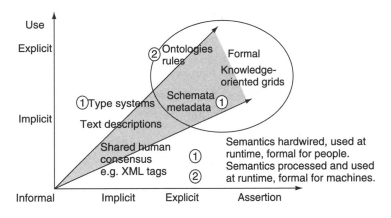

Knowledge and semantics may be implicitly or explicitly asserted and used. The illustration shows where a number of current technologies fit within this spectrum, compared with our goal, which are Grids that explicitly assert and use knowledge.

metadata are suitable only for human consumption, as humans can hope to make sense of knowledge in a wide variety of forms and contexts. Machines need formal, standardized *declarative* representations and formal, standardized reasoning schemes over those representations. The specification must be systematic—formal, precise, expressive, and extensible—and, most important for Grid and Web applications, capable of being used by automated reasoners.

As Figure 23.2 shows, these two requirements are being met to different degrees. At the bottom left of the figure, the only semantics resides in the minds of people or is directly encoded into applications. XML tags belong here; they are an example of *semantics implicitly asserted, implicitly used*. Their meaning entirely depends on an implicit shared consensus about what the tags mean; type declarations for functions are tightly coupled with, and even hardwired within, the computational entity. At the top right of the figure we have *semantics explicitly asserted, explicitly used*. Knowledge-oriented Grids belong here.

All Grids will have knowledge ranging over the entire continuum represented in the figure. However, moving along this continuum implies less ambiguity, greater likelihood of correct functionality, better interoperation, less hardwiring, and more robustness to change. A challenge, then, is enabling the incremental migration of Grids from bottom left to top right. Section 23.6 describes services that become possible at this point; Section 23.7 gives examples of Grid projects taking advantage of the benefits that ensue. To set the stage, we look into architectural implications of knowledge orientation in Grid environments.

23.3   ARCHITECTURES FOR KNOWLEDGE-ORIENTED GRIDS

Jeffery and others (215, 389, 614) have proposed a layered view of Grids in which "knowledge" sits on top of "computation" and "data." However, as argued in Chapter 22 and previously, this view has its limitations: in general, computation, data, and knowledge are inseparable and, in particular, knowledge does not reside only in Grid applications but permeates the full virtual vertical extent of Grid applications and infrastructure. A more accurate architectural view is a component-based one in which the various macrocomponents work together:

✦ *Knowledge networks* of multiple sets of discipline expertise, information, and knowledge that can be aggregated to analyze a problem of scientific, business, or societal interest; for example, individuals and groups, workflows, data repositories, notes, and digital archives (482).

✦ *Knowledge-generating services* that identify patterns, suggest courses of action, and publish results of interest to various individuals and groups (149).

✦ *Knowledge-aware, knowledge-based, or knowledge-assisted Grid services* that are the distributed computational components of the Grid that make use of knowledge, for example, intelligent portals, recommender systems, problem-solving environments, semantic-based service discovery or resource brokering, semantic data integration, and workflow composition planning.

✦ *Grid knowledge services*, the services and technologies for (global) distributed knowledge management to be used by networks, Grid services, and Grid applications. Examples include ontologies for defining and relating concepts in a domain, ontology languages for representing them, and ontology services for querying them or reasoning over them to infer new concepts.

The various components of both the Grid and application layers are placed into service-oriented relationships with one another. This service-oriented view is represented in Figure 23.3 and summarized in the following.

Base services cover data and computational services such as networked access, resource allocation and scheduling, and data shipping between processing resources. Information services respond to requests for computational processes that require several data sources and processing stages to achieve the desired result. These services include distributed query processing, workflow enactment, event notification, and instrumentation management. Base services use metadata associated with the Grid services and entities, but the semantic meaning of that metadata is implicit or missing. For example, the BLASTp and BLASTn algorithms

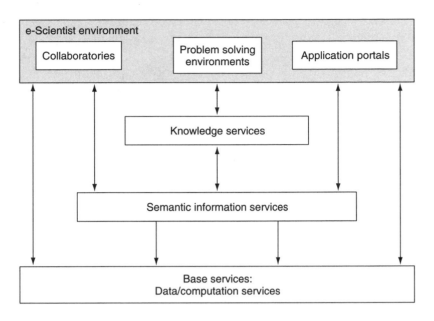

23.3

FIGURE

The relationship between semantic and knowledge services with respect to basic Grid services and applications.

have the same syntactic signature and both take sequence data type; however, one works over proteins, the other over nucleotides, and these are not interchangeable. This is merely implicit in the names of the algorithms, rather than exposed to computational entities that require them.

Semantic information services introduce explicit meaning, for example, that SmithWaterman and BLAST are both homology detection algorithms and are potentially interchangeable over the same data despite the fact they have different function signatures. Semantic descriptions about workflow can lead to automated workflow validation and reasoning about the interchangability of whole or parts of workflows. For example, a workflow using the SwissProt protein database could be substituted with one using the ENZYME database if the data operated over are an ATPase (because it is an enzyme). Semantic database integration requires an understanding of the relative meanings of schemas; for example, the "domain" attribute in the CATH database does not mean the same thing as the "domain" attribute in the SwissProt database. Semantic descriptions about a Grid service explicitly and declaratively assert its purpose and goals, not just the syntax of the data type or the signatures of its function calls, so computational entities can make decisions in light of that knowledge.

Knowledge services are the core services needed to manage knowledge in the Grid, for example, knowledge publication, ontology servers, annotation services, and inference engines. In Section 23.5 we describe such services in greater detail. Knowledge applications use the whole Grid service portfolio to implement intelligent applications and knowledge networks. Section 23.6 offers some case studies of Grid applications that rely on knowledge-oriented processes.

23.4   REPRESENTING KNOWLEDGE

One way to represent knowledge in a knowledge-oriented Grid is as *metadata*. Under this admittedly reductionist view, metadata comprises descriptive statements used to annotate content. Metadata are intended to be machine processible and declarative.

One well-known example of a metadata specification is the Dublin Core Metadata Initiative (10). This is a simple model of 15 properties that have been defined by the digital library community as important for describing digital artifacts. Two of the properties, subject and description, rely on keywords. These keywords are intended to be drawn from ontologies appropriate to the particular community using the specification.

Ontologies comprise (1) *taxonomies*, including *partonomies*, that organize the concepts or terms into hierarchical classification structures (e.g., "calcium-transporting ATPase is-a P-type ATPase"), (2) properties of concepts that relate concepts across classification structures (e.g., "calcium-transporting ATPase has substrate H20"), and (3) axioms (also known as constraints or rules) over the concepts and relationships (e.g., "metal ions and small molecules are disjoint"). Ontologies vary in their expressivity and richness. The most lightweight have only a simple is-a hierarchy. Ontologies are models of concepts rather than instances of those concepts. The combination of an ontology and a set of instances is a *knowledge base*.

Because an ontology is a conceptualization of a domain (see Figure 23.4, which gives an example of an ontology from the biological domain), it provides a shared language for a community of service providers and consumers, be they machines (e.g., agents) or people. An ontology can describe the application domain (e.g., biology, astronomy, engineering) or the Grid system itself (a resource's inputs and outputs, its quality of service, authorization policy, service functionality, provenance, quality assurance criteria, and so on). Ontologies can serve as the conceptual backbone for every task in the knowledge management life cycle. They provide for the structuring and retrieval of information in a comprehensive way

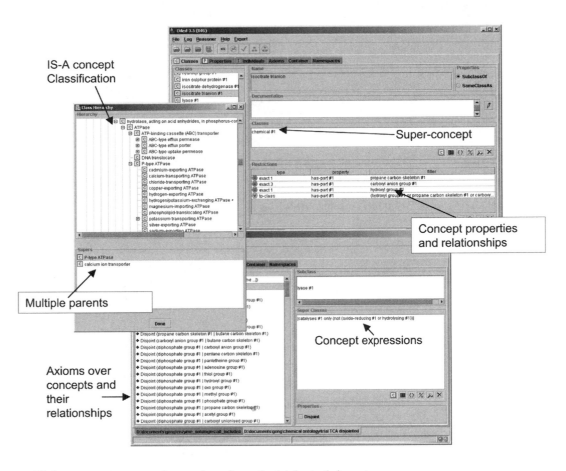

23.4 An example ontology from the biological domain.

FIGURE

and are essential for search, exchange, and discovery. Figure 23.5 summarizes the variety of roles an ontology can play.

As a formal specification, an ontology is open to computational reasoning. Thus, metadata descriptions using terms from the ontology can also be reasoned over so as to infer knowledge implied by, but not explicitly asserted in, the knowledge base. Generally speaking, the traditional trade-off between expressiveness and efficiency holds with respect to ontologies: the more expressive an ontology, the less tractable the reasoning.

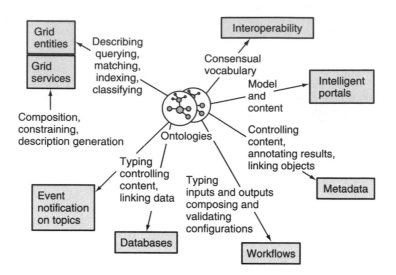

Illustration of the different roles that an ontology can play in the knowledge management lifecycle.

23.5   PROCESSING KNOWLEDGE

To put metadata and ontologies to work, we need methods and tools to support their deployment. As an example of the state of the art in metadata and knowledge representation, we can look to research on the Semantic Web—another distributed computing activity that has knowledge requirements similar to those considered here.

23.5.1   A Semantic Web for E-Science

The Semantic Web (115) and knowledge-oriented Grids have similar requirements for essential knowledge services and components (313, 314). The Semantic Web aims to evolve the Web into one where information and services are understandable and usable by computers as well as humans. The automated processing of Web content requires explicit machine-processible semantics associated with the content but extending more generally to any Web resource, including Web services. The key point is to move from a Web where semantics are embedded in hardwired applications to one where semantics are explicit and available for automated inference. Simple metadata and simple queries give a small but not insignificant improvement in information integration (465). More ambitious ideas are of an environment where software agents are able to discover, interrogate, and interoperate resources dynamically (469), building and disbanding virtual problem-solving environments (115, 357), discovering new facts, and performing sophisticated tasks on behalf of humans.

The core technologies proposed for the Semantic Web recall those identified for a knowledge-oriented Grid. They have their roots in distributed systems and information management. The minimum requirements are as follows:

✦ A unique identity for each resource (e.g., URIs) or data item (e.g., life sciences identifier in the biology domain).

✦ Annotation of resources with metadata describing facts about the resources for subsequent querying or manipulation. Technology proposals include the resource description framework (RDF) (33).

✦ Shared ontologies to supply the terms used by the metadata in order that the applications and people that use it share a common language and a common understanding of what the terms mean (their semantics). Technology proposals include the RDF vocabulary description language (RDF schema, or RDFS) and OWL (662), DAML+OIL (192), and topic maps (120).

✦ Inference over the metadata and ontologies such that new and unasserted facts or knowledge are inferred. Technology proposals include subsumption reasoners such as FaCT (367), Datalog-like deductive databases (166), and rule-based schemes such as RuleML (131).

A primary use of Semantic Web technologies is for the discovery and orchestration of Web services (and Grid services). The Semantic Web itself will be delivered by Web services. Knowledge-oriented Grids, on the other hand, will be delivered by Grid services.

23.5.2 Annotating Resources with Metadata

The metadata describing a computational entity are required to be flexible, expressive, and dynamic. Metadata are themselves data and thus are typically represented as a data model of attributes and values. The Semantic Web uses the resource description framework to represent the metadata needed to describe any kind of Web resource, from a Web page to a Web service. RDF (33) is described as "a foundation for processing metadata; it provides interoperability between applications that exchange machine-understandable information on the Web."

RDF is a simple graph-based data model based on statements in the form of triples (object, attribute, value). It supports additional constructs for handling collections and for reifying triples so that statements can be made about statements. The important point is that the metadata—the assertions that constitute the description of a resource—are held independently of the resource in RDF repositories or as XML documents (since RDF has a carrier syntax in XML). The metadata can be queried through the RDF query languages, and they can be aggregated and integrated by graph-matching techniques. Because they are stored independently of the resource, any number of RDF statements can be made about the resource from different perspectives by different authors, even holding conflicting views. The Dublin Core consortium have been enthusiastic adopters of RDF, and a number of Grid projects are beginning to adopt RDF as a common data model for metadata.

For example, in Figure 23.1, Points 1 and 2 presuppose annotation with provenance metadata, Points 6 and 7 with metadata relating to particular competences and expertise.

23.5.3   Representing Ontologies

Numerous representation schemes for knowledge have been developed over the past four decades, generally falling into two categories. The first comprises *frame-based* (or structured object-based) schemes embodied in tools such as Protégé-2000 (*protege.stanford.edu*) and frameworks such as Ontolingua (255). The second comprises *logic-based* schemes, which are based on fragments of first-order predicate logic such as description logics (e.g., FaCT (367)). Frame-based schemes provide a range of intuitive modeling primitives and have good tools and market penetration. Logic-based schemes, in contrast, have the advantages of well-defined semantics and efficient automated reasoning support. Recent efforts have been made to combine the two to benefit from both (259).

The W3C RDF vocabulary description language (RDF schema, or RDFS) uses a simple object-based model for providing a vocabulary of terms for RDF statements. Because it has limited expressiveness regarding class and property constraints, however, RDFS has proved too limiting for many Web applications.

DAML+OIL is an ontology language specifically designed for the Web, building on existing Web standards such as XML and RDF: the ontologies are stored as XML documents and concepts are referenced by URIs. It is underpinned by an expressive description logic, and its formal semantics enable machine interpretation and reasoning support. DAML+OIL has been adopted in many projects, leading to increasing availability of tools such as parsers and editors. DAML+OIL describes a domain in terms of *classes* and *properties*. DAML+OIL ontologies are compositional, using a variety of constructors that are provided for building class expressions.

DAML+OIL is also the basis of the W3C OWL Web ontology language (662). DAML+OIL/OWL supports two kinds of reasoning task. Given two conceptual definitions A and B, we can determine whether A subsumes B, in other words, whether every instance of B is necessarily an instance of A. In addition, we can determine whether an arbitrary class expression is satisfiable, in other words whether it is logically coherent with respect to the concepts in the ontology. These reasoning tasks mean that a description's place in the classification is inferred rather than asserted. When the description evolves, so does the classification; hence, the classification is always consistent, sound, and complete. We can check whether two descriptions are equivalent, subsume, or (at least partially) match one another or are mutually inconsistent. The usefulness of these capabilities can be gauged with reference to Figure 23.1. Point 6 can link the protein of interest (i.e., P31946, the protein linase C) with the Attwood lab only by explicitly using an inference engine that can deduce that this protein linase is an ATPase enzyme, then that ATPase enzymes are nucleotide-binding proteins, in which the Attwood lab has expertise.

The explicit representation of knowledge in formal languages such as DAML+OIL/OWL opens the door to reasoning about new metadata and new knowledge that are not explicitly asserted. Subsumption inference is not the only kind. Rule-based reasoning of the kind proposed by RuleML (131) and deductive databases are another (166). The latter, in particular, elegantly supports expressive query answering over concept extensions in knowledge bases, for which description logics currently provide insufficient support.

23.6 KNOWLEDGE-ORIENTED GRIDS

The intent of Grid middleware is that new capabilities be constructed dynamically and transparently from distributed services, reusing existing components and information resources. The aim is to assemble and coordinate these components in a flexible manner. If entities are subject to central control, then that control imposes rules of construction and rules of conduct that are shared knowledge with shared protocols of usage. If entities are homogeneous, knowledge and its use can be shared under a priori assumptions and agreements.

A dynamic Grid computational environment, however, is characterized by entity autonomy, heterogeneity, and distribution. It is an environment in which a priori agreements regarding engagement cannot be assumed. Hence, trading partnerships must be dynamically selected, negotiated, procured, and monitored. To achieve the flexible assembly of Grid components and resources requires not just a service-oriented model but information about the functionality, availability, and interfaces of the various components. This information must have an agreed-upon interpretation that can be processed by machines. Thus, the explicit assertion of knowledge and the explicit use of reasoning services—which ontologies and associated ontology reasoners embody—is necessary to allow computational processes to interact fully (390).

Grids already make provision to ensure that certain forms of knowledge are available—resource descriptions (e.g., the Globus Toolkit's resource specification language: Chapter 18) and metadata services (e.g., the Globus Toolkit's monitoring and discovery service), along with computational entities that use this knowledge for decision-making (e.g., the Network Weather Service (682)). We will see more examples in Section 23.6.

Reasoning has a role to play, not just in the creation of the ontologies used to classify services, but also in the matching of services. In Condor, a structural matching mechanism is used to choose computational resources (541). The semantic matching possible through reasoning in languages such as DAML+OIL has been explored in Matchmaker (Chapter 18 and (514, 657)) and myGrid (Chapter 9 and (683)), as we see in Section 23.7.1. In an architecture where the services are highly volatile and configurations of services are constantly being disbanded and reorganized, knowing whether one service is safely substitutable by another is an essential, not a luxury.

The knowledge services layer of Figure 23.3 is expanded in Figure 23.6, taken from Geodise. The services cater to the six challenges of the knowledge life cycle—acquiring, modeling, retrieving, reusing, publishing, and maintaining knowledge. Although research has been carried out on each aspect of this life cycle, in the past each aspect was often developed in isolation from the others. For example, knowledge acquisition was done with little consideration as to how it might be published or used. At the same time, knowledge publishing paid little attention to how knowledge was acquired or modeled. The Grid and the Web have made it apparent that research is needed into how to best exploit knowledge in a distributed environment. Recently, work in the area of knowledge technologies has tried to bring together methods, tools, and services to support the complete knowledge life cycle. Globally distributed computing demands a service-oriented architecture to make it flexible and extensible, easier to reuse and share knowledge resources, and open to making the services distributed and resilient. The approach is to implement knowledge services as Grid services.

Although different knowledge management tasks are coupled together in the architecture, their interactions are not hardwired. Each component deals with

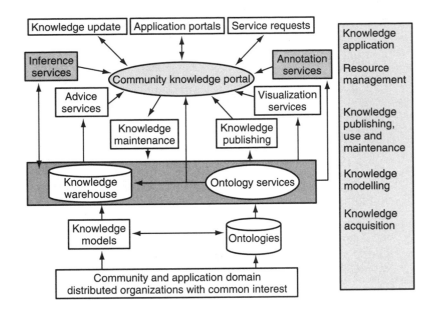

23.6

FIGURE

Expanded view of the knowledge services layer from Figure 23.3.

different tasks and can use different techniques and tools. Each of them can be updated while others are kept intact. Thus, the architecture is robust: new techniques and tools can be adopted at any time, and the knowledge management system will continue working even if some of its components should fail or become unavailable. Knowledge can be added into the knowledge warehouse at any time. It is necessary only to register the knowledge with the community knowledge portal. After registration, all of the services such as publishing and inference can be used to expose the new knowledge for use. Knowledge services can be added in the same way. For example, a data-mining service may be added later for automated knowledge acquisition and dynamic update of knowledge repositories.

The minimal components needed include annotation mechanisms, repositories for annotations and ontologies with associated query and life cycle management, and inference engines that are resilient and reliable and that perform well:

✦ *Annotation services* associate Grid entities with their metadata in order to attach semantic content to those entities. Without tools and methods to annotate entities there will be no prospect of creating semantically enriched material. Point 8 in Figure 23.1 highlights the importance of this.

+ *Ontology services* provide access to concepts in an underlying ontology data model and their relationships. Services include extending the ontology, querying it by returning the parents or children of a concept, and determining how concepts and roles can be combined to create new legal composite concepts. Point 6 in Figure 23.1 highlights the importance of this.

+ *Inference engines* apply different kinds of reasoning over the same ontologies and the same metadata. Figure 23.1 shows how knowledge-oriented Grids rely on inference engines.

In addition, tools are needed for acquiring and managing knowledge. Traditionally, knowledge bases have been small. In contrast, Grid knowledge bases may be large and will require the use of database technology or the use of ontologies indexing the source databases, as described in Section 23.7.4. As the entrance point to an integrated knowledge management system, the knowledge *portal* provides a security infrastructure for authentication and authorization, so that knowledge can be used and updated in a controlled way. Knowledge publishing allows users to register new distributed knowledge and service information; this information is accessed and retrieved in the same way we browse the Web (provided the resources have registered with the portal).

23.7   KNOWLEDGE-ORIENTED GRID CASE STUDIES

We now illustrate five aspects of knowledge-oriented Grids drawn from several Grid projects. These aspects rely on declarative representation of knowledge explicitly held and explicitly used, as characterized in Section 23.1. Hence, such Grid projects are closer to the upper right-hand region of the semantic continuum depicted in Figure 23.2.

Some of the projects described are breaking such new ground. In advance of production-quality software support of the Open Grid Services Architecture, they have adopted comparable standards stemming from the Web services and Semantic Web activities in standardization forums other than the Global Grid Forum. This in no way precludes their replacement by the standards that will emerge from the Grid community.

23.7.1   Service Discovery

The UK e-Science pilot project ᵐʸGrid (Chapter 9) seeks to provide open source high-level Grid middleware for the formulation, management, and sharing of data-intensive *in silico* experiments in bioinformatics. The emphasis is on data integration, workflow, personalization, and provenance.

Resources for ^{my}Grid are OGSA services that can be statically or dynamically combined within a context, for example, the specific user, the cost of execution, the speed of execution, reliability, and the appropriate authorizations available to the user. Finding the right service depends on knowledge of each service. The description of a service is essential for automated discovery and search, selection, (imprecise) matching, composition and interoperation, invocation, and execution monitoring. The services descriptions in the OGSA specification capture the interface syntax, but capturing the meaning is critical for discovery. Not only should the service accept an operation request with a particular signature, but it should also respond "as expected."

Bioinformaticians typically have in hand a particular kind of data for which they need to find a service to operate over to produce a desired outcome, or they have in mind a task to apply to the data. They must express their requirements and match these against available services, taking into account the function of the service, the data it accepts and produces, and the resources it uses to accomplish its goal. Moreover, they must select, from the candidates that can fulfill their task, the one best able to achieve the result within the required constraints. This choice depends on metadata concerning function, cost, quality of service, geographical location, and publisher.

Classification of services based on the functionality they provide is being adopted by diverse communities as an efficient way of finding and indexing suitable services. A classification scheme for a service registry is a consensus as to how the community thinks about these services. For example, the EMBOSS suite of bioinformatics applications and repositories has a coarse classification of tools it contains, and free text documentation for each (557). The bioinformatics integration platforms ISYS (592) and BioMOBY (678) use taxonomies for classifying services.

An assumption of ^{my}Grid is that third-party service registries catalog available bioservices. Additional (personalized) metadata descriptions of the services are asserted by using RDF statements. Providers publish their services, and consumers find and match services, by a range of mechanisms such as name, words, signature, type, and, in particular, ontological description. The ^{my}Grid bioinformatics service ontology is based on the DAML-S service profile and model (211). Service descriptions fall into two categories: the domain coverage of classes of services, and operational metadata (data quality, quality of service, cost, etc.) for invocable instances of services. DAML+OIL provides a vocabulary for expressing service descriptions. Matches are made first on the domain and then the operational properties. Replica services (which are prevalent in biology) have the same domain description but different operational service profiles. Service classes

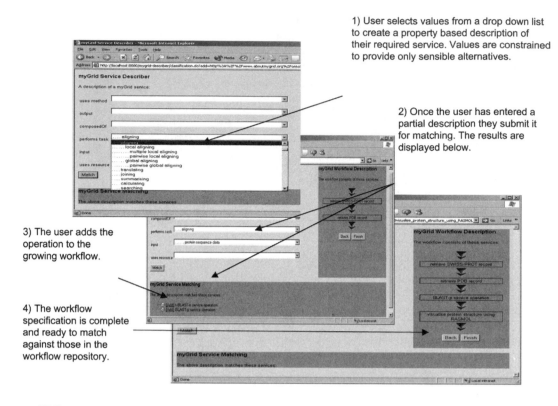

1) User selects values from a drop down list
to create a property based description of
their required service. Values are constrained
to provide only sensible alternatives.

2) Once the user has entered a
partial description they submit it
for matching. The results are
displayed below.

3) The user adds the
operation to the
growing workflow.

4) The workflow
specification is complete
and ready to match
against those in the
workflow repository.

23.7   An early prototype of ᵐʸGrid's service discovery user interface.

FIGURE

and their instances are discovered, matched, and selected before the workflow is executed; instances are also selected dynamically during execution (see (683) for details).

Figure 23.7 shows an early prototype of the service discovery user interface. Service descriptions that characterize the service being sought are formed, guided by the user interface. The service properties displayed on the form and the vocabulary choices for the values of those properties are controlled by the ontology. The form is contextual, since choices of values change, depending on prior choices. The user forms a query description of the service on the fly, which is classified by the FaCT reasoner (367) to give a range of candidate services whose descriptions are logically subsumed by (more specific) or subsume (more general) the query description. Thus, a service can be proposed as a potential, and possibly partial, match and can be substituted for the one required because it is semantically similar (514, 657, 683). This is in contrast to systems such as Condor's ClassAds, where the services are matched using structure (541). It is also a step from matching services based on their syntax or data types as held in their WSDL documents.

23.7.2 Knowledge Annotation, Advice, and Guidance

Geodise seeks to use Grid technologies, design optimization techniques (533), knowledge management technologies, Web services, and ontology techniques to build a state-of-the-art knowledge-intensive design tool consistent with the emerging OGSA infrastructure. Geodise is using knowledge engineering methods (578) to model and encapsulate design knowledge so that new designs of, for example, aero-engine components can be developed more rapidly, and at a lower cost.

One of Geodise's first uses of knowledge has been the semantic enrichment of engineering design workflows through annotation. A key question that Geodise wishes to be able to answer is: What previous designs have been explored, and how can one reuse them? A typical engineering design contains information about the problem definition (the geometry) and the tools used for meshing or breaking the geometric design into units over which an analysis is run. Optimization methods for producing a range of behaviors are applied, and experiments are performed with diverse parameters to produce a range of possible design solutions. All of this information—the step-by-step activity of how the package was used—is recorded in log files. In order to reuse the knowledge contained in these log files most effectively, the Geodise project semantically enriches these files by using terms from the domain ontology.

Figure 23.8 shows a screenshot in which a log file from the OPTIONS design package is being annotated by using the OntoMat annotation tool (350) and the ontologies developed for the Geodise domain. The middle panel contains the specific design workflow for annotation. The left-hand panel contains an ontology, represented in DAML+OIL for the problem domain. Annotation involves marking up fragments of the workflow against this ontology, resulting in an enriched content in RDF format. The aim is to make this process as automated as possible, with the ontology acting as a reference model to enrich workflows as they are built (175).

The resulting semantically enriched log files are built into a knowledge repository, which can then be queried, indexed, and reused. Such a repository can be used to find appropriate solutions to a current design problem based on previous experiences.

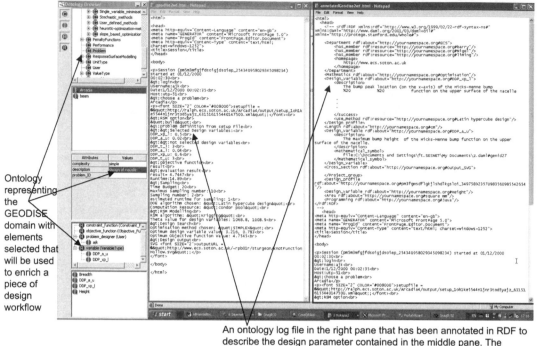

Ontology
representing
the
GEODISE
domain with
elements
selected that
will be used
to enrich a
piece of
design
workflow

An ontology log file in the right pane that has been annotated in RDF to
describe the design parameter contained in the middle pane. The
whole log can be enriched in this way the aim being to automate this
process as far as possible

23.8

FIGURE

A screenshot showing the OntoMat annotation tool is being used to annotate a log
file from the OPTIONS design package.

23.7.3   Workflow Composition

Workflows coordinate and compose services, linking them together through a
systematic plan. Knowledge can be used to constrain and guide the composition
and to validate the configuration.

The myGrid system is used in choosing appropriate operations on user data
and in constraining which operation should sensibly follow another. In myGrid
a task ontology models the workflow process and is used for semantic annotation of the inputs and outputs of services (currently represented in a Web services workflow language). The semantic type of the data must match. For example, a collection of enzymes is permissible as input to BLASTp because enzymes
are a kind of protein and BLASTp takes sets of proteins as an input. Semantic
compatibility is not the same as syntactic. Two services may be semantically the

same but have different signatures and expect data in different formats. Conversely, two services may have the same syntactic signature and operation names but be semantically different. Figure 23.7 shows how the choices of inputs to a service are restricted to those semantically compatible with the previous outputs of a service.

Geodise is also implementing a knowledge-based, ontology-assisted workflow construction assistant, called KOWCA. Generic knowledge about design search and optimization is converted into a rule-based knowledge base. The underlying knowledge-base system checks the consistency of the workflow and gives advice on what should be done next during the workflow construction.

Rather than using knowledge to guide a user in forming workflows, projects such as SCEC (42) and GriPhyN (93) exploit an artificial intelligence planner that uses metadata to generate workflows. The state information used by the planner includes a description of the available resources and files. The input goal description can include (1) a metadata specification of the information the user requires and the desired location for the output file, (2) specific components to be run, or (3) intermediate data products. This approach is being used at the Laser Interferometer Gravitational Wave Observatory, whose objective is to detect gravitational waves predicted by Einstein's theory of relativity. A prototype workflow generator using the planner allows the user to express goals in terms of metadata, or information about the data required, rather than the logical file names. For example, the planner's top-level goal might be a pulsar search in certain areas of the sky for a time period. The planner uses an explicit, declarative representation for workflow constraints (such as program data dependencies), host constraints, and user access constraints. The declarative nature of the planning domain makes it easier to add and modify constraints and to construct applications out of reusable information about the Grid and the hosts available (as described in the next section). Using search heuristics, the planner creates a number of different plans and either returns the best according to some quality criterion or returns a set of choices for the user to consider. The estimated expected run time is used as an initial quality criterion for a workflow (129, 216).

23.7.4   Data Integration

Workflows are one form of service integration. Another is data and metadata integration. By describing metadata in a common model, all the components of an experiment (literature, notes, code, databases, intermediate results, sketches, images, workflows, the persons doing the experiment, the lab they are in, the final paper) can be associated and hence can be reasoned over.

For semantic integration, ontologies play two roles: (1) since a data model is a simple ontology, all databases under the same database management system type either use the same ontology or provide a mapping to a standard ontology, and (2) many intelligent information integration systems use ontologies to represent a canonical model with mappings to the source databases. The user poses requests against the target ontology, which arc then automatically and transparently translated into requests against the source ontologies, that is, the schemata of the source data repositories (315).

The Biomedical Informatics Research Network (Chapter 8) uses a combination of techniques from database mediators and knowledge representation to create model-based mediation (MBM) (453). The mission of MBM is to turn the questions of domain scientists (in this case neuroscientists) into database queries that can be evaluated against multiple sources. For example, a neuroscientist may ask, "What is the cerebellar distribution of rat proteins with more than 70% homology with human NCS-1? Is there any structure specificity? How about other rodents?" These questions could, in principle, be answered by using sources that export protein localization data (ProtLoc), information on calcium-binding proteins (CaProt), morphometry data (Synapse), and so forth. The primary difficulty is that there are semantic gaps between the source data, which need to be filled with "glue knowledge" from the domain experts in order to relate item X from one source with item Y from another source. Ontologies provide a "semantic coordinate system" that acts as a reference mechanism to link source data objects to concepts in the mediator. In MBM, ontologies are used as "domain maps" to provide the terminological glue. A domain map of anatomical structures, ANATOM, has been used to integrate data from different species, scales, and resolutions. Thus, the integration mechanism relies on conformance by data instances to a shared set of concepts. The domain map is a means of semantic browsing and navigation of the multidatabase contents.

If databases export the semantic types of database schema entities, that exported data can be understood in the mediator using rich object-oriented models and Datalog-like languages (e.g., F-Logic), and description logics such as DAML+OIL *can* be used for relating local object models to shared domain maps registered with the mediator. For example, some neuroscience domain knowledge is shown in different forms in Figure 23.9. The domain map graph on the left corresponds to an ontology representing some expert knowledge (upper right). The formal semantics of this graph is given by a description logic fragment (see (453)). Moreover, new concepts can be "situated" relative to

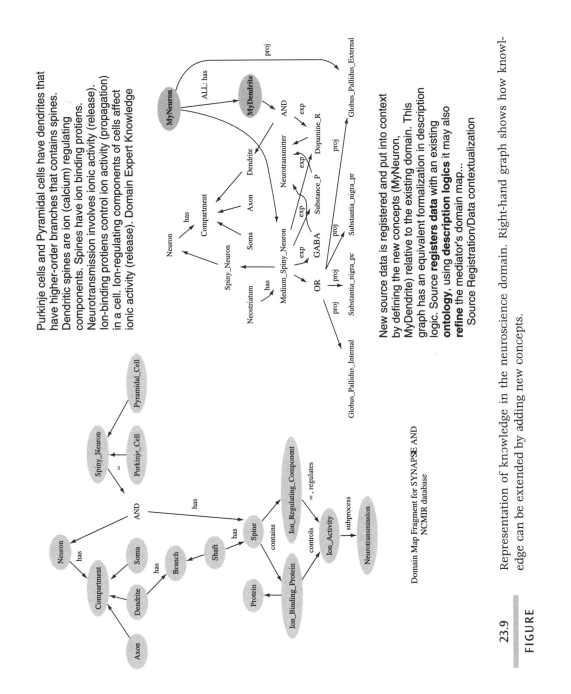

Purkinje cells and Pyramidal cells have dendrites that
have higher-order branches that contains spines.
Dendritic spines are ion (calcium) regulating
components. Spines have ion binding protiens.
Neurotransmission involves ionic activity (release).
Ion-binding protiens control ion activity (propagation)
in a cell. Ion-regulating components of cells affect
ionic activity (release). Domain Expert Knowledge

Domain Map Fragment for SYNAPSE AND
NCMIR database

New source data is registered and put into context
by defining the new concepts (MyNeuron,
MyDendrite) relative to the existing domain. This
graph has an equivalent formalization in description
logic. Source **registers data** with an existing
ontology, using **description logics** it may also
refine the mediator's domain map...
Source Registration/Data contextualization

23.9 Representation of knowledge in the neuroscience domain. Right-hand graph shows how knowledge can be extended by adding new concepts.

FIGURE

existing ones by using description logic axioms (shown in the figure, bottom right).

23.7.5   Collaborative Science

Collaborative meetings involve live exchange of meeting content as well as operational information supporting the conferencing infrastructure. At the simplest level, this information might be slides or remote camera control. New forms of information also may be exchanged, such as speaker queues, distributed voting, minutes taken of the meeting, or annotations on existing documents. In addition, subdiscussions can take place, and these provide knowledge-rich content. As discussed in Chapter 15, sharing and storing this information can significantly enrich the scientific collaboration process.

One approach to supporting the collaborative process is the Access Grid (Chapter 15), which focuses on large-scale distributed meetings and training. Access Grid resources include multimedia display and interaction, notably through room-based videoconferencing (group-to-group), and interfaces to Grid middleware and visualization environments. Access Grid nodes are dedicated facilities that explicitly contain the high-quality audio and video technology necessary to provide an effective user experience.

The CoAKTinG (Collaborative Advanced Knowledge Technologies on the Grid) project is focused on the integration of intelligent meeting spaces, ontologically annotated media streams from online meetings, decision rationale and group memory capture, meeting facilitation, issue handling, planning and coordination support, constraint satisfaction, and instant messaging and presence (589). CoAKTinG requires ontologies for the application domain, for the organizational context, for the meeting infrastructure, and for devices that capture the metadata. In contrast with some other projects, it requires real-time processing and timely distribution of metadata. For example, when someone enters the meeting, other participants can be advised immediately on how their communities of practice intersect.

The combination of Semantic Web technologies with live information flows is highly relevant to Grid computing. Metadata streams may be generated by people, by equipment, or by services, for example, annotation, device settings, and data processed in real time. Instead of a meeting room, the space may be a laboratory, perhaps a "smart lab," with a rich array of devices and multimedia technologies, as explored in the Comb-e-Chem project (5). The need to discover and compose available services when one carries a device into a smart space is closely related to the formation of virtual organizations using Grid services—an important relationship between the worlds of Grid and ubiquitous computing.

23.8   SUMMARY

Grid computing is concerned above all not with accelerating scientific computation but with accelerating the scientific process. Knowledge is the key to facilitating this process. In this chapter we have made the case for knowledge *on* the Grid as well as for knowledge *in* the Grid *for* the Grid middleware infrastructure. For a computational entity to interact fully with any other entity, making informed intelligent and possibly autonomous decisions, it must be able to exploit knowledge about those entities. Rich declarative models of knowledge are relevant to making decisions in the Grid environment and must be uniformly available to the system at any point. Intelligent reasoners access these knowledge sources to make informed decisions about requirements, resources, and processing and to reformulate such decisions in light of changes in the highly dynamic Grid environment, where execution failures and new resources are commonplace.

Knowledge-oriented Grids are needed to enable exciting new scientific outcomes. They also are needed to realize some of the promise of current Grid endeavors and to carry these forward into future projects.

We have explained some of the machinery of knowledge-oriented Grids and have shown that many of the essential ideas and technologies are shared with the Semantic Web. Grid developers already can exploit RDF standards and tools, and the experience of DAML+OIL and OWL in the Semantic Web community enables Grid developers to anticipate the next set of technologies. Ontologies and their associated tools will facilitate *semantic interoperability* on the Grid. As Grid middleware provided a way of dealing with the heterogeneity of computational resources, similarly a knowledge-oriented Grid provides a means of dealing with the heterogeneity of services, information, and knowledge.

Many aspects of knowledge-oriented Grids are active research areas. In some cases the Grid community is well placed to address the challenges. It is motivated by real needs for semantic interoperability, as increasingly we wish to assemble new Grid projects based on components and information from others, and the community has mechanisms in place for establishing and sharing standards. In the short term, we need to establish best practices and gain practical experience relating to performance, scalability (both human and technical), and other aspects such as change management.

Knowledge-oriented Grids are increasingly recognized as an important stage in the evolution of Grid computing, with their promise of semantic interoperability, intelligent automation and guidance, and smart reuse. By exploiting knowledge-rich models of information we hope that Grid middleware will become more flexible and more robust. The techniques we have described in this chapter are a step toward our vision of a Grid with a high degree of easy-to-use and seamless automation and in which there are flexible collaborations and computations on a global scale.

ACKNOWLEDGMENTS

We acknowledge Carl Kesselman, Yolanda Gil, Bertram Ludaescher, and John Brooke, and our coworkers. This work is supported by the Engineering and Physical Sciences Research Council and Department of Trade and Industry through the UK e-Science programme, in particular the myGrid e-Science pilot (GR/R67743), the Geodise e-Science pilot (GR/R67705), and the CoAKTinG project (GR/R85143/01), which is associated with the "Advanced Knowledge Technologies" Interdisciplinary Research Collaboration (GR/N15764/01).

FURTHER READING

For more information on the topics covered in this chapter, see *www.mkp.com/grid2*.

The *Handbook on Ontologies in Information Systems* (605) provides an excellent overview of ontology languages, tools, and applications. Two other books provide early descriptions of the Semantic Web: *Spinning the Semantic Web* (260) and *Towards the Semantic Web: Ontology-Driven Knowledge Management* (214).

IEEE Intelligent Systems acts as the community's magazine, with many relevant articles also in *IEEE Internet Computing*. A major journal is *Web Semantics: Science, Services and Agents on the World Wide Web*, published by Elsevier.

VI

PART

TOOLS

Grid applications can, in principle, be constructed directly by using only low-level mechanisms such as the Internet protocol or (at a somewhat more abstract, but still too primitive level) the Open Grid Services Infrastructure. However, this task is similar to that of developing conventional applications using assembly language: laborious, error-prone, and inflexible. We require higher-level tools that provide more sophisticated abstractions of Grid architecture, perhaps specialized to particular application domains. The Grid programming problem is the subject of Part VI of this book.

The first edition included four chapters on tools: one on application-specific approaches, one on compilers and libraries, one on object-based approaches, and one on "commodity" approaches—that is, the use of then-popular CORBA and Web technologies. We observed that

> [these] four chapters...illustrate the diversity of views regarding how best to program Grid environments. However, some clear directions emerge. Grid-enabled libraries and toolkits will provide a major vehicle for migrating applications and users to Grid environments. Compilers and languages will address Grid issues, and we can expect to see both evolution of existing programming models and the introduction of new approaches. Commodity technologies will play a major role in shaping and constructing Grid environments of the future.

Since that time, considerable progress has been made in this area. The definition of the Open Grid Services Architecture represents, in effect, a successful integration of Grid technologies with a leading "commodity" technology with object features (Web services). This integration defines, albeit still at a low level, a programming and component model for the Grid—and although certainly not "solving" the Grid programming problem, it does put us in a far better position to make progress.

The Open Grid Services Architecture has been discussed in Chapter 17, so we focus in the three chapters in Part VI on various other aspects of the programming problem.

In Chapter 24, "Application-Level Tools," Henri Bal and his colleagues explore tools that application developers can use to write Grid-enabled applications and that users can employ to deploy and run their applications on the Grid. They define requirements for such tools, summarize the state of the art in their development, and use representative case studies to illustrate how such tools can function in practice. Distinguishing between Grid programming models and Grid application execution environments, they present a taxonomy of tools that captures major current activities and trends in Grid application-level tool development.

In Chapter 25, "Languages, Compilers, and Run-Time Systems," Ken Kennedy considers the prospects for development of general-purpose application development support tools that can facilitate the programming process without degrading performance to unacceptable levels. He begins by reviewing application development technologies developed for scalable parallel computers and discusses how these technologies might be extended for heterogeneous distributed systems. He then reviews existing software support for Grid application development, and finally describes a new approach being pioneered by the Grid Application Development Software (GrADS) research project.

Finally, in Chapter 26, "Application Tuning and Adaptation," Daniel A. Reed, Celso L. Mendes, and Charng-da Lu discuss issues relating to the management of performance variability in the Grid environment. They describe the notion of a *performance contract* as a means of representing expectations for application performance demands and resource service capabilities. They present *contract monitoring* techniques that use performance data to verify that expectations are met—and/or to detect when, and diagnose why, performance falls outside acceptable bounds. Finally, they discuss how applications can respond when contracted specifications are not satisfied, and describe adaptive control techniques that an application can use to adapt to a new resource regime.

Two chapters from the first edition that could not be included in the second edition of *The Grid* are somewhat dated in terms of the specific technologies discussed, but contain valuable information on how to structure Grid applications in terms of components—a subject of great relevance within the context of the Open Grid Services Architecture.

In Chapter 1:9, "Object-Based Approaches," Gannon and Grimshaw discuss the role that object-oriented techniques must play in Grids, both as a basis for building applications and as a structuring technique for the services that constitute a Grid software environment. The first part of the chapter reviews object-oriented concepts and relevant commodity client–server technologies, such as CORBA, DCOM, and Java, and also object-oriented composition and container technologies, such as Java Beans. A series of application examples is used to motivate a discussion of ways in which object-oriented methods may be applied and areas in which extensions to current technologies are required. The second half of the chapter discusses the Legion system, an object-oriented software architecture for building Grid applications.

In Chapter 1:10, "High-Performance Commodity Computing," Fox and Furmanski explore the role that commodity software technologies must play in building an operational computational Grid. The concept of a three-tier architecture is introduced, in which middle-tier application servers mediate between sophisticated back-end services and potentially simple front ends. The case is made that this architecture can be adapted for Grid environments quite easily, with alternative implementations of key back-end and middle-tier components being used to meet performance requirements. Approaches to the packaging and implementation of such specialized services are discussed.

24

CHAPTER

Application-Level Tools

Henri Bal, Henri Casanova, Jack Dongarra, and Satoshi Matsuoka

*I*n the early days of Grid computing, most applications were deployed for limited amounts of time (e.g., during a conference) to demonstrate the feasibility of wide-area computing (e.g., (219)). Since then, the number of Grid applications has steadily increased. Collaborations between Grid architects and application teams have led to the re-engineering of large applications that were then deployed on Grid platforms. Several such applications have been presented in Part III of this book, and they provide a convincing demonstration of the benefits and potential of Grid computing.

Despite these successes, the Grid has remained elusive for many users, who often ask: "How do I port my application to the Grid?"; "How do I run my application on the Grid?" or even "Where is the Grid I can use now?" These remain difficult questions to answer. Grid middleware provides fundamental services but is too low level for most application scientists to use directly. For example, application scientists do not have the time, expertise, and motivation to learn the details of Grid information services to retrieve and use resource information as a basis for making resource selection decisions.

Instead, there is a clear need for tools that (1) application developers can use to write Grid-enabled applications and (2) users can employ to deploy and run their applications on the Grid. The more complex, distributed, and large scale the Grid is, the more important such *Grid application-level tools* are to avoid a disconnection between the Grid and its user communities. In this chapter, we define requirements for such tools, summarize the state of the art in their development, and use representative case studies to illustrate how such tools can function in practice. We structure our discussion in terms of the taxonomy depicted in Figure 24.1. We distinguish

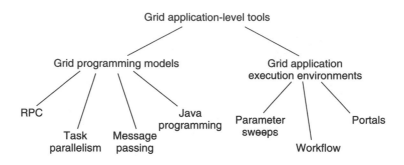

24.1   Taxonomy of Grid application-level tools.

FIGURE

first between Grid programming models and Grid application execution environments, and then further subdivide each of these two high-level categories. This taxonomy is certainly not exhaustive, but it does reflect many of the major current activities and trends in Grid application-level tool development.

24.1   REQUIREMENTS

A Grid application-level tool is software that builds on the base Grid software infrastructure to provide new functionalities and high-level abstractions that allow users to easily write and/or run Grid applications. As such, Grid application-level tools sit above other Grid services in the software stack (Figure 24.2, and see also Figure 4.3).

More specifically, we characterize an application-level tool as a software tool that possesses the following properties.

The tool should build on the Grid software infrastructure.   The base Grid services implement fundamental functionalities needed by most Grid applications. Nevertheless, Grid application developers should not be responsible for implementing each application from the ground up. Instead, it must be possible to use application-level tools that provide higher-level abstractions useful for entire classes of applications. Such abstractions can be implemented as part of programming models and can thus reduce Grid application development time and improve code reuse. In terms of Grid application execution, the end user should not be concerned with the logistics of application deployment. To this end Grid application execution environments must leverage Grid services on behalf of the user and provide the illusion of computing on the desktop.

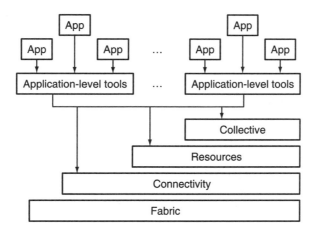

24.2   Grid application-level tools in the Grid software stack.

FIGURE

The tool should isolate users from the dynamics of the Grid hardware infrastructure.
Resources available on the Grid are numerous, diverse, and with fluctuating avail-
abilities. One cannot expect application users to query Grid information services
directly to track and understand the current state of the Grid platform. Instead,
the tool should either take all responsibility to discover, select, and acquire Grid
resources on behalf of the user or provide a simplified view of the platform that
the user can easily browse.

The tool should be generic.   The tool should be applicable to broad classes of applications. This is obviously a strong requirement for tools that enable programming
models. This requirement may be slightly relaxed for application-level tools, as
they have often emerged from application-specific efforts.

The tool should be easy to use.   This subjective notion is difficult to quantify. In the
case of tools allowing users to build applications according to a programming
model, users should ideally need to be concerned only with the programming
model itself (which may be complex) and not with its implementation. For
instance, users who write task-parallel applications for clusters should not experience difficulties in porting their code to the Grid if a Grid task-parallel programming model is provided. In the case of tools allowing users to run and deploy
existing applications, one must ensure that only minimal application modification
is required. Also, the tool should provide a simple interface and should handle
most of the logistics of the application run.

In the rest of this chapter we provide concrete examples of application-level tools, all of which we believe meet the ease-of-use requirement.

24.2   GRID PROGRAMMING MODELS

We use the term *Grid programming models* to denote Grid application-level tools that build on the base Grid infrastructure to provide higher-level abstractions that can be used to write applications. Traditional programming models such as remote procedure call, message passing, and master–worker need to be evolved to take advantage of specific characteristics of the Grid platform. New programming models also need to be developed for emerging classes of Grid applications that pose new challenges (e.g., data-intensive workflow applications (119, 284)). An even more ambitious goal is to provide a complete Grid application software development environment that would support many programming models and achieve high performance on behalf of the user. For example, as described in Chapter 25, the GrADS project (112) is developing a compiler to generate Grid-aware code to be executed by a run-time system that selects appropriate resources and adapts this selection throughout execution.

We describe here work on four different programming models that appear particularly relevant to Grid environments: remote procedure call, task parallelism, message passing, and Java-based models.

24.2.1   Remote Procedure Call

The remote procedure call (RPC) abstraction (121) provides a powerful means of writing simple concurrent client-server applications. RPC-style programming was first successfully implemented and used within single processors or for tightly coupled homogeneous systems. More recently, systems such as CORBA (508) have provided RPC functionality for distributed systems. Several projects have been initiated to specialize the RPC model for Grids, with the goal of enabling users both to specify coarse-grained task parallelism in their program and to access remote computational services available on Grid resources (both hardware and software) in a relatively transparent manner, without concerns for "proper" explicit usage of the underlying Grid services. Other goals of this work are to provide interface description language (IDL) support for the handling of large structured data arrays, efficient argument marshaling and transfer over gigabit/terabit WANs, and automated code management.

NetSolve (153) is a client–agent–server system that enables users to perform computations remotely. The system allows users of FORTRAN, C, Matlab, Mathematica, Octave, or Excel to access both hardware and software computational resources distributed across the Grid. A NetSolve agent searches for computational resources, chooses the best available and, using retry for fault tolerance, performs a computation. NetSolve uses a load-balancing policy to achieve good performance. Ninf (497) provides similar functionality with a different IDL and implementation. The most recent version of Ninf, Ninf-G (626), builds RPC services directly on top of the standard Grid services provided by the Globus Toolkit. Other related projects include RCS (85), PUNCH (398), and NEOS (483). The Grid RPC (496) working group within the Global Grid Forum is working to define a standard RPC model for scientific Grid computing, with the goal of enabling interoperability among these different systems.

The Open Grid Software Architecture (279) (OGSA, Chapter 17) uses the Web Services Description Language (WSDL) (183) for describing Grid services as dynamically coordinated Web services. Thus, OGSA provides basic RPC mechanisms as part of the base Grid infrastructure. These mechanisms can be leveraged to provide a simple Grid RPC programming model for end users when performance is not at a premium. In fact, a recent study (586) has shown that NetSolve/Ninf-like GridRPC systems intended for scientific applications on the Grid can be implemented relatively smoothly, albeit with some remaining technical problems, on a SOAP/WSDL infrastructure. However, the need to optimize for various properties of scientific applications and Grid environments remains. We present a detailed case study of GridRPC systems and technological issues in Section 24.4.

24.2.2   Task Parallelism

Task-parallel applications are so called because parallelism is achieved by partitioning the work to be performed rather than the data to be operated on. In this sense, the RPC programming model provides a mechanism for task parallelism. However, a full-fledged task-parallel programming model must also include functionality for collecting and combining results from application tasks, for automatically partitioning the workload among the tasks, for managing the size of the task pool, and for automatically balancing the load for improved performance. In other words, the programming model must provide abstractions for all the steps needed by a task-parallel application, and not only for the invocation of remote executables. The overwhelmingly popular paradigm for task parallelism is the *master-worker* model in which a master process divides portions of the entire workload among populations of worker processes.

The master-worker paradigm is well suited to the Grid, as application tasks need not be tightly coupled. A profuse literature addresses scheduling and systems issues for master-worker computing, and several Grid efforts provide frameworks that enable this programming. For example, in the master-worker (MW) tool (443), an application is integrated by providing MW with a small number of user-defined functions that implement the core functionality of the application (computation, communication of input, communication of output, etc.). MW has been used for challenging computations, including the solution of open problems in numerical optimization (82).

The AppLeS Master-Worker Application Template (AMWAT) (582) takes a similar approach. AMWAT places a large emphasis on scheduling issues, implementing over 10 different scheduling heuristics, and uses a workflow model to select the best locations for the master and workers. Both MW and AMWAT build on base Grid services for application deployment. They also provide mechanisms for using a hierarchy of masters, which is well adapted to Grid platforms that consist of multiple sites to tolerate high network delays.

Other more specialized and sophisticated task-parallel models have been investigated, such as divide-and-conquer (268, 504) and branch-and-bound (377). For example, the Satin project (504) implements a hierarchical divide-and-conquer task-parallel programming model for Grid computing. We describe Satin as a case study in Section 24.5.

24.2.3 Message Passing

The message-passing programming model is undoubtedly the most general and popular programming model for parallel computing, especially in the high-performance and scientific arenas. The goal is to provide users with primitives that application tasks can use to exchange messages and synchronize. These primitives include point-to-point communication functions, in which a send operation is used to initiate a data transfer between two concurrently executing program components and a matching receive operation is used to extract that data from system data structures into application memory space, and collective operations such as broadcast and reductions that implement operations involving multiple processes.

The message-passing paradigm does not provide the high-level data abstractions of the RPC and the task-parallel programming models and can therefore be more challenging to use. However, it offers greater flexibility, has been tremendously successful for many different parallel applications, is available in many implementations and flavors, and permits (at least in some instantiations) careful control of critical performance issues.

These considerations lead naturally to the idea that one should provide a message-passing programming model for Grid computing. Indeed, the parallel virtual machine (PVM) (305) message-passing system, introduced in 1992, prefigured many key Grid computing concepts. Designed primarily for networks of workstations with the goals of simplicity and portability, PVM allows the dynamic addition of hosts to the virtual machine and provides mechanisms to handle host failures. PVM has been used in many innovative distributed computing experiments (515, 584). However, the simplicity of the PVM model also hindered high-performance implementation, especially on tightly coupled, homogeneous systems.

The message-passing interface (MPI) (601) standard was developed to produce a specification that would allow manufacturers of high-performance MPPs to provide highly optimized and efficient implementations. MPI, introduced in 1994, has been immensely successful and has been implemented by most vendors. A widely used portable implementation, MPICH (334), targets homogeneous platforms, although its ch_p4 device provides limited support for heterogeneity.

Grid-enabled implementations of the message-passing model have been pursued by multiple groups, primarily although not exclusively within an MPI framework. PACX MPI (300) and STAMPI (412) use vendor-supplied MPI inside a Grid node and Grid-based communication between nodes. The Heterogeneous Adaptable Reconfigurable Networked Systems (HARNESS) project (105) extends concepts from PVM to provide a distributed virtual machine (DVM) with enhanced scalability, reliability, and resource-sharing models. MagPIe (409) and Karonis et al. (402) address the efficient implementation of MPI collective communications for wide-area platforms, a critical issue in Grid message passing.

Finally, MPICH-G2 (403) is a Grid-enabled implementation of the MPI standard. The implementation builds on the base Grid software infrastructure provided by the Globus Toolkit (276). MPICH-G2 is unique in the degree to which it hides and manages heterogeneity, as well as in its large user community. Section 24.6 presents a detailed case study involving MPICH-G2.

24.2.4   Java Programming

From its inception, Java had been designed with distributed computing in mind, embodying properties such as Remote Message Invocation (RMI) with object passing, code shipping, a language-integrated security model, and full language and code portability. These characteristics facilitated early proliferation of Java systems for wide-area distributed computing.

Early systems such as JET (593), Javelin (185), and Charlotte (97) used Java applets to implement wide-area compute resource sharing. These systems implemented computational tasks as applets and posted them on Web pages. Compute resource providers would then open the Web pages, thereby downloading the Applet and executing the computations. The Applet security model ensured that the compute resource provider (i.e., the browser) was protected from malicious code. However, the security model, as well as the nonstandard use of browsers as resource providers, also prevented widespread use of such systems, since the scope of applications was quite limited. Furthermore, there was not enough incentive for individuals to maintain their Web browsers pointing to a single page just for computing purposes.

Later and possibly more realistic efforts focused on constructing standalone Java platforms for the Grid, such as IceT (330) and Ninflet (621). These systems implemented their own security models for "uploading" Java code onto servers for safe execution, while allowing greater freedom than the Applet security model, such as the ability for application components to communicate with each other directly. Some also allowed native code to execute on the servers, allowing for greater flexibility while sacrificing some safety. These systems were built from the ground up and generally lacked important functionalities that have been since identified as part of the base Grid infrastructure, such as automated resource allocation, resource discovery, and fault tolerance/checkpointing. Furthermore, these systems lacked interoperability with other "mainstream" Grid middleware efforts, but instead attempted to offer complete infrastructure solutions for wide-area computing.

Recently, the use of Java as a substrate for constructing various Grid systems, while building on the currently available Grid infrastructure, has gained increasing popularity. The Java Commodity Grid (CoG) toolkit (429) provides an object-oriented, encapsulated interface to standard Globus Toolkit (276) (Chapter 4) features such as the Grid Security Infrastructure (280), monitoring and discovery service (204), and Grid resource allocation and management service (205). This support allows the construction of Java frameworks that support Grid application via the use of common Grid middleware services rather than features that are private to Java. One such example is jPoP, a Java framework for various parallel optimizations such as simulated annealing and genetic algorithms. jPoP uses CoG to access Globus Toolkit features while hiding their complexities from the end programmer, whose task is to build subclasses mostly concerned with optimization algorithms and not with the parallel execution on the Grid.

Some existing Grid programming models also provide their own Java interfaces; one example is the GridRPC (NetSolve/Ninf, Section 24.4) Java client API, which allows a client program written in Java to call GridRPC services directly.

Another example is Grid portals (Section 24.3.3), in which Java is used as an implementation language, as in GPDK and the Ninf Portal (618).

The recent shift of underlying Grid services architectures toward OGSA and the natural merger with Web services is further strengthening the utility of Java for the Grid. Many Web services implementations grew out of Java Servlet and its server hosting environments, such as Sun iPlanet and IBM WebSphere. In fact, the prototypes and even the first production implementations of OGSA are being delivered within a Java hosting environment. With such fundamental underlying architecture often being in Java, it is likely that there will be a renewed surge of Java programming frameworks for Grid computing that builds directly on top of OGSA services.

24.3 GRID APPLICATION EXECUTION ENVIRONMENTS

Our second class of Grid application-level tools is what we call *Grid application execution environments:* integrated software tools into which users can "drop" existing applications for execution on the Grid. These tools build on the base Grid infrastructure to provide a computing environment that users can access from the desktop. The tools assume most responsibilities concerning the logistics of resource discovery, resource selection, resource access, application deployment, and application monitoring, thereby providing the illusion of an execution on the desktop.

We describe three classes of such environments: parameter sweep application systems, workflow systems, and portals.

24.3.1 Parameter Sweep Applications

Parameter sweep applications (PSAs) comprise sets of computational tasks that are mostly *independent:* there are few task synchronization requirements or data dependencies among tasks. This simple application model arises frequently in many fields of science and engineering, including computational fluid dynamics, bioinformatics, particle physics (e.g., Chapter 10), discrete-event simulation, computer graphics, astronomy (81), and computational biology.

PSAs are attractive as Grid applications because they are not tightly coupled: tasks do not have stringent synchronization requirements and can thus tolerate high network latencies. In addition, they are amenable to straightforward fault-tolerance mechanisms such as restarting tasks from scratch after a failure.

Despite the simplicity of the PSA model, the development of robust, secure, easy-to-use PSA programs for Grid environments is a nontrivial task because of the need to manage both the hetereogeneity and unreliability of the Grid and the bookkeeping associated with potentially many thousands of tasks. Thus, a variety of approaches have been pursued over the years to automate various aspects of PSA preparation and execution. Systems designed to harness idle desktop systems, such as the Entropia system (180) described in Chapter 11, SETI@home (79), Condor (446) (Chapter 19), and XtremWeb (257) generally focus on achieving high throughput as opposed to performance of an individual application run.

Other systems focus on scheduling and deploying PSAs on resources more available than individually owned desktop PCs, which makes it possible to focus on application performance and integration issues. For example, Nimrod/G (56, 57) supports deadline scheduling as well as the declarative specification of PSAs, ILAB (689) provides a high-level user interface, and APST (156) (presented as a case study in Section 1.7) addresses scheduling issues pertaining to both data and computation.

24.3.2   Workflow Applications

The ability to link and compose diverse software tools and data formats—that is, to define *workflows*—is critical in many application domains. Workflows consist of modules and data filters with well-specified input and output. The modules are connected in order to achieve some desired goal. Workflows arise in many contexts, and the Workflow Management Coalition (WfMC) (51) is an international organization that fosters the use of workflows through the establishment of software standards. Several problem-solving environments (PSEs) that enable users to build and execute large workflows have been developed. It is typical for workflows to be so large, and/or application data and participants to be so distributed, that it is not feasible to run the entire application within a single system or institution (461). Thus, there is a natural affinity between workflow and the Grid. This affinity was recognized early on, and multiple projects have provided successful domain-specific PSEs for executing distributed workflow applications.

Several projects provide generic environments and capabilities for executing workflow applications in a distributed fashion. For instance, TENT (267) is a component-based framework specifically targeted to engineering workflows. It allows engineers to design, automate, control, and steer workflows interactively. It provides a graphical user interface and manages the computation on distributed resources via CORBA services. Globus Toolkit services can be used for Grid execution. Similarly, SciRUN (517) (and see Chapter 1:7) enables users to build and execute workflows. SciRUN places a large emphasis on computational steering and attempts to make it applicable for a broad range of advanced scientific computations. GALE (122) provides an XML-based process definition language by which users can describe their workflow for execution by a workflow management system—in particular, the ASCI Grid Work Management Service.

DAGMan (see Chapter 19) is a popular and successful Grid workflow system that makes it possible to execute workflow applications on the Condor (446) system. DAGMan acts as a metascheduler on top of Condor and manages job dependencies for a directed acyclic graph provided by the user, providing a simple and extremely robust mechanism for mapping workflow applications to Condor pools—or, via Condor-G (291), arbitrary Grid resources. DataCutter (119) is another workflow-oriented system, building on Grid middleware to implement high-performance workflows for data-intensive scientific applications. Chimera (284, 285) (Section 22.6.3) targets DAGMan as its workflow engine and supports the execution of large-scale, data-intensive workflows.

The OGSA trend addresses many of the challenges of integrating services spread across complex virtual organizations, by incorporating Web services into the Grid fabric. Web services are a natural and powerful mechanism by which workflows can be constructed and deployed. In this context, the Web Service Flow Language (WSFL) (439) provides workflow capabilities that are consistent with the Web Service Description Language (WSDL) and allows for recursion. XLANG (641) is used to model business processes as autonomous agents by providing extensions to the standard WSDL operations. In the same spirit, the recent Web services choreography interface (WSCI) (49) aims to provide tighter application-to-application integration than XLANG. The Web Service Conversation Language (WSCL) project (50) adds semantics to WSDL and allows for the specification of an ordering of operations but does not allow recursive composition of Web services, which is often required for Grid computing. More centered on Grid computing, XCAT (420) addresses workflow issues for Grid-based components and makes it possible to connect components dynamically, allowing applications to be built in ways not possible with standard Web services. Leveraging these efforts, the Grid Service Flow Language (GSFL) (421), which enables workflow applications in the OGSA framework with specific Grid computing requirements in mind, has been proposed. A recent critical review reminds us that none of these proposals is necessarily the ultimate solution (53).

24.3.3 Portals

Thin-client (Web) or other graphical interfaces to the Grid can be particularly effective means of gaining user acceptance. Such interfaces are termed *Grid portals*. Grid portals may be linked with middle-tier services that support, for example, secure user authentication with remote resources, the display of resource information obtained from an information service such as the Globus Toolkit's monitoring and discovery service (204; MDS-2, Chapter 20), remote job submission, and the transfer of application data among resources. Portals typically maintain user profile information so that portal users can track and monitor submitted jobs and view results.

Application-specific portals provide a specialized subset of Grid operations within a specific application domain. Many such portals have been developed in fields such as computational chemistry, biomedicine (523), and astrophysics (567). These and many other efforts have proved extremely successful in bringing large scientific communities to the Grid.

Several *general-purpose* portals that provide basic access to Grid resources and services have been developed. For example, the HotPage portal (647), deployed at the National Partnership for Advanced Computational Infrastructure (NPACI), enables researchers to find information about each resource in the NPACI Grid, including technical documentation, operational status, load and current usage, and queued jobs. Researchers with HotPage accounts can access and manipulate their files and data, and submit, monitor, and cancel jobs. UNICORE (Uniform Interface to Computing Resources) (560) is another example of a general-purpose portal infrastructure that provides users with seamless access to HPC resources from a Web browser. Other examples include the Grid Resource Broker (75), Gateway (63), and the NASA IPG Launchpad project.

In addition, several efforts are developing both Grid portal development environments and specific portal-related services. The Grid Portal Development Kit (GPDK) (506) provides both a portal development environment for the creation of new portals and a collection of Grid service "beans" used to accomplish basic operations such as job submission, file transfer, and querying of information services. GPDK uses Java Server Pages (JSP) and Java Beans and is packaged as a Web application as defined by the Java Servlet 2.2 specification, consisting of Web pages (HTML), Java Server Pages, and Java Beans. A client browser wishing to use GPDK services communicates with a GPDK-enabled Web server over a secure HTTP connection. The server can then access other Grid services using the Globus Toolkit infrastructure, via Java client-side interfaces supported by the Java Commodity Grid (CoG) toolkit (429).

Another similar effort, GridPort (646), provides a collection of services, scripts, and tools that allow developers to connect Web-based interfaces to Grid services. These scripts and tools provide consistent interfaces between the underlying infrastructure and security and are based on the Globus Toolkit and standard Web technologies such as CGI and Perl. Originally developed for HotPage, GridPort technology is now being used for other purposes, and is being enhanced with Java components, in a way similar to GPDK.

An important component for all of these systems is the MyProxy online credential repository (507), which allows portal users to access remote resources from anywhere without requiring that their certificate and private key be colocated with the client Web browser.

24.4   GRIDRPC CASE STUDY

In this subsection we present, as the first of four case studies, a description of NetSolve and Ninf, two systems that implement a "GridRPC" model. We introduce this model in the abstract first, and then describe its realization in the NetSolve and Ninf systems.

As noted previously, GridRPC systems seek to provide a familiar and convenient RPC-based programming model. At a high level, this programming model is that of standard RPC plus asynchronous coarse-grained parallel tasking. More specifically, the model should provide the following:

+ Various styles of asynchronous, task-parallel programming on the Grid, along with scalable parallel calls for launching multiple tasks concurrently.

+ "Dynamic" RPC, for example, dynamic interface acquisition and matching, resource discovery, scheduling, and task management.

+ Server-side IDL management, that is, no client-side IDL management and little state left on the client.

+ Support for scientific datatypes in the IDL, including large matrices and files as arguments, call-by-reference, and shared-memory matrix arguments with sections and strides.

GridRPC systems also seek to hide the complex logistics of Grid execution from client programmers, such as issues of resource discovery (both hardware and software), problem decomposition, scheduling, fault recovery, data/file transfer, security, and application code management, while maintaining high performance. This goal can be achieved by building on the base Grid software infrastructure, while having the GridRPC system largely be responsible for management tasks. More specifically, GridRPC should automate the following aspects, which would otherwise be visible for "less capable" RPC systems such as SOAP-RPC:

◆ Job management (suspension/cancellation/monitoring) of medium- to coarse-grained calls, with call durations ranging from a few seconds to more than a week

◆ Referentially transparent array argument serialization and deserialization for call-by-reference argument handling

◆ User file shipping and return shipping of output files

◆ Grid-level security, that is, the ability to make (a successive chain of) calls without the user being directly concerned with details of Grid-level authentication and authorization

◆ Resource selection and scheduling based on library and resource availability

◆ Fault tolerance with checkpoint/rollback and/or retries for failed resources

◆ Efficient bandwidth tuning of networks to maximize WAN transfer efficiency, as well as shipping limited portions of array data for striped usage

GridRPC not only allows individual applications to be distributed but also can serve as the basis for even higher-level software substrates such as distributed, scientific components on the Grid.

24.4.1   GridRPC Software

The NetSolve (153) and Ninf (497) systems both provide features similar to those described previously. We present a simple programming example largely common to both systems. As an example, for multiplying matrices, instead of making a procedure call in a user program,

```
double A[N][N], B[N][N], C[N][N]; // C = A * B, all N by N
matrices
mmul(N,A,B,C);
```

In order to Grid-enable this program, one could easily replace this with

```
double A[N][N], B[N][N], C[N][N]; // C = A * B, all N by N
matrices
grpc_call(mmul_grpc_handle, N,A,B,C);
```

As an example, the defined IDL for Ninf-G, an implementation of GridRPC, would be as follows (abridged):

```
Module mmul;
Define mmul(IN int n, IN A[n][n], IN B[n][n], OUT C[n][n]);
Required mmul.o
```

Note that this programming style is quite different from that of CORBA, in which the IDL generator generates skeletons from IDLs that the user must supplement using CORBA-specific data types. It is also different from SOAP-RPC, where the basic data types are XML—although Web services frameworks such as .NET may feature support of explicit serialization/deserialization of language-level arguments to/from XML. Note also that underlying Grid services, such as authentication and resource management, are not called explicitly in the program but are managed by the GridRPC system, which calls lower-level Grid services automatically.

Because of differences in the protocols and the APIs as well as their functionalities, interoperability between GridRPC systems, including the two systems NetSolve and Ninf, has been poor. There had been crude attempts at achieving interoperability between NetSolve and Ninf using protocol translation via proxy-like adapters (497), but for various technical reasons full support of mutual features proved to be difficult. Thus, a working group has been established within the Global Grid Forum to define a GridRPC standard (496). To date, a standard API has been defined, thus enabling application portability among different GridRPC systems; further work is needed to address run-time features needed to achieve interoperable GridRPC systems. The NetSolve and Ninf teams have implemented the current draft standard, thus establishing feasibility; the former bases the implementation on the original NetSolve, and the latter is the Ninf-G system, a full new implementation that make extensive use of Globus Toolkit features. Other recent work (586) has shown that GridRPC can be effectively built upon future Grid software based on Web services such as OGSA. Figure 24.3 illustrates the architecture of a GridRPC system.

24.4.2 GridRPC Usage

GridRPC systems have demonstrated their viability as easy-to-use Grid programming tools for various applications. For example, the NetSolve farming API was used to develop a simple parallel implementation of the MCell computational neuroscience application (611), which was deployed over hundreds of processors

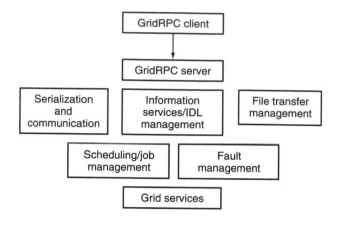

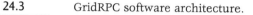

24.3   GridRPC software architecture.

FIGURE

(154). Other examples of NetSolve applications include the IPARS reservoir simulation application (89), the SCIRun environment (517), and the prototyping of the Collaborative Environment for Nuclear Technology Software (CENTS). Ninf has been applied to various branch-and-bound complex optimization problems, such as the BMI eigenvalue problem (62), genetic algorithm, and successive convex relaxation methods (SCRM) (623), as well as a Monte-Carlo weather prediction application. In all cases, Grid-enabling each given existing application was straightforward, involving simply identifying the calls that would benefit from remote execution on the Grid, in particular to exploit task parallelism over abundant computing resources.

24.5   SATIN CASE STUDY

Many applications can benefit from the enormous amount of unused processing power available worldwide. Systems such as Entropia (180) (Chapter 11), Condor (446) (Chapter 19), SETI@home (79), XtremWeb (257), and many others have shown that, at least for some applications, it is indeed feasible to exploit these resources effectively. An interesting question is how general is this approach of distributed computing. Can we also run parallel applications designed for more traditional high-performance computing platforms (supercomputers and clusters) on a Grid? The communication overhead in a wide-area distributed system is orders of magnitude higher than that of the local interconnects used in supercomputers and clusters. The available bandwidth of wide-area networks may improve dramatically, but high latencies will always remain a fundamental obstacle, as they are ultimately limited by the speed of light.

The Albatross project has studied the Grid execution of a range of algorithms and applications. The key insight from this work was that applications should exploit hierarchy by minimizing wide-area communication and/or hiding wide-area latencies. For many applications, simple optimizations such as message combining and caching improved wide-area speedups substantially. The result was that a surprisingly large set of applications could effectively use multiple Grid resources (526, 561).

The goal of Satin is to provide an easy-to-use task-parallel programming environment for Grid computing that supports not just master-worker or embarrassingly parallel applications but the broader class of *divide-and-conquer* applications. This model is chosen not only because of its broad applicability but because it has the advantage of being inherently hierarchical. In principle, we can exploit the insights gained in the Albatross project to map divide-and-conquer applications efficiently onto hierarchical large-scale distributed systems, such as Grids built from clusters or supercomputers.

24.5.1   Satin Software

To ease programming and increase portability, Satin is based on the Java language and provides a straightforward programming model. A Satin program is a single-threaded, sequential Java program extended with simple mechanisms to create subtasks ("divide") and process the results ("conquer"). At the lower level, Satin builds on base Grid infrastructure provided by the Globus Toolkit. The main challenge addressed by Satin is to balance all the subtasks efficiently over the Grid in a way that is transparent to the user.

The Satin programming model is based on the MIT Cilk system (128), implemented in Java. A Satin program is a single-threaded Java program extended with primitives to create subtasks and to wait for the results from subtasks. Figure 24.4 shows a simple example, Fibonacci. The new primitives are expressed in Java using special "marker" interfaces (e.g., ibis.satin.Spawnable), so no language changes are needed.

A task that is spawned can be executed on any processor. However, to reduce communication overhead, most tasks are executed by the processor that spawned them. Nevertheless, any spawned task can in principle be "stolen" by a remote machine. A key problem in running a Satin program efficiently on a Grid is how to partition the subtasks among the different machines. Satin uses a surprisingly

```
interface FibInter extends ibis.satin.Spawnable {
 public long fib(long n);
}

class Fib extends ibis.satin.SatinObject implements FibInter{
 public long fib(long n){
 if(n<2)return n;

 long x=fib(n-1);//Spawn operations, because
 long y=fib(n-2);//fib is tagged in FibInter.
 sync();

 return x+y;
 }

 public static void main(String[]args){
 Fib f=new Fib();
 long res=f.fib(10);
 f.sync();
 System.out.printIn("Fib 10="+res);
 }
}
```

24.4   An example divide-and-conquer program in Satin.

FIGURE

simple, new load-balancing algorithm, called cluster-aware random stealing (CRS)
(504). CRS implements a mix of synchronous and asynchronous work-stealing
strategies to hide the latencies of wide-area links while guaranteeing good load
balance with low overhead.

A major problem in implementing Satin is how to deal with Grid heterogeneity. Satin is based on Java, which (because of its virtual machine technology) is
inherently more portable than compiled languages. To benefit from Java's "write
once, run everywhere" portability, however, the entire Satin system would have
to be written in pure Java, making it difficult to obtain high performance. Satin
solves this dilemma using the Ibis (505) portability layer. Ibis is a communication
system that consists of a pure-Java base system running on any JVM. This base
system uses several important optimizations to obtain reasonable performance.
For example, it uses a bytecode rewriter that takes as input an object class and
adds efficient methods (in bytecode) to serialize and deserialize objects of this
class. These generated class-specific (de)serializers are far more efficient than a
generic (de)serializer that uses run-time inspection. Ibis serialization is further
optimized to avoid memory copies. In addition to this pure-Java base system, Ibis
allows further performance optimizations using native code, such as a native communication library (e.g., for Myrinet) or even a native compiler. At the bottom

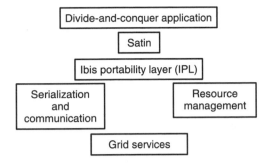

24.5

FIGURE

The software architecture of Satin.

level, Ibis leverages the base Grid software infrastructure provided by the Globus Toolkit (276) (Chapter 4). The entire Satin/Ibis system thus is highly portable, while still allowing low-level performance optimizations and leveraging deployed Grid services. The architecture of the software is depicted in Figure 24.5.

24.5.2   Satin Usage

The Ibis-based implementation of Satin has been tested on several Grid platforms. Satin was initially developed on the Dutch DAS (Distributed ASCI Supercomputer) system and its successor DAS-2, both of which are homogeneous wide-area systems consisting of multiple geographically distributed Pentium/Myrinet clusters. A dozen parallel applications were measured, virtually all of which obtain high speedups, even close to the speedup on a single centralized cluster with the same number of CPUs. These experiments show that divide-and-conquer indeed is a powerful and effective model for writing efficient distributed supercomputing applications on a hierarchical Grid.

Satin was also used on part of the European GridLab testbed, a highly heterogeneous platform. Satin was able to solve a single parallel problem using a Pentium/Myrinet cluster (DAS-2) in Amsterdam, a Pentium/Ethernet cluster in Poznan, a Sparc server in Amsterdam, and an Origin2000 in Potsdam, all at the same time. The Globus Toolkit provided the fundamental capabilities for resource allocation and file transfers. This experiment involved three different CPUs, three different operating systems, and three different countries, showing that Java's "run everywhere" property indeed makes it easier to deal with heterogeneous Grids and can be used effectively in conjunction with base Grid infrastructure.

24.6   MPICH-G2 CASE STUDY

In contrast to some of the other Grid programming tools described in this chapter, the approach described in this section is almost radical in its simplicity. However, it in fact delivers a remarkably sophisticated technology for managing the heterogeneity associated with Grid environments. Specifically, the approach is to use a well-known parallel programming model, the Message Passing Interface (MPI), as a basis for Grid programming. Although not a high-level programming model by any means, MPI incorporates sophisticated support for the management of heterogeneity (e.g., data types), for the construction of modular programs (the communicator construct), for management of latency (asynchronous operations), and for the representation of global operations (collective operations). These and other features have allowed MPI to achieve tremendous success as a standard programming model for parallel computers. The MPICH-G2 system described here and other Grid-enabled MPI implementations make it possible to use these same features to good effect for Grid computing.

The primary interest of MPI from the perspective of Grid computing, apart from its broad adoption, is the care taken in its design to ensure that underlying performance issues are accessible to, not masked from, the programmer. MPI mechanisms such as asynchronous operations, communicators, and collective operations all turn out to be useful in Grid environments. The MPICH-G2 project is focused on providing positive answers to the three following questions: Can one implement MPI efficiently in Grid environments to *hide* heterogeneity without introducing overhead? Second, can one use MPI constructs to enable users to *manage* heterogeneity, when this is required? Third, do users find MPI useful in practice for Grid application development? From a software perspective, one motivation is to provide a standard Grid MPI implementation that leverages the base Grid software infrastructure and can thus be deployed on any Grid resource.

24.6.1   MPICH-G2 Software

MPICH-G2 is a complete implementation of the MPI-1 standard plus the client-server management functions found in Section 5.4 of the MPI-2 standard (333). More specifically, it is structured as Grid-enabled (and Grid-aware) process management and communication modules for the widely used MPICH implementation of MPI (334). These modules use Globus Toolkit mechanisms (276) to address various obstacles to secure, efficient, and transparent execution in heterogeneous, multisite environments, including cross-site authentication, the need to deal with

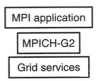

MPICH-G2 software architecture.

multiple schedulers with different characteristics, coordinated process creation, heterogeneous communication structures, executable staging, and collation of standard output. In fact, MPICH-G2 serves as an exemplary case study of how Globus Toolkit mechanisms can be used to create an application-level Grid programming model, as depicted in Figure 24.6.

MPICH-G2 also provides some support for management of heterogeneity, via various mechanisms designed to map low-level systems characteristics into MPI constructs. For example, MPI communicator attributes are used to make system topology information available, while the experimental MPICH-GQ (566) system has demonstrated the ability to achieve high-level management of network quality of service parameters. We refer the reader to technical articles for more details (402, 403, 566).

24.6.2   MPICH-G2 Usage

MPICH-G2 has been used extensively for large-scale application development in a surprisingly wide variety of contexts. One interesting use is to run conventional MPI programs across multiple parallel computers within the same machine room. In this case, MPICH-G2 is used primarily to manage start-up and to achieve efficient communication via use of different low-level communication methods. Other groups use MPICH-G2 to distribute applications across computers located at different sites (72, 99, 524), as described for example in Chapter 16.

Dail et al. (210) report on experiments conducted on a Grid testbed consisting of three sites (University of California, San Diego; University of Tennessee, Knoxville; University of Illinois, Urbana–Champaign) in which MPICH-G2 was used to run several parallel iterative applications. Although the main purpose of the work was to investigate resource selection and application scheduling issues, it provides a clear demonstration that it is straightforward to implement/port MPI applications to MPICH-G2 while benefiting from the Grid software infrastructure (in this case for security/authentication, resource discovery, start-up, monitoring, and control).

MPICH-G2 has also been successfully used as an application-level interface to Grids for nontraditional distributed computing applications, for example, for creating distributed visualization pipelines using MPICH-G2's client-server MPI-2 extensions (333).

24.7   APST CASE STUDY

The APST system that we describe here is concerned with automating the execution of parameter study applications (PSAs) (see Section 24.3.1) in Grid environments. Its goal is to provide for both *transparent deployment* and *automatic adaptive scheduling* of both data and computation. To achieve ubiquitous deployment, APST builds on Grid infrastructure for discovering, using, and monitoring storage, compute, and network resources. To maximize the set of resources that it can use, APST is designed to be able to function with limited numbers of services. For example, if services for resource monitoring are not fully deployed, APST should still function but may likely achieve lower performance. Also, because PSAs are long-running, APST implements fault-detection restart mechanisms for application tasks, and checkpointing for recovery from crashes of APST itself. (See Chapter 19 for further discussion of resilience issues.)

24.7.1   APST Software

APST runs as two distinct processes: a daemon and a client. The *daemon* is in charge of deploying and monitoring applications. The *client* is essentially a console that can be used periodically, either interactively or from scripts. The user can invoke the client to interact with the daemon to submit requests for computation and check on application progress. The user interface is XML-based, does not require modification of the user's application, and could be easily integrated with more sophisticated interfaces available in other Grid application execution environments (56, 689) and Grid portals (506, 646).

Figure 24.7 shows the architecture of the APST software. The computing platform consists of storage, compute, and network resources that are accessible via deployed Grid services, as shown at the bottom of the figure. The central component of the daemon is a *scheduler* that makes all decisions regarding the allocation of resources to application tasks and data. To implement its decisions, the scheduler uses a *data manager* and a *compute manager*. Both components use Grid services to launch and monitor data transfers and computations. In order to

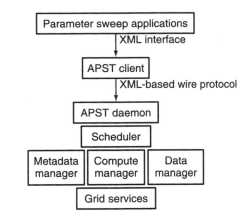

24.7

FIGURE

The APST software architecture.

make decisions about resource allocation, the scheduler needs information about resource performance. As shown in the figure, the scheduler gathers information from three sources. The data manager and the compute manager both keep records of past resource performance and provide the scheduler with that historical information. The third source, the *metadata manager*, uses information services to actively obtain published information about available resources, such as CPU speed information from the Globus Toolkit's monitoring and discovery service (204; see Chapter 20). A predictor, not shown on the figure, compiles information from those three sources and computes forecasts, using techniques from the Network Weather Service (NWS; 682). These forecasts are then used by the scheduling algorithms implemented in APST. The cycle of control and data between the scheduler and the three managers is key for adaptive scheduling of PSAs onto Grid platforms. The scheduling strategies used by APST (155, 156) are completely transparent to the user.

The current APST implementation leverages base Grid services to deploy and monitor applications. We provide a brief description of these capabilities. Compute resources can be accessed via the Globus Toolkit's GRAM (205). Thus, APST inherits the security and authentication mechanisms available from the GSI (280). As a default, APST can use SSH to access individual resources (making it possible to go through firewalls and to private networks). APST can read, copy, transfer, and store application data among storage resources with GASS (117), GridFTP (64), or SRB (100). APST can also use cp, Scp, or FTP. APST can obtain static and dynamic information from the MDS and NWS information services, and also learn about resource performance by tracking past performance when computing application tasks or transferring application data.

Several research articles provide more information on APST, describing and evaluating its scheduling heuristics (155), presenting experimental results obtained on an international Grid (156), describing a computational neuroscience application (151), and discussing the latest APST implementation and usability issues (152).

24.7.2   APST Usage

APST started as a research prototype for exploring adaptive scheduling of PSAs on the Grid platform. Since then, it has evolved into a usable software tool that is gaining popularity in several user communities. The first application to use APST in production was MCell (611), a computational neuroscience application. Since then, APST has been used for computer graphics applications, discrete event simulations (435, 624), and bioinformatics applications (76, 243). There is a growing interest in the bioinformatics community as biological sequence matching applications all fit under the PSA model. APST is currently the base technology used to support the Encyclopedia of Life (EOL) computational biology application.

While interacting with users, we have learned the following lessons. At this stage of Grid computing, many users are more concerned with usability than with performance. A significant number of disciplinary scientists are still running their applications on single workstations just because no particular effort is required, just time. It was surprising to realize that, even for parallel applications as simple as PSAs, there are still many hurdles for users to overcome. APST provides a good solution because it does not require modification of the application, because it requires only a minimal understanding of XML, and because it can be used immediately within a small local area network with default mechanisms. Users can then easily and progressively transition to larger-scale Grids because APST transparently builds on the base Grid software infrastructure. This is a great strength for a Grid application execution environment, as user communities can embrace Grid technology progressively.

24.8   SUMMARY

Our focus in this chapter has been on generic, high-level application programming tools that can be used for writing and deploying applications on Grid platforms. While application- and domain-specific endeavors have provided striking evidence of the potential of Grid computing, generic tools that enable broad classes of applications are critical to widespread acceptance of Grid technology by large user communities. We have identified requirements for these tools. A critical requirement is that they must build on base Grid software infrastructure to implement new functionalities. Also, most tools act as mediators between the user and the Grid infrastructure by providing automated resource discovery, selection, and access, as well as managing all the logistics of application deployment. The tool must be easy to use, in that it provides an implementation of concepts that can be directly manipulated by application developers and users.

We have distinguished between two classes of application-level tools: Grid programming models and Grid application execution environments. Grid programming models provide high-level abstractions that can be used to write applications, along with run-time support for these abstractions. Often, the programming models are inherited from traditional parallel computing and must be extended to accommodate Grid platforms. At the same time, new programming models that take advantage of the specific characteristics of the Grid platform and support emerging classes of Grid applications are being developed. By contrast, Grid application execution environments are integrated software tools in which users can "drop" their applications and have the illusion of a desktop execution while the tool deploys the application on Grid resources automatically and transparently.

We have proposed a taxonomy of Grid application-level tools and, within each subcategory, have listed representative tools and projects in the Grid computing community. We described four classes of Grid programming model—remote procedure call, message passing, task parallelism, and Java programming—and Grid application execution environments for parameter sweep applications, workflow applications, and Grid portals. Finally, we presented four detailed case studies, three involving programming models and one application execution environment.

To ensure a large Grid user community in the future, developers of application-level tools must leverage the still maturing Grid software infrastructure so that end users can benefit from Grid computing today. Many projects described here predate the Open Grid Software Architecture (279) and thus initially provided their own infrastructure. Although much was learned from these works, the current community OGSA standardization effort is an important driving force for wide adoption of Grids in science as well as industry. Thus, many early Grid application-level tools have been or are being redesigned to comply with and build on OGSA infrastructure. We hope that this transition will spur the development of the Grid-enabled debuggers, profilers, code analyzers, and verifiers—and integrated development environments (IDEs) that are currently lacking.

The main goal of Grid application-level tools is to render Grid capabilities accessible to not just individual heroic users but entire end-user communities. To accelerate the development of Grid-enabled tools and applications, we must make it possible for software tool developers and software engineers to leverage existing knowledge of software science and engineering, such as advanced component technologies, program analysis and verification techniques, compiler and run-time optimization techniques, program refactoring, and separation of concerns.

The establishment of OGSA will have a profound impact on application-level tools, as techniques from component-based software engineering have now become eminently applicable. By defining what is in effect a component model for Grid computing, OGSA will foster composability of components and services, an important characteristic for advanced Grid deployment. The programming models that we highlighted in this chapter provide rather low-level abstractions (e.g., RPC). We expect that, because of OGSA and its composition capabilities, new and higher-level programming models will become possible, as described earlier. These models can include domain-specific components that embed domain-specific knowledge.

It is certainly not the case that these advanced software development capabilities come for free just by subscribing to OGSA. Application-level tools that implement these new programming models so that they can be used for next-generation Grid applications are needed. As Grid computing becomes mainstream and Grid applications more diverse—ranging from high-performance scientific computing to business transaction-based computing—increasingly sophisticated software engineering concepts will be needed and will be leveraged by application-level tools.

If the Grid is to become a platform used by a broad user community, it must provide sophisticated application development environments. Although the tools described in this chapter are a first step, the current state of the art of Grid software development support is still in its infancy. We anticipate that application development tools (e.g., compilers, debuggers, profilers, monitors) will be integrated into full-fledged IDEs for Grid applications. These environments will borrow from ideas in the field of traditional parallel computing as well as from currently available environments used in industry, such as Microsoft Visual Studio.

OGSA provides a powerful software abstraction for application development and deployment. However, although its functionality is being carefully established, the question of performance remains somewhat unexplored and may suffer from the presence of many software layers. This situation is natural and has been seen in other large infrastructure developments: first the appropriate concepts are defined and a reference implementation provided, after which the infrastructure is optimized and refined. Although OGSA performance may not be crucial for some applications (e.g., scientific applications that perform most of their communications using other means), it will be a major impediment for transaction-oriented applications common in the business world and emerging in scientific computing. Thus, we anticipate that much application-level tool development work will focus on performance issues so that the base infrastructure can be used efficiently, via for example both static compilation and dynamic optimization techniques.

ACKNOWLEDGMENTS

We acknowledge contributions to this chapter by Rob van Nieuwpoort, Jason Maassen, Thilo Kielmann, Rutger Hofman, and Ceriel Jacobs (Satin); James Hayes and Francine Berman (APST); Hidemoto Nakada, Craig Lee, and Keith Seymour (GridRPC); and Nicholas Karonis and Brian Toonen (MPICH-G2).

FURTHER READING

For more information on the topics covered in this chapter, see *www.mkp.com/grid2.*

Languages, Compilers, and Run-Time Systems

Ken Kennedy

*G*rids pose many new challenges for application developers—challenges that go far beyond those for scalable parallelism. These challenges present so significant a burden for application developers that many are discouraged from considering the Grid as a computational platform. As a result, programming for Grids remains primarily a domain for experts. If the Grid is to realize its potential as a broadly accessible problem-solving platform, application development must be made dramatically easier. To achieve this goal, we need powerful new application development support tools that facilitate the programming process without degrading performance to unacceptable levels.

In this chapter we consider the prospects for the emergence of needed application development tools, focusing in particular on tools to support tightly coupled parallel computations. (See Chapter 24 for a discussion of other Grid programming tools.) We begin by reviewing application development technologies developed for scalable parallel computers and discuss how these technologies might be extended for heterogeneous distributed systems. We also review existing software support for Grid application development. Finally, we describe a new approach pioneered by the Grid Application Development Software (GrADS) research project and the component technologies needed to support the GrADS approach.

25.1 GRID COMPUTING CHALLENGES

Grid computing presents significant new problems and opportunities for programming language designers, compiler implementers, and run-time system developers. As on homogeneous parallel computers, we must deal with concurrency; however, distributed systems also exhibit a number of additional qualities:

+ Distributed systems can be heterogeneous; that is, the components may vary in both power and architecture. Differences may also include data formats.

+ Distributed systems may exhibit long and variable latencies. Latencies can be significantly longer than those of scalable parallel systems and may be variable: Latencies to different nodes may be different in duration, and latencies may vary with network traffic.

+ Distributed systems may have limited and varying bandwidths among components. This characteristic is due to the nature of the networks and variations on the loads that those networks must support.

These differences make development of applications for Grids significantly more complex than for homogeneous parallel computers. Thus, because application developers remain limited in their ability to deal with complexity, we need new and dramatically more powerful ways of supporting the development of Grid applications. The principle that each component should do what it does best suggests the following decomposition of responsibilities between developer and system:

+ The application developer should be free to concentrate on problem analysis and decomposition at a fairly high level of abstraction.

+ The system, including the programming language and compiler, should handle the details of mapping the abstract decomposition onto the computing configuration available at any given moment.

+ The application developer and the system should work together to produce a correct and efficient program through the use of execution monitoring, debugging, and tuning tools.

We concentrate here on the problem of developing tightly coupled applications (i.e., applications that might otherwise run on parallel computers) for Grid platforms that comprise multiple, geographically distributed systems of substantial capability (e.g., parallel supercomputers) interconnected by a high-speed network. At the high end, national-scale systems such as the 1995 I-WAY (219), NASA Information Power Grid (394), German Gigabit Testbed West (246), and NSF-funded TeraGrid (162) are models for this kind of platform. (At the end of 2003, for example, the TeraGrid comprises five parallel computers totaling 20 teraflop/sec peak capability, connected by a 40-gigabit/sec network.) At a more moderate scale, we can point to configurations comprising a set of clusters within a corporation, university campus, or metropolitan area: for example, the Illinois-area Distributed Optical Testbed.

Despite high bandwidths, Grid networks and other resources are likely to be in high demand and so may suffer (from the perspective of any single application) from contention—which, as discussed in Chapter 26, can have a dramatic impact on performance. Thus, we may need to deal with variability in bandwidth, latency, and resource performance both when matching an application to a computing configuration and during application execution.

In order to be truly efficient on the envisioned target configurations, applications need to employ parallelism in several dimensions:

✦ Among the nodes of the computing configuration, which will typically be task or object parallelism.

✦ Within a parallel computer that forms a single node, which corresponds to the parallel computing problem of today.

✦ Within a single processor of a node, used to overlap computing with data access or instructions with one another.

The goal of application development support software is threefold: (1) applications should be easy for the average scientific programmer to develop, (2) applications should be portable to different computing configurations, and (3) applications should achieve performance close to what is possible by an expert programmer using the underlying features of the network and computers forming the configuration. We explore technologies here that might be able to meet these goals in the not-too-distant future. Many of these technologies are extensions of those developed for parallel computing, but new ideas that may bridge the gaps between parallel and distributed computing are beginning to emerge.

The principal problems to be addressed are (1) balancing the load across a heterogeneous configuration in a way that minimizes running time, matching the communication to the underlying network bandwidths and latencies, and (2) dealing with the facilities in the system and network to ensure that performance variability remains within certain bounds. Here we concentrate on the role of the language, compiler, and run-time library in this process, building on the efforts of the system and network designers and implementers.

25.2   LESSONS FROM PARALLEL COMPUTATION

A number of parallel computing technologies need to be explored for potential use in Grid computing configurations: for example, fully automatic schemes, language extensions for data and task parallelism, libraries encapsulating distributed computations and data structures, compiler techniques for latency tolerance and management, and load-balancing schemes.

25.2.1 Automatic Parallelization

Automatic parallelization is an appealing approach for the user: if a fully automatic system could efficiently parallelize applications for distributed heterogeneous networks, the user would be free to concentrate on the application, focusing on *what* is being computed rather than *how* it is being computed. To be successful, a fully automatic scheme must generate code that achieves performance competitive with programs hand-coded by experts.

Automatic parallelization has proved effective for vector computers because the required parallelism was reasonably fine grained (74). However, it has been less successful for asynchronous parallelization, for both shared- and distributed-memory machines. Increasingly complex analysis and optimization technologies have allowed research compilers to parallelize a number of interesting programs (68, 74, 348, 423, 680). However, because of the complexity of the techniques, the long compiler running times, and the small number of successful demonstrations, few commercial compilers attempt to parallelize whole applications on scalable parallel machines. Thus, although this research has yielded important new compilation techniques, automatic parallelization will not by itself solve the parallel programming problem.

Since Grids, with both heterogeneity and variable latencies, are even more difficult to program, there is little hope that fully automatic techniques will suffice. Mechanisms that involve the programmer in design of the parallelization as well as the problem solution are required, just as they have been for parallelization on scalable systems.

25.2.2 Explicit Communication

Given that most scalable parallel machines offer some form of distributed memory and that many require explicit communication through message passing to get data from remote memories, the use of message-passing libraries has emerged as an important programming strategy.

To use such a library, the programmer typically produces a version of the program that runs on each processor, with the code being specialized to the specific processor through the use of environmental inquiry functions. This style of programming, called the *single-program multiple-data (SPMD)* model (212, 396), can be used in a shared-memory environment, but it more commonly requires explicit communication to access data residing in remote memories. In the send-receive model, therefore, the program for each processor must not only determine and receive the data it needs to access on other processors but also determine the data it owns that other processors need, and communicate that data through sends.

The send-receive style of programming was supported on many early parallel systems (287) but proved inadequate for architecture-independent parallel programming because each different machine offered a machine-specific communication interface. With the advent of the parallel virtual machine (PVM) (107), a widely supported de facto standard, and the message-passing interface (MPI) (20, 601), a community-generated standard for message passing on homogeneous machines, it became possible to write send-receive programs in an architecture-independent form.

Some communication systems support a get-put model in which the processor that needs data from a remote memory is able to explicitly get it without requiring explicit action by the remote processor. Active messages (245) are an example of such a system.

In either the send-receive or get-put model, the programmer is responsible for decomposition of the computation and load balancing, the layout of the data and management of latency, and organization and optimization of communication. These requirements make it particularly burdensome even for homogeneous machines. For heterogeneous Grids, the programmer would be required to decompose the program to match the explicit power of the individual processors of the Grid, losing some of the architecture independence and making the problem more difficult. Nevertheless, a Grid-enabled version of MPI, MPICH-G (403), has been developed (see Chapter 24 and Section 25.3).

Although explicit communication is an important tool for application development on Grids, the complexity of using it leads us to consider approaches that will be accessible to a larger community of users. In that sense, explicit communication can be thought of as an assembly language for Grids.

25.2.3 Data-Parallel Languages

Early in the research efforts on parallel computing, Geoffrey Fox and others observed that the key to achieving high performance on distributed-memory machines was to allocate data to the various processor memories to maximize locality and minimize communication. If each computation in a program is then performed on the processor where most of the data involved in that computation resides, the program can be executed with high efficiency.

A second important observation was that if parallelism is to scale to hundreds or thousands of processors, data parallelism must be effectively exploited. Data parallelism is parallelism that derives from subdividing the data domain in some manner and assigning the subdomains to different processors. This strategy provides a natural fit with data layout, because the data layout falls naturally out of the division into subdomains.

These observations are the foundation for data-parallel languages, which provide mechanisms for supporting data parallelism, particularly through data layout. A number of such languages were developed by researchers and companies, including Fortran D (286, 360), Vienna Fortran (171), CM Fortran, C*, and PC++ (170). These research efforts were the precursors of two informal standardization activities leading to high-performance Fortran (HPF) (15) and high-performance C++ (HPC++) (392). Most of these languages provided directives for data layout. These directives have no effect on the meaning of the program. Instead, they merely serve as advice to the compiler on how to assign elements of the program arrays and other data structures to different processors for high performance. This specification is done in a relatively machine-independent fashion, so once the specifications exist, the program can be tailored to run on any of a variety of distributed-memory machines.

The major drawback to the use of data-parallel languages for Grid computing is the same as for message-passing programs: these languages do not allow the user to specify dynamic load balancing of the form needed to adapt to the available compute and communication resources at program launch and execution time.

25.2.4 Task-Parallel Language and System Support

An alternative to data parallelism is task parallelism, in which the components to be run in parallel represent different computations or different functions. The client-server model is an example of task parallelism, as is a multidisciplinary simulation where each discipline simulator runs in parallel with synchronizations to exchange data. Task parallelism is extremely well suited to Grids because different tasks can be allocated to different Grid nodes.

Task parallelism is supported by many Fortran variants, especially those designed for operation in conjunction with threads packages on shared-memory computers. However, task parallelism need not be restricted to such computers.

It can certainly be defined in terms of any communications library, for example. OpenMP (169) specifies extensions to both Fortran and C that support task parallelism in a manner consistent with the directive-based philosophy of HPF: If the task-parallel directives are ignored, the program has the same meaning as it does with the directives taken into account. OpenMP makes it possible to specify a set of cases to be run in parallel with no (or only minor) synchronization until the computation's end. Clearly, such task-parallel extensions to Fortran could serve as a basis for decomposition of tasks for Grid execution. Many problems remain, however, including load matching and communication optimization.

Another interesting source of task parallelism is coarse-grained software integration. One specialized application of this approach is object parallelism, in which different tasks may be methods associated with objects of different classes (432). Another case is the complete application that is not a simple program, but rather a collection of programs that must all run, passing data to one another, before the problem is solved. Typically these programs are integrated through the use of a system-level scripting language, but other approaches may also be used. The main technical challenge of the integration is preventing performance degradation caused by sequential processing of the various programs or tasks in the collection. For distributed heterogeneous processor collections, methods similar to those used for task parallelism can be employed to introduce parallelism into the collection of programs. Each program is viewed as a task, and tasks are collected and matched to the powers of various Grid nodes.

25.2.5 Load Balancing

On current scalable parallel machines, load balancing means spreading the calculations evenly across processors while minimizing communications. A number of useful strategies have been defined, most of which are based on standard numerical optimization procedures including simulated annealing and neural nets (287). Another useful approach is recursive bisection, where at each stage of the load-balancing computation, the work is divided into two equal parts.

On distributed heterogeneous collections, load balancing becomes more difficult because the power of each node in the Grid must be taken into account. Nevertheless, load balancing—or, more precisely, *load matching*—is a critical problem that must be solved before we can reasonably attack the problem of compiling for Grids.

25.2.6   Latency Tolerance and Management

Compiler research has produced two general techniques for dealing with long memory or communication latencies on parallel computers: *latency hiding*, in which data communication is overlapped with computation, and *latency reduction*, in which programs are reorganized to effect better reuse of data in local memories. These techniques have proven very effective in practice (74).

Both techniques are more complex to implement in compilers for the Grid, but latency hiding is especially problematic because Grid latencies are large and variable. This requires that more time be spent on estimating running time and communication delays if we are to be able to determine how far ahead to prefetch variables values. It also means that latency-tolerant algorithms assume increased importance.

25.2.7   Run-Time Compilation

A significant problem with automatic load-balancing schemes is that some needed information, such as loop upper bounds and array sizes, is not known until run time in many applications. This lack of information is also an issue for problems defined on irregular grids, which are difficult to parallelize even on homogeneous parallel machines.

To deal with these problems, Saltz and his colleagues devised the *inspector/ executor method* for run-time compilation (480, 684). In this approach, the compiler subdivides key computations within the program into two parts: an *inspector*, which is executed only a single time once the run-time data are available to establish a plan for efficient execution on a parallel machine, and an *executor*, which is invoked on each iteration of the computation and carries out the plan defined by the inspector.

The idea behind this scheme is to amortize the cost of run-time compilation over many time-steps of a complex computation. In the simple case of unknown loop upper bounds, the inspector would strip-mine loop nests into subloops that matched the powers of the target machines once the values of the upper bounds were known, while the executor would simply carry out the computation in the correct subloop for each machine. For irregular problems, where the inspector must follow a complicated load-balancing step, both the inspector and executor are more complicated.

Run-time compilation can be a powerful tool for tailoring a program for execution on any parallel machine. For heterogeneous distributed computing, it is crucial.

25.2.8   Library Encapsulation

An increasingly important strategy is to encapsulate parallelism in libraries. Two distinct variants of this strategy are in use for scalable parallel machines:

+ The *functional library*, in which parallelized versions of standard functions are applied to user-defined data structures. Examples are ScaLAPACK for dense linear algebra (123), FFTW for fast Fourier transforms (297), and aggregate communication libraries with functions such as shift, global sum, and segmented scan.

+ The *data structure library*, in which a parallel data structure is maintained within the library whose representation is hidden from the users. This approach, which is well suited to object-oriented languages, has been used in the DAGH library (516), which provides a distributed, adaptive grid data structure that is callable from Fortran, along with a number of parallel template libraries usable from C++, including P++. Another example would be a library to build and operate on quad trees for Fortran *N*-body simulations.

Although functional libraries provide much more control to the user program, data structure libraries can encapsulate algorithms that work only on specialized data structures. By combining parallelism in the algorithm with parallelism in the data structure, the data-structure approach provides maximum flexibility to the library builder to manage run-time challenges such as heterogeneous networks, adaptive meshes, and variable latencies.

One drawback of libraries is that current compilers treat them like black boxes. Therefore, with library-defined data structures one cannot take advantage of opportunities to simplify compound calculations. For example, if the program suggests that the transpose of a matrix be multiplied by another matrix, it might be possible to do so without moving data if the underlying implementation can be opened up for examination. This suggests that collaboration between compiler and library might be useful, particularly in an interprocedural compilation environment.

25.2.9   Programming Tools

Both hand programming and compiler- or library-based approaches suffer from significant deficiencies from the viewpoint of the user. Hand programming provides great flexibility but is particularly burdensome on the programmer. Approaches based on powerful compilers and libraries, on the other hand, often do not offer the programmer enough flexibility to identify performance bottlenecks and overcome them. As a result, both approaches benefit from a significant investment in programming support tools. Tools such as Jumpshot (695) and Pablo (550) can identify performance bottlenecks (see Chapters 20 and 26 for further discussion). Low-level programs can then be corrected by hand, whereas more abstract programs will need some additional tools to help restructure programs to improve performance, such as the Parascope Editor (407), a tool that implements "safe" source-to-source transformations, guaranteed to maintain the meaning of the original program.

A particularly promising approach is to employ tight collaboration between tools and compilers. A specific example can be provided in the context of the HPF language described earlier. A joint project between Rice University and the University of Illinois built a tool for performance tuning of HPF that used an HPF compiler to provide information about program transformations and the relationship of program source to the eventual object program (61). After the performance data were collected by Pablo instrumentation, the compiler information was used to map any discovered performance problems back to the original source. Nevertheless, even though this made it much easier to identify performance problems, programmers still needed some way to revise the program to eliminate these problems. In HPF, this typically meant restructuring the program. To address this issue, the project developed tools to carry out advanced source-level transformations that could help overcome performance bottlenecks.

In general, programming tools can be useful in a variety of contexts, helping the user construct correct and efficient programs with less effort. These tools will be even more important for Grids, where flexible parallelism and latency tolerance can have huge effects on the performance of applications.

25.3   PROGRAMMING TOOLS FOR THE GRID TODAY

One popular strategy for implementing Grid applications today is to write message-passing applications on top of the Globus Toolkit infrastructure (276) (Chapter 4) using MPICH-G (275, 403), a Grid-enabled version of the MPI message-passing standard (20). However, although MPICH-G and other tools described in Chapter 24 make it *possible* to write Grid programs, they do not make it *easy*. Most of the hard work of application development—resource selection and mapping, communication management, and adapting to varying loads on Grid resources—is left to the developer. If the Grid is to become broadly accessible to the technical user community, programming support systems must take a much larger portion of the load from the shoulders of the application developer.

Another popular approach involves the use of task farming and workflow systems, of which Condor (444, 446) and Chimera (284, 285) are examples (see Chapters 10, 19, and 24). These systems use the Globus Toolkit infrastructure to map applications expressed as bags of tasks or as directed acyclic graphs to available compute resources. However, they are not designed to deal with more tightly coupled applications.

These considerations lead us to the GrADS project, which is attempting to provide a powerful, integrated approach to building and executing applications on the Grid.

25.4   THE GrADS APPROACH

The *Grid Application Development Software* (GrADS) project (112) seeks to address the fundamental challenge of program development for Grid environments. This project has undertaken since 2000 a coordinated program of research, prototyping, and technology transfer aimed at the central problems of programming models, algorithms, programming systems, and applications.

Underlying and unifying this effort's diverse investigations is a basic assumption: effective application development for Grid environments requires a new approach to the design, implementation, execution, and optimization of applications. A new strategy is needed because the traditional development cycle of separate code, compile, link, and execute stages assumes that the properties of underlying resources are static and relatively simple. In the Grid, this assumption is not valid. (Needless to say, the alternative approach, frequently adopted in distributed computing, of hand coding applications with socket calls or remote procedure calls, is not viable either.) Instead, the Grid requires a software development environment that enables the effects of dynamism to be mitigated and controlled.

In addition, the usefulness of the Grid will be severely limited if application development continues to be as complex and labor intensive as it is today. If the Grid is to become a broadly accessible problem-solving resource, we must raise significantly the level of abstraction at which programs are developed. One long-term vision is to make it possible for scientists and engineers to develop applications in easy-to-use languages such as MATLAB (347). To achieve this goal, we need to provide tools, compilers, and libraries that will help automate the construction of acceptably efficient Grid applications from high-level inputs.

Addressing these two issues is the goal of the GrADS project. GrADS has developed a new program development and execution structure, called GrADSoft (Figure 25.1). In this system, the discrete steps of application creation,

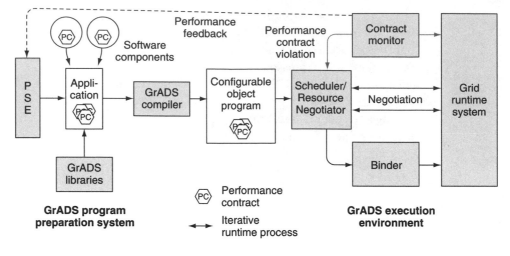

GrADS program preparation and execution architecture.

compilation, execution, and postmortem analysis are replaced with a continuous process of adapting applications to a changing Grid and to a specific problem instance. Two concepts are critical to the working of this system. First, an application must be encapsulated as a *configurable object program*, which can be dynamically mapped for execution on a specific collection of Grid resources that are not known until launch time. Second, the system relies on *performance contracts* (Chapter 26) to specify the expected performance of the application on the available resources. Contracts are used to determine when the performance of an application is enough below expectation to merit a rescheduling step.

The remainder of this section summarizes the key ideas underlying the GrADS effort and explains in detail the technical challenges being addressed and the approach being followed in each area. If the GrADS project succeeds in achieving its long-term goals, it should dramatically reduce the effort required to develop Grid applications and should dramatically broaden the community of users of the Grid itself.

25.4.1   Configurable Object Program

At the heart of the GrADS system depicted in Figure 25.1 is the *configurable object program* (COP), which serves as the standard application format required for GrADS execution. The configurable object program is intended to be a portable program representation that can be executed on many different collections of Grid resources. To make this possible, a COP must contain, in addition to code, components that can be used to help automate mapping and load balancing on collections of resources.

To this end, a configurable object program in the current GrADS framework is based on a parallel application in the form of an MPI program, but also includes two specialized callback routines: a *mapper*, which determines how to map the computation and communication in the application onto a given set of resources (provided as a parameter); and a *performance estimator*, which approximates the performance that the application will achieve on a given set of resources. Note that the performance estimator may invoke the mapper as a preliminary step.

The role of the performance estimator is to serve as an objective function for the scheduler/resource negotiator depicted in Figure 25.1, while the mapper determines how to handle load matching for the best performance.

In a sense, one can view a configurable object program as an application on an abstract parallel machine. This machine takes collections of parallel tasks and automatically handles all the details of matching the loads from the component tasks to the computation and communication resources available at program launch time. The implementation of this abstract parallel machine is within the GrADS execution environment, described in the next section.

25.4.2 GrADS Execution Environment

The principal task of the GrADS execution environment is to automate the process of mapping and executing a configurable object program on an arbitrary collection of Grid resources that fall within the space of resources acceptable to the application. To do this, it must use the callback mapping and performance estimation functions to handle resource allocation and load balancing. In addition it must manage the complex task of adapting the application to the dynamically changing nature of Grid resources.

To this end, when a configurable object program is presented to the execution system, the GrADSoft infrastructure carries out the following steps (depicted in Figure 25.2):

1. The execution system instantiates an application manager to oversee the process of launching and running the application.

2. The application manager, by consulting the program's mapper, provides an initial feasible space of resources to the scheduler/resource negotiator.

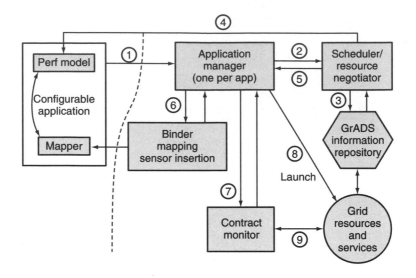

25.2

FIGURE

25.2   Program launch in the GrADS execution system.

FIGURE

3. The scheduler/resource negotiator contacts the GrADS information system to request sets of feasible resources—that is, resources that meet the requirements of the application. The information provided also includes the performance of individual compute resources and the communication links interconnecting those compute resources.

4. The scheduler/resource negotiator then solves an optimization problem using the application's performance estimator as an objective function to find the best match of the application to the available resources.

5. Once the best set of resources is determined, the resources are reserved, and the program launch begins.

6. The binder is invoked to instantiate the mapping and to provide launch-time tailoring of the application to the resources on which it will run. In addition, the binder inserts the sensors and actuators required for the performance monitor, also called the contract monitor.

7. The contract monitor process is launched on the Grid.

8. The application itself is launched on the Grid.

9. During execution, the application continuously communicates with the contract monitor via the inserted sensors. If the contract monitor

determines that performance is falling sufficiently below estimates, it signals that a contract violation has occurred. The application manager can then decide to reschedule or migrate the application onto a different set of resources.

25.4.3   GrADS Program Preparation System

The left-hand side of Figure 25.1 depicts the tools used to construct configurable object programs. The goal is to build tools that free the user from many of the low-level concerns that arise in programming for the Grid today and to permit the user to focus on high-level design and performance tuning for the heterogeneous distributed computing environment.

We expect that most application developers will eventually use high-level problem-solving environments (PSEs) to assemble Grid applications from toolkits of domain-specific components (e.g., MATLAB enhanced with additional domain-specific libraries). Another path will allow developers to build the specialized components that form these PSE toolkits (e.g., a library for solving PDEs on Grids) or to create new modules for their specific problem domain. In either scenario, modules are written in derivatives of standard languages with Grid-specific extensions (e.g., data or task distribution primitives). They are bound together into larger components, libraries, and applications with a coordination language. This process creates malleable modules, annotated with information about their resource needs and predicted performance for a wide variety of resource configurations.

Although the long-term GrADS focus is to achieve this vision of high-level programming, the effort to date has focused on tools that assist the programmer in constructing the performance estimators and mappers that are required components of configurable object programs. This effort is pursuing four general directions:

1. *ClassAD import.* Because Condor ClassAD specifications (see Chapter 19) are so widely used, it should be possible to import mappers and resource selection strategies implemented as ClassADs into the GrADS infrastructure. To accomplish this, the GrADS project has extended the ClassAD language to allow specifications to refer to resource sets (448), a critical capability for Grid scheduling. In addition, the project has implemented an importer tool that translates a performance model and mapper written in the extended ClassAD interface into a GrADS performance estimator and mapper.

2. *Automatic construction of mappers.* A common representation for parallel programs is the *task graph,* in which vertices represent computational tasks and edges represent communication dependences. Task graphs can be used to represent SPMD programs by annotating each task with the set of (virtual) processors that participates in its execution. GrADS research has explored task graph mapping strategies as a way of automatically constructing mappers. The current approach is to use graph-clustering algorithms to eliminate expensive communications or to map them to fast communication links.

3. *Automatic construction of performance estimators.* The GrADS strategy for automating the construction of performance estimators is to use analysis and editing of application binary codes to instrument a program, multiple trial executions to determine the impact of various parameters on performance and the way that performance scales, and curve fitting to produce a final model. In preliminary experiments, this approach has proved extremely successful, with the constructed models often outperforming models hand coded by experts.

4. *Component integration.* If we are to support the development of high-level programming interfaces described earlier, it must be possible to integrate performance estimators and mappers from components written by experts into effective estimators and mappers for whole programs. Although it is too soon to tell how well this will work, evidence suggests that such an approach could be quite effective. If component integration can be carried out successfully in the GrADS framework, it should pave the way for more sophisticated domain-specific problem-solving environments.

25.4.4   GrADS Accomplishments

The GrADS project has succeeded in constructing a prototype execution system that includes all the critical components except rescheduling and migration. This framework was demonstrated at the national high-performance computing conference SC2002. Within that execution framework, GrADS has successfully run six applications:

✦ A version of the ScaLAPACK parallel LU decomposition benchmark (123)

✦ The Cactus numerical relativity toolkit (69, 72) (see Chapter 16)

✦ The sequence-matching application FASTA (522)

✦ A second sequence-matching application that uses the Smith–Waterman algorithm (598)

◆ GrADSAT, a satisfiability application used in circuit design

◆ An HPF version of the SPEC95 benchmark mesh generation program Tomcatv, for which the mapper and performance estimator were automatically constructed

To support evaluation of the application efforts, GrADS researchers have constructed two research testbeds: the *MacroGrid*, which consists of Linux clusters with GrADS software installed, and the *MicroGrid*, a software testbed that permits modifying Grid performance parameters on demand.

The GrADS infrastruture is currently only a prototype, but over the next several years the developers hope to make the system more complete and robust and to spin the key software systems off into Grid middleware to exist on top of the Globus Toolkit.

25.5 COMPONENT TECHNOLOGIES

A number of auxiliary technologies are needed to support the GrADS application development and execution framework. This section discusses some of the research issues that must be dealt with if the component technologies are to suffice for the task.

25.5.1 Performance Estimation

Performance estimation is difficult because it attempts to reason about complex architectures with incomplete information about the program and its data structures. Our target architectures have complicated memory hierarchies with differing cache structures, latencies, bandwidths, and interprocessor communication costs. Furthermore, the target may be executing in a multiprocessing environment in which many applications share the underlying hardware. The problem is made worse by the complexity of the program and the dependence of the performance on various data values that may not be known until run time (399).

These complications lead us to three conclusions. First, performance estimation must be done interprocedurally, so that the entire program can be taken into account. Second, some performance estimation must be done at launch time, when the resources on which the program is to run become known, and some must be done at run time, because assumptions made by the performance estimator about data values must be reconsidered if they are grossly wrong. Finally, the performance estimation may still be inaccurate enough to require that it be modified after the program runs for some period of time. Thus, if the performance estimation was so far off that it is seriously affecting the actual performance, work may need to be migrated from one node in the distributed system to another. Furthermore, the performance of one run may need to be saved to affect the configuration for the next run.

These considerations suggest a level of complication that is far beyond what compilers and systems are able to deal with today. On-demand Grid scheduling will require performance estimators that are up to the task. Thus, automatic construction of performance estimators seems essential to making Grid application development accessible to a broad community of users.

25.5.2   Mapping

Mapping, or more precisely the automatic construction of mappers, is a critical component of the GrADS strategy. The goal of this process is to produce a good match between the computational requirements of the tasks within a computation and the computational power of the underlying compute resources. This matching must also address the issues of communication, which can be critical to the performance of the overall application. In other words, the mapper is responsible for the complex task of load matching to Grid resources.

The overall goal is to produce mappers that assign computation and communication in such a way that the entire computation finishes as early as possible. One approach is to employ classical scheduling techniques. For a task graph, this means using some form of list scheduling, in which tasks on the critical path to completion are scheduled to start at the earliest possible time (104). Although this approach leads to some important insights, list scheduling is not ideally suited to the Grid for two reasons. First, list scheduling maximizes parallelism, which is not always the best way to handle scheduling on the Grid. Second, it fails to handle communication effectively because it tends to assign a fixed delay to each communication, determined by the aggregate data volume to be communicated. Thus, it fails to take into account the possibility that no communication is required if the computations at the source and sink of the communication are scheduled onto the same resource. In other words, it cannot sacrifice parallelism to minimize communication.

These considerations have led GrADS to look at different strategies, based on graph clustering, to build task-graph mappers. The basic idea behind these mappers is to assign the computations at the endpoints of expensive communication edges to the same processor, even if it means sacrificing some parallelism. This suggests a node fusion process that attempts to collapse along the heaviest edges

(405). Additional research is needed to determine the effectiveness of such approaches; however, preliminary experiments in the GrADS project have confirmed the promise of the idea.

25.5.3 Whole-Program Compilation and Integration

Despite much research on whole-program and interprocedural compilation (74, 143, 194), few commercial compilers actually do it systematically, particularly across files. The reason is that whole-program compilation significantly complicates the compilation environment. Although its benefits to program correctness and performance have been well documented (475), most users are unwilling to suffer the associated increases in compile time. In the future, however, the penalties for inefficient compilations will be so large and the compilation problems so great that interprocedural compilation will become a necessity rather than a luxury—particularly when compiling for distributed heterogeneous Grids.

A number of problems remain to be resolved in interprocedural compilation:

✦ An interprocedural compilation system to support the GrADS framework must be able to integrate performance estimators and mappers for the entire application from those same functions for individual components. Thus, interprocedural compilation is needed because an execution model for the entire program must be constructed.

✦ Management of the location of binaries will be an essential function at program launch time. In order to avoid expensive staging of component binaries, it will be important to link program parts against shared component libraries that have been stored in advance on the remote compute resources on which a program will run. Optimizing for this contingency will be a key capability of the interprocedural compilation system.

✦ Management of the recompilation of files in a program will be essential to keep compile times from becoming unacceptably long. Although some research exists on the problem of recompilation analysis, no commercial compiler yet incorporates it.

✦ Recompilation management is even more complicated if run-time information from previous runs is incorporated into the compilation decisions of the current run. The compilation environment will need to be sophisticated enough to manage this process.

✦ Some interprocedural analysis will need to be done at link time and run time. How to effectively manage this process is an open problem.

25.5.4   Run-Time Compilation

Run-time compilation comes in many forms. It may be as simple as reconsidering decisions after some scalar data are read into memory or as complicated as planning communication in an irregular computation whose underlying Grid and location are not known until key data structures are defined.

For Grids, it may be necessary to reconfigure and load balance an entire program at run time, a process likely to be time-consuming, so strategies for minimizing the cost of such steps will be needed. In general, research will be needed on how to minimize the cost of making important, complex decisions at run time, as there are going to be more and more situations in which they will be required.

25.5.5   Libraries

The high-level language strategy that GrADS is pursuing will require extensive libraries of component software to be used by the system to optimize performance. As the HPF experience has demonstrated, all of the standard libraries must be capable of accepting the data types provided in the language—scientific programmers expect no less.

Some high-level programming support strategies being considered by the GrADS project also depend on preprogrammed components for handling computations and managing the data structures. Thus, extensive work will be needed to understand the nature of these libraries and ways to implement them so that they can be effectively integrated and optimized by the interprocedural compiler into a correct and effective configurable object program.

25.5.6   Programming Support Tools

The strategies envisioned for application development establish a complex relationship between the source version of the program and the version that runs on the Grid. Science and engineering users must be able to understand the performance of a given program and to tune the program when performance is unacceptable. Furthermore, the explanation of program behavior must be presented in terms of the source rather than the object version (61). Otherwise, the advantages provided by language abstraction will be lost. This task becomes particularly challenging when some of the compilation process is done at run-time.

The compiler and language must also provide mechanisms that permit program performance to be improved once the bottlenecks have been identified.

Thus, performance-improving changes must typically be made in terms of the program source, lest they be lost before the next run. To support this, the tools must understand the relationship between the structure of the program and typical performance problems, and they must be able to make transformations based on that understanding.

25.6   SUMMARY

Support for application development on Grids presents new challenges to the compiler and run-time system, including load balancing, latency and bandwidth management, and problem decomposition. Although many of the key technologies developed for scalable parallel computation can be applied, these technologies need to be extended and augmented to handle the new challenges presented by heterogeneous distributed computing configurations.

The Grid Application Development Software project is pioneering technologies that will make it easier to develop applications for the Grid without sacrificing acceptable performance. At the heart of the GrADS system is the configurable object program, which includes a mapper and performance estimator in addition to a standard MPI program. The mapper and performance estimator are used by the GrADS execution system to handle resource scheduling and load balancing, two tasks that currently must be carried out by the application developer.

The GrADS effort is also developing tools to help automate the construction of configurable object programs. These tools, which include automatic constructors for performance estimators and mappers, draw on a variety of traditional technologies from parallel computing, including global performance estimation, interprocedural compilation and program management, run-time compilation, libraries, and sophisticated program development tools.

ACKNOWLEDGMENTS

I am particularly grateful to the editors for numerous criticisms and corrections. The ideas underlying the NSF-sponsored GrADS project, including the compilation and execution architectures described in Figure 25.1 and 25.2 were developed in collaboration with many people, including the principal investigators of the GrADS project: Fran Berman, Andrew Chien, Keith Cooper, Jack Dongarra, Ian Foster, Dennis Gannon, Lennart Johnsson, Carl Kesselman, John Mellor-Crummey, Dan Reed, Linda Torczon, and Rich Wolski—and many other researcher in GrADS, especially Dave Angulo, Henri Casanova, Holly Dail, Anshuman Das Gupta, Shridhar Gullapalli, Charles Koelbel, Anirban Mandal, Gabriel Marin, Mark Mazina, Celso Mendes, Otto Sievert, Martin Swany, Satish Vadhiyar, Shannon Whitmore, and Asim Yarkan. Finally, the GrADS program manager at NSF, Frederica Darema, has deeply influenced the philosophy and direction of the project.

FURTHER READING

For more information on the topics covered in this chapter, see *www.mkp.com/grid2* and the following references:

+ The *Sourcebook of Parallel Computing* (237) is an excellent source of information about parallel computing technologies and strategies. In particular, it includes chapters covering HPF, OpenMP, and Co-Array Fortran.

+ *Optimizing Compilers for Modern Architectures* (74) is a comprehensive treatment of compiler technologies for parallel computation, including dependence analysis, vectorization, parallelization, and memory hierarchy management. It includes chapters on interprocedural analysis and compilation of Fortran 90 and HPF.

+ *Parallel Computing Works!* by Fox, Williams, and Messina (287) compiles an enormous amount of information about parallel computation, particularly in the early days of distributed-memory machines.

+ An article by Berman et al. (112) provides a complete overview of the GrADS project.

+ An article by Adve et al. (61) gives an overview of considerations in designing programming tools that are integrated with the language compiler system.

Application Tuning and Adaptation

Daniel A. Reed, Celso L. Mendes, and Charng-da Lu

*G*rid applications often must deliver reliable performance despite the use of distributed resources. As discussed in Chapter 18, one step in addressing this requirement is to allow resource consumers and resource providers to negotiate service-level agreements (SLAs) that define commitments on the part of consumer and provider. Such agreements permit applications and other system components to organize their activities and to provide performance guarantees.

However, SLAs also introduce significant new questions. We need to be able to determine what SLAs should be negotiated, which can often be a nontrivial task, particularly if we wish to express agreements in application-level terms. We must also allow the possibility of SLAs being violated, perhaps by preemption or failure. Thus, we require monitoring mechanisms for detecting SLA violations. Finally, there will always be resources that do not support SLA negotiation. We require mechanisms not only for negotiating SLAs but also for determining application requirements, mapping those requirements to SLAs, detecting violation of SLAs, and adapting to those violations—all with a goal of harnessing resources to deliver reliable application-level performance, even when the performance or availability of those resources may change during application execution.

This chapter describes a number of mechanisms that can be used to address these problems. After a brief illustration of performance variability, we introduce the notion of a *performance contract*, a form of SLA between application and resource that quantifies expectations between application performance demands and resource service capabilities. We present *contract monitoring* techniques that use performance data to verify that expectations are being met—and/or to detect when, and diagnose why, performance falls outside acceptable bounds. Finally, we discuss how applications can respond when contracted specifications are not satisfied, so as to achieve continued satisfactory progress. We describe, in particular, adaptive control techniques that an application can use to adapt to a new resource regime. We conclude with an overview of current challenges and likely next research steps.

26.1   RESOURCE AND PERFORMANCE VARIABILITY

As Grids evolve, we can expect to see increased deployment of resource management interfaces that permit negotiation of service-level agreements, as discussed in Chapter 18. However, the typical Grid environment is still likely to include resources that are subject to contention: for example, computational resources exploited in an opportunistic fashion (e.g., see Chapter 28) and resources (e.g., in many cases, networks and storage systems) that do not support reservations. In addition, even resources that support SLA negotiation can fail or be preempted. Thus variability in the performance and availability of Grid resources is inevitable.

Resource variability can have a major impact on application performance, as we illustrate with results from a computational astrophysics code based on the Cactus package (70) introduced in Chapter 16. This code implements the so-called Wavetoy configuration, which simulates the tridimensional scalar field produced by two orbiting sources. The solution is found by finite differencing a hyperbolic partial differential equation for the scalar field. This simple application is representative of a large class of more complex systems, including Einstein's equations for gravitational interaction, Maxwell's equations for electrodynamics, and the Navier–Stokes equations for fluid flow.

During execution, Wavetoy first reads a configuration file that defines various simulation parameters. Consider a simple Wavetoy execution with 500 iterations and a domain of size $X = 300$, $Y = 150$, $Z = 30$ on a test Grid consisting of two Linux clusters, one at the University of Illinois and the other at the University of California, San Diego. These particular tests are based on an MPICH-G version of Cactus built atop the Globus Toolkit version 2.0 (72, 403).

Table 26.1 shows the execution times of Wavetoy for three different Grid resource scenarios. The first row in the table corresponds to an execution where all the participating nodes were idle. The second row shows the execution time when an external job was concurrently executing on one of the Illinois nodes. The third row shows the time when an external load was induced at both

Grid scenario	Execution time (s)
Nodes exclusively used by Wavetoy	138
One Illinois node shared	245
One Illinois node and one California node shared	446

26.1

Wavetoy Execution Times on Eight Grid Processors under Different Scenarios.

TABLE

sites. We see that even small variations in the environment can dramatically change the observed application performance. Given that such contention is frequently not predictable, we conclude that the only way to pursue high performance in a shared environment is to *adapt* the execution, by either real-locating resources or changing the application behavior given changing resource availability.

26.2   PERFORMANCE CONTRACTS AND ADAPTIVE CONTROL

Given an application and a set of Grid resources with nominal performance characteristics, one might derive models that predict performance under ideal conditions. Such models typically include computational speeds, network latency and bandwidth, and I/O speed, and they have been useful when analyzing performance on parallel systems. However, as we have seen, the dynamic nature of the Grid can result in observed performance that differs from model predictions. Similarly, measurements of application performance are rarely repeatable because, ipso facto, the execution environment is not repeatable. This innate variability exacerbates performance analysis, application tuning, and satisfaction of performance expectations. To deliver "reliable" performance, Grid systems and applications must in general be able to *adapt* dynamically to changing conditions.

Adaptive techniques can include acquiring new resources, reducing solution accuracy, and switching to alternative algorithms. However, a prerequisite for any form of adaptive control is a framework for talking about what performance is acceptable and mechanisms for detecting when adaptation is required.

We describe here how a form of SLA called performance contracts can be used to approach adaptive structures. Intuitively, a performance contract specifies that, given a set of resources with certain characteristics and for particular problem parameters, an application will achieve a specified performance during its execution. The term *contract* is chosen by analogy to civil law. Each party to a contract has certain obligations, which are described in the contract. Case law, together with the contract, also specifies penalties and possible remediations if either or both parties fail to honor the contract terms. Witnesses and evidence provide mechanisms to assess contract validity. Finally, the law recognizes that small deviations from the contract terms are unlikely to trigger major penalties (i.e., the principle of proportional response).

Grid performance contracts are similar. They specify that an application will behave in a specified way (i.e., consume resources in a certain manner) given the availability of the requested resources. Hence, a performance contract can fail to be satisfied because either the application did not behave in the expected way or the resources requested were not available. Equally important, Grid contracts embody the notion of flexible validation. For example, if a contract specifies that an application will deliver 3 gigaflops/processor for 2 hours and measurement shows that the application actually achieved 2.97 gigaflops/processor for 118 minutes, one would probably consider such behavior as satisfying the contract. Intuitively, small perturbations from expected norms, either in metric values or in their expected duration, should be acceptable. Mechanisms for quantifying such discretion are the subject of Section 26.6.

To validate a contract, one must continually monitor both the allocated resources and the application behavior to verify that the contract specifications are met. Hence, the monitoring infrastructure must be capable of monitoring a large number of widely distributed system components without unduly perturbing behavior or performance.

Implicit in performance contracts is the need for an infrastructure to instrument applications and capture performance data amenable to contract verification. This instrumentation must be as automated as possible, or it will not be used. Users should not incur costly procedures to adapt their Grid applications to a contract framework.

In addition, instrumentation should not unduly alter the application's behavior; otherwise, the observed behavior will not be consonant with the actual behavior. Hence, instrumentation must be inserted at the proper level, capturing only those data required to validate the contract. As an example, in a multiply nested loop, it may become too intrusive to collect performance data from the inner loops; data from the outer loop level may be sufficient to characterize the fragment's behavior.

Moreover, one must select the appropriate metrics for contract validation. These metrics should be easy to collect, minimizing perturbation and intrusion, and should clearly characterize the behavior of the application on a given set of

Grid resources. If one considers each of the selected metrics as one axis in a multi-dimensional space, then application execution can be viewed as a trajectory through that space. This trajectory is the *execution signature* of the application on a given set of Grid resources. During contract verification, one must verify that the observed trajectory follows the expected path.

Combining instrumentation and metrics, a contract is said to be violated if any of contract attributes do not hold during application execution (i.e., the application behaves in unexpected ways or the performance of one or more resources fails to match expectations). Any contract validation mechanism must manage both measurement uncertainty and temporal variability (i.e., determining whether the contract is satisfied a sufficiently large fraction of the time to be acceptable). Reported contract violations can trigger several possible actions, including identification of the cause (either application or resource) and/or attempted remediation (e.g., application termination, application or library reconfiguration, or rescheduling on other resources).

Different solutions are potentially applicable, and the specific context will show which one is more appropriate. In some cases, migrating to another set of Grid resources is the right solution, whereas in other cases migration might be too expensive, and a dynamic adjustment of contract parameters might be more convenient. Either way, one needs formal mechanisms to specify, implement, and validate performance contracts. In the remainder of this chapter, we use this notion of performance contract as a basis for discussion of instrumentation techniques, application behavioral characterization, behavioral validation, and performance assessment.

26.3 AUTOMATIC PERFORMANCE INSTRUMENTATION

Measurements of application-intrinsic and system-specific performance metrics during application execution are important both for validating a contract and for identifying the proximate causes for a contract violation. Specifically, one may need to collect performance data from multiple execution sites at differing granularities (e.g., from microseconds to hours) and from multiple system levels (e.g., from hardware performance counters, communication and I/O libraries, and application stimuli). Hence, the infrastructure for collecting performance data must be efficient, scalable, and adaptable. The Grid monitoring architecture described in Chapter 20 is one archetype of such a system. The Autopilot toolkit (555) implements many of these components. Autopilot is a toolkit for real-time application and resource monitoring and control built on the Globus Toolkit

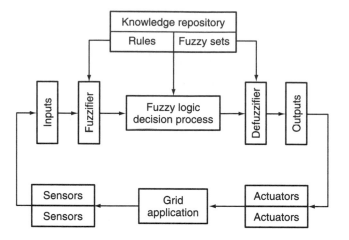

Autopilot performance measurement and control framework.

(Chapters 1:11 and 4). As Figure 26.1 shows, Autopilot includes distributed sensors for performance data acquisition, actuators for implementing performance optimization decisions, and a decision-making infrastructure for evaluating sensor inputs and controlling actuator outputs.

Autopilot sensors can be placed in either application or library code to capture software performance metrics. These sensors also support capture of hardware metrics via the PAPI toolkit (136). When an application executes, the embedded sensors register with an Autopilot directory service for use by contract monitoring software. Sensor clients can then query the directory service to locate sensors with desired properties and attach to those sensors to receive data. Because Autopilot is built atop the Globus Toolkit, the sensors, sensor clients, and directory service can be located anywhere on the Grid.

Autopilot sensors, like all instrumentation, can be inserted in a library, runtime system, or application code in a variety of ways. (These sensors can naturally be expressed as OGSA service data elements, as discussed in Chapter 17.) Traditionally, application developers have instrumented their source code by inserting calls to an instrumentation library. This process can be automated via parsers that locate instrumentable source code constructs and insert the requisite instrumentation calls. As an example, the SvPablo toolkit (223) contains Fortran and C instrumenting parsers that can automatically synthesize instrumentation for loops and procedure calls. The performance data produced during execution is then accessible via Autopilot sensors in real time.

Alternatively, one can use instrumented versions of Grid-aware libraries. For example, an instrumented version of MPICH-G (275, 403) can record wide-area communications among Grid application components. Similarly, instrumented I/O libraries (e.g., PVFS (442)) can provide details on application and file system I/O behavior. Through such library instrumentation, one can identify application performance bottlenecks and implement more intelligent, adaptive libraries.

Consider a set of routines that implements collective MPI operations. Based on observed communication latencies and bandwidths, the library might implement multiple versions of the same operations (e.g., for use across local or distributed resources). During execution, the first call to this library routine would capture current Grid conditions and choose an appropriate implementation for this and for subsequent calls.

One can also directly instrument application executables or compiled libraries. The Wisconsin Dyninst toolkit (139) enables modification of an executable either before or during its execution. By means of Dyninst, one can insert or remove instrumentation throughout application execution, selectively collecting performance data. Similarly, instrumentation can be inserted at specific execution phases, where the behavior is unknown, and removed after some of the data required for intelligent optimization has been obtained.

As an example of these techniques, consider a linear solver based on routines from the ScaLAPACK package, adapted for Grid use (524). The instrumentation techniques described previously can be applied to generate performance data during the solver's execution. One such implementation, which we explore in material to follow, instruments the application's binary code. Just before the application is launched, Autopilot sensors are inserted into the executable, and the code is staged for execution across the Grid.

Once execution begins, Autopilot sensors periodically collect performance data and report to attached clients. Hardware performance metrics are measured by using PAPI hardware performance counters, counts and durations of communication calls are obtained via the MPI profiling interface, and application behavior is monitored by using application-level instrumentation. The resulting data are used to compute execution signatures and to evaluate performance contracts describing expected behavior during execution.

Despite their effectiveness, the instrumentation techniques mentioned previously can produce a huge amount of performance data when applied to large-scale systems. In such cases, some form of data reduction is desirable. Statistical sampling may provide a cost-effective solution. Instead of monitoring each system component, we select a statistically valid subset of components, monitor this subset in full detail, and derive estimates for the whole system based on properties of the subset.

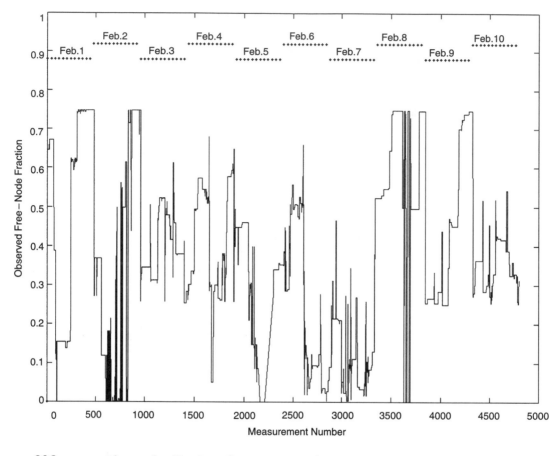

26.2   Observed utilization of NCSA's IA-32 cluster across periodic measurements.

FIGURE

Statistical sampling provides a formal basis for quantifying the resulting accuracy
of the estimation and guides the selection of a subset that meets certain accuracy
and confidence specifications.

As an example of this technique, we analyzed the utilization of NCSA's IA-32
cluster, in which application programs can run on up to 480 compute nodes. Each
node is a dual Pentium III box and is allocated exclusively for a job from one of
the submission queues. We collected periodic snapshots of node status information during the first 10 days of February 2002. For each snapshot, we conducted a
sampling experiment to estimate the number of cluster nodes having a status of
"Available." Figures 26.2 and 26.3 show, respectively, the observed and estimated

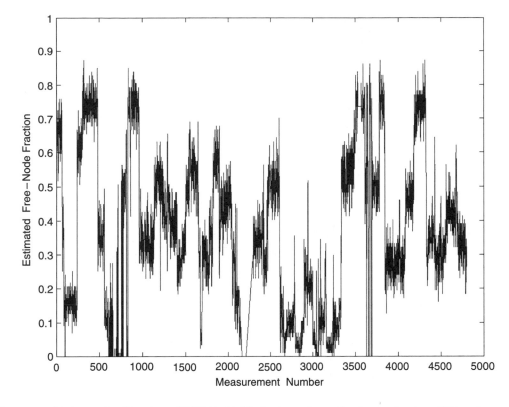

Estimated utilization of NCSA's IA-32 cluster using a fixed sample size of 87 nodes.

utilizations. Using as specifications a confidence of 90% and an accuracy of 8%, we obtain a sample size of 87 nodes; for details, see (472). We see that this sample size, representing less than 20% of the cluster size, is enough to track cluster utilization behavior quite well.

In another example, we simulated a much larger system, comprising 50,000 processors, executing a mix of randomly created jobs. Using the simulation data, we conducted several sampling experiments in which we varied the sampling specifications. For a given confidence/accuracy combination, we sampled the processors on each cycle to estimate the fraction of free processors. Table 26.2 shows the underlying sample sizes required. In all cases, the estimation fell within the specified range of accuracy. The table indicates that using a sample size as small as 106 processors (0.2% of the system size), one can still achieve an effective estimation.

Accuracy	Confidence			
	90%	95%	98%	99%
8%	106	150	211	258
5%	270	382	536	655
3%	741	1045	1460	1778

26.2

TABLE

Sample Sizes, in Number of Processors, for a Simulated System Comprising 50,000 Processors.

26.4   EXECUTION SIGNATURES

Event tracing is the standard measurement approach for obtaining detailed data on the execution dynamics of sequential, parallel, and distributed applications (547). Obtaining detailed data on *long-running distributed* applications, however, poses many challenges. First, the volume of captured performance data may be exorbitant, particularly if one measures fine-grained activities (e.g., procedure calls or intertask communications). Second, causal correlation across distributed resources requires a global time base whose accuracy is commensurate with the granularity of measured events. Conversely, statistical summaries are compact, even for long-running applications; however, such summaries sacrifice insights into temporal variability and causal interactions.

Execution signatures (452) are a lossy compression of trace data that captures performance metric dynamics while minimizing loss of temporal detail. The motivation for performance signatures is quantitative comparison and validation of application execution dynamics across platforms, input datasets, and configurations. In this model, each application has a performance contract that may specify performance expectations, scheduling constraints, and other requirements. When the Grid run-time system loads an application, the corresponding contract can be used by resource brokers to enable dynamic reconfiguration and negotiation between resource providers and the application throughout application execution.

Instrumentation that captures n metrics defines a time-varying trajectory $m(t)$ in an n-dimensional metric space. For each metric, an execution signature is a polyline fit of the trajectory, as shown in Figure 26.4a. The online polyline generation algorithm initially uses one line segment to fit the entire metric trajectory. It attempts to stretch the line segment by fitting as many metric points as possible until the measure of error, a least-squares goodness of fit, exceeds a user-specified error threshold. At this point, the algorithm terminates the current line segment, starts a new line segment, and repeats the previous step until the signature is generated.

Multiple executions of the same application, whether on similar or different platforms, usually result in different trajectories (e.g., because of shared resource use or different hardware capabilities). These perturbations result in nonlinear scaling of the trajectories (i.e., dilation or compression), similarly affecting the polylines fitted to them. Despite the distortion, it is often reasonable to view two polylines as similar even if one is a scaling of the other. Hence, removing the effects of scaling is critical to accurate signature comparison.

One of the simplest approaches to trajectory correlation relies on the insertion of special instrumentation at selected points (e.g., application phase transitions, key procedure invocations, or data movements). This instrumentation emits a "marker" with a unique identifier that the run-time system can use to correlate and compare two signatures, as shown in Figure 26.4b.

One can compare two curves in many ways. For computational efficiency, we have used a template metric $T(p,q)$ for online, quantitative similarity comparison of two signatures $p(t)$ and $q(t)$. The template metric $T(p,q)$ is defined as

$$\int |p(t) - q(t)| \, dt.$$

Geometrically, the template metric is the area difference between p and q, as illustrated in Figure 26.4c. Hence, the smaller the value of $T(p,q)$, the higher the similarity. Using the template metric, we can define the *degree of similarity* (DoS) of a signature q with respect to a baseline signature p:

$$\text{DoS}\,(p,q) = \max(0, 1 - T(p,q)/\int p(t)\,dt).$$

The DoS, which ranges between 0 and 1, is a measure of how close the application behaves in regard to the expected performance. Figure 26.5 illustrates signatures obtained from the Cactus Wavetoy code, using the number of bytes in an I/O request as the time-varying metric. Note that the time dilation across hardware configurations is captured by the markers, enabling signature comparison and correlation across execution contexts. This ability to quantify execution behavior across executions is central to online adaptive performance monitoring and control, as implemented by using fuzzy logic control for contract validation.

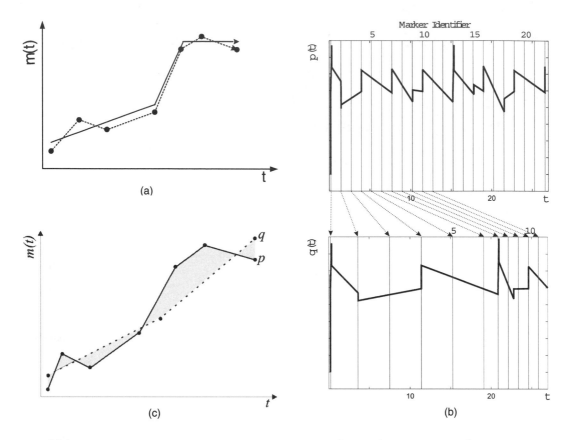

(a)

(c)   (b)

26.4

FIGURE

Execution signature construction and correlation. (a) Performance metric trajectory (dotted line) and the corresponding polyline fit. (b) Correlation of signatures via markers (vertical lines). (c) Similarity comparison of two signatures. The shaded area denotes the template metric $T(p,q)$.

26.5   FUZZY LOGIC CONTROL

Even on dedicated systems, application performance variations can be caused by interactions with operating system services and other applications. Hence, one cannot expect exact matches between observed and predicted performance; some variation is inevitable. As we have seen, the Grid can be an even more dynamic environment, necessitating some mechanisms for reasoning about performance variability.

Classical control techniques and decision tables or trees require in-depth knowledge of the control domain and handle uncertainty awkwardly. In contrast,

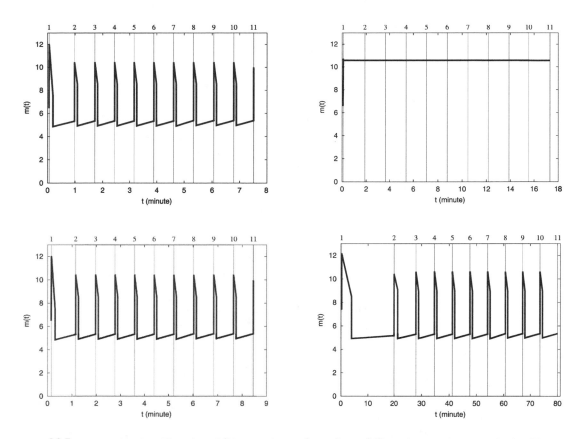

26.5

FIGURE

Cactus Wavetoy I/O signatures from four different execution contexts. Using context 1 as the baseline signature, the degrees of similarity for contexts 2, 3, and 4 are 0.16, 0.99, and 0.98, respectively.

fuzzy logic provides robust mechanisms for treating uncertainty (693, 694). Fuzzy logic allows one to specify behavioral rules qualitatively, rather than with hard quantitative limits (e.g., one should drive approximately 30 mph in a construction area rather than exactly 30 mph). Hence, the appeal of fuzzy logic for contract specification and validation is that violation transitions are smooth, rather than discrete. By analogy, breaking the speed limit is not a binary event, but rather a continuum that acknowledges measurement variability, environmental conditions, and context in determining violation severity.

Formally, fuzzy logic allows one to linguistically state violation conditions that should be represented in a Grid performance contract by means of a set of rules associated with fuzzy truth variables. Unlike Boolean logic values that are either true or false, fuzzy variables can assume a range of values, allowing smooth transitions between areas of acceptance and rejection. Using decision procedures based on fuzzy logic, one can quickly and easily change the rule set describing contract violation conditions to accommodate different modes of operation and levels of tolerance.

To illustrate use of fuzzy logic for Grid performance monitoring, consider a rule base defining two simple fuzzy variables, metricDistance and contractViolation, and linguistic rules for specifying the value of contractViolation based on the value of metricDistance, as follows. Here, the truth value of metricDistance is a function of its crisp input value, which can vary between 0 and 2:

```
var metricDistance (0,2) {
  set trapez LOW (0,0.5,0,0.5);
  set trapez HIGH (1,2,0.5,0);
}
var contractViolation (0,2) {
  set triangle NONE (1,1,1);
  set triangle TOTAL (0,1,1);
}
if(metricDistance == LOW)
  contractviolation = NONE;
if(metricDistance == HIGH)
  violation = TOTAL;
```

These sets and rules could form the knowledge repository for a simple Grid control system, as shown in Figure 26.1. Performance sensors provide measured performance data that can be compared with expected behavior via the knowledge repository, realizing possible behavioral remediations via actuators.

The crisp values for metricDistance result from comparing expected values for a given performance metric with the observed values obtained by means of a measurement sensor. Suppose the expected floating-point performance for an application when executing on a given processor is 5 megaflops. The crisp value of metricDistance would be the absolute difference between the measured performance and the expected value of 5 megaflops.

Depending on such crisp values for metricDistance, the truth values for the fuzzy variables LOW and HIGH are computed and combined to produce the fuzzy truth value of metricDistance. In turn, the rule base enables derivation of a truth value for contractViolation, based on the truth value assumed by metricDistance.

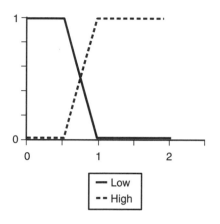

26.6

FIGURE

Fuzzy logic set for the variable metricDistance, defined by the two trapezoidal specifications.

Intuitively, each fuzzy variable has an associated transition function that maps crisp values to a degree of truth for the corresponding fuzzy members. The range of crisp values and the shape of the transition functions are controlled by the numeric values in the rule base. Thus, for each application and metric, one can create an appropriate rule base reflecting the expected execution behavior.

Figure 26.6 illustrates the transition function for the metricDistance variable just defined. Consider a measured (crisp) value of 0.8; both the LOW and HIGH fuzzy variables have some degree of truth. Hence, both linguistic rules mapping metricDistance to contractViolation would be applied, both NONE and TOTAL would each have a degree of truth, and the final violation output would indicate that a partial contract violation had occurred. By adjusting the numeric values in the rule base, one can tune the desired degrees of tolerance. Assuming an expected performance of 5 megaflops, as before, the fuzzy function in Figure 26.6 indicates that there are three possible cases to consider. First, metricDistance values between 0.0 and 0.5 (hence, an observed performance between 4.5 and 5 megaflops) imply no violation, because LOW is 1.0 and HIGH is 0.0. Second, a metricDistance value between 0.5 and 1.0, corresponding to an observed performance between 4.5 and 4.0 megaflops, corresponds to partial violation. Third, metricDistance values of 1.0 or more, corresponding to observed performance levels of 4 megaflops or less, result in total violation, because LOW is 0.0 and HIGH is 1.0.

26.6   ADAPTIVE CONTROL EXAMPLES

To illustrate the effectiveness of fuzzy logic adaptive control for Grid performance monitoring, we present an example showing end-to-end behavior, from application instrumentation, through monitoring and contract evaluation, to final analysis and ideas for remediation. As a test application, we use the Cactus Wavetoy code described in Section 26.1.

This integrated example also relies on the GrADs software infrastructure (112, 406) (Chapter 25). Under the GrADS software framework, an *application manager* performs the Grid equivalent of functions typically done by a linker or a loader on a sequential system. It acts on behalf of the user to prepare the application executable, selects and allocates appropriate Grid resources for application execution, creates and maintains a set of performance contracts, and launches both the application and a contract monitor.

Prior to launching an application, the *application manager* instruments the application code to capture performance data by inserting Autopilot sensors into the binary code. During execution, the sensors periodically send performance data to any connected clients. In this case, the client is a contract monitor task, which accepts sensor inputs, evaluates the rule base using those inputs, and determines whether contract violations exist. These contract outputs are distributed via sensors. A Java interface accepts metric data and contract outputs for real-time visualization.

As an example, Figure 26.7 shows the contract monitor display for the Wavetoy code's execution on two distributed clusters, one at the University of Illinois and another at the University of California, San Diego. Each bar in the figure corresponds to the contract evaluation for a given node, and the envelope over a bar indicates the *high watermark* for that contract. Because contract outputs are fuzzy variables, they can assume any value between 0.0 and 1.0. Values near 0.0 represent no contract violation, whereas values close to 1.0 represent large violations. In the figure, a load has been imposed on one of the distributed computing resources that host the code. This load skews the observed performance, and this delay is propagated across all tasks, resulting in some degree of violation on all processors.

The contract outputs in Figure 26.7 are computed as a fuzzy combination of individual contract outputs for each monitored performance metric. Thus, one can also analyze individual metrics to understand the causes of contract violations. Figure 26.8 shows the individual contract outputs for one processor. Figure 26.9 shows a combined view of the two most affected metrics for the same processor, in a scatterplot form. The bounded regions in the metric

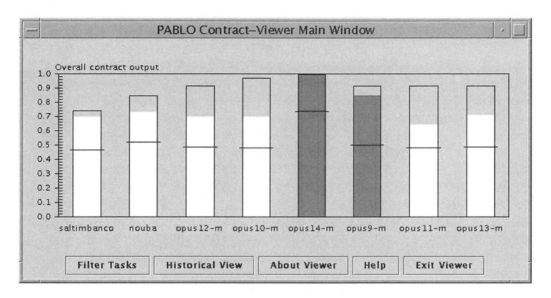

26.7

FIGURE

Pablo contract monitor GUI showing global contract outputs for execution of the Cactus Wavetoy code.

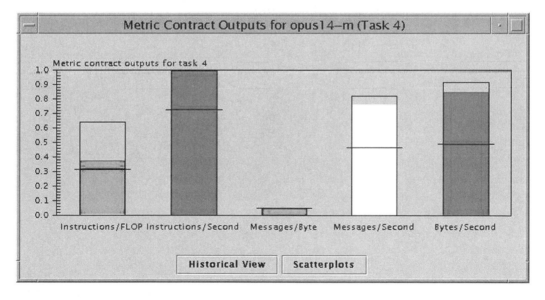

26.8

FIGURE

Pablo contract monitor visualization of Wavetoy contract values for individual performance metrics.

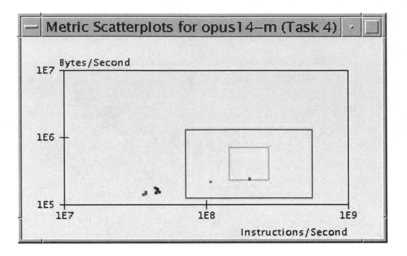

26.9

FIGURE

Pablo contract monitor visualization of contract regions and observed performance for two Wavetoy metrics.

space corresponding to the borders of the contract are codified in the rule base. Points inside the inner rectangle correspond to no contract violation, and points outside the outer rectangle correspond to a total violation. Points that lie between the two rectangles represent partial contract violations for those metrics.

Given this type of real-time contract monitoring, it is possible to redress contract violations, depending on their severity and duration. For example, one might choose to halt the execution. Alternatively, one might choose to migrate and reschedule a portion of the computation on resources not affected by external loads. The ability to stop, migrate, and restart an application requires some degree of application support, typically in the form of check-pointing.

This integrated example highlights both the power of real-time adaptive monitoring and control and the remaining challenges necessary to make it a practical reality. Most notably, current contract monitoring schemes have no mechanism to assess temporal variability and contract violations. Intuitively, a contract remains valid if the performance of most tasks is at or near expected levels most of the time. Formalizing the meaning of "most of the time" and "most tasks" is a critical area of research, as is assessment of control stability and rescheduling mechanisms.

26.7   SUMMARY

The field of performance analysis and optimization for Grid applications is still in its infancy. The need to execute efficiently in the face of resource contention and failure requires nimble, adaptive applications and middleware. Moreover, if Grids are to be widely deployed and embraced by users, these adaptive optimization mechanisms must be automated and largely invisible to application developers.

The performance contract mechanisms introduced here must be extended spatially and temporally. Spatial extension must support analysis and optimization across applications and Grids with potentially thousands of cooperating sites, resources, and services. This capability requires distributed contract validation to ensure contract validation scalability. A monitor corresponding to the entire resource set could combine outputs from distributed contract monitors. Similarly, one must assess the relative importance of violations associated with different resources (e.g., is poor computation performance more, or less, important than poor network performance for this current application?). Moreover, global contract optimization across multiple applications with conflicting resource needs will require new ways of reasoning about system balance and resource availability.

Temporally, several issues must also be explored. The contract outputs in the examples presented here were valid at a given instant without regard to previous application or system status. A more intelligent validation scheme would incorporate previous validations and make decisions based on both current and past states. Temporal logic could provide one formalism whereby contract violations arc charactcrizcd as a pattcrn of consecutive "instantaneous" violations. Such a mechanism would be much more resilient to dynamic variations.

Finally, despite promising early results in adaptive applications (406, 606), much work remains to be done on both basic adaptation techniques and tools to allow these techniques to be incorporated into applications at reasonable cost.

ACKNOWLEDGMENTS

Autopilot and SvPablo are the work of many graduate students, postdoctoral associates, and research staff, notably Ruth Aydt, Luiz DeRose, Pedro DeRose, Randy Ribler, Fredrick Vraalsen, Dan Wells, Shannon Whitmore, and Ying Zhang. This work was supported in part by the National Science Foundation under Grants NSF EIA-99-72884 and ASC 97-20202; by the Department of Energy under contracts DOE W-7405-ENG-36, LLNL B341494, DOE SciDAC DEFC02-01ER41205, and LLNL B505214; and by the NSF Alliance PACI Cooperative Agreement.

FURTHER READING

For more information on the topics covered in this chapter, see *www.mkp.com/grid2* and the following references:

+ An overview of real-time performance monitoring and examples of adaptive control systems (663)

+ An overview of the Autopilot performance monitoring toolkit (556)

+ A general reference on adaptive program control and steering (548) and an annotated bibliography on that area (337)

+ Relevant related works on dynamic optimization (631) and quality-of-service techniques for networked environments (494)

VII

PART

INFRASTRUCTURE

*T*he Grid is, as much as anything, an infrastructure, and its development and deployment are enabled by, and influences, the evolution of key infrastructure components. Hence, the four chapters in Part VII first discuss experiences gained in deploying several major production Grids, and then review the current capabilities and likely evolution of computational elements, peer-to-peer technologies, and basic network technologies.

Chapter 27, "Production Deployment: Experiences and Recommendations," presents a detailed analysis of the practical issues that arise when deploying Grid technologies in "production" environments: that is, Grids developed to enable large-scale scientific research rather than as testbeds for software development or computer science research. William E. Johnston and his coauthors—each a leading participant in one or more major Grid deployments—provide detailed technical descriptions of the technologies involved, discuss the steps involved in deploying and supporting these technologies, and also discuss the interpersonal aspects of a successful deployment.

In Chapter 28, "Computing Platforms," Andrew A. Chien examines the computational elements that act as endpoints in networks. These systems are evolving rapidly, concurrent with networks, protocols, and network interfaces. All computers will soon be multiprocessors. A variety of new interconnection technologies are arising, some similar to those used in wide-area networks and others not. New software systems are being developed to manage and program these increasingly complex computers. System area networks are blurring distinctions between a computer and the Grid of which it is a part. This chapter discusses these trends and their implications for Grids.

In Chapter 29, "Peer-to-Peer Technologies," Jon Crowcroft and his colleagues provide a comprehensive review of work in scalable, self-organizing distributed systems: what are often referred to as peer-to-peer systems. Peer-to-peer systems push the limits of scalablity and robustness, but tend to focus on more homogeneous resources and slower network connections than do contemporary Grids. However, peer-to-peer systems are a potential source of resources for Grid applications, and peer-to-peer research can be a source of scalable and robust algorithms that can be applied to Grid services.

Finally, in Chapter 30, "Network Infrastructure," Joe Touch and Jon Postel discuss the network technologies that tie together the diverse end-system technologies that are connected by the Grid. The next several years will see dramatic improvements in the performance of network components and the number of elements connected by networks. These changes and the new demands of emerging applications will stimulate significant changes in the basic services provided by the networks, beyond the best-effort services offered by today's Internet protocol. This chapter covers past, current, and future network infrastructure, addressing key networking technologies, the future of internetworking infrastructure, and the core services that can be expected in future networks.

Several chapters from the first edition that could not be included in the second edition of *The Grid* remain valuable sources of information.

Chapter 1:18, "Network Protocols," by Melliar-Smith and Moser, discusses advanced network protocols that expand the functionality of a network beyond simple message delivery. Next-generation applications demand a wide variety of enhanced services. Applications as diverse as distributed databases, distributed interactive simulation, and remote education require a variety of multicast services offering different forms of delivery guarantees. Multimedia and instrumentation applications are stimulating development of enhanced streaming protocols. Increased use of networked systems for time-critical applications is increasing demand for soft and hard real-time capabilities.

In Chapter 1:19, "Network Quality of Service," Guérin and Schulzrinne discuss mechanisms for managing network quality of service: the behavior experienced by an application on a network. This problem is challenging because of the substantial "semantic gap" that often exists between the quality-of-service requirements of an application (which may be expressed in terms of such abstract qualities as "teleimmersion fidelity") and the mechanisms actually provided in a network to manage traffic. This material is highly relevant to the discussion of service management in Chapter 18.

In Chapter 1:20, "Operating Systems and Network Interfaces," Druschel and Peterson examine these important components of a Grid and their impact on performance. In many systems today, the end-to-end, process-to-process performance perceived by applications can be degraded significantly relative to that of the network because of inefficient operating system structures, network interfaces, and protocols. Future Grid applications are likely to require new approaches in which networks are integrated with computers and operating systems at a more fundamental level than is the case today. These changes will, in turn, lead to dramatic reductions in network interface overheads and in the performance robustness of networked applications.

Finally in Chapter 1:22, "Testbeds: Bridges from Research to Infrastructure," Catlett and Toole address the important topic of Grid testbeds. Testbeds in which technologies and applications can be integrated and explored have been, and will continue to be, an important engine for progress. A variety of such testbeds have been constructed over the years, of increasing performance and sophistication. Early efforts focused on networking technologies; more recent activities have included substantial application efforts and the deployment of experimental software environments. This chapter reviews U.S. and international attempts to construct such testbeds, notes the lessons that these testbeds have taught us, and suggests approaches for future testbeds. Although the details of specific testbeds are dated, the lessons learned remain highly relevant to the Grids of today.

Production Deployment: Experiences and Recommendations

William E. Johnston, John M. Brooke, Randy Butler, David Foster, and Mirco Mazzucato

We examine experience accrued by those building large-scale Grids for production use: that is, Grids developed to enable large-scale scientific research rather than to be used as testbeds for software development or computer science research. Severe constraints are brought to bear in the construction of such Grids because access to these resources is subject to stringent security and quality-of-service requirements. Furthermore, resources on such Grids may not be designed for or tailored to Grid use. Grid middleware often cannot control policy but must cooperate with site policy and resource management systems. Moreover, ancillary resources, such as telescopes and experimental facilities that are not computational may be involved, may not possess a full operating system, and may have policy and management requirements different from each other and from a computational node.

Even on computational systems, we may encounter multiple architectures, clusters of workstations, specialized parallel machines, clusters of shared-memory nodes, and machines with vector rather than scalar processors. Such machines may run a variety of operating systems, and there may be no common set of software that will work on all.

Grid middleware must combine these diverse resources into a virtual organization, and the Grid building team must solve the resulting engineering challenges. Even within a relatively homogeneous Grid, constraints are imposed by the need to provide reliability, high quality of service, and availability. Thus, monitoring the Grid becomes a vital task.

We attach great importance to abstracting a set of *core Grid functions* that must be implemented in order for the Grid to be productive. Interoperability is a key concept, especially in extending Grids across organizational boundaries. Data are usually at least as important as computation; thus, data-handling and transfer issues must be included in the core functionality.

We structure the chapter as follows. First we summarize the requirements for Grid middleware in a production environment. Then we motivate our identification of core functions. We discuss the engineering requirements necessary for establishing security, reliability, and quality of service. We describe our experience with production Grids, examining policy-based issues crucial to the success of such Grids. We then draw some conclusions and look toward the advent of open Grid services.

27.1   BUILDING LARGE-SCALE GRIDS

Many projects are now building production Grids to provide identified user communities with a rich, stable, and standard distributed computing environment. By "standard" Grids, we specifically mean Grids based on the common practice and standards defined within the Global Grid Forum (GGF). By "production" Grids, we mean Grids having the same levels of reliability and maintainability as traditional large-scale production facilities. Quality-of-service metrics such as 24/7 operation, mean time between failure rates, and throughput should be defined and measurable. Acceptable values for these metrics will depend on the target virtual organization (VO), but in general we require sophisticated user support, engineering support, diagnostic tools, and software release procedures.

This chapter addresses the experiences gained within the following production Grid projects:

✦ The *Information Power Grid* (IPG) project at NASA Ames (394) has integrated the operation of Grids into the NASA Advanced Supercomputing (NAS) production supercomputing environment and the computing environments at several other NASA centers. Together with some NASA "Grand Challenge" application projects, IPG has been identifying and resolving issues that impede application use of Grids.

✦ The *DOE Science Grid* (9) is implementing a prototype production environment at four DOE labs and at the DOE Office of Science supercomputer center, NERSC. It is addressing Grid issues for supporting large-scale, international scientific collaborations and provides services for a variety of Grid projects, including the Particle Physics Data Grid (30) and Earth System Grid (271).

✦ The *EU DataGrid* (12) has integrated a large number of European sites resources providing the infrastructure for high-energy physics, as well as for other sciences such as Earth observation and biology. This Grid is providing access to large-scale data and distributed computing resources to communities of hundreds of scientists throughout Europe and belonging to several tens of different national organizations.

✦ The *Large Hadron Collider* (LHC) Computing Grid is a worldwide production Grid project connecting regional centers that provide resources for processing the data coming from the LHC experiment based at CERN in Geneva, Switzerland.

✦ *EUROGRID* (250) connects major academic and commercial centers in Europe with an emphasis on high-performance applications using specialized architectures, some of which have atypical operating systems and complex architectural configurations.

✦ The *UK e-Science Grid* (Chapter 3) connects major centers of e-science in the UK.

All of these systems are targeted at infrastructure for large-scale, collaborative science and for access to large-scale computing and storage facilities. (Other, equally impressive efforts, which we do not discuss here because of space limitations, include the NSF TeraGrid (162), NEESgrid (Chapter 6), and Asia-Pacific Grid.

27.2   GRID SOFTWARE

This chapter only describes experience gained from deploying a specific set of software: the Globus Toolkit (276) (Chapter 4), Condor (444) (Chapter 19), SRB/MCAT (100), Virtual Data Toolkit (93), PBSPro (31), and a PKI authentication substrate (308). These software suites provided the implementation of the Grid functions used in the Grids described here, with the sole exception of EUROGRID, which used the UNICORE system (560).

The primary software on which these Grids are based is the Globus Toolkit, which provides a clear, strong, and standards-based security model; modular functions (not an all-or-nothing approach) providing all of the core Grid functions except general events; a clear model for maintaining local control of resources incorporated into a Grid; a general design approach that allows a decentralized control and deployment of the software; a demonstrated ability to accomplish large-scale metacomputing (e.g., the SF-Express application in the GUSTO testbed

(138)); presence in supercomputing environments; a clear commitment to open source; and market share. SRB/MCAT (metadata catalog and storage management) and Condor (job manager) were added because they provided specific functionality required for IPG and LCG.

Virtual data technologies (284, 285) are critical for the high-energy physics and astrophysics communities. The virtual data concept encompasses the definition and delivery to a large community of a (potentially unlimited) virtual space of data products derived from experimental data or from simulations (93). In this virtual data space, requests may be satisfied via direct access and/or by (re)computation of simulation data on demand, with local and global resource management, policy, and security constraints determining the strategy used. What is stored in the associated metadata of the data products is not necessarily just descriptions of the data and pointers to that data but prescriptions for generating the data. The Virtual Data Toolkit is providing tools for file naming and location transparency (replica management) and for instantiating data on demand from metadata descriptions.

Grid software beyond that provided by these suites are being defined and implemented by many organizations, and in some cases are being experimented with in the Grids described here (e.g., the EU DataGrid Resource Broker (12)). Nevertheless, the software of the prototype-production Grids described in this chapter is provided primarily by the aforementioned packages, and these provide the context of this discussion.

This chapter recounts lessons learned in deploying these science-oriented Grids. The lessons fall into four general areas: deploying operational infrastructure (what must be managed operationally to make Grids work), establishing cross-site trust, dealing with Grid technology scaling issues, and listening to the users.

27.3   GRID CONTEXT

Production Grids seek to support real work by their community and must operate within the operational and security constraints of existing institutions responsible for complex and valuable resources. The creation of such Grids encompasses (1) uniform core software services that manage and provide access to heterogeneous, distributed resources; (2) a widely deployed infrastructure; and (3) higher-level services such as data Grid tools. The software architecture of such a Grid is depicted in Figure 27.1.

What we call *core Grid functions* constitute the "neck of the hourglass" of Grids and, in the Grids described here, are provided primarily by the Globus Toolkit

Discipline Portals / Frameworks (problem expression; user state management; collaboration services; workflow engines; fault management)
Applications and Utility Services (domain specific and general components)
Language Specific APIs (Python, Perl, C, C++, Java)
Grid Collective Services (resource brokering; resource co-allocation; data cataloguing, publishing, subscribing, and location management; collective I/O, job management)
Core Grid Functions (resource discovery; resource access; authentication and security; event publish and subscribe; monitoring / events)
Communication Services
Security Services
Resource Managers (export resource capabilities to the Grid, handle execution environment establishment, hosting, etc., for compute resources)
Physical Resources (computers, data storage systems, scientific instruments, etc.)

27.1   Grid architecture.

FIGURE

(276) and have been demonstrated in large-scale applications (17). These core functions include a Grid information service (GIS, the basic resource discovery mechanism) (204), a Grid security infrastructure (GSI, the tools and libraries that provide Grid security) (146, 280), a Grid job initiator mechanism (e.g., the Globus Toolkit GRAM (205), Chapter 18), a Grid scheduling function, a basic data management mechanism such as GridFTP (354), and a communications abstraction (e.g., Globus I/O) that incorporates Grid security. To complete this set we need a Grid event mechanism (Chapter 20 discusses issues relating to Grid events, and Chapter 17 describes OGSA notification mechanisms) and a mechanism for authentication (e.g., PKI (146, 308)).

At the resource management level, the capabilities of the individual computing system, data system, or instrument are exposed and may contain specific functionalities necessary for Grid computing. For example, job management systems (e.g., PBSPro (31), Maui) that support advance reservation of resource functions (e.g., CPU sets) are needed to support coscheduling of administratively independent systems. The Grid information service should publish this resource capability information so that only systems with this capability are selected for tasks that require coscheduling.

Beyond these basic common services are associated client-side libraries and tools and other high-level capabilities such as matching job requirements to available resources. Examples include the EU DataGrid resource broker (12), Condor (58) and Condor-G (291) (Chapter 19) for job management, SRB/MCAT (100) (Chapter 15) for federating and cataloging tertiary data storage systems, data Grid tools (Chapter 22) for Grid data management (64, 178), and the Virtual Data Toolkit for file naming and location transparency (replica management) and for instantiating data on demand from metadata descriptions (284, 285).

27.4   ISSUES FOR PRODUCTION GRIDS

Each type of production environment has key issues that must be addressed for success. These issues may include routing agreements and site service-level agreements for networks and user services, accounting and allocation management, and system tuning. In the case of Grids, key operational concerns also must be carefully addressed, if not to ensure success at least to make sure that success is not inhibited. These concerns include the model for the Grid information services, cross-site trust, understanding how and why Grids are scoped, and management of local authorization. We discuss concerns in the following subsections.

27.4.1   Grid Information Service

The GIS provides capabilities for locating resources based on the characteristics needed by a job (OS, CPU count, memory, etc.). The Globus Toolkit's Monitoring and Discovery Service (MDS-2, Chapter 20) (204) is an information service implementation with two components. The Grid Resource Information Service (GRIS) runs on the Grid resources (computing and data systems) and handles the soft-state registration of the resource characteristics. The Grid Information Index Server (GIIS) is a user-accessible directory server that supports searching for a resource or resources by characteristics. Other information may also be stored in the GIIS. The Grid Information Services group of the Global Grid Forum is defining the schema for various objects. Currently a common schema definition and implementation by the Globus Project and EU DataGrid have been achieved for Grid computing element and storage element descriptions.

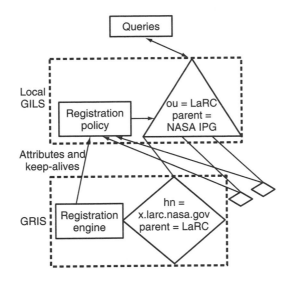

Basic GIS functions. The lines indicate relationships, the arrows information flow, the diamonds resources, and the triangles the information directory.

As illustrated in Figure 27.2, the basic GIS functions, in terms of MDS-2, comprise resource identity, registration target(s), and the registration process. Registration both conveys the resource information to the GIS and has a soft-state maintenance mechanism (the "keep-alives" in the figure).

A GIIS should be planned at each distinct site with significant Grid accessible resources. Such planning is important in order to avoid single points of failure. If one depends on a GIIS at some other site and it becomes unavailable, one will be unable to examine local resources. Depending on the number of local resources, it may be necessary to set up several GIISs at a site in order to accommodate the search load.

An initial GIS model may involve independent GIISs at each site. In this model, either cross-site searches require explicit knowledge of each of the GIISs that must be searched independently, or all resources cross-register in each GIIS (where a resource register is a configuration parameter in the GRISs that run on each Grid resource).

Grid projects should consider early what kind of information needs to be managed. Most of the information available today is *resource specific* (e.g., documenting the operating systems and hardware configuration). This information is useful in understanding the capabilities of the resources at a high level and is likely to be input to higher-level resource brokers that filter all possible candidates against other user criteria. In addition to resource-specific information, however,

Grid users will want information about data storage availability, software versions, job status, and the like. All of this is important to consider when deciding what information to store in the GIS. It is also important to follow the developing schema definition standards to ensure interoperability.

27.4.1.1 Model for the Grid Information System

Directory servers above the local GIISs are an important scaling mechanism for several reasons. An organization may have multiple GIISs at the "local" level for administrative, security management, or load balancing; users will need a single point of entry. The higher-level GIISs expand the resource search space through automated cross-GIIS searches for resources and therefore provide a potentially large collection of resources transparently to users. They also provide the potential for query optimization and query results caching. Furthermore, such directory services provide the possibility for hosting or defining virtual organizations (by storing this nonresource information in the same GIS data hierarchy as the resource characteristics) and for providing federated views of collections of data objects that reside in different storage systems.

Currently, two main approaches are used for building directory services above the local GIISs. One is a hierarchically structured set of directory servers and a managed namespace, usually based on X.500-style naming. The other is a set of "index" servers that provide ad hoc, or VO-specific, views of a specific set of other servers such as a collection of GIISs and data collections, not unlike a project Web page that provides access to all of the information relevant to that project.

Both approaches allow one to "scope" a Grid in terms of the resource search space. The structuring of these higher-level GIISs may provide scoping for a VO or site or may reflect a general structure for an actual organization. In principle, this structure can be fairly complex; indeed, except for the root (no formal root exists today), the situation depicted in Figure 27.3 is not atypical. In particular, individual resources may register with however many (potentially unrelated) GIISs appropriate for their function.

27.4.1.2 X-500-Style Hierarchical Directory Structure

Using an X.500-style hierarchical name component space directory structure has the advantage of organizationally meaningful names that represent a set of "natural" boundaries for scoping searches. It also means that one can (potentially) use commercial metadirectory servers for better scaling. An issue to consider here is the ability to keep the hierarchy up to date if mapped onto a physical organizational structure that may be subject to frequent change. Attaching VO roots, data name

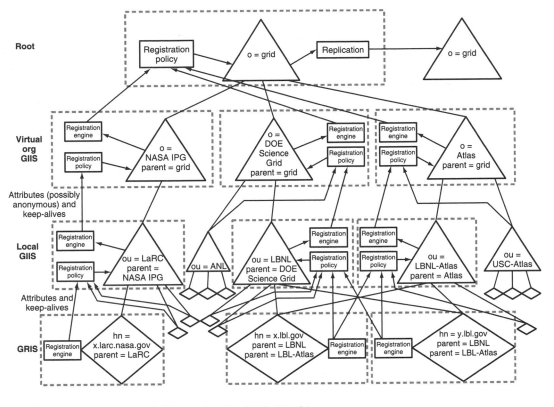

27.3 GIS-encoded organizational relationships.

FIGURE

spaces, and so forth to the hierarchy makes them automatically visible, searchable, and in some sense "permanent" (because they are part of this managed name space).

Those who plan to use this approach should try to involve someone who has some X.500 experience. The directory structures are notoriously hard to get right, a situation compounded if VOs are included in the namespace.

27.4.1.3 Index Server Directory Structure

The Globus Toolkit MDS (204) information system implementation has added to the usual LDAP-based directory service capabilities several features important for Grids.

Of particular note is soft-state registration. This feature provides for autoregistration and deregistration of resources, as well as registration access control. It keeps the information up to date (through a keep-alive mechanism), and it provides for a self-configuring and dynamic Grid. A new resource registering for the first time is essentially no different from an old resource reregistering after a system crash, for example. The autoregistration mechanism also allows resources to participate in multiple information hierarchies, thereby easily accommodating membership in multiple VOs. Moreover, the registration mechanism provides a natural way to impose authorization on those wishing to register with one's GIISs. Every directory server from the GRIS on the resource up to and including the root of the information hierarchy is essentially the same.

Other MDS characteristics include the following:

+ Resources are typically named by using the components of their DNS name, which has the advantage of using an established and managed name space.

+ One must use separate "index" servers to define different relationships among GIISs, VOs, data collections, and so forth. This strategy allows one to establish "arbitrary" relationships within the collection of indexed objects.

+ Hierarchical GIISs (index nodes) are emerging as the preferred approach in the Grids community that uses the Globus Toolkit software.

Apart from the fact that all of the directory servers must be run as persistent services and their configuration maintained, the only real issue is that we do not yet have a lot of experience with scaling this approach to multiple hierarchies with thousands of resources.

27.4.2   Cross-Site Trust Management

Authorizing user access to Grid resources implies several major important steps:

+ Physical identification of the user identity by the registration and certification authorities

+ Attribution of roles and general authorization by virtual organization management

+ Grant of local authorization by the local resource owner and security managers

+ Inclusion (in some cases) of the user into the Grid virtual organization LDAP directory

An important contribution of Grids to supporting large-scale collaboration is the uniform Grid entity naming and authentication mechanisms provided by the Grid Security Infrastructure. For this mechanism to be useful, however, the collaborating sites and organizations must establish mutual trust in the authentication process. Most Grids use the software mechanism of PKI, X.509 identity certificates, and their use in the GSI through TLS/SSL (193). PKI uses both a public and private key to prove—or *authenticate*—that user's identity. Public keys are well known and readily available on Web sites and at other public locations. Private keys are known only by the particular user and are encrypted.

The public key is associated with a named identity in an identity certificate, which is used for Grid authentication. To obtain such a certificate, a user submits the public key half of his private/public key pair, along with the user identity (naming), and a request for a digital certificate, to a third party, called a certificate authority (CA). The CA verifies the identity of the user and the validity of the requested name (which may include organization name elements—e.g., o=Lawrence Berkeley National Lab, ou=Computing Sciences, cn=William E. Johnston—to ensure that the user has not requested a name that makes it look like it is a member of an organization for which the particular CA is not the naming authority) and binds the user's identity to the public key by digitally signing a document—the identity certificate—that contains the public key, the user name, and the identity of the certification authority. This certificate, together with a challenge from the resource that requires the use of the user's private key to satisfy, is the authentication process: the user's proof of identity. If, for example, the user wants to log on to a remote compute resource, he presents this digital certificate and demonstrates possession of the private key as proof of identity. The user interaction is all on the local system; no passwords are sent to the remote machines. The process is accomplished by using the cryptographic protocols of TLS. In most cases, however, the user does not log on to remote systems but creates a proxy certificate that authenticates to the remote resource on behalf of the user when, for example, a batch job is submitted. This proxy mechanism provides a "single sign-on" for the user. The user having authenticated once on the local systems, the proxy mechanism securely carries that authentication to remote systems (146, 280).

The real issue is that of establishing trust in all of the various processes involved in issuing and using the certificate. Typically, the trust issues include the following:

+ The process that each certification authority uses for issuing the identity certificates to users and other entities, such as host systems and services. This involves two steps: (1) "physical" identification of the entities, and a verification of their association with a virtual organization (this usually involves a step where the VO authorizes the CA to issue a certificate, once user identity is established) and (2) issuance of an X.509 certificate. Both of these steps are defined in the CA policy.

✦ The use of the certificate once it is issued, and the management of the user's private key.

These issues are described in more detail in material to follow. In the PKI authentication environment assumed here, the CA policies are encoded as formal documents associated with the operation of the certification authority that issues Grid identity credentials. These documents are called the certificate policy/certification practice statement, which we refer to collectively as "CP" (8).

27.4.3   Trust

The term trust refers to confidence in, or reliance on, some quality or attribute of a person or thing, or the truth of a statement. Cyberspace trust starts with clear, transparent, negotiated, and documented policies associated with identity. When a Grid identity token (X.509 certificate in the current context) is presented for remote authentication and is verified by using the appropriate cryptographic techniques, the relying party has some level of confidence that the person or entity that initiated the transaction is the person or entity expected.

The nature of the policy associated with identity certificates depends a great deal on the nature of particular Grid communities or the virtual organizations associated with those Grids. It is relatively easy to establish policy for homogeneous communities, such as in a single organization, because an agreed-upon trust model is likely to exist already. On the other hand, it is difficult to establish trust for large, heterogeneous virtual organizations, involving people from multiple international institutions, because the shared trust models do not exist. Typical issues related to establishing trust may be summarized as extending across

✦ administratively *similar* systems, for example within an organization, in which case the existing informal trust model can be extended to Grid authentication and authorization;

✦ administratively *diverse* systems, for example across multiple similar organizations (e.g., NASA Centers, DOE labs), in which case the existing formal trust model can be extended to Grid authentication and authorization; and

✦ administratively *heterogeneous* systems, for example across multiple organizational types (e.g., science labs and industry) or international collaborations, in which case a new formal trust model for Grid authentication and authorization must be developed.

Getting a certification authority's CP (and therefore the Grid user's certificates) accepted by other Grids (or even by multisite resources within a Grid) involves identifying and then exchanging CPs with the people who can authorize remote users at all of the sites and organizations that form a virtual organization or collaboration. The CPs are evaluated by each party in order to ensure that local policy for remote user access is met. If it is not, a period of negotiation ensues (the issues involved are indicated in the EU DataGrid Acceptance and Feature matrices (30)). Cross-site trust relationships may be published (see, for example, the EU DataGrid list of acceptable CAs (12)).

Establishing trust is substantially simplified if the sites of interest already have people who are familiar with the PKI CP process and are focused on the scientific community of the institution, rather than on the administrative community. It is vital to get the site security people involved at an early stage in planning and implementation, so that process is appropriately institutionalized.

The policy in the certification authority CP represents a trust model. No single trust model exists for VOs and CAs. The trust model that gives rise to much of what is described here is a model that is appropriate to federal laboratories, mission-oriented organizations, and virtual organizations involved in large-scale science. We probably do not have the experience yet to catalogue trust models, but others clearly will show up in Grids. University-oriented VOs or projects may well find the procedures of the mission-oriented VOs too elaborate or restrictive. Government agencies or corporations that need to protect proprietary information may find them insufficient.

27.4.4   Establishing an Operational Certification Authority

To set up or identify a certification authority to issue Grid X.509 identity certificates to users and hosts, many organizations (e.g., IPG, NCSA, the DOE Science Grid, and the Italian INFN) use the Netscape Certificate Management System software for their operational CA. The CMS software is a mature product that allows a scalable usage model that matches well with the needs of science virtual organizations.

People setting up Grids must take care to understand the issues associated with the CP of their CA. As noted, the CP governs the "nature" of identity verification needed to issue a certificate, and this is a primary factor in determining who will be willing to accept a CA's certificates as adequate authentication for resource access. Changing this aspect of the CP could well mean not just reissuing all certificates but requiring all users to reapply for certificates.

CPs are highly stylized documents, and a standard template should be used. The Global Grid Forum is working on standard CPs that can be used as templates, and the DOE Science Grid has developed a CP that supports international collaborations (8).

CPs must account for the various entities for which the CA will have to issue certificates. These entities typically include human users, hosts (systems), services (e.g., GridFTP), and possibly security domain gateways (e.g., the PKI-to-Kerberos gateway, KX509). Each of these must have a clear policy and procedure described in the CA's CP.

A Grid CP must be established and published as early as possible when one is setting up a Grid, so that issues are exposed as soon as possible. Also, when one is setting up VOs that will have to interoperate with other CAs, the discussions about homogenizing the CPs should begin as soon as possible, since this can be a lengthy process.

Certificates are, as described in the CP, issued for particular purposes. Certificates issued by Grid CAs generally are valid only for authentication. Other potential uses for certificates are general encryption and digital signature by the user of e-mail, documents, and so forth. Encryption and digital signature introduce additional requirements that likely are not to be satisfied by Grid authentication processes, and the Grid CA's CP may explicitly disallow its certificates use for these purposes.

27.4.4.1 Naming

An important issue when developing a CP is the naming of the principals (the "subject," i.e., the Grid entity identified by the certificate). Although there is an almost universal tendency to try to pack a lot of information into the subject name (which is a multicomponent X.500-style name), increasingly there is an understanding that the less information put into a certificate, the better. This simplifies certificate management and reissuance when users forget passphrases (which will happen with some frequency). More important, it emphasizes that *all trust is local*—that is, established by the resource owners and/or when joining a virtual community. The main reason for having a complicated subject name invariably turns out to be that people want to do some of the authorization based on the components of the name (e.g., organization). Doing so, however, usually leads to two problems: People belong to multiple organizations, and the authorization implied by the issuance of a certificate will almost certainly collide with some aspect the authorization actually required at any given resource. Furthermore, the projects, organizations, and affiliations that people are associated with may change frequently, even though they remain members of a VO, and revoking and then reissuing authentication certificates just to change organizational aspects of the names is not an efficient way to handle those changes.

The CA run by ESnet (the DOE Office of Science scientific networks organization) for the DOE Science Grid and the NCSA Alliance CA, for example, serves several dozen different virtual organizations, several of which are international in their makeup. The certificates use what is essentially a flat namespace, with a "reasonable" common name (e.g., a "formal" human name) to which has been added a random string of alphanumeric digits to ensure name uniqueness.

If one does use hierarchical institutional names in certificates, colloquial names for institutions should be avoided, and their full organizational hierarchy should be considered in defining the naming hierarchy. In particular, care should be taken to avoid choosing names that may conflict with the name of anyone else in one's institution working on PKI (most likely in the administrative or business units); if possible, the same hierarchy conventions for naming should be followed within that institution.

We note that CAs set up by the business units of scientific organizations frequently do not have the right policies to accommodate Grid users. This situation is not surprising because the policies are typically aimed at the management of institutional financial transactions.

27.4.4.2   Certification Authority Model

Several models for certification authorities exist. Increasingly, however, collaborations and virtual organizations are funding a single CA provider. The primary reason is that for the trust model described here (mission-oriented VOs), it is a formal and expensive process to operate a CA in such a way that it will be trusted by others, and multiple groups are opting to share the cost of a CA.

One such model has a central CA with an overall CP and has subordinate policies for each of the VOs that it serves. The CA delegates to VOs (via registration agents) the responsibility of deciding who is a member of the particular VO and how the subscriber or user will be identified in order to be issued a VO certificate. Each VO has an appendix in the CP that describes VO-specific issues. VO registration agents are responsible for applying the CP identity policy to their users and other entities. Once satisfied that a user meets the requirements, the registration authority authorizes the CA to issue (generate and sign) a certificate for the subscriber.

This is the model of the DOE Science Grid CA, for example, and it is intended to provide a CA scalable to dozens of virtual organizations and thousands of users. The approach to scalability is the usual divide and conquer, together with a hierarchical organization that maintains the policy integrity. The architecture of the DOE Science Grid CA is indicated in Figure 27.4 and has the following key features. The root CA (which is kept locked up and offline) signs the certificates

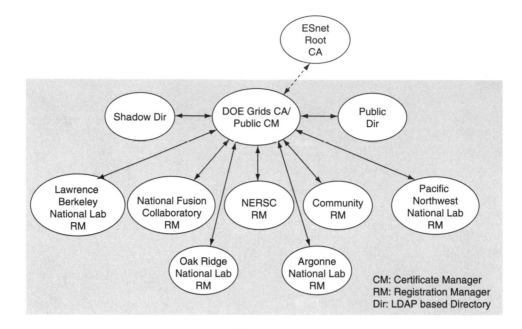

27.4

FIGURE

Software architecture for the May 15, 2002, deployment of the DOE Grids CA. (Courtesy Tony Genovese and Mike Helm, ESnet, Lawrence Berkeley National Laboratory.)

of the CA that issues user certificates. With the exception of the "community" registration manager, all RMs are operated by the VOs that they represent. (The community RM addresses those "miscellaneous" people who legitimately need DOE Grid certificates but for some reason are not associated with a virtual organization.) The process of issuing a certificate to a user ("subscriber") is indicated in Figure 27.5.

ESnet operates the CA infrastructure for DOE science Grids; ESnet does not interact with users. The VO registration agents interface with certificate requestors. The overall policy oversight is provided by a policy management authority, a committee chaired by ESnet and comprising each RA and a few others.

This approach uses an existing organization (ESnet) that is set up to run a secure production infrastructure (its network management operation) to operate and protect the critical components of the CA. ESnet defers user contact to agents within the collaboration communities. In this case, the DOE Science Grid was fortunate in that ESnet personnel were also well versed in the issues of PKI and X.509 certificates, and so they were able to take a lead role in developing the Grid CA architecture and policy.

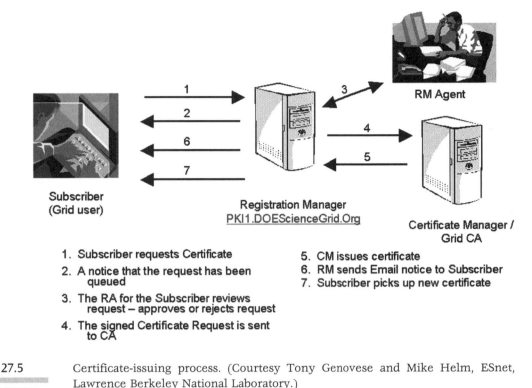

1. Subscriber requests Certificate
2. A notice that the request has been queued
3. The RA for the Subscriber reviews request – approves or rejects request
4. The signed Certificate Request is sent to CA
5. CM issues certificate
6. RM sends Email notice to Subscriber
7. Subscriber picks up new certificate

27.5

FIGURE

Certificate-issuing process. (Courtesy Tony Genovese and Mike Helm, ESnet, Lawrence Berkeley National Laboratory.)

27.4.5   Defining and Understanding the Extent of a Grid

The boundaries of a Grid are determined primarily by three factors. The first concerns the *interoperability of the Grid software*. Many Grid sites run some variation of the Globus Toolkit software, and there has been fairly good interoperability between versions of that toolkit, so most Globus Toolkit sites can interoperate. A basic level of interoperability involving simple jobs to single sites has also been established between the Globus Toolkit and UNICORE; in particular, transfer of UNICORE to Globus Toolkit certificates (and vice versa) has been established. Translation and transfer of more complex requests are being investigated (332). Interoperability between the Virtual Data Toolkit and the European DataGrid technology has also been demonstrated at a basic level. The interoperability issues are being studied as part of the Grid Laboratory Universal Environment (GLUE) project, both at a practical level with today's tools and specifying common schemas that will facilitate interoperability.

The second boundary factor concerns *what CAs the resources of a Grid trust.* This decision is explicitly configured on each Globus Toolkit resource on a per CA basis. The trusted CAs establish the maximum extent of the user population; however, there is no guarantee that every resource in one's Grid trusts the same set of CAs. Each resource potentially has a different space of users; this is a local decision. In fact, this will be the norm if the resources are involved in multiple virtual organizations, as they frequently are, for example, in the high-energy physics experiment data analysis communities.

The third boundary factor concerns *how one scopes the searching of the GII and GIISs or controls the information published in them.* This decision depends on the model chosen for structuring one's directory services.

27.4.6   Local Control and Authorization

Currently, no standard authorization exists for Grids. Almost all Grid software uses some form of access control list (ACL), which is straightforward but typically does not scale well.

The Globus Toolkit mapfile is an ACL that maps from Grid identities (the subject names in the identity certificates) to local UIDs on the systems where jobs are to be run. The Globus Toolkit gatekeeper (205) replaces the usual log-in authorization mechanism for Grid-based access and uses the mapfile to authorize access to resources after authentication. Therefore, managing the contents of the mapfile is the basic Globus Toolkit user authorization mechanism for the local resource. The mapfile mechanism is good in that it provides a clearcut way for locally controlling access to a system by Grid users. It is bad, however, in that for a large number of resources—especially if they all have slightly different authorization policies—it can be difficult to manage.

The first step in the mapfile management process is usually to establish a connection between user account generation on individual platforms and requests for Globus Toolkit access on those systems. That is, generating mapfile entries is done automatically when the Grid user goes through the account request process. If Grid users are to be automatically given accounts on several different systems with the same usage policy, it may make sense to centrally manage the mapfile and periodically distribute it to all systems. Unless the systems are administratively homogeneous, however, a nonintrusive mechanism, such as an e-mail to the responsible system administrators to modify the mapfile, is best. The NCSA Alliance has developed a transaction-based account management system that supports account management and Grid mapfile management in a virtual organization that spans administrative domains. This system is now being extended through an NSF NMI (26) grant.

The Globus Toolkit mapfile also allows a many-to-one mapping so that, for example, a group of Grid users can be mapped to a single account. Whether the individual identity is preserved for accounting purposes typically depends on whether the batch queuing system can pass the Grid identity (which is carried along with a job request, regardless of the mapfile mapping) back to the accounting system. PBSPro provides this capability (see Section 27.4.9).

One way to address the issues of mapfile management and disaggregated accounting within an administrative realm is to use the Community Authorization Service (CAS) (519).

As a secondary check on authorization, administrators can tailor the CA naming policy to ensure that only certificates with an appropriate name structure are validated. This is a blanket check applied to all certificates.

27.4.7   Site Security Issues

Incorporating any computing resource into a distributed application system via Grid services involves using a collection of IP communication ports that are otherwise not used. If one's systems are behind a firewall, these ports are almost certainly blocked, and one will have to negotiate with the site security staff to open the required ports.

The Globus Toolkit can be configured to use a restricted range of ports, but it still needs several tens or so (depending on the level of usage of the resources behind the firewall) in the mid-700 range. A Globus Toolkit "port catalogue" explains what each Globus Toolkit port is used for and provides other information that site security staff will want to know. The catalogue also helps one to estimate how many ports must be opened (how many per process, per resource, etc.). Additionally, GIS/GIIS needs some ports open, and the CA typically uses a secure Web interface (port 443). The Globus Toolkit port catalogue provides the basis for defining a Grid firewall policy document that, one hopes, will serve the same role as the CA Certificate Practices Statement: it lays out the conditions for establishing trust between the Grid administrators and the site security staff responsible for maintaining firewalls for site cyber protection.

It is important to develop tools and procedures for periodically checking that the ports remain open. Unless one has a clear understanding with the network security staff, the Grid ports will be closed by the first network engineer that looks at the router configuration files and has not been told why these nonstandard ports are open. This is another example of why the various administrators of the systems and networks need to embrace the Grid and see it as part of their responsibility to support it.

An alternative approach to firewalls has various service proxies to manage the intraservice component communication so that one, or no, new ports are used. An interesting version of this approach has been developed for the Globus Toolkit 1.1.2 (627, 628).

27.4.8   High-Performance Communications Issues

If one anticipates high data-rate distributed applications, whether for large-scale data movement or for process-to-process communication, the help of a WAN networking specialist should be enlisted, and the network bandwidth should be checked and refined end-to-end by using large-sized packet test data streams. (Many problems that can affect distributed applications do not show up when pinging with 32-byte packets.) Problems are likely between application and host and site LAN/WAN gateways, WAN/WAN gateways, and any path that traverses the commodity Internet.

The DOE Science Grid has developed tools and techniques for detecting and correcting high-performance communication problems. End-to-end monitoring libraries and toolkits such as Iperf (654), NetLogger (339), and pipechar (391) are invaluable for application-level distributed debugging. Iperf is a tool for measuring maximum TCP bandwidth, allowing the tuning of various parameters and UDP characteristics; it reports bandwidth, delay jitter, and datagram loss. NetLogger, in particular, is used extensively in DOE Grids and has been used to identify a variety of dramatic performance problems in distributed applications (393, 650, 651, 653). It provides for detailed data path analysis, top to bottom (application to NIC) and end to end (across the entire network path). It is also being incorporated into some components of the Globus Toolkit.

If at all possible, network monitors that monitor specific TCP flows and return that information to the application should be provided. Such information can be used for performance debugging (340). TCP algorithms also can be tuned to achieve high performance in high-speed wide area networks. Increasingly, techniques for automatic or semiautomatic setting of various TCP parameters based on monitored network characteristics are being used to relieve the user of having to deal with this complex area of network tuning that is critical for high-performance distributed applications (242, 431, 649).

27.4.9   Schedulers

Although Grid middleware can mask differences between different local site resources, and even enhance the capabilities of those resources in some regards, there are some important functions that cannot easily be emulated by Grid middleware: for example, advance reservation capabilities in schedulers. Thus, as part of the NASA IPG project, advance reservation features were added to PBS (31).

Users can become attached to the syntax of a specific scheduling system. Thus, NASA IPG also arranged for PBS to be modularized, and its user interfaces and client-side process manager functions were packaged separately and interfaced to the Globus Toolkit for job submission. This approach enables PBS-managed jobs to run on Globus Toolkit-managed systems, and vice versa. Thus, users familiar with PBS can use the PBS front-end utilities (submit via PBS *qsub* command-line and *xpbs* GUI, monitor via PBS *qstat* and control via PBS *qdel*, etc.) to run jobs on remote systems managed by the Globus Toolkit. In a similar fashion, Condor-G (291) provides a Condor interface to Globus.

PBS also provides time-of-day-based advance reservation. It actually is a queue that "owns" the reservation. As such, all the access control features (allowing or disallowing specific users or groups) can be used to control access to the reservation. It also allows one to submit a string of jobs to be run during the reservation. The existing job-chaining features in PBS may be used to do complex operations such as "Run X; if X fails, run Y; if X succeeds, run Z."

PBS passes the Grid user ID back to the accounting system. This feature is important for allowing, for example, the possibility of mapping all Grid users to a single account (and thereby not having to create actual user accounts for Grid users) but at the same time maintaining individual accountability, typically for allocation management.

Moreover, PBS supports access-controlled, high-priority queues. This feature is of interest in cases where a project must "commandeer" a lot of resources in a hurry to address a specific, potentially emergency, situation. Consider, for example, that a collection of Grid machines has been designated for disaster response. To accomplish an immediate response requires high-priority queues accessible to a small number of people preauthorized to submit jobs that preempt all other jobs. PBS has such full preemption features that, combined with the existing access control mechanisms, provide this sort of "disaster response" scheduling capability. There is a configurable "preemption threshold": if a queue's priority is higher than the preemption threshold, then any jobs ready to run in that queue will preempt all running work on the system with lower priority. In other words,

multiple levels of preemption are possible. The preemption action can be configured to try to checkpoint, suspend, or kill and requeue, in any order. For access
control, every queue in PBS has an access control list that can include and exclude
specific users and groups.

27.4.10 MyProxy Service

A frequent Grid user complaint relates to the constant management of GSI
credentials and the frequent necessity of generating proxy credentials so that
Grid work can proceed. A related, and functionally more serious, issue is that
in order to minimize the risk of the relatively unprotected proxy credentials their
lifetimes are kept relatively short (typically 12 h). This restriction can create
significant problems when, for example, large jobs take longer than that to
execute on remote computing systems or when the batch queues are long and
the proxies expire before execution starts. In either case the job is likely to fail.

The MyProxy service (507) alleviates these problems and eases the problem
of trying to move the user's permanent identity credential to all of the systems
from which the user will want to access the Grid. MyProxy provides for creating
and storing intermediate lifetime proxies that may be accessed by Web-based portals, job schedulers, and the like on behalf of the user. Extensions to the service
are planned so that it can manage the user's permanent identity credential.
MyProxy provides client tools that let the user create, store, and destroy proxies,
and it allows programs acting on the user's behalf to obtain valid (short-term)
proxies. The user can create a proxy with a lifetime of a week, or a few weeks,
and store that proxy on a MyProxy server. The user and the MyProxy service
establish a shared secret, and the user passes that secret to processes that need to
obtain proxies on the user's behalf. In this way, a Grid service such as the Globus
Toolkit job initiator or the Condor job manager can, after getting the user's access
secret for MyProxy, contact the MyProxy service each time that a short-term
proxy is needed to perform a task. When a Grid job manager finds that a job's
proxy is about to expire, it can ask the MyProxy service for a new proxy without
user intervention.

The user must still supply proxy generating authority to MyProxy, but much
less often than to a usual Grid task. An analysis (67) finds that the security risks
not only are acceptable compared with direct user management of the short-lived
proxies, but may even be less risky because the process is less prone to user
error.

A key operational issue is that the MyProxy server must be managed not only
as a persistent service but also as a *secure* persistent service. Hence, it should

probably be in a controlled physical environment (e.g., a controlled-access machine room), should be a strictly single-purpose system, and should be behind a content-filtering firewall.

27.5   BUILDING A MULTISITE GRID

Like networks, successful Grids involve almost as much sociology as technology. Good working relationships among all people involved are essential.

The concept of an engineering working group (WG) has proven successful as a mechanism for promoting cooperation and mutual technical support among those who will build and manage the Grid. The WG should be driven by a well-defined set of goals, milestones, and responsibilities and should meet weekly via teleconference. A designated WG lead should be responsible for setting the agenda and managing the discussions. There should also be a WG mail list that is archived and indexed by thread. Notes from the WG meetings should be mailed to the list; such notes provide a living archive of technical issues and the state of the Grid.

The WG should involve Grid deployment teams at each site, including resource administrators, applications developers, and those who can set or interpret site policies (since interactions between organizations are bounded by site policies that are often difficult to decipher). If possible, the WG should also involve Grid technology experts, at least during the first several months while people are coming up to speed.

Grid software involves not only root-owned processes on all of the resources but also a trust model for authorizing users. In this model, local control of resources is maintained but is managed a bit differently from current practice. It is therefore important to set up liaisons with the system administrators for all systems that will provide computation and storage resources for the Grid—whether or not these systems are within one's organization.

We often find that system, network, and security administrators are not well integrated with Grid deployment teams. This is a critical flaw. These administrators must buy into the Grid concept and see the deployment and support of the Grid as a high priority. Configurations on these systems change frequently, and it is easy to overwrite or otherwise negate Grid services previously deployed through system upgrades. Furthermore, the whole Grid concept may conflict directly with an organization's security profile. The security team must embrace the goals of the Grid and work proactively to meet both the needs dictated by site security and the Grid.

27.5.1   Physical Resources

As early as possible, one should identify the computing and storage resources to be incorporated into one's Grid. Such identification requires sensitivity to the fact that opening up systems to Grid users may turn lightly or moderately loaded systems into heavily loaded systems. Batch schedulers may have to be installed in order to manage the increased load.

Choosing a batch scheduler requires careful consideration of coscheduling. Many potential Grid applications need this capability, for example, to run cross-system MPI jobs or support pipelined applications across systems. Only a few schedulers (notably, PBSPro and Maui) currently provide the advance reservation mechanism used for Grid coscheduling on heterogeneous systems. Several schedulers that purport to support coscheduling in fact do so only among schedulers of the same type or within administratively homogeneous domains.

In addition, the Grid pushes the operational requirements of the resources so that they may support usage on an extended operational window. Remote access may include the need to support the usage of these resources across time zones and indeed may require that the resources be operationally supported 24 /7.

27.5.2   Initial Testbed

For initial testbed use, one should use PKI authentication and certificates from the Globus Toolkit certification authority, or almost any other CA that will issue certificates for a test environment. (The OpenSSL CA may be used for this testing. Also see (28).) One should issue certificates for the Globus Toolkit and the testers; these are "toy" certificates that will be used simply to get an initial configuration up and running.

The Globus Toolkit, the host certificates, and the CA naming policy files should be installed on at least two different systems. The mapfile should also be populated. One should then install (or gain access to) the Globus Toolkit at two or more sites. If one's site has firewalls, this is good time to look at the Globus Toolkit port catalogue and to start talking with whoever controls the firewall policy.

Access to, and operation of, the GIS/GIISs must be validated at all sites, and local and remote job submission must be tested.

27.5.3   Transition to a Prototype-Production Grid

To transition to a prototype-production Grid, one must set up, or identify, one's production CA as described previously; issue host certificates for all the computing and data resources; and then establish procedures for installing those certificates and their associated CA naming policy files. One must also issue user certificates, recognizing that all the certificates will probably have to be revoked and reissued at least once before going operational (especially if one had not previously operated a CA).

The Grid mapfile and certificate revocation procedures must be worked out and tested. Similarly, certificates issued by the Grid CA must be used to validate correct operation of the Grid Security Infrastructure (GSI) (146, 280), GSS libraries, GSI-SSH, and GSI-FTP or GridFTP (64) at all sites. A testing monitor should be installed that periodically tests each critical service and reports the result in a Web page.

To ensure success, a Grid application support team should be trained on this prototype.

27.5.4   Preparing for Users

A key task of the Grid support team is to find problems before the users do. To this end, test and validation suites must be designed and used to exercise the Grid in the same way that actual applications are likely to use the Grid. Such tests should include distributed applications that require reasonable bandwidth and should be run across as many widely separated systems in the Grid as possible. Such test cases must, of course, be rerun every time something changes in the system configuration.

User help mechanisms are imperative, including a Grid user e-mail list and a trouble ticket system. User-oriented Web pages should include pointers to documentation, such as the Globus Toolkit "Quick Start Guide" modified to one's specific Grid (starting with a Grid "hello world" example).

27.5.5   Testing on Production Grids

Once the Globus Toolkit, GIS/MDS, and the security infrastructure are operational on the testbed system(s), the Globus Toolkit should be installed on at least two production computing platforms at two different sites. A distinction must be made regarding the relationship between the Globus Toolkit job submission and the local batch schedulers (one queue, several queues, a Globus Toolkit queue, etc.), and this configuration should be validated.

27.5.6   Grid Systems Administration Tools

Grids present special challenges for system administration because of the administratively heterogeneous nature of the underlying resources. A Grid configuration tool called *Gridconfig* (developed at the San Diego Supercomputer Center) presents a unified interface to all Grid software including the Globus Toolkit, Condor, and NWS. Gridconfig is part of the NMI Release 2 (26). In the DOE Science Grid, monitoring tools are built as pyGlobus (386) modules for the NetSaint (25) system monitoring framework. These tools currently allow testing GSIftp, MDS, and the Globus Toolkit gatekeeper; and a GUI tool that will use these modules to allow an administrator to quickly test functionality of a particular host is planned. The NCSA Grid-in-a-Box effort has developed a simple Grid service monitor that has proven to be effective.

The harder issues in Grid administrator tools involve authorization and privilege management across site boundaries. So far, work in these areas has concentrated on tools for *identifying* problems. When problems are located, the current way to correct them is to e-mail a privileged local user on the broken machine in order to fix things. Clearly, a framework that uses a more autonomic model for continuous monitoring and restart of services is needed. To this end, in several Grids, tools and techniques are being developed for extending trouble-ticket-based problem-tracking systems to the Grid environment. Grid account systems must evolve to track Grid user usage across a large number of machines and to manage allocations in accordance with (probably varying) policy on the different systems (477).

27.5.7   Data Management and the Grid Service Model

A Grid service model is needed for moving data between *all* of the systems involved in a Grid. Such a service model must be validated to ensure that all required data paths work correctly (see Figure 27.6). GridFTP servers should be deployed on the Grid computing platforms and on the Grid data storage platforms. This task presents special difficulties when data reside on user systems that are not usually Grid resources, and it emphasizes the importance of defining the Grid service model precisely. One must determine what services are outside one's core Grid resources (e.g., GridFTP on user data systems) but are needed to achieve a Grid that is useful for applications. One must then determine how these services will be supported.

If individual groups manage their experimental data on their own systems, GridFTP servers must be installed on those systems so that the data can be moved between the user system and the user job on the computing platform. Managing long-lived or root access Grid components on user systems can be tricky, however, and may require providing some level of system administration on user systems.

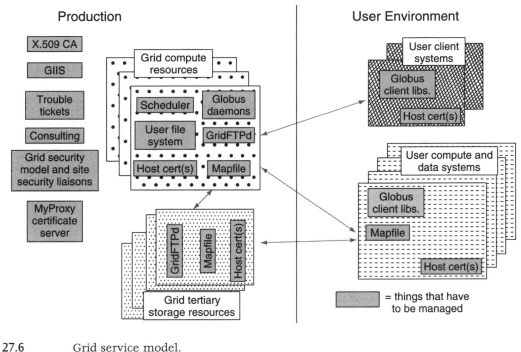

27.6

Grid service model.

FIGURE

27.5.8 User Assistance

A Grid application specialist group should be running sample jobs as soon as the testbed is stable, and certainly as soon as the prototype production system is operational. The group members should be able to assist generally with building Grid distributed applications, and specifically should serve as the interface between users and the Grid system administrators in order to solve Grid-related application problems.

Grid application specialists should encourage and assist early users in getting jobs running on the Grid. An approach that has been successful in the IPG and DOE Science Grid is to encourage the porting of applications frameworks to the Grid. This task typically is not too difficult because these frameworks often already have some form of built-in resource management that is easily replaced or augmented with Grid resource management functions. Examples of such frameworks deployed in the IPG and DOE Science Grid are NPSS (265, 450), Cactus (see Chapter 16), and Ninf (Chapter 24).

One current impediment is that extant Grid functions are relatively primitive (i.e., low level). This issue is being addressed by Grid middleware at various levels that provide aggregate functionality, more conveniently packaged functionality, toolkits for building Grid-based portals, and so forth. Examples of such work in progress include Web services (e.g., the Open Grid Services Architecture (278), diverse interfaces to Grid functions (e.g., PyGlobus (386), CoG Kits (429)), and the Grid Portal Development Kit (506)). Also useful are Grid job-tracking and monitoring portals, such as IPG's LaunchPad and NPACI's HotPage (647) (see Chapter 24).

27.6   SUMMARY

We have summarized experiences gained in building several production Grids, and we have provided some global context for this work. As the reader may imagine, there were many false starts, refinements to the approaches and to the software, and several substantial integration projects (e.g., the NASA-sponsored SRB and Condor integration with the Globus Toolkit) to get where we are today. We hope that this material makes it substantially easier for others to build production Grids so that we can move rapidly toward the vision of a common cyberinfrastructure for science.

The work described in this chapter represents actual experiences based on specific architectural and software choices made during design and implementation. These choices were dictated by the criteria laid out in the first section. However, the foundation choices of Globus Toolkit, SRB, and Condor would not be significantly different today from what they were four years ago.

Some of us have experience in building production Grids based on software other than the Globus Toolkit (specifically, UNICORE (560)). We find that the lessons are fundamentally the same as those we have outlined for Globus Toolkit-based Grids, thus providing a useful point of reference for confirming the common core functions approach, since both the Globus Toolkit and UNICORE can be viewed as implementations of a subset of the core functions and can be made to interoperate (e.g., in the Grid Interoperability Project, GRIP (332)).

Our focus here has been on *how* to build Grids, not *why* one should want to build one, a topic that is addressed elsewhere (e.g., see Chapters 3 and 4, and the application descriptions in Part III). We point out, however, that one significant (if unexpected, at least by us) success of Grids is that they are providing the security and directory infrastructure required to support the ever-increasing size and complexity of science collaborations. The uniform security infrastructure of the Globus Toolkit and the emerging cross-site trust agreements for identity authorities and resource usage that result from the use of the Globus Toolkit are having a major positive effect on large-scale scientific collaboration.

ACKNOWLEDGMENTS

We thank Tony Genovese and Mike Helm for their contributions to Section 27.4.4, Keith Jackson and Stephen Chan for Section 27.5.6, and Bill Nitzberg for Section 27.4.9.

The experience presented in this chapter is the result of much hard work by the Grid teams in the authors' organizations.

The principals at NASA IPG are Tony Lisotta, Chair, Warren Smith, George Myers, and Judith Utley, all of the NASA Ames Research Center, and Isaac Lopez of the NASA Glenn Research Center. This project is led by William Johnston, Tom Hinke, and Arsi Vaziri of the NASA Ames Research Center.

The principals in the DOE Science Grid Engineering team are Keith Jackson, Chair, Lawrence Berkeley National Laboratory; Tony Genovese and Mike Helm, ESnet; Von Welch, Argonne National Laboratory; Steve Chan, NERSC; Kasidit Chanchio, Oak Ridge National Laboratory; and Scott Studham, Pacific Northwest National Laboratory. This project is led by William E. Johnston, Lawrence Berkeley National Laboratory; Ray Bair and Ian Foster, Argonne National Laboratory; Al Geist, Oak Ridge National Laboratory; and William Kramer, NERSC.

IPG work is funded by NASA's Aero-Space Enterprise, Computing, Information, and Communication Technologies (CICT) Program (formerly the Information Technology), Computing, Networking, and Information Systems Project. Eugene Tu, Jerry Yan, and Cathy Schulbach are the NASA program managers.

The DOE Science Grid work is funded by the U.S. Department of Energy, Office of Science, Office of Advanced Scientific Computing Research, Mathematical, Information, and Computational Sciences Division, under Contract DE-AC03–76SF00098 with the University of California. This program office is led by Walt Polansky. Mary Anne Scott is the Grids program manager and George Seweryniak the ESnet program manager.

The architects of UNICORE have done much to identify critical issues in Grids. Dave Snelling and Sven van der Berghe of Fujitsu European Laboratories developed the notion of an abstract job object. Jon MacLaren of the University of Manchester demonstrated that EUROGRID CA certificates can interoperate between different Grid middleware systems. This work is funded by the European Union and the German BMBF. The partners in EUROGRID, UNICORE-PLUS, and

GRIP have all contributed. Dietmar Erwin of FZ Jülich is the project manager, and the software integrators are Pallas GmbH under Karl Solchenbach and Hans-Christian Hoppe.

The UK e-Science program, funded by the DTI and involving the major UK Science Research Councils, was initiated by John Taylor the Director-General of the Research Councils and is directed on behalf of EPSRC by Tony Hey.

The European DataGrid work is funded by the European Union and is led by Fabrizio Gagliardi and Bob Jones. The work package leaders are Francesco Prelz, Peter Zoltan Kunszt, Steve Fisher, Olof Barring, John Gordon, François Etienne, Pascale Primet, Frank Harris, Luigi Fusco, Christian Michau, and Maurizio Lancia.

FURTHER READING

For more information on the topics covered in this chapter, see *www.mkp.com/grid2*.

28 Computing Elements

CHAPTER

Andrew A. Chien

Given that distributed computing systems are constructed by integrating diverse end systems, it is important to understand key characteristics of these systems with respect to both current and expected future capabilities. This chapter characterizes end systems as basic elements and simple composite elements. In fact, the similarity between a national-scale Grid and simple composite elements reflects the "fractal nature" of Grids. Hence, it is interesting to review and contrast the solutions adopted.

We begin by discussing basic elements, including computing elements, computer systems (e.g., processors and memory), communication elements (e.g., networks), and storage elements (e.g., attached disk and network-attached storage). Subsequently, we describe simple composite elements (SCEs), which are collections of basic elements, aggregated with software and sometimes special hardware, to provide a qualitatively different interface and capability. Examples of simple composite elements include high-throughput, high-reliability, dedicated high-performance, and shared controllable SCEs. These composite elements can be employed in functions suited to their capabilities—reliable SCEs as name servers, for example—in Grids. We describe each element type in turn, outlining the current state of the art and outstanding research challenges.

28.1 BASIC ELEMENTS

The capabilities of basic elements—building blocks for all computing systems—have improved at geometric rates for the past three decades (see Figure 28.1 for microprocessor trends). Such rapid change produces not only tremendous quantitative

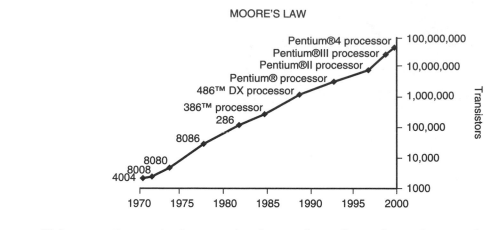

MOORE'S LAW

28.1

FIGURE

Geometric increase in the number of transistors integrated on a single microprocessor chip (Courtesy, Intel). Intel's 64-bit microprocessors—Itanium (2001) and Itanium2 (2002)—now exceed 221 million transistors.

changes in capability (1,000–10,000 times) but also qualitative changes in capability. Computer systems were once multiton behemoths the size of a small building and now are wristwatch-sized gadgets. Multiplying the revolutionary changes enabled by size reductions are equally dramatic increases in storage, compute power, and networking capability. We briefly outline here the continuing revolutionary changes in the technology of basic computing elements.

28.1.1   Computing Elements

Computing elements, the power sources for a Grid, have evolved at a tremendous rate over the past 20 years and are expected to continue their rapid evolution over the next 10 years. Since the introduction of the Intel 4004 microprocessor in 1971, the scale of integration, transistor count, and clock speed have increased rapidly in accord with Gordon Moore's observation in 1965, now commonly known as Moore's law, that the number of transistors would increase exponentially:

$$\text{Transistors} = 20 * 2^{(\text{year}-1965)/1.5}.$$

This law predicts continued doublings every 18 months in our capability to integrate transistors onto a single chip. Compounded over 20 years, this geometric increase in performance has brought us from microprocessors such as the Intel 8080 in 1975 with 4,500 transistors to the Pentium II in 1997 with 7.5 million

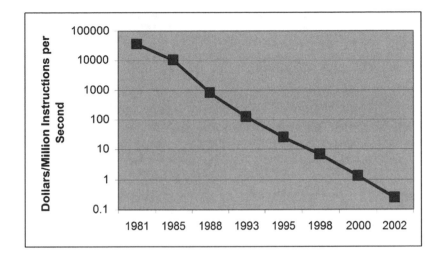

Technology improvements and high-volume markets drive the geometric decrease in system cost-performance (based on personal computer prices).

transistors to the Pentium IV and Itanium2 with 221 million transistors—hundreds of times more transistors than the total number in all computer systems in the 1970s. The geometric increase in integration capability has fueled a rapid increase in microprocessor performance, where delivered performance (as measured by MIPS or SpecMarks) increases by 1.5 times each year. Over the past 20 years, microprocessor performance has increased from approximately 100,000 instructions per second in 1975 to nearly 8 billion instructions per second today. Advances in price-performance have been even more dramatic; technology advancements coupled with high-volume production (tens to hundreds of millions of units) have driven processor prices down rapidly.

Advances in microelectronics and packaging not only have fueled increased processor performance but also have produced geometric improvements in system price-performance. System capacities—main memory capacity, disk capacity, and internal system bandwidths—have all increased dramatically. In addition, system prices have plummeted, producing an explosion in volume for computers with Pentium IV systems retailing under $500 and PC volumes exceeding 120 million units in annual sales. The rapid progress shows no sign of abating in the next decade (92); technological advances in microelectronic feature size and new markets (home computers, handheld devices, wireless devices, embedded computers, and worldwide markets) continue to drive a virtual cycle of lower cost and higher volume (see Figure 28.2).

In the past 15 years, high-performance systems have also leveraged the advantages of high-performance microprocessors. Massively parallel processors such as the Intel iPSC, Ametek 2010, Transputer Arrays, Thinking Machines CM-5, Intel Paragon, IBM SP-2, Cray T3D/T3E, and a series of ASCI Red, Blue, White, Q, and Purple machines all exploit ensembles of low-cost, high-performance microprocessors to deliver high performance. In addition, commercial systems have made heavy use of large-scale shared-memory multiprocessors, Hewlett–Packard's Superdome and TruServer, and Sun's Ultra Enterprise systems, built from high-performance microprocessors to deliver performance on database and other commercial applications. These systems all benefit from the continued rapid improvement in underlying microprocessor technologies.

Computing performance for microprocessors over the next 10 years will continue to improve at a geometric rate (92). This improvement will be further accelerated by increasingly effective use of large-scale parallelism in high-end server systems. To view this increase merely as a continuation of the past trends, however, understates the rate of change: after 25 years of increase, the base is much larger. Thus, in quantitative terms, the relative size of increase in hardware resources and capability will be much greater. For example, in the next 10 years, we will go from microprocessors with 200 million transistors to those with nearly 20 billion transistors (92); from volume production of memory chips with 256 megabytes to 16 gigabytes; and from systems that can manipulate rich text and simple two-dimensional graphics to systems that easily manipulate a range of complex data and real-world inputs, generating rich, high-modality outputs (e.g., three-dimensional immersive virtual reality, Chapter 1:6). In short, the large quantitative change will push computational capability through many thresholds, producing a large qualitative change in system capabilities.

28.1.2   Communication Elements

Communication technologies have also improved geometrically over the past 25 years, producing communication elements with breathtaking capabilities. Gigabit networks are now widespread, and the technology base for networking elements with terabit performance is available (see Figure 28.3). The rate of adoption of such technologies has been slowed, however, both by its cost and by the fundamental nature of communication to involve multiple parties. Thus, communication depends on an infrastructure of links, routers, switches, and metainformation structures such as name servers. Infrastructures evolve slowly, as they require large-scale systematic upgrading and investment. Consequently, deployed network performance lags significantly behind technological capability.

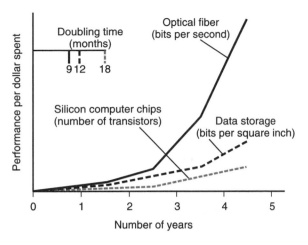

28.3

FIGURE

Geometric increases in communication technology far outstrip growth in other capabilities such as computing, memory, and storage (courtesy *Scientific American*). Deployed technology lags demonstrated technology by a number of years.

Rather than focus on wide-area issues that are well covered in Chapter 30, we focus on localized networks that can evolve rapidly in response to local needs. These are most germane to the design of simple composite elements. In particular, we focus on technologies for cluster networks, which are rapidly finding their way into local-area, metropolitan-area, and corporate intranet infrastructures. These localized networks form subgrids that could be incorporated into national-scale Grids. In this area, we expect deployment of revolutionary technology over the next 10 years.

After many years of modest advances, over the past few years we have seen a rapid advance from shared 100-megabit/sec networks to 100-megabit/sec switched to 1000 megabit/sec (gigabit networks), with 10-gigabit/sec Ethernet just recently finding initial deployment. This change is being driven by file service, e-mail, peer-to-peer file sharing, multimedia, and Web surfing. We expect this change to accelerate with the increasing use of wide-area information systems catalyzed by the Web and Grid. Future transitions will be driven by rich video content and perhaps novel applications not yet extant. Increasingly widespread adoption of gigabit/sec Ethernet onto system motherboards, combined with low-cost switches and networks (attributable in part to the adoption of copper interfaces) and 10-gigabit/sec technologies (appearing in network-interface cards but expected to quickly ramp to large-scale adoption) portends continuing rapid increases in the available communication bandwidth for Grid systems.

Innovation in cluster networks and system area networks has produced novel link, interface, and software layer technologies. Cluster networks are physically localized, high-speed, and generally low-volume products. Because they are part of a system and therefore are subject to weaker requirements of compatibility, innovation is more rapid. In addition, because their performance is tightly coupled to cluster applications and systems, innovations in network interface design can directly improve system performance. To give an idea of the networking capabilities that underlie current cluster research, we describe a number of networking interfaces.

A few years ago, low-cost clusters employed 100BaseT networking because 100BaseT network interfaces were incorporated on computer motherboards and 100BaseT switches were low cost. At the time of this writing (January 2003), 1000BaseT networking interfaces are just beginning to be incorporated in server motherboards and will soon become common on desktop systems as well. For example, the Intel SE7500WV2 server motherboards include dual Pentium IV processors as well as dual 1000BaseT connections. At the same time, 1000BaseT switches have also become inexpensive, with 24-port switches retailing for well below $100 per port.

At these price points, a 1000BaseT network forms the low-cost baseline for performance and latency of a clustered system. With TCP/IP and an open-source messaging library such as MPICH (334) or LAM-MPI (144), latencies of ~100 microseconds and peak bandwidths of 300 to 500 megabit/sec can be achieved. More aggressive interconnects such as those available from Myricom and Quadrics provide lower latencies and higher bandwidths at higher price points as shown in Table 28.1.

All of these systems use a sophisticated microprocessor on the network-interface card, which offloads the processing from the host processor and efficiently moves data to and from memory. The order-of-magnitude reduction in latency is achieved by using OS-bypass technologies (45, 245, 513), which allow

Interconnect type	Short message latency (microsec)	Peak bandwidth (megabytes/sec)	Bidirectional bandwidth (megabyte/sec)	Approximate cost per port
Gigabit Ethernet (TCP/IP)	100	~65 (varies)	~130 (varies)	$100
Myrinet	9	280	500	$1000
Quadrics QSNet	5	300	500	$3000

28.1

TABLE

A Variety of Interconnects and Delivered Latency and Bandwidth for MPI in a 32-node Cluster.

the application to directly access the high-speed network. With optimized paths, both low latency and high bandwidth can be achieved at modest levels of host processor load. Other interconnects such as Infiniband and Fibrechannel offer similar link speeds, but with different emphasis in architecture, since both were designed primarily as a storage device interconnect or storage area network.

28.1.3 Storage Elements

Storage elements (magnetic disk and tape) (317, 382) continue to improve in both capability and price-performance at an exponential rate. Because the trends for magnetic disk and tape are similar, we focus only on magnetic disk here. The rate of capacity and performance improvement over the past five years has accelerated. After a steady rate of improvement in density (the number of bits stored per unit area) of approximately 29% a year from 1970 to 1988, recent technology breakthroughs have accelerated the rate of improvement to nearly 60% per year. These improvements, combined with mechanical and packaging improvements (e.g., rotational speeds), have accelerated cost-per-byte improvements for hard disks from 40 to over 100% per year in personal computer systems. Thus, in succession, 500 megabytes (1995), 2 gigabytes (1997), 8 gigabytes (1998), 30 gigabytes (2000), and 100 gigabytes (2002) have become standard low-cost disk configurations. With continued dramatic growth in the deployment of information technologies, there is every indication that this trend will continue.

Although cost per byte and available capacity have improved at nearly 100% per year, performance factors for disk drives have failed to improve at that rate. Peak transfer rates continue to improve rapidly, tied to increases in areal density and small increases in rotational speeds, with current disks such as Seagate's 15,000-rpm Cheetah delivering 60–80 megabyte/sec. Seek times, however, are improving more slowly, coupled to improvements in mechanical technologies and gradual shrinking of the platters (and therefore the seek distances involved). Average seek times of 3–5 milliseconds remain typical. Thus, in the face of geometric performance improvements in other elements of computing systems, disk access times are essentially constant and therefore a bottleneck of increasing importance.

The rapid decrease in the cost of storage has significant implications for Grids. Not only do technology improvements make it possible and cost-effective to store large quantities of data, but the exploding storage capability in lowest-cost systems dictates that huge amounts of storage will be available on networks of any size, and the improving capabilities of high-speed networks will enable Grids to use that storage flexibly. For example, in our local PC-workgroup at the University of California, San Diego, the file server is configured with 500 gigabytes of disk. However, the

	Device type	Network connection	Capacity	Comment
EMC CX200	Storage-area network	Fibrechannel, up to 4 gigabit/sec	Up to 2 terabytes	Block-oriented
EMC CX600	Storage-area network	Fibrechannel, up to 16 gigabit/sec	Up to 17.5 terabytes	Block-oriented
Dell Powervault 715N	Network-attached storage using various protocols (IP, NetBeui, IPX)	Dual 100-megabit/sec Ethernet	160–480 gigabytes	Network file-sharing protocol-oriented (e.g., NFS, Netware, CIFS/SMB)
Dell Powervault 775N	Network-attached storage using various protocols (IP, NetBeui, IPX)	Dual gigabit Ethernet	16.4 terabytes	Network file-sharing protocol-oriented (e.g., NFS, Netware, CIFS/SMB)

28.2

TABLE

A Variety of Network-Attached Storage and Storage-Area Network Devices.

30 desktop and laptop machines associated with that server contain a far larger quantity—several terabytes. If one includes the local compute clusters, the number rises to 10 terabytes. This trend reflects the new reality that much of the real cost of storage is administration and backup. Thus, uses of storage will change. In our workgroup laboratory, only the file server's disks are archived each night; the majority of online storage is considered scratch space. Clearly, current management and administration techniques will change to exploit this excess capability. Further discussion of this topic and its relation to Grids can be found in Chapter 29.

An increasingly popular trend in storage is network-attached storage, based on either IP networks or storage-area networks (SANs) running proprietary protocols. These storage devices typically implement multiple network file-sharing protocols and provide additional functionality in volume virtualization and management, as well as sophisticated file-system snapshotting and backup. Some representative products with their capacities and interfaces are shown in Table 28.2.

28.1.4   Basic Elements of the Future

To get a perspective on the dramatic exponential improvement of capabilities in basic elements, one can extrapolate the growth rates to five- and ten-year horizons. Table 28.3 shows the basic capabilities of our personal computers and

Machine	Computing	Memory	Disk	Network
Today's machines (2003)				
Personal computer	8 gigaop/sec	512 megabyte	128 gigabyte	1 gigabit/sec
Supercomputer	80 teraop/sec	50 terabyte	1,280 petabyte	10 terabit/sec
5-year machines (2008)				
Personal computer	64 gigaop/sec	16 gigabyte	2 terabyte	10 gigabit/sec
Supercomputer	640 teraop/sec	160 terabyte	20 petabyte	100 terabit/sec
10-year machines (2013)				
Personal computer	512 gigaop/sec	256 gigabyte	32 terabyte	100 gigabit/sec
Supercomputer	5 petaop/sec	2.6 petabyte	320 petabyte	1 petabit/sec

28.3

TABLE

Future Capabilities of Personal Computers and Supercomputers Based on Recent Growth Rates.

supercomputers (10,000-processor parallel machines) in the years 2008 and 2013 if recent historical growth rates in performance and capability continue.

The extrapolations for networks are probably the least accurate, since technology is readily available but technology deployment rates are unpredictable. The networking rates are based on estimated network interface speeds in standard high-volume configurations. Thus, they form an upper bound and reflect the likely available performance in local area networks, with accessible performance in metropolitan area and wide-area networks limited by advances in national and global initiatives in infrastructure efforts such as Internet II (597) and its successors (see also Chapter 30) as well as in research projects such as OptIPuter. For networks within supercomputer configurations, the available network bandwidths may be 5–10 times greater because of the use of specialized hardware.

28.2 SIMPLE COMPOSITE ELEMENTS: LOCAL GRIDS

Simple composite elements (SCEs) are richly connected, relatively homogeneous collections of basic system elements (compute, memory, communication, and storage). They are often housed within single administrative domains and in many cases are already thought of as a single system. As illustrated in Figure 28.4, SCEs (or

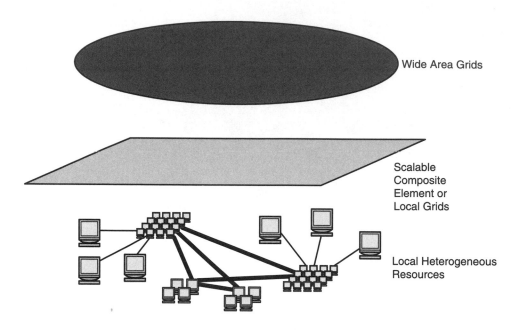

Wide Area Grids

Scalable
Composite
Element or
Local Grids

Local Heterogeneous
Resources

28.4

FIGURE

SCEs nested in a larger Grid. Each type of SCE can play a unique role in providing a cost-effective Grid.

clusters as they are commonly called) are building blocks for wide-area, national, and international Grids. SCEs are worthy of particular study for several reasons.

◆ Local Grid technologies can reduce the number of problems higher-level Grids must solve.

◆ Local Grids use resources and software to implement the external properties of the composite element affecting its utility or integration into larger Grids.

◆ Local Grids form the basis for larger Grids. Thus, their evolution is an integral part of the challenges in building larger Grids.

Together, these integral relationships make understanding technologies for SCEs and their capabilities a crucial element of understanding issues in building Grids. For example, in a national Grid, reliable composite elements can be used to provide management (access control and scheduling) and basic services (naming and routing). Other composite elements can provide resource pools with distinct capabilities such as network data caching, persistent storage, and predictable computation power. Composing two SCEs together may be challenging, however, if they correspond to different administrative domains or employ distinct data representations or different network protocols.

In the following subsections, we first describe the two key distinguishing features of SCEs: their external interfaces and guarantees and their hardware requirements. External interfaces and guarantees affect the use and utility of SCEs in the larger Grid context. Hardware requirements determine the SCE capabilities that can be exploited for building Grids. Then we describe a series of state-of-the-art SCEs and technologies: high-throughput clusters, reliable clusters, dedicated high-performance clusters, and shared controllable-performance clusters.

28.2.1   Capabilities and Requirements

SCEs are defined by their external interfaces and guarantees, by their internal hardware requirements, and by their ability to deliver efficient, flexible use of their internal capabilities to applications. Since other chapters discuss managing interfaces and guarantees in Grids (see Chapters 1:19 and 18), we focus here on providing a classification of these interfaces and guarantees. In addition, because an SCE technology's internal hardware requirements and capabilities are integrally related to its applicability, we also provide a classification of hardware requirements. Together, the two classifications delineate both current-day SCE systems and many other systems under study.

External interfaces and guarantees define how SCEs are used by applications and how they can be integrated into larger Grids. Five attributes capture the important distinctions among a wide range of SCEs: capacity, aggregate performance, reliability, predictability, and sharability. *Capacity* corresponds to the total throughput of the SCE in dimensions of compute, memory, communication, and storage. *Aggregate performance* corresponds to the SCE's ability to deliver compute, memory, communication, and storage performance. *Reliability* reflects the likelihood of unavailability of resource or unavailability or loss of data. *Predictability* captures an application's ability to predict the delivered capacity or performance. *Sharability* refers to whether the SCE can be shared, integrating a number of computations on one resource for tighter coupling or simply multitasking.

Hardware requirements and capabilities distinguish the range and capability of the technologies used to build an SCE. These constrain the range of an SCE and distinguish it from higher-level Grids. Five attributes capture many important distinctions in applicability: heterogeneity, networking requirements, distributed resources, changes in constituent systems, and scalability. *Heterogeneity* in compute, networking, and storage elements influences the inclusiveness of an SCE environment and its ability to encompass both legacy and new systems. *Networking requirements*—special hardware, link length limited, high bandwidth, and so on—all limit the locales and cost constraints under which an SCE technology can be deployed. Whether an SCE technology can exploit *distributed resources* (links tens of meters or thousands of kilometers) limits the geographical extent of the SCE. Whether an SCE technology requires *changes in its constituent systems* has a significant effect on the deployment requirements and technology insertion cost, and therefore on deployability of a technology. *Scalability* of a system influences the number of nodes that can be deployed and the SCE's ability to manage and deliver their performance.

In the following, we use a two-part framework—external interfaces and hardware requirements—to understand and distinguish the wide range of cluster systems and systems that have been built by both researchers and commercial vendors. Each type has distinct capabilities and provides different challenges and advantages for integration into a Grid environment. They include high-throughput, high-reliability, and dedicated high-performance SCEs.

28.2.2 High-Throughput SCEs or Desktop Grids

In high-throughput computing or desktop Grid systems, pooled resources are used to achieve high throughput on a set of compute jobs (446, 702). Such systems allow large numbers of machines to be added as a single resource in a higher-level Grid system, achieving significant benefits in reduced management effort and Grid complexity. Systems such as Entropia, Condor, and LSF manage clusters of workstations as pooled resource servers, with the primary application being compute-bound sequential jobs. Although all three systems provide cluster access and resource management facilities, Entropia and Condor also increase the pool of available resources by allowing desktop machines to be added as resources and by ensuring that those resources can be gathered without interfering with the desktop users. Whereas early definitions of high throughput involved only long-running (multiday) jobs, more recent systems such as Entropia have focused on achieving rapid turnaround to enhance scientific or engineering productivity.

The key elements in a desktop Grid system include physical node management, resource scheduling, and job scheduling. In addition, systems that also support data-intensive computations include facilities for data management. We briefly describe the Entropia system as an example. More information on the Condor system can be found in Chapter 19; see also the discussion of parameter study applications in Chapter 24 for a summary of other systems.

28.2.2.1 Requirements for Desktop Grids

Desktop Grid systems aggregate large numbers of machines (tens of thousands to millions) into a single high-throughput SCE. Such systems allow the desktop systems to be incorporated into a larger Grid at a low management effort. Desktop Grid systems begin with a collection of computing resources—heterogeneous in hardware and software configuration, distributed throughout a corporate network and subject to varied management and use regimens—and aggregate them into an easily manageable and usable single resource. Furthermore, a desktop Grid system must do this in a fashion that ensures there is little or no detectable impact on the use of the computing resources for other purposes. For end users of distributed computing and higher-level Grids, the aggregated resources must be presented as a simple-to-use, robust resource that can be easily integrated into larger-scale Grids. A matrix of key requirements for desktop Grids is shown in Table 28.4.

The Entropia system architecture consists of three layers: physical management, scheduling, and job management (see Figure 28.5). The base, the physical node management layer, provides basic communication and naming, security, resource management, and application control. The second layer is resource scheduling, providing resource matching, scheduling, and fault tolerance. Users can interact directly with the resource-scheduling layer through the available APIs or alternatively through the third layer management, which provides management facilities for handling large numbers of computations and files. Entropia provides a job management system, but existing job management systems can also be used. An example of how these layers participate in the execution of an application is shown in Figure 28.6.

Physical node management. The desktop environment presents numerous unique challenges to reliable computing. Individual client machines are under the control of the desktop user or IT manager. As such, they can be shut down, rebooted, reconfigured, and disconnected from the network. Laptops may be offline or just off for long periods of time. The physical node management layer of the Entropia system manages these and other low-level reliability issues. The physical node management layer provides naming, communication, resource management, application control, and security. The resource management services capture a wealth of node information (e.g., physical memory, CPU speed, disk size and free space, software version, data cached) and collect it in the system manager. This layer also provides basic facilities for process management including file staging, application initiation and termination, and error reporting. In addition, the physical node management layer ensures node recovery, terminating runaway and

Requirement	Description
Efficient	A desktop Grid should harvest virtually all of the idle resources available. For example, the Entropia system gathers over 95% of the desktop cycles unused by desktop user applications.
Robust	Computational jobs must complete with predictable performance, masking underlying resource failures. The Entropia Grid tolerates job, machine, and network failures and includes a variety of mechanisms for ensuring timely completion of a larger job in the presence of such failures.
Secure	The system must protect the integrity of the distributed computation (tampering with or disclosure of the application data and program must be prevented). In addition, the desktop Grid system must protect the integrity of the desktops, preventing applications from accessing or modifying desktop data. We provide a more complete description of this problem and several solutions elsewhere (180).
Scalable	Desktop Grids must scale to the 1,000s, 10,000s, and even 100,000s of desktop PCs deployed in enterprise networks. Systems must scale both upward and downward, performing well with reasonable effort at a variety of system scales.
Manageable	With thousands to hundreds of thousands of computing resources, management and administration effort in a desktop Grid cannot scale up with the number of resources. Desktop Grid systems must achieve manageability that requires no incremental human effort as clients are added to the system. A key leverage for including desktop Grids as single entities in larger Grids is to reduce the management effort.
Unobtrusive	Desktop Grids share resources (computing, storage, and network resources) with other usage in the corporate IT environment. The desktop Grid's use of these resources should be unobtrusive, so as not to interfere with the primary use of desktops by their primary owners and networks by other activities.
Open/easy to integrate application	Desktop Grid software is a platform that supports applications that in turn provide value to the end users. Distributed computing systems must support applications developed with varied programming languages, models, and tools—all with minimal development effort.

28.4

Requirements for Desktop Grids.

TABLE

poorly behaving applications. The security services employ a range of encryption and binary sandboxing technologies to protect both distributed computing applications and the underlying physical node. Application communications and data are protected with high-quality cryptographic techniques. A binary sandbox controls the operations and resources visible to distributed applications on the physical nodes in order to protect the software and hardware of the underlying machine.

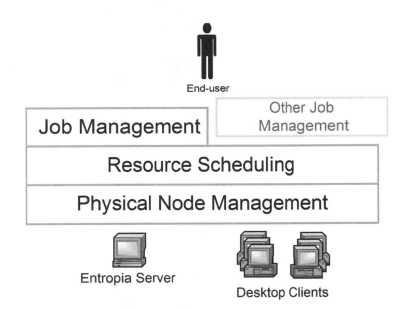

End-user

| Job Management | Other Job Management |
| Resource Scheduling |
| Physical Node Management |

Entropia Server

Desktop Clients

28.5

FIGURE

Architecture of the Entropia distributed computing system. The physical node management layer and resource-scheduling layer span the servers and client machines. The job management layer runs only on the servers. Other (non-Entropia) job management systems can be used with the system.

The binary sandbox also regulates the usage of resources by the distributed computing application. This ensures that the application does not interfere with the primary users of the system—it is unobtrusive—without requiring a rewrite of the application for good behavior.

Resource scheduling.   A desktop Grid system consists of resources with a wide variety of configurations and capabilities. The resource-scheduling layer accepts units of computation from the user or job management system, matches them to appropriate client resources, and schedules them for execution. Despite the resource conditioning provided by the physical node management layer, the resources may still be unreliable (indeed the application software itself may be unreliable). Therefore, the resource-scheduling layer must adapt to changes in resource status and availability and to high failure rates. To meet these challenging requirements, the Entropia system supports multiple instances of heterogeneous schedulers. This layer also provides simple abstractions for IT administrators, abstractions that automate the majority of administration tasks with reasonable defaults but allow detailed control as desired.

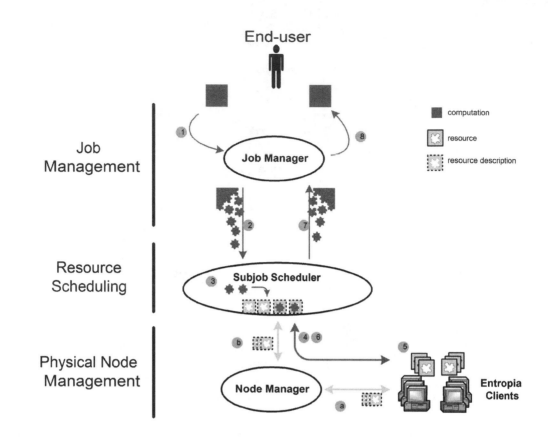

End-user

Job
Management

Resource
Scheduling

Physical Node
Management

Job Manager

Subjob Scheduler

Node Manager

Entropia
Clients

computation

resource

resource description

28.6

FIGURE

Application execution on the Entropia system. (1) The user submits a computation to job management. (2) The job manager breaks up the computation into many independent "subjobs" and submits the subjobs to the resource scheduler. In the meantime, (a) the available resources of a client are periodically reported to the node manager, (b) which informs the subjob scheduler using the resource descriptions. (3) The subjob scheduler matches the computation needs with the available resources and (4–6) schedules the computation to be executed by the clients. (7) Results of the computation are sent to the Job Manager, (8) put together, and handed back to the end user.

Job management.   Distributed computing applications often involve large overall computation (thousands to millions of CPU hours) submitted as a single large job. These jobs consist of thousands to millions of smaller computations and often arise from statistical studies (e.g., Monte Carlo or genetic algorithms), parameter sweeps, or database searches (bioinformatics, combinatorial chemistry, etc.). Because so many computations are involved, tools to manage the progress and status of each piece—in addition to the performance of the aggregate job in order to provide short, predictable turnaround times—are provided by the job management layer. The job manager provides simple abstractions for users, delivering a high degree of usability in an environment where it is easy to drown in the data, computation, and the vast number of activities.

Entropia's three-layer architecture provides a wealth of benefits in system capability, ease of use by users and IT administrators, and internal implementation. The physical node layer manages many of the complexities of the communication, security, and management, allowing the layers above to operate with simpler abstractions. The resource-scheduling layer deals with unique challenges of the breadth and diversity of resources but need not deal with a wide range of lower-level issues. Above the resource-scheduling layer, the job management layer deals with mostly conventional job management issues. Finally, the higher-level abstractions presented by each layer simplify application development. This process is highlighted in the next section.

28.2.2.2 External Interfaces and Guarantees

A high-throughput cluster provides high computational capacity and is a sharable resource. Its interface might be presented by the job manager or resource scheduler in the Entropia system. In fact, most such systems share resources with interactive users, and some include elaborate mechanisms for ensuring good interactive response. While these systems provide no special support for aggregate performance, interfaces for loosely coupled parallel computing such as PVM (305) are now becoming available. No special support for reliability or predictability is provided.

28.2.2.3 Hardware Requirements

High-throughput SCEs have minimal hardware requirements, running on a wide range of processor and network environments and tolerating both processor and network heterogeneity in type and speed. High-throughput systems are also used on widely distributed resources, such as for pooling workstation resources across the worldwide sites for a corporation. In addition, high-throughput SCEs do not require significant change to the underlying systems (depending only on some common job controls and special system libraries) and can scale to larger numbers of processors (hundreds to thousands) with little difficulty.

28.2.2.4 High-Throughput SCEs in Grids

High-throughput SCEs are flexible, powerful systems for achieving high throughput on large numbers of sequential jobs. Thus, they are well-matched Grid elements for such tasks. These SCEs manage a wide range of heterogeneity automatically (instruction set, memory configuration, network, etc.) and schedule compute resources efficiently to reduce turnaround time for jobs. In addition, effective sharing of resources with interactive users increases the pool of resources available to the SCE dramatically. The primary benefit of using desktop Grids to organize large numbers of small resources is that the complexity of the higher-level Grid is reduced (dramatically fewer SCEs), and the usability of the small resources is enhanced through the sophisticated management that the high-throughput SCE software provides.

However, because high-throughput SCEs primarily focus on processing large numbers of small but compute-bound jobs, such SCEs do little to efficiently aggregate resources for larger computations, enhance reliability, or improve performance predictability. Each of these issues is addressed by at least one of the other types of SCEs described next.

28.2.3   High-Reliability SCEs

High-reliability SCEs provide computational resources with extremely low probability of service interruption and data loss (327). In high-reliability SCEs, commonly called *reliable clusters*, additional computing resources are deployed to replicate the state of an application, and responsibility for the computation is "failed over" automatically in the case of software, hardware, or any other failure. An example of a reliable cluster is shown in Figure 28.7. Failover transfers responsibility for the computation to the additional hardware, which takes up the task seamlessly, so clients see no interruption of service. This approach, typified by Tandem's Guardian system (327), has been adopted by a wide variety of vendors for highly available systems.

28.2.3.1   *External Interfaces and Guarantees*

Reliable clusters use replication for reliability but can also add resources for scalability for many kinds of applications. With the exception of a few large data manipulation applications, however, the scalability is generally used to increase system capacity, not to scale to support large jobs. Of course, reliable clusters provide a reliability guarantee to applications and are generally sharable resources. Because of failover delays and dynamic load sharing, most reliable systems do not provide strong guarantees of predictable response.

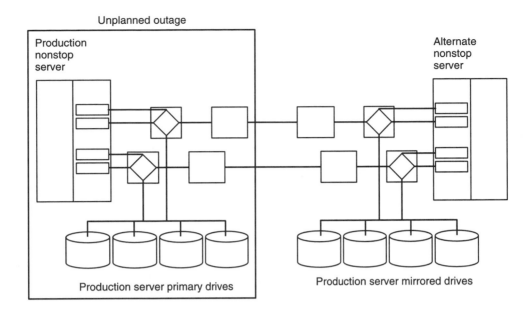

28.7   A Tandem failover cluster with mirrored disks.

FIGURE

28.2.3.2   Hardware Requirements

Reliable clusters generally prefer compatible hardware to enable failover, data
sharing, and convenient restoration from checkpoints. For cold standbys, however, less powerful configurations can be deployed to reduce cost, provided lower
performance is tolerable in a failover situation. Custom networking is employed
among cluster nodes and between primaries and standbys to ensure fault detection and isolation at the earliest possible time. Reliable clusters can be physically
localized or distributed over a wide-area network. Traditionally, reliable systems
use special operating systems (e.g., Tandem—now Hewlett–Packard's—NonStop
kernel), but many recent systems have been implemented as a middleware layer,
so a specialized operating system is no longer required. Finally, reliable clusters
can also include multiple nodes for scalability in capacity.

28.2.3.3   High-Reliability SCEs in Grids

High-reliability elements are a natural choice for simple composite elements. The
internal substructure of such elements is encapsulated, allowing them to be
viewed as reliable, high-capacity systems. Such systems can provide a wealth of

important services reliably, facilitating rigorous reasoning about operation, bootstrap procedures, reconfiguration, failure modes, and so on for Grid systems.

28.2.4   Dedicated High-Performance SCEs

Dedicated high-performance SCEs merge basic elements into a single resource pool for computing, memory, and storage, allowing these resources to be applied to a single computation. Since microprocessors have become the fastest processors available, collections of microprocessors (massively parallel processors) or entire systems (scalable clusters or networks of workstations) have become an attractive and cost-effective way to achieve high performance (29, 80, 106, 181, 331, 600). By employing standard workstation or PC building blocks and scalable networks, these dedicated high-performance clusters can be scaled to arbitrarily large configurations. These systems were initially applied to supercomputing tasks and were operated as dedicated systems, with space sharing used to run two or more applications simultaneously. To connect hundreds or thousands of nodes together with high efficiency, dedicated high-performance systems employ high-speed custom networks with limited physical extent (tens of meters). These networks employ parallel data links and custom signaling to deliver high performance, as with the custom cluster networks described in Section 28.1.2.

For example, the IBM Blue Horizon machine uses high-volume microprocessors as their basic computation engines. It employs 8-processor SMP servers as the basic building blocks, with custom interconnects delivering ~350 megabit/sec of network bandwidth to each node in the system and latencies as low as 20 microseconds. The IBM Blue Horizon system uses a standard AIX (IBM's UNIX) workstation operating system and a collection of middleware to provide job scheduling, program loading, file input/output, and so on. Allowing a single job on each node enables high performance on dedicated jobs—direct access to networks, management of local memory, and so on. Operating system services such as file access and external network input/output are hosted on system service nodes.

The predominant programming model on these systems is explicit message passing, typically via a standard interface such as MPI. This model enables the achievement of high performance at the price of explicit programmer management of naming and data movement. Higher-level interfaces, such as HPF and distributed shared memory, are used to a lesser degree. For a wide range of applications, high-performance MPI implementations have been constructed, so for these applications, dedicated high-performance SCEs can effectively aggregate their compute performance. These systems provide single-system image (uniform monitoring, resource usage, file system access, etc.). Distributed shared-memory systems have demonstrated techniques for efficient memory pooling (244, 440), although significant questions remain about how to manage and share such pools as well as how to best implement virtual memory in such an environment. Efficient scheduling remains a difficult challenge, as schedulers typically focus on processors, utilizing memory, network, disk, and other resources poorly.

28.2.4.1 Beowulf Clusters

An increasingly popular dedicated high-performance SCE is a PC cluster, commonly known as a Beowulf cluster (106). Beowulf clusters consist of high-volume products such as dual-processor desktop or server systems, networked by low-cost, commodity fast Ethernet or gigabit Ethernet networking. These systems are predominantly Linux based, with Redhat, Debian, and Suse being popular variants, and there are a wide variety of both commercial and research/academic software systems for assembling and managing such cluster systems. Commercial systems include Scyld, Scali, Platform Computing, VA Cluster, and Score. Research and academic systems include Oscar and NPACI Rocks. Although the functionality in these systems varies widely, they all address elements of the key challenges in building dedicated high-performance elements from commodity components: configuration management, scheduling, single-system image, and a shared file system. These software packages allow a Beowulf cluster to be viewed as an aggregate resource with a single point of access for inclusion as a dedicated, high-performance SCE into the Grid. Typical Beowulf cluster systems are anywhere from 8 to about 128 nodes, with the majority of the systems being in the range of 16 to 64 nodes. Above 64 nodes, the complexity of physical machine maintenance, configuration management, and even network wiring becomes significant, and the advantages of custom-engineered systems are more pronounced. Even at 64 nodes, however, Beowulf systems can have substantial compute, memory, and storage capabilities.

28.2.4.2 Commercial Resource Virtualization Systems

Recently, a number of commercial vendors have introduced resource virtualization systems that increase the manageability of resources and the applications deployed on them. Examples of such commercial systems include IBM's Oceano (84), Hewlett–Packard's Utility Data Center (322), and Sun Microsystem's N1. (See also Chapter 14.) Although public information on these systems is limited at present, each of these systems purports to support "wire once" approaches to hardware in large server complexes, automated deployment of applications, monitoring, provisioning, and evolution as application needs evolve. Many of these systems are advertised as providing a single-system view of an entire data center, much as cluster software packages provide a single-system view of a cluster. As the commercial virtualization systems become more widespread, they will not only support dedicated high-performance SCEs as Grid elements but will also extend their capabilities to include dynamic deployment of applications.

28.2.4.3 External Interfaces and Guarantees

Dedicated high-performance SCEs aggregate resources to speed up individual computations and are scalable to hundreds or thousands of nodes. Thus, they provide both pooled capacity for sequential jobs and high performance for parallel computations. In fact, many scheduling systems such as Sun's Grid Engine, IBM's LoadLeveler, and Platform Computing's LSF will schedule in combination both uniprocessor and dedicated parallel jobs. Because they focus on highest single-job performance (supercomputing), however, dedicated SCEs have not delivered reliability or predictability and are not generally sharable (other than via space partitioning). We note that many commercial reliable cluster products have an element of scalability but generally do not deliver the levels of performance described for dedicated high-performance SCEs.

28.2.4.4 Hardware Requirements

In dedicated high-performance SCEs, aggregate performance is the primary objective, so scalability to hundreds or thousands of nodes is supported. Hardware attributes (e.g., heterogeneity) that degrade performance are not generally included. Software features (e.g., process pairing for reliability) that reduce performance are also not included. In addition, because the SCE is viewed as a single system, changes to the underlying systems (operating system and motherboard) are sometimes required. Networks and interfaces are virtually always customized. Recently, under pressure from low-cost, high-volume products, many vendors have chosen to use unmodified workstations and operating systems, differentiating only with modest scheduling and middleware software.

28.2.4.5 Dedicated High-Performance SCEs in Grids

Dedicated high-performance SCEs can be assets in a Grid environment. Indeed, many such systems are deployed in production Grids today. However, their dedicated-use model significantly reduces their effectiveness. This observation provides a major impetus for the development of shared controllable-performance systems. Broadening the model of use is essential both for improving resource utilization and for supporting a broader class of resource-intensive online and interactive applications for the future.

28.3 SUMMARY

In this chapter, we have focused on the capabilities of basic elements and SCEs. The capabilities of basic computation, communication, and storage elements continue to improve geometrically, producing a Grid rich in resources and capable of rich sharing because of the availability of high-bandwidth links. Simple composite elements provide both aggregate capabilities and qualitatively different capabilities, such as reliability (summarized in Table 28.5). These capabilities will determine the role and contribution of SCEs to larger Grids.

Grids based on the Globus Toolkit are now moving from a resource to a services model in which all capabilities are presented as network "Grid services" (279). In such a model, SCEs can provide compute resources, data/storage resources, and application services. As compute resources, they will form dynamic Grid application servers, allowing compute-oriented applications to be dynamically instantiated and provide Grid compute application services. As data/storage resources, they will provide a wealth of data Grid services. As these capabilities are combined with the increasingly popular commercial resource virtualization systems, applications will increasingly be expressed in a fashion independent of the detailed platform environment. That is, if they do not need the greatest possible performance or access to unique services, they can be expressed against a virtualized interface. Such an approach will further increase the liquidity of applications

Element type	Capacity	Aggregatable	Reliable	Predictable	Sharable
Basic compute	Fixed	—	No	No	Yes
Basic storage	Fixed	—	No	No	Yes
Basic network	Fixed	—	No	No	Yes
High-throughput SCE	Scalable	No	Partial	No	Yes
Reliable SCE	Limited scaling	No	Yes	No	Yes
Dedicated high-performance SCE	Scalable	Yes	No	No	No

28.5   Unique Capabilities of Each SCE Type.

TABLE

and their flexible deployment, enabling further progress in achieving the Grid vision of computing and application services as a fungible resource.

Several important challenges arise in building bridges from useful SCEs to large-scale Grids. Three major elements of these challenges are composition (interfacing), performance guarantees, and security and data integrity.

Composing both basic and SCEs into larger Grids is a complex challenge, requiring directory services, protocols, compatible services and data representations, and conversion where necessary. Although a general solution must involve all element types, special problems are raised here by simple composite elements. They include interfaces, semantics, scheduling, and management for aggregated memory resources, aggregated persistent storage resources, aggregated communication resources, and migration/interoperation. The distinct challenges for SCEs here include developing interfaces to aggregate resources that provide simple semantics and high performance yet reflect the fact that, even within an SCE, the hardware elements come and go dynamically. A number of lower-level issues are also critical: how to map aggregated resources to the disjoint basic elements within an SCE (e.g., where do the I/O requests and computations go?), whether such mappings are static or dynamic, and how users can manage their usage of the resources.

Another important challenge is enabling Grid computations to achieve reasonable global performance. In most current approaches, this is predicated on some ability to reserve (or guarantee) performance from Grid elements. However, such techniques must be reconciled with local resource management policies designed to achieve local resource and computational efficiency. Thus, challenges for SCEs in Grids include the following:

+ Mechanisms to ensure predictable performance for memory, computation, and storage both for basic and for aggregated resources

+ Techniques for coordinated scheduling across basic (within an SCE) and global memory, computation, and storage resources

+ Policies for predictable performance, which manage the needs of global and local computations against available resources

Finally, if users are to achieve high productivity in a computing environment spanning numerous physical resources and administrative domains, they must be insulated from a wealth of security and data integrity concerns. For example, users may wish to use remote storage facilities for performance or even cost advantages. However, if they must worry about unauthorized data disclosure or unexpected loss of data, users are likely to be scarce. Thus, important challenges for SCEs in Grids include providing secure access to resources and data security for participating computations, and providing data integrity guarantees for data, independent of availability or failure of any individual data repository.

ACKNOWLEDGMENTS

This work has been supported in part by the Defense Advanced Research Projects Administration through U.S. Air Force Rome Laboratory Contracts AFRL F30602-99-1-0534 and the National Science Foundation through NSF EIA-99-75020 Grads and NSF Cooperative Agreement ANI-0225642 (OptIPuter) to the University of California, San Diego. Support from Hewlett–Packard is gratefully acknowledged.

FURTHER READING

For more information on the topics covered in this chapter, see *www.mkp.com/grid2* and also the following references:

+ Pakin et al. (513) and Chun et al. (188) describe fast communication methods.

+ Chien et al. (180) describe the Entropia desktop Grid system in greater detail.

+ Gray and Reuter (327) provide information relevant to reliable SCEs.

+ Sterling (609) discusses Beowulf PC clusters.

+ Snir et al. (600) describes a dedicated high-performance SCE, the IBM SP.

29

Peer-to-Peer Technologies

Jon Crowcroft, Tim Moreton, Ian Pratt, and Andrew Twigg

*P*eer-to-peer (P2P) systems are Internet applications that harness the resources of a large number of autonomous participants. In many cases, these peers form self-organizing networks that are layered on top of conventional Internet protocols and have no centralized structure. Inspired by the successes of early P2P systems such as Napster, Gnutella, and SETI@home, a large and active research community continues to explore the principles, technologies, and applications of such applications.

P2P and Grid computing are both concerned with enabling resource sharing within distributed communities. However, different base assumptions have led to distinct requirements and technical directions (273) (see Figure 29.1). P2P systems have focused on resource sharing in environments characterized by potentially millions of users, most with homogenous desktop systems and low-bandwidth, intermittent connections to the Internet. As such, the emphasis has been on global fault-tolerance and massive scalability. Grid systems have arisen from collaboration between generally smaller, better-connected groups of users with more diverse resources to share.

Despite these differences, the long-term objectives of P2P and Grids seem likely to converge at least in some regard, as Grids expand in scale and incorporate more transient services and resources and as P2P researchers consider a broader class of applications (273). Our goal in this chapter is to take a step toward this reconciliation of approaches, first by introducing the reader to key P2P concepts and technologies and second by pointing out areas in which P2P results appear particularly likely to find application in the Grid context. We discuss, for example, how P2P results may apply to challenges faced by the Open Grid Services Architecture

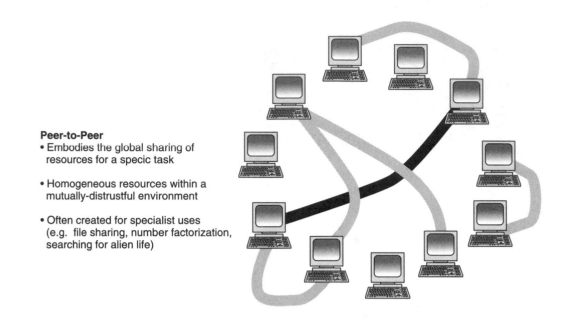

Peer-to-Peer
- Embodies the global sharing of resources for a specic task

- Homogeneous resources within a mutually-distrustful environment

- Often created for specialist uses (e.g. file sharing, number factorization, searching for alien life)

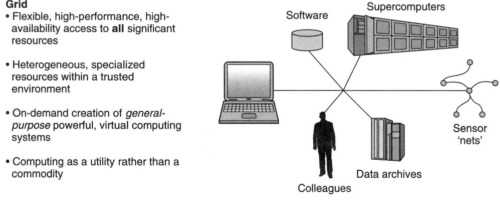

Grid
- Flexible, high-performance, high-availability access to **all** significant resources

- Heterogeneous, specialized resources within a trusted environment

- On-demand creation of *general-purpose* powerful, virtual computing systems

- Computing as a utility rather than a commodity

29.1   Comparing peer-to-peer and Grid computing styles.

FIGURE

(OGSA, Chapter 17) (279), in such areas as resource discovery, scalable load balancing, and highly available storage and data distribution systems.

The chapter is arranged as follows. After reviewing the history of P2P computing, we examine P2P middleware and three broad application areas: storage, computation, and searching. We investigate the relationship between P2P and

Grid computing, and conclude by looking at possible future developments that build on P2P and Grid approaches.

29.1 A BRIEF HISTORY

P2P networking has divided research circles. The traditional distributed computing community views these young technologies as "upstarts with little regard for, or memory of, the past"; evidence supports this view in some cases. Others welcome an opportunity to revisit past results and to gain practical experience with large-scale distributed algorithms. An early use of the term "peer-to-peer computing" is in IBM's Systems Network Architecture documents on LU6.2 Transactions, over 25 years ago. The term, which we shall use interchangeably with P2P, came to the fore publicly with the rise and fall of Napster. Although prior systems did exist in the evolutionary phase of distributed computing (e.g., Eternity), we limit our survey to the period from Napster to now (i.e., 1998–2003).

29.1.1 Beyond the Client-Server Model

P2P systems can be contrasted with asymmetric *client-server* systems, in which a *server*—usually a more powerful and better-connected machine—runs for long periods of time and delivers storage and computational resources to some number of *clients*. Thus, the server emerges as a performance and reliability bottleneck. To mitigate these problems, server sites may use such solutions as replication, load balancing, and request routing, so that one conceptual server is made up of many distinct machines. A natural evolution of this thinking is to include the clients' resources in the system, an approach that becomes increasingly attractive as the performance gap between desktop and server machines narrows and broadband networks dramatically improve client connectivity.

Thus, P2P systems evolve from client–server systems by removing the asymmetry in roles: a client is also a server that allows access to its resources. Clients, now really *peers*, contribute their own resources in exchange for the use of the service. Work (be it message passing, computation, storage, or searching) is partitioned between all peers, so that a peer consumes its own resources on behalf of others (acting as a server), while asking other peers to do the same for its own benefit (acting as a client). As in the real world, this cooperative model may break down if peers are not provided with incentives to participate. We look into trust, reputation, and economically grounded approaches in Section 29.3.3.

It is sometimes claimed that P2P systems have *no* distinguished node and thus are highly fault tolerant and have good performance and scaling properties. Although there is some truth to this claim, many P2P systems do have distinguished nodes, and many have performance limitations. In fact, the fault-tolerance claims are hardly borne out in early P2P systems: availability figures in Napster, Gnutella (558), and Freenet (190) do not compare favorably with even the humblest Web sites. Second- and later-generation systems, however, may indeed provide the claimed functionality and performance gains. We see promising results in Pastry (564), Chord (613), and CAN (546); and even more recent work building applications and services over these systems shows great potential gains.

One can also compare and contrast classical client–server and modern P2P systems on another axis, namely, statefulness. Despite successes with stateless servers, many Web servers use cookies, script-driven repositories, and Web services to maintain state over various transactions with a client. In a P2P system, since a peer rarely knows directly which node is able to fulfill its request, each peer keeps track of a soft-state set of neighbors (in some sense) in order to pass requests, messages, or state around the network. While soft state is also a long-recognized technique in Grid computing (176, 204, 278) (and see Chapter 19), Grid services themselves are often inherently stateful during their (explicitly managed) lifetimes.

Yet another viewpoint from which one can dissect these systems is the use of *intermediaries*. The Web (and client–server file systems such as NFS and AFS) uses caches to reduce average latency and networking load, but these caches are typically arranged statically. P2P systems partition work dynamically among cooperative peers to achieve locality-oriented load balancing. Content distribution systems such as PAST (565) and Pasta (485) use demand-driven strategies to distribute data to peers close in the network to that demand. Similarly, Grid systems are starting to explore the dynamic provisioning of distributed computation close to data sources, in proportion to the time and parallelization demands (544, 636).

The classical distributed systems community would claim that many of these ideas were present in early work on fault-tolerant systems in the 1970s. For example, the Xerox Network System's name service, *grapevine* (579), included many traits mentioned here. Other systems that can be construed as P2P systems include Net News (NNTP is certainly not client–server) and the Web's intercache protocol, ICP. The Domain Name System also includes zone transfers and other mechanisms that are not part of its normal client–server resolver behavior.

29.1.2   Deploying Internet Services by Overlaying

New Internet network-level services such as IP QoS in the form of integrated services and differentiated services, as well as novel service models such as multicast and mobility, have proved notoriously hard to build and deploy in their native forms. Thus, network researchers, frustrated in their attempts to deliver new network services within the context of traditional telecommunications or Internet networks, have built experimental infrastructures by constructing *overlay* systems: developing new infrastructures using services of and layering on the existing infrastructure, rather than by complementing or replacing it.

An overlay may be as simple as a collection of static IP-in-IP tunnels or as complex as a full dynamic VPN (virtual private network). Some such systems are in use in the active networks research community. Clearly, overlaying is a relative term. The nature of the overlay and the underlay depends on the infrastructure being developed. Grid systems use overlaying to provide unified (virtualized) interfaces to all aspects of service management, with the aim of integrating underlying native platforms and protocols. In contrast, P2P systems have focused on the use of overlaying to provide an abstraction for *addressing* between peers spread throughout the Internet.

IP was originally an overlay service, implemented above other layered communications systems: the PSTN, ARPANET, and X.25 circuit switched networks. Indeed, this overlay model keeps reemerging as network operators deploy faster switched infrastructures such as Frame Relay, ATM and WDM, and PONS (Pure Optical Networked Systems) core networks.

In the Resilient Overlay Network system (77, 78), sites collaborate to find a longer "IP level" path that has better properties (such as throughput or loss) at the application level, by dynamically routing via a set of dynamically created tunnels. Similar approaches have been used for multicast (186, 187, 585), multimedia conferencing systems (387), streaming media (224), anycast (696), and server selection (351).

29.1.3   Napster

The Napster *file-sharing system* allowed users to search for and download music files held on other Napster users' hard drives. When the application was started, metadata for a user's shared songs were transferred into a global directory. When other users searched for a song using keywords in this metadata, the directory returned a list of clients sharing songs matching the query. The end machines (peers, in this sense) cooperated to transfer the song directly between themselves.

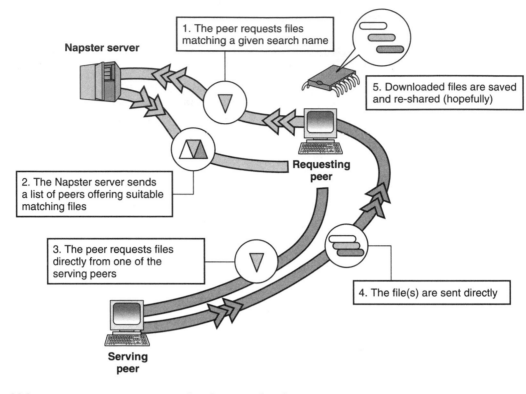

1. The peer requests files matching a given search name

Napster server

5. Downloaded files are saved and re-shared (hopefully)

Requesting peer

2. The Napster server sends a list of peers offering suitable matching files

3. The peer requests files directly from one of the serving peers

4. The file(s) are sent directly

Serving peer

29.2

FIGURE

Napster—an example of a centralized peer-to-peer system.

Each took a client or server role, depending on whether a song was being downloaded or uploaded (see Figure 29.2).

Opinions differ as to whether Napster was truly P2P because its directory is stored on central servers. However, by distributing the bandwidth and storage requirements, the system ameliorated its initial perceived scalability and performance bottlenecks. Further, the real utility of the network—the diversity of music that was available—was certainly a property of its constituent peers.

Technically, the program suffered from a simple interface, and the poor reliability and bandwidth of other clients' connections often hampered users' attempts to retrieve songs. However, because it dramatically simplified the task of obtaining music on the Internet, Napster became immensely popular, having at its peak approximately 1.6 million simultaneous users. Over time, Napster's centralized directory became both a severe bottleneck and a single point of failure for legal, economic, and political attacks; Napster was eventually shut down by court order for helping users infringe copyright.

29.1.4   In Napster's Wake

Napster's success was attributable to online music sharing being a "killer application." Moreover, it demonstrated the potential in harnessing client resources to satisfy their need for a service. With the demise of Napster, there arose a desire within the music-sharing community for a fully decentralized service that would not be susceptible to a similar legal attack. The projects that rose to the challenge stimulated important technical developments in distributed object location and routing, distributed searching, and content dissemination.

29.1.4.1   The Second Generation: Full Decentralization

Gnutella is a distributed search protocol adopted by several file-sharing applications that dispensed with the centralized directory and instead broadcast search queries between a peer's neighbors (Figure 29.3). Despite measures to limit and restrict queries, several studies and user experience found that the volume of query and control traffic caused excessive network load, limiting the size of the network, the chance of satisfying a given query, and the amount of a client's bandwidth left for actual file transfers (558, 574).

Other systems for locating content, including Freenet (190), added mechanisms to route requests to a node where the content is likely to be, in a best-effort partial partitioning of the networks' content. Systems for file sharing such as Kazaa (436) and recent Gnutella evolutions (595) added structure to P2P file-sharing networks by dynamically electing nodes to become *super-peers*, caching and serving common queries or content. These schemes take advantage of the observed Zipf-like distribution of object popularity and mitigate the difficulties of passing queries through hosts on high-latency, low-bandwidth dialup connections.

29.1.4.2   The Third Generation: Efficient Routing Substrates

Although the range of applications for P2P techniques remained limited by the end of 2001, a common requirement had emerged. For each peer to make a useful contribution to the global service, a reliable way of partitioning workload and addressing the node responsible was needed. Further, the emphasis on scalability—and the corresponding observation that in a global-scale system peers will be joining, failing, and leaving continually—required that these functions be

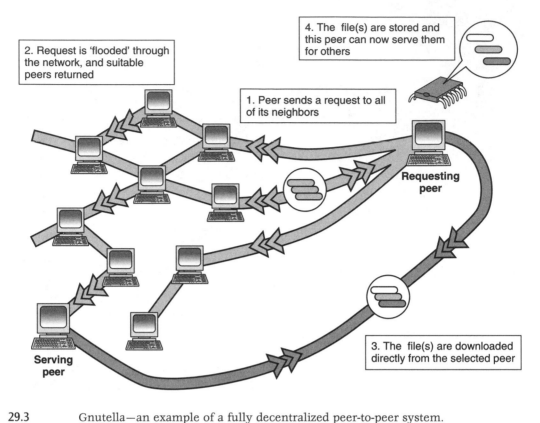

2. Request is 'flooded' through the network, and suitable peers returned

4. The file(s) are stored and this peer can now serve them for others

1. Peer sends a request to all of its neighbors

Requesting peer

3. The file(s) are downloaded directly from the selected peer

Serving peer

29.3   Gnutella—an example of a fully decentralized peer-to-peer system.

FIGURE

performed with knowledge of only a fraction of the global state on each peer, maintained with only a low communication overhead in the underlying network.

This architectural separation inspired a generation of *P2P routing substrates* that provided a distributed message-passing object or key location service. The most popular approach adopts a distributed hash table (DHT), in which nodes are assigned a unique pseudo-random identifier that determines their position in a key space (Figure 29.4). Messages are routed to points within the same key space and are delivered eventually to the closest node. According to the way in which applications use this service, a message destined for a given key represents a request to provide a given service with respect to that key. As requests' keys must be mapped onto the key space pseudo-randomly (usually using some secure hash function such as SHA-1 (262)), DHTs offer effective partitioning of the work

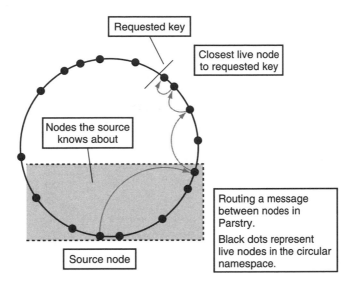

Requested key

Closest live node
to requested key

Nodes the source
knows about

Routing a message
between nodes in
Parstry.

Black dots represent
live nodes in the circular
namespace.

Source node

29.4

FIGURE

Routing a message between nodes in Pastry, a distributed hash table (DHT). Black dots represent live nodes in the circular key space.

between peers. Variants of this basic approach differ as to the structure of information on nodes and the way messages (or sometimes requests for routing information) are passed between peers.

The presence of DHT substrates that offer routing services, node management, and a simple interface led to a rise in the number and variety of P2P applications. Systems for event dissemination and overlay multicast, file archive, file systems, and replacements for DNS have emerged; we survey these areas in Section 29.2.

29.1.5   Future Directions for P2P Systems

P2P systems are still an active area of research, and progress is steady. We outline in the following technical issues facing the research community, before describing them and their application to Grid architectures in more detail in Section 29.3.

Although DHTs introduced an essential split between P2P middleware and applications, they have limitations that are providing an impetus for more flexible schemes. Further, each proposal for a new routing substrate contains convincing evaluation results from large-scale simulations, but no Internet deployment has tested their properties under real-world conditions—with respect to failure and latency, in particular. Such analysis will play an important part in directing research.

The scale of P2P systems means that participants are typically individuals and organizations without an out-of-band trust relationship. This key characteristic is not currently shared by Grid computing but takes on increasing significance as Grid architectures scale up. This property generates interesting work in the area of trust, reputation systems, economic incentives, and detection of malicious participants.

Indeed, many of the lessons learned from studies of second-generation deployments concern human behavior. Most P2P applications rely on a cooperative model of node interaction. Participants join the network and use the service: in return, they are expected to contribute their own resources, although doing so yields no direct benefit to them. Even the mutual benefits of cooperation will not stop people from defecting (59), and thus incentives through economic (677) and trust (484) models form an important part of ongoing research.

Much progress has been made in the security and censor-resistant aspects of some applications (157), including an important general result in the impossibility of preventing *pseudo-spoofing* (238) (owning more than one virtual identity) without a trusted link to a real-world identity.

As P2P computing matures, we will see a diversification in its applications. As Grid systems scale up and P2P techniques begin to capture shared use of more specialized resources, and as users are able to specify location, performance, availability, and consistency requirements more finely, we may see a convergence of techniques in the two areas. We describe this view further in Section 29.4.

29.2   APPLICATIONS

We partition P2P projects into routing substrates and the main classes of applications that run on them: systems for storage, computation, and searching.

29.2.1   Routing Substrates

Routing substrates are P2P middleware that facilitates communication between and management of a network's constituent nodes. We categorize these substrates as *unstructured* or *structured*, the essential difference being whether the neighbors that each peer maintains are organized in such a way as to allow deterministic location of a piece of content or a node.

29.2.1.1 Unstructured Routing

When joining a P2P network, a new node needs knowledge of at least one peer already present in the network from which to obtain its initial routing table entries. Nodes in unstructured systems tend to maintain these same neighbors, replacing their entries only if the node in question has failed. Hence, the topology of the network grows in an arbitrary, unstructured manner; it becomes difficult to bound the maximum path length and guarantee even connectivity between groups of nodes. This situation impacts performance and reliability: Unintentionally, some nodes may become bottlenecks.

So far, such systems have not allowed efficient searching (either for keys or for more complicated metadata queries). Gnutella uses a flooding-based search in which a query is broadcast to each of its neighbors, which in turn pass it on to each of their neighbors; each peer tracks the queries that it has seen to prevent routing loops. Unfortunately, the buildup of traffic from each query is exponential—to such an extent that unless the search breadth and depth are low, the system will not scale. More efficient schemes have borrowed from conventional data structures, including iterative deepening techniques (688) (incrementally considering the nodes at a given number of hops from the requester) and random walks (456).

A concept of *direction* seems essential, however, in pruning the potential search space and in routing efficiently. In Freenet (190), a publishing network where peers cooperatively participate in caching and retrieving documents, each node maintains a data store that locally caches the data and key associated with a document, as well as the node from which it was originally obtained. Entries for evicted documents are maintained, but without the attached data. Upon receiving a request for a key where no cache entry exists, a node finds the entry for the document with the key *numerically closest* to that sought, and forwards the request to the node from which it was obtained. In this way, Freenet nodes over time may come to specialize in portions of the keyspace, and other nodes' knowledge of this gives direction to searches. Because this scheme relies on uniform local knowledge of the keyspace, however, it suffers poor worst-case lookup performance (364) and cannot guarantee success.

29.2.1.2 DHTs and Structured Routing

Structured routing substrates (approximately synonymous with DHTs at present) organize their peers so that any node can be reached in a bounded number of hops, typically logarithmic in the size of the network. Although subtly different, all of the main schemes operate similarly. Pastry maintains per node routing

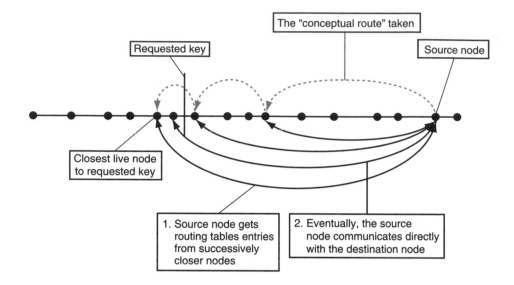

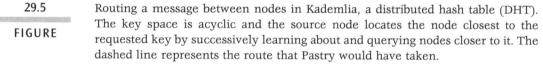

29.5

FIGURE

Routing a message between nodes in Kademlia, a distributed hash table (DHT). The key space is acyclic and the source node locates the node closest to the requested key by successively learning about and querying nodes closer to it. The dashed line represents the route that Pastry would have taken.

tables organized by the length of the entries' shared address prefix. Tapestry (700) nodes each maintain an inverted index organized, again, by prefix. Kademlia (464) routes according to distance between IDs using the XOR metric (Figure 29.5). In Chord (613), each peer is arranged in a circular ID space and maintains links with its immediate predecessor and successor, and a number of "chords" to other nodes whose distances are arranged in an exponential fashion. CAN (546) uses several hashes to map into a multidimensional ID space; queries are passed along the axes of this space.

The class of DHTs derived from Karger's work on consistent hashing (401) and Plaxton's distributed data structure (527) are mathematically described in (91), which gives upper and lower bounds on the query time in DHTs. The results are similar to the empirical results from CAN and Chord. As an alternative underlying technique, Distributed Tries (290) use a trie, and so the same lookup(key)-> value as DHTs, but they may offer lower average-case message overhead. Each node holds a trie: By using a backtracking search, they query nodes that are known to contain other parts of the trie, which in turn may return the object or more up-to-date or detailed parts of the trie. In the worst case this scheme degenerates to broadcast search.

An inherent difficulty with DHTs relates to the uniform partitioning of work. Since data (be it content, blocks to store, or multicast topics) are associated with pseudo-random keys, a user cannot control which peer is responsible for a particular data item. Locality of reference is broken: an essential property of P2P computing is to offer the performance seen by conventional client–server models. Significantly, though, SkipNet (356) offers a hybrid architecture based on skip lists that can route and store within explicit administrative domains.

29.2.2   Content Distribution and Storage Systems

P2P techniques first found their niche in *file-sharing systems*. We distinguish such applications from *distributed file systems* (e.g., NFS (572)). The former allow users to obtain specific well-defined content, usually based on a metadata search; the latter expose local file-system hierarchies to remote users, may be writable, and may implement access control or consistency semantics. We also describe *distributed archival storage systems*, in which insertion and retrieval operations are coarse grained (i.e., documents at a time) and storage is durable, long term, and often focused on censor resistance or anonymity. Additionally, we consider storage requirements in Grid computing applications.

29.2.2.1   File Sharing

Recall that Napster, while partly centralized, applied P2P techniques to file sharing by distributing the high-bandwidth requirement of transfers: files were passed directly between peers. However, in this setup the performance and reliability of file retrieval are dependent on the peer with which a user is transacting, preventing the system from implementing any quality-of-service guarantees. Frequently, transfers may be aborted when the sender cancels or disconnects or when the network partitions. The rate at which transfers proceed depends on the relative positions of the endpoints, their latency, and their bandwidths.

Swarm distribution in systems such as Kazaa improves load balancing and reduces a transfer's dependence on individual nodes by naming the file by the secure hash of its contents. If a transfer aborts, another peer sharing the same file may be identified and the transfer resumed. Further, subdividing the file into portions and naming these allows different parts of the file to be transferred from multiple sources at once, improving performance for well-connected machines. By allocating small portions to dial-up peers and larger portions to others, each node contributes according to its ability.

Recent P2P applications based on DHTs offer content streaming and effective content dissemination by replicating data in proportion to demand for it, close in the network to that demand. These applications include CFS (209) and Pasta (485), file systems, and SplitStream (158) for streaming media.

The difficulty of performing arbitrary metadata searches and obtaining deterministic results in a fully decentralized environment is limiting file sharing. Many systems are restricted to specific areas (in particular media and software distribution) where the search-space for users is well defined; typically, users "discover" content by out-of-band means.

29.2.2.2 Archival Storage Systems

The Eternity service proposed a design for a system that offers censor-resistant, durable storage to users for a specific time period by replicating and scattering data across servers in a distributed system. Although Eternity is a design and does not specify any of the mechanisms by which P2P applications are now characterized, its ambitions were reflected in many early P2P systems.

Free Haven (231), a document storage system, implements a variation on Eternity. Its primary aim is to offer anonymity to publishers of documents and to provide plausible deniability to server owners. Documents are stored on a P2P network of mutually distrustful servers, called a *servnet*: queries and publication requests are broadcast to the whole group. Much early work on the nature of peer behavior is present in Free Haven's design. It makes pairs of servers mutually accountable for files that they store using a buddy system, and uses a reputation system to report complaints from "buddies": Servers over time develop trust for other servers according to their reputation. An economic system of trading reputation capital for resources on other servers provides an incentive to participate and minimizes the damage caused by individual malicious entities.

PAST (565) is an experimental archival utility built over the Pastry DHT. Storage and retrieval operations are performed at the granularity of whole files. No human-readable naming scheme is supported; rather, a fileID associated with the insertion must be passed by other means. Inserted files are immutable until withdrawn by their owner.

29.2.2.3 Global-Scale File Systems

Network file systems were one of the first great successes of client–server distributed systems. Sun RPC and NFS were ubiquitous from the mid-1980s in research, and education labs and many small organizations use Samba to share storage resources.

Recent distributed file-system designs aim more ambitiously to present a unified view of storage resources of any Internet-connected system, while offering secure reliable storage, better-defined, application-variable concurrency guarantees, and efficient content distribution. The current cost of management and organization of storage tends to exceed the cost of the physical media. This situation has led to the adoption of P2P techniques for managing large, dynamic sets of unreliable hosts, replacing brittle, location-dependent mutual client–server systems (such as NFS) and high-maintenance organization-centric client–server systems, such as AFS.

The Cooperative File System (CFS) (209) is implemented over Chord. Files are split into fixed-size blocks, which are identified by their secure hash, then distributed to nodes. Storage can be guaranteed for a set time period enabled by per node storage limits based on IP addresses. Users arrange files hierarchically in a "file system," which forms a per-publisher, decentralized namespace. CFS offers coarse-grained file mutability; but since each publisher manages its own file system, collaborative file manipulation is not possible. No cache consistency or concurrent update control scheme is proposed.

Pasta (485), a prototype P2P file system operating over Pastry (564), offers a persistent, mutable shared storage and content distribution service to a potentially large collection of mutually distrustful users. It integrates closely with local file systems through a loopback NFS. Users store data as a series of immutable blocks, referenced through mutable index blocks that store fragments of decentralized namespace. By replicating and maintaining blocks across peers, Pasta offers persistent and reliable storage. Widespread localized caching in proportion to demand provides an efficient content distribution system by preventing hot spots and migrating data to the source of requests. Files are split into blocks in terms of their contents, to exploit commonality between sections of files; this arrangement allows Pasta to store different versions of a file efficiently and to modify them on a copy-on-write basis. A scheme of storage quotas, enforced in a distributed fashion, regulates consumption. Ongoing work on Pasta focuses on a scheme whereby privately owned data may be collaboratively modified by untrusted users. Through namespace overlays, users may appear to share and organize each other's stored data; modifications to files or namespace are seen as in a versioning file system, and third parties form a view by choosing which modifications to trust.

OceanStore (422) is an infrastructure for providing persistent data storage in a global-scale ubiquitous computing environment, although its current prototype, Pond (554), shares more with the systems discussed previously. It uses a variant of Plaxton's distributed hierarchical data structure (527) to locate stored data efficiently. The system caches data widely for performance and availability and performs distributed cache consistency management. For each file, a primary tier of replica-carrying nodes use a Byzantine agreement protocol (159) to commit modifications. A conflict resolution scheme resolves concurrent updates as in Bayou (635).

29.2.2.4 Data Access in Grids

Requirements for data access and movement in Grid computing, where computation is performed at a remote site, may motivate applications that combine techniques from both content distribution and P2P file systems. Several P2P file system designs, including OceanStore (422) and Pasta (485), might be suitable for the task—and also offer fault-tolerant, highly available long-term storage. They provide schemes to support location independence of data on a global scale, allowing data to be gathered from a variety of sites and sensors or from dynamically established caches, while being named in a unified way. Although many systems offer only limited concurrency semantics, this is all that most Grid file access patterns require. Such systems also use conventional file-system interfaces, necessary to minimize rewriting of applications for a Grid setting.

As discussed in Chapters 19 and 22, Grid applications require flexible caching of input files and output files for rerunning computational tasks with different parameters or for comparing results. Systems such as CFS and Pasta incorporate caching schemes suitable for this purpose. The size of some datasets, however, may necessitate files being stored across different nearby sites, then streamed; moreover, streaming of diagnostic data back to the client site is essential for tracking progress. Data movement issues such as these may benefit from swarm distribution and other techniques developed for P2P file-sharing applications.

29.2.3   Distributed Computation

Several hundred million personal computers and workstations are now on the public Internet, each with hundreds of MIPS going unused every second. Attempts to exploit this vast processing resource, however, have been limited for several reasons. The granularity of computations required in many applications is small, individual nodes are unreliable, and external code and data distribution is hampered by relatively poor latency and bandwidth. The computations that make sense are those that can be broken into many relatively small pieces that require long individual processing times but perform little communication.

Numerous P2P computing systems have been developed and have seen considerable success for computations that are able to use large numbers of processors that may vary in job throughput but are homogeneous in that they offer no specialized functionality. "Philanthropic computing" projects continue to thrive in such domains as large-scale signal processing (e.g., SETI@Home (79, 615)), genome searching, Astrogrid, and code cracking. Since many peers in such systems are home users with slow and intermittent connections, such projects have typically involved highly parallelizable tasks. Recent consideration of inter-node proximity in P2P systems may, however, lead to the use of clustering, allowing more tightly coupled computations of the sort commonly run on Grid systems (e.g., see Chapter 10). These technologies have also been applied in corporate settings, where higher connectivity allows for more tightly coupled applications (e.g., see Chapter 11).

29.2.4 Distributed Searching

In addition to key-based searching and file name metadata searching, researchers have tried to offer *generalized metadata search functionality* over DHTs. Systems having this functionality operate within the context of resource discovery and may suggest directions for similar service discovery mechanisms in Grid computing. Examples include PlanetP (200), pSearch (630)/Sedar (457), and Multi-Dimensional Pastry (604). These systems use the vector space model to represent documents, which maps complex searches to similarity searches in a vector space. Searches are carried out in pSearch by using a CAN (546) network to route requests, and in PlanetP by summarizing using Bloom filters (127) and "gossiping" using the "name dropper" algorithm (353). XenoSearch (604) extends Pastry's lookup to multiple dimensions; its operation is shown in Figure 29.6.

29.2.5 Developing P2P Software

The symmetric nature of P2P software makes such software systems harder to write than client–server systems. Many of the issues discussed in Chapter 19 arise in this context. One must pay great attention to synchronization effects: one cannot separate concerns as in client–server systems. (However, the separation of concerns that can often be achieved between routing substrate and application can reduce development complexity.) In addition, the P2P programmer must cope with the types of erroneous requests that only server (rather than client)

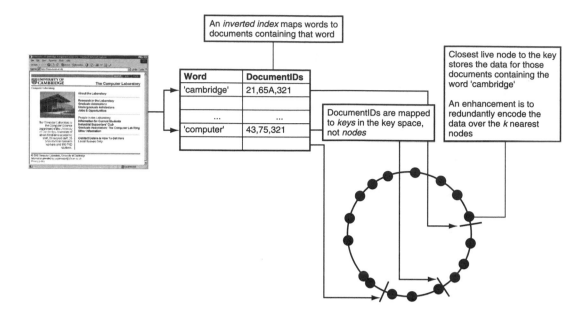

29.6

FIGURE

Distributing an inverted index over a distributed hash table, such as Pastry's circular key space. An inverted index maps keywords to documents containing those words. A Web page containing certain keywords is found by intersecting (using bloom filters passed between peers) the sets of possible documentIDs.

application programmers must deal with. Thus, P2P programming is currently an expert systems-programmer task.

Nevertheless, the widespread use of Java in some research projects, combined with the observation that there are enough common components in P2P development activities, has motivated development of a few toolkits. One example is Sun's JXTA toolkit. SEDA (674) provides a framework that supports event-drvien programming in Java and has been used in OceanStore (422) to build event-driven systems. Also, of course, OGSA (279) (Chapter 17)—as realized, for example, in the Globus Toolkit (276) (Chapter 4)—provides many relevant primitives.

29.3 PROPERTIES AND ISSUES

We now explore various properties of P2P computing, some aspects of which are present in current systems, while some are still the subject of ongoing work. In each case, we discuss the relevance to Grid computing.

29.3.1   Harnessing Resources

The P2P fault model of an unreliable infrastructure and mutually distrustful participants leads P2P systems to treat resources as *homogeneous* and peers as *individually dispensable*. Therein lie many of the strengths and weaknesses of the approach. DHT designs embody these assumptions. Any node is equally likely to be responsible for one particular key, so it is assumed to be equally suitable to carry out a task related to it. Nodes carry similar numbers of keys, so it is assumed that their resources for storing or managing these keys are also equal.

Peers, however, are unlikely to have similar resources—either in quantity or in quality. Nor are peer resources likely to have similar reliability characteristics. Systems that recognize these facts benefit in terms of performance and availability. For example, superpeering in file-sharing systems takes advantage of well-connected nodes to implement distributed caching and indexing schemes.

Unfortunately, properties of a DHT routing substrate can hinder an application's ability to recognize the heterogeneity of resources. In CFS (209), for example, each node offers a globally fixed amount of disk space as storage for blocks inserted by other nodes. Nodes with substantially more spare capacity can run separate *virtual nodes* on the same physical machine, each offering the same fixed unit. CFS employs routing table "snooping" to avoid increased lookup path lengths (because virtual nodes effectively increase the size of the network), but this approach weakens assumptions about independent failure of nodes.

Grid systems, on the other hand, tend to comprise fewer, more varied, more specialized resources; each resource's properties are described and published, and individual work units are matched to a provider based on their own description (e.g., see Chapter 19).

29.3.2   User Connectivity

The nature of a peer's network connection is an essential consideration when designing P2P systems for practical use in established user communities. The problem is twofold: in many contexts, mean connection quality is low but also has high variance, because of differences between dial-up, broadband, and connections from academic or corporate networks. Thus, the scope for generic internode communication is severely limited, and applications must consider the heterogeneity of their peers' connections.

Another source of difficulty results from peers that cannot accept incoming connections, either because their ISP uses NAT and as such have no externally recognized IP address or because they are behind a separately administered firewall.

Additionally, most broadband connections have unequal provisioning of upstream and downstream bandwidth, and many impose "caps" on permanent connections. These factors all complicate attempts to understand routing behavior in real deployments.

Existing Grids tend to comprise participants connected by well-administered, reliable academic networks. However, as generic Grid services begin to incorporate more diverse peers, these issues may become more important.

29.3.3   Collaboration and Trust

In Grids and P2P systems, participants constitute a virtual organization defined by common interests. However, the nature of these common interests and associated trust relationships can span a broad spectrum, with Grid systems tending to feature "intra-VO" bonds stronger than those in P2P systems. The following features tend to be more common in P2P systems than in Grids:

+ *Nonexistent trust relationships.* The owner of one peer in a P2P system frequently has no real-world knowledge of the owner of other peers.

+ *Poor administration.* Peers in P2P systems are more likely to be *run by individuals than corporations.* This property has implications for uptime and reliability, leading to the observed power law up-time distributions for Gnutella and the relatively small number of hosts reliably available.

+ *Operated with no prior agreement between peers.* Consider a typical Grid computing task, such as processing a large amount of (possibly confidential) data. Before submitting the task to a Grid compute service, the submitter (consumer) often agrees on some terms and conditions with the service provider (Chapter 18).

+ *Composed of nodes that act in their own interests.* In P2P systems, one must assume a mutually distrustful environment and must assume that, without incentive to participate, a node will use the service without returning anything to it. In fact, such free riding is the norm rather than the exception in Gnutella.

In particular, although many P2P services rely on a cooperative model of interaction among nodes, they provide little incentive for nodes to collaborate.

One approach to addressing this situation is to use economic models to realign nodes' incentives to participate in P2P systems. Such models assume variable demand for services. For example, Geels and Kubiatowicz (304) argue that replica management in global-scale storage systems should be organized as an economy. Nodes trade off the cost of storing data blocks with the value they are able to charge for access to them. In this context, a variable demand for blocks is essential. However, whereas variable-demand properties may hold for human-valued commodities such as information stored or shared in a P2P system, such demands may not hold for routing table entries. Since DHTs typically determine the allocation of items to nodes pseudo-randomly, requests for keys will also be distributed evenly. Hence, no particular value can be conferred on any particular destination.

The lack of a scalable, low-overhead, fully decentralized digital cash system has hampered adoption of economic models. Mojo Nation (677), a distributed file storage and trading system, used a currency "mojo" to discourage free-riding and to obtain load balancing at servers by congestion charging; however, it relied on a centralized, trusted third party to discourage double spending.

Acqusti et al. (58) have developed an incentive model for a distributed application that offers anonymity to its participants. They take a game-theoretic approach to analyzing node behavior and attacks in various system models. Trust is considered only as a means to ameliorate pseudo-spoofing attacks, rather than as a means to provide incentives to peers.

Aberer and Despotovic (54) have devised a system for managing trust in a P2P system using a complaint-based metric. Nodes can make "complaints" regarding interactions they have had with other nodes. A threshold technique checks whether a node is untrustworthy, based on the difference between its recommendations and the average view. This system presents a rather brittle and almost binary view of trust, however, which is often difficult to reason about explicitly. Taking a different thrust, the NICE system (433) aims to identify rather than enforce the existence of cooperative peers. It claims to "efficiently locate the generous minority [of cooperating users], and form a clique of users all of whom offer local services to the community." The system takes a novel approach: rather than using economics to model trust, it proposes using trust to model expected service prices.

Many approaches to enforcing or encouraging collaboration have been proposed based on rather arbitrary measures. We believe that, instead, a collaborative service should have two properties: *avoidance*, whereby dishonest nodes are "routed around" by those using the service (which is often the desired case for a hedonistic node), and *exclusion*, whereby dishonest nodes are unable to use the service because others refuse to carry out work for them (e.g., not forwarding packets). We have developed a trust and security architecture (484) for a routing and node location service that uses a *trust protocol*, which describes how honest nodes perform, and a distributed, explicit trust model that allows reasoning about trust in the network. This system is resistant to a number of attacks, including collusion.

29.3.4   Scalability

P2P systems often add resources as they add customers. Thus, they should scale (at least at the computing and storage resource level, if not networking) linearly, or better, with the number of peers. Of course, many networks are designed assuming client–server traffic, and so it is possible that performance scaling properties may not be achieved transparently. Indeed, some claim that the "small world" models of human behavior and interaction, combined with the preferential way in which people link to known locations, lead to power law structures in connectivity.

Scalability is not a trivial consideration. While, for example, hops in a DHT may vary as $\log(n)$ with the number n of nodes in the network, acceptable access latency is constant and bounded by the user. Thus, P2P designs must make good use of proximity information to balance load between nodes and to maintain state efficiently as nodes join and fail. For file-system applications, this means exploiting caching, predictive prefetching, and the apparent Zipf-like power law distribution in content popularity.

Forming a structured topology is important in most P2P systems to provide bounds on latency and performance of internode communication. Approaches that structure and partition the keyspace tend to allow deterministic node location and better load balancing.

29.3.5   Proximity

Latency is an important consideration when routing in P2P systems. Poor proximity approximation in DHTs can result in a message traveling around the globe many times to reach its final destination. Several distributed applications aim to automate the gathering of relevant proximity information, and Zhang et al. (699) assure us that point-to-point latency is constant enough over time to allow such systems to provide good approximations. Current systems include IDMaps (288), GNP (502), Lighthouse (525), King (338), and geographical position estimates (512).

Issues of "stretch" (distance traveled relative to the underlying network) become increasingly important in file sharing or storage systems in which large quantities of data must be transferred between peers. Furthermore, to minimize the load on the network and increase the rate at which data may be obtained, data must be stored near the place they are accessed. A system simply storing blocks across a DHT is at odds with this approach. Since nodes and keys tend to have pseudo-random identifiers, blocks will be assigned to a node regardless of that node's position. However, when replicating data across k neighbors, which are likely to diverse in location, a DHT that takes into account locality (and so is likely to route through the *nearest* of these k nodes) provides some means of obtaining content from nearby peers.

29.3.6   Load Balancing

Pseudo-random assignment of nodes and keys tends to create an imbalance in the allocation of keys to nodes, with the maximum load at any node being $\log(n)$ times the mean load in an n-node network. Of course, this analysis assumes that any resources associated with keys are homogenous, making the same requirements of their destination node.

In PAST, an archival storage system, whole files are associated with a key and inserted into an underlying DHT. Because the size distribution of files is heavily skewed, this imbalance mentioned in the preceding paragraph is exacerbated, and a complicated scheme of storage management is required in which replicas are diverted to nodes with more storage space. The net effect is an increase in the average hop count (and so latency) required to retrieve files.

In an environment of heterogeneous resources and competing job requirements, load balancing is difficult and requires a trade-off between the best allocation of job to resource and the rate at which job and resource properties are distributed.

29.3.7   Availability

P2P networks experience a high rate of nodes joining and leaving both because of their scale and because of the nature of their user communities. Hence, individual peers cannot be relied on to maintain any essential state on their own.

For purposes of redundancy, most DHTs replicate state at the k nodes with identifiers numerically closest to the associated key. This replication invariant is maintained by local node cooperation, despite nodes joining or failing. If surrounding nodes maintain their routing tables correctly, this offers automatic failover: If the nearest node to a key fails, requests are automatically rerouted to the next closest node, which will also maintain state for that node.

At the application level, erasure coding schemes have been shown to offer the same availability for an order-of-magnitude lower overhead compared with deployed replication schemes. Data are encoded into n unique fragments; the coding ratio determines the proportion m/n of unique fragments required to recover the original data. Since each fragment is unique, however, a simple local maintenance scheme does not suffice to maintain a data item's availability as different nodes fail.

The nature of network failures in the Internet is an important consideration for any practical system. Networks tend to fail along administrative boundaries, close to users, because of individual router or link failures. Conversely, individual peers are assumed to fail randomly (although other patterns also occur). Although most DHTs perform suitably under the latter failure model, a network failure of the former type tends to render most of the keyspace inaccessible (most likely, all of it, unless locality is taken into account when choosing routing table entries).

SkipNet (356) is a routing substrate based on a data structure similar to a *skip list* and offers DHT-like data distribution, load balancing, and routing at various administrative levels. Keys specify using a reverse-DNS notation of the domain of peers over which they may be placed, allowing items to be distributed solely across nodes in the same organization. Furthermore, a request for a key specifying an organizational domain will never be routed through nodes outside the same domain; thus, access to that data is maintained even if a network failure separates that organization from the rest of the Internet.

Little attention has been paid to the effect of network partitions on systems in which partially or wholly independent fragments of systems are formed, update their own state, and then rejoin. Quorum systems (e.g., (159)) have been used to enforce state consistency between peers updating replicated data (422), but the overhead of these schemes is prohibitive for use across a whole network. Instead, techniques from the literature on reconciliation of divergent file replicas may inform the semantics of P2P systems under network partition. One exception is Ivy (488), a P2P file system where participants each maintain a log of the updates they make to the global state. Log entries have per-log sequence numbers and are tagged with version vectors, detailing the latest log entry seen for each other log in the system. Later, as each update carries sufficient information to determine the exact view of the global state at that time, conflict resolution can be performed to combine these states.

29.3.8   Anonymity and Censorship Resistance

Some P2P systems offer privacy by masking user identities. Some go further and mask content so that peers exchanging data do not know who delivered or stores which content. True anonymity is typically two layer, requiring some form of anonymous IP routing system (e.g., onion routing) and application layer mechanisms to protect privacy. Eternity and subsequent P2P file systems withstand censorship by several means.

Partition.   A file is split into component parts to ensure that no single site carries the whole file, and a denial-of-service attack must run over multiple sites. Later systems made clever use of techniques such as Rabin fingerprinting or other techniques for finding common elements of objects. These techniques can also exploit overlapping content between multiple files to reduce storage costs.

Replication.   Blocks of a file are replicated over multiple sites to provide higher availability. This strategy can be combined with locality information to reduce latency and increase file-sharing throughput, at some cost in terms of consistency in update.

Encryption.   File blocks are encrypted to ensure not only that disclosure is unlikely but also that a node can deny knowledge of the actual content it carries. Again, P2P exploits mutual benefit: The argument is that "I might not approve of this content, but I approve of the ability to hide my content in a set of peers, so I will live with what I do not know here." This is often termed "plausible deniability" and is used by service providers to align themselves with the "common carrier'" defence against legal liability for content, as telephony and postal providers can do.

"Anonymization."   The identities of request sources and sinks are masked, thus protecting *users* from the potential *censor* or unsavory *agency*. Location information must be masked as well as identifiers; otherwise, a traffic analysis may effectively reveal identities, and thus some form of onion routing is also usually required.

29.4   FUTURE DIRECTIONS

We examine several areas in which additional research questions can be identified, based on problems and shortcomings in current P2P systems. In describing these areas, we try to keep history in mind and to consider how some problems relate to those past, present, and possibly future in Grid computing.

29.4.1   Sharing Computation

Two systems epitomize the sum use of P2P technology thus far: Napster file sharing and the SETI@home coarse-grained distributed computing system. P2P systems have been successful in supporting the former, but the latter represents the tip of the iceberg in distributed computing.

A critical difference between sharing files (and file transfers) and sharing computation is that the former are static, and hence are partitioned easily. Transferring one file is independent of another. Computation is notoriously hard to distribute, yet there are some interesting cases that are well understood; these are situations with a low communication overhead compared with the computation required.

Work is required in two areas in order to broaden the range of computational tasks that can be treated with a massive distributed P2P system. First, the infrastructure needs to handle tightly coupled distributed computation better, by exploiting self-organizing properties, staging and timing, and using innovative data transfer schemes to minimize communication overhead. Second, algorithms should be *designed* to exploit P2P properties, by using, for example, asynchronous schemes to reduce dependency on low-latency communication links.

29.4.2   Auditing and Accounting

SETI@home relies on users simply volunteering their CPU resources. Introducing an economic model whereby resources are bought and sold adds a new complication: accounting for their use.

The motivations for file and CPU resource sharing are not the same: it is not clear how to apply the mutual benefit arguments that work for file sharing to cycle sharing. The network connections of file sharers typically have some degree of separation in capacity provisioning that allows them to upload and download independently; to some extent, cooperation does not disadvantage them. The bursty nature of interactive use, however, means the same is not true for any third-party sharing of a local CPU. Fine-grained accounting for resource sharing is required to limit, prioritize, and arbitrate between sharers. However, how does one measure and enforce relative resource usage between different services?

The Xenoserver project (549) takes one approach. Its goal is to deploy machines running a *hypervisor* that performs accounting of commodities such as CPU cycles and network bandwidth. Principals may use these machines to deploy high-level services, paying server operators for each service's use of low-level resources. In turn, other principals may be charged for accessing high-level services. Xenoservers might be used as a platform for both P2P and Grid services, but their accounting scheme has direct application in all distributed computation systems.

P2P systems make accounting difficult in general, because of the coarse nature of jobs, the mutual distrust assumed between participants (the lack of an out-of-band trust relationship), and the possible short-term network presence of pseudonymous participants. Accounting in a Grid environment is easier: one possible approach and the associated issues are investigated by GSAX (103) (Grid Services Accounting Extensions), an extension to the OGSA standard. Accounting, and ultimately charging for, services at the application level suits the Grid computing paradigm because OGSA embraces a notion of *virtualization*, exposing resources as services.

29.4.3   Local Solutions to Achieve a Global Optimum?

Recent P2P systems select preferred neighbors to fill routing table entries by *proximity*. Although it has been shown (e.g., in Pastry (564)) that making peering decisions locally can improve global routing properties (i.e., by minimizing "stretch," routing distance relative to IP), such an approach is error prone. More important, it leads to a succession of local optimizations, rather than a solution *optimized* for global performance. In the future, results from location services may be obtained and cached locally to improve proximity estimates and inform routing decisions.

We have a long way to go before we can provide performance guarantees within large-scale distributed systems, whether via adaptive techniques that respond to congestion (e.g., via explicit congestion notification or a pricing mechanism) or via an engineered solution based on some type of signaling. In particular, high-level composite interactions in a P2P system often rely on the coordination of many peers, so it is difficult to base solutions purely on local decisions. However, as measurement projects produce more results to characterize peer behavior, we may be able to obtain good solutions through localized traffic engineering, admission control, and scheduling algorithms.

The problem is related to providing incentives to participants. If we apply a market economy model, in which each peer is free to set its own prices for resources and a stable global equilibrium is reached based on supply and demand, will an "invisible hand" mechanism globally optimize resource supply and utilization? How do we ensure fairness? Lessons from economics and distributed algorithmic mechanism design (258) will play an increasingly large part in the design of such systems.

29.4.4   Locality versus Anonymity

P2P networks with large sets of participants offer an opportunity for obfuscating the activities of individual nodes. Indeed, many early projects capitalized on this. Yet practical P2P systems struggle with the apparently inherent contradiction between offering anonymous sharing of resources and the localization of service offers. A number of factors are reducing the anonymity characteristic of P2P systems; at the very least, their immunity to traffic analysis is being lost as such techniques become more sophisticated.

Increasingly, anonymity-preserving features may be implemented as an overlay on top of P2P applications or middleware. Crowds (552) and onion routing already take this approach to the Web and e-mail, respectively. Of course, the extent of the trade-off with performance lies in different users' requirements and the degree to which particular applications need to exploit locality to obtain this.

29.4.5   From Overlay to Infrastructure

Many successful overlay systems migrate over time into the infrastructure itself, often to maximize the efficiency of the protocols but also to handle application-level security concerns. Indeed, a recent report (191) recommended looking at overlay systems as a general approach to building research infrastructures. As the nature of P2P networks and infrastructures become well understood, the techniques may migrate into the infrastructure, just as the handling logic for IP traffic has migrated from overlay networks into native services such as routers.

Many P2P systems are complex, however, and devising a minimal service enhancement in the lower levels that would support their algorithms is an interesting challenge. The IETF FORCES working group has been working on remote IP router control (separating out packet forwarding and packet routing). Yet more is needed if general P2P intermediary functions are to be performed within time insignificant relative to packet transmission time. Furthermore, complex filtering and processing of content keys will be needed to maintain a global-scale distributed hash table at the infrastructure level—not to mention the many hashes and signatures used in many current schemes. Such hopes show that we do not really understand what P2P actually means.

29.4.6   P2P Systems and Ad Hoc Wireless Network Duality

A defining characteristic of P2P systems is their ability to provide efficient, reliable, and resilient routing between their constituent nodes by forming structured ad hoc topologies. In this respect, we can draw useful parallels with ad hoc wireless networking.

Resilient P2P mechanisms for content distribution services have been proposed, but the effect of these systems on global network utilization is not well understood. Studies show that high overheads for topology maintenance and message routing prohibit the use of such systems on wireless ad hoc networks, which suffer stringent power requirements and highly transient network connectivity.

An application of P2P techniques to mobile wireless ad hoc networks would involve making peers "load aware," by distributing load information and implementing a distributed congestion control scheme. To handle mobility, a topographical metric might be used for nodes to specify their own location. An *anycast* routing scheme, allowing a request to specify a set of satisfactory destinations, would be one approach to reducing message-passing overhead.

Next-generation P2P systems will probably use actual location and scope information to influence routing functions so that content is initially placed and requests are routed to copies that have proximity on a number of quality-of-service axes—often including delay, throughput, and packet loss, but perhaps also battery considerations for wireless users. Thus, the distribution of replicas in a content delivery or storage infrastructure will evolve to meet the user demand distribution, optimizing use of the scarce wireless resources to better match user concerns.

29.5   SUMMARY

P2P computing has had a dramatic effect on mainstream computing, even blurring the distinctions between computer science, engineering, and politics. An unfortunate side effect is that due consideration often has not been given to the classic research in distributed systems. We hope that this chapter has shed light on the nature of P2P computing, the reasons for its successes (and failures) to date, and the interesting relationships that exist between P2P and Grids. As depicted in Figure 29.7, we see considerable potential for a synthesis between the two approaches—although we certainly do not yet claim to understand how this synthesis could be achieved.

We are entering the age of massively distributed, global-scale computing and storage systems in which computing will change from a *commodity* to a *utility*. We hope that this chapter can stimulate both the P2P and Grid communities to identify how ideas from P2P and Grid computing can best be synthesized to influence and ultimately realize this vision of utility computing.

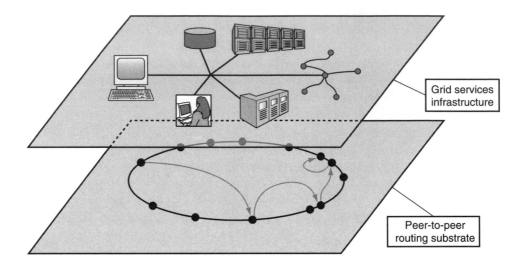

Grid services
infrastructure

Peer-to-peer
routing substrate

29.7

FIGURE

A P2P Grid computer could combine the varied resources, services, and power of Grid computing with the global-scale, resilient, and self-organizing properties of P2P systems. A P2P substrate provides lower-level services on which to build a globally distributed Grid services infrastructure. Issues such as trust that are lacking in P2P systems need to be managed between the layers.

FURTHER READING

For more information on the topics covered in this chapter, see *www.mkp.com/grid2*.

Network Infrastructure

Joe Touch and Jon Postel[1]

Network infrastructure describes the overall interconnection fabric that provides the foundation on which Grids are built. The organization and architecture of the network define the interactions over which computational, storage, data, and other Grid services and facilities are layered. Network infrastructure is a composition of local-area and wide-area transport services, which in turn are composed of transport protocols and services, layered on routing protocols and network services, layered over link protocols and physical media. The most famous current example of this infrastructure is the Internet.

In many ways, the Internet can be considered a preliminary attempt at building a Grid, in which the basic services focus on data delivery rather than computation. The core Internet protocols (e.g., TCP/IP) define a common, ubiquitous interface that already spans the globe and provides a level of shared access, which even current electrical power grids only hope to eventually achieve. For example, a laptop still requires electrical power converters because voltage and line frequency are not standardized among different countries. Yet local network connections do not require adapters, and the user need not carry "power converters" for IP.

Networking infrastructure, using the Internet as its canonical example, is a good place to learn the lessons of providing a ubiquitous infrastructure. In the beginning, the Internet leveraged the lesson of providing a minimal, common interface to promote ubiquity. With few options and simple, strict requirements, a single pervasive infrastructure is a likely result.

---

[1]Dr. Postel was co-author of this chapter in the first edition and is included here posthumously to acknowledge his substantial contributions that are kept in this revision.

The current Internet is beginning to show the challenge of ubiquity, of supporting a wide range of host and network capabilities in a single framework. Internet infrastructure is remarkably stable, providing a consistent base on which new services can be deployed, but it also is slow to incorporate new features. In the past 20 years, since TCP/IP was deployed in 1983, the core IP service has changed little, despite continually emerging capabilities. Services that appeared to be on the near horizon only five years ago—notably multicast, network resource reservation, and quality of service—have fallen out of favor. The only wide-scale new application protocols are peer-to-peer file sharing and instant messaging. This is not to say that new services or protocols are never deployed, but that Internet infrastructure evolves comparatively slowly.

The evolutionary pace of the Internet is both a lesson and a challenge for the Grid. A stable set of core functions is essential to achieving ubiquity, yet care must be taken with respect to extensibility if the infrastructure is to keep pace with rapidly changing requirements. The challenge is that as the Grid evolves, it expands the network capability beyond those of transport, to become a functional resource. The Grid as a distributed functional resource has the ability to become more useful than its local equivalent (multiprocessor computing), just as the Internet is so much more than a data link between two computers. In the process, the Grid will challenge the principles on which the Internet is based. These principles, discussed in detail later, include best-effort delivery, fixed global endpoint labels, variable-length messages, and an assumption that data are addressed at the endpoints but that routing is handled inside the network.

The punctuated evolution of the Internet is representative of the evolution of computers in general (*"interogeny* recapitulates *computogeny*"?—with apologies to Ernst Haeckel, of "Ontogeny recapitulates phylogeny" fame) because both are characterized by plateaus of capability (Figure 30.1). At each jump in capability,

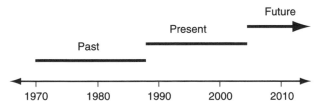

30.1   Timeline of network infrastructure.

FIGURE

a corresponding new application is enabled, which further fuels the jump until a new plateau is reached. The first jump was basic connectivity among mainframe computers, terminals, and backbones, which enabled e-mail. The current jump is due to increased capacity and ubiquitous connectivity among PCs and multiple service providers, enabling the Web and file sharing. The future may be characterized by reliability and location independence among personal digital assistants (PDAs) and network computers (NCs), enabling applications we cannot imagine.

This chapter describes three phases in the development of network infrastructure, based on examples from the evolution of the Internet. The Internet is currently in its second phase of evolution and appears to be entering its third. The first phase was characterized by the origin and development of the Internet as ubiquitous infrastructure. During this period, its growth was governed largely by researchers and driven by e-mail and file transfer applications. The second phase of the Internet is characterized by ubiquity within the research community and by growth into the general population, driven by distributed hypermedia (the Web). The third phase will be characterized by ubiquity within the general population, driven by services beyond that of data transfer and access. These phases are discussed in subsequent sections, as follows:

+ *Phase 1*. Section 30.1, "The Past (1969–1988)," describes the origins of ubiquitous network infrastructure, based on the origins of the ARPANET.

+ *Phase 2*. Section 30.2, "The Present (1988–2005)," describes the current state of the Internet, the common infrastructure and services that define global networking infrastructure.

+ *Phase 3*. Section 30.3, "The Future (2005–)," makes some predictions for the evolution of the Internet, based on current issues and advances anticipated within the near term.

Each phase is characterized by the technological capabilities available, including network technologies, protocols, and services. In addition, the overall system organization also drives the composition and aggregation of these systems to form large-scale shared systems. It is important to understand the driving application of each phase. Hence, we organize our presentation of each phase in terms of the following topics:

+ *Driving application*. The "killer application" that drove the technology or pushed the capabilities to a new level. Killer applications, rather than the network itself, are key to defining the phases of network evolution.

+ *Network technology.* The physical components that support network infrastructure, including basic link and router technologies, as well as local area, long-haul, and home access variants. Note that specific link technologies are not described in detail, because they present a rapidly moving target and good network architectures should transcend such details.

+ *Protocols and services.* The software organization, presenting a user and programmer interface to the network, as well as their in-network capabilities.

+ *System integration.* The system management issues that enable the integration of components to form a coherent whole.

We also discuss the implications of these predictions. As difficult as the future is to picture in detail, several issues will be key to the evolution of network infrastructure and are likely to constrain its capabilities. Such issues include scale, complexity, and the fundamental limits of networking. Some of these issues are only now being exposed as engineering limitations are gradually overcome.

30.1   THE PAST (1969–1988)

Modern computer networking infrastructure came into existence only about 25 years ago. The canonical example is the ARPANET (559), with its 56-kilobit/sec lines. Over the years, networks have grown in scope, speed, and interconnections. Two trends interact to allow this growth: the increasing bandwidth of affordable links, and increasing computer processing power (Chapter 28).

In the era of mainframe time-sharing systems and access via teletype terminals, the ARPANET began as a bold attempt to prove the concepts of resource sharing and remote access via a network. One of the key problems to be solved was that users of multiple systems had to have multiple terminals, one for each system.

Because the trend of increasing computer power was ahead of the trend of increasing bandwidth, the key to modern data communications is to use computing power to manage the bandwidth effectively. Such power is used in two places: at the edges in end systems (often called host computers) and internal to the system in interconnecting devices called gateways, or routers.

The basic strategy of network communication systems has been to identify a layer in the system structure and to design and use a fixed simple interface, protocol, and function at that level. In the ARPANET this was the interface message processor (IMP), and in the Internet this is the router. This strategy leaves a great deal of flexibility for the lower layers of the network infrastructure and the higher layers of applications in the end systems.

Having a common set of link technologies for over 20 years provided a stable base from which to develop and deploy advanced services such as routing, reliable congestion-controlled transport, and self-configuration protocols. Conversely, many current protocols retain artifacts of this common infrastructure, which hinder their deployment on nontraditional technology.

Other network infrastructures that did not have a common underlay did not advance as quickly or with as much success (for example, OSI, X.25). Other competitors defeated ubiquity by remaining proprietary, for example, DECNET. The lesson here is that picking a single common infrastructure freed upper-layer services to deploy advanced features, rather than constantly shifting to regain a foothold on a changing foundation.

Characteristics that fueled the growth of TCP/IP protocols and the Internet included the following:

✦ Freely available protocol documentation (online, colloquial prose)

✦ Readily available source code, for at least a few implementations

✦ Software "bundled" with workstations and servers

✦ Use of the ARPANET/Internet architecture and TCP/IP protocol family for teaching examples—a natural extension of much of their initial development having been done in university research labs

✦ A sense of community ownership, a culture arising from the protocols being developed in groups of organizations, rather than being promoted by a single company, university, or government agency

30.1.1 Driving Application

At the beginning of the ARPANET, the driving applications were electronic messaging (e-mail), remote file access, and remote job control. These applications put less demand on the network technology and more on the basic protocols and system organization. The latter provided seamless remote services, enabling adoption by a scattered and diverse user community.

One of the earliest formal justifications for the ARPANET was remote access to limited, localized resources. At the time, mainframe computers were scarce, and there was a desire to share them among geographically distributed researchers. Remote job entry and control would avoid costly travel, as well as enable more efficient sharing, not limited to those already on site.

In the background, however, a less dramatic but more important application was considered. Remote messaging services, such as teletype, paging, and fax, were already available, but costly. If messaging were cheap, rapid, and common, user communities would develop beyond the confines of organizations. This idea hearkens back to the Royal Societies, where researchers met frequently and exchanged letters to debate their work. Such convenient, colloquial exchanges overcome the tendency to wait for publication, which often took (and still takes) years after work was completed.

30.1.2   Network Technology

The wide-area network links were long lines leased from the telephone companies, starting in the ARPANET with 56 kilobit/sec, and progressing to 1.5 megabit/sec, and finally to 45 megabit/sec in the NSFNET. The lines can be thought of as point-to-point copper wires providing digital transmission (though some microwave technology was used). These long-haul links were used to interconnect packet switches, and the IMPs of the ARPANET, or the routers of the NSFNET, ESnet, NSI, and the rest of the Internet.

The ARPANET was conceived to interconnect the mainframe computers at research centers to share their often-unique computational resources. Its essential features were the use of an independent device, the IMP, to manage the networking tasks, and the development of a set of protocols between the hosts to embody a consistent model of communication. The IMP implemented packet switching in the network to provide for sharing the lines of the network and the routing of data between sources and destinations that might be separated by several hops. The IMP provided all the essential features of what we now call a router.

At first there were no local area networks (LANs), but this situation soon changed with the pioneering work of the Xerox Palo Alto Research Center (PARC), which created the experimental (3 megabit/sec) Ethernet and the prototype Alto workstation. As the ARPANET grew, the number of machines at each location connected to the network did also. Many of these additional machines were minicomputers, especially DEC PDP-11's, supporting specialized research systems.

Long-haul network lines became faster over time; and although there were several early LAN technologies, including IBM's token ring, the Ethernet quickly emerged as the de facto standard LAN technology. Early Ethernets used a 3-megabit/sec shared coaxial cable, later replaced by the 10-megabit/sec standard (474). Thick Ethernet with "vampire taps" gave way to thin net, yielding to twisted pair. Repeaters and bridges gave way to intelligent bridges.

These early LAN technologies were motivated by the emergence of what we now call workstations (e.g., Sun, Apollo, Symbolics). The more successful workstations came with the Internet standard protocols as a bundled part of the product. Later, as PCs became more powerful, and as the Ethernet was extended to simpler and cheaper wiring and interfaces, these relatively low-cost computers could be full Internet participants.

Initially, the interconnections between networks were made through a general-purpose computer with two (or more) interfaces to different networks. This computer (in the early days called a gateway and now called a router) acted to each network as if it were an end-user host computer. One popular hardware choice for such a gateway was the PDP-11. In addition, these gateways exchanged information about which other networks they could reach using a routing protocol called the "gateway-to-gateway protocol" (or GGP).

Although the earliest personal computers were not powerful enough to participate in the computer networks of their day, not even the early LANs, the situation changed rapidly. Networks were simplified, the costs of interfaces dropped, and PCs became more powerful. The model of computing changed from terminals and mainframes to PCs or workstations and LANs. Mainframes did not disappear, though LANs were connected to mainframes, too, and the mainframes became known as servers.

Soon enough, though, PCs became powerful enough to implement wide-area network protocols, and the rapid growth of internetworking began. The existence of TCP/IP provided the model, and often the implementation, for linking PCs and workstations into large-scale networks. Even though these wide-area protocols provided features little used in a local environment, the appeal and benefits of doing networking the same way in all cases proved overwhelming. One early use of PCs was interconnecting the LAN with the wide area network, that is, acting as the gateway or router.

30.1.3   Protocols and Services

The early popular protocols of the ARPANET—telnet (531) for remote login, the file transfer protocol (FTP) (530) for transferring files, and e-mail (532) for electronic mail—were the mainstays of network usage until quite recently.

The first applications were motivated by the ways computers were used at the time: access to time-sharing systems via terminals, access to files, and job submission to batch processing by mainframes. Telnet solved the problem of using the local terminal to access a remote system over the network as if one were there. FTP solved the problem of moving files between computers. There was quite a bit of work on, and use of, remote job entry protocols, mainly adding semantics to file transfer techniques, to allow the submission of batch jobs and retrieval of results.

However, electronic mail was the first true network application. Although most time-sharing systems had a means for leaving an online message for one or more other users, these were treated in a casual fashion (except for the NLS system at SRI International). The interconnection of these message systems into a network-wide electronic mail system via a feature of FTP established the basis for a new mode of long-distance communication.

The underlying transport protocol—initially the network control protocol (NCP) and later Internet TCP (529)—provided a model of interprocess communication based on the notion of a stream of bytes. Such streams, or connections, could be opened or closed, and data could be sent or received. Data were always received in the order in which they were sent.

The host-to-host protocol implemented a simple model of process-to-process stream-style communication. This provided a base for protocols for remote terminal access (telnet), transferring files (FTP), and electronic mail. The development of a model of interprocess communication that could be used consistently across all the systems connected to the ARPANET was remarkable because of the wide variety of machine architectures and operating systems. For example, machines had a variety of word sizes (8, 16, 18, 32, 36, 60, 64 bits), and characters could be any of 6, 7, 8, or 9 bits. In most operating systems, processes were to be isolated from one another, and all communication with processes was via input from or output to a file.

While the U.S. Department of Defense Advanced Research Projects Agency (ARPA, now called DARPA) was building the ARPANET, it was also experimenting with other networking technologies, including packet radio and packet satellite networks. The desire to demonstrate end-to-end communication over an interconnected system of multiple networks of different technologies is one of the motivations for the development of a model for internetworking and ultimately the TCP/IP family of protocols.

Some of the ubiquity of Internet protocols is due to the underlying stability of the link and LAN technologies. Having a common topology and link layer provided a basis for raising the level of service (Figure 30.2). Today we live with the artifacts of this ubiquity. Many protocols assume Ethernet's broadcast characteristics (e.g., BOOTP). Other protocols, such as the address resolution protocol (ARP), were originally designed only for shared-access media (e.g., Ethernet) and later required extension to operate over point-to-point or switched media.

The routers used GGP to exchange information about the networks they could reach. This was a distance vector single-level protocol. Several techniques were used to map the Internet addresses to the physical-layer addresses of hosts. In some cases, such as the ARPANET, the actual physical address was carried as a

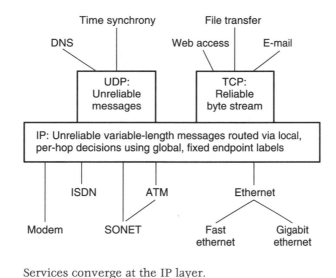

Services converge at the IP layer.

component of the Internet address. In other cases, such as Ethernets, a dynamic mapping was provided through ARP.

From the earliest days users referred to the various computers on the network with names such as MIT-AI or UCLA-NMC. Each computer kept a list of all the other computers with the name, numeric address, computer type, and other information for each. A master copy of this list was maintained by the Network Information Center (NIC) at SRI International and copied (via FTP) by each computer periodically.

This simple system was replaced by the Domain Name System (DNS) (481). The DNS is a large hierarchical distributed redundant database where data can be found by using a structured name. The early simple "file of names" method began to be problematic when there were about 300 host computers. There are now about 30 million hosts.

One important exception to the use of names was a special type of computer used in the ARPANET called a TIP (terminal IMP). This device combined the functions of an IMP and a multiline terminal controller with 64 lines. The TIP implemented the NCP and the user or client part of the telnet protocol to provide remote terminal access to the computational resources on the ARPANET. The TIP did not have a file of host names, however, so users had to know the numeric addresses of the hosts they wanted to access.

30.1.4   System Integration

The components of networking architectures—the links, the computers, the protocols, and so on—came together in several different ways for different system architectures. All of these systems have evolved or transformed to become part of the Internet.

The main line of development starts with the ARPANET. Although the network was designed to be robust in operation and to adjust automatically to outages, there was an assumption that policy matters would be decided by DARPA and that there would be a central network operations center. The scale of the ARPANET was small in today's terms. At first the system was envisioned to be only 15 sites, though it later grew to several hundred.

The notion of a hierarchical system was introduced with the NSFNET. The early NSFNET interconnected about half a dozen supercomputer sites, and the later NSFNET was never more than about a dozen sites. However, the important notion of a top-level central backbone network connecting to second-level regional networks that then connect to third-level campus networks provided an organizing principle to connect far more sites into the Internet than the ARPANET technology could support.

The fundamental feature of this main line of development was the underlying use of packet switching to optimize the shared use of the expensive resources that are the communication lines. Also, as time has gone by, the computing resources have become cheaper and much faster than the communications lines, thus furthering the advantages of packet switching.

Other lines of development included the ISO OSI protocols and hop-by-hop dial-up systems such as UUCP, BITNET, CSNET, and FidoNet. The OSI protocol family was based primarily on X.25, a type of packet switching that used virtual circuits. Virtual circuits require complicated connection establishment steps and, because they are state oriented, also complicate recovery from system outages. Perhaps more significantly, OSI protocol specifications were in controlled-distribution, difficult-to-understand documents and in expensive, separately priced implementations. Further, there was a lack of overall coordination of the user community.

The dial-up systems, such as UUCP, did well for a time because the cost of a local phone call in the middle of the night is fairly low; but as the system grew, the load of information to be transmitted grew faster, and the concentration of distribution on a few centers made the cost for those centers high. As Internet connectivity became available, the dial-up paths were replaced by Internet connections to save costs. Now nearly all UUCP network traffic uses Internet connections.

30.1.5 Summary of the Past

One clear lesson of this past is that packet switching is a winning strategy because the cost of computing drops much faster than the cost of communication links, so the use of computing to optimize the use of communication lines pays off.

Another lesson, perhaps not so clear, is that the widespread use of a single communication model is a winning strategy because the power of a communications system is related to the number of others that can be reached by using it. Thus, the convergence on the use of the Internet and the TCP/IP family of protocols is a big win. Building new applications on the base of TCP/IP provides an instant ubiquity of access.

30.2 THE PRESENT (1988–2005)

The current Internet, with a multiplicity of backbone networks and regional networks connected in myriad ways, is far more complex than anything imagined by the early designers of its component technologies. The most significant change from the past to the present is the vastly increased role of the private sector in the implementation and operation of the Internet and the comparatively small role of the government agencies that created and fostered the technology. Today, the key players in the system are the service providers.

The growth of the Internet is now governed by a pair of feedback loops. The positive feedback is that ubiquity breeds ubiquity: the more people join the Internet, the more services are made available, and thus the more attractive it is to join. The negative feedback is that capacity usually lags subscription: the more people join, the worse the service will be because capacity is shared by more people. Because service providers are competing to sign up customers, however, each service provider is motivated to upgrade its capacity to provide its customers good service.

Other significant changes in the context of the Internet are the continuing increases in the speed of backbone communication lines and the increasing diversity of computing and LAN options, including laptops and wireless LANs. The increased level of service available to the typical user has made possible some applications that have dramatically changed the nature of the Internet and the nature of computing in general.

The primary significant development in the present Internet is the Web. The impact of the Web has been so extraordinary that there is hardly any aspect of life today that does not have some reference to the Web. It has driven Internet technology out of the academic and research community into a pervasive commodity market. During this period, a number of additional capabilities have arisen, some still waxing, and a few waned or are waning. It is equally important to note that although the Web drove the Internet to its current ubiquity, and certain changes were needed to make that possible, the Internet architecture has remained largely unchanged for over 20 years. New capabilities continue to appear, but none has significantly changed the architecture yet.

30.2.1   Driving Application

In the current Internet, the driving application is graphical access to remote data, that is, interactive distributed information access. The current common example is the Web, with its embedded hypertext links. Earlier examples include Archie (a distributed information search service) and Fetch (a collection of graphical remote file access facilities).

The Web is given substantial credit for the popularization of the Internet. This credit is deserved, but it is not always obvious what characteristics of the Web drive this logic. It is clear that the Web provides great power by embedded links and the ability to chain data together. It is perhaps less clear, though no less important, that the Web provides a graphical interface to facilities that existed years before. It also scripts and automates tasks that researchers had been happy to toil over, such as the repetitive sequence of opening and closing FTP connections.

There is a second class of killer applications for the present Internet, which are somewhat less ubiquitous. With the increases in host capability and link bandwidth comes the opportunity to use network infrastructure as an audio/visual communications medium. Individuals can now become radio or television broadcasters, although on a smaller scale, or use their digital links to provide analog telephony service. For decades this assumed video on demand, or live streaming of video, but the more ubiquitous use has been file sharing, notably digitized audio (MP3s) (Chapter 29). The desire to share digitized music results in an increased average file size, from 6 kilobytes for a Web page, to 60 kilobytes for an animated Web page, to 6 megabytes per song in a compressed MP3 file (100x the size of animated Web pages). This increase drives the desire for higher bandwidth, both in the network core and at the access points. Home users are no longer satisfied with 56-kilobit/sec dial-up lines (which were the core of the ARPANET originally); they demand 1-megabit/sec DSL or cable modem connections.

30.2.2   Network Technology

Data communications link technology is currently in crisis. The backbone and many regional networks built systems of dedicated 45-megabit/sec lines (T3) two or three years ago. A significant upgrade in capacity is urgently needed, but the costs are far too high, and the technology is not ready yet.

The next steps available from the telephone companies involve using ATM technology (629). Earlier telephony links, such as T1 and T3, delivered data as a continuous bitstream between two customers. In ATM, the telephone company accepts the variable-sized IP packets (typically 500–1,500 bytes) as a stream of chopped-up components, each small and fixed in size (48 bytes of payload), known as ATM cells. These cells are typically delivered to the telephone company in a large SONET frame (hundreds of cells per frame). Unlike the T-series, neither ATM nor SONET indicates a specific data rate; SONET is an hierarchy of rates, in powers of 2 of approximately 155 megabit/sec, for example, OC-3 at 155 megabit/sec, OC-12 at 622 megabit/sec.

Although ATM provides some interesting flexibility in rapid reconfiguration, it does so at a substantial cost in performance. The ATM cells impose a 5-byte overhead on each 48 bytes of payload, over 10%. Also the initial service available at 155 megabit/sec (OC-3) is too small a step in capacity to be worth all the equipment changes. As a result, most links today use IP directly over SONET, avoiding the ATM layer altogether.

Some service providers installed many parallel 45-megabit/sec T3 lines and a much richer network topology to improve service. The major service providers require multigigabit/sec backbone links. At such speeds, direct router-to-router dedicated SONET links make more sense than T3 lines. As the backbone service providers led the way to higher capacity, the regional networks and the local service providers have increased the variety of connection services and provide every imaginable case (fractional T1, T3, frame relay, etc.). Satellite delivery is being used in particular markets, notably remote areas, as well as for some user access systems; its high latency and limited return channel make it suitable primarily for bulk downloads (mirror updates, cache push).

Optical networks are also now being deployed. In these networks, a single fiber carries multiple, independent channels on separate wavelengths, each capable of supporting tens of gigabit/sec transfer rates. For example, the TeraGrid project (162) uses four wavelengths to provide a 40-gigabit/sec network backbone between participating sites. The data on these optical channels are transparently (independent of the data bits) switched based on wavelength only. These networks rely on connection establishment protocols to create paths of a single wavelength in the network, a wavelength version of a circuit. Optical protocol design is beginning to recapitulate the evolution of electronic switching, such as ATM, beginning with circuit switching (wavelength paths), to recent tag/flow switching (burst switching), resulting (one hopes) in packet switching, the Internet's native mode.

To service providers the aggregate capacity matters. They see little likelihood that individual end-to-end user data streams will be noticeable in the overall level of traffic. However, some of the applications forecast in this book (for example, management of large-scale datasets as in Chapter 22), or even emerging music-sharing systems, challenge that assumption. Furthermore, the typical data rate per user is creeping up as users obtain faster "last mile" connections by using by clever modems (33.6–56 kilobit/sec), integrated services digital network (ISDN, 56–128 kilobit/sec), digital subscriber lines (xDSL, 1–10 megabit/sec), or cable modem technologies and engage in higher-demand interactive applications (629). Modems are simple and inexpensive but require 1–2 minutes to establish initial connections and are limited because of analog-to-digital translation. The telephone company's ISDN is a somewhat faster, all-digital telephone service with millisecond connect times but is less widely available. Newer xDSLs are emerging, such as asymmetric (ADSL), symmetric DSL, and hybrid DSLs, providing even higher bandwidth; but these technologies are available only in limited markets. Cable modems provide bandwidths similar to xDSL over shared television cable infrastructure.

The current state of LAN technology is also poised for a transition. Many current workstation and PC systems are connected to a standard (10–100 megabit/sec) Ethernet. Gigabit Ethernet (1 gigabit/sec) is already available, although internal host limitations (backplane bandwidth capacities) may limit its becoming as ubiquitous as the 100-megabit/sec Ethernet. We are at a point of transition for university and corporate users of the Internet from roughly megabit technology to roughly gigabit technology.

We also now have technology that promises to free users from the tie of a physical connection. LAN technologies that allow a user to move a computer (typically a laptop), around within a building, communicating all the while (802.11 wireless), are now deployed. Other technologies allow such freedom of movement within cities. Many airports are now covered by such systems so that travelers may use their laptop computers with Internet connectivity up to the moment they board their plane.

General-purpose routers have been replaced by specialized devices optimizing the fastest possible packet-forwarding function. The design of ever faster routers is an important area of concern. Routers with processing speed to match the next generation of gigabit-speed networks are needed now.

The appropriate roles of routers, bridges, and gateways seem to have been sorted out, with bridges being used mainly as a convenient aid in the layout of local (building-sized) area networks. Routers have come to the fore as the main interconnection technology, especially with commodity products from vendors (such as

Cisco and Nortel). Gateways, or firewalls, have also become more prominent as security devices to protect private corporate networks from the possibility of inappropriate access from the public Internet.

With the deployment of serial line protocols (such as SLIP and PPP) and the ubiquity of Ethernet, nearly all machines are Internet host computers. That is, the machine with a keyboard that a person types at (including laptops) is much more likely to be an Internet host computer than a terminal connected to a mainframe or time-sharing system.

30.2.3   Protocols and Services

A basic change in applications between the past and the present is the transition from text-oriented user interfaces to graphical user interfaces (GUIs). There are GUIs to file transfer (Fetch) and e-mail (Eudora). The contents of the information communicated have also changed to include graphics, audio, video, and other non-textual data. Basic e-mail procedures have been extended to allow messages to include a variety of data types using the MIME protocol extensions (289).

The phenomenal new application is the Web. The Web provides a service that is in many ways an augmented, automated file transfer. The Web uses a data structure that specially identifies pointers (or links) to other files. This feature was present in earlier systems (such as NLS in the late 1960s). The Web also allows some of those pointers, even though they look like pointers to files, to actually invoke programs or other ways to return data computed at the time of access. This feature was also present in earlier systems (such as Unix's named pipes in the early 1980s and the Prospero file system (499) in the late 1980s). The Web, however, brought these features together with a user-friendly interface (Mosaic in the early 1990s) at a time when the raw network capacity had just been upgraded to a higher plateau of performance.

To use the Web is to understand the joy of browsing a vast body of information and opinion (and perhaps misinformation) with a point-and-click interface. It is to also to experience the frustration of less-than-instantaneous response time. The Web has led to a significant change in the way companies, government agencies, and other organizations think about information they have that could or should be made publicly available.

Other components to file sharing have further increased what the Web provides. Search engines such as Google and hierarchical indices such as Yahoo! provide an additional resource discovery capability. Other resource location systems, some based on distributed protocols, find types of files of particular interest; for instance, Gnutella (Chapter 29) finds both music files and programs.

Another application area that has emerged is multimedia conferencing and audiovideo presentations. Touted as the "killer application" since the early 1980s, the related remote video playback (video on demand) has not taken off as a network application. The pioneer teleconferencing programs were vat, nv, sd, and cu-see-me in the early 1990s. These are being replaced with commercial products such as those from Precept, which tend to be focused more at conference room than desktop use. These applications make additional demands on the network, namely, reduced jitter and limited loss, which have required some examination and reengineering of the network transport protocols. Some fine-tuning and extension to the implementation of TCP have made possible increased performance; emerging approaches, such as DCP, are tuned to reducing jitter rather than prohibiting loss. This situation has been especially true as the understanding of flow and congestion control has improved.

The model of the network for the purposes of routing has also evolved. Networks are grouped into routing domains (identified as autonomous systems). Some routing protocols provide a two-level scheme: routing between routing domains, and then routing within each routing domain. Another change in routing is the introduction of classless interdomain routing (CIDR (299)), also called "supernetting." Basically, this extends the old notion of Class A, B, and C Internet networks (which were on byte boundaries) to networks configured on any bit boundary. CIDR allows address blocks to be aggregated at any appropriate point to reduce as much as possible the number of routing table entries.

The use of multicast and real-time protocols, which are based on IP but not TCP, is pushing the vendors and network service providers to include these protocols in their products and service offerings (Figure 30.3). We may see a dramatic increase in applications that make use of these underlying protocols in the future. A transition is in progress in the support of multicast in the Internet from the handcrafted experimental M-Bone to the native multicast routing protocols. An early protocol, DVMRP, uses more resources than necessary because it does not prune unused branches of the multicast tree. The newer PIM protocol, which does prune unused branches, is now being deployed, albeit slowly because of other scaling issues and challenges to existing charging and billing models. These protocols were gaining momentum in the late 1990s, but their deployment has stalled, being replaced by application-layer multicast, which does not rely on in-network capabilities and can be billed via conventional means but is less efficient.

"Plug-and-play" installation of new computers on the Internet has not yet been achieved, but strides have been made in that direction with the development of configuration management and autoconfiguration protocols such as RARP, BOOTP, DHCP, and dynamic DNS. For at least the end user, most devices are configured automatically when connected to the network. Such automation has not

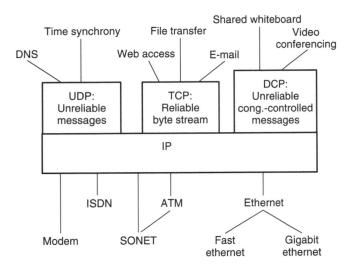

30.3
FIGURE

Services converge at higher layers (e.g., UDP, TCP, and DCP).

yet provided similar capabilities further up in the network and can be fraught with peril even for the end system. Network address (and port) translators (NATs/NAPTs), allow groups of machines to masquerade as a single machine, automating the configuration of that group but breaking many protocols and creating other problems in the process.

Although the DNS has been a feature of the Internet for some time, it has come to the fore today as considerations are made for the expansion of the naming structure. The DNS is a large-scale replicated and distributed database system for looking up a few kinds of data associated with structured names. The database is distributed so that managers in each organization can maintain the part of the database pertaining to their organization. It does not provide any means for searching the database for a close match, and as such it is not suited to be a general directory system. DNS is good at what it was designed to do: provide the numeric Internet address of a computer with a particular name.

More recently, a number of protocols have appeared, while others have waned dramatically. Augmented IP capabilities providing security (IPsec) or extending the address space (IPv6 (218)) are emerging, while resource reservation (RSVP) (697), quality of service (QoS), and multicast are waning. The successful protocols are driven by user demand, such as IPsec for private networks. Less successful protocols (such as RSVP and multicast) are examples of the perils of scalability; once their deployment or management was shown to have difficulty scaling as the number of connections increased, their deployment stalled. Other protocols (such as IPv6 and QoS) lack user demand.

Some core Internet protocols are showing their age, demanding extension or modification. TCP, originally a reliable byte-stream protocol that used simple windowing for reliability, was augmented with sophisticated congestion control. Its feedback algorithms are being stressed by the incredible dynamic range over which they are expected to operate—from 1 kilobit/sec to 10 gigabit/sec, over seven orders of magnitude. Extensions are being developed to enable TCP to saturate gigabit, high-latency channels under moderate packet loss, as well as to enable zero-copy, direct placement of received data into application memory (608). Other modifications, already being deployed, enable TCP to react to explicit congestion feedback from routers, rather than merely inferring it from packet loss.

Some network protocols were supplanted or replaced by application-layer services. Network multicast gave way to application-layer multicast. IPsec is challenged by secure transport connections, such as the Secure Socket Layer (SSL). Application-layer protocols even provide the capabilities of an entire network, including naming, forwarding, and routing; these "peer-to-peer" systems are gaining ground for focused domains, such as music file sharing (Chapter 29).

30.2.4   System Integration

In the past, at conferences and meetings someone always had a diagram of the Internet; that does not happen anymore. The Internet has grown to the point that it is impossible to show even the most important connections and components in any simple diagram. The Internet now has thousands of components, perhaps approaching one million, and well over one million users. The Internet is also now an international system, and control is diffuse.

The role of government agencies as policymakers has been supplanted by the combination of the engineering community (mostly from vendor companies) and the operations staff of large network service providers. In a sense, the Internet is watched over by a priesthood of engineers.

The evolution of the Internet design is in the hands of the IETF, which consists of over a thousand people working in about a hundred working groups on various enhancements and extensions to the Internet protocols and operational procedures. One of the principles of the IETF is "test before standardizing," which provides an opportunity for techniques that work to become ad hoc standards that are formalized later. Competing service providers must also work together to provide their customers with Internet service and have made a "gentleman's agreement" among themselves to accomplish this task.

The explosive growth of the Internet and the commercial opportunity have led to a large number of network service providers competing for customers. Several types of service are available, and many of these companies are in several or all of the types. One type is backbone service; only about a dozen companies are significant players in this business. Then there are regional networks, where a region can be the size of several states or just a large city. Also there are metropolitan networks, which typically serve a single city and mainly provide dial-up connections. Another type of business is providing facilities for information servers (Web farms). The government does have a role in enabling experiments in advanced technology and applications through projects such as the NSF's TeraGrid, DOE's ESnet, DARPA's ATDnet, and NASA's NSI. The emergence of commercial radio-based metropolitan networks for mobile wireless Internet access from laptop computers may have a profound effect on the nature of computing by substantially increasing the possibility of ubiquitous access.

30.2.5   Summary of the Present

In the early design of the basic protocols, a goal was to use the simplest mechanism to achieve the desired function. The amazing growth of the Internet and the extension of these basic protocols to performance ranges far beyond their initial design criteria demonstrate the fundamental wisdom of keeping things simple. Within that framework, however, performance tuning has been important as the application mix has changed.

The big point about the current networking infrastructure is that it is overwhelmingly driven by commercial interests to provide good service to the average user. The good news is that the average user still wants a higher-performance system than currently exists. The bad news is that any experiments with services substantially different from those available will need special resources. To have a long-term impact, however, any special systems that are developed must provide a way to fold their results back into the common Internet system.

30.3   THE FUTURE (2005–)

Predicting the future of network infrastructure is as popular as predicting the weather, with as much likelihood of success. Although the Internet has been around for over 30 years, few would have predicted its current growth and ubiquity. Whatever the future network technology is, regardless of how it is built, it will continue to be called "the Internet." It's like Fortran in that regard. This future vision may be shaped by the development of a Grid, and it may affect our current vision of that Grid. It may also include features and services that are not even seen as useful today. Yet there are several aspects of the future that we can safely assume.

This future Internet will have a much higher aggregate capacity, including multigigabit and terabit links. It will include automated management and configuration, and it will support fault tolerance. It will also support services independent of location, much like voicemail from the telephone company. It is also likely to include aspects of the Grid, such as parameterized service location and distributed processing capabilities.

Some aspects are harder to predict. It is not clear whether the hosts on this network will continue to be PCs or include reductionist architectures such as PDAs, NCs, toasters, and light bulbs. They will certainly include high-definition displays, including opaque and volumetric 3D imaging. This variety challenges a Grid to support a variety of host capabilities, at once both higher and lower in capability than those of today.

The future Internet will support some form of mobility, some form of reconfigurability, some reprogrammability, and some adaptivity. We will see more reliable, more pervasive access, supporting dependable service as a feature of the network infrastructure. Networking will be available in places we would never have considered before: cars, laptops without special-purpose LANs, and so on. In fact, LANs may disappear altogether, being replaced by per host links as routing becomes cheaper and more ubiquitous.

In the end, we will probably have a higher level of services, but will also be much less aware of details. For example, a few years ago, knowledge of FTP commands was required to surf the Internet. Today, knowledge of URLs is required, but no one knows the HTTP commands that result from accessing that URL. URLs themselves are being replaced by the use of ever more powerful search engines, such as Google. In the future, we will do more asking for what we want, and less memorizing of magic incantations. This view of the future Internet supports the Grid goal of ubiquity and universal access, depending less on application support for such features. Infrastructure support for these services avoids per application idiosyncrasies that steepen the user learning curve and impede access.

The Internet of today also gives us a hint at one additional future requirement. The Web is the latest demonstration that a single, graphical, semantic-action user interface drives technology acceptance. The commercial acceptance of PCs has rocketed with the advent of graphical user interfaces (MacOS,

Windows), which also standardize interfaces available earlier within each application. The Web similarly drove existing Internet capability into public acceptance with mouse-based navigation. For future network technologies to be rapidly deployed and ubiquitously accepted, they will require "do what I mean" interfaces as well.

30.3.1   Driving Application

The driving application of the future is impossible to predict. Such an application emerges only after new services are available and a new plateau is reached. There have been some notable predictions, reviewed here, although they are no more convincing now than when they first appeared years ago.

Some predict that applications will be driven by a convergence of media, of telephony, cable television, radio, and the Internet. They predict "video on demand," which already exists as "pay per view" cable. Internet telephony exists, though hampered by complexity of use and lack of aggregate capacity. Video conferencing is no longer touted as the "killer application" it once was. It is available near the core of the Internet (there is no backbone, but there is a high-bandwidth center) and is used to augment conference room capabilities, but its desktop use has not grown as quickly as anticipated.

The advanced capabilities of the future Internet will give rise to true distributed applications, whose fundamental nature is the result of a congregation of resources. The Web is a database version of such an application; that is, the Web is not located in any one place. Gnutella is another such application, where end users both participate in the infrastructure and drive the deployment of a service. In the future, other applications will be as hard to locate. In this way, the Grid extends the notion of the Internet as a distributed database (the Web) or for exchange of messages (e-mail); a true Grid promotes distributed computation and supports such advanced applications as teleimmersion and online control of scientific instruments.

30.3.2   Network Technology

The phase changes of the past Internet were driven by changes in the capability of network technology. In the next five years, it is not clear whether evolution or revolution will dominate this landscape, driving predictable growth or another phase change. In either case, Grid capabilities will be affected by the capabilities of the network technology.

One certainty is that both link and LAN bandwidths will continue to grow; 40 gigabit/sec IP over SONET bandwidth is nearing experimental deployment (16x what was emerging in 1998, during this text's first edition), and a 10-gigabit/sec Ethernet is used commercially. In the LAN, we are nearing the limits of electrical signaling, and optical components are already near commodity prices. Together, these technologies have already shifted the bandwidth bottleneck from the network itself to the host interface and operating system; high-end PCs are taxed to saturate 1-gigabit/sec links. These technologies extend the host out into the LAN, and the Grid can help extend that even further to take advantage of phenomenal WAN link capacities.

Link technologies are favoring less layering of services, largely avoiding ATM altogether, and using IP over SONET directly, to avoid ATM's high overhead (over 10%). ATM is already being considered less of an end-to-end protocol and more of a reconfigurable link layer, used for dynamic provisioning. New backbones and local loop technologies, such as AT&T's cable-television-based network and the telephone company's DSL, will continue to drive end-user capacities upward, beyond the current 1 megabit/sec. These technologies encourage ever more dynamic network topologies, which can be used to support the dedicated, high-availability services that Grids require.

LANs will begin to include dynamic (reconfigured between static periods) and mobile (connected while moving) services. Wireless last hops are already common. For the local loop, digital wireless (PCS) services will support ISDN bandwidths for mobile users. Satellite systems may augment these services, although they increase end-to-end latency in the process and are falling out of favor somewhat. The result will obviate the LAN, replacing it with routed links to the last hop.

Grids will be challenged to accommodate this flattening of the network hierarchy. Clients are connected directly to wide-area access networks to provide increased bandwidth. This architecture also allows the infrastructure to be amortized more effectively, bypassing the so-called last-mile costs usually associated with telephone companies. The problem is that with this increased capability comes an increase in the LAN latency because the LAN has been replaced with a metropolitan-sized (or larger) interconnect. The optimizations currently assumed within the LAN will have to be reconsidered in such an architecture; for example, at these latencies, remote file service may not be appropriate for casual use.

Even as the capabilities of these networks increase, the capabilities of user access points may decrease. Simpler devices, including PDAs and NCs, will increase the demands on the network capabilities to fill the void. There is even talk of IP addresses for toasters and light bulbs, to extend network services to include burnt-bulb signaling. This will result in an increased diversity in the requirements on the networking infrastructure.

For example, current Internet protocols contain parameters tuned to its size and bandwidth capabilities, such as maximum segment (packet) lifetime (MSL). The original value for the MSL was based on 56-kilobit/sec links, 10 hops, and 200-millisecond round-trip propagation latencies, all reasonable bounds in 1969. It might be expected that, in the current days of 10-gigabit/sec links, the MSL would decrease accordingly. Instead, the hops per route have increased to accommodate the global infrastructure, as well as the richness in local infrastructure, often reaching 15–20. The round-trip latency has increased by the inclusion of geosynchronous satellites, often reaching 500 milliseconds. Finally, the bandwidth on any of these links often includes devices, such as PDAs, which continue to use low bit rates, for example, 2.4 kilobit/sec. As a result, the MSL has not changed much, although the expected segment lifetime has become ever more diverse. Consequently, the current "least common denominator" service of the Internet needs to give way to an adaptive interaction, to allow high-performance resources to interact with low-performance interfaces.

These changes provide both opportunities and challenges for a Grid. Increases in bandwidth can change the trade-offs in the distribution of resources. We are already encountering applications that prefer high-bandwidth transmission to compression, to reduce the overall latency and local computation requirements. In the future, we will trade bandwidth for latency, computation, or even storage. All these trade-offs may require much more elaborate coordination of services, especially including mapping of resources to the underlying topology and network capabilities.

We note that details about these technologies are not considered in this chapter. Such details are liable to present a moving target that, at best, would be outdated by the time of publication. Besides, a good architecture takes into account only generalizations of technologies, in order to provide a flexible framework. Such a framework should apply as well in the next few years as in a future whose capabilities are difficult to imagine. Architecture must be independent of such specifics; it is the component of a distributed system that persists the longest.

30.3.3   Protocols and Services

In the near term, protocols will be dominated by the deployment and refinement of recent revisions in the basic Internet paradigm, IP, and subsequent advanced services provided by an enriched address space. Transport protocols will support a broader class of services as well, including efficient support for ordered transactions. Finally, these richer services will be provided to the application with ever-simpler interfaces, including address and service registries based on resource discovery.

Although overexposure of DNS names (www.joe.com) is more noticeable, IP numbers are being depleted more rapidly than even telephone numbers. Current IPv4 addressing supports a worldwide total of 2 billion addresses, but only a fraction of that number is available (10–100 million) because of partitioning of the space for administrative purposes. The current version, IPv4, will be replaced with IPv6, with its larger address space. This new IP provides additional addressing paradigms, akin to multicast, that enrich the overall architecture as well.

IPv6 (218) solves that problem by providing an increased address space that should serve for decades to come, capable of supporting 10^{38} addresses. Even with administrative partitioning and reservation of part of the space for advanced services, that is roughly 1 billion billion addresses per square millimeter on the surface of the earth (including oceans).

In the past, security has been left as something to be added on later; but in the design of the IPv6 protocol, security has been a key element all through the development. The IETF is also developing a robust security framework and infrastructure (IPsec) that is already coming into use (see Chapter 21).

The provisioning of multiple services levels or quality of service may need to emerge as well. The first widespread attempt, RSVP, was a success as a distributed soft-state protocol, but its use for path provisioning did not scale well with the number of connections and thus had deployment difficulties.

IPv6's advanced services include addressing support for anycasting and sub-host networks. *Anycast* is the request for anyone to respond. It is a broadcast question but requires only a single response and can be used for service location. *Subhost networks* allow components within a PC to have their own network addresses, and the interior of a host to be, in a sense, a network. This strategy allows network-based control of the interaction between the components within the host. Additionally, mobile IP is under development and expected to be deployed shortly.

End-to-end transport will be advanced with the deployment of new service classes, including reliable, partially ordered transactions; unreliable, congestion-controlled datagrams (DCP); direct data placement; and reliable multicast protocols. New transaction protocols will allow more effective Web access, permitting client–server interaction to be governed by data dependencies, rather than the whims of a socket layer. It is not clear, however, which of these protocols will be deployed at the network or transport levels, or overtaken by more easily managed application-layer equivalents, as has already occurred with multicast.

Routing will advance to include policy-based control. This will encourage multiaccess hosts, which increase reliability without compromising the ability to use resources based on preferences. Multicast, currently an overlaid service, had been becoming a native network function and, because of scaling limitations, is now being pushed into applications. Active networking, where packets include their own programs, although not so successful as anticipated, may result in some dynamically deployed in-network services, such as caching and data transcoding.

These advanced routing services enhance the network capability as presented to the application. In the existing Internet, the endpoint alone determines the route, and that route is provided by the network. This provides a powerful and simple interface for the programmer by hiding path information. In the future, applications may want control over some aspects of the path, for example, latency or jitter properties; or they may want use of in-network services directly by the application; or they may even want to allow applications to control the forwarding path itself, as in peer-to-peer networks (Chapter 29).

Network names will evolve, no longer indicating a specific machine on the network. The current name service, DNS, is a name indirection service (name-to-number lookup) overloaded with service location (domain names as directory information, such as www.ford.com for the car company). Two types of name need to appear to address this overload. People will have network names not bound to any one location or computer; and services will have network names located at the time of a request and based on the availability and capability of resources and their associated cost.

30.3.4   System Integration

As the size and scope of the Internet grow, the scale grows also. It is becoming clear that the number of entities on the network will reach the billions. Of necessity, there will be fewer entities whose name we care about; hence, the explosive growth of the network may precipitate changes that make it more comprehensible, not less. A similar phenomenon occurred in telephony and, more recently, in television. Early telephone networks taxed the recall of even the most accomplished operator; but as the network grew, so grew the number space organization, such as directories, lookup services (1-800-Dentist), and aggregations (800/888 numbers, area codes, country codes). Similar aggregation and indirection may relieve the current cacophony.

Network operations and control are already evolving out of the hands of the engineers who design networks and into an apprenticeship community. This situation in turn will evolve to a trade association model. Provisioning is already evolving to include more virtual networking, necessitated by the growth of commercial services and the corresponding hesitation to support a strictly separate infrastructure for research or dedicated services. Virtual networks support dynamic, rapid deployment and reconfiguration of resources, sharing infrastructure among production, experimental, and reserved services. This virtualization can occur at any level, in any protocol, in link-specific protocols, or in the IP layer (as in USC/ISI's X-Bone (656)).

Virtualization complicates management because each virtual network can have its own (competing) requirements and management. The so-called tragedy of the commons challenges their use to optimize routing topologies. They may evolve and include ever more diverse components; automated management will become a critical requirement. Grid applications can use this virtual network infrastructure to provide per application networks, which will help isolate and manage the control of the network components by the application. Virtualization also helps extend local high-performance dedicated networks into the global infrastructure in a controlled fashion.

Network virtualization has two competing approaches: overlays and peer-to-peer networks. Overlays use tunnels at the network layer, providing a virtual Internet; when used to attach a remote host or network to an existing managed network over the public infrastructure, these are called VPNs. Peer-to-peer networks are application-layer overlays, having the advantage of being able to forward data based on application data, but the disadvantage of needing to reimplement most network-layer services at the application layer.

Finally, the notion of end nodes in the Internet is also due for a change. As noted earlier, low-end clients (PDAs, NCs) will enter the equation. In addition, user stations will also begin to add capability to the network, as file servers, cache agents, or compute engines. In exchange for this service, users will receive reduced rates for network access, just as users generating power can now sell it back to the electric company. As a result of this additional capability, network services will evolve that, like the Web, cannot be described as confined to a single location.

30.3.5   Summary of the Future

The network infrastructure of the future will be much larger in scale and scope but will include more virtual components. Services will be located by type, rather than by name or location. End stations will add value, rather than benefiting only from the value of servers. The dynamic range of bandwidth, latency, and capability will continue to expand. The challenges of this future are those of service location, virtualization, and automated management.

In the future, the LAN will be a less discernible feature of the infrastructure, with clients being directly connected to a metropolitan or wide area network. This situation will change the trade-offs for which local cluster systems are optimized, for example, for networked file systems.

Finally, the extraordinary capabilities of the future infrastructure and end systems will be complicated by their increasing diversity. The advent of gigabit and terabit links will not mitigate the need to support kilobit access, as network capability devolves down to the appliance level.

30.4 CHALLENGES

A few underlying themes continue to challenge the evolution of the network infrastructure:

+ *Scale.* As the number of network components, distance between the components, and speed of communication increase, other aspects of the network increase, sometimes exponentially (or worse). These include the costs of management and performance overheads (e.g., routing).

+ *Complexity.* Although scale increases complexity, new protocol and network features further complicate networking. Advanced transport services include multicast, ordered messaging, reliable multicast, real time, and mobility.

+ *Fundamental limits.* Advances in network technology are approaching fundamental limits of communication, including speed-of-light latency and bandwidth over copper media. In addition, advances in protocols are now exposing these limits, which were previously masked by other performance limits.

In this section we discuss these impediments to our vision of the future outlined earlier. We address how each issue impacts our goal of a ubiquitous infrastructure and how that goal may itself address some of these impediments.

30.4.1 Scale

"Scale" means many things to many people. Networks scale as the number of hosts, routers, users, and so on increases. They scale in distance as distances decrease, moving networked components inside a host, and increase to include low- and high-orbit satellites. They scale in bandwidth as it decreases to support light bulbs, toasters, and beepers and increases to support ADSL, cable modems, and OC-3072 to the user.

Scale can increase the number of components and thus complexity of the network. As the number of routers and links increases, so too does the number of redundant paths. Such an increase is hyperexponential (factorial, in this case).

Other increases in complexity are exponential or linear. In any case, increases in complexity necessitate simplifying organizations, such as encapsulations or hierarchies.

Numeric scale brings about a need for a real directory service and automated network management and configuration. DNS will no longer be useful as a locator service; Web search engines will similarly fail when thousands of servers are located in response to a query. Summarization services will be required to reduce the redundancy in search responses—for example, to provide a single, canonical entry for *ford.com*, rather than listing every Web page at Ford. With the advent of larger numbers of servers and services, property-based service location will be required. Locating a server by name will not be as important as locating one by capability, availability, cost, or performance metrics.

In other cases, scale can increase the dynamic range over which a network operates. Bandwidth supports both higher- and lower-speed devices. Latencies increase to include 200-millisecond hops (high-orbit satellites) or LANs with 10-millisecond latencies (low-orbit systems), beyond the typical 1- to 2-millisecond latencies now supported.

Increased dynamic range requires increased adaptability in transport protocols, network management, and configuration, and eventually in applications. Systems will need to adjust to the range of latencies and bandwidths supported, rather than denying service to less capable users. PDAs and NCs on telephone links should not have to wait 10 minutes for fancy graphics they cannot render; rather, responses tuned to the capability of the host and network will be required.

In the past five years, scale—or, more precisely, the inability of certain protocols to scale—has stalled the deployment of a number of protocols. Multicast IP and RSVP both had difficulty scaling as the number of connections (multicast groups, reservations) increased. This contributed significantly to their disuse. Peer-to-peer networks deployed rapidly, often despite their architecture's lack of scale, but some were eventually sufficiently encumbered by scaling challenges to disappear.

30.4.2   Functional Complexity

Scale complexity is compounded by an increase in the complexity of network services. Basic network protocols are being augmented to include larger address spaces (IPv6), multicast, and mobility. In addition, new network-oriented versions of service location are being coupled to routing and addressing mechanisms, notably anycasting.

Augmented transport protocols are looking to the interior of the network to provide state or computational support, such as ordered groups, reliable multicast, and real time. These services will require additional function in the routers, such as real-time scheduling, sliding-window queuing, and reordering of buffers.

New features may be supported via *active networking* (634) code that accompanies the packets to the routers. This approach allows new features and services to be implemented inside the network on the fly, such as inserting data-dependent forward error correction over wireless links. Two of the more promising applications for this technology are intelligent caching and data transcoding. Intelligent caching moves temporary data storage inside the network, near natural aggregation points on high-capacity links, closer to the user access. Transcoding can be used to avoid transmitting multiple encodings at the source and to use time-efficient encodings over fast links, space-efficient encodings over slow links, and user-dependent encodings over the last hop to the host.

Many previous predictions suggested that protocols would move from overlays into the core, including multicast. More recently, it has become evident that such overlays and virtual network components may persist as part of a richer, hierarchical Internet structure, including network overlays and application overlays (peer-to-peer networks). An ongoing tension exists between the quick fix of end-system application solutions and the more judicious, deliberate design of the core network and Internet as a whole. The field is clearly becoming more complex in the near term, as the barrier to deployment is lowered and protocol development is less the domain of a closely knit "priesthood."

30.4.3 Fundamental Limits

Networking has always coped with the fundamental limits of communication. As technology progresses, these limits become more significant in the overall architecture. They change the architectural trade-offs of bandwidth, processing, latency, and storage and can impact the design of efficient protocols matched to network characteristics, although they are general to the design of any protocol subject to those limits.

Bandwidth is limited by the physical encoding and by transmission media and devices. Gigabit Ethernet supports both copper and optical fiber media, but higher speeds are more likely to require fiber. Wireless systems are limited by frequency allocations and power constraints, both those regulatory and those due to portability and battery properties. Optical systems are limited by electro-optical conversion speeds, which limit the single-link bandwidth to the host. Striping (parallelization) techniques are being used to virtualize a single link from multiples, such as WDM for optics, and dynamic configuration of stripes is likely to be required.

Latency is limited by the speed-of-signal propagation speed, serialization, and packetization delays. Store-and-forward routing may be replaced by sub-packet (cut-through) switching, reducing the per-hop switching latency. The inclusion of satellite systems changes the fundamental propagation latency of hops, from submillisecond for LANs and 100 milliseconds for WANs, to tens of milliseconds for LANs and 500 milliseconds for WANs. This change is coupled with an ever-increasing assumption that even remote or distributed applications should behave as if they were local; users often complain that Netscape's Navigator Web browser does not respond like Microsoft Word. Recently, the Interplanetary Internet research group changed its name to show its focus: it is now called Delay-Tolerant Networking.

Given higher bandwidth and latency, feedback will become ever more difficult. The increase in dynamic range, as well as in scale, of the network increases the unpredictability and complicates feedback protocols.

Overall, what users *can* do may begin to be limited by the combination of *what* they want to do and *where* they want to do it. The future where distributed simulations include games between people anywhere on the planet is unrealistic; there are simply some levels of interaction that require physical proximity, if not in the same room, then maybe in the same city.

The speed of both communication and computation is steadily increasing, but propagation latency remains constant, an effect of the nature of the speed of light. As a result, in the future infrastructure, applications will be required to handle this latency appropriately and directly, though it is masked by other inefficiencies at present. For example, some video-based applications compress their output prior to network transmission; in the future, avoiding the latency of this extra computation may be more important than the additional bandwidth wasted as a result.

30.4.4   General Summary

The future of the network infrastructure, as predicted by some expected future aspects of the Internet, is certain to include higher bandwidth and more hosts. It will include a higher level of in-network services and capabilities—some, such as policy routing and resource discovery, are motivated by current deficiencies. Other changes, such as new trade-offs enabled by these new capabilities, may challenge the assumptions on which our current systems are based. The key issues of scale, complexity, and limits must be taken into account, as the success and failure of many components attest.

30.5   SUMMARY

Overall, network infrastructure is currently dominated by the infrastructure of the Internet. The Internet is a reasonable model for the Grid, providing both an early version of its services and a platform from which to evolve. As a starting point, we need to examine the successes—and failures—of the Internet and try to predict what the future Internet holds and how to make the two futures converge.

The Internet has one powerful underlying assumption: first and foremost, "keep it simple." The simplicity of the basic Internet architecture and infrastructure has let it be integrated into a wide variety of hosts and used in a diverse arena of applications. The selection of a single architecture provides a commonality that ensures interoperation. If only one version exists, everything interoperates. The Internet eschews customization in favor of this simplicity, from picking a single byte order within words to picking a single address space.

Part of why the Internet succeeds as a network infrastructure is that it has made some other assumptions, some of which must be reexamined to move forward. A great number of its protocols, notably for routing and configuration management, assume LANs with shared access media and WAN connections that are dedicated and point to point. Shared links, used for virtualization, and asymmetric access systems such as satellite networks break these models and are difficult to support in the current Internet. These assumptions need to be challenged and replaced with adaptable components.

Another of the Internet's successful characteristics is that of "do it simple first." Internet protocols do not attempt to be everything to every system. They are not the most efficient mechanism for transport over some technologies. They are adaptable, however; and when they fail to achieve high performance, they do not fail to achieve basic connectivity.

Designing a Grid out of the Internet requires augmenting the Internet—mostly ways it is already evolving and in other, new ways. However, the Internet also challenges the Grid to provide ubiquity and a common interface that is as global as IP (Figure 30.4).

The Internet is an example of how consistency engenders ubiquity; the common IP interface is largely responsible for its current worldwide acceptance. The development of a Grid should follow this lead in selecting simple common interfaces, to provide the consistency that promotes ubiquity (see Table 30.1).

The Internet is already being challenged in its area of greatest weakness, that of reliability. A Grid further challenges that goal, requiring dependability of not only transport but also computational and other in-network services.

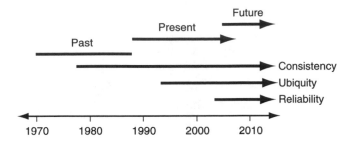

30.4

FIGURE

Timelines of the Internet and Grid goals compared.

	Consistency	Ubiquity	Reliability
Internet past	Yes	No	No
Internet present	Yes	Yes	No
Internet future	Yes	Yes	Yes
Grid	Yes	Yes	Yes

30.1

TABLE

Goals of the Grid and How the Internet Addresses Them.

This chapter has used the Internet to illustrate the evolution of network infrastructure. In the past, the Internet proved the concept of packet switching, based on the assumption that computing costs drop more rapidly than communication link costs, such that sharing a link by multiplexing packets is more effective than providing new links. The result was a single model that enabled global ubiquity. With these principles having evolved, the current Internet now focuses on performance rather than only on simplicity. It is driven by service to the user, directed at benefiting the majority of users. In the future, the scale of the infrastructure will increase but may be affected more by the resulting diversity than the size or scope of any one component.

The Internet is likely to be dominated in the next few years by the following changes:

✦ *Diverse hosts*. From PDAs, NCs, and toasters to 3D visualization environments, the only certainty is that the dynamic range of capability will widen.

✦ *Dynamic infrastructure*. Mobility and satellite links, together with virtual infrastructure, will increase the dynamic range and volatility of transport capabilities.

- *GUIs for network manipulation and control.* Just as windowed OSs and graphical browsers opened elitist communities to the masses, a GUI for the infrastructure will raise the capability of the infrastructure.

- *Fewer assumptions.* It will no longer be safe to assume shared-media LANs or point-to-point WAN links. New trade-offs will become economically feasible, such as trading increases in computation or bandwidth to reduce latency.

- *Capability-based naming.* URLs will cease to be useful or even notable; search engines, organization services, and capability-based directories will replace fixed strings.

- *New protocols and network capabilities.* Policy-based routing, reliable ordered transactions, and overlays will enable new network services, and emerging protocols (IPv6) and experimental protocols (DCP) will become mainstream. A distributed operating system will eventually emerge, akin to the Web's distributed database, that enhances our local operating systems.

Many of these changes foster the development of Grid capabilities. A more dynamic, more capable infrastructure will encourage new in-network services, including computational servers. In addition, the reliability requirement of a Grid challenges the Internet to evolve as a dependable system, even in the presence of these other advances. The Grid can indeed become as significant as the Internet, as it applies the lessons of the Internet: use of standardization and consistency to drive ubiquity rather than customization to drive performance. In this way, the two systems cooperate to provide ever-increasing and exciting capabilities.

FURTHER READING

For more information on the topics covered in this chapter, see *www.mkp.com/grid2* and the following references:

- Hafner and Lyon's historical account of the development of the Internet includes a discussion of key issues of Internet design philosophy (346). In a sense, it is a retrospective on the Internet, in the way this text is a prospective on the Grid.

- A special issue of *Scientific American* devoted to the Internet also contains many articles on related services (165).

✦ Bush's seminal article (145) contains the genesis of several key ideas, including the reasons for national funding of scientific research. It includes a few visions of future technologies, one of which foreshadows the Web.

✦ Tanebaum's text (629) is an introduction to networking and includes discussions of network technologies, such as ATM, SONET, xDSL, and ISDN.

✦ Smith and Weingarten's report presents a vision for the next generation of the Internet—and, by way of context, describes what is currently possible in the Internet and where Internet research is likely to lead (597).

Glossary

Accounting

The process of tracking, limiting, or charging for the consumption of resources in a system.

Active networks

Networks with dynamically reprogrammable resources. The programs can be loaded one time or can prepend the data of individual packets.

Adaptation

Set of mechanisms used by applications to adjust their behavior based on the current availability of network resources, so as to maximize application-specific performance measures.

Advanced reservation

A service level agreement (qv) in which the conditions of the agreement start at some agreed-upon time in the future.

Assurance

A means by which the user of a service or program determines that the service provider or the program meets specific criteria for trustworthiness, security, reliability, or similar characteristics.

ATM (Asynchronous Transfer Mode)

A telephone company service using a packet-switching-like technique with very small packets, called *cells*, of 48 data bytes.

Auditing

The process of recording a history of the actions taken by a system component. Auditing is often used to collect the information needed for accounting.

Authentication

The process of verifying the identity of a participant to an operation or request.

Authorization

The process of determining whether a client may use or access an object or resource, and the type of access allowed.

Autonomous system (AS)

A routing domain. In general, control is designed to be exchanged more frequently, with fewer restrictions, within an AS than between different ASs.

Bandwidth

The amount of information that can be sent across a channel in a unit time. It is usually measured in bits per second and powers thereof.

Best effort

Attempt by the Internet Protocol to deliver each packet (or datagram) of data to the destination, but if this cannot be done because of a lack of routing information, because time-to-live is exceeded, or because of a variety of other reasons, the datagram is discarded, and no further effort is made.

Bridge

A device used to interconnect two separate instances of a single network technology. Data is transferred between the two networks by examining the link layer information only. Contrast with *router* and *gateway*.

Broker

An entity that acts as a intermediary between one or more service providers and a service consumer. A broker may isolate the consumer from complex decisions, such as end-to-end scheduling, or may virtualize the underlying services, hiding their existence from consumer.

BSLA (Binding Service Level Agreement)

A service level agreement in which an agreement to provide capability is bound to an agreement to perform a task.

C#

An object-oriented programming language based on C++ and containing features similar to Java.

CBR

Case-based reasoning.

Cell

A small, fixed-sized *packet*, such as in ATM.

Certificate

A data object signed by an issuer (e.g., a certification authority) binding the name and possibly other characteristics of a principal with an encryption key issued to or selected by the principal.

Certification authority (CA)

The third party that attests to the validity of a *certificate* and the binding of the attributes and encryption key it contains by applying a digital signature to the certificate.

CIDR (classless interdomain routing)

A way of grouping sets of addresses that avoids the byte boundaries of "classful" routing. CIDR has been credited with avoiding the exhaustion of the IPv4 address space.

CIM (common information model)

An object-oriented information model defined by the Distributed Management Task Force (DMTF). CIM defines a meta-model, as well as a set of detailed classes for management of resources such as computers, networks, and storage systems.

COM (common object model)

Microsoft's Windows object model, which is being extended to distributed systems and multi-tiered architectures. ActiveX controls are an important class of COM, which implement the component model of software. The distributed version of COM is called DCOM.

Complexity

A measure of the internal relationships of the components of a system. A complex system has more internal relationships than that of a simple one.

Contract violation

An observed failure, on the part of a Grid resource or application, in presenting the expected performance that was expressed in a predefined contract.

Contracts

A set of statements indicating how a certain Grid resource or application is expected to perform during operation on the Grid. Each statement should contain a metric and the domain of acceptable values for such metric.

CORBA (Common Object Request Broker Architecture)

An approach to cross-platform cross language distributed objects developed by a broad industry group, the Object Management Group (OMG). CORBA specifies basic services (such as naming, trading, persistence) that are run over the protocol IIOP and is developing higher-level facilities that are object architectures for specialized domains such as banking.

Co-scheduling

A scheduling approach in which two or more resources are scheduled to be used at the same time.

Credential

A piece of information that is used to prove the identify of a subject.

DAG (directed acyclic graph)

Data structure used to represent workflows in the virtual data toolkit.

DAML+OIL

A language used to represent ontologies and knowledge bases in semantic Web applications.

Data access and integration (DAI)

A Global Grid Forum (GGF) standard that defines a common mechanism for data access regardless of the underlying technology used to store the data.

Data consistency

A property that defines the extent to which multiple distributed copies of data are kept up to date. Strong data consistency requires that any data updates be propagated so that the same data value is seen at every copy, while weak data consistency allows older copies to exist.

Data federation

A data management system in which multiple storage systems are integrated with respect to access mechanisms, data model, policy, consistency, or other aspects.

Data-intensive application

A class of application that is primarily driven by the need to access and process data.

Data mediation

A technique used to federate data sources with different data models. Data mediation converts one data model to another, or perhaps to a third more universal data model.

Data provenance

Information about the history of a piece of data included information such how, when, and who generated the data in question.

Database management system (DBMS)

A system for reliably storing data and supporting queries and updates on that data, typically via a standardized language or APIs.

Delay jitter

Variation in end-to-end delay experienced by the receiver.

Delegation

The process of granting a delegate the right to act as another principal (the grantor). In delegation of identity, the delegate may assume the identity of the grantor when authenticating to a server. In delegation of authority, the delegate is granted the right to perform certain functions that were available to the grantor, but without assuming the identity of the grantor.

Digital library

A set of services for creating, protecting, viewing, and manipulating data stored in collections.

Digital signature

The encryption of a message (or *message digest*) using the originator's private key, so that the integrity and origin of the message can be verified by decryption with the originator's public key.

Directory service

A system for finding information about a named object by searching based on the name, on a fuzzy match for the name, or on the values of keywords that may be indexed. The current Web search engines could be configured as powerful directory systems.

Distributed hash table

A peer-to-peer routing substrate in which nodes are assigned a unique pseudo-random identifier that determines their position in a key space.

DNS (Domain Name System)

A replicated distributed database that maps global names (foo.example.com) to global numbers (192.0.2.0). The DNS provides a lookup service but not a directory service, since it is not searchable. A recent survey indicates that the database contains information for over 30 million names.

DP

Diagnosis and prognostic.

Dublin core

A specification of core metadata elements to associate with published data.

Dynamic range

The ratio between the largest and smallest scale of a property. Often, it is not the scale but the dynamic range that presents the most difficulty. It is not hard to build either kilobit-per-second or gigabit-per-second networks; it is hard to build a single system with the dynamic range to cope with bandwidths of both.

Encryption

A transformation that scrambles data in a way that varies based on a secret parameter, called an encryption key, so that the data cannot be interpreted (unscrambled or decrypted) without the corresponding *decryption* key. The scrambled data is called *ciphertext*, and the original or subsequently unscrambled data is called *plaintext*.

Encryption key

See *key*.

End-to-end

Concerned with a complete path across a system, not just a single component: hence, end-to-end security, end-to-end monitoring, end-to-end provisioning, and so forth.

Enterprise JavaBeans

JavaBeans enhanced for server-side operation with capabilities such as multiuser support.

eScience

A term coined to refer to global collaboration science and the infrastructure that enable this collaboration.

ESnet

The Department of Energy's Energy Sciences Network, a high-speed network designed to support research applications across the United States.

Ethernet

The most common local area network technology, developed at Xerox PARC in the 1970s. It originally used a shared bus media, such as coax cable, but now relies typically on twisted-pair lines that are interconnected by bridges.

EU DataGrid (EDG)

A European Union–funded project operating from 2001 to 2004 with the goal of building a production Grid infrastructure focused on a range of data-intensive applications.

Execution signature

A compressed representation of the events observed during application execution, which characterizes the application's dynamic behavior.

Fast Ethernet

Ethernet operating at 100 megabit/sec.

Firewall

A computer placed between two networks through which only specifically authorized communication may proceed or through which specifically prohibited communication is prevented.

Flow

A group of packets from one sender to one or more receivers, grouped by destination network address, protocol, or transport protocol multiplexing identifier (port number).

Frame

A fundamental unit of transfer at the network physical layer.

FTP (File Transfer Protocol)

The application for moving files among computers.

Fundamental limit

A property, such as bandwidth or latency, that has a physical limit, such as the speed of light, or the Shannon coding limit.

Gantt chart

A two-dimensional plot where the y-axis enumerates a set of tasks and the x-axis represents time. The point (x,y) on a Gantt chart shows the state of task number x at time y.

Gateway

A device used to interconnect two networks, using application-level information. Contrast with *router* and *bridge*.

Gigabit Ethernet

Ethernet operating at 1 gigabit/sec.

Gigabyte

A thousand megabytes.

Global Grid Forum (GGF)

An international standard organization for specifications related to Grids.

Globus Toolkit®

The open source Grid software that provides the basis for many Grid deployments worldwide.

GRAM (Grid Resource Allocation Manager)

Part of the *Globus Toolkit*. GRAM defines protocols for creating and interacting with a managed job. GRAM jobs are typically associated with computational resources.

Grid

A distributed computing infrastructure that supports the creation and operation of virtual organizations by providing mechanisms for controlled, cross-organizational resource sharing.

Grid Service Handle (GSH)

A OGSI construct. A GSH is a long-term name for a Grid service.

Grid Service Reference (GSR)

An OGSI data structure that contains all information needed to interact with a Grid service. GSRs are created by passing a GSH to a resolver service.

Grid service

A Web service that supports the Open Grid Services Infrastructure (OGSI) standard.

Grid Security Infrastructure (GSI)

A service used by the Globus Toolkit for secure authentication and communication over an open network. GSI services include mutual authentication and single sign-on.

Guaranteed service

A network service that provides lossless transmissions and hard delay upper bounds to packets from applications that conform to their specified traffic contract.

Histograms

Representations using horizontal or vertical bars to plot the magnitude of each of one or more variables.

Hosting environment

A language- and programming-specific environment within which service implementations execute.

Hourglass model

Approach to network system design in which heterogeneous system components (the base of the hourglass) are integrated by adapting them to provide a small number of basic functions (the neck of the hourglass). Using these basic functions, a wide range of complex system behaviors can be created (the top of the hourglass).

HTTP (Hyper Text Transport Protocol)

A stateless transport protocol allowing control information and data to be transmitted between Web clients and servers.

IETF (Internet Engineering Task Force)

The standards development body of the Internet. The IETF is an open organization of volunteers, primarily network software engineers from research labs, universities, and vendor companies. The principle of the IETF is "test before standardize," and decisions are made by "rough consensus," rather than by strict voting.

IIOP (Internet Inter-ORB Protocol)

A stateful protocol allowing CORBA ORBs to communicate with each other and to transfer both the request for a desired service and the returned result.

Information Repository

A service that supports the storage, discovery, and retrieval of archival data elements.

Instant messaging

A messaging system that provides immediate exchange; contrast to e-mail, which users receive only when they check their mailbox, and which may be arbitrarily delayed.

Integrity

A characteristic of data, a message, or a system or program of being unmodified from its original or correct value.

Intelligent caching

The sharing and reuse of data based on hints in the data stream and sophisticated analysis of access patterns, often on a wider scale than a single cache.

Interactive distributed information access (IDIA)

Another name for Web-like services, in which a user is involved in real-time, online access to shared information that is distributed.

Interface definition language (IDL)

A special-purpose programming language designed to describe the interfaces to a remote service. Typically, language-specific remote procedure call interfaces are automatically generated from IDL.

Internet

The public access interconnected set of networks using the Internet Protocol.

Internet-II

A program sponsored by major universities to provide high-capacity network service to university researchers.

Information Power Grid (IPG)

A production Grid deployment project in the United States designed to support the activities of the National Aeronautics and Space Administration (NASA).

J2EE

A popular Java-based hosting environment.

Java

A software language for implementing applications. Java is often used to write mobile and portable programs.

JavaBeans

A software mechanism for supporting exchange of control information to coordinate presentation across multiple systems.

JDBC (Java DataBase Connectivity)

A set of interfaces (Java methods and constants) in the Java 1.1 enterprise framework, defining a uniform access to relational databases. JDBC calls from a client or server Java program link to a particular driver that converts these universal database access calls (establish a connection, SQL query, etc.) to the particular syntax needed to access essentially any significant database.

Job scheduler

A software component that is responsible for determining when a requested action, or job, is performed.

Key

When used in the context of a security system, refers to a parameter to an *encryption* (*decryption*) function that changes the transformation of *plaintext* to *ciphertext* (ciphertext to plaintext). This key is sometimes called a secret key when used with a symmetric cryptosystem. A session key is a key generated for short-term use in a particular exchange. In a public key cryptosystem, the public and private keys form a pair, where one key is used to decrypt the ciphertext generated by encryption with the other key. Also used to refer to a unique identifier (e.g., hash key, database key) generated by computing a function on some data attribute.

Knowledge network

The collective application of experts, resources, and data repositories for the solution of a discipline-oriented task.

Large Hadron Collider (LHC)

A high-energy particle accelerator located at CERN, the European Particle Physics Laboratory. Several experiments are being run at LHC, each of which has a distributed, international team of scientists and each of which generates hundreds of terabytes of data per year.

Latency

The time from message origination at the source to message delivery at the destination (sec). In communication, it is the sum of transmission and propagation latencies.

LDAP (Lightweight Directory Access Protocol)

A directory service standard for organizing information using hierarchical structure.

Lifetime management

The mechanisms associated with the creation and destruction of a service. In the case of OGSA, lifetime management also refers to the softstate mechanisms used to keep a service alive.

Link protocol

The protocol used on a link or single step (or hop) in the network. A commonly used link protocol is PPP.

Load balancing

The assignment of equivalent amounts of work to processors that will execute concurrently.

Mass storage system (MSS)

A storage system optimized for volume of data, rather than access speed. Typically MSS involves the use of tape for storing data, sometimes in coordination with spinning disks to provide low-latency caching of data.

Master/worker

A job scheduling and load balancing strategy in which a computation is split into independent subtasks and each subtask is assigned by a master computation of available worker processing nodes for execution.

Matchmaker

A system scheduling component in which work is assigned to a computational node by matching attributes of the work to be done with attributes of the capability provided by the computational node.

Message Passing Interface (MPI)

A widely used standard API for developing message passing parallel programs.

Metadata

Attributes describing data, information, or resources.

Metadata schema

An organization of metadata attributes into a table structure within a database.

MIB (management information base)

A set of variables that describe the namespace of objects controlled by an SNMP agent. Information such as packets per second through a router can be specified using the MIB.

MIME (Multipurpose Internet Mail Extensions)

A standard that allows e-mail to include multimedia components.

Monitoring and Discovery Service (MDS)

Part of the Globus Toolkit. MDS is a distributed service for publishing and discovering dynamic information about distributed resources.

MRO

Maintenance, repair, and overhaul.

MSL (maximum segment lifetime)

A parameter in the TCP protocol. Internet protocols assume that no packet will persist inside the network for longer than one MSL. MSL is typically set to 2 minutes.

Multicasting

A mechanism that allows for efficient delivery of information to several destinations with a single transmission, avoiding separate transmissions to each destination. In one-to-many multicasting, a single sender sends to multiple destinations. In many-to-many multicasting, multiple senders send to multiple destinations at the same time.

Multiplexing (muxing)

The overall process of several virtual channels sharing a single physical channel. Specifically, several source channels alternately share, or are multiplexed onto, a single shared channel. At the destination, the shared channel is demultiplexed, or dispersed appropriately, onto multiple outgoing channels. That is, multiplexing is performed first, then demultiplexing. Its converse is *striping*.

Network infrastructure

The combined equipment, lines, hardware, software, and management of a network.

Network service

The performance of the network as experienced by the end user.

Network-aware applications

Applications that adapt their own behavior and demands on the network to reflect the current network load, latency, or rate of message loss.

NGI (Next Generation Internet)

A late-1990s U.S. government research program to spur development of advanced network architectures and protocols.

NOC (network operations center)

The network management and problem-solving facility, often staffed 24 hours a day, 7 days a week.

NTP (Network Time Protocol)

A protocol to allow clocks connected by a computer network to be synchronized. For LANs it is possible to keep clocks synchronized within 1 millisec using NTP.

OC-3

A telephone company service with a data rate of 155 megabit/sec. OC services are typically available over SONET links and also typically provide ATM carrier services.

OC-12

A telephone company service with a data rate of 622 megabit/sec. OC services are typically available over SONET links and also typically provide ATM carrier services.

OGSA data access and integration (OGSA-DAI)

Global Grid Forum working group that is defining service-oriented interfaces for manipulating distributed data sources.

on-demand

A scheduling approach in which resources are made available in "real time," immediately after the request for the resource is made.

Ontology

Concepts used to define a structure to organize knowledge.

Open Grid Services Architecture (OGSA)

An integration of Grid and Web services technologies that defines standard interfaces and behaviors for distributed system integration and management.

Open Grid Services Infrastructure (OGSI)

A Global Grid Forum (GGF) standard that defines the core semantics of a transient Web service, including naming, lifetime, and exposing service state.

Overlay network

A network in which some nodes are implemented as paths or subnets of a larger network. Typically, overlays use protocol encapsulation to perform this embedding. Also known as a virtual network.

Packet

A variable-sized unit of data transfer. The term packet is used generically at any level of the protocol hierarchy.

Packet switching

A technique of grouping the data to be transmitted in variable-sized blocks, or packets, and sending them interleaved with packets to other destinations over a single line. This often requires intermediate systems, called routers, to forward the packets from one line to another before the packets reach their destination.

PDA (personal digital assistant)

A hand-held, hand-sized computer.

Peer to Peer

A protocol or distributed system in which all components are equivalent; contrast to client-server, where one the server has most of the information, and a group clients initiate requests through routers that forward those requests. In peer-to-peer, a party may concurrently act as client, server, and router.

Performance contract

A service level agreement whose terms are focused on program performance metrics.

Performance instrumentation

The mechanism used to extract performance metrics from a program in execution. Although usually implemented via the insertion of subroutine calls or inline code that records performance information, performance instrumentation can also exploit internal or external hardware.

Performance steering

A technique by which an external agent, either human or intelligent software, manipulates program or operating system parameters and policies during application execution to achieve performance improvements.

Performance

The manner in which a mechanism performs. Performance is measured by optimizing a cost model that provides a means of comparing and ranking alternatives within that model.

Petabyte

One thousand terabytes, or one million gigabytes.

Pileup (PU)

Overlay (or pileup) events resulting from multiple particle interactions occurring so close together in time that they are difficult to identify separately.

Policy

The set of terms and conditions under which a service or capability is made available for user.

Portal

A Web-browser-based user interface to a network based application. Often, a portal is targeted toward a specific application domain or class of user, with the intention of providing simplified access to a complex underlying system.

portType

WSDL language construct that allows one to define a collection of related operations. A portType is used to define a basic interface to a service and serves as the basic conceptual building block for defining OGSA-based services.

PPP (Point to Point Protocol)

A protocol that allows mixing communication streams over a single point-to-point line or interface. PPP has largely replaced SLIP because PPP is more general.

Principal

An entity whose identity is verified through *authentication* and on whose authority an operation is performed or authorized.

Private key

See *key*.

Propagation latency

A measurement of the time one bit takes to travel a distance. It is usually directly related to distance and the properties of the transmission medium.

Protocol

A communication procedure with specific rules about the language used and the sequences of statements that are allowed.

Provisioning

Reserving or setting aside some amount or resource or service capability to ensure that the requirements of a client are met. Provisioning is typically achieved by establishing a service level agreement.

Public Key Infrastructure (PKI)

A security system based on the use of asymmetric (i.e., public key) cryptograpy to prove the identity of a subject. Identity established by having a user encrypt a challenge with a private key. If it can be decrypted with the public key, then the identity of the user is established. The veracity of a user's public key is ensured by having a trusted third party (a certificate authority) cryptographically sign a data structure containing the user's name and public key.

Public key

See *key*.

QoS (quality of service)

The bandwidth, delay, delay jitter, and packet loss (and possibly other measurements) experienced by a receiver. Also known as GoS (grade of service).

Real-time measurement

The acquisition of performance data from a Grid application or system concurrently with its normal operation.

Relational database management system (RDBMS)

A DBMS where the abstraction is relational tables and the query language is relational algebra.

Resource Description Framework (RDF)

An XML-based language for representing the relationships between objects. RDF was defined by the W3C as a means to represent the semantics of Web content; however, RDF makes it possible to represent general graph structure in XML, and can be applied to a range of modeling tasks.

Resource scheduler

A scheduler that optimizes the performance of a particular resource. Performance may be measured by such criteria as fairness (to ensure that all requests for the resource are satisfied) or utilization (to measure the amount of the resource used).

RMI (Remote Method Invocation)

A somewhat controversial part of Java 1.1 in the enterprise framework that specifies the remote access to Java objects with a generalization of the Unix RPC (Remote Procedure Call).

RSLA (Resource Service Level Agreement)

A service level agreement that provisions capability within a service or resource.

RMON

A protocol to allow the remote monitoring of network performance via an SNMP agent.

Router

A device to interconnect heterogeneous network technologies, using the most general information possible. Routers examine packet information that is link independent (to support heterogeneous networks), but also data independent (to support heterogeneous applications). Contrast with *bridge* and *gateway*.

Routing protocol

The communication used between routers to update the information they use to decide the best path for a packet to take on its way from the source to the destination. There are two broad classes of routing protocols: the distance vector and the link state.

RSVP (ReSerVation Protocol)

Resources reservation protocol for IP networks. RSVP allows applications to request, from both hosts and networks, that resources be set aside to ensure specific service guarantees to their data.

RTP (Real-Time Transport Protocol)

A transport protocol for carrying data, such as audio and video, with realtime constraints. It provides timing, sequencing, loss detection, and QoS monitoring.

Scale

The magnitude of a property of a system, such as the number of hosts or the bandwidth. Scale generally focuses on relative size and is given in powers of 10.

Scatter plot

A mapping of the values of one variable to the x-coordinate of a plotted point, a second to its y-coordinate, and (optionally) a third to its z-coordinate. This seemingly simple representation has countless variants, including use of semilog and log-log scaling, contouring, surface and iso-surface plots, color mappings, and a wide variety of glyphs and line markers.

Scheduling

The assignment of work to resources within a specified timeframe.

Secret key

See *key*.

Semantic Web

An extension of the current Web aimed at giving information well-defined meaning.

Semantics

The meaning of metadata and their relationship to data.

Service

An entity that provides a capability over a network. A service provides its capability in response to sending it messages to which it may respond by sending back messages. By defining interactions with a service only in terms of these messages (i.e., protocol), the implementation of the service is completely hidden from the consumers of the capabilities that it provides.

Service Data Element (SDE)

The OGSI construct that is used to publish information about the state of a service. A SDE provides a name and an arbitrary piece of XML. The value of a specific SDE can be retrieved by FindServiceDateElement, a operation that must be provided by any OGSI compliant service.

Service Level Agreeement (SLA)

An agreement between a service provider and a service consumer that defines the terms under which a capability offered by a service can be used. The terms under which an SLA is established may constrain both the provider and consumer as thus provides a level of guarantee about how both the provider and consumer are expected to behave.

Service-oriented architecture

An approach to distributed system design in which every system component is a service. Service-oriented architecture enables a system to be constructed in a way that is independent of both the implementation and location of the system components.

Session key

See *key*.

Simple Object Access Protocol (SOAP)

A XML-based W3C standard that defines how the information required to invoke a remote procedure call is packaged for transport to a remote service. SOAP is defined so that the encoded messages can be moved using a variety of transport protocols including HTTP, TCP, and e-mail.

SLIP (Serial Line Internet Protocol)

A protocol that describes the framing and control needed to manage serial line transmission of the Internet Protocol.

SNMP (Simple Network Management Protocol)

A protocol to allow hosts to control and monitor network devices such as hosts, links, hubs, and routers.

Softstate

An approach to state management in which information is discarded after a specified period of time unless it is explicitly refreshed.

Storage Resource Broker (SRB)

A data access and federation technology.

Striping

The aggregation of several channels to act as a single virtual channel (the converse of *multiplexing*). Striping involves first demultiplexing, then multiplexing.

Structured data

Any data that is organized in a well-defined manner such as via a database schema, file format, or tabular.

Supernetting

The process by which multiple routing entries are aggregated, a technique at the core of CIDR. It permits more efficient use of the IP address space, allowing the space to be delegated on bit boundaries rather than byte boundaries.

T1

A telephone company service with a data rate of 1.5 megabit/sec.

T3

A telephone company service with a data rate of 45 megabit/sec.

TCP/IP (Transmission Control Protocol/Internet Protocol)

Layered protocols in which TCP handles the functions dealing with guaranteed delivery and IP the functions dealing with addressing and forwarding messages through the network.

Task Service Level Agreement (TSLA)

A service level agreement associated with performing a specified activity or task.

Telepresense

The ability to interact with a device or piece of equipment remotely. Telepresense can include teleobservation, the ability to see, hear, feel everything that is occurring at the remote location, and telecontrol, the ability to direct or interact with the remote location.

terabyte

A thousand gigabytes.

TeraGrid

An NSF-funded project that is interconnecting five multi-teraflop compute clusters with a 40 gigabit/sec network and using a Grid-based software infrastructure to facilitate sharing of these resources between the sides and the end-user community.

Throughput

The number of user data bits communicated per second.

Transaction protocol

A protocol for communicating an operation or event such as a purchase, banking deposit, or other database update where confirmation is needed that the operation was completed successfully.

Transcoding

Transcoding is the translation of one data format into another.

Transient service instance

A dynamic service, one that may be created and destroyed. Basic Web service standards do not have any concept of service creation, or dynamics, while the Open Grid Services Infrastructure (OGSI) defines what it means for a service to be transient.

Transmission latency

The time it takes to emit an entire message. Related to the bandwidth of a channel, but not at all related to the distance of the channel.

Transport protocol

The operating-system-level protocol that delivers data from a source process to a destination process. The data may be thought of as a stream (as in TCP) or as distinct messages (as in UDP).

Trust

The extent that one entity can depend on another to behave as expected.

Trust domain

A set of entities that all have the same level of trust. Behavior in this case is typically defined in terms of a policy that all members of the trust domain are expected to conform to.

UDP (User Datagram Protocol)

A transport protocol that provides unordered, unreliable message delivery.

URL (Universal Resource Locator)

A naming convention for accessing pages on the Web by concatenating the IP address with the data set name.

URN (universal resource name)

A generalization of URLs to remove dependence on host name for location of the dataset.

Virtual data

An approach to data intensive applications in which data products may be 'materialized' on demand from more fundamental data. Data is virtualized in that the end user does not care if the desired data products actually existed or were created on demand to respond to their request.

Virtual Data Toolkit

Product of the NSF's GriPhyN project that integrates a variety of data management and analysis technologies including the Globus Toolkit, Condor, and Chimera.

Virtual databases

A distributed database that looks like a single unified database from the perspective of data model (schema), and query.

Virtual network

See *overlay network*.

Virtual organization

A collaboration whose participants are both geographically and organizationally distributed.

Virtual private network (VPN)

A network implemented using the shared physical infrastructure of the Internet, but where communication is permitted only between participating nodes in the private network and where encryption is used to protect messages from disclosure and modification by nodes that are not participants.

Virtualized service

A service whose implementation consists primarily of passing requests on to other, potentially distributed services, thus providing a single virtualized access to the underlying services.

Web clients

Clients that originally displayed HTML and related pages but now support Java applets that can be programmed to provide the necessary capabilities to support general enterprise computing. The support of signed applets in recent browsers has removed crude security restrictions, which handicapped previous use of applets.

Web servers

Servers that originally supported HTTP requests for information: basically HTML pages but also the invocation of general server-side programs using the simple but arcane CGI (Common Gateway Interface). A new generation of Java servers have enhanced capabilities, including server-side Java program enhancements (servlets) and support of stateful permanent communication channels.

Web Services Description Language (WSDL)

A W3C standard that defines a standard interface description language. Based on XML, a WSDL specification specifies the functions implemented by a Web service in terms of typed message exchange. WSDL groups these message exchanges into operations and interfaces, and then describes the representation of the message content in a specific transport mechanism, such as HTTP, TCP, or even e-mail.

Web services

A widely used set of standards specifying how to define, discover, and access network-accessible services.

Workflow

An ordered sequence of tasks whose completion accomplishes some higher-level activity. Workflows are typically specified by some workflow description language, and execute by a specialized system that sequences the execution of the individual tasks.

Workload

The set of activities tasked to a system component. Within enterprise systems, workloads often form the basis for scheduling resource use.

Worldwide Web Consortium (W3C)

The standards body that has defined many of the standards for the World Wide Web, including the Hypertext Transfer Protocol (HTTP), the eXtensible Markup Language (XML), the core Web services standards, and core standards for the Semantic Web.

X.500

An access protocol standard for directories.

X.509

A standard that defines the format of a certificate utilizing public-key cryptology. Defined as part of the X.500 directory standard.

XML (eXtensible Markup Language)

A W3C standard that defines a basic syntax for expressing structure in documents. XML is the basis for virtually all of the newer W3C standards activities including Web services and the Semantic Web.

Bibliography

[1]   AstroGrid Project: *www.astrogrid.org*.

[2]   Astrophysical Virtual Observatory: *www.euro-vo.org*.

[3]   AURA-G, DAME York Development Team Report. University of York, ACAG, 2002.

[4]   Biomedical Informatics Research Network (BIRN): *www.nbirn.net*.

[5]   Comb-e-Chem Project: *www.combechem.org*.

[6]   Cone Service Definition Web Site: *www.us-vo.org/metadata/conesearch*.

[7]   *DECchip 21064 and DECchip21064A Alpha AXP Microprocessors—Hardware Reference Manual*, 1994.

[8]   DOE Science Grid PKI Certificate Policy and Certification Practice Statement, 2002: *www.doegrids.org*.

[9]   DOE Science Grid Project: *www.doesciencegrid.org*.

[10]   Dublin Core Metadata Initiative (DCMI): *dublincore.org*.

[11]   European Southern Observatory: *www.eso.org*.

[12]   European Union DataGrid (EU DataGrid) Project: *www.eu-datagrid.org*.

[13]   Extensible Access Control Markup Language (XACML) Specification v1.0. OASIS, 2003.

[14]   Extensible Rights Markup Language: *www.xrml.org*.

[15]   High Performance Fortran Forum, High Performance Fortran language specification, *Scientific Programming* 2(1–2), 1–170, 1993.

[16]   *IBM Load Leveler: User's Guide*, September 1993.

[17]   International Virtual Observatory Alliance: *www.ivoa.net*.

[18]   Intrinsic Graphics: *www.intrinsic.com*.

[19]   Jabber Server: *www.jabber.com.*

[20]   Message Passing Interface Forum, MPI-2: A message passing interface standard,
           International Journal of High Performance Computing Applications **12**(1–2), 1–299, 1998.

[21]   National Virtual Observatory: *www.us-vo.org.*

[22]   *NCSA HDF Reference Manual, Version 4.1*, 2001. Available at *hdf.ncsa.uiuc.edu/
           doc.html.*

[23]   NDL Homepage: *www.ndl.com.*

[24]   *NetCDF User's Guide, Version 2.4*, UCAR/Unidata Program Center, Boulder, CO, 1996.
           Available at *www.unidata.ucar.edu/packages/netcdf.*

[25]   NetSaint, 2002: *www.netsaint.org.*

[26]   NSF Middleware Initiative (NMI): *www.nsf-middleware.org.*

[27]   Open Grid Services Architecture Data Access and Integration (OGSA-DAI) Project:
           www.ogsa-dai.org.uk.

[28]   *Open-Source PKI Book*, 2000: *ospkibook.sourceforge.net.*

[29]   *Paragon (XP/S) Product Overview*. Intel Corporation, 1991.

[30]   Particle Physics Data Grid (PPDG) Project: *www.ppdg.net.*

[31]   Portable Batch System: *www.pbspro.com.*

[32]   Portable Operating System Interface (POSIX), IEEE Computer Society
           Technical Committee on Operating Systems and Applications Environment,
           New York, 1990.

[33]   *Resource Description Framework (RDF) Model and Syntax Specification.* Available at
           www.w3.org/TR/REC-rdf-syntax.

[34]   *Realizing the Information Future: The Internet and Beyond.* National Academy Press,
           Washington, DC, 1994.

[35]   RenderWare Homepage: *www.renderware.com.*

[36]   Research and Technological Development for a TransAtlantic Grid (DataTAG)
           Project: *www.datatag.net.*

[37]   *Revolutionizing Science and Engineering through Cyberinfrastructure: Report of the
           National Science Foundation Blue Ribbon Advisory Panel on Cyberinfrastructure.* NSF,
           2003. Availabe at *www.communitytechnology.org/nsf_ci_report.*

[38]   The Rocks Homepage: *www.rocksclusters.org.*

[39]   *Salutation Service Discovery in Pervasive Computing Environments.* Available at
           www-3.ibm.com/software/pervasive/tech/whitepapers/salutation.shtm.

[40]   *Security Association Markup Language (SAML) Specification v.1.0.* OASIS, 2002.
           Available at *www.oasis-open.org/committees/security.*

[41]   *Simple Object Access Protocol (SOAP) 1.1*, W3C, Note 8, 2000. Available at
           www.w3.org/TR/SOAP.

[42]   Southern California Earthquake Center (SCEC): *www.scec.org.*

[43]   StarLight: *www.startap.net/starlight.*

[44]   UDDI: Universal Description, Discovery and Integration: *www.uddi.org.*

[45]   *The Virtual Interface Architecture Specification Version 1.0.* Promoted by Intel, Compaq, and Microsoft, 1997.

[46]   Visible & Infrared Survey Telescope for Astronomy (VISTA) Project: *www.vista.ac.uk.*

[47]   Vizier Web Site: *vizier.u-strasbg.fr/cgi-bin/VizieR.*

[48]   Votable Web Site: *cdsweb.u-strasbg.fr/doc/VOTable.*

[49]   *Web Service Choreography Interface (WSCI) 1.0 Specification.* Sun Microsystems Corporation. Available at *wwws.sun.com/software/xml/ developers/wsci.*

[50]   *Web Services Conversation Language (WSCL) 1.0.* Hewlett–Packard Corporation, 2002. Available at *www.w3.org/TR/wscl10.*

[51]   The Workflow Management Coalition Web Site: *www.wfmc.org.*

[52]   *XML Signature Syntax and Processing.* OASIS, 2002. Available at *www.w3.org/ TR/xmldsig-core.*

[53]   Aalst, W. v. d., Don't go with the flow: Web services composition standards exposed, *IEEE Intelligent Systems* (Jan/Feb), 2003.

[54]   Aberer, K., and Despotovic, Z., Managing trust in a P2P information system, in *ACM Conference on Information and Knowledge Management*, Assoc. Comput. Mach. Press, New York, 2001.

[55]   Abiteboul, S., Buneman, P., and Suciu, D., *Data on the Web. From Relations to Semistructured Data and XML.* Morgan Kaufmann, Los Altos, CA, 1999.

[56]   Abramson, D., Giddy, J., and Kotler, L., High performance parametric modeling with Nimrod/G: Killer application for the global Grid?, in *International Parallel and Distributed Processing Symposium, Cancun, Mexico*, IEEE Computer Society Press, Los Alamitos, CA, 2000, pp. 520–528.

[57]   Abramson, D., Sosic, R., Giddy, J., and Hall, B., Nimrod: A tool for performing parameterised simulations using distributed workstations, in *5th IEEE International Symposium on High Performance Distributed Computing*. IEEE Computer Society Press, Los Alamitos, CA, 1995.

[58]   Acquisti, A., Dingledine, R., and Syverson, P., *On the Economics of Anonymity.* Available at *freehaven.net/doc/fc03/econymics.pdf.*

[59]   Adar, E., and Huberman, B., Free riding on Gnutella, technical report. Xerox PARC, 2000.

[60]   Advanced Computer Architectures Group: The AURA Project Web Site: *www.cs.york.ac.uk/arch/nn.*

[61]   Adve, V., Wang, J. C., Mellor-Crummey, J., Reed, D., Anderson, M., and Kennedy, K., An integrated compilation and performance analysis environment for data parallel programs, in *Supercomputing '95*. Assoc. Comput. Mach. Press, New York, 1995.

[62]   Aida, K., Futaka, Y., and Hara, S., High-performance parallel and distributed computing for the BMI eigenvalue problem, in *16th IEEE International Parallel and Distributed Processing Symposium*, IEEE Computer Society Press, Los Alamitos, CA, 2002.

[63]   Akarsu, E., Fox, G., Haupt, T., and Youn, C., The gateway system: Uniform Web based access to remote resources, *Concurrency: Practice and Experience* **12**, 629–642, 2000.

[64]   Allcock, W., Bester, J., Bresnahan, J., Chervenak, A., Foster, I., Kesselman, C., Meder, S., Nefedova, V., Quesnel, D., and Tuecke, S., Data management and transfer in high-performance computational Grid environments, *Parallel Computing* **28**(5), 749–771, 2002.

[65]   Allcock, W., Bester, J., Bresnahan, J., Chervenak, A., Liming, L., and Tuecke, S., *GridFTP: Protocol Extension to FTP for the Grid*. Global Grid Forum, 2001.

[66]   Allcock, W., Bester, J., Bresnahan, J., Chervenak, A. L., Foster, I., Kesselman, C., Meder, S., Nefedova, V., Quesnel, D., and Tuecke, S., Secure, efficient data transport and replica management for high-performance data-intensive computing, in *18th IEEE Symposium on Mass Storage Systems, San Diego, CA*, 2001.

[67]   Allcock, W., Foster, I., Nefedova, V., Chervenak, A., Deelman, E., Kesselman, C., Lee, J., Sim, A., Shoshani, A., Drach, B., and Williams, D., High-performance remote access to climate simulation data: A challenge problem for data Grid technologies, in *SC'2001*. Assoc. Comput. Mach. Press, New York, 2001.

[68]   Allen, F. E., Burke, M., Charles, P. and Cytron, R., An overview of the PTRAN analysis system for multiprocessing, *Journal of Parallel and Distributed Computing* **5**, 617–640, 1988.

[69]   Allen, G., Angulo, D., Foster, I., Lanfermann, G., Liu, C., Radke, T., Seidel, E., and Shalf, J., The Cactus worm: Experiments with dynamic resource selection and allocation in a Grid environment, *International Journal of High Performance Computing Applications* **15**(4), 345–358, 2001.

[70]   Allen, G., Benger, W., Goodale, T., Hege, H., Lanfermann, G., Merzky, A., Radke, T., Seidel, E., and Shalf, J., The Cactus code: A problem solving environment for the Grid, in *9th IEEE International Symposium on Performance Distributed Computing, Pittsburgh*, IEEE Computer Society Press, Los Alamitos, CA, 2000, pp. 253–262.

[71]   Allen, G., Davis, K., Dolkas, K. N., Doulamis, N. D., Goodale, T., Kielmann, T., Merzky, A., Nabrzyski, J., Pukacki, J., Radke, T., Russell, M., Seidel, E., Shalf, J., and Taylor, I., Enabling applications on the Grid: A GridLab overview, *International Journal of High Performance Computing Applications*, **17**(3), 2003.

[72]   Allen, G., Dramlitsch, T., Foster, I., Goodale, T., Karonis, N., Ripeanu, M., Seidel, E., and Toonen, B., Supporting efficient execution in heterogeneous distributed computing environments with Cactus and Globus, in *SC'2001*. Assoc. Comput. Mach. Press, New York, 2001.

[73]   Allen, G., Goodale, T., Lanfermann, G., Seidel, E., Benger, W., Hege, H.-C., Merzky, A., Mass'o, J., Radke, T., and Shalf, J., Solving Einstein's equation on supercomputers, *IEEE Computer* **32**(12), 52–59, 1999.

[74]   Allen, R., and Kennedy, K., *Optimizing Compilers for Modern Architectures*. Morgan Kaufmann, San Francisco, 2002.

[75]   Aloisio, G., and Cafaro, M., Web-based access to the Grid using the Grid Resource Broker Portal, *Concurrency and Computation: Practice and Experience*, **14**(13–15), 1145–1160, 2002.

[76]   Altschul, S., Madden, T., Schaffer, A., Zhang, J., Zhang, Z., Miller, W., and Lipman, D., Gapped BLAST and PSI-BLAST: A new generation of protein database search programs, *Nucleic Acids Research* **25**, 3389–3402, 1997.

[77]   Anderson, D., Balakrishnan, H., Kaashoek, F., and Morris, R., The case for resilient overlay networks, in *8th Annual Workshop on Hot Topics in Operating Systems*, 2001.

[78]   Anderson, D., Balakrishnan, H., Kaashoek, F., and Morris, R., Resilient overlay networks, in *18th ACM Symposium on Operating Systems Principles, Lake Luise, Canada*, Assoc. Comput. Mach. Press, New York, 2001.

[79]   Anderson, D. P., Cobb, J., Korpella, E., Lebofsky, M., and Werthimer, D., SETI@home: An experiment in public-resource computing, *Communications of the ACM* **45**(11), 56–61, 2002.

[80]   Anderson, T., Culler, D., and Patterson, D., A case for NOW (networks of workstations), *IEEE Micro* **15**(1), 54–64, 1995.

[81]   Annis, J., Zhao, Y., Voeckler, J., Wilde, M., Kent, S., and Foster, I., Applying Chimera virtual data concepts to cluster finding in the Sloan Sky Survey, in *SC2002, Baltimore, MD*, 2002.

[82]   Anstreicher, K., Brixius, N., Goux, J.-P. and Linderoth, J. T., Solving large quadratic assignment problems on computational Grids, *Mathematical Programming* **91**(3), 563–588, 2002.

[83]   Antonioletti, M., and Jackson, M., *OGSA-DAI Product Overview*, 2003. Available at www.ogsa-dai.org.uk/downloads/docs/OGSA-DAI-USER-M3-PRODUCT-OVERVIEW.pdf.

[84]   Appleby, K., Fakhouri, S., Fong, L., Goldszmidt, G., Kalantar, M., Krishnakumar, S., Pazel, D., Pershing, J. and Rochwerger, B., Oceano—SLA based management of a computing utility, in *7th IFIP/IEEE International Symposium on Integrated Network Management*, IEEE Computer Society Press, Los Alamitos, CA, 2001.

[85]   Arbenz, P., Gander, W., and Oettli, M., The remote computation system, *Parallel Computing* **23**, 1421–1428, 1997.

[86] Arbree, A., Avery, P., Bourilkov, D., Cavanaugh, R., Katageri, S., Graham, G., Rodriguez, J., Voeckler, J., and Wilde, M., Virtual data in CMS production, in *Computing in High Energy Physics*, 2003.

[87] Arends, R., Austein, R., Larson, M., Massey, D., and Rose, S., DNS security introduction and requirements. Internet Engineering Task Force, Internet Draft, 2003.

[88] Armstrong, R., Gannon, D., Geist, A., Keahey, K., Kohn, S., McInnes, L., and Parker, S., Toward a common component architecture for high performance scientific computing, in *8th IEEE International Symposium on High Performance Distributed Computing*. IEEE Computer Society Press, Los Alamitos, 1999.

[89] Arnold, D., Lee, W., Dongarra, J., and Wheeler, M., Providing infrastructure and interface to high-performance applications in a distributed setting, in *High Performance Computing 2000*, 2000, pp. 248–253.

[90] Aslakson, E., Bunn, J., Iqbal, S., Newman, H., Singh, S., Steenberg, C., Afaq, M. A., Aziz, S., Bauerdick, L. A. T., Ernst, M., Graham, G., Kaiser, J., Ratnikova, N., Wenzel, H., Wu, Y., Branson, J., Disk, I., Letts, J., Arbree, A., Avery, P., Bourilkov, D., Cavanaugh, R., Rodriquez, J., Katagari, S., Couvares, P., DeSmet, A., Livny, M., Roy, A., and Tannenbaum, T., The CMS Integration Grid Testbed. CMS Collaboration, CMS Note, 2003.

[91] Aspnes, J., Diamadi, Z., and Shah, G., Fault-tolerant routing in P2P systems, in *Twenty-First ACM Symposium on Principles of Distributed Computing, Monterey, CA*, 2002, pp. 223–232.

[92] *The National Technology Roadmap for Semiconductors*. Semiconductor Industry Association, 1994.

[93] Avery, P., and Foster, I., The GriPhyN Project: Towards petascale virtual data Grids, Technical Report GriPhyN-2001-14, 2001. Available at *www.griphyn.org*.

[94] Avery, P., Foster, I., Gardner, R., Newman, H., and Szalay, A., An international virtual-data Grid laboratory for data intensive science, Technical Report GriPhyN-2001-2, 2001. Available at *www.griphyn.org*.

[95] Bajorath, J., Virtual screening in drug discovery: Methods, expectations and reality, in *Current Drug Discovery*, 2002.

[96] Baker, F., Requirements for IP version 4 routers. Internet Engineering Task Force, RFC 1812, 1995. Available at *ietf.org/rfc/rfc1812.txt*.

[97] Baratloo, A., Karaul, M., Kedem, Z., and Wyckoff, P., Charlotte: Metacomputing on the Web, in *9th International Conference on Parallel and Distributed Computing Systems*, 1996.

[98] Barish, B. C., and Weiss, R., LIGO and the detection of gravitational waves, *Physics Today* 52(10), 44, 1999.

[99] Barnard, S., Biswas, R., Foster, I., Larsson, O., Wijngaart, R. V. d., Yarrow, M., and Zechter, L., Large-scale distributed computational fluid dynamics on the Information Power Grid using Globus, in *7th Symposium on the Frontiers of Massively Parallel Computation*, 1999, pp. 60–67.

[100]   Baru, C., Moore, R., Rajasekar, A., and Wan, M., The SDSC storage resource
          broker, in *8th Annual IBM Centers for Advanced Studies Conference, Toronto,
          Canada*, 1998.

[101]   Basney, J., Livny, M., and Mazzanti, P., Utilizing widely distributed computational
          resources efficiently with execution domains, *Computer Physics Communications* **140**,
          2001.

[102]   BEA, IBM, Microsoft, and SAP, Web Services Policy Language (WS-Policy), OASIS,
          2002.

[103]   Beardsmore, A., Hartley, K., Hawkins, S., Laws, S., Magowan, J., and Twigg, A.,
          GSAX Grid service accounting extensions. Global Grid Forum, Draft. Available at
          www.ggf.org/Meetings/ggf6/ggf6_wg_papers/ggf-rus-gsax-01.doc.

[104]   Beaumont, O., Boudet, V. and Robert, Y., A realistic model and an efficient heuristic
          for scheduling with heterogeneous processors, Research Report 2001-3. Laboratoire
          de l'Informatique du Parallélisme, École Normale Supérieure de Lyon, 2001.

[105]   Beck, M., Dongarra, J., Fagg, G., Geist, A., Gray, P., Kohl, J., Migliardi, M., Moore, K.,
          Moore, T., Papadopoulous, P., Scott, S., and Sunderam, V., HARNESS: A next
          generation distributed virtual machine, *International Journal on Future Generation
          Computer Systems* **15**(5–6), 571–582, 1999.

[106]   Becker, D., Sterling, T., Savarese, D., Dorband, J., Ranawak, U., and Packer, C.,
          Beowulf: A parallel workstation for scientific computing, in *International Parallel
          Processing Symposium*, IEEE Computer Society Press, Los Alamitos, CA, 1995.

[107]   Beguelin, A., Dongarra, J., Geist, A., Manchek, R., and Sunderam, V., Opening the
          door to heterogeneous network supercomputing, *Supercomputing Review* **4**(9), 44–45,
          1991.

[100]   Beiriger, J., Johnson, W., Bivens, H., Humphreys, S., and Rhea, R., Constructing the
          ASCI Grid, in *9th IEEE International Symposium on High Performance Distributed
          Computing*. IEEE Computer Society Press, Los Alamitos, CA, 2000.

[109]   Belani, E., Vahdat, A., Anderson, T. and Dahlin, M., The CRISIS wide area security
          architecture, in *8th Usenix UNIX Security Symposium*, 1998.

[110]   Benger, W., Foster, I., Novotny, J., Seidel, E., Shalf, J., Smith, W., and Walker, P.,
          Numerical relativity in a distributed environment, in *9th SIAM Conference on Parallel
          Processing for Scientific Computing*, 1999.

[111]   Bent, J., Venkataramani, V., LeRoy, N., Roy, A., Stanley, J., Arpaci-Dusseau, A. C.,
          Arpaci-Dusseau, R. H., and Livny, M., Flexibility, manageability, and performance in
          a Grid storage appliance, in *11th IEEE International Symposium on High Performance
          Distributed Computing*. IEEE Computer Society Press, Los Alamitos, CA, 2002.

[112]   Berman, F., Chien, A., Cooper, K., Dongarra, J., Foster, I., Gannon, D., Johnsson, L.,
          Kennedy, K., Kesselman, C., Mellor-Crummey, J., Reed, D., Torczon, L., and
          Wolski, R., The GrADS project: Software support for high-level grid application
          development, *International Journal of High Performance Computing Applications*
          15(4), 327–344, 2001.

[113]   Berman, F., Fox, G., and Hey, T. (Eds.), *Grid Computing: Making the Global Infrastructure a Reality*. Wiley, New York, 2003.

[114]   Berman, F., Wolski, R., Figueira, S., Schopf, J., and Shao, G., Application-level scheduling on distributed heterogeneous networks, in *Supercomputing '96*, 1996.

[115]   Berners-Lee, T., Hendler, J., and Lassila, O., The Semantic Web, *Scientific American* **284**(5), 34–43, 2001.

[116]   Bernstein, D., Bolmarcich, A., and So, K., Performance visualization of parallel programs on a shared memory multiprocessor system, in *International Conference on Parallel Processing, University Park, PA*, 1989.

[117]   Bester, J., Foster, I., Kesselman, C., Tedesco, J., and Tuecke, S., GASS: A data movement and access service for wide area computing systems, in *6th ACM Workshop on I/O in Parallel and Distributed Systems*, Assoc. Comput. Mach. Press, New York, 1999.

[118]   Beynon, M., Ferreira, R., Kurc, T., Sussman, A., and Saltz, J., in DataCutter: Middleware for filtering very large scientific datasets on archival storage systems, in *17th IEEE Symposium on Mass Storage Systems, San Diego, CA*, IEEE Computer Society Press, Los Alamitos, CA, 2000, pp. 119–133.

[119]   Beynon, M., Kurc, T., Catalyurek, U., Chang, C., Sussman, A., and Saltz, J., Distributed processing of very large datasets with DataCutter, *Parallel Computing* **27**(11), 1457–1478, 2001.

[120]   Biezunski, M., Bryan, M., and Newcomb, S. R., Information technology—SGML applications—Topic maps, ISO/IEC13250:2000, 1999.

[121]   Birrell, A., and Nelson, B., Implementing remote procedure calls., *ACM Transactions on Computing Systems* **2**, 39–59, 1984.

[122]   Bivens, H., and Beiriger, J., GALE: Grid access language for HPC environments. Sandia National Laboratory. Available at *vir.sandia.gov/drmweb/docs/gale.pdf*.

[123]   Blackford, L. S., Choi, J., Cleary, A., D'Azevedo, E., Demmel, J., Dhillon, I., Dongarra, J., Hammarling, S., Henry, G., Petitet, A., Stanley, K., Walker, D., and Whaley, R. C., *ScaLAPACK Users' Guide*, Philadelphia, PA, 1997.

[124]   Blake, S., Black, D., Carlson, M., Davies, E., Wang, Z., and Weiss, W., An architecture for differentiated services. Internet Engineering Task Force, RFC 2475, 1998. Available at *ietf.org/rfc/rfc2475.txt*.

[125]   Blakley, B., Burrows, W., Clark, G., Murdoch, A., and Siebenlist, F., Authorization (AZN) API- generic application interface for authorization frameworks, Technical Standard C908. Open Group Technical Standard, 2000. Available at *www.opengroup.org/onlinepubs/009609199*.

[126]   Blaze, M., Feigenbaum, J., Ionnidis, J., and Keromytis, A. D., The Keynote trust management system. Internet Engineering Task Force, RFC 2704, 1999. Available at *ietf.org/rfc/rfc2704.txt*.

[127]   Bloom, B., Space/time trade-offs in hash coding with allowable errors, *Communications of the ACM* **13**(7), 422–426, 1970.

[128]   Blumofe, R., Joerg, C., Kuszmaul, B., Leiserson, C., Randall, K., and Zhou, Y., Cilk: An efficient multithreaded runtime system, in *5th ACM SIGPLAN Symposium on Principles and Practice of Parallel Programming*, 1995, pp. 207–216.

[129]   Blythe, J., Deelman, E., Gil, Y., and Kesselman, C., Transparent Grid computing: A knowledge-based approach, in *15th Annual Conference on Innovative Applications of Artificial Intelligence IAAI, Acapulco, Mexico*, 2003.

[130]   Bolcer, G. A., and Kaiser, G. E., SWAP: Leveraging the Web to manage workflow, *IEEE Internet Computing* **3**(1), 85–88, 1999.

[131]   Boley, H., Tabet, S., and Wagner, G., Design rationale of RuleML: A markup language for Semantic Web rules, in *1st International Semantic Web Working Symposium, Stanford*, 2001.

[132]   Borovikov, E., Sussman, A., and Davis, L., An efficient system for multi-perspective imaging and volumetric shape analysis, in *Workshop on Parallel and Distributed Computing in Image Processing, Video Processing, and Multimedia*. IEEE Computer Society Press, Los Alamitos, CA, 2001.

[133]   Braden, R., Clark, D., and Shenker, S., Integrated services in the Internet architecture: An overview. Internet Engineering Task Force, RFC 1633, 1994. Available at *ietf.org/rfc/rfc1633.txt*.

[134]   Bray, T., Paoli, J., and Sperberg-McQueen, C. M., The extensible markup language (XML) 1.0, 1998.

[135]   Brazma, A., et al., Minimum information about a microarray experiment (MIAME)—Toward standards for microarray data, *Nature Genetics* **29**(4), 365–371, 2002.

[136]   Browne, S., Dongarra, J., Garner, N., London, K., and Mucci, P., A scalable cross-platform infrastructure for application performance tuning using hardware counters, in *SC 2000, Dallas*, 2000.

[137]   Brunett, S., Czajkowski, K., Fitzgerald, S., Foster, I., Johnson, A., Kesselman, C., Leigh, J., and Tuecke, S., Application experiences with the Globus Toolkit, in *7th IEEE International Symposium on High Performance Distributed Computing*, IEEE Computer Society Press, Los Alamitos, CA, 1998, pp. 81–89.

[138]   Brunett, S., Davis, D., Gottschalk, T., Messina, P., and Kesselman, C., Implementing distributed synthetic forces simulations in metacomputing environments, in *Heterogeneous Computing Workshop*, IEEE Computer Society Press, Los Alamitos, CA, 1998, pp. 29–42.

[139]   Buck, B., and Hollingsworth, J., An API for runtime code patching, *Journal of High Performance Computing Applications* **14**(4), 317–329, 2000.

[140]   Buneman, P., Khanna, S., Tajima, K., and Tan, W.-C., Archiving scientific data, in *ACM SIGMOD International Conference on Management of Data*, Assoc. Comput. Mach. Press, New York, 2002.

[141]   Buneman, P., Khanna, S., and Tan, W.-C., Why and where: A characterization of data provenance, in *8th International Conference on Database Theory*, Springer-Verlag, Heidelberg, 2001.

[142]   Burger, M., Kielmann, T., and Bal, H. E., TOPOMON: A monitoring tool for Grid network topology, in *International Conference on Computational Science*, Springer-Verlag, Heidelberg, 2002.

[143]   Burke, M., and Cytron, R., Interprocedural dependence analysis and parallelization, in ACM *SIGPLAN Symposium on Compiler Construction, New York*, Assoc. Comput. Mach. Press, New York, 1986.

[144]   Burns, G., Daoud, R., and Vaigl, J., LAM: An open cluster environment for MPI, in *Supercomputing '94*, 1994, pp. 379–386.

[145]   Bush, V., As we may think, *Atlantic Monthly* 534–541, 1945.

[146]   Butler, R., Engert, D., Foster, I., Kesselman, C., Tuecke, S., Volmer, J., and Welch, V., A national-scale authentication infrastructure, *IEEE Computer* 33(12), 60–66, 2000.

[147]   Buttler, D., Coleman, M., Critchlow, T., Fileto, R., Han, W., Liu, L., Pu, C., Rocco, D., and Xiong, L., Querying multiple bioinformatics data sources: Can Semantic Web research help?, *SIGMOD Record* 31(4), 2002.

[148]   Camarinha-Matos, L. M., Afsarmanesh, H., Garita, C., and Lima, C., Towards an architecture for virtual enterprises, *Journal of Intelligent Manufacturing* 9(2), 189–199, 1998.

[149]   Cannataro, M., and Talia, D., The knowledge Grid, *Communications of the ACM* 46(1), 89–93, 2003.

[150]   Carr, L., Bechhofer, S., Goble, C. A. and Hall, W., Conceptual linking: Ontology-based open hypermedia in *Tenth World Wide Web Conference, Hong Kong*, 2001.

[151]   Casanova, H., Bartol, T., Stiles, J., and Berman, F., Distributing MCell simulations on the Grid, *International Journal of High Performance Computing Applications* 14(3), 243–257, 2001.

[152]   Casanova, H., and Berman, F., Parameter sweeps on the Grid with APST, in *Grid Computing: Making the Global Infrastructure a Reality* (F. Berman, G. C. Fox, and A. J. G. Hey, eds.). Wiley, 2003.

[153]   Casanova, H., and Dongarra, J., NetSolve: A network server for solving computational science problems, *International Journal of Supercomputer Applications and High Performance Computing* 11(3), 212–223, 1997.

[154]   Casanova, H., Kim, M., Plank, J. S., and Dongarra, J., Adaptive scheduling for task farming with Grid middleware, *International Journal of Supercomputer Applications and High Performance Computing* 13, 231–240, 1999.

[155]   Casanova, H., Legrand, A., Zagorodnov, D., and Berman, F., Heuristics for scheduling parameter sweep applications in Grid environments, in *9th Heterogeneous Computing Workshop, Cancun, Mexico*, IEEE Computer Society Press, Los Alamitos, CA, 2000, pp. 349–363.

[156]   Casanova, H., Obertelli, G., Berman, F., and Wolski, R., The AppLeS parameter sweep template: User-level middleware for the Grid, in *SC2000: High Performance Networking and Computing*, 2000.

[157]   Castro, M., Druschel, P., Ganesh, A., Rowstron, A., and Wallach, D., Security for structured P2P overlay networks, in *Proceedings of the 5th Symposium on Operating Systems Design and Implementation*, Boston, Dec. 2002.

[158]   Castro, M., Druschel, P., Kermarrec, A. M., Nandi, A., Rowstron, A., and Singh, A., SplitStream: High-bandwidth content distribution in a cooperative environment. in *2nd International Workshop on Peer-to-Peer Systems, Berkeley, CA*. Springer-Verlag, Heidelberg, 2003.

[159]   Castro, M., and Liskov, B., Practical Byzantine fault tolerance, in *ACM Conference on Operating System Design and Implementation*, 1999.

[160]   Catalyurek, U., Beynon, M. D., Chang, C., Kurc, T., Sussman, A., and Saltz, J., The virtual microscope, in *IEEE Transactions on Information Technology in Biomedicine*. 2002.

[161]   Catlett, C., In search of gigabit applications, *IEEE Communications Magazine* (April), 42–51, 1992.

[162]   Catlett, C. The TeraGrid: A primer, 2002. Available at *www.teragrid.org/about/TeraGrid-Primer-Sept-02.pdf.*

[163]   Catlett, C., and Smarr, L., Metacomputing, *Communications of the ACM* **35**(6), 44–52, 1992.

[164]   *CCITT Recommendation X.509: The Directory—Authentication Framework*, 1988.

[165]   Cerf, V., Networks. *Scientific American*, Special Issue: Communications, Computers, and Networks, 72–81, 1991.

[166]   Ceri, S., Gottlob, G., and Tanca, L., *Logic Programming and Databases*. Springer-Verlag, Berlin, 1990.

[167]   Chadwick, D. W. *Understanding X.500—The Directory*, 1996. Available at *www.isi.salford.ac.uk/staff/dwc/X500.htm.*

[168]   Chadwick, D. W., and Otenko, A., The PERMIS X.509 role based privilege management infrastructure, in *7th ACM Symposium on Access Control Models and Technologies*, Assoc. Comput. Mach. Press, New York, 2002.

[169]   Chandra, R., Kohr, D., Menon, R., Dagum, L., Maydan, D. and McDonald, J., *Parallel Programming in OpenMP*. Morgan Kaufmann, San Francisco, 2000.

[170]   Chandy, K. M., and Kesselman, C., PC + + : A declarative concurrent object oriented programming language, Technical Report CS-TR-92-01. California Institute of Technology.

[171]   Chapman, B., Mehrotra, P., and Zima, H., Programming in Vienna Fortran. *Scientific Programming* **1**(1), 31–50, 1992.

[172]   Chapman, B. M., Sundaram, B., and Thyagaraja, K., EZGrid system: A resource broker for Grids. Available at *www.cs.uh.edu/~ezgrid.*

[173] Chase, J. S., Anderson, D. C., Thakar, P. N., Vahdat, A., and Doyle, R. P., Managing energy and server resources in hosting centres, in *Symposium on Operating Systems Principles*, 2001, pp. 103–116.

[174] Chen, K., Kutzko, M., and Rimovsky, T., *Multicast Beacon Server v0.8x (Perl)*, 2002: dast.nlanr.net/Projects/Beacon/.

[175] Chen, L., Cox, S. J., Goble, C., Keane, A. J., Roberts, A., Shadbolt, N. R., Smart, P., and Tao, F., Engineering knowledge for engineering grid applications, in *EuroWeb2002—The Web and the Grid: From E-science to E-business, Oxford, UK*, 2002, pp. 12–25.

[176] Chervenak, A., Deelman, E., Foster, I., Guy, L., Hoschek, W., Iamnitchi, A., Kesselman, C., Kunst, P., Ripenu, M., Schwartzkopf, B., Stockinger, H., Stockinger, K., and Tierney, B., Giggle: A framework for constructing scalable replica location services, in *SC2002: High Performance Networking and Computing*, 2002.

[177] Chervenak, A., Deelman, E., Kesselman, C., Pearlman, L., and Singh, G., A metadata catalog service for data intensive applications, SC2003, 2003.

[178] Chervenak, A., Foster, I., Kesselman, C., Salisbury, C., and Tuecke, S., The data Grid: Towards an architecture for the distributed management and analysis of large scientific data sets. *Journal of Network and Computer Applications* **23**, 187–200, 2001.

[179] Cheswick, W. R., and Bellovin, S. M., *Firewalls and Internet Security: Repelling the Wily Hacker*. Addison-Wesley, Reading, MA, 1994.

[180] Chien, A., Calder, B., Elbert, S., and Bhatia, K., Entropia: Architecture and performance of an enterprise desktop Grid system. *Journal of Parallel and Distributed Computing*, **63**(5), 597–610, 2003.

[181] Chien, A., Pakin, S., Lauria, M., Buchanan, M., Hane, K., Giannini, L., and Prusakova, J., High performance virtual machines (HPVM): Clusters with supercomputing APIs and performance, in *Eighth SIAM Conference on Parallel Processing for Scientific Computing, Minneapolis, MN*, 1997.

[182] Childers, L., Disz, T., Olson, R., Papka, M. E., Stevens, R., and Udeshi, T., Access Grid: Immersive group-to-group collaborative visualization, in *4th International Immersive Projection Technology Workshop*, 2000.

[183] Christensen, E., Curbera, F., Meredith, G., and Weerawarana, S., Web *Services Description Language (WSDL) 1.1*, W3C, Note 15, 2001. Available at *www.w3.org/TR/wsdl*.

[184] Christian, D., et al., The multimission archive at space telescope, in *Astronomical Data Analysis Software and Systems VIII* (D. M. Mehringer, R. I. Plante, and D. A. Roberts, eds.), ASP Conference Series, Vol. 172, p. 233. Astron. Soc. Pac., San Francisco, 1999.

[185] Christiansen, B., Cappello, P., Ionescu, M., Neary, M., Schauser, K., and Wu, D., Javelin: Internet-based parallel computing using Java, in *1997 Workshop on Java in Computational Science and Engineering*, 1997.

[186]   Chu, Y., Rao, S., Seshan, S., and Zhang, H., Enabling conferencing applications on the Internet using an overlay multicast architecture, *ACM SIGCOMM, San Diego, CA*. Assoc. Comput. Mach. Press, New York, 2001.

[187]   Chu, Y., Rao, S., and Zhang, H., A case for end system multicast, *ACM SIGMETRICS International Conference on Measurement and Modeling of Computer Systems, Santa Clara, CA*, Assoc. Comput. Mach. Press, New York, 2000, pp. 1–12.188. Chun, B., Mainwaring, A., and Culler, D., Virtual network transport protocols for Myrinet, in *Hot Interconnects Symposium V*. IEEE Computer Society Press, Los Alamitos, CA, 1997.

[189]   Clark, D. D., The design philosophy of the DARPA Internet protocols, in *ACM SIGCOMM Symposium on Communications Architectures and Protocols*, Assoc. Comput. Mach. Press, New York, 1988, pp. 106–114.

[190]   Clarke, I., Sandberg, O., Wiley, B., and Hong, T.W., Freenet: A distributed anonymous information storage and retrieval system, in *International Workshop on Designing Privacy Enhancing Technologies, Berkeley, CA*. Springer-Verlag, Heidelberg, 2000.

[191]   Committee on Research Horizons in Networking. Looking over the fence at networks: A neighbor's view of networking research. Computer Science and Telecommunications Board, National Research Council, 2001.

[192]   Connolly, D., van Harmelen, F., Horrocks, I., McGuinness, D. L., Patel-Schneider, P. F., and Stein, L. A. DAML+OIL reference description. W3C, Note 18, 2001. Available at *www.w3.org/TR/daml1oil-reference*.

[193]   Cooper, A., and Postel, J., The US Domain. Internet Engineering Task Force, RFC 1480, 1993. Available at *ietf.org/rfc/rfc1480.txt*.

[194]   Cooper, K. D., Hall, M. W., Kennedy, K., and Torczon, L., Interprocedural analysis and optimization, *Communications in Pure and Applied Mathematics* 48, 1995.

[195]   Cornell, M., et al., GIMS—A data warehouse for storage and analysis of genome sequence and functional data, in *2nd IEEE International Symposium on Bioinformatics and Bioengineering*, IEEE Press, New York, 2001, pp. 15–22.

[196]   Cranor, L., Langheinrich, M., Marchiori, M., Presler-Marshall, M., and Reagle, J., The platform for privacy preferences 1.0 (P3P1.0) specification. W3C, Recomendation 16, 2002. Available at *www.w3.org/TR/P3P*.

[197]   Croes, G. A., On AIPS++, a new astronomical information processing system, in *Astronomical Data Analysis Software and Systems II* (R. J. Hanisch, R. Brissenden, and J. Barnes, eds.), ASP Conference Series, Vol. 52, p. 156. Astron. Soc. Pac., San Francisco, 1993.

[198]   Cronon, W., *Nature's Metropolis: Chicago and the Great West*. W.W. Norton, New York, 1991.

[199]   Cruz-Neira, C., Sandin, D. J., DeFanti, T. A., Kenyon, R. V., and Hart, J. C., The CAVE: Audio visual experience automatic virtual environment. *Communications of the ACM* 35(6), 65–72, 1992.

[200]   Cuenca-Acuna, F. M., and Nguyen, T. D., Text-based content search and retrieval in ad hoc P2P communities, 2002.

[201]   Curtis, P., Dixon, M., Frederick, R.. and Nichols, D. A., The Jupiter audio/video architecture: Secure multimedia in network places, in *ACM Multimedia 95—Electronic Proceedings*, 1995.

[202]   Curtis, P., and Nichols, D. A., MUDs grow up: Social virtual reality in the real world, in *3rd International Conference on Cyberspace, Austin, TX*, 1993.

[203]   Czajkowski, K., Demir, A. K., Kesselman, C., and Thicbaux, M., Practical resource management for Grid-based visual exploration, in *10th IEEE International Symposium on High Performance Distributed Computing*. IEEE Computer Society Press, Los, Alamitos, CA, 2001.

[204]   Czajkowski, K., Fitzgerald, S., Foster, I., and Kesselman, C., Grid information services for distributed resource sharing, in *10th IEEE International Symposium on High Performance Distributed Computing, San Francisco*, IEEE Computer Society Press, Los Alamitos, CA, 2001, pp. 181–184.

[205]   Czajkowski, K., Foster, I., Karonis, N., Kesselman, C., Martin, S., Smith, W., and Tuecke, S., A resource management architecture for metacomputing systems, in *4th Workshop on Job Scheduling Strategies for Parallel Processing* Springer-Verlag, Heidelberg, 1998, pp. 62–82.

[206]   Czajkowski, K., Foster, I., and Kesselman, C., Co-allocation services for computational Grids, in *8th IEEE International Symposium on High Performance Distributed Computing*. IEEE Computer Society Press, Los Alamitos, CA, 1999.

[207]   Czajkowski, K., Foster, I., Sander, V., Kesselman, C., and Tuecke, S., SNAP: A protocol for negotiating service level agreements and coordinating resource management in distributed systems, in *8th Workshop on Job Scheduling Strategies for Parallel Processing, Edinburgh, Scotland*, 2002.

[208]   Czerwinski, S. E., Zhao, B. Y., Hodes, T. D., Joseph, A. D. and Katz, R. H., An architecture for a secure service discovery service, in *International Conference on Mobile Computing and Networking, Seattle, WA*, 1999.

[209]   Dabek, F., Kaashoek, M. F., Karger, D., Morris, R., and Stoica, I., Wide-area cooperative storage with CFS, in *Symposium on Operating Systems Principles*, 2001, pp. 202–215.

[210]   Dail, H., Berman, F., and Casanova, H., A decoupled scheduling approach for Grid application development environments, *Journal of Parallel and Distributed Computing*, **63**(5), 505–524, 2003.

[211]   DAML services coalition, DAML-S: Web service description for the Semantic Web, in *1st International Semantic Web Conference*, 2002, pp. 348–363.

[212]   Darema, F., George, D. A., Norton, V. A. and Pfister, G. F., A single-program-multiple-data computational model for EPEX/FORTRAN, *Parallel Computing* **7**(1), 11–24, 1988.

[213]   Davidson, S. B., Crabtree, J., Brunk, B. P., Schug, J., Tannen, V., Overton, G. C., and Stoeckert, C. J., Jr., K2/Kleisli and GUS: Experiments in integrated access to genomic data sources, *IBM Systems Journal* **40**(2), 512–531, 2001.

[214]   Davies, J., Fensel, D., and Harmelen, F. v. (eds.), *Towards the Semantic Web: Ontology-Driven Knowledge Management*. Wiley, New York, 2003.

[215]   De Roure, D., Jennings, N., and Shadbolt, N., Research agenda for the Semantic Grid: A future e-science infrastructure. UK National eScience CenterUKeS-2002–02, 2001. Available at *www.semanticgrid.org*.

[216]   Deelman, E., Blythe, J., Gil, Y., Kesselman, C., Mehta, G., Vahi, K., Blackburn, K., Lazzarini, A., Arbree, A., Cavanaugh, R., and Koranda, S., Mapping abstract workflows onto Grid environments, *Journal of Grid Computing* **1**(1), 25–39, 2003.

[217]   Deelman, E., Kesselman, C., Mehta, G., Meshkat, L., Pearlman, L., Blackburn, K., Ehrens, P., Lazzarini, A., Williams, R., and Koranda, S., GriPhyN and LIGO, building a virtual data Grid for gravitational wave scientists, in *11th IEEE International Symposium on High Performance Distributed Computing, Edinburgh, Scotland*, IEEE Computer Society Press, Los Alamitos, CA, 2002.

[218]   Deering, S., and Hinden, R., Internet protocol, version 6 (IPv6) specification. Internet Engineering Task Force, RFC 2460, 1998. Available at *ietf.org/rfc/rfc2460.txt*.

[219]   DeFanti, T., Foster, I., Papka, M., Stevens, R., and Kuhfuss, T., Overview of the I-WAY: Wide area visual supercomputing, *International Journal of Supercomputer Applications* **10**(2), 123–130, 1996.

[220]   DeFanti, T., and Stevens, R., Teleimmersion, in *The Grid: Blueprint for a New Computing Infrastructure* (I. Foster and C. Kesselman, eds.). Morgan Kaufmann, San Francisco, 1999, pp. 131–155.

[221]   Degermark, M., Kohler, T., Pink, S., and Schelen, O., Advance reservations for predictive service in the Internet, *ACM/Springer Verlag Journal on Multimedia Systems* **5**(3), 1997.

[222]   DeRose, L. A., and Reed, D. A., SvPablo: A multi-language architecture-independent performance analysis system, in *International Conference on Parallel Processing, Wakamatsu, Japan*, 1999.

[223]   DeRose, L. A., Zhang, Y., and Reed, D., SvPablo: A multi-language performance analysis system, in *10th International Conference on Computer Performance Evaluation— Modeling Techniques and Tools—Performance Tools'98, Palma de Mallorca, Spain*, 1998, pp. 352–355.

[224]   Deshpande, H., Bawa, M., and Garcia-Molina, H., Streaming live media over a peer-to-peer network, Technical Report, 2001.

[225]   Desktop Management Task Force. Alert Standard Format Specification, 2002. Available at *www.dmtf.org/standards/documents/ASF/DSP0136.pdf*.

[226]   Diachin, D., Freitag, L., Heath, D., Herzog, J., Michels, W., and Plassmann, P., Remote engineering tools for the design of pollution control systems for commercial boilers, *International Journal of Supercomputer Applications* **10**(2), 208–218, 1996.

[227]   Dieberger, A., and Frank, A. U., A city metaphor to support navigation in complex information spaces, *Journal of Visual Languages and Computing* 9, 597–622, 1998.

[228]   Dierks, T., and Allen, C., The TLS protocol version 1.0. Internet Engineering Task Force, RFC 2246, 1999. Available at *ietf.org/rfc/rfc2246.txt*.

[229]   Dinda, P., et al., The architecture of the Remos System, in *10th IEEE International Symposium on High Performance Distributed Computing, San Francisco, CA*. IEEE Computer Society Press, Los Alamitos, CA, 2001.

[230]   Dinda, P., and O'Hallaron, D., An evaluation of linear models for host load prediction, in *8th IEEE International Symposium on High Performance Distributed Computing*. IEEE Computer Society Press, Los Alamitos, CA, 1999.

[231]   Dingledine, R., Freedman, M., and Molnar, D., The Free Haven Project: Distributed anonymous storage service, in *Workshop on Design Issues in Anonymity and Unobservability*, 2000.

[232]   Distributed Management Task Force. Common Information Model (CIM) specification, 1999. Available at *www.dmtf.org/standards/documents/CIM/DSP0004.pdf*.

[233]   Distributed Management Task Force. Common information model (CIM) standards, 2002. Available at *www.dmtf.org/standards/standard_cim.php*.

[234]   Disz, T. L., Evard, R., Henderson, M. W., Nickless, W., Olson, R., Papka, M. E., and Stevens, R. Designing the future of collaborative science—Argonne's Futures Laboratory. *IEEE Parallel and Distributed Technology* 3(2), 14–21, 1995.

[235]   Disz, T. L., Judson, I., Olson, R., and Stevens, R., The Argonne Voyager multimedia server, in *6th IEEE International Symposium on High Performance Distributed Computing, Portland, OR*. IEEE Computer Society Press, Los Alamitos, CA, 1997.

[236]   Disz, T. L., Papka, M. E., Pellegrino, M., and Stevens, R., Sharing visualization experiences among remote virtual environments, in *International Workshop on High Performance Computing for Computer Graphics and Visualization*, 1995, pp. 217–237.

[237]   Dongarra, J., Foster, I., Fox, G., Gropp, W., Kennedy, K., Torczon, L., and White, A., *Sourcebook of Parallel Computing*. Morgan Kaufmann, San Francisco, 2002.

[238]   Douceur, J., The Sybil attack, in *1st International Workshop on Peer-to-Peer Systems, Cambridge, MA. LNCS* 2429, Springer-Verlag, Heidelberg, 2002.

[239]   Douglis, F., and Ousterhout, J., Transparent process migration: Design alternatives and the Sprite implementation. *Software Practice and Experience* 21(8), 757–785, 1991.

[240]   Dowell, R. D., Jokerst, R. M., Day, A., Eddy, S. R., and Stein, L., The distributed annotation system, *BMC Bioinformatics* 2(1), 7, 2001.

[241]   Dunham, M. H. *Data Mining: Introductory and Advanced Topics*. Prentice Hall, Englewood Cliff, NJ, 2003.

[242]   Dunigan, T., Mathis, M., and Tierney, B., A TCP tuning daemon, *IEEE Supercomputing, Baltimore, MD*, IEEE Computer Society Press, Los Alamitos, CA, 2002.

[243]   Durbin, R., Eddy, S., Krogh, A., and Mitchison, G., *Biological Sequence Analysis: Probabilistic Models of Proteins and Nucleic Acids*. Cambridge Univ. Press, Cambridge, UK, 1998.

[244]   Dwarkadas, S., Cox, A. L., and Zwaenpoel, W., An integrated compile-time/run-time software distributed shared memory system, in *Architectural Support for Programming Languages and Operating Systems (ASPLOS-VII), Cambridge, MA*, 1996.

[245]   Eicken, T. v., Culler, D., Goldstein, S., and Schauser, K., Active messages: A mechanism for integrated communication and computation, in *19th International Symposium on Computer Architecture*, 1992, pp. 256–266.

[246]   Eickermann, T., Wunderling, P., Niederberger, R., and Völpel, R., Aufbruch ins Jahr 2000—Start des Gigabit Testbed West, *DFN-Mitteilungen, Heft* **45** (Nov.), 13–15, 1997.

[247]   Ellison, C., Franz, B., Lampson, B., Rivest, R. L., Thomas, B. M., and Ylonen, T., SPKI certificate theory. Internet Engineering Task Force, RFC 2693, 1999. Available at *ietf.org/rfc/rfc2693.txt*.

[248]   Elmasri, R., and Navathe, S. B., *Fundamentals of Database Systems*. Addison-Wesley, Reading, MA, 2000.

[249]   EU DataGrid. *VOMS Architecture v1.1*, 2003. Available at *grid-auth.infn.it/docs/VOMS-v1_1.pdf*.

[250]   EUROGRID. *Grid for HPC Applications on Heterogeneous Architectures*. Available at www.eurogrid.org.

[251]   European Bioinformatics Institute. *Sequence Retrieval System*. Available at *srs.ebi.ac.uk*.

[252]   Ewing, T. J. D., and Kuntz, I. D., Critical evaluation of search algorithms for automated molecular docking and database screening. *Journal of Computational Chemistry* **9**, 1175–1189, 1997.

[253]   Fallside, D. C., XML schema part 0: Primer. W3C, Recommendation, 2001. Available at *www.w3.org/TR/xmlschema-0*.

[254]   Fan, L., Cao, P., Almeida, J., and Broder, A. Z., Summary cache: A scalable wide-area Web cache sharing protocol. *IEEE/ACM Transactions on Networking* **8**(3), 281–293, 2000.

[255]   Farquhar, A., Fikes, R., and Rice, J., The Ontolingua server: A tool for collaborative ontology construction, *International Journal of Human-Computer Studies* **46**(6), 707–727, 1997.

[256]   Farrell, S., and Housley, R., An Internet attribute certificate profile for authorization. Internet Engineering Task Force, RFC 3281, 2002. Available at *ietf.org/rfc/rfc3281.txt*.

[257]   Fedak, G., Germain, C., Néri, V., and Cappello, F., XtremWeb: A generic global computing system, in *Workshop on Cluster Computing and the Grid*, IEEE Computer Society Press, Los Alamitos, CA, 2001.

[258]   Feigenbaum, J., and Shenker, S., Distributed algorithmic mechanism design: Recent results and future directions, in *6th International Workshop on Discrete Algorithms and Methods for Mobile Computing and Communications, New York*. Assoc. Comput. Mach. Press, New York, 2002.

[259]   Fensel, D., Harmelen, F. v., Horrocks, I., McGuinness, D., and Patel-Schneider, P. F., OIL: An ontology infrastructure for the Semantic Web. *IEEE Intelligent Systems* **16**(2), 38–45, 2001.

[260]   Fensel, D., Hendler, J., Lieberman, H., and Wahlster, W. (eds.), *Spinning the Semantic Web: Bringing the World Wide Web to Its Full Potential*. MIT Press, Cambridge, MA, 2002.

[261]   Ferrari, D., Gupta, A., and Ventre, G., Distributed advance reservation of real-time connections. *ACM/Springer Verlag Journal on Multimedia Systems* **5**(3), 187–198, 1997.

[262]   FIPS Secure Hash Standard. Federal information processing standards, Technical Report Publication 180–1. NIST, U.S. Deparment of Commerce, 1995.

[263]   Fisher, S., and WP3. Information and monitoring services architecture. *Design, Requirements and Evaluation Criteria*, 2001.

[264]   Fitzgerald, S., Foster, I., Kesselman, C., Laszewski, G. v., Smith, W., and Tuecke, S., A directory service for configuring high-performance distributed computations., in *6th IEEE Symposium on High-Performance Distributed Computing*, IEEE Computer Society Press, Los Alamitos, CA, 1997, pp. 365–375.

[265]   Follen, G., Kim, C., Lopez, I., Sang, J., and Townsend, S., A CORBA-based development environment for wrapping and coupling legacy codes, in *10th IEEE International Symposium on High Performance Distributed Computing, San Francisco*. IEEE Computer Society Press, Los Alamitos, CA, 2001.

[266]   Ford, W., Hallam-Baker, P., Fox, B., Dillaway, B., LaMacchia, B., Epstein, J., and Lapp, J., XML key management specification (XKMS). W3C Note, 2001. Available at *www.w3.org/TR/xkms*.

[267]   Forkert, T., Kersken, H.-P., Schreiber, A., Strietzel, M., and Wolf, K., The distributed engineering framework TENT, in *Vector and Parallel Processing (VECPAR 2000)*, 2000, pp. 38–46.

[268]   Foster, I. Automatic generation of self-scheduling programs. *IEEE Transactions on Parallel and Distributed Systems* **2**(1), 68–78, 1991.

[269]   Foster, I. The Grid: A new infrastructure for 21st century science. *Physics Today* **55**(2), 42–47, 2002.

[270]   Foster, I. The Grid: Computing without bounds. *Scientific American* **288**(4), 78–85, 2003.

[271]   Foster, I., Alpert, E., Chervenak, A., Drach, B., Kesselman, C., Nefedova, V., Middleton, D., Shoshani, A., Sim, A., and Williams, D., The Earth System Grid II: Turning climate datasets into community resources, in *Annual Meeting of the American Meteorological Society*, 2002.

[272]   Foster, I., Fidler, M., Roy, A., Sander, V., and Winkler, L., End-to-end quality of service for high-end applications, *Computer Communications*, 2003.

[273]   Foster, I., and Iamnitchi, A., On death, taxes, and the convergence of peer-to-peer and Grid computing, in *2nd International Workshop on Peer-to-Peer Systems, Berkeley, CA. LNCS*, Springer-Verlag, Heidelberg, 2003.

[274]   Foster, I., Insley, J., Laszewski, G. v., Kesselman, C., and Thiebaux, M., Distance visualization: Data exploration on the Grid. *IEEE Computer* 32(12), 36–43, 1999.

[275]   Foster, I., and Karonis, N., A Grid-enabled MPI: Message passing in heterogeneous distributed computing systems, in *Supercomputing'98, Orlando*, 1998.

[276]   Foster, I., and Kesselman, C., Globus: A metacomputing infrastructure toolkit, *International Journal of Supercomputer Applications* 11(2), 115–129, 1998.

[277]   Foster, I., Kesselman, C., Lee, C., Lindell, R., Nahrstedt, K., and Roy, A., A distributed resource management architecture that supports advance reservations and co-allocation, in *International Workshop on Quality of Service*, 1999, pp. 27–36.

[278]   Foster, I., Kesselman, C., Nick, J., and Tuecke, S., The physiology of the Grid: An Open Grid Services Architecture for distributed systems integration (extended version of Grid services for distributed system integration). Open Grid Service Infrastructure WG, Global Grid Forum, 2002.

[279]   Foster, I., Kesselman, C., Nick, J. M., and Tuecke, S. Grid services for distributed systems integration. *IEEE Computer* 35(6), 37–46, 2002.

[280]   Foster, I., Kesselman, C., Tsudik, G., and Tuecke, S., A security architecture for computational grids, in *5th ACM Conference on Computer and Communications Security*, Assoc. Comput. Mach. Press, New York, 1998, pp. 83–91.

[281]   Foster, I., Kesselman, C., and Tuecke, S., The anatomy of the Grid: Enabling scalable virtual organizations, *International Journal of Supercomputer Applications* 15(3), 200–222, 2001.

[282]   Foster, I., Papka, M., and Stevens, R., Tools for distributed collaborative environments: A research agenda, in *5th IEEE International Symposium on High Performance Distributed Computing*, IEEE Computer Society Press, Los Alamitos, CA, 1996, pp. 23–28.

[283]   Foster, I., Roy, A., and Sander, V., A quality of service architecture that combines resource reservation and application adaptation, in *8th International Workshop on Quality of Service*, 2000.

[284]   Foster, I., Voeckler, J., Wilde, M., and Zhao, Y., Chimera: A virtual data system for representing, querying, and automating data derivation, in *14th International Conferemce. on Scientific and Statistical Database Management, Edinburgh, Scotland*, 2002.

[285]   Foster, I., Voeckler, J., Wilde, M., and Zhao, Y., The virtual data Grid: A new model and architecture for data-intensive collaboration, in *Conference on Innovative Data Systems Research*, 2003.

[286]   Fox, G., Hiranandani, S., Kennedy, K., Koelbel, C., Kremer, U., Tseng, C., and Wu, M., Fortran D Language Specification. (TR90-141), 1990.

[287]   Fox, G., Williams, R., and Messina, P. *Parallel Computing Works!* Morgan Kaufmann, San Francisco, 1994.

[288]   Francis, P., Jamin, S., Jin, C., Jin, Y., Raz, D., Shavitt, Y., and Zhang, L., Idmaps: A global Internet host distance estimation service, in *IEEE/ACM Transactions on Networking*, 2001, pp. 525–540.

[289]   Freed, N., and Borenstein, N., Multipurpose Internet mail extensions. Internet Engineering Task Force, RFC 2045, 1996. Available at *ietf.org/rfc/rfc2045.txt*.

[290]   Freedman, M. J. and Vingralek, R., Efficient P2P lookup based on a distributed trie, in *1st International Workshop on Peer-to-Peer Systems, Cambridge, MA. LNCS 2429*, Springer-Verlag, Heidelberg, 2002.

[291]   Frey, J., Tannenbaum, T., Foster, I., Livny, M., and Tuecke, S., Condor-G: A computation management agent for multi-institutional Grids. *Cluster Computing* 5(3), 237–246, 2002.

[292]   Frey, J., Tannenbaum, T., Foster, I., Livny, M., and Tuecke, S., Condor-G: A computation management agent for multi-institutional Grids, in *10th IEEE International Symposium on High Performance Distributed Computing*, IEEE Computer Society Press, Los Alamitos, CA, 2001, pp. 55–66.

[293]   Friedlander, A., *Emerging Infrastructure: The Growth of Railroads.* Corporation for National Research Initiatives, Reston, VA, 1995.

[294]   Friedlander, A., *In God We Trust; All Others Pay Cash: Banking as an American Infrastructure 1800–1935.* Corporation for National Research Initiatives, Reston, VA, 1995.

[295]   Friedlander, A., *Power and Light: Electricity in the U.S. Energy Infrastructure: 1870–1940.* Corporation for National Research Initiatives, Reston, VA, 1996.

[296]   Friedlander, A., *U.S. Telecommunications Infrastructure 1837–1940.* Corporation for National Research Initiatives, Reston, VA, 1995.

[297]   Frigo, M., and Johnson, S.G., FFTW: An adaptive software architecture for the FFT, in *1998 International Conference on Acoustics, Speech, and Signal Processing (ICASSP)*, 1998, pp. 1381–1384.

[298]   Fuchs, H., Beyond the desktop metaphor: Toward more effective display, interaction, and telecollaboration in the office of the future via a multitude of sensors and displays, in *Advanced Multimedia Content Processing*, 1999, 30–43.

[299]   Fuller, V., L, T., Yu, J., and Varadhan, K., Classless inter-domain routing (CIDR): An address assignment and aggregation strategy, RFC 1519, 1993. Available at *ietf.org/rfc/rfc1519.txt*.

[300]   Gabriel, E., Resch, M., Beisel, T., and Keller, R., Distributed computing in a heterogenous computing environment, in *EuroPVM/MPI'98*, 1998.

[301]   Gambetta, D. (ed.), *Trust: Making and Breaking Cooperative Relations*, electronic ed. Department of Sociology, University of Oxford, 2000.

[302]   Gardner, M.K., et al. MAGNET: A tool for debugging, analysis and reflection in computing systems. Los Alamos National Laboratory, Technical Report LA-UR 02–7170, 2002.

[303]   Gasser, M., and McDermott, E., An architecture for practical delegation in a distributed system, in *IEEE Symposium on Research in Security and Privacy*, IEEE Computer Society Press, Los Alamitos, CA, 1990, pp. 20–30.

[304]   Geels, D., and Kubiatowicz, J., Replica management should be a game, in *SIGOPS European Workshop*, 2002.

[305]   Geist, A., Beguelin, A., Dongarra, J., Jiang, W., Manchek, R., and Sunderam, V., *PVM: Parallel Virtual Machine*. MIT Press, Cambridge, MA, 1994.

[306]   Geist, G. A., Heath, M.T., Peyton, B.W., and Worley, P.H., *PICL—A Portable Instrumented Communication Library*. Oak Ridge National Laboratory Technical Report, ORNL/TM-11130, 1990.

[307]   Gemmell, J., Multicast distributed powerpoint add-in, in *Microsoft Research*, San Francisco, 2000.

[308]   Genovese, T., and Helm, M., ESnet's SciDAC PKI & Directory Project—Homepage. DOE Energy Sciences Network, 2002. Available at *envisage.es.net/*.

[309]   Giacomini, F., Prelz, F., Sgaravatto, M., Terekhov, I., Garzoglio, G., and Tannenbaum, T., Planning on the Grid: A status report, Technical Report PPDG-20. Particle Physics Data Grid Collaboration, 2002. Available at *www.ppdg.net/docs/documents_and_information.htm*.

[310]   Gleeson, B., Lin, A., Heinanen, J., Finland, T., Armitage, G., and Malis, A., IP based virtual private networks. Internet Engineering Task Force, RFC 2764, 2000. Available at *ietf.org/rfc/rfc2764.txt*.

[311]   Global Grid Forum. *Grid Information Systems and Performance Area Website*. Available at *https://forge.gridforum.org/projects/rgis-rg*.

[312]   Global Grid Forum. Grid Monitoring Architecture Working Group, 2002. Available at *www-didc.lbl.gov/GGF-PERF/GMA-WG*.

[313]   Goble, C. A., and De Roure, D., The Grid: An application of the Semantic Web, *SIGMOD Record* **31**(4), 2002.

[314]   Goble, C. A., and De Roure, D., The Semantic Web and Grid computing, in *Real World Semantic Web Applications* (V. Kashyap, ed.). IOS Press, 2002.

[315]   Goble, C. A., Stevens, R., Ng, G., Bechofer, S., Paton, N., Baker, P., Peim, M., and Brass, A., Transparent access to multiple bioinformatics information sources, *IBM Systems Journal* **40**(2), 532–551, 2001.

[316]   Goland, Y. Y., Cai, T., Leach, P., Gu, Y., and Albright, S., Simple service discovery protocol/1.0. Internet Engineering Task Force, Internet Draft, 1999.

[317]   Goldstein, S., Storage performance—An eight year outlook. IBM Santa Teresa Laboratory, Technical Report TR 03.308, San Jose, 1987.

[318]   Goodale, T., Allen, G., Lanfermann, G., Massó, J., Radke, T., Seidel, E., and Shalf, J., The Cactus Framework and Toolkit: Design and applications, in *Vector and Parallel Processing: VECPAR'2002, 5th International Conference*. Springer-Verlag, Heidelberg, 2003.

[319]   Graham, G. E., MCRunjob: A metadata based workflow manager for the Grid, in *Computers in High Energy Physics 2003, San Diego, CA*, 2003.

[320]   Graham, S., Simeonov, S., Boubez, T., Daniels, G., Davis, D., Nakamura, Y., and Neyama, R., *Building Web Services with Java: Making Sense of XML, SOAP, WSDL, and UDDI*. Sams, 2001.

[321]   Grandison, T., and Sloman, M., A survey of trust in Internet applications, *IEEE Communications Surveys*, 3(4), 4–7, Oct.–Dec., 2000.

[322]   Graupner, S., Kotov, V., Trinks, H., and Andrzejak, A., Control architecture for service Grids in a federation of utility data centers, Technical Report HPL-2002-235. HP Labs, 2002.

[323]   Gray, C. G., and Cheriton, D. R., Lease: An efficient fault-tolerant mechanism for distributed file cache consistency, in *12th ACM Symposium on Operating System Principles*, 1989, pp. 202–210.

[324]   Gray, J., The transaction concept: Virtues and limitations, in *5th Symposium on Reliability in Distributed Software and Database Systems*, 1981, pp. 144–154.

[325]   Gray, J., Chong, W., Barclay, T., Szalay, A. S., and Vandenberg, J., TeraScale SneakerNet: Using inexpensive disks for backup, archiving, and data exchange, MSR TR 2002-54, 2002.

[326]   Gray, J., McJones, P., Blasgen, M., Lindsay, B., Lorie, R., Price, T., Putzolu, F., and Traiger, I., The recovery manager of the System R database manager. *ACM Computing Surveys* 13(2), 223–242, 1981.

[327]   Gray, J., and Rueter, A., *Transaction Processing: Concepts and Techniques*. Morgan Kauffman, San Mateo, CA, 1993.

[328]   Gray, J., Szalay, A. S., Thakar, A. R., Kunszt, P. Z., Malik, T., Raddick, J., Stoughton, C. and vandenBerg, J., The SDSS SkyServer—Public access to the Sloan Digital Sky Server Data, in *ACM SIGMOD*, 2002, pp. 1–11.

[329]   Gray, J., Szalay, A. S., Thakar, A. R., Stoughton, C., and Vandenberg, J., Online scientific data curation, publication, and archiving, in *SPIE Astronomy Telescopes and Instruments, Waikoloa, HI*, 2002, pp. 103–107.

[330]   Gray, P., and Sunderam, V., The IceT environment for parallel and distributed computing, in *1997 International Scientific Computing in Object-Oriented Parallel Environments Conference, LNCS 1343*, Springer-Verlag, Heidelberg, 1997.

[331]   Greenberg, D., Brightwell, R., Fisk, L., McCabe, A., and Riesen, R., A system software architecture for high-end computing, in *Supercomputing '97*, IEEE Computer Society Press, Los Alamitos, CA, 1997.

[332]   *GRIP: GRid Interoperability Project (Globus and UNICORE)*, 2002: *www.grid-interoperability.org.*

[333]   Gropp, W., Huss-Lederman, S., Lumsdaine, A., Lusk, E., Nitzberg, B., Saphir, W., and Snir, M., *MPI—The Complete Reference: Volume 2, The MPI-2 Extensions.* MIT Press, Cambridge, MA, 1998.

[334]   Gropp, W., Lusk, E., Doss, N., and Skjellum, A., A high-performance, portable implementation of the MPI message passing interface standard, *Parallel Computing* 22(6), 789–828, 1996.

[335]   Grosof, B. N., and Horrocks, I., Description logic programs: Combining logic programs with description logic, 2002. Available at *ebusiness.mit.edu/bgrosof/paps/dlp-wp-v19.pdf.*

[336]   Groth, R., *Data Mining, A Hands-On Approach for Business Professionals.* Prentice Hall, Englewood Cliffs, NJ, 1997.

[337]   Gu, W., Vetter, J., and Schwan, K., An annotated bibliography of interactive program steering, *SIGPLAN Notices* 29(9), 140–148. 1994.

[338]   Gummadi, K. P., Saroiu, S., and Gribble, S. D., King: Estimating latency between arbitrary Internet end hosts, in ACM *SIGCOMM Internet Measurement Workshop, Marseille, France*, Assoc. Comput. Mach. Press, New York, 2002.

[339]   Gunter, D., Tierney, B., Crowley, B., Holding, M., and Lee, J., NetLogger: A toolkit for distributed system performance analysis, in *IEEE Mascots 2000: Eighth International Symposium on Modeling, Analysis and Simulation of Computer and Telecommunication Systems*, IEEE Computer Society Press, Los Alamitos, CA, 2000.

[340]   Gunter, D., Tierney, B., Jackson, K., Lee, J., and Stoufer, M., Dynamic monitoring of high-performance distributed applications, in *11th IEEE International Symposium on High Performance Distributed Computing, HPDC-11.* IEEE Computer Society Press, Los Alamitos, CA, 2002.

[341]   Gupta, A., Ludäscher, B., and Martone, M., Knowledge-based integration of neuroscience data sources, in *12th International Conference on Scientific and Statistical Database Management Systems, Berlin*, 2000, pp. 39–52.

[342]   Gupta, S., *Logging in Java with the JDK 1.4 Logging API and Apache log4j.* APress, 2003.

[343]   Guy, L., Kunszt, P., Laure, E., Stockinger, H., and Stockinger, K., Replica management in data Grids. *Global Grid Forum* 5, 2002.

[344]   Haas, L. M., Schwarz, P. M., Kodali, P., Kotlar, E., Rice, J. E., and Swope, W. C., DiscoveryLink: A system for integrated access to life sciences data sources, *IBM Systems Journal* 40(2), 489–511, 2001.

[345]   Hadida, M., Kadobayashi, Y., Lamont, S., Braun, H. W., Fink, B., Hutton, T., Kamrath, A., Mori, H., and Ellisman, M. H., Advanced networking for telemicroscopy, in *10th Annual Internet Society Conference, Yokohama, Japan*, 2000.

[346]   Hafner, K., and Lyon, M., *Where Wizards Stay Up Late*. Simon & Schuster, New York, 1996.

[347]   Hahn, B., *Essential MATLAB for Scientists and Engineers*. Arnold, Sevenoaks, CA, 1997.

[348]   Hall, M. W., Murphy, B. R., and Amarasinghe, S. P., Interprocedural analysis for parallelization: A case study, in *7th SIAM Conference on Parallel Processing for Scientific Computing, San Francisco*, 1995.

[349]   Hand, D., Mamilla, H., and Smyth, P., *Principles of Data Mining*. MIT Press, Cambridge, MA, 2001.

[350]   Handschuh, S., and Staab, S., Authoring and annotation of Web pages in CREAM, in *11th World Wide Web Conference, Honolulu, HI*, 2002.

[351]   Hanna, K. M., Natarajan, N., and Levine, B., Evaluation of a novel two-step server selection metric, Technical Report, 2001.

[352]   Hapner, M., Burridge, R., Sharma, R., Fialli, J., and Stout, K., Java Message Service (version 1.1). Sun Microsystems, 2002.

[353]   Harchol-Balter, M., Leighton, F. T., and Lewin, D., Resource discovery in distributed networks, in *Symposium on Principles of Distributed Computing*, 1999, pp. 229–237.

[354]   Hardcastle-Kille, S. E., X.500 and domains. Internet Engineering Task Force, RFC 1279, 1991. Available at *ietf.org/rfc/rfc1279.txt*.

[355]   Hardman, V., Sasse, A., and Kouvelas, I., Successful multi-party audio communication over the Internet. *Communications of the ACM* 41(5), 74–80, 1995.

[356]   Harvey, N., Jones, M. B., Saroiu, S., Theimer, M., and Wolman, A., SkipNet: A scalable overlay network with practical locality properties, in *4th USENIX Symposium on Internet Technologies and Systems*, 2003.

[357]   Hendler, J., Agents and the Semantic Web, *IEEE Intelligent Systems Journal* 16(2), 30–37, 2001.

[358]   Hey, A., and Trefethen, A., The UK e-Science Core Programme and the Grid, *Future Generation Computer Systems* 18(8), 1017–1031, 2002.

[359]   Hey, A. J. G., and Trefethen, A., The data deluge: An e-science perspective, in *Grid Computing: Making the Global Infrastructure a Reality* (F. Berman, G. C. Fox, and A. J. G. Hey, eds.). Wiley, New York, 2003.

[360]   Hiranandani, S., Kennedy, K., and Tseng, C. W. Compiling Fortran D for MIMD distributed memory machines, *Communications of the ACM* 35(8), 66–80, 1992.

[361]   Hirschman, L., Park, J. C., Tsujii, J., Wong, L., and Wu, C. H. Accomplishments and challenges in literature data mining for biology, *Bioinformatics* 18(12), 1553–1561, 2002.

[362]   Hollingsworth, J. K., and Miller, B. P., An adaptive cost model for parallel program instrumentation, in *Euro-Par'96, Lyon, France*, Springer-Verlag, Heidelberg, 1996.

[363]   Hong, N. P. C., Krause, A., Malaika, S., McCance, G., Laws, S., Magowan, J., Paton, N. W., and Ricardi, G., Grid database services specification. Global Grid Forum, 2003.

[364]   Hong, T., Performance, in *P2P: Harnessing the Power of Disruptive Technologies* (A. Oram, ed.), O'Reilly, 2001.

[365]   Horn, P., *The IBM Vision for Autonomic Computing*, 2001. Available at *www.research.ibm.com/autonomic/manifesto*.

[366]   Horrocks, I., DAML + OIL: A reasonable Web ontology language, in *8th International Conference on Extending Database* Technology, 2002.

[367]   Horrocks, I., The FaCT System automated reasoning with analytic tableaux and related methods, in *International Conference Tableaux'98*, Springer-Verlag, Heidelberg, 1998, pp. 307–312.

[368]   Hoschek, W., Jaen-Martinez, J., Samar, A., Stockinger, H., and Stockinger, K., Data management in an international data Grid project, in *International Workshop on Grid Computing*. Springer-Verlag, Heidelberg, 2000.

[369]   Housley, R., Polk, W., Ford, W. and Solo, D. Internet X.509 Public Key Infrastructure Certificate and Certificate Revocation List (CRL) Profile. Internet Engineering Task Force, RFC 3280, 2002. Available at *ietf.org/rfc/rfc3280.txt*.

[370]   Howard, J. H., Kazar, M. L., Menees, S. G., Nichols, D. A., Satyanarayanan, M., Sidebotham, R. N., and West, M. J., Scale and performance in a distributed file system. *ACM Transactions on Computer Systems* 6(1), 51–81, 1988.

[371]   Howell, J., and Kotz, D., End-to-end authorization, in *2000 Symposium on Operating Systems Design and Implementation*. USENIX Association, 2000.

[372]   Howes, T. A., and Smith, M. C., A scalable, deployable directory service framework for the Internet, Technical Report, Center for Information Integration, University of Michigan, 1995.

[373]   Humphrey, M , Knabe, F., Ferrari, A., and Grimshaw, A., Accountability and control of process creation in metasystems, in *2000 Network and Distributed System Security Symposium*, 2000.

[374]   Humphreys, G., Buck, I., Eldridge, M., and Hanrahan, P., Distributed rendering for scalable displays, in *Supercomputing 2000*.

[375]   Humphreys, K., Demetriou, G., and Gaizauskas, R., Bioinformatics applications of information extraction from scientific journal articles. *Journal of Information Science* 26(2), 75–85, 2000.

[376]   Hunt, E., Atkinson, M. P., and Irving, R. W., Database indexing for large DNA and protein sequence collections. *VLDB Journal* 11(3), 2002.

[377]   Iamnitchi, A., and Foster, I., A problem-specific fault-tolerance mechanism for asynchronous distributed systems, in *International Conference on Parallel Processing*, 2000.

[378]   IBM and Microsoft Security in a Web Services World: A Proposed Architecture and Roadmap (version 1.0), 2002. Available at *www-106.ibm.com/developerworks/library/ws-secmap/*.

[379]   IBM, Microsoft, RSA Security and VeriSign Web Services Secure Conversation
         Language (WS-SecureConversation) Version 1.0, 2002. Available at
         www-106.ibm.com/developerworks/library/ws-secon/.

[380]   IBM, Microsoft, RSA Security and VeriSign Web Services Trust Language
         (WS-Trust), 2002. Available at *www-106.ibm.com/developerworks/
         library/ws-trust/*.

[381]   IBM, Microsoft and VeriSign Web Services Security Language (WS-Security),2002.
         Available at *www-106.ibm.com/developerworks/library/ws-secure/*.

[382]   IEEE Storage Systems Standards Working Group. *Reference Model for Open Storage
         Systems Interconnection*. IEEE, 1994.

[383]   Imamura, T., Dillaway, B., and Simon, E., XML encryption syntax and
         processing. W3C, Recommendation, 2002. Available at *www.w3.org/TR/
         xmlenc-core*.

[384]   ITU-T X.509 (03/00): Information technology—Open systems interconnection, the
         directory: Authentication framework. ITU, Recommendation, 2002.

[385]   Jackson, D., Snell, Q., and Clement, M., Core algorithms of the Maui scheduler, in
         7th Workshop on Job Scheduling Strategies for Parallel Processing, 2001.

[386]   Jackson, N., pyGlobus: a Python interface to the Globus Toolkit, *Concurrency and
         Computation: Practice and Experience* 14(13–15), 1075–1084, 2002.

[387]   Jannotti, J., Gifford, D. K., Johnson, K. L., Kaashoek, M. F., and O'Toole, J. W.,
         Overcast: Reliable multicasting with an overlay network, Technical Report, 2000.

[388]   Jarke, M., Lenzerini, M., and Vassiliou, Y., *Fundamentals of Data Warehousing*.
         Springer-Verlag, Heidelberg, 2000.

[389]   Jeffery, K. G., Knowledge, information and data, CLRC technical report. Council for
         the Central Laboratory of the Research Councils, 1999.

[390]   Jennings, N. R., Faratin, P., Lomuscio, A. R., Parsons, S., Sierra, C., and Wooldridge, M.
         Automated negotiation: prospects, methods and challenges. *International Journal of
         Group Decision and Negotiation* 10(2), 199–215, 2001.

[391]   Jin, G., Pipechar network characterization service, 2001. Available at
         www-didc.lbl.gov/NCS.

[392]   Johnson, E., Gannon, D., and Beckman, P., HPC++: Experiments with the parallel
         standard template library, in *1997 International Conference on Supercomputing, Vienna,
         Austria*, 1997.

[393]   Johnston, W., Greiman, W., Hoo, G., Lee, J., Tierney, B., Tull, C., and Olson, D.,
         High-speed distributed data handling for on-line instrumentation systems, in
         ACM/IEEE SC97: High Performance Networking and Computing, 1997.

[394]   Johnston, W. E., Gannon, D., and Nitzberg, B., Grids as production computing
         environments: The engineering aspects of NASA's information power Grid, in *8th
         IEEE International Symposium on High Performance Distributed Computing*. IEEE
         Computer Society Press, Los Alamitos, CA, 1999.

[395] Jones, G., Willett, P., Glen, R. C., Leach, A. R., and Taylor, R., Development and validation of a genetic algorithm for flexible docking, *Journal of Molecular Biology* **267**, 727–748, 1997.

[396] Jordan, H. F., The force, in *The Characteristics of Parallel Algorithms* (L. H. Jamieson, D. B. Gannon, and R. J. Douglass, eds.). MIT Press, Cambridge, MA, 1987.

[397] Kanehisa, M., Goto, S., Kawashima, S., and Nakaya, A., The KEGG Databases at GenomeNet, *Nucleic Acids Research* **30**, 42–46, 2002.

[398] Kapadia, N., and Fortes, J., An architecture for Web-enabled wide-area network-computing, *Journal of Networks, Software Tools and Applications* **2**(2), 153–164, 1999.

[399] Kapadia, N. H., Fortes, J. A. B., and Brodley, C. E., Predictive application-performance modeling in a computational Grid environment, in *8th IEEE International Symposium on-Performance Distributed Computing*, IEEE Computer Society Press, Los Alamitos, CA, 1999.

[400] Karavanic, K. L., and Miller, B. P., Experiment management support for performance tuning, in *SC'97, San Jose, CA*, 1997.

[401] Karger, D. R., Lehman, E., Leighton, F. T., Panigrahy, R., Levine, M. S., and Lewin, D., Consistent hashing and random trees: Distributed caching protocols for relieving hot spots on the World Wide Web, in *Symposium on Theory of Computing*, Assoc. Comput. Mach., New York, 1997, pp. 654–663.

[402] Karonis, N., Supinski, B. d., Foster, I., Gropp, W., Lusk, E., and Bresnahan, J., Exploiting hierarchy in parallel computer networks to optimize collective operation performance, in *14th International Parallel and Distributed Processing Symposium*, IEEE Computer Society Press, Los Alamitos, CA, 2000, pp. 377–384.

[403] Karonis, N., Toonen, B., and Foster, I., MPICH-G2: A Grid-enabled implementation of the message passing interface, *Journal of Parallel and Distributed Computing*, **63**(5), 551–563, 2003.

[404] Kaufmann, W. J., and Smarr, L. L., *Supercomputing and the Transformation of Science*. Scientific American Library, New York, 1993.

[405] Kennedy, K., Fast greedy weighted fusion, *International Journal of Parallel Programming* **29**(5), 463–491, 2001.

[406] Kennedy, K., Mazina, M., Mellor-Crummey, J., Cooper, K., Torczon, L., Berman, F., Chien, A., Dail, H., Sievert, O., Angulo, D., Foster, I., Gannon, D., Johnsson, L., Kesselman, C., Aydt, R., Reed, D., Dongarra, J., Vadhiyar, S., and Wolski, R., Toward a framework for preparing and executing adaptive Grid programs, in *14th International Parallel Distributed Processing Symposium*, 2002.

[407] Kennedy, K., McKinley, K. S., and Tseng, C., Analysis and transformation in the ParaScope editor, in *ACM International Conference on Supercomputing, Cologne, Germany*, 1991.

[408] Kent, S., and Atkinson, R., Security architecture for the Internet protocol. Internet Engineering Task Force, RFC 2401, 1998. Available at *ietf.org/rfc/rfc2401.txt*.

[409]   Kielmann, T., Hofman, R., Bal, H., Plaat, A., and Bhoedjang, R., MagPIe: MPI's collective communication operations for clustered wide area systems, in *7th ACM SIGPLAN Symposium on Principles and Practice of Parallel Programming*, Assoc. Comput. Mach. Press, New York, 1999, pp. 131–140.

[410]   Kim, K., and Nahrstedt, K., A resource broker model with integrated reservation scheme, in *IEEE International Conference on Multimedia*, IEEE Computer Society Press, Los Alamitos, CA, 2000, pp. 859–862.

[411]   Kim, Y., Mazzocchi, D., and Tsudik, G., Admission control in peer groups, *MC2R* **6**(4), 2002.

[412]   Kimura, T., and Takemiya, H., Local area metacomputing for multidisciplinary problems: A case study for fluid/structure coupled simulation, in *International Conference on Supercomputing*, 1998, pp. 145–156.

[413]   Kistler, J. J., and Satyanarayanan, M., Disconnected operation in the code file system, *Operating Systems Review* **23**(5), 213–225, 1989.

[414]   Klebe, G. (Ed.), *Virtual Screening: An Alternative or Complement to High Throughput Screening?* Kluwer Press, Norwell, MA, 2000.

[415]   Kleinrock, L., UCLA Press Release, July 3, 1969.

[416]   Knorr Cetina, K., *Epistemic Cultures. The Cultures of Knowledge Societies*. Harvard Univ. Press, Cambridge, MA, 1999.

[417]   Kornievskaia, O., Honeyman, P., Doster, B., and Coffman, K., Kerberized credential translation: A solution to Web access control, in *10th Usenix Security Symposium*, 2001.

[418]   Kossmann, D., The state of the art in distributed query processing, *ACM Computing Surveys* **32**(4), 422–469, 2000.

[419]   Kotov, V., On virtual data centers and their operating environments, HP LabsHPL-2001–44, 2001.

[420]   Krishnan, S., Bramley, R., Gannon, D., Govindaraju, M., Indurkar, R., Slominski, A., Temko, B., Alkire, R., Drews, T., Webb, E. and Alameda, J., The XCAT science portal, in *SC'01: High Performance Networking and Computing, Denver, CO*, 2001.

[421]   Krishnan, S., Wagstrom, P., and Laszewski, G. v., GSFL: A workflow framework for Grid services, ANL/MCS-P980-0802. Argonne National Laboratory, 2002.

[422]   Kubiatowicz, J., Bindel, D., Chen, Y., Czerwinski, S., Eaton, P., Geels, D., Gummadi, R., Rhea, S., Weatherspoon, H., Weimer, W., Wells, C., and Zhao, B., OceanStore: An architecture for global-scale persistent storage, in *9th International Conference on Architectural Support for Programming Languages and Operating Systems*, 2000.

[423]   Kuck, D., Kuhn, R., Padua, D., Leasure, B., and Wolfe, M. J., Dependence graphs and compiler optimizations, in *8th ACM Symposium on the Principles of Programming Languages, Williamsburg, VA*, 1981.

[424]   Kurc, T., Catalyurek, U., Chang, C., Sussman, A., and Saltz, J., Exploration and visualization of very large datasets with the active data repository, *IEEE Computer Graphics and Applications* **21**(4), 24–33, 2001.

[425]   Kurc, T., Chang, C., Ferreira, R., Sussman, A., and Saltz, J., Querying very large multi-dimensional datasets in ADR, in *SC'99: High Performance Networking and Computing, Orlando, FL*. Assoc. Comput. Mach. Press, New York, 1999.

[426]   Kurowski, K., Nabrzyski, J. and Pukacki, J., User preference driven multiobjective resource management in Grid environments, in *1st International Symposium on Cluster Computing and the Grid*, 2001, p. 114.

[427]   Lai, C., Medvinsky, G., and Neuman, B. C., Endorsements, licensing, and insurance for distributed system services, in *2nd ACM Conference on Computer and Communication Security*, 1994.

[428]   Lamport, L., Time, clocks, and the ordering of events in a distributed system, *Communications of the ACM* 21(7), 558–564, 1978.

[429]   Laszewski, G. v., Foster, I., Gawor, J., and Lane, P., A Java Commodity Grid Toolkit, *Concurrency: Practice and Experience* 13(8–9), 643–662, 2001.

[430]   Leake, D. B., *Case-Based Reasoning: Experiences, Lessons, and Future Directions*. MIT Press, Cambridge, MA, 1996.

[431]   Lee, J., Gunter, D., Tierney, B., Allock, W., Bester, J., Bresnahan, J. and Tuecke, S., Applied techniques for high bandwidth data transfers across wide area networks, in *Computers in High Energy Physics, Beijing, China*, 2001.

[432]   Lee, J. K., and Gannon, D., Object oriented parallel programming: Experiments and results, in *Supercomputing, Albuquerque, NM*, 1991, pp. 273–282.

[433]   Lee, S., and Bhattacharjee, B., Cooperative peer groups in NICE, in *IEEE Infocom*, IEEE Computer Society Press, Los Alamitos, CA, 2003.

[434]   Lefebure, V., and Wildish, T., The spring 2002 DAQ TDR production, CMS Note 034, 2002.

[435]   Legrand, A., Marchal, L., and Casanova, H., Scheduling distributed applications: The SimGrid simulation framework, in *3rd IEEE International Symposium on Cluster Computing and the Grid, Tokyo, Japan*, IEEE Computer Society Press, Los Alamitos, CA, 2003.

[436]   Leibowitz, N., Ripeanu, M., and Wierzbicki, A., Deconstructing the Kazaa network, in *3rd IEEE Workshop on Internet Applications, San Jose, CA*, IEEE Computer Society Press, Los Alamitos, CA, 2003.

[437]   Leigh, J., Johnson, A., and DeFanti, T. A., CAVERN: A distributed architecture for supporting scalable persistence and interoperability in collaborative virtual environments, *Virtual Reality: Research, Development and Applications* 2(2), 217–237, 1997.

[438]   Levine, D., Wirt, M., and Whitebook, B., *Practical Grid Computing for Massively Multiplayer Games*. Charles River Media, 2003.

[439]   Leymann, F., *Web Services Flow Language (WSFL 1.0)*. IBM Corporation, 2001. Available at *www-3.ibm.com/software/solutions/webservices/pdf/WSFL.pdf*.

[440]   Li, K., and Hudak, P., Memory coherence in shared virtual memory systems, *ACM Transactions on Computer Systems* 7(4), 321–359, 1989.

[441]   Licklider, J. R., Man–computer symbiosis, *IRE Transactions on Human Factors in Electronics, HFE-1*, 4–11, 1960.

[442]   Ligon, I. W., and Ross, R., An overview of the parallel virtual file system, in *Extreme Linux Workshop, Monterey*, CA, 1999.

[443]   Linderoth, J., Kulkarni, S., Goux, J.-P., and Yoder, M., An enabling framework for master–worker applications on the computational Grid, in *9th IEEE International Symposium on High Performance Distributed Computing*, IEEE Computer Society Press, Los Alamitos, CA, 2000, pp. 43–50.

[444]   Litzkow, M., and Livny, M., Experience with the Condor distributed batch system, in *IEEE Workshop on Experimental Distributed Systems*, IEEE Computer Society Press, Los Alamitos, CA, 1990.

[445]   Litzkow, M., Tannenbaum, T., Basney, J., and Livny, M., Checkpoint and migration of UNIX processes in the Condor distributed processing system, University of Wisconsin—Madison Computer Sciences 1346, 1997.

[446]   Litzkow, M. J., Livny, M., and Mutka, M. W., Condor—A hunter of idle workstations, in *8th International Conference on Distributed Computing Systems*, 1988, pp. 104–111.

[447]   Liu, C., and Foster, I., A constraint language approach to Grid resource selection. University of Chicago, Department of Computer Science, 2003.

[448]   Liu, C., Yang, L., Angulo, D., and Foster, I., Design and evaluation of a resource selection framework for Grid applications, in *11th IEEE International Symposium on High Performance Distributed Computing, Edinburgh, Scotland*, IEEE Computer Society Press, Los Alamitos, CA, 2002.

[449]   Livny, M., and Raman, R., High-throughput resource management, in *The Grid: Blueprint for a New Computing Infrastructure* (I. Foster and C. Kesselman, eds.), pp. 311–337. Morgan Kaufmann, San Francisco, 1999.

[450]   Lopez, I., Follen, G., Gutierrez, R., Foster, I., Ginsburg, B., Larsson, O., Martin, S., and Tuecke, S., NPSS on NASA's IPG: Using CORBA and Globus to coordinate multidisciplinary aeroscience applications, in *NASA HPCC/CAS Workshop*. NASA Ames Research Center, 2000.

[451]   Lowekamp, B., Miller, N., Sutherland, D., Gross, T., Steenkiste, P., and Subhlok, J., A resource query interface for network-aware applications, in *7th IEEE International Symposium on High Performance Distributed Computing*. IEEE Computer Society Press, Los Alamitos, CA, 1998.

[452]   Lu, C., and Reed, D., Compact application signatures for parallel and distributed scientific codes, in *SC'2002, Baltimore, MD*, 2002.

[453]   Ludaescher, B., Gupta, A., and Martone, M. E., Model-based mediation with domain maps, in *17th International Conference on Data Engineering, Heidelberg, Germany*, IEEE Computer Society Press, Los Alamitos, CA, 2001.

[454]   Lumb, I., and Smith, C., Scheduling attributes and platform LSF, in *Grid Resource Management* (J. Nabrzyski, J. Schopf, and J. Weglarz, eds.) Kluwer Academic, Norwell, MA, 2003.

[455]   Lumpp, J. E., Models for recovery from software instrumentation intrusion. Ph.D. thesis, Department of Electrical and Computer Engineering, University of Iowa, 1993.

[456]   Lv, Q., Cao, P., Cohen, E., Li, K., and Shenker, S., Search and replacement in unstructured P2P networks, in *16th ACM International Conference on Supercomputing*, Assoc. Comput. Mach. Press, New York, 2002.

[457]   Mahalingam, M., Tang, C., and Xu, Z., Towards a semantic, deep archival file system, Technical Report. Hewlett–Packard Research Labs, 2002.

[458]   Malik, T., Szalay, A. S., Budavari, T., and Thakar, A., SkyQuery: A Web-service approach to federate databases, in *Conference on Innovative Database Research*, 2003.

[459]   Malony, A., Reed, D. Models for performance perturbation analysis. *1991 ACM/ONR Workshop on Parallel and Distributed Debugging, Santa Cruz, CA*, Assoc. Comput. Mach. Press, New York, 1991, pp. 15–25.

[460]   Mann, R., Williams, R., Atkinson, M. P., Brodlie, K., Storkey, A., and Williams, C., Scientific data mining, integration and visualisation, UK e-Science Report UKeS-2002-06, 2002. Available at *umbriel.dcs.gla.ac.uk/NeSC/general/technical_papers*.

[461]   Marinescu, D., *Internet Based Workflow Management: Towards a Semantic Web*. Wiley, New York, 2002.

[462]   Mathis, M., Heffner, J., Reddy, R., Raghunarayan, R., Saperia, J., TCP extended statistics MIB. Internet Engineering Task Force, 2003.

[463]   Mathisen, T., Pentium secrets. *Byte* **19**(7), 191–192, 1994.

[464]   Maymounkov, P., and Mazieres, D., Kademlia: A P2P information system based on the Xor metric, in *1st International Workshop on Peer-to-Peer Systems, Cambridge, MA*. LNCS 2429, Springer-Verlag, Heidelberg, 2002.

[465]   McBride, B., Four steps towards the widespread adoption of a Semantic Web, in *1st International Semantic Web Conference, Sardinia, Italy*, 2002, pp. 419–422.

[466]   McBrien, P., and Poulovassilis, A., Schema evolution in heterogeneous database architecture, a schema transformation approach, in *14th International Conference on Advanced Information Systems Engineering, Toronto, Canada*, LNCS 2348, Springer-Verlag, Heidelberg, 2002, pp. 484–499.

[467]   McCanne, S., and Jacobsen, V., Vic: A flexible framework for packet video, *ACM Multimedia* 511–522, 1995.

[468]   McIlraith, S., and Martin, D., Bringing semantics to Web services, *IEEE Intelligent Systems* **18**(1), 90–93, 2003.

[469]   McIlraith, S. A., Son, T. C., and Zeng, H., Semantic Web services, *IEEE Intelligent Systems* **16**(2), 46–53, 2001.

[470]   Meder, S., Welch, V., Tuecke, S., and Engert, D., GSS-API extensions, draft. Global Grid Forum, 2002. Available at *www.ggf.org/security/ggf4_2002-02/draft-ggf-gss-extensions-05.doc*.

[471]   Mehringer, D. M., Plante, R. L., and Roberts, D. A. (Eds.), *Astronomical Data Analysis Software and Systems VIII*, ASP Conference Series, Vol. 172. Astron. Soc. Pac., San Francisco, 1998.

[472]   Mendes, C., and Reed, D., Monitoring large systems via statistical sampling, in *LACSI Symposium, Santa Fe, NM*, 2002.

[473]   Messina, P., Brunett, S., Davis, D., Gottschalk, T., Curkendall, D., Ekroot, L., and Siegel, H., Distributed interactive simulation for synthetic forces, in *11th International Parallel Processing Symposium*, IEEE Computer Society Press, Los Alamitos, CA, 1997.

[474]   Metcalfe, R., and Boggs, D., Ethernet: Distributed packet-switching for local computer networks, *Communications of the ACM* **19**(7), 395–404, 1976.

[475]   Metzger, R., and Stroud, S., Interprocedural constant propagation: An empirical study, *ACM Letters on Programming Languages and Systems* **2**(14), 213–232, 1993.

[476]   Mewes, H. W., Frishman, D., Güldener, U., Mannhaupt, G., Mayer, K., Mokrejs, M., Morgenstern, B., Münsterkötter, M., Rudd, S., and Weil, B., MIPS: A database for genomes and protein sequences, *Nucleic Acids Research* **30**, 31–34, 2002.

[477]   Meyer, N., and Wolniewicz, P., Virtual user account system. Poznan Supercomputing and Networking Center, 2002. Available at *www.man.poznan.pl/ metacomputing/cluster*.

[478]   Miller, B. P., Callaghan, M. D., Cargille, J. M., Hollingsworth, J. K., Irwin, R. B., Karavanic, K. L., Kunchitkapadam, K., and Newhall, T., The Paradyn parallel performance measurement tools, *IEEE Computer* **28**(11), 37–46, 1995.

[479]   Mills, D. L., Improved algorithms for synchronizing computer network clocks, in *ACM SIGCOMM, London, U.K.*, Assoc. Comput. Mach. Press, New York, 1994.

[480]   Mirchandaney, R., Saltz, J., Smith, R., Nicol, D., and Crowley, K., Principles of runtime support for parallel processors, in *2nd International Conference on Supercomputing, St. Malo, France*, 1988.

[481]   Mockapetris, P. V., and Dunlap, K., Development of the Domain Name System, in *ACM SIGCOMM*, Assoc. Comput. Mach. Press, New York, 1988, pp. 123–133.

[482]   Moore, R., Knowledge-based Grids, in *18th IEEE Symposium on Mass Storage Systems, San Diego, CA*, IEEE Computer Society Press, Los Alamitos, CA, 2001.

[483]   More, J., Czyzyj, J., and Mesnier, M., The NEOS Server, *IEEE Journal on Computational Science and Engineering* **5**, 68–75, 1998.

[484]   Moreton, T., and Twigg, A., Enforcing collaboration in P2P routing services, in *1st International Conference on Trust Management*, 2003.

[485]   Moreton, T. D., Pratt, I. A., and Harris, T. L., Storage, mutability and naming in Pasta, in *International Workshop on P2P Computing and Networking, Pisa, Italy*, 2002.

[486]   Mukhi, N., *Web Service Invocation sans SOAP*, 2001. Available at *www.ibm.com/developerworks/library/ws-wsif.html*.

[487]   Mulligan, J., and Patrovsky, B., *Developing Online Games: An Insiders Guide*. New Riders Games, 2003.

[488]   Muthitacharoen, A., Morris, R., Gil, T., and Chen, B., Ivy: A read/write P2P file system, in *5th USENIX Symposium on Operating Systems Design and Implementation*, 2002.

[489]   Mutka, M., and Livny, M., Profiling workstations' available capacity for remote execution, in *12th Symposium on Computer Performance*, 1987, pp. 529–544.

[490]   Nabrzyski, J., Schopf, J., and Weglarz, J. (eds.), *Grid Resource Management*. Kluwer Academic, Norwell, MA, 2003.

[491]   Nagaratnam, N., Janson, P., Dayka, J., Nadalin, A., Siebenlist, F., Welch, V., Foster, I., and Tuecke, S., Security architecture for Open Grid Services, 2002. Available at *www.globus.org/ogsa/Security/draft-ggf-ogsa-sec-arch-01.pdf*.

[492]   Nahrstedt, K., Chu, H., and Narayan, S., QoS-aware resource management for distributed multimedia applications, *Journal on High-Speed Networking* 8(3–4), 227–255, December 1998.

[493]   Nahrstedt, K., and Smith, J. M., The QoS broker, *IEEE Multimedia* 2(1), 53–67, 1995.

[494]   Nahrstedt, K., Xu, D., and Wichadakul, D., QoS-aware middleware for ubiquitous and heterogeneous environments, *IEEE Communication Magazine* 39(11), 140–148, 2001.

[495]   Nairac, A., Townsend, N., Carr, R., King, S., Cowley, P., and Tarassenko, L., A system for the analysis of jet engine vibration data, *Integrated Computer-Aided Engineering* 6, 53–65, 1999.

[496]   Nakada, H., Matsuoka, S., Seymour, K., Dongarra, J., Lee, C., and Casanova, H., An overview of GridRPC: A remote procedure call API for Grid computing, in *Grid Computing Workshop, Baltimore, MD*, 2002.

[497]   Nakada, H., Sato, M., and Sekiguchi, S., Design and implementations of Ninf: Towards a global computing infrastructure, *Future Generation Computing Systems*, Metacomputing Issue, 15(5/6), 649–658, 1999.

[498]   National Library of Medicine PubMed Web Site: *www.ncbi.nlm.nih.gov/PubMed*.

[499]   Neuman, B. C., The Prospero file system: A global file system based on the virtual system model, *Computing Systems* 5(4), 407–432, 1992.

[500]   Neuman, B. C., Proxy-based authorization and accounting for distributed systems, in *13th International Conference on Distributed Computing Systems*, 1993, pp. 283–291.

[501]   Neuman, B. C., and Ts'o, T., Kerberos: An authentication service for computer networks, *IEEE Communications Magazine* 32(9), 33–88, 1994.

[502]   Ng, E., and Zhang, H., Predicting Internet network distance with coordinates-based approaches, in *INFOCOM'02, New York*, 2002.

[503]   Nick, J. M., Moore, B. B., Chung, J.-Y., and Bowen, N. S., S/390 cluster technology: Parallel Sysplex, *IBM Systems Journal* 36(2), 172–201, 1997.

[504]   Nieuwpoort, R. v., Kielmann, T., and Bal, H., Efficient load balancing for wide-area
          divide-and-conquer applications, in *8th ACM SIGPLAN Symposium on Principles and
          Practice of Parallel Programming*, 2001, pp. 34–43.

[505]   Nieuwpoort, R. v., Maassen, J., Hofmen, R., Kielmann, T., and Bal, H., Ibis: An
          efficient Java-based Grid programming environment, in *ACM JavaGrande ISCOPE
          2002 Conference, Seattle, WA*, 2002.

[506]   Novotny, J., The Grid portal development kit, *Concurrency and Computation: Practice
          and Experience* **14**(13–15), 1145–1160, 2002.

[507]   Novotny, J., Tuecke, S., and Welch, V., An online credential repository for the
          Grid: MyProxy, in *10th IEEE International Symposium on High Performance
          Distributed Computing, San Francisco, CA*. IEEE Computer Society Press, Los
          Alamitos, CA, 2001.

[508]   Object Management Group. *Common Object Request Broker Architecture: Core
          Specification (V3.0.2)*. Object Management Group, Formal Specification 2002/12/02,
          2002. Available at *www.omg.org/technology/documents/formal/
          corba_iiop.htm*.

[509]   Object Management Group. *Common Warehouse Metamodel*. Available at
          www.omg.org/technology/cwm.

[510]   Oinn, T. M., Talisman—Rapid application development for the Grid, in *11th Inter-
          national Conference on Intelligent Systems for Molecular Biology, Brisbane, Australia*,
          2003.

[511]   Olson, G. M., and Olson, J. S., Distance matters, *Human–Computer Interaction* **15**,
          139–179, 2000.

[512]   Padmanabhan, V. N., and Subramanian, L., An investigation of geographic mapping
          techniques for Internet hosts, in *ACM SIGCOMM*, Assoc. Comput. Mach. Press,
          New York, 2001.

[513]   Pakin, S., Karamcheti, V., and Chien, A. A., Fast messages: Efficient, portable
          communication for workstation clusters and MPPs, *IEEE Concurrency* **5**(2), 60–73,
          1997.

[514]   Paolucci, M., Kawamura, T., Payne, T. R., and Sycara, K., Semantic matching
          of Web services capabilities, in *1st International Semantic Web Conference*, 2002.

[515]   Papadopoulos, P. M., and Geist, G. A., Wide-area ATM networking for large-scale
          MPPS, in *SIAM conference on Parallel Processing and Scientific Computing*, 1997.

[516]   Parashar, M., and Browne, J. C., A computational infrastructure for parallel adaptive
          methods, in *Symposium on Parallel Adaptive Methods, 4th U.S. Congress on
          Computational Mechanics, San Francisco*, 1997.

[517]   Parker, S. G., Weinstein, D. M., and Johnson, C. R., The SCIRun computational
          steering software system, in *Modern Software Tools in Scientific Computing* (E. Arge,
          A. M. Bruaset, and H. P. Langtangen, eds.), pp. 1–44. Birkhauser Press,
          Basel, 1997.

[518] Paton, N. W., Atkinson, M. P., Dialani, V., Pearson, D., Storey, T., and Watson, P., Database access and integration services on the Grid, UK e-Science Technical Report UKeS-2002-03. UK National e-Science Center, 2002. Available at *www.nesc.ac.uk/technical_papers*.

[519] Pearlman, L., Welch, V., Foster, I., Kesselman, C., and Tuecke, S., A community authorization service for group collaboration, in *IEEE 3rd International Workshop on Policies for Distributed Systems and Networks*, IEEE Computer Society Press, Los Alamitos, CA, 2002.

[520] Pearson, D., Data requirements for the Grid scoping study report. UK Grid Database Taskforce, 2002. Available at *www.cs.man.ac.uk/grid-db/documents.html*.

[521] Pearson, D., The Grid: Requirements for establishing the provenance of derived data, in *Data Derivation and Provenance Workshop, Chicago*, 2002.

[522] Pearson, W. R., Flexible sequence similarity searching with the FASTA3 program package, *Methods in Molecular Biology* **132**, 185–219, 2000.

[523] Peltier, S. T., Lin, A. W., Lee, D., Mock, S., Lamont, S., Molina, T., Wong, M., Dai, L., Martone, M. E. and Ellisman, M. H., The telescience portal for tomography applications, *Journal of Parallel and Distributed Computing*, **63**(5), 539–550, 2003.

[524] Petitet, A., Blackford, S., Dongarra, J., Ellis, B., Fagg, G., Roche, K., and Vadhiyar, S., Numerical libraries and the Grid: The GrADS experiments with ScaLAPACK, *International Journal of High Performance Computing Applications* **15**(4), 359–374, 2001.

[525] Pias, M., Crowcroft, J., and Wilbur, S., Lighthouse: A QoS metric space to maintain network proximity, unpublished, 2002.

[526] Plaat, A., Bal, H., and Hofman, R., Sensitivity of parallel applications to large differences in bandwidth and latency in two-layer interconnects, *5th International Symposium on High Performance Computer Architecture*, IEEE Computer Society Press, Los Alamitos, CA, 1999, pp. 244–253.

[527] Plaxton, C. G., Rajaraman, R., and Richa, A. W., Accessing nearby copies of replicated objects in a distributed environment, in *ACM Symposium on Parallel Algorithms and Architectures*, Assoc. Comput. Mach. Press, New York, 1997, pp. 311–320.

[528] Popek, G. J., Guy, R. G., Thomas W., Page, J., and Heidemann, J. S., Replication in Ficus distributed file systems, *Workshop on Management of Replicated Data*, IEEE Computer Society Press, Los Alamitos, CA, 1990, pp. 20–25.

[529] Postel, J., Transmission control protocol. Internet Engineering Task Force, RFC 793, 1981. Available at *ietf.org/rfc/rfc793.txt*.

[530] Postel, J., and Reynolds, J., File transfer protocol. Internet Engineering Task Force, RFC 959, 1985. Available at *ietf.org/rfc/rfc959.txt*.

[531] Postel, J., and Reynolds, J., Telnet protocol specification. Internet Engineering Task Force, RFC 854, 1983. Available at *ietf.org/rfc/rfc854.txt*.

[532]   Postel, J. B., Simple mail transfer protocol. Internet Engineering Task Force, RFC 821, 1982. Available at *ietf.org/rfc/rfc821.txt*.

[533]   Pound, G. E., Xu, F., Wason, J. L., Tao, F., Shadbolt, N. R., Keane, A. J., Jiao, Z., Eres, M. H., and Cox, S. J., CFD based design search and the Grid: Architecture, environment and advice, *International Journal of High Performance Computing Applications*, 2002.

[534]   Pruyne, J. C., *Resource Management Services for Parallel Applications*, Ph.D. thesis. University of Wisconsin, 1996.

[535]   Rajasekar, A., and Moore, R., Data and metadata collections for scientific applications. *High Performance Computing and Networking, Amsterdam*, 2001.

[536]   Rajasekar, A., Wan, M., and Moore, R., MySRB & SRB—Components of a data Grid, in *11th IEEE International Symposium on High Performance Distributed Computing, Edinburgh, Scotland*. IEEE Computer Society Press, Los Alamitos, CA, 2002.

[537]   Ramakrishnan, R., and Gehrke, J., *Database Management Systems*. McGraw Hill, New York, 2000.

[538]   Raman, R., *Matchmaking Frameworks for Distributed Resource Management*, Ph.D. thesis. University of Wisconsin, 2000.

[539]   Raman, R., Livny, M., and Solomon, M., Matchmaking: distributed resource management for high throughput computing, in *7th IEEE International Symposium on High Performance Distributed Computing*. IEEE Computer Society Press, Los Alamitos, CA, 1998.

[540]   Raman, R., Livny, M., and Solomon, M., Policy driven heterogeneous resource co-allocation with gangmatching, in *12th IEEE International Symposium on High-Performance Distributed Computing, Seattle, WA*, IEEE Computer Society Press, Los Alamitos, CA, 2003.

[541]   Raman, R., Livny, M., and Solomon, M., Resource management through multilateral matchmaking, in *9th IEEE International Symposium on High Performance Distributed Computing*, IEEE Computer Society Press, Los Alamitos, CA, 2000, pp. 290–291.

[542]   Raman, S., and McCanne, S., A model, analysis, and protocol framework for soft state-based communication, *ACM SIGCOMM Computer Communication Review* 29(4), 15–25, 1999.

[543]   Ranganathan, K., and Foster, I., Decoupling computation and data scheduling in distributed data-intensive applications, in *11th IEEE International Symposium on High Performance Distributed Computing, Edinburgh, Scotland*. IEEE Computer Society Press, Los Alamitos, CA, 2002.

[544]   Ranganathan, K., and Foster, I., Simulation studies of computation and data scheduling algorithms for data Grids, *Journal of Grid Computing*, 1(1), 53–62, 2003.

[545]   Ranganathan, K., Iamnitchi, A., and Foster, I., Improving data availability through dynamic model-driven replication in large peer-to-peer communities, in *Global and Peer-to-Peer Computing on Large Scale Distributed Systems Workshop*, 2002.

[546]   Ratnasamy, S., Francis, P., Handley, M., Karp, R., and Shenker, S., A scalable content addressable network, in *ACM SIGCOMM*. Assoc. Comput. Mach. Press, New York, 2001.

[547]   Reed, D., Aydt, R., DeRose, L., Mendes, C., Ribler, R., Shaffer, E., Simitci, H., Vetter, J., Wells, D., Whitmore, S., and Zhang, Y., Performance analysis of parallel systems: Approaches and open problems, in *Joint Symposium on Parallel Processing, Nagoya, Japan*, 1998, pp. 239–256.

[548]   Reed, D., Elford, C., Madhyastha, T., Smirni, E., and Lamm, S., The next frontier: Interactive and closed loop performance steering, in *1996 ICPP Workshop on Challenges for Parallel Processing, Bloomingdale, IL*, 1996, pp. 20–31.

[549]   Reed, D., Pratt, I., Menage, P., Early, S., and Stratford, N., Xenoservers: Accountable execution of untrusted programs, in *7th Workshop on Hot Topics in Operating Systems, Rio Rico, AZ*. IEEE Computer Society Press, Los Alamitos, CA, 1999.

[550]   Reed, D. A., Aydt, R. A., Noe, R. J., Roth, P. C., Shields, K. A., Schwartz, B. W., and Tavera, L. F., Scalable performance analysis: The Pablo performance analysis environment, in *Scalable Parallel Libraries Conference*, IEEE Computer Society Press, Los Alamitos, CA, 1993, pp. 104–113.

[551]   Reed, D. A., Padua, D. A., Foster, I. T., Gannon, D. B., and Miller, B. P., Delphi: An integrated, language-directed performance prediction, measurement, and analysis environment, in *7th Symposium on the Frontiers of Massively Parallel Computation*, 1999.

[552]   Reiter, M., and Rubin, A., Crowds: Anonymity for Web transactions, *ACM Transactions on Information and System Security* **1**(1), 66–92, 1998.

[553]   Resnick, P., Zeckhauser, R., Friedman, E., and Kuwabara, K., Reputation systems, *Communications of the ACM* **43**(12), 45–48, 2000.

[554]   Rhea, S., Eaton, P., Geels, D., Weatherspoon, H., Zhao, B., and Kubiatowicz, J., Pond: The OceanStore prototype, in *2nd USENIX Conference on File and Storage Technologies FAST '03*, 2003.

[555]   Ribler, R., Simitci, H., and Reed, D., The Autopilot performance-directed adaptive control system, *Future Generation Computer Systems* **18**(1), 175–187, 2001.

[556]   Ribler, R. L., Vetter, J. S., Simitci, H., and Reed, D. A., Autopilot: Adaptive control of distributed applications, in *7th IEEE International Symposium on High Performance Distributed Computing*. IEEE Computer Society Press, Los Alamitos, CA, 1998.

[557]   Rice, P., Longde, I., and Bleasby, A., EMBOSS: The European Molecular Biology Open Software Suite. *Trends in Genetics* **16**(6), 276–277, 2000.

[558]   Ripeanu, M., Foster, I., and Iamnitchi, A., Mapping the Gnutella network: Properties of large-scale peer-to-peer systems and implications for system design, *IEEE Internet Computing* **6**(1), 50–57, 2002.

[559]   Roberts, L., *Nerds: A Brief History of the Internet*. TV Books, New York, 1998.

[560]   Romberg, M., The UNICORE Architecture: Seamless access to distributed resources, in *8th IEEE International Symposium on High Performance Distributed Computing*. IEEE Computer Society Press, Los Alamitos, CA, 1999.

[561]   Romein, J., Bal, H., Schaeffer, J., and Plaat, A., A performance analysis of transposition-table-driven work scheduling in distributed search, *IEEE Transactions on Parallel and Distributed Systems* 13(5), 447–459, 2002.

[562]   Rose, M., *The Simple Book: An Introduction to Internet Management*. Prentice Hall, Englewood Cliffs, NJ, 1994.

[563]   Roussos, M., Johnson, A., Leigh, J., Valsilakis, C., Barnes, C., and Moher, T., NICE: Combining constructionism, narrative, and collaboration in a virtual learning environment, *Computer Graphics* 31(3), 62–63, 1997.

[564]   Rowstron, A. I. T., and Druschel, P., Pastry: Scalable, decentralized object location, and routing for large-scale peer-to-peer systems, *Middleware* 329–350, 2001.

[565]   Rowstron, A. I. T., and Druschel, P., Storage management and caching in PAST, a large-scale, persistent P2P storage utility, in *Symposium on Operating Systems Principles*, 2001, pp. 188–201.

[566]   Roy, A., Foster, I., Gropp, W., Karonis, N., Sander, V., and Toonen, B., MPICH-GQ: Quality-of-service for message passing programs, in *IEEE/ACM SC'2000*, IEEE Computer Society Press, Los Alamitos, CA, 2000.

[567]   Russell, M., Allen, G., Daues, G., Foster, I., Seidel, E., Novotny, J., Shalf, J., and Laszewski, G. v., The astrophysics simulation collaboratory: A science portal enabling community software development, *Cluster Computing* 5(3), 297–304, 2002.

[568]   Ruzicka, D., What's going on?: Network management with Nagios, NetSaint's successor, *Linux Magazine*, 2003.

[569]   Ryutov, T., Neuman, C., Zhou, L., and Kim, D., Integrated access control and intrusion detection for Web servers, in *23rd International Conference on Distributed Computing Systems*, 2003.

[570]   Saltzer, J., Reed, D., and Clark, D., End-to-end arguments in system design, *ACM Transactions on Computer Systems* 2(4), 277–288, 1984.

[571]   Saltzer, J. H., The protection of information in computer systems, *Proceedings of the IEEE* 63(9), 1278–1308, 1975.

[572]   Sandberg, R., Goldberg, D., Kleiman, S., Walsh, D., and Lyon, B., Design and implementation of the Sun network filesystem, in *Summer USENIX Conference*, June 1985, pp. 119–130.

[573]   Sander, V., Adamson, W., Foster, I., and Roy, A., End-to-end provision of policy information for network QoS, in *10th IEEE International Symposium on High Performance Distributed Computing*, IEEE Computer Society Press, Los Alamitos, CA, 2001, pp. 115–126.

[574]   Saroiu, S., Gummadi, P. K., and Gribble, S. D., A measurement study of peer-to-peer file sharing systems, in *Multimedia Computing and Networking Conference, San Jose, CA*, 2002.

[575]   Schiano, D. J., Lessons from LambdaMOO: A social, text-based virtual environment, *Presence* 8(2), 127–139, 1997.

[576]   Schneier, B., *Applied Cryptography*. Wiley, New York, 1996.

[577]   Schneier, B., *Secrets and Lies: Digital Security in a Networked World*. Wiley, New York, 2000.

[578]   Schreiber, G., Akkermans, H., Anjewierden, A., de Hoog, R., Shadbolt, N. R., Van de Velde, W., and Wielinga, B., *Knowledge Engineering and Management*. MIT Press, Cambridge, MA, 2000.

[579]   Schroeder, M. D., Birrell, A. D., and Needham, R. M., Experience with Grapevine: The growth of a distributed system, *ACM Transactions on Computer Systems* 2(1), 3–23, 1984.

[580]   Schwingenschlogl, C., and Heigl, A., Development of a service discovery architecture for the Bluetooth radio system, in *EUNICE 2000, Sixth EUNICE Open European Summer School, Twente, Netherlands*, 2000.

[581]   Seidel, E., Allen, G., Merzky, A., and Nabrzyski, J., Gridlab: A Grid application toolkit and testbed, *Future Generation Computer Systems* 18, 1143–1153, 2002.

[582]   Shao, G., *Adaptive Scheduling of Master/Worker Applications on Distributed Computational Resources*. Ph.D. thesis, University of California—San Diego, San Diego, 2001.

[583]   Sharma, R., Java API for XML based remote procedure call (JAX-RPC) specification. Sun Microsystems, 2002.

[584]   Sheehan, T., Shelton, W., Pratt, T., Papadopoulos, P., LoCascio, P., and Dunigan, T., Locally self consistent multiple scattering method in a geographically distributed linked MPP environment, *Parallel Computing* 24(12–13), 1827–1846, 1998.

[585]   Shi, S., and Turner, J., Routing in overlay multicast networks, in *IEEE Infocom*, IEEE Computer Society Press, Los Alamitos, CA, 2002.

[586]   Shirasuna, S., Nakada, H., Matsuoka, S., and Sekiguchi, S., Evaluating Web services based implementations of GridRPC, in *11th IEEE International Symposium on High Performance Distributed Computing, Edinburgh, Scotland*. IEEE Computer Society Press, Los Alamitos, CA, 2001.

[587]   Shoshani, A., Sim, A., and Gu, J., Storage resource managers: Essential components for the Grid, in *Grid Resource Management* (J. Nabrzyski, J. Schopf, and J. Weglarz, eds.), Kluwer Academic, Norwell, MA, 2003.

[588]   Shoshani, A., Sim, A., and Gu, J., Storage resource managers: Middleware components for Grid storage, in *19th IEEE Symposium on Mass Storage Systems, San Diego, CA*, IEEE Computer Society Press, Los Alamitos, CA, 2002.

[589]   Shum, S. B., De Roure, D., Eisenstadt, M., Shadbolt, N., and Tate, A., CoAKTinG: Collaborative advanced knowledge technologies in the Grid, in *2nd Workshop on Advanced Collaborative Environments, Edinburgh, Scotland*, 2002.

[590]   Siebenlist, F., and Hemsath, D., DCE 1.2.3 public key certificate login. The Open Group, RFC 68.4, 1998. Available at www.opengroup.org/tech/rfc/ rfc68.4_d08.pdf.

[591]   Siebenlist, F., Welch, V., Tuecke, S., Foster, I., Nagaratnam, N., Janson, P., Dayka, J., and Nadalin, A., Roadmap towards a secure OGSA. Global Grid Forum, draft, 2002.

[592]   Siepel, A. C., Tolopko, A. N., Farmer, A. D., Steadman, P. A., Schilkey, F. D., Perry, B. D., and Beavis, W. D., An integration platform for heterogenous bioinformatics software components, *IBM Systems Journal* 40(2), 570–591, 2001.

[593]   Silva, L., Pedroso, H., and Silva, J., The design of JET: A Java library for embarrassingly parallel applications, in *WOTUG'20—Parallel Programming and Java Conference*, IOS Press, Amsterdam, 1997, pp. 210–228.

[594]   Silverston, L., *The Data Model Resource Book*. Wiley, New York, 2001.

[595]   Singla, A., and Rohrs, C., *Ultrapeers: Another Step towards Gnutella Scalability*, 2002: Available at *www.limewire.com/developer/Ultrapeers.html*.

[596]   Smith, J., Gounaris, A., Watson, P., Paton, N. W., Fernandes, A. A. A., and Sakellariou, R., Distributed query processing on the Grid, in *3rd International Workshop on Grid Computing*. Springer-Verlag, Heidelberg, 2002.

[597]   Smith, J. E., and Weingarten, F. W., Research challenges for the next generation Internet. Computing Research Association, 1997.

[598]   Smith, T. F., and Waterman, M. S., Identification of common molecular subsequences, *Journal of Molecular Biology* 147, 195–197, 1981.

[599]   Smith, W., A framework for control and observation in distributed environments. NASA Advanced Supercomputing Division, NASA Ames Research Center, 2001. Available at *www.nas.nasa.gov/~wwsmith/papers.html*.

[600]   Snir, M., Hochschild, P., Frye, D. D., and Gildea, K. J., The communication software and parallel environment of the IBM SP2, *IBM System Journal* 34(2), 205–221, 1995.

[601]   Snir, M., Otto, S., Huss-Lederman, S., Walker, D., and Dongarra, J., *MPI: The Complete Reference*. MIT Press, Cambridge MA, 1998.

[602]   Solomon, M., and Litzkow, M., Supporting checkpointing and process migration outside the UNIX kernel, in *Winter USENIX Conference*, 1992, pp. 283–290.

[603]   Spellman, P. T., et al., Design and implementation of microarray gene expression markup language (MAGE-ML), *Genome Biology* 46, 41–49, 2002.

[604]   Spence, D., and Harris, T., XenoSearch: Distributed resource discovery in the Xenoserver open platform, in *12th IEEE International Symposium on High Performance Distributed Computing*. IEEE Computer Society Press, Los Alamitos, CA, 2003.

[605] Staab, S., and Studer, R. (Eds.), *Handbook on Ontologies in Information Systems*. Springer-Verlag, Heidelberg, 2003.

[606] Steenkiste, P., Adaptation models for network-aware distributed computations, in 3rd International Workshop on Communication, Architecture, and Applications for Network-based Parallel Computing, LNCS 1602, Springer-Verlag, Heidelberg, 1999.

[607] Steiner, M., Tsudik, G., and Waidner, M., Key Agreement in Dynamic Peer Groups, *IEEE Transactions on Parallel and Distributed Systems*, **11**(8), 769–780, 2000.

[608] Sterbenz, J., and Parulkar, G., Axon: A distributed communication architecture for high-speed networking, in *Infocomm '90*, 1990, pp. 415–425.

[609] Sterling, T., Salmon, J., Becker, D. J., and Savarese, D. F., *How to Build a Beowulf: A Guide to the Implementation and Application of PC Clusters*. MIT Press, Cambridge, MA, 1999.

[610] Stevens, R., Woodward, P., DeFanti, T., and Catlett, C., From the I-WAY to the national technology Grid, *Communications of the ACM* **40**(11), 50–61, 1997.

[611] Stiles, J. R., Bartol, T. M., Salpeter, E. E., and Salpeter, M. M., Monte Carlo simulation of neuromuscular transmitter release using MCell, a general simulator of cellular physiological processes, *Computational Neuroscience* (J. M. Bower, ed.), pp. 279–284. Plenum Press, New York, 1998.

[612] Stockinger, H., Samar, A., Allcock, W., Foster, I., Holtman, K., and Tierney, B., File and object replication in data Grids, in *10th IEEE International Symposium on High Performance Distributed Computing*, IEEE Computer Society Press, Los Alamitos, CA, 2001, pp. 76–86.

[613] Stoica, I., Morris, R., Karger, D., Kaashoek, F., and Balakrishnan, H., Chord: A scalable peer-to-peer lookup service for Internet applications, in *ACM SIGCOMM, San Diego, CA*, Assoc. Comput. Mach. Press, New York, 2001, pp. 149–160.

[614] Stork, H.-G., Webs, Grids and knowledge spaces—Programmes, projects and prospects, in *I-KNOW '02 International Conference on Knowledge Management, Graz, Austria*, 2002.

[615] Sullivan, W., Werthimer, D., Bowyer, S., Cobb, J., Gedye, D., and Anderson, D., A new major SETI Project based on Project SERENDIP data and 100,000 personal computers, in *Astronomical and Biochemical Origins and the Search for the Life in the Universe*, 1997.

[616] Sun Microsystems, Java 2 Platform, Enterprise Edition (J2EE): *java.sun. com/j2ee*.

[617] Sundaram, B., and Chapman, B. M., Policy engine: A framework for authorization, accounting policy specification and evaluation in Grids, in *GRID2001, 2nd IEEE Workshop on Grid Computing, Denver, CO*, IEEE Computer Society Press, Los Alamitos, CA, 2001, pp. 143–153.

[618] Suzumura, T., Nakada, H., Saito, M., Matsuoka, S., Tanaka, Y., and Sekiguchi, S., The Ninf portal: An automatic generation tool for the Grid portals, in ACM *Java Grande, Seattle, WA*, 2002, pp. 1–7.

[619]   Szalay, A., and Gray, J., The World-Wide Telescope, *Science* **293**, 2037–2040, 2001.

[620]   Szalay, A. S., Kunszt, P. Z., Thakar, A., Gray, J., Slutz, D., and Brunner, R. J., Designing and mining multi-terabyte astronomy archives: The Sloan Digital Sky Survey, *SIGMOD Record* **29**(2), 451–462, 2000.

[621]   Takagi, H., Matsuoka, S., Nakada, H., Sekiguchi, S., Satoh, M., and Nagashima, U., Ninflet: A migratable parallel objects framework using Java, *ACM Workshop on Java for High-Performance Network Computing*, 1998, pp. 151–159.

[622]   Takaoka, A., Yoshida, K., Mori, H., Hayashi, S., Young, S. J., and Ellisman, M. H., International telemicroscopy with a 3MV ultrahigh voltage electron microscope, *Ultramicroscopy* **83**(1/2), 93–101, 2000.

[623]   Takeda, A., Fujisawa, K., Fukaya, Y., and Kojima, M., Parallel implementation of successive convex relaxation methods for quadratic optimization problems, *Journal of Global Optimization* **24**(2), 237–260, 2002.

[624]   Takefusa, A., Matsuoka, S., Nakada, H., Aida, K., and Nagashima, U., Overview of a performance evaluation system for global computing scheduling algorithms, in *8th IEEE International Symposium on High Performance Distributed Computing*, IEEE Computer Society Press, Los Alamitos, CA, 1999, pp. 97–104.

[625]   Tamches, A. and Miller, B. P., Fine-grained dynamic instrumentation of commodity operating system kernels, in *3rd Usenix Symposium on Operating Systems Design and Implementation, New Orleans, LA*, 1999.

[626]   Tanaka, Y., Nakada, H., Sekiguchi, S., Suzumura, T., and Matsuoka, S., Ninf-G: A reference implementation of RPC based programming middleware for Grid computing, *Journal of Grid Computing*, **1**(1), 41–51, 2003.

[627]   Tanaka, Y., Sato, M., Hirano, M., Nakada, H., and Sekiguchi, S., Performance evaluation of a firewall-compliant Globus-based wide-area cluster system, in *9th IEEE International Symposium on High Performance Distributed Computing*, IEEE Computer Society Press, Los Alamitos, 2000, pp. 121–128.

[628]   Tanaka, Y., Sato, M., Hirano, M., Nakada, H., and Sekiguchi, S., Resource manager for Globus-based wide-area cluster computing, in *1st IEEE International Workshop on Cluster Computing*, IEEE Computer Society Press, Los Alamitos, CA, 1999, pp. 237–244.

[629]   Tanenbaum, A. S., *Computer Networks*, 3rd ed. Prentice-Hall, Upper Saddle River, NJ, 1996.

[630]   Tang, C., Xu, Z., and Mahalingam, M., PSearch: Information retrieval in structured overlays, in *1st Workshop on Hot Topics in Networking*, 2002.

[631]   Tapus, C., Chung, I. H., and Hollingsworth, J. K., Active harmony: Towards automated performance tuning, in *SC'2002, Baltimore, MD*, 2002.

[632]   Taylor, C. F., et al., A systematic approach to modelling, capturing and disseminating proteomics experimental data, *Nature Biotechnology* **21**(3), 247–254, 2003.

[633]   Team, G. D. Ganglia: Distributed Monitoring and Execution System, 2002: *ganglia.sourceforge.net.*

[634]   Tennenhouse, D. L., Smith, J. M., Sincoskie, W. D., Wetherall, D. J., and Minden, G. J., A survey of active network research, *IEEE Communications Magazine* **35**(1), 80–86, 1997.

[635]   Terry, D., Theimer, M., Petersen, K., Demers, A., Spreitzer, M., and Hauser, C., Managing update conflicts in Bayou, a weakly connected replicated storage system, in *15th Symposium on Operating Systems Principles, Cooper Mountain, CO*, 1995.

[636]   Thain, D., Basney, J., Son, S.-C., and Livny, M., The Kangaroo approach to data movement on the Grid, in *10th IEEE International Symposium on High Performance Distributed Computing*, IEEE Computer Society Press, Los Alamitos, CA, 2001, pp. 325–333.

[637]   Thain, D., Bent, J., Arpaci-Dusseau, A., Arpaci-Dusseau, R., and Livny, M., Gathering at the well: Creating communities for Grid I/O, in *SC'2001*. IEEE Computer Society Press, Los Alamitos, CA, 2001.

[638]   Thain, D., and Livny, M., Multiple Bypass: Interposition agents for distributed computing, in *9th IEEE International Symposium on High Performance Distributed Computing*, IEEE Computer Society Press, Los Alamitos, CA, 2000, pp. 79–85.

[639]   Thain, D., and Livny, M., Bypass: Interposition agents for distributed computing, *Journal of Cluster Computing* **4**, 39–47, 2001.

[640]   Thain, D., Tannenbaum, T., and Livny, M., Condor and the Grid, in *Grid Computing: Making the Global Infrastructure a Reality* (F. Berman, G. Fox, and A. Hey, eds.). Wiley, New York, 2003.

[641]   Thatte, S., XLANG, Web services for business process design Web site, Microsoft Corporation. *www.gotdotnet.com/team/xml_wsspecs/xlang-c/default.htm.*

[642]   Object Management Group, Common Secure Interoperability version2 (CSIv2). 2001. Available at *www.omg.org/cgi-bin/doc?ptc/2001-03-02.*

[643]   The Open Group, DCE 1.1: Security Services and Authentication. Available at *www.opengroup.org/products/publications/catalog/c311.htm.*

[644]   The Open Group, *OpenPegasus CIM Object Broker Manual*, 2001. Available at *www.opengroup.org/management/pegasus.*

[645]   The Open Group, *Systems Management: Application Response Measurement (ARM)*, Technical Standard C807, 1998. Available at *www.opengroup.org/publications/catalog/c807.htm.*

[646]   Thomas, M., Mock, S., Boisseau, J., Dahan, M., Mueller, K., and Sutton, S., The GridPort Toolkit Architecture for building Grid portals, in *10th IEEE International Symposium on High Performance Distributed Computing*. IEEE Computer Society Press, Los Alamitos, CA, 2001.

[647]   Thomas, M. P., Mock, S., and Boisseau, J., Development of Web toolkits for computational science portals: The NPACI HotPage, in *9th IEEE International Symposium on High Performance Distributed Computing*. IEEE Computer Society Press, Los Alamitos, CA, 2000.

[648]   Thompson, M., Johnston, W., Mudumbai, S., Hoo, G., Jackson, K., and Essiari, A., Certificate-based access control for widely distributed resources, in *8th Usenix Security Symposium*, 1999.

[649]   Tierney, B., TCP tuning guide for distributed applications on wide area networks, *Usenix; login Journal 33*, 33, 2001.

[650]   Tierney, B., Gunter, D., Becla, J., Jacobsen, B., and Quarrie, D., Using NetLogger for distributed systems performance analysis of the BaBar data analysis system, in *Computers in High Energy Physics, Padova, Italy*, 2000.

[651]   Tierney, B., Johnston, W., Crowley, B., Hoo, G., Brooks, C., and Gunter, D., The NetLogger methodology for high performance distributed systems performance analysis, in *7th IEEE International Symposium on High Performance Distributed Computing*, IEEE Computer Society Press, Los Alamitos, CA, 1998.

[652]   Tierney, B., Johnston, W., Lee, J., and Hoo, G., Performance analysis in high-speed wide area IP over ATM networks: Top-to-bottom end-to-end monitoring, *IEEE Network* **10**(3). 1996.

[653]   Tierney, B., Lee, J., Crowley, B., Holding, M., Hylton, J., and Drake, F., A network-aware distributed storage cache for data intensive environments, in *8th IEEE International Symposium on High Performance Distributed Computing*. IEEE Computer Society Press, Los Alamitos, 1999.

[654]   Tirumala, A., Qin, F., Dugan, J., Ferguson, J., and Gibbs, K., *Iperf 1.7.0*. National Laboratory for Applied Network Research, 2002: *dast.nlanr.net/Projects/Iperf*.

[655]   Tody, D., *A Reference Manual for the IRAF Subset Preprocessor Language*, 1983. Available at *iraf.noao.edu/iraf/docs/spp.txt.Z*.

[656]   Touch, J., Dynamic Internet overlay deployment and management using the X-Bone, *Computer Networks* **36**(2/3), 117–135, 2001.

[657]   Trastour, D., Bartolini, C., and Preist, C., Semantic Web support for the business-to-business e-commerce lifecycle, in *11th International World Wide Web Conference, Honolulu, HA*, Assoc. Comput. Mach. Press, New York, 2002, pp. 89–98.

[658]   Trumbo, J., Spatial memory and design: A conceptual approach to the creation of navigable space in multimedia design, *Interactions* **5**(4), 26–34, 1998.

[659]   Tuecke, S., Czajkowski, K., Foster, I., Frey, J., Graham, S., Kesselman, C., Maguire, T., Sandholm, T., Snelling, D., and Vanderbilt, P., Open Grid Services Infrastructure Version 1.0. Global Grid Forum, Draft draft-ggf-ogsi- gridservice-29, 2003. Available at *www.ggf.org/documents/Drafts*.

[660]   Tuecke, S., Engert, D., Foster, I., Thompson, M., Pearlman, L., and Kesselman, C., Internet X.509 public key infrastructure proxy certificate profile. Internet Engineering Task Force Draft, draft-ietf-pkix-proxy-01.txt, 2001.

[661]   Tung, B., Ryutov, T., Neuman, C., Tsudik, G., Sommerfeld, B., Medvinsky, A., and
          Hur, M., Public key cryptography for cross-realm authentication in Kerberos,
          Internet draft, draft-ietf-cat-kerberos-pk-cross-05.txt, 1997.

[662]   van Harmelen, F., Hendler, J., Horrocks, I., McGuinness, D. L., Patel-Schneider, P. F.,
          and Stein, L. A., OWL Web ontology language reference. W3C, Working Draft, 2003.
          Available from *www.w3.org/TR/owl-ref.*

[663]   Vetter, J. S., and Reed, D. A., Real-time performance monitoring, adaptive control,
          and interactive steering of computational Grids, *International Journal of High
          Performance Computing Applications* 14(4), 357–366, 2000.

[664]   Visualware Inc., *VisualProfile Enterprise Edition 2.0 User's Manual*, 2002. Available
          from *www.visualware.com/visualprofile.*

[665]   Vyssotsky, V. A., Corbató, F. J., and Graham, R. M., Structure of the Multics
          supervisor, in *Fall Joint Computer Conference*, 1965.

[666]   Wahl, M., Howes, T., and Kille, S., Lightweight directory access protocol (v3).
          Internet Engineering Task Force, RFC 2251, 1997. Available at *ietf.org/
          rfc/rfc2251.txt.*

[667]   Waldbusser, S., Remote network monitoring management information base. Internet
          Engineering Task Force, RFC 1757, 1995. Available at *ietf.org/rfc/rfc1757.txt.*

[668]   Waldo, J., The Jini Architecture for network-centric computing, *Communications of
          the ACM* 42(7), 76–82, 1999.

[669]   Waldrop, M. M., J.C.R. Licklider: Computing's Johnny Appleseed, *MIT Technology
          Review* 66–71, 2000.

[670]   Walters, W. P., Stahl, M. T., and Murcko, M. A., Virtual screening: An overview, *Drug
          Discovery Today* 3, 160–178, 1998.

[671]   Welch, V., Siebenlist, F., Foster, I., Bresnahan, J., Czajkowski, K., Gawor, J.,
          Kesselman, C., Meder, S., Pearlman, L., and Tuecke, S., Security for Grid services, in
          *12th IEEE International Symposium on High Performance Distributed Computing, Seattle,
          WA*, IEEE Computer Society Press, Los Alamitos, CA, 2003.

[672]   Welch, V., Siebenlist, F., Meder, S., and Pearlman, L., Use of SAML for OGSA
          authorization. Global Grid Forum, Draft, 2003. Available at *www.globus.org/
          ogsa/security.*

[673]   Wells, D. C., Greisen, E., and Harten, R. H., FITS: A flexible image transport system,
          Astronomy and Astrophysics Supplement Series 44, 363–370, 1981.

[674]   Welsh, M., Culler, D., and Brewer, E., SEDA: An architecture for well-conditioned,
          scalable Internet services, in *18th Symposium on Operating Systems Principles, Banff,
          Canada*, 2001.

[675]   Westphal, C., and Blaxton, T., *Data Mining Solutions: Methods and Tools for Solving
          Real-World Problems*. Wiley, New York, 1998.

[676]   Whitten, A., and Tygar, J. D., Why Johnny can't encrypt: A usability evaluation of
          PGP 5.0, in *USENIX Security Symposium*, 1999.

[677]   Wilcox-O'Hearn, B., Experiences deploying a large-scale emergent network, in *1st International Workshop on Peer-to-Peer Systems, Cambridge, MA. LNCS* 2429, Springer-Verlag, Heidelberg, 2002.

[678]   Wilkinson, M. D., and Links, M., BioMOBY: An open-source biological Web services proposal, *Briefings in Bioinformatics* 3(4), 331–334, 2002.

[679]   Williams, R., *Virtual Sky*: *virtualsky.org*.

[680]   Wolfe, M. J., *Optimizing Supercompilers for Supercomputers*. MIT Press, Cambridge, MA, 1989.

[681]   Wolski, R., Forecasting network performance to support dynamic scheduling using the Network Weather Service, in *6th IEEE International Symposium on High Performance Distributed Computing, Portland, OR*. IEEE Computer Society Press, Los Alamitos, CA, 1997.

[682]   Wolski, R., Spring, N., and Hayes, J., The Network Weather Service: A distributed resource performance forecasting service for metacomputing, *Future Generation Computer Systems* 15(5–6), 757–768, 1999.

[683]   Wroe, C., Stevens, R., Goble, C. A., Roberts, A., and Greenwood, M., A suite of DAML + OIL ontologies to describe bioinformatics Web services and data, *International Journal of Cooperative Information Systems*, special issue on bioinformatics data and data modelling, 12(2), 197–224, 2003.

[684]   Wu, J., Saltz, J., Hiranandani, S., and Berryman, H., Runtime compilation methods for multicomputers, in *International Conference on Parallel Processing, St. Charles, IL*, 1991.

[685]   Wu, X., and Taylor, V., Design and development of Prophesy performance database for distributed scientific applications in *10th SIAM Conference on Parallel Processing for Scientific Computing, Virginia*, 2001.

[686]   Wu, X., Taylor, V., and Stevens, R., Design and implementation of Prophesy automatic instrumentation and data entry system, in *13th IASTED International Conference on Parallel and Distributed Computing and Systems, Anaheim, CA*, 2001.

[687]   Wulf, W. A., Wang, C., and Kienzle, D., A new model of security for distributed systems, Technical Report CS-95-34. University of Virginia, 1995.

[688]   Yang, B., and Garcia-Molina, H., Efficient search in P2P networks, in *22nd IEEE International Conference on Distributed Computing Systems*, IEEE Computer Society Press, Los Alamitos, CA, 2002.

[689]   Yarrow, M., McCann, K., Biswas, R., and Van der Wijngaart, R., An advanced user interface approach for complex parameter study process specification on the Information Power Grid, in *GRID 2000, Bangalore, India*, 2000.

[690]   Ylonen, T., Kivinen, T., Saarinen, M., Rinne, T., and Lehtinen, S., SSH protocol architecture. Internet Engineering Task Force, Draft, 2001.

[691]   Zacharia, G., and Maes, P., Trust management through reputation mechanisms, *Applied Artificial Intelligence* 14, 881–907, 2000.

[692]   Zacharia, G., Moukas, A., and Maes, P., Collaborative reputation mechanisms in electronic marketplaces, in *32nd Hawaii International Conference on System Sciences* IEEE Press, New York, 1999.

[693]   Zadeh, L. A., Commonsense knowledge representation based on fuzzy logic, *IEEE Computer* 16(10), 61, 1983.

[694]   Zadeh, L. A., Fuzzy logic=computing with words, *IEEE Transactions on Fuzzy Systems* 2, 103–111, 1996.

[695]   Zaki, O., Lusk, E., Gropp, W., and Swider, D., Toward scalable performance visualization with Jumpshot, *International Journal of High Performance Computing Applications* 13(3), 277–288, 1999.

[696]   Zegura, E., Ammar, M., Fei, Z., and Bhattacharjee, S., Application-level anycasting: A server selection architecture and use in a replicated Web service, Technical Report, 2000.

[697]   Zhang, L., Deering, S., Estrin, D., Shenker, S., and Zappala, D., RSVP: A new resource ReSerVation protocol, *IEEE Network* 7(5), 8–18, 1993.

[698]   Zhang, X., Freschl, J. L., and Schopf, J. M., A performance study of monitoring and information services for distributed systems, in *12th IEEE International Symposium on High Performance Distributed Computing.* IEEE Computer Society Press, Los Alamitos, CA, 2003.

[699]   Zhang, Y., Paxson, V., and Shenker, S., The stationarity of Internet path properties: Routing, loss, and throughput. ACIRI, Technical Report, 2000.

[700]   Zhao, B. Y., Kubiatowicz, J., and Joseph, A., Tapestry: An infrastructure for fault-tolerant wide-area location and routing, Technical Report UCB/CSD-01-1141. University of California—Berkeley, 2001.

[701]   Zhou, S., LSF: Load sharing in large-scale heterogeneous distributed systems, in *Workshop on Cluster Computing*, 1992.

[702]   Zhou, S., Zheng, X., Wang, J., and Delisle, P., Utopia: A load sharing facility for large, heterogeneous distributed computer systems, *Software: Practice and Experience* 23(12), 1305–1336, 1993.

[703]   Zimmerman, P., *The Official PGP User's Guide.* MIT Press, Cambridge, MA, 1995.

Contributors

Gabrielle Allen (*allen@aei.mpg.de*) leads the Cactus Code research and development team at the Max Planck Institute for Gravitational Physics in Potsdam, Germany. Her research interests include programming frameworks, tools, and techniques for large-scale computing, and numerical relativity.

Malcolm Atkinson, FRSE (*mpa@nesc.ac.uk*) is the Director of the UK National e-Science Centre and a Professor at the Computing Science Department, University of Glasgow and the Informatics School at the University of Edinburgh. He leads the OGSA-DAI project and the e-Science Institute programme. His research concerns the integration of programming and databases to deliver large-scale and long-lived systems.

Jim Austin (*austin@cs.york.ac.uk*) is the Chair of neural computation in the Computer Science Department at the University of York, UK, where he leads the Advanced Computer Architectures Group. His research interests are Grid computing, neural networks, image analysis, and high-performance pattern matching architectures.

Henri Bal (*bal@cs.vu.nl*) is a Professor at the Faculty of Sciences of the Vrije Universiteit Amsterdam where he heads research groups on parallel programming and physics-applied computer science. His interests include parallel and distributed programming and applications, Grid computing, interactive visualization, and programming languages.

Fran Berman (*berman@sdsc.edu*) is Professor and holder of the Endowed Chair in High Performance Computing at the University of California, San Diego. She serves as Director of the San Diego Supercomputer Center and Director of the National Science Foundation's National Partnership for Advanced Computing Infrastructure. She is also one of the Principal Investigators of the TeraGrid project. Her research focuses on Grid and high-performance computing, in particular in the areas of adaptive middleware and programming tools and environments.

Alan Blatecky (*alan@sdsc.edu*) is Executive Director at the San Diego Supercomputing Center. His interests include high-performance networking and distributing computing, collaboration technologies, and the development and management of virtual organizations and loosely coupled dynamic research programs.

John Brooke (*j.m.brooke@man.ac.uk*) is Co-Director of the UK North-West eScience Centre (ESNW) and leads the eScience team at Manchester Computing. His research concerns high-performance computing, visualization, and the dynamics of complex systems.

Randy Butler (*rbutler@ncsa.uiuc.edu*) is Senior Associate Director of Networks, Security, and Middleware at the National Center for Supercomputing Applications at the University of Illinois at Urbana-Champaign. His experience and focus are on applying and supporting Grid and security technologies for scientific research.

Henri Casanova (*casanova@cs.ucsd.edu*) is an Adjunct Professor of Computer Science and Engineering, a Research Scientist at the San Diego Supercomputer Center, and the director of the Grid Research and Development Laboratory, all at the University of California, San Diego. His research interests are in the area of high-performance distributed computing with emphases on modeling and scheduling.

Richard Cavanaugh (*Richard.Cavanaugh@cern.ch*) is a Postdoctoral Research Assistant with the Physics Department at the University of Florida. He is Deputy Coordinator for the GriPhyN Project and Coordinator for the US-CMS Grid Testbed. His current interests include applying virtual data, data mining, and mathematical modeling techniques to data-intensive scientific computing.

Ann Chervenak (*annc@isi.edu*) is Research Team Leader in the Center for Grid Technologies at the Information Sciences Institute (ISI) of the University of Southern California (USC) and Research Assistant Professor in the USC Computer Science Department. Her research concerns services for data management in Grids, including replica management and metadata services.

Andrew A. Chien (*achien@cs.ucsd.edu*) is the SAIC Chair Professor in the Computer Science and Engineering Department at the University of California, San Diego. He also serves as a Senior Fellow and Strategic Advisor for the San Diego Supercomputer Center and is a member of the Global Grid Forum's Steering Group. He is also the Chief Technology Officer and co-Founder of Entropia, Inc., a desktop Grid software company. His research interests include desktop Grids, parallel computer architecture, clusters, networking, routing networks and network interfaces, object-oriented languages and implementations, and large-scale computing.

Peter Couvares (*pfc@cs.wisc.edu*) is an Associate Researcher in the Computer Sciences Department at the University of Wisconsin-Madison, where he works on the Condor Project. His research focus is on software to help scientists take advantage of distributed and Grid computing environments.

Peter Cowley (*peter.cowley@rolls-royce.com*) is Chief Scientist—Research and Technology for Rolls-Royce plc and a Visiting Professor at Manchester University. He is interested in emerging technologies likely to have a large impact on aerospace, marine, and energy systems.

Jon Crowcroft (*jon.crowcroft@cl.cam.ac.uk*) is the Marconi Professor of Networked Systems in the Computer Laboratory at the University of Cambridge. Prior to that he was professor of networked systems at UCL in the Computer Science Department. He is a fellow of the ACM and the Royal Academy of Engineering. His research is on the functionality and performance of communications systems.

Karl Czajkowski is Scientist at the Information Sciences Institute (ISI) of the University of Southern California (USC). His research focuses on architectural requirements for high-performance distributed computing in complex policy environments.

Robert Davis is a Research Associate in the Advanced Computer Architectures Group at the University of York. His current research interests include real-time and performance aspects of simple binary neural networks—known as Correlation Matrix Memories (CMMs). Rob is investigating how novel representations and compression techniques can be applied to CMMs with the aim of improving performance for very large datasets.

David De Roure (*dder@ecs.soton.ac.uk*) is a Professor of Computer Science in the Intelligence, Agents, Multimedia Group within the Department of Electronics and Computer Science at University of Southampton, UK, where he leads Grid and pervasive computing research. His research interests include the application of knowledge technologies within distributed systems infrastructure and applications.

Alan De Smet (*adesmet@cs.wisc.edu*) is a Systems Programmer for the Condor Project at the University of Wisconsin-Madison. His work has focused on the Globus Toolkit and Condor-G.

Jack Dongarra holds an appointment as University Distinguished Professor in the Computer Science Department at the University of Tennessee. He specializes in numerical algorithms in linear algebra, use of advanced-computer architectures, programming methodology, and tools for parallel computers. He was involved in the design and implementation of the open source software packages EISPACK, LINPACK, the BLAS, LAPACK, ScaLAPACK, Netlib, PVM, MPI, NetSolve, ATLAS, PAPI, and Harness and is currently involved in the design of algorithms and techniques for high-performance computer architectures. He is a Fellow of the AAAS, ACM, and IEEE and a member of the National Academy of Engineering.

Mark Ellisman (*mark@ncmir.ucsd.edu*) is Professor of Neurosciences and Bioengineering and the Director of the National Center for Microscopy and Imaging Research at the University of California, San Diego.

Alvaro A. A. Fernandes (*alvaro@cs.man.ac.uk*) is a Lecturer in the Department of Computer Science of the University of Manchester in the UK. His research interests include knowledge discovery and distributed, adaptive query processing in computational Grids.

Martyn Fletcher (*martyn.fletcher@cs.york.ac.uk*) is the Software Manager for the Distributed Aircraft Maintenance Environment (DAME) Project based at The University of York. His interests include requirements capture and software design/modeling.

David Foster (*david.foster@cern.ch*) is a Senior Scientist at the European Laboratory for Nuclear Research (CERN) where he is a lead Technologist on the LHC computing Grid project. He is a specialist in the technologies of distributed systems management. His research interests include modeling Grid systems as a managed infrastructure, organizational behavior, the human relationship to technology, and complexity management.

Wolfgang Gentzsch (*wolfgang.gentzsch@sun.com*) is Director of Grid Computing at Sun Microsystems, Inc. in Menlo Park, California. He joined Sun in July 2000, with Sun's acquisition of Gridware. He was cofounder and CTO of Gridware and founder and president of its predecessor Genias Software. From 1985 to 2000, he was a professor of mathematics and computer science at the University of Applied Sciences in Regensburg, Germany, and a consultant for vector, parallel, and distributed computing companies.

Carole Goble (*carole@cs.man.ac.uk*) is a Professor in the Department of Computer Science at the University of Manchester where she co-leads the Information Management Group. Her research concerns interests include hypermedia, intelligent information and knowledge management, ontologies, and semantic-based information integration with particular application to the semantic web, bioinformatics and e-Science.

Gregory Graham (ggraham@fnal.gov) leads the Distributed Processing Environment effort for the USCMS Software and Computing Project at Fermi National Accelerator Laboratory. His research focuses on bringing the incredible resources made available by Grid technology to bear upon specific research problems for scientists around the world.

Jim Gray (*gray@microsoft.com*) is a Distinguished Engineer in Microsoft's Scaleable Servers Research Group.

Chris Greenhalgh (c.greenhalgh@cs.nott.ac.uk) is a Reader in the Department of Computer Science at Nottingham University. He is a designer of multiuser virtual reality systems, especially system-level distributed graphical systems.

Junmin Gu (*JGu@lbl.gov*) is a Computer Science Engineer in the High Performance Computing Research Department at Lawrence Berkeley National Laboratory. She is a member of the Scientific Data Management Group. She is the main designer and developer of Disk Storage Resource Manager and its application to various scientific domains. Her interests are in object data models, query languages, federated databases, and Grid technology.

Tony Hey (*Tony.Hey@epsrc.ac.uk*) is Director of the UK's e-Science Core Programme at the Engineering and Physical Sciences Research Council (EPSRC) and Professor of

Computation at the University of Southampton. He has worked in the field of parallel and distributed computing and has research interests in performance engineering for Grid applications and the development of the next-generation Grid middleware as well as experimental explorations of quantum computing and quantum information theory. He is also the author of a number of popular science books such as *Einstein's Mirror* and *The New Quantum Universe*.

Jeffrey K. Hollingsworth (*hollings@cs.umd.edu*) is an Associate Professor of Computer Science at the University of Maryland. His research interests include instrumentation and measurement tools, resource-aware computing, and high-performance distributed computing. Dr. Hollingsworth's current projects include the dyninst runtime binary editing tool, and harmony—a system for building adaptable, resource-aware programs.

Zane Zhenhua Hu received his Ph.D. in Computer Science from Huazhong University of Science and Technology and is Senior Product Architect at Platform Computing.

Tom Jackson (*tom.jackson@cs.york.ac.uk*) is a Senior Researcher in the Advanced Computer Architectures Group at the University of York, UK, and is the Project Coordinator for the DAME e-Science project. He is responsible for the research coordination of the DAME project.

Mark Jessop (*mark.jessop@cs.york.ac.uk*) is a Research Associate in the Department of Computer Science at The University of York, England. His primary research interests are in the area of building service-orientated Grid applications, with a particular interest in porting existing systems and technologies to the Grid/service paradigm.

William E. Johnston (*wejohnston@lbl.gov*) is a Senior Scientist and head of the Distributed Systems Dept. in the Computational Research Division of Lawrence Berkeley National Laboratory, and program manager for the Information Power Grid project at NASA Ames Research Center. His research interests include high-speed, widely distributed computational and data Grids and wide area network-based distributed systems, Public Key cryptography-based security architectures and authorization systems, and use of the global Internet to enable remote access to scientific instrumentation.

Ken Kennedy (*ken@rice.edu*) is the John and Ann Doerr University Professor of Computer Science and Director of the Center for High Performance Software Research (HiPerSoft) at Rice University. His research focuses on software for the support of high-level programming in science and engineering, with a particular emphasis on scalable parallel computers and the Grid.

Peter Kunszt (*Peter.Kunszt@cern.ch*) is Staff Member at the European Organization for Nuclear Research CERN in the Database Group of the IT Division. His interests includes data and resource management, data access optimization and databases.

David Levine is the President and CEO of Butterfly.net, the leading provider of computing Grids for massively multiplayer online games. He is the author of one of the first books on the Java programming language, *Live Java, Database to Cyberspace,* and was the keynote speaker at the first NASA Java Day in Cape

Canaveral. In addition to his interest in technology, he has been an active essay-ist, poet, and songwriter. He recorded four CDs for European music labels, pro-duced a video for MTV, and toured extensively in the United States, Canada, and Europe. He has received grants to pursue these interests from the National Endowment for the Humanities, the National Endowment for the Arts, NCR, and Shell Oil. He earned a B.A. in Philosophy from Yale University and was a Rackham Memorial Fellow in Poetry at the University of Michigan.

Wayne Biao Liu received his Ph.D. in Electrical Engineering from the University of Waterloo and is Senior Developer on Platform Symphony.

Peter Lobner (*peter.r.lobner@ds-s.com*) is a Vice President and Director, Technology at Data Systems & Solutions, where he works with the business unit managers and their chief engineers to maximize the alignment of DS&S research and devel-opment programs with the company's business plan. He also initiates corporate-sponsored research and development efforts that lead to common solutions intended to improve integrated system and services delivered by DS&S.

Weihong Long received his Ph.D. in Computer Science from Northwestern Polytechnical University in China and is product manager, Platform Symphony.

Charng-da Lu (*clu2@uiuc.edu*) is a Ph.D. student at the University of Illinois at Urbana-Champaign. His interests include computer performance analysis and fault tolerance.

Miron Livny (*miron@cs.wisc.edu*) is Professor of Computer Science at the University of Wisconsin-Madison. His research focuses on high-throughput computing and data management, visualization, and exploration systems.

Satoshi Matsuoka (*matsu@is.titech.ac.jp*) is Professor of Mathematical and Computing Sciences at the Tokyo Institute of Technology. His primary interests are high-performance software systems in general, including large-scale commodity clus-tering, global-scale Grid computing, as well as use of object-oriented technologies in high-performance settings.

Mirco Mazzucato (*mirco.mazzucato@pd.infn.it*) is Director of Research in the Italian Istituto Nazionale di Fisica Nucleare (INFN). His expertise is focused on distrib-uted computing and software development. He had for about 10 years the respon-sibility of the management of the offline computing activities of the large DELPHI HEP experiment at CERN. He was Chairman of the CERN LHC Computing Committee from 1996 to 2000. He is responsible for the INFN Grid project and member of the EU DataGrid and DataTAG Management Boards.

Celso Mendes (*cmendes@cs.uiuc.edu*) is Research Scientist at the Department of Computer Science of the University of Illinois at Urbana-Champaign. His research interests focus on tools and techniques for performance analysis of parallel and distributed systems.

Tim Moreton (*tim.moreton@cl.cam.ac.uk*) is a Ph.D. student in the Computer Laboratory at the University of Cambridge, UK. His research interests include distributed storage and peer-to-peer systems.

Nataraj Nagaratnam (*natarajn@us.ibm.com*) is a Senior Technical Staff Member at IBM and the lead security architect for IBM WebSphere product and IBM OGSA infrastructure. He is a core member of the IBM Web services security architecture team and is a co-author of Web services security specifications and JSRs related to J2EE security.

Inderpal Narang (*narang@almaden.ibm.com*) is a Distinguished Engineer at the IBM Almaden Research Center in San Jose, California. His research includes architecture and algorithms for parallel, distributed data systems. Several of his inventions have been included in the IBM's database products.

Norman W. Paton (*norm@cs.man.ac.uk*) is a Professor of Computer Science at the University of Manchester, where he co-leads the Information Management Group. He works principally on databases and distributed information management. Current activities include the development of distributed and service-based query processing technologies for the Grid in the OGSA-DAI and ᵐʸGrid projects, and the design and implementation of spatio-temporal data models and query languages in the Tripod project. He also works on genome data management, in particular exploring the use of data integration techniques for making better use of functional genomic data. He is Co-Chair of the Database Access and Integration Services Working Group of the Global Grid Forum.

Dave Pearson (*Dave.Pearson@oracle.com*) is a senior director at Oracle and leads its Grid initiatives in the UK. His interests include information architecture, and data access and integration.

Steven Peltier (*peltier@ncmir.ucsd.edu*) is Executive Director of the National Center for Microscopy and Imaging Research, UCSD. His interests include remote instrumentation, automation, and collaboration environments.

Steve Pettifer (*srp@cs.man.ac.uk*) is a Lecturer in the Department of Computer Science at the University of Manchester, UK. His research interests include collaborative visualization, virtual environments, distributed systems, and human computer interaction.

Ian Pratt (*ian.pratt@cl.cam.ac.uk*) is a leader of the Systems Research Group in the University of Cambridge Computer Laboratory and Fellow of King's College, Cambridge. His research interests cover a broad range of topics including operating systems, communications, and computer architecture.

Thomas Prudhomme (*tip@ncsa.uiuc.edu*) is Senior Associate Director for the Cybercommunities Division of the National Center for Supercomputing Applications at the University of Illinois at Urbana-Champaign. His research is focused on the design and use of distributed community collaboratories supporting team-oriented research, policy development, and decision making.

Daniel A. Reed (*reed@ncsa.uiuc.edu*) is Director of the National Center for Supercomputing Applications (NCSA), where he leads the National Computational Science Alliance and is one of two principal investigators for the NSF TeraGrid. He is also the Edward William and Jane Marr Gutgsell Professor of Computer Science at the University of Illinois. His research interests include performance analysis of high-performance systems, Grid software, adaptive control systems for parallel and Grid environments, and virtual environments.

Edward Seidel (*eseidel@aei.mpg.de*) leads the Computational Science and Numerical Relativity research groups at the Max Planck Insitute for Gravitational Physics in Potsdam, Germany, and has adjunct positions at Illinois astronomy and physics departments and the NCSA. His research interests include topics in general relativity, astrophysics, and computational science.

Nigel Shadbolt (*nrs@ecs.soton.ac.uk*) is Professor of Artificial Intelligence (AI) in the Department of Electronics and Computer Science at Southampton University. He is a member of the Intelligence, Agents, Multimedia Group. His research concentrates on knowledge technologies and biorobotics in artificial intelligence.

Arie Shoshani (*shoshani@lbl.gov*) is a Senior Staff Computer Scientist in the High Performance Computing Research Department at Lawrence Berkeley National Laboratory. He heads the Scientific Data Management Group. His research interests include semantic data models, temporal data, statistical and OLAP databases, efficient access from tertiary storage, distributed storage and data management, and database techniques for scientific database applications.

Frank Siebenlist (*franks@mcs.anl.gov*) is a Software Architect in the Distributed Systems Laboratory of the Mathematics and Computer Science Division at Argonne National Laboratory. His research interests include distributed computing and security.

Alex Sim (*ASim@lbl.gov*) is a Computer Science Engineer in the High Performance Computing Research Department at Lawrence Berkeley National Laboratory. He is a member of the Scientific Data Management Group. He is the main designer and developer of Tertiary Storage Resource Manager and its application to various scientific domains. His interests are in system architecture, security, and Grid technology.

Larry Smarr (*lsmarr@ucsd.edu*) is the founding Director of the California Institute for Telecommunications and Information Technology, which spans the Universities of California at San Diego and Irvine. Prior to moving to California, Dr. Smarr was founding director of the National Center for Supercomputing Applications at the University of Illinois at Urbana-Champaign and directed the NCSA for fifteen years. He conducted research for many years in observational, theoretical, and computational-based astrophysical sciences.

Rick Stevens (*stevens@mcs.anl.gov*) is Director of the Mathematics and Computer Science Division at Argonne National Laboratory, where he also leads the Futures Laboratory, and Professor of Computer Science at the University of Chicago. His research concerns high-performance and parallel computing, advanced collaboration and visualization technologies, and computational science.

Robert Stevens (*robert.stevens@cs.man.ac.uk*) is a lecturer in bioinformatics at the University of Manchester. His research concerns the development and use of ontologies within the bioinformatics domain. Of particular interest is the encoding of biological content and description of services over those data in order to support analysis of biological data through shared understandings that may be reasoned over computationally.

Alexander Szalay is the Alumni Centennial Professor of Astronomy and Professor of Computer Science at the Johns Hopkins University. He is a cosmologist, working on the statistical measures of the spatial distribution of galaxies and galaxy formation. He is the architect for the Science Archive of the Sloan Digital Sky Survey. He is Project Director of the NSF-funded National Virtual Observatory.

Douglas Thain (*thain@cs.wisc.edu*) is a Ph.D. student at the University of Wisconsin—Madison. His research interests include distributed systems, domain-specific languages, complexity management, and fault tolerance.

Brian L. Tierney is a Staff Scientist and group leader of the Data Intensive Distributed Computing Group, which is part of the Distributed Systems Department at Lawrence Berkeley National Laboratory. His research interests include data-intensive distributed computing, high-speed networking issues, and distributed system performance monitoring and analysis.

Joe Touch (*touch@isi.edu*) is Director of the Postel Center for Experimental Networking at USC/ISI and a Research Associate Professor in the USC Computer Science Department. His research interests include virtual Internets, network and protocol architecture, high-speed networks, latency reduction and protocol performance, automatic network configuration and management, and optical Internets.

Steven Tuecke (*tuecke@mcs.anl.gov*) is a Software Architect in the Distributed Systems Laboratory in the Mathematics and Computer Science Division at Argonne National Laboratory and a Fellow in the Computation Institute at the University of Chicago. He plays a leadership role in many of Argonne's research and development projects in the area of Grid computing and directs the efforts of both Argonne staff and collaborators in the design and implementation of the Globus Toolkit and Open Grid Services Architecture. He is also the co-director of the Global Grid Forum (GGF) Security area and co-chair of the GGF Open Grid Services Infrastructure working group. He received *Technology Review* magazine's TR100 award in 2002, recognizing him as one of the world's top 100 young innovators.

Andrew Twigg (*andrew.twigg@cl.cam.ac.uk*) is a Ph.D. student in the Computer Laboratory at the University of Cambridge, UK. When not trying to be a musician, he finds Internet-scale computation mechanisms interesting.

Paul Watson (*Paul.Watson@newcastle.ac.uk*) is Professor of Computer Science at the University of Newcastle, UK, and Director of the UK's North East Regional e-Science Centre. His research is focused on the design of scalable, high-performance systems, particularly for data-intensive computations.

Von Welch (*welch@mcs.anl.gov*) is a Software Architect with the University of Chicago and the Globus Project. His research interests include the security of distributed systems.

Mark Conway Wirt (*mark.wirt@butterfly.net*) is the co-founder and Chief Technology Officer of Butterfly.net Inc., a company that focuses on networking technologies for massively multiplayer on-line games. His experience includes the modeling of cosmic ray extensive air showers, architectural analysis and Monte Carlo modeling of strategic defense systems, and network performance/vulnerability modeling and assessment.

Irving Wladawsky-Berger (*irving@us.ibm.com*) is IBM's General Manager, e-business on demand. As such, he is responsible for IBM's companywide e-business on demand initiative intended to bring together deep business expertise with advanced IT capabilities and thus help organizations achieve whole new dimensions in productivity. In conjunction with this, he leads IBM's Grid computing efforts. Among other things, he led the revival of the company's supercomputing and parallel computing businesses, including the transformation of IBM's large commercial systems to parallel architectures. He has managed a number of IBM's businesses, including the large systems software and UNIX systems divisions.

Ming Xu received his Ph.D. in Computing Science in the area of Parallel Discrete Event Simulation Protocols from the University of Exeter, England, and is Principal Product Architect at Platform Computing.

Index